INDUSTRIAL STRENGTH JAVA

Luke Cassady-Dorion

Matthew Brumbaugh

Shirani Maheshwari

Jon Wright

Dan Brookshier

Ben Last

Jim Mathis

New Riders

New Riders Publishing, Indianapolis, Indiana

Industrial Strength Java

By Luke Cassady-Dorion
Dan Brookshier
Matthew Brumbaugh
Ben Last
Shivani Maheshwari
Jim Mathis
Jon Wright

Published by:
New Riders Publishing
201 West 103rd Street
Indianapolis, IN 46290 USA

Copyright © 1997 by New Riders Publishing

Printed in the United States of America 1 2 3 4 5 6 7 8 9 0

Library of Congress Cataloging-in-Publication Data

CIP data available upon request

Warning and Disclaimer

This book is designed to provide information about the Java computer language. Every effort has been made to make this book as complete and as accurate as possible, but no warranty or fitness is implied.

Publisher	Don Fowley
Publishing Manager	Sean Angus
Marketing Manager	Mary Foote
Managing Editor	Carla Hall

Product Development Specialist
Chris Cleveland

Acquisitions Editor
Nancy Maragolio

Software Specialist
Steve Flatt

Senior Editor
Sarah Kearns

Development Editor
Chris Cleveland

Project Editor
Cliff Shubs

Copy Editors
Dan Axelrod, Gina Brown
Larry Frey, Krista Litwiller
Carrie Peterson, Molly Warnes

Technical Editors
Eugene W. Sotirescu, Greg Guntle,
Joseph R. Kiniry

Acquisitions Coordinator
Tracy Turgeson

Administrative Coordinator
Karen Opal

Cover Designer
Sandra Schroeder

Cover Production
Aren Howell

Book Designer
Gary Adair

Production Manager
Kelly Dobbs

Production Team Supervisors
Laurie Casey, Joe Millay

Graphics Image Specialists
Debra Bolhuis, Kevin Cliburn,
Wil Cruz, Daniel Harris,
Oliver Jackson, Laura Robbins

Production Analysts
Jason Hand, Erich J. Richter

Production Team
Diana Groth, Maureen Hanrahan,
William Huys Jr., Christopher
Morris, Rowena Rappaport,
Elizabeth SanMiguel,
Pamela Woolf

Indexer
Eric Brinkman, Sandy
Henselmeier, Greg Pearson

About the Authors

Luke Cassady-Dorion heads client/server development at Odyssey Systems Corporation near Philadelphia, PA. His work centers around the development of databases for web sites. Additionally he is finishing a degree in computer science at Drexel University also in Philadelphia, PA. In addition to acting as lead author on this book, he was a contributing author on Que's *Special Edition Using Java*, and *JavaScript by Example*. His journal publications include the *Java Developer's Journal*, and *Web Informant*. He loves to answer questions about his work (although response time may take a while) and can be reached at luke@luke.org.

Dan Brookshier is a Senior Software Consultant who has worked in the defense, oil & gas, insurance, and telecom industries. Dan graduated with a B.S. degree in Engineering from the California Polytechnic University in Pomona (Cal Poly U). When not writing Java programs, Dan kayaks and juggles torches, knives, and rubber chickens. Dan can be reached through e-mail at turbogek@cluck.com.

Jim Mathis is a freelance Java and JavaScript consultant by night and a communications systems architect by day. He has been active in the Internet community from its very beginnings and wrote one of the first implementations of TCP/IP. He received his B.S. from Stanford University in Electrical Engineering during that most interesting time when the Internet was being born.

Shivani Maheshwari is a graduate student in the Department of Computer Science at the University of Georgia at Athens, GA. She completed her Bachelor of Engineering degree in Computer Technology from the University of Bombay in 1994. Her fields of interest in computer science are Object-Oriented Programming, Java, CORBA, and related technologies.

Matt Brumbaugh is finishing his B.S. in Computer Science at Marquette University in Milwaukee, Wisconsin. He is employed when not in school by Control Data Systems, Inc. as a software developer. He is interested in computer networks and distributed computing.

Ben Last works for Anchor Computer Systems, based on the island of Anglesey, North Wales (UK), both as a project leader on a major Internet site incorporating database, CGI and Java programming, and as head of software development overseeing the development of systems targeted at the automotive and related markets. He has been programming since before his teens and has suffered many different operating systems and languages in that time, including all of those from Microsoft, some from Apple, and many different species of Unix. He has been on the Internet for many years and has wasted more time in USENET than is generally advisable.

He is married to Margaret who tolerates him having a room filled with computers, guitars, synthesizers, and general studio equipment. Their baby daughter Elizabeth contributed to the book by enthusiastically pressing random keys while her father was away from the computer. This led to the most frustrating two hours of debugging he has ever spent. You can visit his Hypereality Systems web site at `http://www.hypereality.co.uk/`.

Jon Wright, a senior software engineer, is involved in the design and construction of a large CORBA-based network management system for NEC Australia in Melbourne. He can be reached via the home page of his software development site at `http://www.mycelium.com/`.

Dedications

Dedicated to Luann, and James, Marietta and Alexander; a wonderful family.
—Jim Mathis

To my father and grandfather—may I work as hard in my life as you have in yours.
—Matt Brumbaugh

Acknowledgments

First and foremost to my parents and family who always knew (even when I didn't) that I would live out my dreams. To my friends who still make social calls even though I have spent the past few months in hiding while finishing this book. Yes, Matt, this does mean that I can go out next Wednesday ;-). To Nancy, Eugene, Greg, Cliff, Chris, my contributing authors, and everyone at New Riders for making this book a reality. To John Dhabolt, Natural Intelligence, the participants on the java-mac and advanced-java list-serves, and everyone on comp.lang.java for providing me with ideas and answers to my many, many questions. —Luke Cassady-Dorion

Dedicated to my Mom and Dad who never said a discouraging word about writing or programming. To Bill Brosche and Jeff Fitzgerald, co-workers and friends, who made me realize that I could write great books. To the Java development team for finally developing a language that doesn't give me gray hairs. —Dan Brookshier

I wish to thank my family and friends for their love and support. Their understanding has helped me try to achieve all that I want. Rajesh Nair, a graduate student at the University of Georgia, Athens, and also my best friend, has made valuable contributions to my chapter. I take this opportunity to express my gratitude to him for the support he has always given me. My major professor, Dr. John A. Miller, has given and continues to give me valuable direction and insights in my chosen field of study, distributed object management. I am deeply grateful for that. —Shivani Maheshwari

Trademark Acknowledgments

All terms mentioned in this book that are known to be trademarks or service marks have been appropriately capitalized. New Riders Publishing cannot attest to the accuracy of this information. Use of a term in this book should not be regarded as affecting the validity of any trademark or service mark.

Warning and Disclaimer

This book is designed to provide information about the inner workings of Java technology. Every effort has been made to make this book as complete and as accurate as possible, but no warranty or fitness is implied.

The information is provided on an "as is" basis. The authors and New Riders Publishing shall have neither liability nor responsibility to any person or entity with respect to any loss or damages arising from the information contained in this book or from the use of the disks or programs that may accompany it.

Contents at a Glance

Table of Contents

6   Advanced AWT   173

7   Beginning Data Structures: Taking Advantage of java.util   197

8 Advanced Data Structures   231

9 Input/Output: Using Streams   277

13   Thinking in Terms of Threads   503

15 Java Beans 677

16 Jeeves and Java Servlets 709

17   JDBC   757

Chapter 1

Industrial Strength Java: For the Industry's Strongest Developers

For the past 20 years, software prophets have been talking about a mythical day when all software will be capable of running on any computer without it being necessary to make any modifications whatsoever. Developers bought into this idea with a hope that one day they would wake up to find that their user base had increased ten fold! They could then look at titles Egghead Software has to offer and not even bother to check whether they run on their computer.

This dream became a reality with the development of a new programming language from Sun Microsystems called Java. When Java was in late beta form in late 1995, it was implemented on very few platforms and was scarcely used to build applications.

It is understandable why Java was embraced by developers. It came at a time when the web's popularity was growing exponentially and when developers were looking for an answer to the ever-growing problem created by a diverse platform environment. It is completely amazing how this language was embraced so completely by developers. Programmers rarely change development languages; this is one of the main reasons there are so many COBOL programmers.

Developers usually find a language that they like and then stick with it. After Java was announced, developers using C++ or Smalltalk ran like lemmings to Java. In fact, Java has even made the move from geekdom to mainstream, and not only are people moving from C++ to Java, but many developers now choose Java as their first language.

Despite Java's versatility, there are few business solutions currently in existence that have been developed in Java. In fact, most of the language's publicity has come from glorified animated GIFs, which amount to nothing more than bandwidth-wasting applets. This is all very interesting considering it is business solutions (such as database front ends or spreadsheets) that often prove a language. However, solutions being written in Java are increasing, and with the help of this book, you may be among the first people to develop real-world solutions entirely in Java.

The Industrial Strength Reading Audience

The *Industrial Strength* series at New Riders is catered toward intermediate to advanced developers. As an intermediate Java developer, you should already know most of the language's syntax and have developed a few applets and applications. This book is designed to take you beyond this point by providing you with discussions of advanced Java topics. After all, if you're looking at this book, you know that Java is the coolest language out there, but, unfortunately, you need to convince your boss of this before he or she will let you develop in Java. This book not only provides you with fodder for you boss, but it shows you what it means to develop full-force applications in Java.

Computer books often focus only on the actual coding process of an application but neglect to discuss the planning stages involved. How many times have you looked at a piece of code and said, "Oh, well that makes sense now that I see it. I would have never thought of that myself though." *Industrial Strength Java* not only shows you an application's finished code, it discusses application design. And yes, if you flipped though this book, those are Booch diagrams you saw!

Industrial Strength Java serves a dual purpose. The first is to educate you about real-world software development in Java. Here you will want to clear off your calendar and curl up in front of your computer with this book. In addition to teaching you about development in

Java, this book is designed to serve as that one reference that sits on your lap while you code. This is not to say that you will find the same annotated API that is featured in every other book on Java, but rather you will find detailed instructions on how to use different aspects of Java in various situations.

The Focus of the Book

As was stated at the beginning of this chapter, Java owes much of its fame to silly band-width-wasting applets. Although this "applet craze" did a tremendous service to the language by propelling it into the developer community, the craze has also given the language a bad name.

Many people feel that Java is great for spicing up web sites, but it can never compete with C++. To counter this belief, this book is designed to show you how Java is capable of producing business solutions. These solutions are almost all applications, and you will find very little applet code in this book.

This, of course, is not to say that applets are meaningless garbage because there are many examples of companies that have a totally applet-based intranet. Applets do have a great distribution model, and, in many situations, they are the best way to solve a problem. However, applets suffer due to a draconian security sandbox. This "security sandbox" keeps users safe, but it makes developers jump through hoops when building complex applications.

If you are using Java to develop applets, this book is a great resource for you. The book is not limited to the larger topic of application development. If you are using the book as an applet developer, however, note that some code presented may violate the security sand-box. If this is the case, adaptations to the material may be necessary. You should note that code signing will probably become common soon, resulting in the need for a config-urable security manager. Chapter 4, "Applets," discusses applet development in greater detail, including a discussion of how you can develop powerful applications within the security sandbox.

Contents of the Book

Developing a book about a topic as large as business solutions in Java is not an easy task. You have what professionals in the field consider to be 1,000 pages of the most important, available material. However, were we given the time (and trees), we could have written volumes on this topic.

The topics that today's professional Java developers feel are the most important in the Java environment are outlined in the chapter descriptions that follow.

Chapter 2, "Object-Oriented Programming"

If it has been a while since you last wrote code in an object-oriented language, use Chapter 2 as a jump-start. This chapter discusses the most important step in application development—design. Chapter 2 focuses on what it means to design applications from an object-oriented perspective.

Chapter 3, "Planning Your Application"

Chapter 2 provides the framework for Chapter 3, which gets into the nitty-gritty details of application development. This chapter looks at Booch diagrams as planning tools and discusses the different forms that your code can take.

Chapter 4, "Applets"

Chapter 4 examines applet development in Java. Topics of interest in this chapter include the following:

- Taking advantage of the applet distribution model
- Surviving within the security sandbox
- Applet-specific methods and related HTML references

Chapter 5, "AWT Basics"

This chapter is an indispensable resource to the AWT API package. In this chapter, two applications are developed:

- An application that shows you how to use AWT components to build complex screens

- An application that shows you how each layout manager deals with the same set of components.

Both applications are interactive and not only show you the code required to implement the application, but how to choose between different components and layout managers.

Chapter 6, "Advanced AWT"

This chapter expands upon the coverage of the AWT API package discussed in Chapter 5 It also taught you how to build a graphical user interface (GUI) application framework that can be subclassed to provide an instant graphical front end to an existing text-based application. You will find that the framework is a great starting point for new applications.

Chapter 7, "Beginning Data Structures: Taking Advantage of java.util"

Data structures are the core of any application, and this chapter introduces them painlessly through the use of the java.util package. The chapter covers what is provided by the package and explains some slight modifications you can use to make preexisting data structures act like others.

Chapter 8, "Advanced Data Structures"

This chapter moves beyond the basic data structures introduced in Chapter 7 and covers building data structures from the ground up. This chapter addresses the enigma of the lack of pointers in Java.

Chapter 9, "Input/Output: Using Streams"

Chapter 9 is a class-by-class reference to the java.io package. This chapter teaches you not only how to provide communication into and out of your application, but it instructs how streams can be used for communication between applications.

Chapter 10, "Introducing Networking"

Chapter 10 introduces one of the main features built into Java from day one—networking. This chapter discusses different networking protocols, and how they can be built using

Java. Additional coverage includes interaction with the Common Gateway Interface (CGI) using HTTP-GET and HTTP-POST.

Chapter 11, "Advanced Networking"

Understanding the minute details of an application that takes advantage of Java's rich networking features is often the key to its success. This chapter expands on the networking coverage found in Chapter 10 with the development of a complete server framework written totally in Java. Additionally, you will learn how to build a complete e-mail client and server application that uses the SMTP, POP, and HTTP protocols.

Chapter 12, "Distributed Computing with Java"

Currently, many business solutions are built as client/server applications. This is changing, however, and a "new wave" of computing is taking over. Distributed computing is the process by which application tasks are spread out over multiple machines. This chapter focuses on the Object Management Group's (OMG) CORBA standard for distributed object technology.

Chapter 13, "Thinking in Terms of Threading"

Regardless of which language you use, if execution time matters at all, you will need to build a multithreaded application. Fortunately, this is easy in Java. Chapter 13 briefly introduces the syntax needed to write threaded code and delves into the details of how and when to use threads in your application.

Chapter 14, "Interfacing C/C++ and Java"

Although Java is much more fun to work with when compared to C++, the sad truth is that there are times when a platform-specific language is needed. This occurs frequently when some sort of direct-to-hardware communication is needed. This chapter shows you how to build a library that enables a Java application to access serial ports on a Windows 95 or NT machine.

Chapter 15, "Java Beans"

Java Beans, JavaSoft's component architecture for Java, has the potential to alter the manner in which software is written. Code that complies with the Java Beans standard is benefited with increased reuse, a logical event model, and easier testing patterns. This component architecture is the focus in Chapter 15.

Chapter 16, "Jeeves and Java Servlets"

Chapter 16 focuses on JavaSoft's Jeeves Java-based web server, particularly on the implementation of servlets. Of interest is the servelet implementation of popular web CGIs, such as a shopping basket and a hit counter.

Chapter 17, "JDBC"

Chapter 17 focuses on the Java Database Connectivity Standard, an API that facilitates database integration in Java. This chapter is of huge interest to anyone wanting to move from C++ to Java as a front end development tool.

Development of the Book

It goes without saying that there is a lot of material jammed into this book. It is the product of a small team of developers getting together to produce a book we ourselves have always wanted. Although the authors live in different parts of the world and use different compilers on different machines, the final product is a highly polished piece of work that applies to you regardless of compiler or platform choices.

For the curious, a majority of the book was developed using Natural Intelligence's Roaster on a PowerBook 5300cs. Other authors used every other platform and compiler imaginable, from vi and the JDK on one level, to an IDE such as Symantec Café on another. Of course, all examples were tested using the JDK as a reference.

Enjoy and learn from this book! If you ever have any questions, feel free to e-mail me at `luke@luke.org`. Please note that although I may not answer your question right away, I will get back to you.

Chapter 2

Object-Oriented Programming

Programming in an object-oriented language can be a lot of fun. It can also be a huge headache. Headaches are obviously a result of not fully understanding the environment, and having fun is a result of entirely grasping the environment. Most Java books provide an overview of terms such as encapsulation, inheritance, and polymorphism, but few really teach you how to visualize your application as a whole. Being able to visualize your application is the most important step in the entire software development process. By fully planning your application, the coding process becomes smoother, and most importantly, your debug time decreases exponentially. As a reminder (and to serve as a reference), this chapter briefly covers object-oriented programming terminology and then jumps right into a discussion of the process used to design an application; in fact, you will use this process to design a complete application.

One of the most important points of this chapter is that object-oriented design mirrors human communication. As an example of this, parallel a human dialogue to an object-based information transfer. The human dialogue is constructed by stringing together a series of phrases, which either tell the one individual about the other or ask questions of one individual.

When two objects need to perform an exchange of information, one object either calls an information-retrieval method in the other object or a set-information method in the other. Learning to program with objects, therefore, does not require that you learn any new concepts; it only means that you must approach application development in a different manner.

Object-Oriented Programming Terminology

Every object contains a series of methods. Access to these methods is strictly controlled, and without the proper permissions, one object cannot use another object's methods. Most objects offer some methods that any other object can access and some methods that can be accessed only by certain objects.

Allowing the outside world to access only a small part of your data is called *encapsulation*. Because object interaction parallels human interaction, the discussion on encapsulation is detailed with an object-to-human analogy. It could be stated safely that there are two levels of human communication. We communicate with ourselves (thinking), and we communicate with others (talking, typing, signing, and so on).

When thinking, we access parts of our brain that are only "viewable" by ourselves. This is very similar to an object, which limits certain data and methods to itself. To mark such data and methods as such, the *private* keyword is used.

Communicating with other objects is similar to the manner in which two humans interact. When two humans talk, data is shared, and when two objects communicate, some data is shared. Methods and data that can be shared between two objects are referred to as *public*.

Inheritance

Although information transfer between two objects can be viewed as sharing data that results from a computation, another form of object communication that passes along the skills necessary to perform those computations is called *inheritance*.

As an example, if you needed to know the square root of 42, you could either ask me for the answer or you could ask me how to compute the answer. If an object supports a public method called getSquareRoot(int n), for example, any other object could call that method and find out the square root of 42. However, an object could also inherit (or extend) off the object that contains the getSquareRoot(int n) method, and then both objects would know how to compute square roots.

Objects that take on methods of other classes can accomplish this method gain by inheriting from those classes. For example, whenever you develop an applet, that applet is actually a subclass of the Applet class contained in the java.applet package, which is why the init() method is automatically called when your applet loads.

As humans, we inherit certain traits from our parents. These traits are so deeply embedded in who we are that fighting them is pointless. For example, many people believe that the ability to breathe is passed from the mother to child during pregnancy. Have you ever tried to just stop breathing for a while? I doubt that you will be successful. Objects are the same way. When one object extends another object, it carries along certain methods. The child object can do nothing about the fact that it now has access to those methods; it must simply accept them.

Polymorphism

If you are experienced with developing code in structured programming languages, then you are accustomed to writing functions that accept one value and return another. These functions are far from versatile and support input/output for a fixed data-set, which is rather odd when you consider that there are few models in the universe that follow the same pattern. Can you imagine what humans would be like if they could react to only one type of input and then produce only one type of output based on it? Fortunately, this is not the case with humans or in object-oriented programming.

Imagine, for example, that humans were only programmed to answer one question: Do you want pepperoni on that? And these same humans only knew one answer: Sure, my cholesterol is rather low today! This situation could get pretty sticky when dealing with people who have high cholesterol or are vegetarians. In structured programming, a function is a lone block of code that serves a totally unique data-set.

Polymorphism ("many forms") is the process by which objects are able to respond to different environments. As humans, polymorphism enables us to inform the bearer of the pepperoni that we are vegetarians. An object-based example is an object that can evaluate a mathematical expression stored on a stack or on a parse tree and produce a correct result in each situation.

Applying Object-Oriented Theory to Application Design

Most explanations of object-oriented programming (OOP) are incomplete because they often do not show how OOP concepts are put to use. Many books on Java simply introduce the concepts early and then teach you Java syntax without much regard for how theory applies to application development.

To properly develop industrial-strength applications, you should have a full grasp on OO theory. To reinforce this fact, most examples in this book are complete applications, and before their code is revealed, you are given a detailed understanding of how and why the code was developed.

Remember that by designing your application before you begin coding, you can reduce errors and ensure the success of your application. The end of this chapter discusses the design of a working application. In the discussion of the design, the full outline of a project is developed. By the end of this chapter, you will have little trouble understanding how to take the outline and make it a full-fledged application.

The application outlined in this chapter is a simple contact book (addresses, phones numbers, and so forth). Due to space constraints, the application is not developed to a point where it could compete with a product such as Now Software's Now Contact, but you will see how the application's potential for expansion includes a comparable feature set.

Contact-By-Contact: Allowing for the Existence of Each Contact

On the most basic level, the contact book needs to hold data about all of your contacts. The information about each contact is contained in a separate instance of the Contact object. Figure 2.1 shows a representation of the Contact object made while developing this application.

The notation for the Contact object is quite easy to understand. It has public methods for getting and setting quantities, such as first name, phone, fax, and e-mail. Another method, streamEncoded(), is of particular interest because it provides a common method by which other objects can get the entire contents of a Contact object.

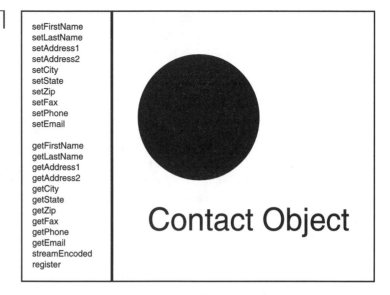

FIGURE 2.1

The Contact object. Note the coverage and grouping of all methods.

setFirstName
setLastName
setAddress1
setAddress2
setCity
setState
setZip
setFax
setPhone
setEmail

getFirstName
getLastName
getAddress1
getAddress2
getCity
getState
getZip
getFax
getPhone
getEmail
streamEncoded
register

Contact Object

Before you try to comprehend the use of the streamEncoded() method, compare this method to the manner in which web-based form submissions are managed.

NOTE

Allowing for the existence of this method has rather broad implications. If a standard method for storing and retrieving contact data is formed, then not only can the Contact object be used by this contact book, but now they can also be used by other applications that need to manage a contact file.

A user on a PC running Windows 3.11 hits a web page with the AOL web browser, fills in a form, submits it, and has his results processed in the same way that someone running Netscape Navigator under SGI IRIX has her results processed. These identical results are a result of the fact that although all browsers operate differently, they all comply with certain standards. With form usage, these standards apply to the manner in which the data is sent from browser to server. The user does not need to have any knowledge of these inner workings; one simply takes advantage of the fact that everything works correctly.

The streamEncoded() method acts exactly the way that form submissions do. Any object can ask a Contact object for its entire contents, and the Contact object can stream its contents to the object that requests the data.

Additionally, there is a method in the Contact object called register(). The underlying processes behind this method is detailed in the next section. For now simply understand that this method notifies a global repository that a new Contact object has been instantiated (or created).

Tracking Contact Objects

Although it is perfectly fine to have zillions of Contact objects existing in random memory locations, they are practically useless if you can't track them. To track each Contact object, you need to create a Registry object. The Registry object publishes a set of methods by which various Contact objects can notify the Registry Object of their existence.

The Registry object (see fig. 2.2) is notified by a Contact object that the Contact object has been created. The Contact object performs this notification (see the Note) by calling the registerObject() method contained in the Registry object. This method accepts as a parameter a reference to a Contact object. After this method finishes executing, the Contact object passes a reference to itself so that the Registry object can allow any object that it interacts with to have access to a Contact object.

You should pay special attention to the retrieve(), store(), and delete() methods as described in the following list.

- **retrieve().** Enables the Registry object to search for a specific object and return a reference to that object to whomever has requested the object.

- **store().** Enables the Contact references to be stored in some manageable fashion.

- **delete().** Enables the Registry object to remove a reference to a specific Contact object.

Building a Library of Contact Objects

Now that you can create and manage a large contact file, you need to learn how to add and subtract from that file. Because addition must come before subtraction, take a look at the AddContact object, as shown in figure 2.3.

The AddContact object has a series of equally important methods, which are discussed here in the order in which they are called. First is the promptForInput() method, which draws a form to the screen (see fig. 2.4) that prompts the user for information, such as the contact's name, address, and phone and fax numbers.

FIGURE 2.3

FIGURE 2.3

The Registry object keeps track of all Contact objects.

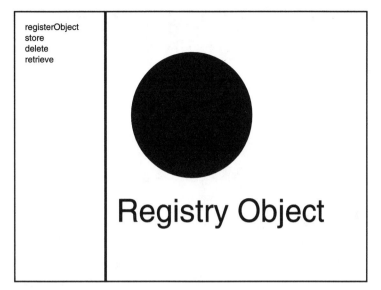

registerObject
store
delete
retrieve

Registry Object

FIGURE 2.4

The AddContact object can accept use input and turn this input into a Contact object.

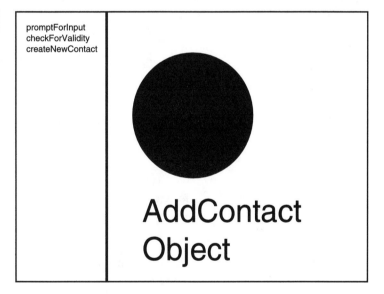

promptForInput
checkForValidity
createNewContact

AddContact Object

After the user has finished inputting the data and the Add button has been clicked, the information contained in the form is submitted to the AddContact object. The AddContact object in turn generates a Contact object.

FIGURE 2.5

*Using a form to
collect data.*

The form in figure 2.4 shows how the user can click the Add button
to transfer the information. In this application, the Add button serves
two purposes. First of all, it calls the checkForValidity() method
to ensure that the user has entered valid information (for example,
did the user leave the name fields blank); next, it calls the
createNewContact() method. Without delving into too much detail,
the createNewContact() method grabs all information from the
current fields and uses it to create a new Contact object.

To recap, the classes that have been developed so far do the
following:

1. Create new contacts.

2. Act as the contacts themselves.

3. Act as a global registry for all contacts.

   Having developed the above functionality, your contact
   book is almost complete. However, three rather important
   features still need to be implemented:

   ■ Deleting existing contacts

   ■ Displaying a list of all contacts

   ■ Saving the contacts to a file

Building the Interface

Now that the back end is shaping up, it is time to begin designing the front end. The front
end for this application comes in the form of the Display object, shown in figure 2.5.

Display is in charge of displaying on screen a list of all available entries in the contact book. Display is responsible for managing all user interaction, such as allowing the user to create and delete entries, saving the contact file to disk, and retrieving full information on a contact.

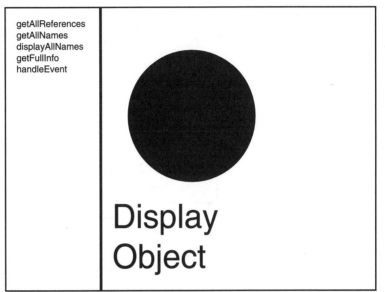

FIGURE 2.6

The Display object manages all user interaction.

getAllReferences
getAllNames
displayAllNames
getFullInfo
handleEvent

Display Object

The Display object functions by asking the Registry for a list of all registered contacts. After this information has been obtained, the values of each Contact object's firstName and lastName variables are displayed. The firstName and lastName fields are used again later in the program's execution as search criteria when a user wants to view a full information on a contact. The flowchart in figure 2.6 documents not only this process, but the entire flow of execution that the program exhibits.

The flowchart shows that the when the application begins, it streams in the contents of a file that contains all contact information. Information on each contact is parsed out of the file and used to create a series on Contact objects. As each Contact object is created, it registers itself with the Registry object. After the file is fully processed, the Display object is created and consequently creates an interface through which the user may interact with the application. At this time, the application basically stops and waits for input from the user. Figure 2.7 shows the application at this point.

FIGURE 2.7

A flowchart of the Contact Book application.

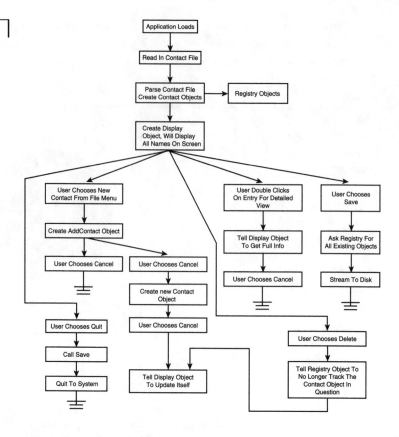

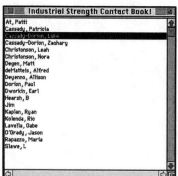

Now that display has been implemented, the only additional features that need implementation are the saving of the entire data to a file and the deletion of contacts from the contact book.

As shown in figure 2.6, the contact book saves data via the following steps:

1. The Registry object is asked for a list of all Contact objects.
2. The data from those Contact objects is written to a file.

When you look over the two steps for saving data and the steps taken when data needs to be displayed, the process used to delete a contact becomes obvious. If the Registry object does not have a contact object registered, then it cannot be accessed and, effectively, does not exist. Therefore, the steps to delete a Contact object are as follows:

1. Tell the Registry object not to track the object that needs to be deleted.
2. Redisplay the data contained in the Registry object.

Lines in Object diagrams often indicate inheritance. Here they are used to indicate object interaction.

For a final overview of the entire application, see figure 2.8, which uses cloud-like shapes to indicate the existence of all objects in the application. Objects that interact with each other have interconnecting lines. Instead of detailing all methods, only those that are of importance to the interaction between the objects are indicated.

FIGURE 2.9

An overview of the entire Contact Book application.

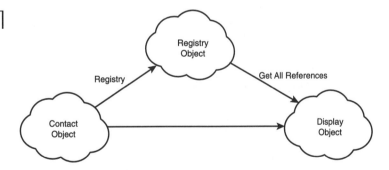

Summary

You have stepped through your first object-oriented application. Was it as bad as you thought it would be? As the book progresses, you will see how planning an application aids in the development process.

Code introduced throughout the book occurs in one of two formats. On one level, code snippets serve as quick teaching tools and as references after you are finished with the book. On a more advanced level, these examples help you to develop actual applications. The applications developed throughout this book are designed with the same level of detail provided for the contact book, except that in these cases you will actually code the application.

Chapter 3

Planning Your Application

This chapter covers the Java-specific issues of planning applications. Planning is often overlooked as a step in the design process. Planning should not be confused with design. *Design* is the mechanics of creating an application. *Planning* is how you decide what to design. Planning includes understanding the following:

What is needed? The problem domain and its requirements. Understanding these goals and priorities creates a framework that the application will be designed to meet.

What is possible? The technology mapped to the problem. What's "possible" is the technology at hand. Technology is the development environment, code libraries, and the staff creating the application. The technology is the context in which the design is built and the building blocks that are pulled from the shelf or designed from scratch.

What is easier? The easily implemented features, either by their nature or because of the technology. Understanding what is easy can be used to set priorities of easy functions early in a project to give the application the most utility as quickly as possible.

What is harder? Features requiring the most design and coding. By understanding what is hard, risks and the critical functions can be planned for.

These four basic questions, when understood for a particular application, can be used to create the design and implementation details required for programming the application. Not knowing the answers can lead to failure. For instance, not understanding requirements leads to creating the wrong application. Not knowing what is possible could lead to a design that is impossible. Not knowing what is easy can lead to doing what is hard while never implementing what could be easily implemented and in use far before the hard functions are ready.

Without thorough planning you may be faced with a great deal of functional, but ultimately useless, code. This chapter's purpose is to cover how to answer the questions and to put them into the context of Java programming techniques and limitations. The following subjects are covered:

1. Evaluate pre-development issues, which affect how you start designing, such as the problems and benefits of network based-computing.

2. Learn the mechanics of specific Java language features and how to use them to create better applications.

3. Discover how Java incorporates the object-oriented design model discussed in the previous chapter. Lots of code and Booch diagrams are included to help you visualize the object-oriented structure of Java.

4. Become knowledgeable about delivery issues such as ZIP files and the basic features of the Java Documentation utility.

This information not only helps you write better Java programs, but it can also help you complete successful applications.

Java, the Web, and Intranets: The New Programming Environment

Java brings us a new way of creating applications, although it is not quite a revolutionary leap forward. Nonetheless, Java represents a large step toward a better way of programming. Compared to C++, the previous language of choice for object-oriented programming, Java has many advantages:

C++: Pointer arithmetic is unsafe, with no bound checking or validation that pointers are accurate.

Java: No pointers or pointer arithmetic. References are used to access objects.

C++: Arrays in C++ are unsafe and code could run off the ends.

Java: Arrays cannot overflow without trapping.

C++: Complex syntax with C roots (for compatibility to legacy C code).

Java: Language designed from scratch. Syntax similar to C and C++ only to reduce the learning curve of existing programmers. Many rarely used C++ features removed to reduce language complexity.

C++: Casting is not validated.

Java: Casting between types is only valid between compatible types.

C++: Threads are implementation dependent and not part of the language.

Java: Threads are integrated into the language and into the Java VM.

C++: GUI is vendor or platform dependent.

Java: One GUI model for all platforms, the AWT.

C++: Libraries performing the similar functions are usually not standard between vendors.

Java: Popular libraries have standard APIs. APIs are used by all vendors.

Java may not double production time or eliminate bugs, but generally, experienced Java developers are more productive than C++ programmers. Java programmers don't need to worry about cleaning up memory or platform dependencies because Java has friendly features, including garbage collection, standard libraries, networking, multitasking, and cross-platform compatibility. Java also eliminates many common bugs, such as arrays going out of bounds and misbehaving pointers.

The Internet

The Internet has created a whole new way of thinking about software and users. Many of the changes have improved the delivery of software. Before the Internet, there was a long process that had to be executed before a program could reach users. Many of these tasks have been shortened or eliminated as the list below shows:

- Software can be delivered in minutes instead of days or weeks.
- New versions can be distributed to every user as they are released.
- Bug fixes can be delivered to all users immediately.
- No disks need to be copied.

- No packages need to be shipped.
- No manuals need to be printed.
- Inventory of old versions does not need to sell before releasing a newer version.

The networks have problems too. A new list of problems must be overcome. Network environments have a distinct disadvantage because communication is so quick and easy that new problems occur while classic problems become frequent occurrences.

- The cycle between new versions can be days or weeks rather than years. Users want the latest technology today, not tomorrow.
- The competition is on the same virtual shelf at the electric shopping mall. Marketing may be half of your development cost.
- Users may report bugs to everyone on the net. Damage and rumor control becomes an everyday occurrence.
- Users expect bugs to be fixed sooner. Even during holidays.
- The competition can watch every move you make—and counter them faster than ever before.

These challenges are difficult, but they can all be handled if you are aware that they are there. Plan to deal with them because they will eventually affect you. Unexpected problems can still be corrected.

The most important part of this new mode of business is user support. Customers have much more influence than ever before. Customers can complain to thousands of other customers and your potential customers, simply by posting a message to a news group or writing their experiences on their web page. There are also consumer-oriented web pages where individuals publish information about a range of products. The information that gets to the web depends on how well you satisify customers, both through good products and good support.

You must be very responsive to user problems. Your support also needs to be concerned with how customers are handled. The worst words a user support representative can ever use are "I don't know." Better ones are, "I don't know, but I'll find out and get back to you ASAP!" To do otherwise could quickly degrade customer loyalty and possibly generate bad press on the web.

Intranet Software

Intranets are like the Internet, except that an intranet network is comprised only of the interconnections within a corporation. Because the intranet is within the corporation, the network has access to corporate resource's databases, as well as much better network speeds than can be had through a 28.8 modem. The network can be made secure to the outside world, which is very important when secure data flows across the network.

Corporate intranets are usually made of different brands and models of computers. Each computer has its own software and sometimes dissimilar hardware features. In other words, corporate intranets are a mix of dissimilar computers. Because of the hardware mix, a mix of software is needed to run these machines, as well. This mass of software and hardware has become a large and expensive part of a corporation's operating budget.

The total cost for software in large corporations can be huge. The types of software include general office software, such as spreadsheets, editors, and scheduler tools. The rest of the software consists of specialized programs that are oriented specifically to the business. Such software is either created in-house or by other companies on contract. The software could be anything from petroleum-prospecting software used by oil companies to special planning software used by telephone companies. General business and specific industry or company software must be inexpensive to obtain or create, and inexpensive to maintain.

Unfortunately, because of multiple hardware platforms, software becomes expensive to maintain. The solution is a corporate intranet and software written in Java. Many companies have diverse networks of varying brands of hardware and operating systems. Using Java to write a single cross-platform application for every computer in the corporation greatly reduces in-house development costs. In addition, many in-house software programs are unavailable to users in other departments because of network incompatibility. Now, the intranet is used to bridge the gap. Using Java to write a single Java cross-platform application for every computer in the corporation can also greatly reduce in-house development costs.

Libraries

Software projects that used to take years to write are quickly becoming out-dated. Software can now be built by combining application-specific programming with generic libraries. Many truly generic functions have been implemented by libraries, reducing the time and work required to deliver complete applications. For instance, printing has long been a major effort of many software development organizations. Just making an application print on two different printers could be a significant stumbling block. Libraries and operating system services such as the Windows printing system now enables programmers to focus more energy on their specific applications.

At this time, a Java developer's access to libraries is just starting to multiply. Java cannot yet print in version 1.0, but third-party companies have implemented printing solutions for some specific platforms. Sun's 1.1 version of Java supports generic printing. Sun also is developing API specifications for industry standard libraries, such as database access and 3D graphics libraries. Some libraries, such as the Telephone Application Interface (TAPI) and multimedia libraries, have only recently come into use.

Because of the corporate commitment to Java, many companies are developing libraries that implement Sun's APIs as quickly as possible. Before developing a project, it is wise to survey the current state of these specifications and the libraries that are supplied by Sun and third-party developers. These libraries help reduce the total code developers have to design and write. For some applications, this could be the difference between a month of development with libraries and several years without.

Design Goals and Incremental Delivery

Determining exactly what you want your application to do and when you want to deliver it to customers are important design considerations. A source of problems that can affect delivery is the time wasted developing functions that the user does not need or are too inadequate to use. Preventing this mismatch by creating applications that users want and can use is accomplished with a design process called incremental delivery.

Incremental Delivery Design Model

Incremental delivery is a good way to both increase the success of an application and reduce development risks. Incremental delivery starts when a customer makes a specific request to a developer. Then the developer begins the design of a base application that will perform the minimum functions required. The user can then verify that the base meets everyone's expectations or give the developer information of the application's short-comings. This process continues with the addition of new features, each verified before the next is designed and built.

Compare the steps in classic top-down design in figure 3.1 to the steps of incremental delivery in figure 3.2. There are a few extra steps in incremental delivery, but an important difference between the two is the loop that feeds information from users testing back into the design. In top-down design the cycle, test, and redesign happens at the end of development. Top-down code is designed and written before a customer can see it. In the incremental delivery model, small, deliverable pieces are designed and delivered to users for testing and possible use. The steps of incremental delivery are shown in figure 3.2.

These two types of development are valid, but they have different outcomes. The incremental delivery approach is better because the feedback loop of design, development, and testing occurs multiple times, reducing the risk that an error was made in customer requirements or in how developers interpreted the requirements. Top-down only receives feedback after the design and development have been completed. You may need to modify or redesign a lot of code because mistakes made to the basic design can affect most of the code written. Incremental delivery proceeds in stages. Each stage creates a version of the application that has increased functionality. For example, an editor design would have dozens of functions targeted for the final design. The first incremental version would have just simple file I/O and primitive text editing. Version 2 would implement cut and paste. Version 3 would add font control. More versions are added until the application is considered complete. Each function is added to the base application and delivered to the user for testing or actual use.

The incremental delivery process is very accurate.The user is periodically validating the current state of the product. Users can determine quickly when a feature may be incorrect or not as originally envisioned. Developers benefit greatly from this process because each step is verified or fixed before development continues. Problems are fixed in code written in the past week instead of code that was written six months ago, as it would be with top-down design. Incremental design also prevents designers from creating extra functionality that may never be used. The user is always informed about what is going on so that only the user's immediate needs are implemented.

FIGURE 3.1

A top-down design cycle.

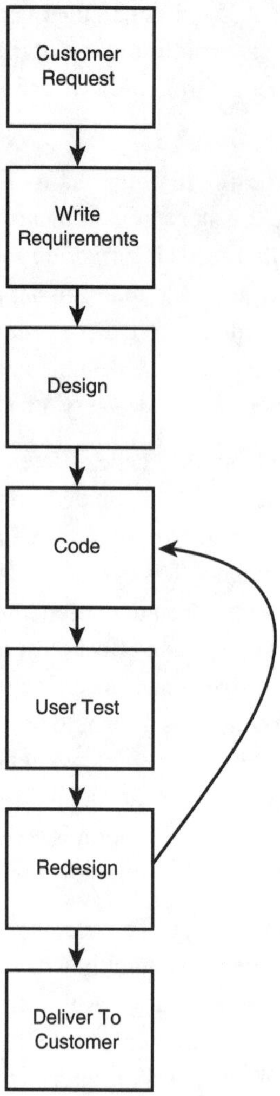

```
        ┌──────────────┐
        │  Customer    │
        │  Request     │
        └──────┬───────┘
               │
               ▼
        ┌──────────────┐
        │   Write      │
        │ Requirements │
        └──────┬───────┘
               │
               ▼
        ┌──────────────┐
        │   Design     │
        └──────┬───────┘
               │
               ▼
        ┌──────────────┐
        │    Code      │◄─────────┐
        └──────┬───────┘          │
               │                  │
               ▼                  │
        ┌──────────────┐          │
        │  User Test   │          │
        └──────┬───────┘          │
               │                  │
               ▼                  │
        ┌──────────────┐          │
        │  Redesign    │──────────┘
        └──────┬───────┘
               │
               ▼
        ┌──────────────┐
        │ Deliver To   │
        │ Customer     │
        └──────────────┘
```

This may seem like the user is completely in the driver's seat. This is somewhat true because, after all, the user is the customer who needs to be satisfied. Communication between developer and user is not unidirectional. The developer must also make sure that the user actually requires certain functions and uses them when they are supplied. The developer is responsible for knowing what is difficult or simple to design, too. The developer should work with the user to prove each solution is viable before it ever becomes part of the application.

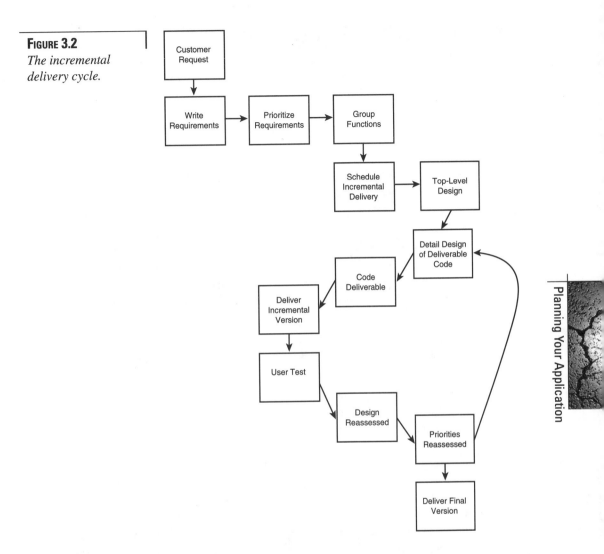

FIGURE 3.2

The incremental delivery cycle.

When the results of each stage of development are in use by users between each cycle, the developer can simply look to determine whether features are actually being used. Information about usage can be used as a measurement of how accurate the design is versus how it is used or if it is even required. Features that are not used can be removed so that maintenance can be avoided in the future. Removing unused functions also reduces documentation and training tasks. It is important to remember that the biggest of all bugs is unused software!

Identifying User Requirements

As features are developed, some may become more important than others, and some may prove to be unnecessary. A few simple steps help developers and customers create a specification of features and their importance. They help you to avoid useless functions and features, and as an added benefit, they help schedule incremental deliveries. This process also helps to loosen up reluctant customers who have difficulty defining their requirements.

1. List the major tasks requested by the customer.

2. Have the customer use this list to prioritize each feature and task (this helps to perform the next step).

3. Determine the core functions. These are the tasks that the customer *must* have in the first delivery. Be careful to distinguish between "nice to have" and "I cannot do my work without it." The first delivery should be as small as possible, but still be adequate. If it is too large, break the development into stages that the user can successfully verify as correct. This helps to ensure that you are still on the right track.

4. Write clear descriptions of every function. Include both the "must have" group and each of the lesser functions. Include their perceived complexity and probable design times along with the customer's specified judgments of importance.

5. Create a schedule of phased deliveries. Each phase can be as small as a single, testable function or a group of tightly coupled functions. Try to avoid delivery increments of greater than a month. The preferred delivery cycle is one to two weeks. Remember that the smaller the cycle, the lower the development risk. Having to throw away a week of work is far cheaper than losing two months.

At the end of this process, you should have enough information to begin an object-oriented analysis. The target model should be the only set of features designed in detail. Attempting to model the entire set of deliverable features could be a waste of time. The initial model should take into account key features that may affect future deliveries. Certain key classes may need to be designed from the start to ensure success later on.

For instance, an employee database may be designed to hold the name, address, and a picture of the employee. The code for loading the picture from the employee database is required. Code for displaying the picture of the employee can be added in a future version.

The first analysis should not attempt to make the first delivery overly generic. A program enabling additional functionality in the future sometimes takes much more time to produce. It may be more effective to simply rewrite small portions as the program evolves. The trap hidden in many plug-and-play features is that they usually limit the features to be added or grow too large because developers attempt to cover too many possibilities.

Java does have a way for developers to easily implement a simple plug-and-play interface. See the section "Dynamic Class Loading" later in this chapter.

Pick Your Environment

There are several Java runtime models that can be used to accomplish various tasks (see table 3.1). It is important to understand the details of these models because they each dramatically change the design of your application.

TABLE 3.1

Common Runtime Models

Application Model	Environment	Advantages	Disadvantages	Uses
Applet	Runs in applet or web browser.	Very secure. Loaded via browser.	Integrates with HTML content. Only one copy used by all users. No access to local resources. No read or write of local files. Reloaded on each use. Must have a browser to use.	Live content for HTML pages. Front end (client) for client server.
Windows	Class files loaded from the local file system are run in a Java VM. User interacts with the application with AWT windows and dialogs.	Access to local resources. Can use native methods to access hardware or integrate with non-Java applications.	Unsecured access to local resources. Users must have a local copy to use.	Can be used like any window application.

continues

TABLE 3.1

Continued

Application Model	Environment	Advantages	Disadvantages	Uses
Console	Class files loaded from the local file system are run in a Java VM. User interacts via command line prompts (if at all).	Access to local re-sources. Can use native methods to access hard-ware or integrate with non-Java applications.	Unsecured access to local resources. Users must have a local copy to use.	Used where user interaction is simple or unnecessary. Can be used as a server for client server applications.
Client/Server	One application, the server, runs on a host. The host controls access to information and resources. Another application, the client, interacts with the server to use and control information and resources.	Multiple lightweight clients can access resources on a single server, decreasing need for client-side resources. Server consolidates control of resources. Security access can be controlled by the server, limiting access to resource to a single, controllable point.	Client and server applications must be maintained. Server is a single point of failure for multiple users. Communication between client and server can be monitored.	Multiuser applications.

Application Model	Environment	Advantages	Disadvantages	Uses
Socket to Socket	Two applications that communicate and cooperate via sockets. Like client with communications via sockets. Applications can be on different computers and written in dissimilar languages.	Sockets are independent of hardware platform or computer language, allowing the mix of C/C++ with Java.	Server and client must both implement sockets.	Similar to client server. For instance, an Applet may communicate via sockets to a database server written in C++. Also used to bridge other languages to Java.

The Applet

Applets are a common way of writing Java applications. Integrating web-based sound and graphics into applications is simplified by using methods in the Applet class. Applets are essentially programs that run from within a web browser. They appear as a part of HTML documents in the same way that pictures are presented. The major difference is that instead of a static graphic, the Java applet is a complete running program. An applet is just like a window application, but without a classic window frame. The range of programs that can be written as an applet are reduced because of security limitations imposed by the target browser.

Applets only run from within Java-enabled browsers such as Netscape, Hot Java, and

FIGURE 3.3
Booch diagram of an applet.

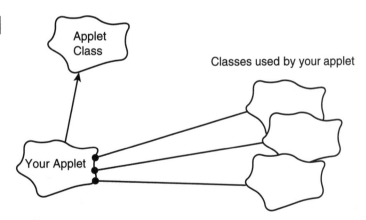

Applet Class

Classes used by your applet

Your Applet

Internet Explorer. This means that a user's machine must have a properly configured browser to execute Java applets. Because more users have these browsers, even within corporations, the number of potential users is growing quite large.

The Applet Class

In order for a Java program to be an applet, the starting class for the application must inherit from the Applet class. The Applet class is very useful because it contains methods that make accessing the Internet very easy. The following sections detail specific applet class methods of which you should be aware.

getDocumentBase()

The getDocumentBase() method retrieves the directory from which your applet was loaded. This could be on your local machine or an HTTP server. This function is used as a base point for opening streams, loading pictures with getImage(), or playing sounds with play(). From the document base, any subdirectory and file can be specified.

start(), stop(), and destroy()

These three methods are called when the applet starts, stops, or gets destroyed. If the applet needs to know when any of these actions occur, they must overload in the main class, and specific code must be added.

getParameter() and getParameterInfo()

These two methods provide access to the Applet parameter tags. This enables you to perform the equivalent of command-line options. The getParameter() method retrieves a specific parameter. getParameterInfo() returns an array of strings describing the parameters that are understood by this applet.

getImage()

The getImage() method loads a JPEG or GIF image that is displayable on the Applet's panel.

getDocumentBase()

The getDocumentBase() function is used to determine the base directory from which to load sounds and images. For applets loaded from an HTTP server, the document base is the root directory from which the applet is allowed to access. The applet cannot access directories below this point for security reasons. For example, an applet loaded from

/documents/myJava could load images from /documents/myJava/images but could not load any files from /documents/personal.

getAudioClip() and play()

These methods enable your applet to play sound files. GetAudiClip() loads a clip into an AudioClip class that can be played later. The play() method loads and plays in one step.

The Advantages of Applets

There are several advantages to using applets. The most obvious is that you only need one copy of your production class files on an HTML server. This reduces the nightmare of distributing and installing software by tape or disk. Internet and intranet-based software also reduces the problems of LAN access to software. Instead of accessing a disk by way of a network mounted disk (not always possible between departments or company divisions) files are accessed through HTTP and FTP.

Web pages can also be used as a method of presenting help to your users as well as keeping them informed about the latest changes to your programs. This enables you to keep in constant touch with your users.

The Disadvantages of Applets

Running your application from a web browser is not necessarily a good thing. Target users must be running a version of a web browser that supports Java. It also helps if users have an Internet connection of 28.8K or higher on relatively fast computers.

Another large problem is local file access. If the applet was loaded from an HTTP server, no local files can be read or written to on the client's machine. This can be alleviated by loading the applet from the user's local disk storage, but this defeats many of the web-based applet advantages mentioned earlier.

Applets have reduced network access. If an applet is loaded from a networked machine, only that machine can be communicated with via a socket connection. This prevents the applet from communicating to other machines on the web. This security restriction is alleviated if the applet is loaded from the user's local disk.

Applets may have reduced memory access. From within a web browser there may be a limitation on the memory space that applets are allowed to access. If the application uses a large amount of memory, developers must force users to modify options in their web browser before they can run the applet. Also some browsers may not support JVM memory environment changes, if it does at all.

Another, relatively new disadvantage of Java is the control over thread priority. The latest version of the Netscape Navigator 3.0b6 does not allow applets to change priority. Netscape created this security enhancement to prevent applets from changing priorities to a point where they take over the machine and prevent other functions from running.

Applets have a limited capability to communicate information to a host machine. Host communication is required for saving data or controlling host software. To currently achieve this, there must be cooperating software on the HTTP server. For more information on these options, refer to the section on client/server applications that follows.

Stand-Alone Java Applications

Java applications are similar to running an applet from within a web browser. Instead of running in a virtual machine supplied by the browser, the application executes in a stand-alone version of the Java VM. The application also is loaded from the local file system. Because it is assumed that users loaded the application to the local file system, there are fewer file and network security restrictions imposed.

An important advantage for large applications is that the memory space can be controlled. From the Java JVM you can control initial limits for the stack and heap. If your application uses a large amount of memory, you will have complete control of these settings.

Stand-alone applications must also provide their own connection to resources, such as pictures and sound. With applets, the connections are provided through the Applet class.

The other problem with windows applications is that they do not run from web browsers. As was discussed previously, the web browser reduces problems with delivering applications by making them available on HTTP servers.

It is possible to launch this type of application from an icon. You have the option of running with a console window or without. To launch with a console, use the standard Java VM. To launch without a console, use javaw.

Windows Applications

Windows applications are similar to running an applet from within a web browser. The main difference is that there are fewer file and network security restrictions. Stand-alone Windows applications must also provide their own connection to resources such as pictures and sound.

Windows applications can also contain menus. This makes a Java application behave like most other Windows-based programs (see fig. 3.4).

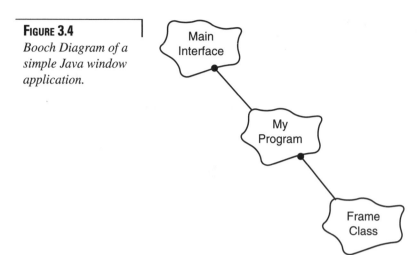

FIGURE 3.4
Booch Diagram of a simple Java window application.

There are two disadvantages to windows applications. The first problem is the windows themselves. Having a window on the screen may not be desired for some applications that require no user input or need to display status. Applications that only display simple text should be written as console applications.

Console Applications

Console applications are executed from the command line. No windows are opened and all communication to the user is accomplished with System methods, such as System.out.println() and System.in.readln(). Like a stand-alone application, console applications have few security restrictions placed on file or network access (see fig. 3.5).

FIGURE 3.5
Booch Diagram of a simple Java console application.

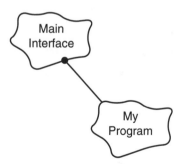

Client/Server Applications

A *client* is a program that uses another program (usually running on another machine) to perform functions. A *server*, simply defined, is a software application that performs functions at the behest of a client application. The goal is to centralize common data and tasks on the server, while client-specific data and functions are performed on the client's machine (see fig. 3.6).

FIGURE 3.6

Your basic client/ server Internet application flow chart.

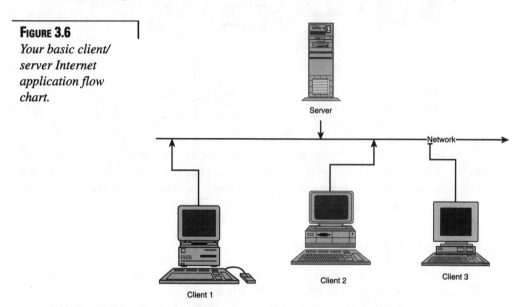

There are many different ways of implementing client/server applications. The following sections briefly describe most of the current alternatives.

Socket-to-Socket Applications

In the socket-to-socket model the client talks to the server via a socket stream. The server and client code can be written in any language that supports streams. This is discussed in detail in Chapter 9, "Input/Ouput: Using Streams."

Socket Communication from Java Clients to CGI on a Server

In this model, the client talks to the server via a socket stream on an HTTP server. The specific socket only communicates via the CGI protocol. CGI programs can be written in most languages and currently do most of the specific server-side functions for web sites. There are many CGI-based applications that already exist on many web sites. These CGI programs perform a variety of tasks, from database access to form input. Java can use CGI to communicate to a server to access files, databases, and other programs.

Servlets and Agents

Servlets are Java applications that run on an HTTP server. Servlets are similar to CGI applications, but they are cross-platform because of their Java environment. Servlets can essentially do all the work that is now done by CGI programs, including the generation of HTML text to browsers, form processing, and database access.

Servlets can also be sent from the client and run on the server. The client-to-server servlet model is often referred to as a software agent. Software *agents* are built by the client to accomplish tasks on multiple servers or to roam from server to server until a task is complete.

A good example of a software agent is a web crawler agent. The web crawler agent is sent to a HTTP server where it queries the local system for certain information held in HTML pages. After the information is found, the agent sends the information back to the client.

Software agents use less network bandwidth than simple HTTP queries and, unlike CGI, can be tailored by the client to perform client-specific processing. Unfortunately, software agents also require CPU and memory resources on the HTTP server.

The current way to run servlets is through JavaSoft's HTTP server, Jeeves. Jeeves performs the normal tasks of an HTTP server and additionally handles servlet management, security, and communications. There is also a public domain HTTP server called Jigsaw with similar features.

Common Object Request Broker Architecture (CORBA)

Java implements the Common Object Request Broker Architecture through the Java IDL API. The Java IDL system enables you to define remote interfaces in the interface definition language (IDL), which is an industry standard defined by the Object Management Group (OMG). CORBA is becoming more important as more companies release libraries of CORBA objects that can be used by developers.

CORBA lets a program pass data to a CORBA object on another machine as if it were just an object at the local machine. This client/server approach is at the object level rather than at an application level.

The mapping from IDL to Java is defined in the Java IDL language mapping specification defined by JavaSoft. The idlgen program, JavaSoft's IDL stub generator tool, is used to generate Java interface definitions and Java client and server stubs. Along with idlgen there is an IDL library used to access CORBA objects.

CORBA and IDL are best suited for Java applications that require access to CORBA objects. CORBA can also be used to interface distributed legacy applications to Java code.

Remote Method Invocation (RMI) and Object Serialization

The Remote Method Invocation API and the Object Serialization API are classes utilities and rules that allow a developer to create and access objects running on separate machines. This is similar to CORBA except that it is pure Java. It is also similar to the socket-to-socket model except that access is done by calling functions rather than encoding and decoding a data stream. RMI still uses a stream, but all of the encoding and decoding is done by serializing objects.

Using the RMI model, a client and a remote object interact with each other by sending serialized object data across a network. This type of client/server model should be relatively easy for Java developers to use.

RMI can be used in any application that communicates across a network to other Java applications. The RMI API is used in Jigsaw and Jeeves to control servlets.

Transmitter/Receiver (Castinet)

Castinet, from Marima, is a new distribution model that applies the transmitter and reciever concepts of radio and television to the distribution of software and data.

The *transmitter* is a Java application that runs on a server or multiple servers. It distributes Java applications to receivers on other machines via a network. *Receivers* are Java programs running on client machines that receive Java applications from transmitters. After an application is received, it is run localy in the Java VM. Each application is given access to its own file space but not to the entire machine, reducing security problems.

Each time a user runs an application, the version on the transmitter is checked to determine whether a new copy is available. If the user agrees, the new copy is downloaded to the client's machine.

This technology is important because it automates the distribution of software and data, which is very important due to the slow speeds and volatility of the World Wide Web.

In addition to transmitters and receivers, there are repeaters. A *repeater* is used to distribute applications and data from a source transmitter to another server. This secondary server becomes a transmitter of identical content of the original transmitter. This concept is similar to mirror sites. *Mirror sites* are used to reduce the bottleneck of muliple users attempting to access a single machine for content. The advantage of repeaters is that content is automatically updated.

The transmitter/receiver model supports distribution through a concept called *channels*, which are data or programs that a user tunes to with the reciever. For instance, the user tunes to the document editor to receive the program or to execute the local copy. To retrieve data, the user could tune to the stock exchange to receive either a summary of the day's events or live data feed.

Java Blocks: Classes, Interfaces, and Packages

Java uses classes, interfaces, and packages to organize a program's structure. Using these constructs, Java programs can be written in an object-oriented structure. The following sections show you how this is done and relate this structure to Booch method class notation. This section also expands the information covered in Chapter 2.

Classes

Classes are the basic building blocks of object-oriented programming with Java. A Java class can contain data or methods or both data and methods.

Inheritance

The following example designs chess pieces for a chess game, as illustrated in figure 3.7. Chess pieces are very easily represented as an inheritance tree.

The Piece class in the diagram has an "A" within an inverted triangle. This designates that Piece is an abstract class. The arrows drawn from the classes, such as Queen or Pawn, designate that they inherit from the class Piece. Arrows point to parent classes.

FIGURE 3.7

*A Booch diagram of
class inheritance
with a chess piece
model.*

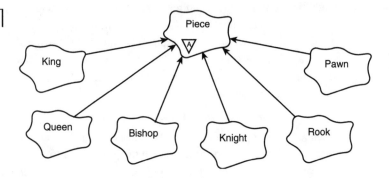

The lack of the abstract symbol on specific chess pieces, such as the Queen, designates that they are concrete classes.

The code in listing 3.1 shows the class specification for the class Piece. (The ➡ symbol indicates a line that would fit on the previous line were this a computer screen.) The listing was produced by the javap tool, which dumps information from a class file. The listing shows the public class definition that can be accessed by other classes. The javap class disassembler also prints the fully qualified names of classes used. In other words, the package that a type comes from is included.

Listing 3.1 The Piece Class, Public Definition

```java
public abstract class Piece extends java.lang.Object {
    private boolean captured;
    private java.awt.Color color;
    private int value;
    private int id;

    public abstract java.util.Vector
generateMoves(Board);

    public Piece(int,java.awt.Color,int);

    protected final boolean addMove
    ➥(java.util.Vector,Board,java.awt.Point,java.
    ➥awt.Point);

    public final boolean isMoveValid(Board,Move);
    public final int ID();
    public final void voidCapture();
    public final void setCaptured();
    public final boolean isCaptured();
    public final java.awt.Color getColor();
}
```

Notice that the generateMoves() method is abstract. Because of this one abstract method, the entire class becomes abstract and the compiler forces you to use the abstract modifier on the class, before it can be compiled.

The class also inherits from the java.lang.Object class. The javap disassembler added this information to the listing even though the class did not specify it. All classes inherit from java.lang.Object.

Another interesting method is addMove(). This method is used exclusively by child classes to perform part of the functionality of the generateMoves() method. Because it is exclusive to the child class, its access is set to protected private to make it only accessible from child classes.

Limiting access is done to prevent other classes not inheriting this class from calling the function. By being protected private, the Piece class specifies that the method is specific to the class and has nothing to do with any other class. Additionally, the addMove() method could depend on the current state of the object. This is very important in the Piece class because moves are added based on internal state.

The rest of the methods are public final, preventing these methods from becoming redefined by child classes. This is done as a precaution and to clarify the intent behind the design of the base class. By being final, it prevents programmers from inadvertently rewriting the method and changing its meaning. The intent that this is the "final" implementation also informs the programmer that there is no need to reimplement the method because its design is complete and its meaning will not change. These methods are used only to access private fields. Between the final modifier on these methods and the private modifiers used on the fields, you have effectively prevented any bugs from being created in the child classes by method overloading. This is probably overkill, but it costs very little to make this class hierarchy safer. Also, the use of the final modifier should enable the compiler to generate faster code (see the following discussion on final). Listing 3.2a shows the source code for class Piece.

Listing 3.2a   Piece Class: Imports, Class Definition and the Abstract Method generateMoves()

```
/** Piece.java
    This class is an abstract base class for chess pieces.
*/
import Move;
import Board;
import java.awt.Color;
import java.awt.Point;
import java.util.*;
public abstract class Piece{
    // Abstract function specific to each piece
    public abstract Vector generateMoves(Board board);
```

The constructor for the Piece class is implemented in listing 3.2b. This constructor does all the busy work that is required to set up basic information about a piece. A child class calls this method with the super() method call. Super, in the case of this constructor, would have the definition of void super(int id, Color color, int value);.

Listing 3.2b   Class Constructor for the Piece Class

```
public Piece(int id, Color color, int value){
        // Set up piece points and ID
        this.id = id;
        this.color = color;
        this.value = value;
        // Set default capture state
        captured = false;
    }
```

To help make the definition of this method easier to read, the names of the values passed into the method are the same as those used to define the private members of the class. The "this" is a reference to the current object, used to distinguish the difference between the fields in the method definition and those of the class.

Because "this" is a base class, it implicitly inherits from the java.lang.Object class, so this class has all additional methods that are not visible here. An implicit call to super() creates an Object class instance.

This function is used to lower the work load of generateMoves(). It checks to see whether the piece can be put at this position. If it is okay, then add it to a move vector and return true, else return false.

Listing 3.2c Piece Class: The Implementation for the addMove() Method

```
protected final boolean addMove(Vector moved,Board board,Point
➡from,Point to){
    Piece capturedPiece = board.getPiece(to);
    if (capturedPiece == null){
        moved.addElement(new Move(this,from,null,to));
    }else{
        if (capturedPiece.getColor() != color){
            //Capturing a piece
            moved.addElement(new Move(this,from,capturedPiece,to));
        }else{
            // Move was blocked by my own color
            return (false);
        }
    }
    return (false);
}
```

The isMoveValid() method, shown in listing 3.2d, is used to validate that a move is possible. This method would normally be used when a user moves a piece on the board, which is done by first generating a list of moves with generateMoves(), which creates a list of valid moves for the piece, given the context of the current board. The most important feature of this method is that it is a generic function that works for all types of chess pieces. By calling generateMoves(), an abstract method, you are guaranteed that the moves returned will be for the current class of piece. If the class was Pawn and extends the class Piece, and the program calls isMoveValid() for a pawn, this method will call the generateMoves() for the class Pawn.

Listing 3.2d   Piece Class: The Implementation for the isMoveValid() Method

```
public final boolean isMoveValid(Board board, Move move){
   // Check to see if we are moving this piece
   if (move.movedPiece.ID() != id){
      return(false);
   }
   // Generate a list of moves to check against
   Vector moves = generateMoves(board);
   for (Enumeration e = moves.elements() ; e.hasMoreElements() ;) {
      Move temp = (Move)e.nextElement();
      if (move.equals(temp)){
         return(true);
      }

   }
   // If we got here then there were no matching moves.
   return (false);

}
```

Many programmers not used to object-oriented programming find the concepts of such behavior quite perplexing. The key to understanding is to remember that the call to generateMoves() is actually seen as "this. generateMoves()." The "this" is a reference to the current object and its type, so the result is that the method belonging to the object is called.

The remaining implementations of the class are the accessor methods and the private fields that define the state of a Piece object.

Listing 3.2e   Piece Class: The Implementation for Public Accessor Methods and Private Data

```
public final int ID(){
         return(id);
   }

   public final void voidCapture(){
         captured = false;
   }

   public final void setCaptured(){
         captured = true;
   }
```

```
public final boolean isCaptured(){
        return(captured);
}

public final Color getColor(){
    return (color);
}
// private protected data
private  boolean captured; // true if captured
private  Color color; // Black or White piece color
private  int value; // Point value
private  int id; // ID of piece
}
```

To understand why the class Piece was created as an abstract base, observe the class definition in listing 3.3a for the Pawn class.

Listing 3.3a   Class Pawn: Imports, Class Definition, and Constructor

```
/** Pawn.java
    Implementation for a Pawn Piece.
*/
import Piece;
import Move;
import Board;
import java.awt.Color;
import java.awt.Point;
import java.util.*;
class Pawn extends Piece{
    Pawn(int id,Color color){
        super(id,color,15);
    }
```

Notice first that class Pawn extends class Piece. The "extends" keyword is used to show that the class on the left, Pawn, inherits the class on the right, Pawn. The word "extends" is used rather than "inherits" because, unlike biological inheritance, we will always be extending the functionality of the parent.

The constructor, as discussed earlier, calls super(), which is the constructor for the class Piece. The keyword "super" designates that the next superior class's constructor in the inheritance tree is to be called. In this example, the next super class is Piece. Remember that there are actually three classes in this class hierarchy. The first, and most base class, is java.lang.Object.

The abstract method generateMoves() is implemented in listing 3.3b. The method first determines what square it is on by asking the board for its position. A vector is next created in which to return moves, followed by the actual generation of the moves. The base class method addMove() is used to ensure that the move will be valid.

Listing 3.3b   Class Pawn: Imports, Class Definition, and Constructor

```
public Vector generateMoves(Board board){
    Point point = board.getPointForPiece(ID());
    // validate that piece was on board
    if (point == null){
        // Piece was not on board, escape!
        return null;
    }
    // Create a Vector to hold moves
    Vector vector = new Vector();
    Point tempMove;
    if (getColor() == Color.white){
        tempMove = new Point(point.x,point.y+1);
        addMove(vector,board,new Point(point.x,point.y),tempMove);
        tempMove = new Point(point.x+1,point.y+1);
        addMove(vector,board,new Point(point.x,point.y),tempMove);
        tempMove = new Point(point.x-1,point.y+1);
        addMove(vector,board,new Point(point.x,point.y),tempMove);
    }else{
        tempMove = new Point(point.x,point.y-1);
        addMove(vector,board,new Point(point.x,point.y),tempMove);
        tempMove = new Point(point.x+1,point.y-1);
        addMove(vector,board,new Point(point.x,point.y),tempMove);
        tempMove = new Point(point.x-1,point.y-1);
        addMove(vector,board,new Point(point.x,point.y),tempMove);
    }

    return vector;
    }
}
```

There is overall very little code in class Pawn. Pawn only needs a constructor and an implementation of the abstract class generateMoves(). Note that there is a lot of code saved by using the addMove() method from the base class.

This example features many advantages to the inheritance. First, common generic functions that work for any class inheriting from the base do not require reimplementing base functionality. Also, the benefit gained by addMove() when writing the generateMoves()

method greatly decreases the amount of code required. The definition of generateMoves() as an abstract method also means that any class inheriting from class Piece can be operated on generically, as seen by the use of the abstract method from within the isMoveValid() method.

Interfaces

Interfaces are Java's way of implementing safe multiple inheritance. Interfaces add pure abstract methods and constants to classes. The class must implement the abstract functions in the same way that a child class implements abstract functions of abstract classes. This is better than classic multiple inheritance because it avoids the common problem of name clashing and multiple copies of inherited base classes. It does this by treating the inheritance only as an interface and not as an implementation.

A class can have only one inherited class and any number of interface classes. Each interface implemented in a class enables it to cast as an object of that class. Once cast to the interface class, methods or constants within the interface definition can be used.

Interfaces are quite useful; they enable classes to communicate with each other as uniform classes. In other words, an interface can act as a class translator between different classes. The observer example that follows is a classic representation of this concept.

Bypassing Multiple Inheritance Problems

Multiple inheritance is often described as dangerous because multiple inheritance can make classes very complex, which is especially true with C++ because there is little control over which parts of classes are inherited. But there are other reasons. Inherited classes have multiple constructors and destructors, creating hard-to-follow sequences that affect the state of an object. Data in base classes can be similar or duplicated, making it confusing for a child class to use the data. There are ways to fix these problems in C++, but the designers of Java decided that they were not worth the trouble.

Just to prove that Java interfaces are better solutions, look at the following very nasty inheritance problem. This is an example of an employee information program. Notice that all the inheritance arrows for Project Consultant and for Temporary Secretary both end up eventually leading to the Employee class, despite the fact that they should only inherit from Temporary! There is also a problem with the Project Consultant and Director classes because each of these may only need certain parts of the Manager class. The Project consultant handles the project-side of management and the Director only handles the people-side of Manager.

The problem here is the visibility of multiple inherited classes, Employee and Temporary (see fig. 3.8). For example, Project Consultant has a copy of both the Employee class and the Temporary class, which means that the project consultant might have access to the employee insurance and retirement plan!

FIGURE 3.8

A C++ model of company employees.

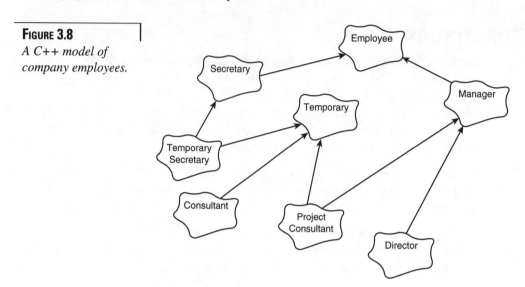

Unfortunately, this implementation happens to be perfectly valid in C++. Inexperienced programmers, when faced with this problem, may design it just this way (*or worse*).

This class structure is logically incorrect and needs to be rewritten. In fact, the same model can be implemented with pure abstract classes similar to the Java version below.

The Java solution is much cleaner, and the designer is forced into a particular structure because true multiple inheritance is impossible. In the Java example shown in figure 3.9, there is no way that a Project Consultant and a Temporary Secretary could become both a Temporary and an Employee. Also, the problems between Director and Project Manager are reduced because they only need to implement the Manager interface, and that implementation can be tailored as is required for each management type.

Multiple inheritance is a very useful metaphor in many programming problems; however, as was demonstrated, C++ could be easily abused, creating more problems than it was worth. The designers of the Java language saw that the only safe method for multiple inheritance was to limit the programmer to inherit one regular class and multiple pure abstract classes, which are now known as interfaces. Interfaces have become an important part of the Java language. They make several programming problems easy to understand and develop.

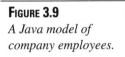

FIGURE 3.9
A Java model of company employees.

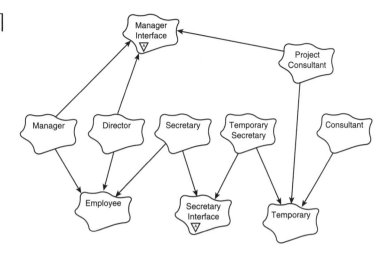

Decoupling Classes

Interfaces can also be used to decouple classes from their environments (see fig. 3.10). For instance, a class of Employee can use an interface called Database. The Database interface contains a method called getNextEmployee() that returns employee information. The getNextEmployee() method can be implemented by the OracleDatabase class or FlatFileDatabase class or even an EmployeeDialog class. The Employee class does not care which other class is doing the work—it just calls the supplied object's method and uses the results.

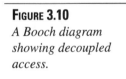

FIGURE 3.10
A Booch diagram showing decoupled access.

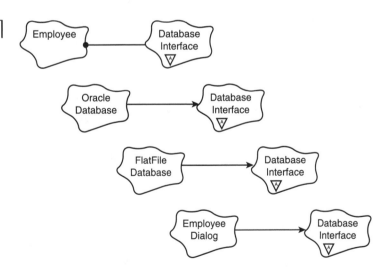

The Myth of Mixed Inheritance (Making Pigs Fly)

Genetic inheritance is often used to describe object-oriented programming. In Chapter 2, human inheritance was used to explain some of these very concepts. However, genetic inheritance is often used inappropriately. To understand why and to show by example what can happen, the example of crossing a pig with a bird is discussed. First, you need a quick review of high school biology.

Genetic inheritance is accomplished when an egg and sperm, each carrying one half of a strand of DNA, are integrated and (soon) form the first cell of a new individual. The halves, representing the list of attributes that make up the individual, are combined, creating a "list" of instructions that are used to build the animal. The instructions on the chromosomes are position-dependent, and each of the chromosomes contains different codes. The cell contains the machinery needed to read the instructions encoded in the DNA, and a factory needed to produce more cells and chemicals that create the individual.

Now to the example of mating a pig with a bird. Nature does not allow these two very different species to produce offspring. Exactly why not is a mystery, but there are many clues. The most obvious reason is the integration of the DNA to create the offspring.

The sequencing and positioning of the instructions is very dependent on the species. Many are identical. For instance, instructions for building cells that make up bones, skin,and organs are almost identical. But, in the case of wings and feathers of a bird, there is no clear position that can be used to replace some of the parts of the pig with those of the bird. Some sequences that describe wings and other features, such as hollow bones and feathers, are possibly in areas of a pig's DNA that may describe its legs or curly tail. Even if they were in the same place, they probably do not take up the same amount of information on the chromosome. Because of the position dependence of the chromosome data, mixing a pig with a bird would create some very unpredictable results.

For example, if the DNA data were represented as the names of the parts, you could see where a problem might occur. In the following example, the positions are the same for the heart and lung, but the remaining part of the string have different lengths, so were they to be mixed, the information would become almost random.

Bird DNA string:	Heart|Lung|Wings|Feather|Beak
Pig DNA string:	Heart|Lung|Leg|Skin|Tail|Hair
Bird/Pig:	Heart|Lung|Win|skfeather|Beak

The resulting "birdpig" would have a heart, lung, and beak, but the legs, skin, and tail of the pig would be randomly mixed with the wings and feathers of the bird. The probability of a flying pig from this combination is quite low.

Comparing this type of mixed species inheritance is impossible to do. If there were a class Bird and a class Pig, with the combination designated as a class of FlyingPig, it would become a class with an identity crisis. For instance, the FlyingPig would have a snout and a beak, four stubby pig legs and an extra pair of clawed feet, a brain that knows how to fly, and a brain that likes to rut in the mud. The FlyingPig class could isolate or replace certain methods to create a reasonable flying pig, but that could entail a lot of work.

The alternative is to evolve a pig into a flying pig. This is much closer to the genetic inheritance model. In normal inheritance, children are like their inheritance with only slight differences and possibly mutations. This means you use mutation to create a pig that has a set of wings. In programming terms, you simply create a flying pig class that inherets from pig, which adds a new method called fly().

Simply adding a fly() method is the simplistic answer. A more useful way of creating the new FlyingPig class is to implement a Flyer interface. The interface has the method fly(), which the class implements. The reason for the interface becomes obvious if the FlyingPig and the Bird class are used in the same program. In this case, the Bird class would also implement the Flyer interface. Now both animals can be operated on as class of Flyer.

The Java Interface model, in contrast to inheritance, is more like a learned behavior. By implementing specific interfaces, a class can interact via the interface methods and its specifically programmed (learned) behavior.

Interfaces are also decoupling. In other words, if a pig implemented the interface Flyer, the users of the Flyer interface would never realize that they were making a pig fly. The class only expects that when the Flyer.fly() method is called, it flies, just not very far in the case of our pig.

More Multiple Inheritance: Simple Observer

This next example uses an interface called DataChanged. It is an Observer interface. Observers are used to notify interested classes of data changes in one class without physically knowing about that class's specific implementation. The observer model is often used to integrate a class with a GUI representation of its state.

The DataChanged interface is implemented by the NameLabel class. The Name class uses an object of the NameLabel class as a cast to DataChanged. This method of sharing of information allows the Name class to treat the NameLabel class as a DataChanged class. What has been accomplished is that the Name class does not require access to any methods of the NameLabel class! This is sometimes called decoupling. *Decoupling* classes reduces interdependencies between classes, making them less susceptible to design changes. For instance, if either NameLabel or Name changes anything about the way that their classes are designed, as long as the DataChanged Interface is implemented, the two classes will not change their behavior with respect to the DataChanged behavior.

In figure 3.11, you can see the decoupling of the Name and NameLabel classes. Both classes use the DataChanged interface. The NameLabel class implements it, whereas DataChanged interface is a member of the Name class. The code that makes this all work is in the SimpleObserver class, which connects the NameLabel to Name by setting the DataChanged member of Name with the NameLabel object cast as a DataChanged type. These classes are defined in listing 3.4.

A simple example of these classes's use is also described so that the relationships can be understood. Listing 3.4 is the DataChanged interface. It defines an abstract method dataChanged(), which takes a string as an argument. This function will be called by the originator of data and be a part of the observer's implementation.

Listing 3.4   Name Class: Imports, Class Definition, and Constructors

```
interface DataChanged{
    void dataChanged(String newData);
}
```

FIGURE 3.11
A Booch diagram for a simple observer example.

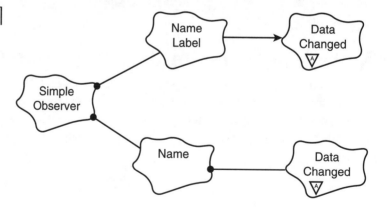

Listing 3.5a is the beginning of the Name class. This class extends the java.awt.TextField class. In this section of the class listing, one of the constructors for the TextField is implemented so that an object can be created. There is also a field defined as "observer," which is a DataChanged interface type.

Listing 3.5a   Name Class: Imports, Class Definition, and Constructors

```
/** Name.java
    * Name widget that informs a DataChanged observer
    of the current contents after each key press.
*/
import DataChanged;
import java.awt.*;
class Name extends TextField{
    DataChanged observer;
public Name(int columns){
        super(columns);

}
```

Listing 3.5b defines a method that will set the DataChanged observer. After this method is called, setting the interested observer the next time a character is typed causes the observer to be called with the current contents of this text field.

Listing 3.5b   Name Class: The setObserver() Method

```
void setObserver(DataChanged observer){
        this.observer = observer;
    }
```

Listing 3.5c shows the handleEvent() method, which is waiting for a key release event. If one occurs and the observer is not null, then the observer is called with the current contents of the string. Because this is the end of listing 3.5, notice that there has been no mention of what the observer is. All this class is associated with is the DataChanged interface, which is treated as an object. Any class that implemented the DataChanged interface could have been passed in the setObserver() method.

Planning Your Application

Listing 3.5c   Name Class: The handleEvent() Method

```
public boolean handleEvent(Event event) {
    if (event.id == Event.KEY_RELEASE &&
        event.target == this &&
        observer != null) {
            observer.dataChanged(getText());
    }
    return super.handleEvent(event);
}
}
```

The NameLabel class in listings 3.6a and 3.6b is the observer in this example. The class definition in 3.6a shows that the class extends the java.awt.Label class so that it can represent the observed data as a label on a window. The class also implements the DataChanged interface.

Listing 3.6a   NameLabel Class: Imports, Class Definition, and Constructors

```
import DataChanged;
import java.awt.*;
class NameLabel extends Label implements DataChanged{
    public NameLabel(String contents){
        super(contents);
    }
}
```

The final method in this class is the implementation of the DataChanged.dataChanged() method. The method sets the current displayed contents to the value of the string parameter newData. Again, decoupling is evident because the class does not have any reference to the data source. The class only has a method that can be used by any data source.

Listing 3.6b   NameLabel Class: The dataChanged() Method

```
/** Called by class Name when its contents are updated */
public void dataChanged(String newData){
    setText(newData);
}
}
```

The next class is an extension of the Frame class for use as the main window of an application. It is the thrust of this example and has both the Name and NameLabel classes.

The final connection of the observer to the data source takes place after an instance of Name class is created. The setObserver() method is called, with the instance of NameLabel cast as DataChanged. This finally couples the observer to the observed.

Listing 3.7a   SimpleObserver Class: Imports, Class Definition, and Constructors

```java
import Name;
import NameLabel;
import DataChanged;
import java.awt.*;

public class SimpleObserver extends Frame {

    public SimpleObserver() {

        super("SimpleObserver window");

        setLayout(null);
        addNotify();
            resize(insets().left + insets().right + 348, insets().top +
            ➡insets().bottom + 164);
            label2=new Label("Simple Observer Demonstration",
            ➡Label.CENTER);
            add(label2);
            label2.reshape(insets().left + 44,insets().top + 10,250,16);

    // Label that observed Name field

            nameLabel=new NameLabel("");
        add(nameLabel);
            nameLabel.reshape(insets().left + 12,insets().top +
            ➡42,318,26);

    // Name field that talks to the label

        nameField=new Name(39);

    // NameLable connected to nameField
        nameField.setObserver((DataChanged)nameLabel);

        add(nameField);

            nameField.reshape(insets().left + 6,insets().top +
            ➡81,324,26);

        show();
    }
```

Listings 3.7b through 3.7e have the remaining code that completes the example by implementing the remaining methods needed by the frame class. The show() method moves the display to 50,50 and causes the frame to appear.

Listing 3.7b   SimpleObserver Class: The show() method

```
public synchronized void show() {
        move(50, 50);
        super.show();
}
```

The method handleEvent() traps the WINDOW_DESTROY event to close the frame.

Listing 3.7c   SimpleObserver Class: The handleEvent() Method

```
public boolean handleEvent(Event event) {
        if (event.id == Event.WINDOW_DESTROY) {
            hide();              // hide the Frame
            dispose();           // tell windowing system to free resources
            System.exit(0); // exit
            return true;
        }
        return super.handleEvent(event);
}
```

The main() method is called when the class is run.

Listing 3.7d   SimpleObserver Class: The main() Method

```
public static void main(String args[]) {
        new SimpleObserver();
}
```

Listing 3.7e   SimpleObserver Class: Field Definitions

```
        Label label2;
        NameLabel nameLabel;
        Name nameField;
}
```

Packages

Packages are used to group several interacting or similar classes into a single logical unit. Packages are used for several reasons. The first is for ensuring unique name spaces. The package name is prefixed to the class names in the package in order to form a unique sequence of characters. This prevents name collisions when two different collections of classes have identical names.

Name Collision Avoidance

The possibility of name collision becomes obvious when you imagine that you are writing an application that would design houses. Because this would be a window application, you use the AWT package. As part of a house designer, you need to create several classes that will be used to form the pieces of the house. Some of these classes, such as Door, Roof, and Bathroom, will not cause any problems. Other classes, however, will have the same names as those found in the AWT. Classes such as Frame, Window, and Button (a base class for lights and doorbells) can cause the compiler to generate errors because of name duplication.

Packages solve the house problem because the package java.awt holds the AWT classes, thus making them unique and not confusable with the classes in the house designer application. When the classes that are from the AWT and the house designer are used in the same class, the package name can be added to the AWT classes to prevent name collision.

For instance, in listing 3.8, the house Window class is used in the DisplayHouse class. Additionaly, because DisplayHouse is used to render the house in an AWT window, the java.awt.Window class must also be used.

The class will compile correctly because the Window class is fully qualified by prefixing AWT's package name to the Window class name.

Listing 3.8   DisplayHouse Class: Field Definitions

```
import java.awt.*;
import Window;
class DisplayHouse{
    DisplayHouse(java.awt.Frame frame){
        Window frontWindow = new Window();
        java.awt.Window displayWindow = new  java.awt.Window(frame);
    }
}
```

Package Name Conventions

Name collisions can happen between code libraries or even major sections of your own code. When any group of classes can be placed in a logical grouping or are to be delivered to other users as utilities, they should be placed in packages. This prevents problems that occur when other utility classes are used or when new code is written that has the same name for classes.

Because packages should be used to prevent collisions, the package names themselves need to be free from ambiguity. The standard is to prefix your company's Internet domain name, followed by the name for the group of classes. If, for instance, your company's domain was cluck.com and the package was serialToolbox, the full package name should be cluck.com.serialToolbox. Because domain names are somewhat unique, the probability that anyone will have the same name is quite low.

If you are part of a major corporation, there could be a problem with many programmers developing packages. To prevent problems, the group name or project name can be added to the package name. What if there were a Macintosh team and a Sun team developing serialToolBox packages? The package names could become cluck.com.mac.serialToolbox and cluck.com.sun.serialToolbox.

Visibility Control

Another reason to package groups of classes is to hide classes and methods that only interact within a group of classes and that should not be accessed outside of the group. This is useful when there are many classes that make up a system but only a few that are accessed by other classes. Programmers only see some of the classes and methods when they use them, preventing them from using inappropriate classes and reducing the need to understand a complete package beyond its visible members.

For example, imagine that part of the house designer consists of a group of classes that could be used to make up the structure of the house frame. These functions would include calculations for determining where structural members would be placed and the amount of material required. The actual interface to this group of functions would specify only the layout of the house, then ask for the blueprint and list of materials. Exposing the classes that make the calculations would make the package appear more complex than it is. Because the package would be used to hide all the calculation details, only the simpler interaction of specifying the layout and printing information is required. This helps reduce to just one simple class the amount of documentation and training that is required to use a potentially complex system.

The default visibility of a package is protected. Classes in a package can interact with any method or field in any other class in the same package, unless it has been specifically modified to be private. Foreign classes—those not in the same package—can only access classes, methods, and fields that are specifically labeled public.

The following code example shows how packages protect unmodified classes, while being accessible to classes within the same package. The main() method can only access ClassA1 and ClassA2 because they were specifically declared public. The publicMethod() in each of these classes is also visible to main(), but the defaultMethod() is not accessible.

From within the packages the defaultMethod() methods are visible and can be executed. This method is used to attempt calling the other methods in each class in the example. The code that has been commented out are methods that would fail because the methods they are attempting to access are invisible from their class.

Listing 3.9 shows the ClassA1 class of package1. The class has a public method called publicMethod(), which is visible to all classes in all packages. The method creates an instance of ClassA2 and calls its defaultMethod().

Listing 3.9   The Class package1.ClassA1

```
/** ClassA1.java
*/
package package1;
// public class modifier
public class ClassA1{
    public void publicMethod(){
        System.out.println("package1.ClassA1: This is a public method");
        ClassB1 b1 = new ClassB1(); // class visible within package
        b1.defaultMethod(); // method visible within package
    }
    void defaultMethod(){
        System.out.println("package1.ClassA1: This is a default
        ➥method");
    }
}
```

Listing 3.10 shows the ClassB1 class of package1. The class has a public method, publicMethod(), which is visible to all classes in all packages. The method creates an instance of ClassB2 and calls its defaultMethod(). Like the default method in ClassA1, the defaultMethod() in this class prints a string to the console acknowledging that it was called.

Listing 3.10   The Class package1.ClassB1

```
/** ClassB1.java
*/
package package1;
// default class modifier
class ClassB1{
    public void publicMethod(){
        System.out.println("package1.ClassB1: This is a public method");
        ClassA1 a1 = new ClassA1(); // class visible within package
        a1.defaultMethod(); // method visible within package
    }
    void defaultMethod(){
        System.out.println("package1.ClassB1: This is a default
method");
    }

}
```

The classes in listings 3.11 and 3.12 are almost identical to those of 3.9 and 3.10. The only differences are in the names of the classes and the fact that they only attempt to call the defaultMethod() of classes within package2.

Listing 3.11   The Class package2.ClassA2

```
/** ClassA2
*/
package package2;
// public class modifier
public class ClassA2{
    public void publicMethod(){
        System.out.println("package2.ClassB2: This is a public method");
        ClassB2 b2 = new ClassB2(); // class visible within package
        b2.defaultMethod(); // method visible within package
    }
    void defaultMethod(){
        System.out.println("package2.ClassB2: This is a default
method");
    }
}
```

Listing 3.12   The Class package2.ClassB2

```
package package2;
/** ClassB2
*/
// default class modifier
class ClassB2{
    public void publicMethod(){
        System.out.println("package2.ClassB2: This is a public method");
        ClassA2 a2 = new ClassA2(); // class visible within package
        a2.defaultMethod(); // method visible within package
    }
    void defaultMethod(){
        System.out.println("package2.ClassB2: This is a default
method");
    }

}
```

In listing 3.13, the testing is done to prove that the visibility is correct, and the proper information about the method call sequence is printed by each method called. When this method was first compiled, the code line that attempted to call defaultMethod() of each of the packaged classes failed. They were commented in order to compile the final application.

Listing 3.13   The Class pkg_test: Tests Java Package Visibility

```
/** pkg_test.java
*/
import package1.*;
import package2.*;
import java.awt.*;
import java.io.IOException;

public class pkg_test {

    public static void main(String args[]) {
        System.out.println("package test");
        System.out.println("");

        ClassA1 pA1 = new ClassA1();
        //ClassB1 pB1 = new ClassB1(); - not visible to this class
```

continues

Listing 3.13   Continued

```
        ClassA2 pA2 = new ClassA2();
        //ClassB2 pB2 = new ClassB2(); - not visible to this class
        pA1.publicMethod();
        //pA1.defaultMethod();- not visible to this class
        pA2.publicMethod();
        //pA2.defaultMethod();- not visible to this class

        System.out.println("");
        System.out.println("(press Enter to exit)");
        try {
            System.in.read();
        } catch (IOException e) {
            return;
        }
    }
}
```

Directory Structure

Packages are stored in directories that have the same name and case as the package. Packages are searched from the base of each class path directory. For example, the code in listing 3.9 through 3.13 was stored as follows:

Listing 3.14   A Directory Listing Showing File Locations of Packages

```
d:\java\industrial\pkg_test\    <- root directory of the application
d:\java\industrial\pkg_test\pkg_test.class
d:\java\industrial\pkg_test\package1\ClassA1.class
d:\java\industrial\pkg_test\package1\ClassB1.class
d:\java\industrial\pkg_test\package2\ClassA2.class
d:\java\industrial\pkg_test\package2\ClassB2.class
```

From the application root directory, two additional directories make up each of the two packages that were compiled. The class files of each of these packages were stored by the compiler into their respective directories. Because the application was executed from the pkg_test directory, the Java VM searched the tree for the package1 and package2 directories when imports of the packages were made inside of the pkg_test.class file. If the package1 and package2 packages were used by an application in another directory, the CLASSPATH environment variable would need to have the directory d:\java\industrial-\pkg_test\ appended to the existing path string.

Dynamic Class Loading

Dynamic class loading enables a new object of a class to be instantiated from object code that was not specified when the program was first compiled. This becomes useful for several software constructs, like object persistence or plug-and-play libraries. The class creating the new object will still need to have a way of casting the new objects to a class where the interface is understood. The minimum functionality is a class of Object. This enables you to load any public class and perform the same functions that can be done on any object class.

Loading a class dynamically can be a powerful tool to create versatile programs. A good example why a class would be loaded at runtime is a graphics editor that supports differing image formats that can be purchased separately. The code to read and write the formats would be supplied as class files. In this model, the editor would know about the base class of these new classes and the interfaces that they support. When the graphics editor requires a specific format, the class loader loads a copy of the class by name. Once in memory, new instances can be created from the class.

Normally, use this facility with a useful base class that a group of classes extends or with classes that implement specific interfaces.

There are a few restrictions to the types of classes that can be loaded:

- The class must have at least one constructor that requires no arguments.
- The class must be accessible to the class that loads it.

The code in listing 3.15a dynamically loads two classes, creates an object of that class, and prints Object and Class information.

Listing 3.15a   The Class ClassLoad: Imports, Class Definition, and the main() Method

```
import java.awt.*;
import java.io.IOException;

public class ClassLoad {

    public static void main(String args[]) {
        new ClassLoad();
    }
}
```

Listing 3.15b defines the ClassLoad class contructor to run a test.

Listing 3.15b   The Class ClassLoad

```
ClassLoad(){
    try{
        System.out.println("demonstration of class load.");
        System.out.println();
        System.out.println("Creating an object of Foo");
        Object foo = getObjectOfClass("Foo");
        objectAnalyze(foo);
        System.out.println();
        System.out.println("Creating an object of Bar");
        Object bar = getObjectOfClass("Bar");
        objectAnalyze(bar);
        System.out.println();
        System.out.println("(press Enter to exit)");
    } catch(Exception ex){
        System.out.println("Class load failed.");
    }

    try {
        System.in.read();
    } catch (IOException e) {
        return;
    }
}
```

Listing 3.15c defines the helper function getObjectOfClass() used for loading classes.

Listing 3.15c   The Class ClassLoad

```
public Object getObjectOfClass(String className)
    throws IOException
{
    Object anObject;
    try{
        Class aClass = Class.forName(className);
        anObject = aClass.newInstance();
    } catch(Exception ex){
        throw new IOException(ex.toString());
    }

    return anObject;
}
```

Listing 3.15d defines the objectAnalyze() method that demonstrates available class information.

Listing 3.15d   The Class ClassLoad

```
// Prints information about an object
void objectAnalyze(Object target){
    System.out.println("Name: "+target.getClass().getName());
    System.out.println("Super Class:"+target.getClass().
    ➥getSuperclass());
    System.out.println("isInterface():"+target.getClass().
    ➥isInterface());
    //Get any implemented interfaces
    Class interfaces[] = target.getClass().getInterfaces();
    //Print interface names if they exist
    if (interfaces.length != 0){
        for ( int  i=0 ; i < interfaces.length ;  i++  ){
            System.out.println("ImplementsInterface:"+interfaces[i].
            ➥getName());
        }
    }
    System.out.println("Objet.hashCode():"+target.hashCode());
    System.out.println("Objet.toString():"+target.toString());
}

}
```

Listing 3.16 defines the PlugInterface interface.

Listing 3.16   PlugInterface Interface

```
interface PlugInterface{
    void plug();
}
```

Listing 3.17 defines the SocketInterface interface.

Listing 3.17   SocketInterface Interface

```
interface SocketInterface{
    void socket();
}
```

Listing 3.18 defines the test class, Foo, that extends a base class and implements interfaces.

Listing 3.18   Class Foo

```
class Foo extends Bar implements PlugInterface, SocketInterface{
    Foo(){// Contructor with no arguments
        super();
    }
    public String toString(){
        return("this is an object of class Foo saying hello!");
    }
    // Interface implementations.
    public void plug(){}
    public void socket(){}
}
```

Listing 3.19 defines the base class, Bar.

Listing 3.19   Class Bar

```
class Bar{
    Bar(){}// Contructor with no arguments
    public String toString(){
        return("this is an object of class Bar saying hello!");
    }
}
```

Access Modifiers

There is a lot of power in the different ways that classes can be defined. If you are moving from another language to Java, you may not initially realize the reasoning behind many of these language features. They may seem limiting to some programmers, but they are intended to create robust and easily maintainable programs. Many of the language's features prevent mistakes that may be made by teams of programmers and users of code libraries. Whether you use these access modifiers or not, they are still worth learning because Sun's libraries and others use these constructs. Table 3.2 summarizes them.

	Access Modifier	Type	Description
TABLE 3.2 **Access Modifiers**	"none"	Access Modifier	Package classes have access to member
	public	Access Modifier	All classes have access
	Private	Access Modifier	Only the class has access
	protected	Access Modifier	Package, class, and child classes have access
	private protected	Access Modifier	Class and child classes have access
	abstract	Declaration	Defines class or methods as abstract
	static	Declaration	Defines methods or fields as the only instance in a class
	final	Declaration	Defines class, method, or field as the final definition in a class tree
	volatile	Declaration	Marks a field for special handling
	transient	Declaration	Marks a field as non-serializable

"none" (Also Called Package)

The default method modifier is "package." Classes in the same package can access any method or field that is not explicitly restricted to private. This default is similar to "friend" in C++. None is the default because it makes it easy to write collections of interdependent classes without resorting to adding access modifiers, except to make some classes and members public. This is simpler than the C++ default, which is private.

It is important to remember that any class that is not in a package becomes part of the default package. Unless you explicitly declare a method private, it will be visible to all other package-less classes.

If a future application is grouped into packages, it is best to do it from the very beginning. This ensures that all your code tests these functions for visibility from the start of the development process.

public

The public modifier causes a class method or field to be visible to any other class in an application regardless of package membership. Only use public for methods that are meant to be called by classes outside of packages.

private

This is the most restrictive modifier. It absolutely bars access to methods and fields in a class. This prevents client or child classes from inappropriately accessing a class's internal data and methods.

It is good practice to make all data and methods private until it is an absolute certainty that another class will require it.

protected

Protected members are accessible by child classes and by classes in the same package. The types of methods that have this modifier should be those that are utilities used by the public interface. For example, a package that implements a text editor would have its classes for manipulating the class as public, but the classes that do the actual drawing of the text on a panel would be protected. These protected classes could be inherited from the user to add new implementations such as adding languages like French or Chinese.

private protected

Private protected methods and fields are accessible by child classes. Fields and methods that are only used within the class and necessary for child classes should be declared private protected.

In the chess piece example, the base class Piece contains a method called addMove(), which is used by all child classes to perform some of the actions required in the abstract method generateMoves(). There is no reason for addMove() to be accessed by any other class in the chess package or the rest of the program. This protection ensures that another class will not use it out of context of its intended function. Marking the method in this way also documents the fact that it is used by creators of child classes. Your knowing this helps programmers design to the intent specified for children of the class.

abstract

An abstract method is a method definition without a body. The class cannot be initialized. The class must be subclassed with all abstract methods overloaded with non-abstract functions. Methods in interfaces are defaulted to abstract.

The abstract method was used earlier in the chapter in the chess piece example. Listing 3.20 shows some code from that example. Notice that the class is labeled as abstract, as well as the generateMoves() method. If any method is marked as abstract, the class must also be marked as abstract. This helps document the class.

Listing 3.20   Class Piece Showing the Abstract() Method

```
public abstract class Piece{
    // Abstract function specific to each piece
    public abstract Vector generateMoves(Board board);

        ...

}
```

As mentioned in the chess piece example, abstract methods are used to define common interfaces to classes without defining their implementations. Abstract classes are used when the base class method has no meaning. For instance, the base class of Piece cannot have an implementation because it only represents the concept of a generic piece and not a real piece. After the piece is subclassed, as a King for example, the information for movement is implemented in the generateMoves() method.

Abstract methods also help to enforce proper implementation of child classes. Abstract methods "must" be implemented, so the programmer cannot depend on a default method to handle the new instance. This was important in the chess example because all pieces move differently and no default is possible or allowed.

static

Static methods and fields are accessible as a class and do not depend on an object of the class being initialized. A good example of a static method is the main() method that starts all console and window application classes. Another use for statics is for storing data that is relevant to objects in the same class.

Static methods and fields are also called class methods and class fields. They are associated with the class instance and not the instance of objects of the class.

Statics are used to hold and access information such as object counters that are used to count the number of objects created by a class, or to limit the number of objects that may be created by the class. Statics can be used to hold information, such as values last used by any one of the classes, or sequence information that all objects need access to.

Because statics are associated with the class, you must understand the effects they can have. The following sections describe their behavior in different situations.

Static Initializer Block

Static method variables can be initialized in a special parameter-less method called a static initializer block. The *static initializer block* is similar to a constructor, except that it gets executed when a class is loaded. Also, static initializer blocks, like static methods, cannot access anything but static members. Here is an example class that uses a static array to hold pre-calculated powers of 2.

Listing 3.21a shows the static initializer block used to fill the table. Note that it takes no functions—it is never called from within the program like a method. Only the class loader can call the static block.

Listing 3.21a   Class StaticInit: Imports, Class Definition, Static Variables, and Static Block

```
/** StaticInit.java
    Demonstation of static initializer block
*/
import java.awt.*;
import java.io.IOException;

public class StaticInit {
    // Static array to be initialized
    static int [] powersOf2;
    static final int maxPower = 16;
    // Static initializer gets called when class is loaded
    static{
        // Create an array of powers of 2
        powersOf2 = new int[maxPower];
        for (int i = 0;i<maxPower;i++){
            powersOf2[i] = (int)Math.pow(2,i);
        }


    }
```

Listing 3.21b defines the main() method, which is always static because it does not depend upon an instance of the class being in existence. In fact, the main() method, as it is used here, creates an instance of the StaticInit class. It is important to note that the static block has already been called before main() is called. It would have to have been called by the class loaded before the main() method can be called.

Listing 3.21b   Class StaticInit: The main() Method

```
public static void main(String args[]) {
    new StaticInit();
}
```

The constructor for this class simply prints the contents of the static variable (see listing 3.21c). This is done to validate that they were correctly initialized.

Listing 3.21c   Class StaticInit: The Class Constructor

```
StaticInit(){
    System.out.println("Demonstation of static initializer block");
    System.out.println("");

    System.out.println("Powers of 2 initialized when class was
    ➥loaded:");
    for (int i = 0;i<maxPower;i++){
        System.out.println("2^"+i+"="+powersOf2[i]);
    }
    System.out.println("");
    System.out.println("(press Enter to exit)");
    try {
        System.in.read();
    } catch (IOException e) {
        return;
    }


}
}
```

Statics and Inheritance

Statics should be used with care when classes are inherited. The output in listing 3.22 was generated by the StaticJava.java test. This application shows what happens when statics are inherited. Notice that the Counter and SonOfCounter have the same object count because when SonOfCounter extends Counter, it does not get a new copy of the static field count.

Listing 3.22　Output of the StaticJava Test Program

```
Demonstration of class counter
Object count at start
There are 0 copies of class Counter
There are 0 copies of class SonOfCounter
There are 0 copies of class SonOfCounter
There are 0 copies of class SecondSonOfCounter

Object count after new Counter() & new SonOfCounter()
There are 2 copies of class Counter
There are 2 copies of class SonOfCounter
There are 0 copies of class SecondSonOfCounter

Object count after new SonOfCounter()
There are 3 copies of class Counter
There are 3 copies of class SonOfCounter
There are 1 copies of class SecondSonOfCounter

Object count after SonOfCounter a dereferenced  & b finalized
There are 2 copies of class Counter
There are 2 copies of class SonOfCounter
There are 1 copies of class SecondSonOfCounter
```

In order to fix this problem, the field count and the methods getCount() and finalize() must be overloaded. In addition the constructor must also control the incrementing of the count. Notice that this is still not a good solution because even SecondSonOfCounter, which overloads the static access, still causes the other classes to increment because of the implicit call to super (which increments the static for Counter) (see fig. 3.12).

To add to the woes of statics, the programmer must be careful to call the objects finalizer to ensure that the object count is decremented.

To begin this example, the class Counter is created (see listing 3.23). It is a simple example of a class that counts its instances. Note that the counter is set to zero where the count field is defined. The count is incremented when its constructor is called and decremented when the finalizer is called.

Listing 3.23　A Class Counter

```
class Counter{
    private static int count = 0;
    public static int getCount(){
        return (count);
```

```
    }

    Counter(){
        count++;
    }
    public static void printStatus(){
        System.out.println("There are "+getCount()+" copies of class
 Counter");
    }
    protected void finalize() throws Throwable{
        super.finalize();
        count--;
    }

}
```

FIGURE 3.12

*A Booch diagram for
a static counter test.*

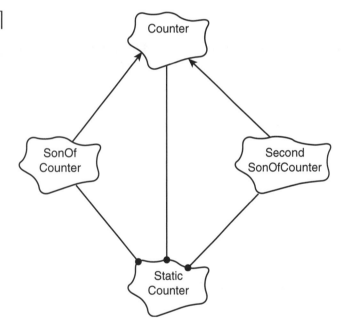

The next class to be defined is the SonOfCounter class (see listing 3.24). As the name
implies, it is a child of the Counter class. The class only implements the constructor and
the printStatus() method. Note that the constructor calls super() as is required.

Listing 3.24   The Class Counter

```
class SonOfCounter extends Counter{
    SonOfCounter(){
        super();
    }
    public static void printStatus(){
        System.out.println("There are "+getCount()+" copies of class
    SonOfCounter");
    }
}
```

The next class to be defined is SecondSonOfCounter. This class takes measures to count instances only of this class. You do this by creating an instance of count and incrementing and decrementing it, similar to the original Count class. In the constructor, you do not call super(), but its call is implied and made by default as described in the Java language specification.

Listing 3.25   The Class SecondSonOfCounter

```
class SecondSonOfCounter extends Counter{
    private static int count = 0;
    SecondSonOfCounter(){
      count++;
    }
    public static void printStatus(){
        System.out.println("There are "+getCount()+" copies of class
    SecondSonOfCounter");
    }
    public static int getCount(){
        return (count);
    }
    protected void finalize()throws Throwable{
        super.finalize();
        count--;
    }
}
```

Listing 3.26a is the main class for this test. It first prints the counter status of each of the three counting classes. The results are that all of the counters are zero because not all instances have been created.

Listing 3.26a Class StaticCounter: Imports, Class Definition, Static Variables, and the main() Method

```
/** StaticCounter.java
    This demonstrates usage and problems with
    static methods and fields. It also
    show inheritance problems with statics.
*/

import java.awt.*;
import java.io.IOException;

public class StaticCounter {

    public static void main(String args[]) {
        new StaticCounter();
    }
StaticCounter(){
        System.out.println("Demonstration of class counter");
```

The class diagram shown in figure 3.12 shows the layout of the StaticCounter example. The StaticCounter class contains instances of the Counter, SonOfCounter, and SecondSonOfCounter classes (see listing 3.26b). As you can see, SonOfCounter and SecondSonOfCounter are child classes of Counter. SonOfCounter is used in the obvious way, but works incorrectly. SecondSonOfCounter has been properly written.

Listing 3.26b The Class StaticCounter: Constructor Continues

```
System.out.println("Object count at start");
Counter.printStatus();
SonOfCounter.printStatus();
SecondSonOfCounter.printStatus();
System.out.println("");
```

Next an instance of Counter and SonOfCounter are created and the current state of the counters is printed. The problems because of inheritance can be seen at this point because both the Counter and SonOfCounter objects believe that there are two instances counted, despite the fact that only one each was created. The SecondSonOfCounter, however, because it reimplemented the counting mechinism, was able to correctly print a zero because no instances have been created for it yet (see listing 3.26c).

Listing 3.26c   The Class StaticCounter: Constructor Continues

```
Counter a = new Counter();
SonOfCounter b = new SonOfCounter();
System.out.println("Object count after new Counter() & new
 SonOfCounter()");
Counter.printStatus();
SonOfCounter.printStatus();
SecondSonOfCounter.printStatus();
System.out.println("");
```

Next an instance of SecondSonOfCounter is created (see listing 3.26d). At this point the problems of statics and inheritance become worse. The value of SecondSonOfCounter does show the correct count of its instances; however, Counter and SonOfCounter now show three instances! The reason for this is that the static field in the Counter class is still being incremented by its constructor when a new instance of SecondSonOfCounter is created.

Listing 3.26d   Class StaticCounter: Constructor Continues

```
SecondSonOfCounter c = new SecondSonOfCounter();
System.out.println("Object count after new SecondSonOfCounter()");
Counter.printStatus();
SonOfCounter.printStatus();
SecondSonOfCounter.printStatus();
System.out.println("");
```

To complete this example, the remaining code derefrences the instance of Counter and finalizes the reference to the SonOfCounter (see listing 3.26e). The information about the respective counts shows that there was only one decrement of the base class. The reason for this is that simply setting a reference to null does not mean that the finalize() method is called. The finalize() method will be called, but only when garbage is collected. It is good practice that whenever statics are used, always to call the finalize() method explicitly before the object is deleted or goes out of reference. This ensures that the count will be set to the correct value.

Listing 3.26e   Class StaticCounter: Constructor Continues

```
        a=null;
        try{
            b.finalize();
```

```
    }catch(Throwable x){
    }
    System.out.println("Object count after SonOfCounter a
    ➥dereferenced & b finalized");
    Counter.printStatus();
    SonOfCounter.printStatus();
    SecondSonOfCounter.printStatus();
    System.out.println("");
    System.out.println("(press Enter to exit)");
    try {
        System.in.read();
    } catch (IOException e) {
        return;
    }
  }
}
```

The only way out of these problems is not to get into a situation where classes with statics must keep track of separate class type instances. One way to do this is to place the static counter mechanism only in the child class. This totally eliminates the problem.

final

Final has the equivalent functionality of a C++ constant. Any function or variable declared final cannot be changed. Finals can be used to prevent accidental modifications to constant data, and they prevent classes from being inherited and methods from becoming overloaded. Private method and static method fields are also final without having to specify the final keyword. In addition, if a class is declared as final, all method fields declared within a class are also final.

Final Methods and Classes Increase Security

There are several reasons for stopping a class or method from being overridden. The first benefit is security. The example in listing 3.27 uses the final modifier on the PasswordDialog class to protect the methods and data from being overridden. This is important if you do not want another class to break into your application by simply overriding your methods or classes. The resultant Password dialog box is shown in figure 3.13.

FIGURE 3.13

FIGURE 3.13

The Password dialog box.

This is a final class, and nothing may be inherited from it. This protects all the methods from being overloaded. PasswordStatus interface is used to inform a client of the status of the password comparison.

Listing 3.27   Class PasswordDialog

```
/** PasswordDialog.java
    PasswordDialog
import java.awt.*;
import PasswordStatus;
public final class PasswordDialog extends Frame{

    // Observer of the result of a password test.
    private PasswordStatus statusObserver;

    // This holds that password that is compared.
    private final String validPassword = "password";

    public PasswordDialog(PasswordStatus observer) {
        super("Enter Password");
        // Record the observer of the password status;
        statusObserver = observer;

        //{{INIT_CONTROLS
        setLayout(null);
        addNotify();
        resize(insets().left + insets().right + 379
                     , insets().top + insets().bottom + 180);
        label1=new Label("Enter your password"
                                    , Label.CENTER);
        label1.setFont(new Font("Dialog",Font.BOLD,14));
        add(label1);
        label1.reshape(insets().left + 12,insets().top
                                        + 13,350,28);

        password=new TextField(30);
        add(password);
```

```
            password.reshape(insets().left + 61,insets().top
                                                + 62,252,26);

        button1=new Button("OK");
        add(button1);
        button1.reshape(insets().left + 142,insets().top
                                                + 112,82,29);

        //}}

        // Prevent other users from seeing the
            // password while it is typed.
        password.setEchoCharacter('*');

}

    public synchronized void show() {
        move(50, 50);
        super.show();
    }

    public boolean handleEvent(Event event) {
        if (event.id == Event.ACTION_EVENT && event.target == button1) {
            clickedButton1();
            return true;
        }
        else
        if (event.id == Event.WINDOW_DESTROY) {
            hide();
            return true;
        }
        return super.handleEvent(event);
    }

    //{{DECLARE_MENUS
    //}}

    //{{DECLARE_CONTROLS
    Label label1;
    TextField password;
    Button button1;
    //}}
    public void clickedButton1() {
        String text = password.getText();
        if (text.equals(validPassword)){
            //Password is OK.
```

continues

Access Modifiers

Planning Your Application

Listing 3.27   Continued

```
                statusObserver.passwordStatus(true);
        }else{
            //Bad password.
            statusObserver.passwordStatus(false);
        }
    }
}
```

The class in listing 3.28 is an applet that tests the password dialog. It implements PasswordStatus to retrieve password entry status.

Listing 3.28   Class Password

```
import java.awt.*;
import java.applet.*;
import PasswordDialog;
import PasswordStatus;

public class Password extends Applet implements PasswordStatus{
    PasswordDialog passwordDialog;

    public void init() {

        super.init();

        //{{INIT_CONTROLS
        setLayout(null);
        resize(292,117);
        button1=new Button("Logon");
        add(button1);
        button1.reshape(110,68,70,30);
        label1=new Label("Password Test", Label.CENTER);
        label1.setFont(new Font("Dialog",Font.BOLD,16));
        add(label1);
        label1.reshape(0,6,294,21);
        statusText=new Label("Press Logon Button", Label.CENTER);
        statusText.setFont(new Font("Dialog",Font.BOLD|Font.ITALIC,
        12));
        add(statusText);
```

```
            statusText.reshape(20,37,252,23);
            //}}
    }

    public boolean handleEvent(Event event) {
        if (event.id == Event.ACTION_EVENT
&& event.target == button1) {
                clickedButton1();
                return true;
        }

        return super.handleEvent(event);
    }

    //{{DECLARE_CONTROLS
    Button button1;
    Label label1;
    Label statusText;
    //}}

    public void clickedButton1() {
        passwordDialog = new PasswordDialog((PasswordStatus)this);
        passwordDialog.show();
    }
    // passwordStatus implementation.
    public void passwordStatus(boolean isValid){
        if (isValid){
            //Password is OK.
            statusText.setText("Password OK");
        }else{
            //Bad password.
            statusText.setText("Password failed (hint:try 'password')");
        }
        passwordDialog.dispose();
    }
}

/** PasswordStatus.java

    Used to pass to an observer, the status of the
    password validation.
*/
```

Listing 3.29 defines the PasswordStatus interface.

Listing 3.29   Interface PasswordStatus

```
interface PasswordStatus{
    void passwordStatus(boolean isValid);
}
```

Final Methods May Be Faster

Because final methods prevent inheritance and overloading, the compiler can generate faster code. The compiler knows that final methods have nothing overloaded so any runtime search for overloaded functions is avoided. This can save time for some applications.

Dynamic method lookup is the default for calling methods in Java. The runtime environment must look for the correct method of classes that, through inheritance, have their methods overloaded.

The example FinalTest, found on the book's CD, shows a simple test that calculates the timing differences between final and normal methods. Figure 3.14 of the final application shows that there does not seem to be much difference in timing for this example (Windows 95, 32 MB memory with Symantec's V1.51 with JIT compiler). If you are running complex code that takes several minutes or hours to run, there may be some benefit, but sometimes speed gains may be quite small. Some Java VMs are written to recognize when an object's methods can be considered final because of context. When this happens, a shortcut is made to the method, rather than checking the class first and looking up the method for the class.

FIGURE 3.14

Output window of the FinalTest application.

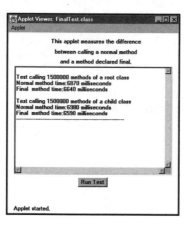

Three: Planning Your Application

volatile

The volatile modifier is used to cause the compiler to generate code that retrieves the most recent value of a class field. This prevents problems caused by compiler optimization in code that uses multiple threads. The volatile modifier will be discused further in Chapter 13, "Thinking in Terms of Threads."

Documenting Your Design with javadoc

The javadoc utility is used to read Java files and produce class documentation. It produces HTML documentation that is suitable for additions to web sites or for including with a delivered application. If javadoc comments and tags are used, the javadoc tool can produce very useful class documentation.

The javadoc tool only documents public and protected methods and fields. All others are ignored. This is important to remember, because the default for fields and methods is protected. Because protected methods are only available from within a package, javadoc assumes that the document reader does not need to know about them.

Java documentation looks for javadoc comment pairs like these: /** */. If the comments are above class definitions, public or private methods and fields, the javadoc generator places the contents into the documentation file for the class.

javadoc Tags

Additional documentation can be added by using javadoc tags. The javadoc tool adds additional sections to the document based on the tag and the text that follows the tag. Table 3.3 lists each of the available tags and their descriptions.

TABLE 3.3	Tag	Description
javadoc Tags	@author [author info]	Used to designate author for the class or method.
	@exception [class]	Used to create a section that shows the exception produced by the method.

continues

TABLE 3.3

Continued

Tag	Description
@return [return information]	Used to create a section describing the return value of a method.
@see [className]	Used to create a hyperlink reference to another class.
@see [className#methodName]	Used to create a hyperlink reference to another class method.
@version [version information]	Used to create a section that describes version information.

It is very important that there be no more than one space between the asterisk and a parameter tag. Any other character or tab will cause the parameter tag to be ignored.

javadoc Input

The javadoc utility takes java files as inputs and compiles them for package, method, and field information. In addition it embellishes the output by using the text and tags in the javadoc comments.

Listing 3.30 shows class Pawn from the previous example with some of the javadoc tags added. Note the asterisk on each line of the comment. This asterisk is required by javadoc to find the parameter tag.

Listing 3.30   The Pawn Class Annotated with javadoc Comments and Tags

```
/** Pawn.java
 * @version 1.0
 * @author New Riders
 *
 * Implementation for a Pawn Piece.
 */
 :

    :
    :
/**
    * Constructor for class Piece.
    * @param id ID number for this piece.
    * @param color Color for this piece.
    */
    public Pawn(int id,Color color){
        super(id,color,15);
```

```
    }
    /**
     * Implementation for abstract function in Piece.
     * @param board The board that this piece is played on.
     * @return A vector of move objects or null if no moves
     * were possible.
     * @see Piece
     */
    public Vector generateMoves(Board board){
        :
        :
        :
}
```

javadoc Output

The results of javadoc are four or more files. There are three files that are always generated.

■ The first file is AllNames.html, which contains an index of all the names of classes, methods, and fields for the documented classes.

■ The next file, tree.html, which contains a tree layout of the classes. The tree is also hypertext-enabled so that it can be used to navigate to the class descriptions themselves.

■ The third file is packages.html, which contains references to the packages that were documented.

Any remaining files are the actual documentation generated for each class. Table 3.4 shows each of these files and their contents.

TABLE 3.4	*javadoc Output File*	*Functionality*
javadoc Output Files	AllNames.html	Index of all public and protected fields and methods
	Tree.html	Class Tree of all classes
	Packages.html	Index of all packages
	[ClassName].html	An individual HTML file for each documented class

The resulting HTML files can be found on the book's CD-ROM. Figure 3.15 shows an example of the HTML file produced for the Pawn class as it appears when viewed by a web browser.

FIGURE 3.15

Constructor and Method output from javadoc for Pawn class.

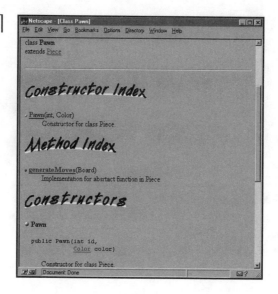

ZIP Files

ZIP files can be used to hold collections of Java classes. The style of ZIP file that the Java class loader accepts represents the full file name, has no compression turned on, and contains directory information.

ZIP File in the CLASSPATH

In order to use ZIP files for applications, the ZIP file must be listed in the CLASSPATH as a fully qualified directory and file name. For instance, if the standard Java ZIP file is listed in c:\java\lib\classes.zip, then the CLASSPATH must be .;c:\java\lib\classes.zip.

ZIP Files from HTTP Servers

Since the introduction of Netscape Navigator 3.0, you can specify an uncompressed .zip file as an addition to the code base of your application. By specifying a ZIP file, the browser will load your applet's classes from a specified ZIP file before it searches the code base.

```
<APPLET archive="zipfile.zip" CODE="myclass">
```

This ZIP can improve applet download time by reducing the number of HTTP connections required to fetch applet code. This could save time when network connectivity is slow. As an added benefit, Netscape caches the single ZIP file so that it will not reload your applet unless the date of the ZIP file has changed.

This could be a disadvantage only if you have a large application and if a user accesses only a few of the many classes. Using a single ZIP file causes the user to load the whole application, when only part is required. You can avoid this problem by loading a ZIP file with only the classes that are frequently used, while keeping rarely accessed files in your code base.

Summary

It is now even more important that your design is accurate, flexible, and robust. Competition is everywhere on the World Wide Web, so you need a design that is easy to extend and debug. It must be more reliable and resistant to crashes or catastrophic errors. Simply put, your software needs to be held to the highest standards of planning, design, and development.

This chapter covers many of the pre-development issues that affect how you design an application. Also introduced is the idea of incremental delivery—a simple procedure of obtaining requirements from customers and incrementally developing applications with less effort and reduced development risks.

Many of the language features of Java have also been covered with an emphasis on how they relate to the object-oriented framework. Also exposed are some good design techniques such as observers and object decoupling. Important information in the chapter discusses how to avoid design problems such as inheriting from classes with static variables.

Finally, this chapter provided some information about how to use javadoc and ZIP files to help you deliver your application.

You are now well on the way toward writing advanced applications in Java.

Chapter 4

Applets

Because this book is geared toward application development, you might be surprised that it contains a chapter about applets. Indeed, other chapters focus more heavily on application code than applet code, but although application development numbers among the more powerful uses for Java, certain projects require the implementation of applets. Applets employ a distribution medium that most people recognize, eliminate the headache associated with distributing software upgrades, and enable users to interact in an area of familiarity.

This chapter serves primarily as an applet development reference. The following sections discuss an applet's required characteristics, as well as how to properly implement these requirements. In addition, the chapter concludes with a detailed discussion on how to decide whether to develop your project as an applet or as an application. If you plan to undertake any applet development in the future, keep this chapter on hand as a reference.

Applets versus Applications

When developing an applet, you must work within the "Java applet security sandbox." This sandbox is the result of the high-level security restrictions the browser places on the applet. These restrictions exist for good reason—without them, malicious applets could damage a host machine. Developing within the sandbox can be very annoying, however, and sometimes you might feel as though you are jumping through hoops to produce a working solution. With all the headache involved, the big question remains: Why develop an applet?

Applets offer many advantages over an application, which you can exploit to produce a successful business solution. These advantages prove useful in two distinct categories: distribution and administration.

The Applet Distribution Model

In the past year, the World Wide Web has become a household name for many reasons. The Internet has moved from something that "geeks" kept as a little secret to something that even their moms turn to for entertainment or information. This means that although many people are not familiar with the steps involved in the local installation of a remote application, virtually everyone understands the steps involved in downloading a web page. Now that Java applets can be distributed through web pages, users of your software can click on one link and begin using your software within a short time frame.

Currently, the major browsers download new copies of an applet's class files every time they are needed. In the future, however, browsers might download applets once and then access them from a local file. When this happens, applet authors most likely will stamp each applet with a version signature, in which case the applet will be downloaded only if the server has a version with a more recent version number.

Because of Javasoft's intense marketing during the past year, you probably already recognize this concept. This topic, however, should not be taken lightly. If you distribute your software to thousands of people, you should consider developing it as an applet. Installing software on thousands of machines costs money, and allowing your users to install the software themselves saves both time and money.

Administration of Applets

Depending on your occupation, you might find administration to be one of your biggest headaches. If you oversee hundreds of computers, you would need to work day and night to even hope to keep all software fully updated. With business applications, however, it is usually necessary to keep up with the most recent versions. If your staff uses a custom-developed application to access the company Oracle database, for example, your staff most likely will need the updated software before it is available. With applets, the most recent versions are downloaded every time a client uses them. Therefore, distributing a new version is as simple as placing that new version on the company intranet web server.

Inside Applets

This chapter covers virtually every aspect of applet development. As with any new topic, it is important to build a stable foundation before diving too deep into the topic. The next few sections teach you about embedding an applet in HTML, some methods specific to applet development, and also the form that an applet takes.

Developing Applets

This book does not intend to provide a detailed analysis of the applet development cycle; its focus remains the development of large projects. However, you can use the text as a reference and model for applet implementation.

Although applets do suffer greater restrictions than applications, the two are not radically different. In fact, most of the topics covered in this book apply to applets as well as applications.

The development of a complete applet reference involves the following steps:

1. Coverage of the appropriate HTML used to call an applet from a web page

2. Coverage of certain methods to which only applets have access to

3. The building of two applet frameworks

Calling an Applet via HTML

You don't need magic to place an applet on a web page. In fact, the process appears similar to the process of inserting an image. At the most basic level, an applet joins a web page with the <APPLET CODE="xxx.class"></APPLET> container tag, where xxx.class is the name of the class file that extends java.applet.Applet. However, as with images, the tag can accept additional attributes. Table 4.1 describes these attributes in detail. If you plan to develop applets, mark this page for future reference.

TABLE 4.1	<APPLET> Attribute	Function
Attributes applicable to the <APPLET> container tag	CODEBASE	The directory that contains your class files. If this parameter is not used, the system will honor the default of the directory that houses the host HTML.
	WIDTH	The default width (in pixels) that the web browser allocates to the applet.
	HEIGHT	The default height (in pixels) that the web browser allocates to the applet.
	VSPACE	The number of pixels to be used as a margin above and below the applet.
	HSPACE	The number of pixels to be used as a margin to the left and right of the applet.
	ALIGN	The alignment of the applet on the page itself. ALIGN can take on nine values: LEFT, RIGHT, MIDDLE, BOTTOM, TOP, ABSMIDDLE, ABSBOTTOM, TEXTTOP, and BASELINE.
	PARAM	Any additional information passed into the applet from the web page. This is discussed in detail in the following section.
	NAME	The name attribute of an applet, used mainly for inter-applet communication.
	ARCHIVE	Enables you to specify a .zip file to be downloaded instead of a series of .class files. New to Netscape Navigator 3.0, this attribute proves useful when many .class files exist and can be downloaded faster all at once.

Listing 4.1 illustrates an example of a web page that uses many of these attributes. Note that a browser that contains the capability to display applets displays an applet named "MyApplet.class," located in the Applets directory, in a 300×300 square to the right of the web page. This applet includes a 10-pixel margin on all sides. If a browser that does not support Java (such as Lynx) loads the page, the screen displays the words, "Either your browser does not support applets, or display has been disabled."

Listing 4.1   Sample HTML Used to Lay Out a Web Page with One Applet

```
<HTML>
<HEAD><TITLE>Applet Layout 101</TITLE></HEAD>
<BODY BGCOLOR="FFFFFF">
```

Four: Applets

```
Welcome to my Web page. Take a look at all of the fun Java that I
➥learned to develop by reading Industrial Strength Java.<br><br>
<APPLET CODE="MyApplet.class" CODEBASE="Applets" WIDTH=300 HEIGHT=300
➥VSPACE=10 HSPACE=10 ALIGN=RIGHT>
<PARAM NAME="text" VALUE="Applets can be cool!">
<PARAM NAME="red" VALUE="0">
<PARAM NAME="green" VALUE="0">
<PARAM NAME="blue" VALUE="0">
Either your browser does not support applets, or display has been
➥disabled.
</APPLET>
</BODY>
</HTML>
```

Parameters are very useful when you want to distribute your applet in byte-code form only. You can treat parameters like a configuration file common to many stand-alone applications.

Although table 4.1 provides adequate details for most of the information specific to the <APPLET> container tag, you must understand the PARAM attribute in greater depth. This attribute enables the HTML to pass certain information to the applet. Figure 4.1, for example, illustrates the web page generated by the code in listing 4.1. The applet contained in MyApplet.class receives parameters that contain information on the text to display and how to color that text. Now—without recompiling—you can use that same applet to display any string of any color. Simply modify the parameters and you are all set!

FIGURE 4.1

The web page built in listing 4.1 as viewed in Netscape 3.0 for MacOS.

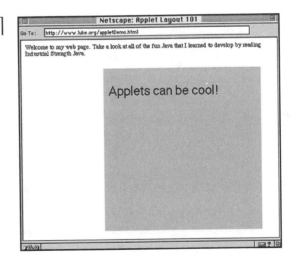

Applet-Specific Methods

Although an applet is little more than a different form of your Java code, it does contain methods that only an applet can access. These methods basically enable the applet to communicate with the host browser.

Retrieving Parameters with Applet-Specific Methods

The first applet-specific method you will want to study is the getParameter() method contained in class java.applet.Applet. This method enables you to fetch the value attribute of a <PARAM> tag of the HTML page which hosts the applet. The Java code for the applet pictured in figure 4.1 is shown in listing 4.2b. Note specifically the section of the applet singled out in listing 4.2a where parameters are read in from the HTML page.

Listing 4.2a   The getParameter() Method Allows Your Applet to Read In Data from an HTML Page

```
myString = this.getParameter("text");
myFont =  new Font("Helvetica", Font.PLAIN, 24);
red = Integer.parseInt(this.getParameter("red"));
green = Integer.parseInt(this.getParameter("green"));
blue = Integer.parseInt(this.getParameter("blue"));
myColor = new Color(red, green, blue);
```

Listing 4.2b   Sample Applet that Reads in Parameters from Its Host Web Page

```
import java.awt.*;
public class MyApplet extends java.applet.Applet {
        String          myString;
        Font            myFont;
        int             red;
        int             green;
        int             blue;
        Color           myColor;

    //this method is required, and called when the applet is loaded
    public void init() {
        myString = this.getParameter("text");
        myFont =  new Font("Helvetica", Font.PLAIN, 24);
        red = Integer.parseInt(this.getParameter("red"));
        green = Integer.parseInt(this.getParameter("green"));
```

Four: Applets

```
        blue = Integer.parseInt(this.getParameter("blue"));
        myColor = new Color(red, green, blue);
    }


        //this method will be called when the applet draws itself
        //here it is setting to font and color as per the values of
        //the <PARAM> tags. The last line of the method prints the text
        //to the screen.
    public void paint(Graphics g) {
        g.setFont(myFont);
        g.setColor(myColor);
        g.drawString(myString, 10, 50);
    }
}
```

If you look up java.applet.Applet.getParameter() in your handy API reference, you will note that it returns a String object in all cases. This often poses a problem for beginning developers, who assume that it is okay to read in a parameter with value "42.606" as a float. Doing so causes a compile-time error because no automatic data-type coercion occurs. To work within this return value, however, you can take advantage of methods such as those that appear in listing 4.2a. Within the code that reads in the red, green, and blue integers, you will note that although the parameter is returned as a String, it is passed immediately to the Integer.parseInt() method, which returns a String as an int.

Although studying an applet reading in parameters offers a useful example of an applet-specific method, this by no means constitutes the only applet-specific method on the market. Other methods of this type enable the applet to ask the browser to attend to certain tasks. These tasks include retrieving and displaying images and sound clips, and also changing the current web page.

Retrieving Images with Applet-Specific Methods

To grab an image in an application is not difficult, and the methods used make sense in the context of an application. However, an applet is a different medium and uses a retrieval system that fits in logically with the web. The process by which applets receive images is based on the current process by which a web page gains an image—through an URL reference. To grab an image from the host server in Java, simply create an instance of the URL class that references the image. Then pass that URL to the method java.applet.Applet.getImage().

Two additional methods exist: getCodeBase() and getDocumentBase(). These methods prove useful when creating URL objects because each returns an URL of some sort. The getCodeBase() method returns the complete URL to the applet's class files, whereas getDocumentBase() returns the complete URL to the HTML page that houses the applet. Frequently, you can take advantage of the overloaded version of getImage(), which accepts a base URL and a String indicating a relative path. For example, if you ask the browser to get an image named "sillyGit.gif," located in the directory named "gifs," which in turn was located in the same folder as your web page, simply write the following instructions:

```
Image myImage = getImage(getDocumentBase(), "gifs
➥sillyGit.gif")
```

Retrieving Audio Clips with AppletSpecific Methods

To ease the developers' burden of learning Java syntax, Java's designers created methods for accessing audio files similar to the methods used for accessing images.

You can retrieve audio clips using the same URL notation used for retrieving images. The following example returns the audio clip nnnniii.au, located in the audio directory that exists in the same directory as your applet class files.

```
AudioClip myAudioClip =getAudioClip
➥(this.getCodeBase(), "audio nnnniii.au")
```

Using Applet-Specific Methods to Control the Browser

In addition to asking the browser to fetch multimedia files for your applet, you can ask the browser to display a different page of HTML. Applets are only one small part of the whole web page. It is to your advantge to use the browser space to discuss the applet. Figure 4.2, for example, displays a simple database query applet.

FIGURE 4.2

*Providing user
directions for applets
in browser windows.*

The web page consists of two different frames: one houses the applet, and the other houses directions for use. If you squint and look toward the bottom of the applet, you notice some buttons that offer different help screens. These buttons do not bring up a Java window with help information, but rather instruct the lower frame to display a different help screen. The HTML changes occur when the applet tells the browser to load a different HTML file into the bottom frame.

The applet in figure 4.2 uses JDBC to connect to a large database developed as an intranet-based solution for a large retail store. Because the entire applet is rather large, it is not possible to display all the code here. However, you should learn how the buttons control the HTML on the bottom frame.

Frame HTML

Obviously, you must understand frame layout before beginning any level of development. Frames were first introduced as a part of Netscape Navigator 2.0 and have since been incorporated into Microsoft Internet Explorer. The HTML in listing 4.3 creates the layout for the web page, which figure 4.2 illustrates.

Listing 4.3   HTML to Generate the Frame Layout Shown in Figure 4.2

```
<HTML>
<HEAD><TITLE>Intranet Database Server Access Point</TITLE></HEAD>
<FRAMESET ROWS="50%, 50%">
<FRAME SRC="DatbaseAccess.html" NAME="applet">
<FRAME SRC="Direction.html" NAME="directions">
</FRAMESET>
</HTML>
```

Of particular note in the HTML for listing 4.3 is the NAME attribute, which each frame uses to identify itself. NAME attributes exist as targets when you ask the browser to load a new URL. Before you actually begin the code for the buttons, you should understand the process that occurs when the browser is asked to display a new web page. First, the applet must obtain its AppletContext by placing a call to getAppletContext(). Afterwards, the applet simply must ask the browser to show the new document, which the showDocument() method manages.

Two versions of showDocument() actually exist. Calling it simply with an URL, as in showDocument("http://www.luke.org"), loads that URL into the current web page. This often produces a less-than-desirable situation, however: After you jump to a new page, you lose your applet. If you intend to send the user away for good, you can definitely use this version.

More often, you should use the second version, which targets the location of the new page. This version uses a string as a second parameter, which identifies the target for the new URL. In the case of the HTML frame layout above, for example, use the NAME attribute of one of the frames. In addition to the targets defined by the user when building a framed page, four additional targets (detailed in table 4.2) can be used.

TABLE 4.2	Target Parameter	Purpose
Acceptable Targets When Using showDocument() to Change the Current HTML Page	_Self (default)	Shows the document in the current window
	_Parent	Shows the document in the parent frame; if called from a page that is a frame in a larger layout, this will display in the page that actually defines the frame layout
	_Top	Shows the document in the top-most frame
	_Blank	Shows the document in a new window or frame

Four: Applets

These target parameters should appear familiar to you—they are the same ones used when targeting frames in standard HTML.

Further Use Of Targets

Now take a peek at the code for the database query applet in listings 4.4a and 4.4b. This code catches button actions and calls methods to display the proper HTML pages in the directions frame.

Listing 4.4a   Controlling the Web Browser with an Applet

```
//The following show methods will display a specific document in the
//directions frame. They take advantage of Netscape 2.0 Frames, and the
//overloaded version of showDocument() which allows a target for the
//new document to be specified.
public void showAbout() {
      try{     URL newLocation = new URL(getDocumentBase(),
      ➥"about.html");
                  this.getAppletContext().showDocument(newLocation,
                  ➥"directions");
      }
      catch(Exception e) { this.showStatus("ERR: Issues With File"); }
}
public void showSearching() {
      try{     URL newLocation = new URL(getDocumentBase(),
      ➥"searching.html");
                  this.getAppletContext().showDocument(newLocation,
                  ➥"directions");
      }
      catch(Exception e) { this.showStatus("ERR: Issues With File"); }
}
public void showFAQ() {
      try{     URL newLocation = new URL(getDocumentBase(), "faq.html");
                  this.getAppletContext().showDocument(newLocation,
                  ➥"directions");
            }
      catch(Exception e) { this.showStatus("ERR: Issues With File"); }
}
public void showMore() {
      try{     URL newLocation = new URL(getDocumentBase(),
      ➥"moreHelp.html");
                  this.getAppletContext().showDocument(newLocation,
                  ➥"directions");
            }
      catch(Exception e) { this.showStatus("ERR: Issues With File"); }
}
```

Listing 4.4b   Trapping a Users Action and Showing the User the Desired Web Page

```
//deal with client clicks
public boolean action (Event evt, Object arg) {
    if ("About".equals(arg)) {
        this.showAbout();
        return true;
    }
    else if ("Searching".equals(arg)) {
        this.showSearching();
        return true;
    }
    else if ("FAQ".equals(arg)) {
        this.showFAQ();
        return true;
    }
    else if ("More Help".equals(arg)) {
        this.showMore();
        return true;
    }
    return false;
}
```

Putting Your Knowledge to the Test

Before moving on to developing applet frameworks, stop for a minute and apply the previous information. Here, write a small applet that enables the user to find out information about a dog named Shaker. The applet enables the user to click buttons to look at a picture and to hear the dog bark. Additionally, the applet enables the user to click on different buttons that ask the browser to show different web pages about the dog.

From this applet description, note the options that must be offered to the user:

- See a picture
- Hear a sound
- View different web pages

The information provides biographical data about Shaker, and additional links offer connections to other dog-related sites. Recall listing 4.4a and 4.4b where you learned to use the showDocument() method to display differnt web pages based on button clicks.

Here you will take advantage of that code and write the Shaker applet with all options offered as buttons.

Because the applet relies on a frame's NAME attribute, you must name each frame. Listing 4.5 illustrates the HTML layout for the page that houses both the applet and the information about Shaker. Note that "theApplet.html" is an HTML page that loads an applet and the page. "Shaker.html" is a default page that includes basic information about Shaker. In the same folder, two additional HTML files exist: "bio.html," which loads when someone requests Shaker's biographical data, and "links.html," which loads when the client asks for links to other dog sites.

After deciding which HTML files you need, you can begin coding this applet.

Many people consider the ability to spawn multiple frames to be a security risk. With little trouble, you could spawn an entirely new window and make it look like an actual web browser. You could then wait for the user to give information, such as credit card numbers, to a web site and snatch it right away. As a preventative measure, the browser appends the string "Unsigned Java Applet Window" to the frame when a Java applet spawns a new frame.

When displaying the image of Shaker, you could either load it onto the main page or load the image into a separate frame. For purely aesthetic reasons, you will choose the latter. Users then can place the frame anywhere on their page, or even close it if they are finished looking at it. In fact, users can create many different image frames on the same screen.

Now that this chapter has covered the applet's procedure and specific methods, get ready to write some code! This applet is rather small and contains only two classes. One extends java.applet.Applet, and the other both extends java.awt.Frame and displays the picture of Shaker. The event-handling code is a slight modification of the code from listing 4.4b. Listings 4.5a through 4.5d illustrate the completed applet.

Listing 4.5a A Simple Applet Demonstrating Three Applet-Specific Methods

```
import java.net.*;
import java.awt.*;
import java.applet.*;

public class ShakerNET extends java.applet.Applet {
    //image of shaker
    Image           shaker1;
    //his bark
    AudioClip       bark;
    //MediaTracker is used to make sure that the
    //image is fully loaded
```

continues

Listing 4.5a   Continued

```
MediaTracker      theTracker;

//called when the applet is loaded
    public void init() {
        //get the bark
        bark = getAudioClip(this.getDocumentBase(), "audio
        ➥bark.au");

        //get the image
        shaker1 = this.getImage(this.getDocumentBase(), "gifs
        ➥shaker.gif");
        theTracker = new MediaTracker(this);

        //add the image to the MediaTracker object
        theTracker.addImage(shaker1, 0);

        //halt execution until after the image is fully loaded.
        //Users expect a slight wait when the applet is loading, but
        //do not expect one when a button is clicked.
        try{       theTracker.waitForID(0); }
        catch(    InterruptedException ie) { showStatus("error
        ➥loading image"); }
        //draw the screen
        Panel buttonPanel = new Panel();
        buttonPanel.setLayout(new GridLayout(4, 1, 20, 20));
        buttonPanel.add(new Button("See Shaker Pics"));
        buttonPanel.add(new Button("Hear Shaker"));
        buttonPanel.add(new Button("Read His Bio"));
        buttonPanel.add(new Button("Links To Other Dog Sites"));

        //add the buttons to the actual screen
        this.add(buttonPanel);
    }
```

In listing 4.5b are the methods called when different buttons are clicked. The action() method in listing 4.5c calls each of these methods when the user requests it.

Listing 4.5b   Methods that Control the Web Browser as Instructed by the User

```
//create a new window and show a shaker picture
public void showShaker() {
    Frame pictureFrame = new ImageFrame("Shaker", shaker1);
    pictureFrame.show();
```

```
        }
        //play the .au file of shaker barking
        public void bark() {
                bark.play();
        }

        //display Shaker's bio in the bottom frame
        public void showBio() {
                try{     URL newLocation = new URL(getDocumentBase(),
                ➥"bio.html");
                        this.getAppletContext().showDocument(newLocation,
                        ➥"information");
                }
                catch(Exception e) { this.showStatus("ERR: Issues With
File"); }
        }
        //display Shaker's bio in the bottom frame
        public void showLinks() {
                try{     URL newLocation = new URL(getDocumentBase(),
                ➥"links.html");
                        this.getAppletContext().showDocument(newLocation,
                        ➥"information");
                }
                catch(Exception e) { this.showStatus("ERR: Issues With
File"); }
        }
```

The code in listing 4.5b traps the event that is sent when a user clicks on a button. A method associated with each button is called when the the click occurs.

Listing 4.5c   Calling the Method Associated with Each Button

```
        //deal with client clicks
        public boolean action (Event evt, Object arg) {
                if ("See Shaker Pics".equals(arg)) {
                        this.showShaker();
                        return true;
                }
                else if ("Hear Shaker".equals(arg)) {
                        this.bark();
                        return true;
                }
                else if ("Read His Bio".equals(arg)) {
```

continues

Listing 4.5c   Continued

```
                  this.showBio();
                  return true;
          }
          else if ("Links To Other Dog Sites".equals(arg)) {
                  this.showLinks();
                  return true;
          }
          return false;
    }
}
```

Listing 4.5d creates a class that will display an image in a frame.

Listing 4.5d   Code to Display an Image in a Frame

```
//will create a new Frame displaying an image
class ImageFrame extends Frame {
    Image theImage;

    public ImageFrame(String title, Image newImage) {
          super(title);
          theImage = newImage;
          this.resize(125, 100);
    }

    public boolean handleEvent(Event e) {
          if(e.id == Event.WINDOW_DESTROY) {
                  this.hide();
                  return true;
          }
          return super.handleEvent(e);
    }

    public void paint(Graphics g) {
          g.drawImage(theImage, 0, 0, this);
    }
}
```

Figure 4.3 illustrates the applet in action. Note the warning attached to the spawned window.

Applet Frameworks

So far, now that you have witnessed the development of two applets, you probably want to create applets of your own. To facilitate your development, this next section examines the two basic forms that an applet can take: a single-threaded model and a multithreaded model.

The Single-Threaded Applet Model

Due to a bug in Netscape's implementation of Java, the spawned window on the Macintosh will not correctly display the image. As a workaround, you may want to force a redraw of the image when the frame is resized.

Although this book has not covered threads yet, you are probably familiar with them. If you think of a thread as a task that executes on its own, you understand the basic concept. An application that must process multiple requests at the same time simply spins each task onto a separate thread. Usually, you will develop multithreaded applets (and applications), but at times you must create a quick-and-dirty applet that does not require the power of threads. The two applets created in the beginning of this chapter are examples of these single-threaded applets.

Applets

Certain structural methods are defined by the applet's parent or interface, and these methods control the execution of the applet. Other methods exist that your applet should support to provide particular functionalities. The following list details the suite of methods required by a single threaded applet:

- init()
- start()
- stop()
- destroy()
- paint()
- action()
- handleEvent()

The init() Method

Sound and image files set up using the getAudioClip() and getImage() methods (respectively) are not loaded into memory. The applet instead checks that the files actually exist where you indicate. In the case of the image file, loading was forced with the aid of the MediaTracker class. At some point in the future, Sun claims that this class will be modified to deal with audio files, but at this point, no easy way exists to force audio files to load into memory.

The init() method basically serves as an applet's form of constructor and is called when you initialize the applet. It is here that you will want to perform any initialization code that your applet may require. Listing 4.5a, for example, used the init() method to load the sound and image files. The listing also used this method to draw your screen. Placing code from 4.5a in the init() method assures that, before anything else can happen in the applet, the screen, image, and sound files are ready to go.

The start() Method

After an applet finishes with the init() method, it is ready to begin its full course of execution. Execution begins in the start() method, and from there you can branch to any other methods or classes. The only way to alter this flow of execution is to design your applet to respond to events. The ShakerNET applet developed in listing 4.5 classifies as such an applet. In fact, this applet did nothing beyond drawing the initial screen until the user took some action.

The action() and handleEvent() Methods

If your applet responds to any type of user events, you must support either the action() or handleEvent() methods, depending on the requirements of your applet.

When an event is generated by a user, that event is sent to the handleEvent() method contained in the component that the event occurred in. handleEvent() acts as a dispatcher and will pass most events on to action(). It is commonplace for an applet to override handleEvent() if—and only if—the needed event is not passed to action(). This logically concludes that it is commonplace for an applet to override action() and manage the event through that method.

Events passed to action() include events such as those that occur in buttons or pull-down menus. One event not passed to action() that you will have to handle in handleEvent() is WINDOW_DESTROY. The event is passed to handleEvent() when a window's close box is clicked.

In the ShakerNET applet, you will override both the action() and handleEvent() methods. In action() you will process the events generated when a user clicks on a button. However, in handleEvent(), you will process the event generated when a user clicks on the close box.

The paint() Method

You should now understand how to create and run an applet, and you should understand how to write applets that respond to user-generated actions. However, you must also become familiar with the paint() method or the means by which an applet produces its on-screen drawing.

When the applet senses that it needs to be redrawn (or when you tell the applet to redraw), the applet will pass the current Graphics object to the paint() method. The Graphics object represents the available drawing area, and, in the paint method, does all of its drawing on the Graphics object.

Albeit counter-intuitive, proper protocol for telling an applet to redraw itself is not to call paint() directly, due to the fact that housekeeping tasks need to be taken care of by the browser before this method should be called. Additionally, the current Graphics object needs to be discovered and passed to paint(). If you call repaint(), repaint() will discover the current Graphics object and pass it to a method called update(), which clears the screen and passes the Graphics object to paint() for painting. If you know that your entire screen does not need to be redrawn, you will want to override update() to call only call paint() and not perform any clearing of the screen. This can be done by incorporating the following code into your application:

```
public void update(Graphics g) {
        paint(g);
}
```

Providing Closure for Your Applet

This chapter now has covered everything your applet needs to start up, run a static course of action, and run a user-defined course of action. The following sections detail the process that must occur when the user finishes with your applet.

There are two conditions that are satisfied with the word "done." The first condition occurs when a user leaves the web page that hosts your applet. In this situation, you can anticipate that the user might return to your applet at some time in the very near future. In this situation, you will usually not want to end all processes associated with the applet.

If the user quits his browser, you can assume that the user will not be returning to your applet, and you will institute more permanent closing of the applet.

The stop() Method

The system calls an applet's stop() method every time that a user leaves your web page. If you play music in the background, for example, you must stop that music in the stop() method. If you do not, then the music continues playing as the user further explores the web. In addition to stopping any obvious interference, you also should halt any intensive processing that might slow the machine.

The destroy() Method

The system calls the destroy() method when the browser shuts down, and with this method you will want to release any resources that you have allocated to your applet. It is often difficult to decide what aspects this method should encompass. Java does offer automatic garbage collection, so any allocated memory-dependent resources will be taken care of for you. If you allocate a resource, such as a window handle, that does not depend on memory, you should dispose of it here.

Single-Threaded Applet Code

As you have seen, applets follow a pretty static framework. From this statement, a logical choice is to develop a set of standard frameworks that can be used when you develop applets. To finish up coverage of applets, you will develop two applet frameworks. One of a single-threaded model, and one of a multithreaded model.

Threads are discussed further in Chapter 13, "Thinking in Terms of Threads." However, for now you should understand that a thread represents a single task executing at the same time as n other tasks. The variable n can vary from 0, where your applet has but one course of execution, to infinity (given infinite hardware), where multiple processes occur at the same time.

Our first framework is for a single-threaded applet (where n = 0).

The code in listing 4.6 demonstrates the basic single-threaded applet framework just discussed.

Listing 4.6   A Simple Framework for a Single-Threaded Applet

```
import java.applet.*;
public class <applet name> extends java.applet.Applet {

        //The init method is called whenever the applet is loaded. Place
        //all initialization code here. Use this method as you would use
        //a constructor in any other class.
        public void init() {
                //code
        }


        //The start method will be called immediately after the init
        //method finished executing. From here your applet is free
        //to branch to other methods and classes.
        public void start() {
                //code
        }


        //The handleEvent method will allow your applet to respond to
        //user events. In case your applet is not event driven I have
        //added a call to pass the event to the applet's parent.
        public boolean handleEvent(Event e) {
         //remove this line if you wish to deal with the event yourself
         return super.handleEvent(e);
    }

        //The action method also allows your applet the ability to
        //respond to user actions. In case your applet is not event driven
        //I have added a call to pass the event to the applet's parent.
        //The decision to use either handleEvent or action will be
        //dictated by your applet.
        public boolean action (Event evt, Object arg) {
                //remove this line if you wish to deal with the event yourself
                return super.action(evt, arg);
        }
```

continues

Listing 4.6   Continued

```
//The paint method is called whenever your applet needs to paint
//itself. Here you will place code that needs to draw images,
//polygons, etc...
public void paint(Graphics g) {
    //code
}
 //The update method is automatically called when your applet
 //needs to repaint itself. Its usual purpose is to clear the
 //main screen and then call paint. Here we have overloaded it to
 //simply call paint. This will help to minimize screen "flicker".
public void update(Graphics g) {
    paint(g);
}


//The stop method is called when a user leaves your Web page. It
//should take care to stop any intensive processing.
public void stop() {
    //code
}
//The destroy method is called when a user quits his browser. It
//should take care to free any non-memory dependent resources.
//All memory dependent resources will be taken care of by the
//garbage collector.
public void destroy() {
    //code
}

}
```

Building a Multithreaded Applet Framework

Few applets are logically designed with a single thread of execution. You usually will want to separate different tasks off into their own thread.

Threads enable your applet to manage concurrent tasks. For example, a small applet with three different animations happening at the same time should allow each animation to occur on its own thread. Most computers can process only one task at a time. If a machine deals with one animation, therefore, it cannot consider any others. If you place each animation in its own thread, however, the VM grants each thread a slice of the processor's time. This processor time-slicing occurs in a fair order, enabling each thread (or animation, in this example) to appear as if it executes at the same time as all other threads.

Multithreading Support

Multithreading sounds very cool, but it also sounds like a high level of operating system knowledge is needed to properly manage threading. This is not the case at all. If you program in a language such as C, you might spend a lot of time trying to properly thread your application. However, Java offers built-in support for threads.

This support comes in the form of a Thread class that your projects can extend, as well as a Runnable interface that your projects can implement. Because Java does not support multiple inheritance, and because all applets must extend java.applet.Applet, all applets that need to be multithreaded must implement Runnable.

Migrating from Single-Threaded to Multithreaded Applets

Moving the single-threaded framework to a multithreaded one is not that difficult. Methods such as init(), paint(), stop(), and destroy() serve the same purpose. In fact, the only method that includes a different purpose is start(). An additional method—run()—will also need to be added; here the majority of the classes' processing will occur.

The start() method in the single-threaded model holds the body of the applet code. In the multithreaded model, you move the code from start() to run(), which grants start() the capability to tell run() to begin processing. At this point, the situation becomes more complex. The start() method does not directly tell run() to begin; instead, start() creates and starts a new thread based on the current applet. This new thread executes a method called run(), which your class implements. It is in this method that the bulk of your procesing is done. Listing 4.7 illustrates the revised version of the start() method.

Listing 4.7   A Revised Version of start(), which Supports Multithreading

```
Thread appletThread = null;
public void start() {
        if(appletThread == null) {
                appletThread = new Thread(this);
                appletThread.start();
        }
}
```

Multithreaded Applet Code

After rewriting start, our framework is basically complete. Remember to place the body of the code in the run() method, however. Listing 4.8 contains the multithreaded framework:

Listing 4.8   A Mulithreaded Applet Framework

```java
import java.applet.*;

public class <applet name> extends java.applet.Applet implements
Runnable {

    //The init method is called whenever the applet is loaded. Place
    //all initialization code here. Use this method as you would use
    //a constructor in any other class.
    public void init() {
        //code
    }


    //The start method will be called immediately after the init
    //method finished executing. The purpose of this method is to
    //create and start a new thread.
    Thread appletThread = null;
    public void start() {
        if(appletThread == null) {
            appletThread = new Thread(this);
            appletThread.start();
        }
    }


    //The run method will be called when the start method creates
    //and starts a new thread. It should contain the bulk of your
    //code.
    public void run() {
        //code
    }


    //The handleEvent method will allow your applet to respond to
    //user events. In case your applet is not event driven I have
    //added a call to pass the event to the applet's parent.
    public boolean handleEvent(Event e) {
    //remove this line if you wish to deal with the event yourself
     return super.handleEvent(e);
    }
```

```
//The action method also allows your applet the ability to
//respond to user actions. In case your applet is not event driven
//I have added a call to pass the event to the applet's parent.
//The decision to use eitherhandleEvent or action will be
//dictated by your applet.
public boolean action (Event evt, Object arg) {
      //remove this line if you wish to deal with the event
      //yourself
      return super.action(evt, arg);
}


//The paint method is called whenever your applet needs to paint
//itself. Here you will place code that needs to draw images,
//polygons, etc...
public void paint(Graphics g) {
      //code
}
 //The update method is automatically called when your applet
 //needs to repaint itself. Its usual purpose is to clear the
 //main screen and then call paint. Here we have overloaded it to
 //simply call paint. This will help to minimize screen "flicker."
public void update(Graphics g) {
      paint(g);
}


//The stop method is called when a user leaves your web page. It
//should take care to stop any intensive processing.
public void stop() {
      //code
}
//The destroy method is called when a user quits his browser. It
//should take care to free any non-memory dependent resources.
//All memory dependent resources will be taken care of by the
//garbage collector.
public void destroy() {
      //code
}


}
```

Differentiating Applets from Applications

Applets can basically accomplish the same procedures as applications, and you can apply the techniques for working with applications to applet development. However, certain differences do exist between applets and applications.

If you prefer tiny details, you probably could write an entire book about the differences between applets and applications. The primary differences, however, have one distinct theme—security.

Security Issues

An applet's functionality is limited by one major factor; the security manager. The security manager basically gets to play God over your applets by instituting a set of pre-defined rules to which your applets must conform. The security manager stops an applet's attempts to violate any rule.

Although security often ranks as the chief source of headaches for programmers, it does keep users safe. Remember that an applet is an independent program that you allow to run on your system. Without restrictions on applets, they could cause huge security holes. Imagine, for example, loading what you thought to be a simple animation applet and instead finding that the applet scans your hard drive for credit card numbers and uploads that data somewhere else!

Obviously, the need exists for some level of applet security, but the level to which this security is implemented remains an item of debate. Currently, the restrictions are very strict, but this might change at some point in the future.

Restricting Access to a File System

As one of the more obvious restrictions, applets cannot access the local file system. This means that not only can an applet not scan your hard drive for financial data, but it also cannot create directories, write files, or even check the attributes of a known file. This creates problems when you attempt to write applets that retain information about its user in a preferences file. Incidentally, a preferences file allows your favorite word processor to remember your favorite font every time you load the application. To avoid this problem, you usually must store all user information server-side and then force the user to "log-in" every time he uses the applet.

Restricting Access to Outside Servers

Moving beyond the local file system, the applet's potential external connections are also limited. Although Java contains rich networking features, applets can load data only from the server that hosts the pages. Many developers are confused by this restriction. After all, if a web browser can access a web site anywhere in the world, why does an applet not gain this freedom? Simply, a standard web page consists of text that does not contain the ability to actually take any action, such as reading files from your hard drive. Careful readers now point out, however, that web pages used to be text, but now they can contain Java applets. Users of a web browser have the freedom to load any web page they desire, and those web pages can contain any number of Java applets.

To cut to the chase, the issue involves trust. When you load a web page that contains a Java applet, you load that web page from a known host. You can decide whether you trust that host and either download the web page or cancel the download. If you load a Java applet from a known (trusted) web site, and if that Java applet extends to a different (untrusted) source for data input, the applet could load a new class from a host that you do not trust.

Granted, "trust" is a term that is not too technical and deserves further explanation. It is not always a safe practice to randomly download files to your hard drive (or RAM cache). It is a rare occurance that an HTML page or Java applet contained on an HTML page could cause problems, but the chance is there.

This trust in Java applets is currently being examined as a source for a more flexible security manager. This proposed security manager is based on code-signing, in which developers finish an applet and then "sign" it. This digital signature would not guarantee that an applet is not malicious, but it would guarantee the source of the applet. Thus, if you download an applet from java.sun.com, you can be confident that both the true source of the applet is java.sun.com and that no one has modified the applet since the Sun engineers finished with it.

As a user, you could set up rules based on digital signatures. For example, you could allow all applets developed as part of your corporate intranet total unabridged access to your machine and all external machines. However, you also could institute a rule that treats applets from servers different from those maintained internally. This system currently exists for Microsoft's ActiveX.

In the ShakerNET applet developed earlier in the chapter, the new window bore the stamp "Unsigned Java Applet Window." This stamp acts as part of the security manager and prohibits a developer from tricking a user into thinking that an applet is actually their standard web browser.

Applets

As the last restriction that could affect you as a developer, your applets do not contain access to any threads outside their own group. This is actually very logical as if an applet were able to toy with Threads belonging to another applet or to another application, a very dangerous situation might develop.

Summary

This chapter provides an excellent resource on applets, and the rest of the book details developing powerful Java code. Some of this code violates the applet security manager and thus cannot be used in applet development. However, you can use most of the code in any applet. Remember that applets are not limited to silly animations or scrolling texts: You can develop a very powerful applet that can solve many business issues. In fact—supported by the points at the beginning of this chapter—applet development often emerges as a more logical choice than application development.

Chapter 5

AWT Basics

Gone are the days when all applications had a simple text interface. Most operating systems have graphical user interfaces (GUIs), and users demand that all applications come equipped in the same fashion, which is great for the user because properly designed GUIs make applications easier to use. To the developers, however, this new wave of computing generates mixed feelings. Sure, the user base increases when applications are easy to use; development time, however, increases if you have to build a pretty front end to the application. Now developers not only have to spend time writing powerful applications, but also developing an easy-to-use interface. Fortunately, it has become increasingly easy to develop a GUI; powerful code generation tools are available, and most operating systems provide a "windowing toolkit" consisting of pre-written code.

Widget, woodget, willit? Confused? Like most terms in computing, "widget" is a little confusing; not to mention silly. The term applies to GUI components: buttons, scrollbars, windows, title bars, and so on.

Although it is relatively easy to make decisions regarding the development of a platform-dependent toolkit, it is not as easy to do the same in platform-independent terms because GUI widgets vary from operating system to operating system—a button in MacOS looks very different from a button on IRIX.

Because Java is a platform-independent language, the necessity for a platform-independent toolkit obviously exists.

Java's creators have provided the developer community with the Abstract Window Toolkit (AWT). There has been mixed response to the AWT because it is lacking many important features, but it does serve its purpose. This chapter begins with the AWT as a topic for discussion, including the pros, cons, and future design plans. The chapter then moves on to some development with the AWT. In the development sections, you will build a small application by using many standard AWT components, and some that you build yourself.

The Great Cross-Platform GUI

Like most of the Java language, the AWT exists at basically two levels. At one are the components that most developers use in their applications. This level enables you to build any screen or form that your application requests. There are classes for scrollbars, menus, buttons, and so on. All these components are based on the next level of AWT—*peer classes*. These classes are primarily compromised of native methods and actually provide the visual implementation of the components. Peer classes are native because each operating system deals with widgets in a unique fashion. Because the actual visual feel is created by native methods, you will find that the same piece of Java code generates a screen with a "Windows feel" when run under Windows NT, and a screen with a "Mac feel" when run under MacOS.

In addition to providing a Java interface to the native windowing system, Java provides screen layout tools called *layout managers*. If you are accustomed to developing with native windowing toolkits, chances are you are familiar with laying out screens in terms of pixels. If your code is going to offer the luxury of functionality across multiple platforms, you cannot afford to layout screens in terms of pixels. After all, what would happen if you created a screen that looked great on systems where buttons are oval, and then ran that same screen on a system where buttons are square? Chances are that one screen would have overlapping components.

A native method is defined as a platform-dependent piece of code usually written in C.

Instead of providing a standard of pixel-based screen layout, Java provides a series of LayoutManager classes that enable you to build screens in terms of relative positioning. In a nutshell, this means that instead of telling the VM to place a button at (0, 0) and another at (0, 10), you tell the VM to place one button to the right of the other. In addition, you can do things such as tell the VM to place components at relative screen positions—one button at the top of the screen and one button on the left side. This topic is discussed later in the section on the LayoutManager classes provided by the AWT.

Function versus Aesthetics of the AWT

It is true that the AWT fulfills its promise of providing a cross-platform GUI toolkit. Unfortunately, the manner in which it does this is clanky, and complex screens are hard to build properly. As you work with the AWT more, you will likely become frustrated with it as a whole. On the positive side, improvements are always being worked on; JavaSoft does not claim to have provided a perfect implementation.

One of the biggest drawbacks to the AWT is the level of difficulty required to build screens that are visually appealing on all platforms. It is easy to build a functional screen, but as stated earlier, an application's success often hinges on its GUI; an awkward hard-to-use GUI rarely sells. Developers often struggle with screen building because only one layout manager gives you the control you need over your screens, and this layout manager—GridBagLayout—is not the easiest thing to learn.

Event Management in Java

The manner in which events are managed in a Java application is a topic which deserves much discussion. Up until the Java 1.1 release, a hierarchical event model was used. However, Java 1.1 brings a delegation-based event model. The two are very different, and some discussion on the topic is needed.

In a hierarchical event model, events propagate from the component where the event occurred up the inheritance hierarchy; stopping when a method processes the event. In a delegation-based event model, events propagate from their source directly to registered listeners.

In covering the AWT, it is tricky to decide which event model to employ in ones code. On one hand, it is important to cover the Java 1.0 hierarchical model because it is in place on thousands of systems. Developers working on preexisting systems will most likely be working with the Java 1.0 model. However, the Java 1.1 delegation-based model is much more efficient and deserves discussion as well.

AWT Basics

Developing Applications with AWT

The sad truth about AWT is that unless you have the time to rewrite it yourself, you're just going to have to learn to love it. In this chapter you will accomplish two things:

1. Learn about the components that ship with the AWT.
2. Learn to create your own components.

In the process of learning about the AWT, you will build an application that demonstrates using each AWT component. This application will be built as the chapter's coverage of the AWT develops and will serve as a code reference that you will be able to take advantage of during application development.

Frames, Panels, and Canvases

The AWT components can be divided into two basic categories:

- Components which are placed on other components
- Components on which other components are placed

Of all the components that have the ability to "house" other components, the Frame class is one you will probably deal with in every application. A Frame is a top-level window with a title, border, and (if desired) a menu bar. Most GUI applications contain either an instance of the Frame class or an instance of a class that extends Frame. Frame supports two constructors—one that enables you to create a Frame without a title, and one that enables you to create a Frame with a title. Listing 5.1 is a small class that produces a new Frame when you create a new instance of it. Pay careful attention to this code because it is the foundation for most of what will be developed in this chapter.

Listing 5.1   A Simple Class that Creates a New Frame

```
package industrial;
import java.awt.*;
public class FileFrame extends Frame {

    //Constructor, accepts a title as a parameter
    public FileFrame(String title) {
```

```
        //set the background to white
        setBackground(Color.white);
        //resize the frame
        resize(300, 200);
        //set the title
        setTitle(title);
        //show the Frame
        show();
    }


    //Constructor creates a title-less Frame
    public FileFrame() {
        setBackground(Color.white);
        resize(300, 200);
        setTitle("New Frame");
        show();
    }


    //provide a border around the frame
    public Insets insets() {
        return new Insets(10, 10, 10, 10);
    }


    //handleEvent must be overidden to catch Event.WINDOW_DESTROY
    //this will close this main window if the user clicks on the close
    //button
    public boolean handleEvent(Event e) {
        if(e.id == Event.WINDOW_DESTROY) {
            this.hide();
            return true;
        }
        return super.handleEvent(e);
    }
}
```

Two other high-level components often used in screen-building are the Canvas and Panel classes.

The Canvas class is useful when building any sort of screen that needs to be painted. This class will be explored in a later section on building a class that scrolls an image.

The Panel class is useful for grouping different components together. For example, you create a subclass of Panel called ButtonPanel that contains five different buttons. To add those five buttons to an application, you would simply have to add a new instance of ButtonPanel. This class will be discussed in a later section on Layout Managers.

The Dialog Class

The Dialog class provides a manner for creating modal and modeless dialog boxes.

A modal dialog box blocks the user from working with the current application until he dismisses the dialog box. A modal dialog box is useful when the current application cannot continue until a critical information exchange occurs between the application and the user.

In any GUI, it is common to use dialog boxes, and you will want to have a series of flexible children classes of Dialog that can be used when needed. One of the more common uses for a dialog box is to tell the user that he made some sort of error. For example, if you were to create a front end to an ordering database, you would want to examine the contents of a form before inserting it into the products database. If an entry from the U.S.A. was submitted and the phone number contained only five digits, you would want to tell the user before even passing the data to the server.

An error dialog box of this type basically needs to support two features:

1. It must be able to display some sort of message.

2. It must offer some method by which the user can dismiss it when he acknowledges the error.

Listing 5.2 contains a small class called ModalOK. Its constructor accepts a string to display and also a frame to act as the dialog's owner. The class displays the string in the dialog and also a button that the user can use to dismiss the dialog box. The dialog is made modal so the user must acknowledge the comment before he can continue using the application. To ensure consistent placement of both the string and the button, the GridBag-Layout layout manager is used. This layout manager enables the greatest flexibility when building screens. It is examined later in this chapter.

Listing 5.2   A Small Class that Displays an Error Message to a User

```java
package industrial;
import java.awt.*;
//the error dialog
public class ModalOK extends Dialog {
        private Button okButton; //the button which the user will
                                 //click to dismiss the box

        public ModalOK(Frame parent, String theMessage) {
                super(parent, true); //tell Dialog that we are modal
```

Five: AWT Basics

```
        //set the layout manager
        GridBagLayout gb = new GridBagLayout();
        GridBagConstraints constraints = new GridBagConstraints();
        ➥setLayout(gb);

        //create the widgets
        okButton = new Button("OK");
        Label message = new Label(theMessage);

        //place the widgets on the screen
        constraints.fill = GridBagConstraints.NONE;
        constraints.anchor = GridBagConstraints.CENTER;
        constraints.ipadx = 20;
        constraints.ipady = 20;
        constraints.weightx = 1.0;
        constraints.weighty = 1.0;
        constraints.gridwidth = GridBagConstraints.REMAINDER;
        constraints.gridheight = GridBagConstraints.RELATIVE;

        gb.setConstraints(message, constraints);
        add(message);

        constraints.ipadx = 0;
        constraints.ipady = 0;
        constraints.weightx = 0.0;
        constraints.weighty = 0.0;
        constraints.gridwidth = 1;
        constraints.gridheight = GridBagConstraints.REMAINDER;

        gb.setConstraints(okButton, constraints);
        add(okButton);

        //force our dialog box to take minimum of space
        pack();
    }

    //trap the ok click
    public boolean action(Event e, Object arg) {
        //if the user clicked on the OK button close the dialog box
        if(e.target == okButton) {
            hide();
        }
        return true;
    }
}
```

Check Boxes and Radio Buttons

Two methods of prompting a user to choose between a series of options are by using check boxes and radio buttons. Radio buttons allow a user to pick one option from a set of mutually exclusive options, and check boxes allow a user to pick from a number of options from a group. Although functionally different, the code used to implement them is similar. Figure 5.1 shows a series of check boxes along the left side of the screen and a pair of radio buttons on the right.

FIGURE 5.1

Two methods of obtaining input from a user: check boxes and radio buttons.

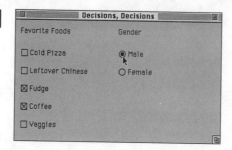

If you have a group of items from which the user must select only one, you would choose to represent these items as a series of radio buttons. The radio buttons in figure 5.1, for example, enable the user to choose his or her gender. Gender status is mutually exclusive; you are either male or female (note that, like gender, it is possible to change the selected radio button).

Often the options presented to a user are from a group in which the user can select more than one. With the check boxes in figure 5.1, the user is presented with a choice of foods and asked to select those foods he likes. Note that the user is not asked for his favorite food (that would involve radio buttons, as you can only have one favorite) but to choose which foods he likes.

In noting the details of both radio buttons and check boxes, it is important to realize that any one screen can have multiple groups of radio buttons that are all mutually exclusive at the group level.

Because they have totally different uses, you might conclude that they are built using different code, but you would be wrong. Check boxes are created by placing a series of Checkbox objects on-screen, and radio buttons are created by placing a series of Checkbox objects on-screen, and then grouping them together with the aid of a CheckboxGroup object.

Having stated that the Checkbox and CheckboxGroup classes are used to create check boxes and radio buttons on-screen, it is obvious that a greater understanding of these classes will have to be developed.

Five: AWT Basics

When simply passed a string, the Checkbox class creates a new check box with the string as a label. This label can be altered later using the setLabel() method. If you want to create a group of radio buttons, you first need to create an instance of the CheckboxGroup class and then pass that class as a second parameter to the Checkbox constructor. Note that this constructor also accepts a Boolean value to indicate the initial state (checked or unchecked).

Listing 5.3 shows the code behind the majesty of figure 5.1. Note the creative use of blank Label objects that act as placeholders in the GridLayout class. The blank Label objects are used to show one rapid way to work within the limitations of the AWT layout managers. All layout manager classes in the AWT are discussed later in this chapter.

Listing 5.3   The Code Used to Create Figure 5.1

```
//set the layout
this.setLayout(new GridLayout(6, 2));

//create the checkbox group
CheckboxGroup myCheckboxGroup = new CheckboxGroup();

//create the radio buttons
Checkbox male = new Checkbox("Male", myCheckboxGroup, false);
Checkbox female = new Checkbox("Female", myCheckboxGroup, false);

//create the check boxes
Checkbox chinese = new Checkbox("Leftover Chinese");
Checkbox pizza = new Checkbox("Cold Pizza");
Checkbox fudge = new Checkbox("Fudge");
Checkbox coffee = new Checkbox("Coffee");
Checkbox veggies = new Checkbox("Veggies");

//add the components
this.add(new Label("Favorite Foods"));
this.add(new Label("Gender"));
this.add(pizza);
this.add(male);
this.add(chinese);
this.add(female);
this.add(fudge);
this.add(new Label());
this.add(coffee);
this.add(new Label());
this.add(veggies);
this.add(new Label());
```

The ability to place some radio buttons and check boxes on a screen is nice, but besides impressing your friends, the code is pretty useless. Now you will take your new knowledge of creating radio buttons and check boxes and add it to what has already been covered in this chapter. You will create a simple frame that poses the question, "What is your favorite color?" The user is presented with a series of choices, and after he makes up his mind, the application uses the ModalOK class (from listing 5.4) to tell the user the color that he chose. In the spirit of Monty Python's *The Holy Grail*, you will allow the user to say "I don't know." The code to create this Frame with radio buttons is presented in listings 5.4a through 5.4c.

The code in listing 5.4a builds the screen that is displayed when the application loads. Note how the Checkbox objects are grouped with a CheckboxGroup object to form radio buttons.

Listing 5.4a   Communicating with a User by Using Check Boxes and Dialog Boxes

```
package industrial;
import java.awt.*;
public class RadioDemo extends Frame {
        //all GUI components
        private          Label              text;
        private          CheckboxGroup      myCheckboxGroup;
        private          Checkbox           red;
        private          Checkbox           cyan;
        private          Checkbox           yellow;
        private          Checkbox           pink;
        private          Checkbox           dontKnow;

        //Constructor
        public RadioDemo(String title) {
                //set the title
                super(title);

                //create a new CheckBoxGroup
                myCheckboxGroup = new CheckboxGroup();

                //actually create all components. For good measure the color
                //of a radio button is set to match its label
                text = new Label("What Is Your Favorite Color?");
```

```
red = new Checkbox("Red", myCheckboxGroup, true);
red.setBackground(Color.red);

cyan = new Checkbox("Cyan", myCheckboxGroup, false);
cyan.setBackground(Color.cyan);

yellow = new Checkbox("Yellow", myCheckboxGroup, false);
yellow.setBackground(Color.yellow);

pink = new Checkbox("Pink", myCheckboxGroup, false);
pink.setBackground(Color.pink);

dontKnow = new Checkbox("I Don't Know", myCheckboxGroup,
➥false);

//add the components
this.setLayout(new GridLayout(6, 1));
this.add(text);
this.add(red);
this.add(cyan);
this.add(yellow);
this.add(pink);
this.add(dontKnow);

//cause the frame to show its face
this.show();
}
```

Listing 5.4b contains the doResponse() method which our code will call when a radio button is clicked. This method creates a new instance of the ModalOK class and displays in that dialog box the label corresponding to radio button that was clicked.

Listing 5.4b   Telling the User Which Button was Clicked

```
public void doResponse(String arg) {
        ModalOK          theResponse = new ModalOK(this, arg);

        theResponse.pack();
        theResponse.show();
    }
```

Listing 5.4c contains the action() method, which is called when a radio button is clicked. This method is passed a parameter that corresponds to the label of the clicked radio button.

Listing 5.4c   Trapping the Event Generated After the User Clicks on a Radio Button

```java
public boolean action(Event evt, Object arg) {
    //did the event occur in a checkbox
    if(evt.target instanceof Checkbox) {
        this.doResponse("You Chose:
        ➥"+((Checkbox)evt.target).getLabel());
        return true;
    }

    //if not let our parent deal with the event
    return super.action(evt, arg);
}
}
```

Figure 5.2 shows the class in action. Note the consequences are not as harsh as the ones imposed in *The Holy Grail*.

FIGURE 5.2

The RadioDemo class presents a user with a list of colors and asks that he choose one as his favorite.

Although it might seem logical to use radio buttons when asking someone his favorite color, the truth of the matter is that most people cannot decide on one color that they identify as their favorite. To accommodate these users you will rewrite your RadioDemo class, this time using check boxes. Due to the similarity between the classes, this transition is possible to perform by simply altering a few lines of code. The code for the Checkbox-Demo class is in listing 5.5, and an example of the output is contained in figure 5.3.

Listing 5.5   Communicating with a User via Radio Buttons and Dialog Boxes

```java
package industrial;
import java.awt.*;
public class CheckboxDemo extends Frame {
    //all GUI components
    private         Label               text;
```

```
private       Checkbox        red;
private       Checkbox        cyan;
private       Checkbox        yellow;
private       Checkbox        pink;
private       Checkbox        dontKnow;
//Constructor
public CheckboxDemo(String title) {
      //set the title
      super(title);

      //actually create all components. For good measure we set the
      //color of a checkbox to match its label
      text = new Label("What Is Your Favorite Color?");

      red = new Checkbox("Red");
      red.setBackground(Color.red);

      cyan = new Checkbox("Cyan");
      cyan.setBackground(Color.cyan);

      yellow = new Checkbox("Yellow");
      yellow.setBackground(Color.yellow);

      pink = new Checkbox("Pink");
      pink.setBackground(Color.pink);

      dontKnow = new Checkbox("I Don't Know");
      //add the components
      this.setLayout(new GridLayout(6, 1));
      this.add(text);
      this.add(red);
      this.add(cyan);
      this.add(yellow);
      this.add(pink);
      this.add(dontKnow);
      this.show();
}

//tell the user what checkbox he clicked
public void doResponse(String arg) {
      ModalOK        theResponse = new ModalOK(this, arg);

      theResponse.pack();
      theResponse.show();
}
```

AWT Basics

continues

Listing 5.5 Continued

```
        //this will trap the event generated when the user actually clicks
        //on a checkbox
        public boolean action(Event evt, Object arg) {
                //did the event occur in a checkbox
                if(evt.target instanceof Checkbox) {
                        this.doResponse("You Chose:
                        ➥"+((Checkbox)evt.target).getLabel());
                        return true;
                }

                //if not let our parent deal with the event
                return super.action(evt, arg);
        }
}
```

FIGURE 5.3

The class created in listing 5.4 running on the MacOS.

Menuing

Although placing user options on a frame in the form of some sort of button often is a logical choice, you can place only so many options in a single frame without "crowding" it. An application usually places some specific options in a Frame but provide access to that Frame through a menu option. In Java, a menu is attached to a Frame; all instances of that Frame and all classes that extend that class have access to the menu.

Creating a menu is a three-step process.

1. First an instance of the MenuBar class is created. This object acts as an actual menubar; each Frame may have one.

2. To this MenuBar multiple instances of the Menu class are added; one for each different menu that needs to be added to the menu bar. For example, most applications have at least two instances of this class; one for the File menu and one for the Edit menu.

3. Finally, to each instance of the Menu class instances of the MenuItem class are added. These objects are the options each menu displays.

If you are at all confused by these steps, run to your computer and look at the way a standard Edit menu is implemented. Options are provided for undoing the last action, cutting, copying, and pasting. Some applications may offer additional options, but these are the basic ones. After you have a good idea of how your Edit menu looks, go over listing 5.6 showing the Java code required to implement this Edit menu. Note how the MenuBar, Menu, and MenuItem classes are used to create the Edit menu you just saw on your computer.

Listing 5.6   A Java Code Snippet Used to Create an Edit Menu

```
//create the components
MenuBar myMenuBar = new MenuBar();
Menu editMenu = new Menu("Edit", true);
MenuItem undo = new MenuItem("Undo");
MenuItem cut = new MenuItem("Edit");
MenuItem copy = new MenuItem("Copy");
MenuItem paste = new MenuItem("Paste");

//add them together
editMenu.add(undo);
editMenu.addSeparator();
editMenu.add(cut);
editMenu.add(copy);
editmenu.add(paste);
myMenuBar.add(editMenu);

//create new frame and assign it the menu bar which we just created.
Frame newFrame = new Frame("Edit Menu Demo");
newFrame.setMenuBar(myMenuBar);
```

Creating Pull-Down Menus

Now that you have the basic form of the menu down, you should learn how to add pull-down menus to the CheckboxDemo and RadioDemo Frames. You can add them in the two ways described in the following paragraphs.

Writing a bunch of menuing code and adding it to both the CheckboxDemo and Radio-Demo classes, which works, and is pretty cumbersome. If the application contained 100 different Frames, you would have to reproduce the code 100 times.

A better way to deal with this situation is to write a parent class that contains a menu structure and then modify all current classes to extend the parent class. To this parent class, add code to set the default background color (white in this case), show the window after it is drawn, and also deal with the user clicking on the close box. Basically, you identify all features that the different Frame classes have in common and move them up to the parent class. In fact, because both classes need access to the doResponse() method, you can even bring this method up the parent class.

The code for the parent Frame is in listings 5.7a through 5.7e. Note that it makes reference to a few classes that have yet to be developed. Don't worry, there's a lot more fun to come, and everything is fully developed by the time you finish this chapter.

Listing 5.7a is set up of all member data, and also both constructors. The constructors are charged with the following:

- Setting the title
- Setting the background color
- Setting the default size
- Calling initMenus() to build the menu structure
- Displaying the Frame

Listing 5.7a   Grouping Common Information in a Parent Class

```
package industrial;
import java.awt.*;
import java.awt.image.*;
import java.io.*;


//parent class to all classes developed in our application
//provides common menus, and access to common methods
public class FileFrame extends Frame {
        //create menu componets
        private              MenuBar         myMenuBar;

        private              Menu            fileMenu;
        private              MenuItem        fileNew;
        private              MenuItem        fileOpen;
        private              MenuItem        fileSave;
        private              MenuItem        fileQuit;
        private              Menu            componentMenu;
        private              MenuItem        componentButton;
```

Five: AWT Basics

```
private            MenuItem          componentRadio;
private            MenuItem          componentCheckbox;
private            MenuItem          componentTextField;
private            MenuItem          componentTextArea;
private            MenuItem          componentChoice;
private            MenuItem          componentList;

private            Menu              customMenu;
private            MenuItem          customScrolling;

//constructor, creates a new Frame with the title "Untitled Frame"
public FileFrame() {
       super.setBackground(Color.white);
       super.resize(300, 200);
       super.setTitle("Untitled Frame");
       this.initMenus();
       super.show();
}

//constructor, creates a new Frame with the title passed as a
//parameter
public FileFrame(String title) {
       super.setBackground(Color.white);
       super.resize(300, 200);
       super.setTitle(title);
       this.initMenus();
       super.show();
}

//set up a border around the Frame ... asthetic reasons only
public Insets insets() {
       return new Insets(10, 10, 10, 10);
}
```

Listing 5.7b contains the code necessary for menu creation. New instances of the Menu, MenuBar, and MenuItem classes are created and added to the Frame.

Listing 5.7b   Creating All Menus and Adding Them to the Menu Bar

```
private void initMenus() {
       //create the menus
       myMenuBar = new MenuBar();
       fileMenu = new Menu("File", true);
       componentMenu = new Menu("AWT Components", true);
```

continues

AWT Basics

Listing 5.7b   Continued

```
customMenu = new Menu("Custom Components", true);

//create choices for the file menu
fileNew = new MenuItem("New Frame");
fileOpen = new MenuItem("Open...");
fileSave = new MenuItem("Save...");
fileQuit = new MenuItem("Quit");

//add choices to the file menu
fileMenu.add(fileNew);
fileMenu.add(fileOpen);
fileMenu.add(fileSave);
fileMenu.add(fileQuit);

//add the file menu
myMenuBar.add(fileMenu);

//create the choices for the component menu
componentButton = new MenuItem("Button Demo...");
componentRadio = new MenuItem("Radio Button Demo...");
componentCheckbox = new MenuItem("Checkbox Demo...");
componentTextField = new MenuItem("Text Field Demo...");
componentTextArea = new MenuItem("Text Area Demo...");
componentChoice = new MenuItem("Choice Demo...");
componentList = new MenuItem("List Demo...");

//add choices to the component menu
componentMenu.add(componentButton);
componentMenu.add(componentRadio);
componentMenu.add(componentCheckbox);
componentMenu.add(componentTextField);
componentMenu.add(componentTextArea);
componentMenu.add(componentChoice);
componentMenu.add(componentList);

//add the component menu
myMenuBar.add(componentMenu);

//create the choices for the custom menu
customScrolling = new MenuItem("Scrolling Frame...");

//add choices to the custom menu
customMenu.add(customScrolling);
```

```
        //add the custom menu
        myMenuBar.add(customMenu);

        //add the menubar to the frame
        this.setMenuBar(myMenuBar);
}
```

Listing 5.7c contains three useful methods:

- createNewFrame(), which creates a new instance of the current frame
- createOpenDialog(), which creates an Open File dialog box
- createSaveDialog(), which creates a Save dialog box

In most situations you will override these methods in child classes.

Listing 5.7c   Creating a New Frame, and an Open and a Save Dialog Box

```
//create a new frame
public void createNewFrame() {
        FileFrame newFrame = new FileFrame("AWT Demo");
        newFrame.resize(300, 200);
        newFrame.show();
}


//create open dialog
public void createOpenDialog() {
        FileDialog myDialog = new FileDialog(this, "Open File",
        ➡FileDialog.LOAD);
        myDialog.setDirectory(".");
        myDialog.setFile("openFile.txt");
        myDialog.show();
}


//create save dialog
public void createSaveDialog() {
        FileDialog myDialog = new FileDialog(this, "Save File As",
        ➡FileDialog.SAVE);
        myDialog.setDirectory(".");
        myDialog.setFile("newFile.txt");
        myDialog.show();
}
```

Listing 5.7d contains the doResponse() method, and the action() method. The doResponse() method has already been discussed, and from your knowledge of the action() method, it is easy to figure out that it will be called when an event occurs, and will then call a proper method.

Listing 5.7d   Display the String arg in a Modal Dialog Box

```
public void doResponse(String arg) {
    ModalOK          theResponse = new ModalOK(this, arg);

    theResponse.pack();
    theResponse.show();
}



//catch menu choices
public boolean action(Event evt, Object arg) {
    if("New Frame".equals(arg)) {
            this.createNewFrame();
             return true;
    }
    else if("Open...".equals(arg)) {
            this.createOpenDialog();
                return true;
    }
    else if("Save...".equals(arg)) {
            this.createSaveDialog();
                return true;
    }
    else if("Button Demo...".equals(arg)) {
            Buttons myButtons = new Buttons("Button Demo");
             return true;
    }
    else if("Radio Button Demo...".equals(arg)) {
            RadioDemo myRadioDemo = new RadioDemo("Radio Button
            ➥Demo");
             return true;
    }
    else if("Checkbox Demo...".equals(arg)) {
            CheckboxDemo myCheckBoxDemo = new
            ➥CheckboxDemo("Checkbox Demo");
             return true;
    }
    else if("Text Field Demo...".equals(arg)) {
```

```
                    TextFieldDemo myTextFieldDemo = new
                    ➥TextFieldDemo("Textfield Demo");
                     return true;
            }
            else if("Text Area Demo...".equals(arg)) {
                    TextAreaDemo myTextAreaDemo = new TextAreaDemo("Text
                    ➥Area Demo");
                     return true;
            }
            else if("Choice Demo...".equals(arg)) {
                    ChoiceDemo myChoiceDemo = new ChoiceDemo("Choice
                    ➥Demo");
                     return true;
            }
            else if("List Demo...".equals(arg)) {
                    ListDemo myListDemo = new ListDemo("List Demo");
                     return true;
            }
            else if("Scrolling Frame Demo...".equals(arg)) {
                    ScrollingFrame myScrollingFrame = new
                    ➥ScrollingFrame("Scrolling Frame Demo");
                     return true;
            }
            else if("Quit".equals(arg)) {
                    System.exit(0);
                     return true;
            }
            return false;
    }
```

Listing 5.7e contains the handleEvent() method which catches a click on a Frame's close box, and closes the frame.

Listing 5.7e   handleEvent Must be Overidden to Trap Event.WINDOW_DESTROY

```
public boolean handleEvent(Event e) {
        if(e.id == Event.WINDOW_DESTROY) {
                this.hide();
                return true;
        }
        return super.handleEvent(e);
    }
}
```

Merging the Menu Support with the AWT Screens

Now that you have the parent class hammered out, you can begin implementing the classes that are accessed via the menus. Actually, you have already written two. Look back to the code that you wrote to demonstrate radio buttons and check boxes. All you need to do to add menuing support to these classes is change their parent from Frame to FileFrame and remove any redundant code. The redundant code includes the line this.show() in the constructor and the doResponse() method. If you want to see an in-progress version of your application, simply comment out the part of the action method where you reference classes that have not been written, edit the RadioDemo and CheckboxDemo classes, create a driver (or use the one in listing 5.8), and you are ready to rock-n-roll. After you get your own version up and running, take a look at figure 5.4. Note that the menu bar includes the AWT Components and Custom Components menus.

Listing 5.8   A Driver for the AWT Demo Application

```
import industrial.*;
//create a new FileFrame
public class AWTDemo {
      public static void main(String args[]) {
            FileFrame myFileFrame = new FileFrame();
      }
}
```

FIGURE 5.4

An in-progress version of your AWT demo application.

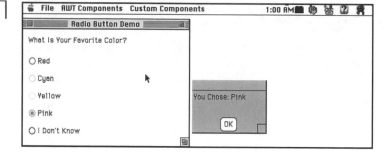

Creating Buttons

One of the more common AWT widgets used in application development is some form of button. Buttons were used previously in the ModalOK class (see listing 5.2) to wait for user acknowledgment before continuing, and can be used to prompt a user to answer some question.

A button in Java is generated by creating a new instance of the Button class and adding it to a screen. The Button class constructor accepts a String that is used as the text of the button. If you take a look at listing 5.9, you will note the next class in this chapter's ever-growing AWT demo application. The class uses the GridBagLayout class to place a series of buttons on the screen. Again you ask the user the question, "What is your favorite color?"

Listing 5.9   The Buttons Class Adds Additional Features to the AWT Demo Class

```
package industrial;
import java.awt.*;
//class to demonstrate the Button class
public class Buttons extends FileFrame {
        //screen widgets. a label, and (of course) a series of buttons
        private        Label        text;
        private        Button       red;
        private        Button       cyan;
        private        Button       yellow;
        private        Button       pink;
        private        Button       dontKnow;


        //constructor, will set the title of the frame to equal the title
        //parameter
        public Buttons(String title) {
                super(title);

                //use the GridBagLayout manager class to give us flexibility
                //when placing components on the screen
                GridBagLayout myLayout = new GridBagLayout();
                GridBagConstraints constraints = new GridBagConstraints();

                this.setLayout(myLayout);

                text = new Label("What Is Your Favorite Color?");

                red = new Button("Red");
                red.setBackground(Color.red);

                cyan = new Button("Cyan");
                cyan.setBackground(Color.cyan);
```

continues

Listing 5.9   Continued

```
yellow = new Button("Yellow");
yellow.setBackground(Color.yellow);

pink = new Button("Pink");
pink.setBackground(Color.pink);

dontKnow = new Button("I Don't Know");

constraints.gridx = 0;
constraints.gridy = 0;
constraints.gridwidth = 5;
constraints.gridheight = 1;
myLayout.setConstraints(text, constraints);
this.add(text);
constraints.gridy = 1;

constraints.gridwidth = 1;
constraints.gridheight = 1;
myLayout.setConstraints(red, constraints);
this.add(red);

constraints.gridx = 1;
constraints.gridwidth = 1;
constraints.gridheight = 1;
myLayout.setConstraints(cyan, constraints);
this.add(cyan);
constraints.gridx = 2;
constraints.gridwidth = 1;
constraints.gridheight = 1;
myLayout.setConstraints(yellow, constraints);
this.add(yellow);
constraints.gridx = 3;
constraints.gridwidth = 1;
constraints.gridheight = 1;
myLayout.setConstraints(pink, constraints);
this.add(pink);
constraints.gridx = 4;
constraints.gridwidth = 1;
constraints.gridheight = 1;
myLayout.setConstraints(dontKnow, constraints);
this.add(dontKnow);
}


//trap the button click
public boolean action(Event evt, Object arg) {
```

```
        //did the event occur over a button
        if(evt.target instanceof Button) {
                super.doResponse("You Chose: "+(String)arg);
                return true;
        }
        return super.action(evt, arg);
    }
}
```

If you uncomment the section of the FileFrame class that creates a new instance of the Buttons class and add in this code, you will be able to generate a screen similar to that shown in figure 5.5.

FIGURE 5.5
The Buttons class in action.

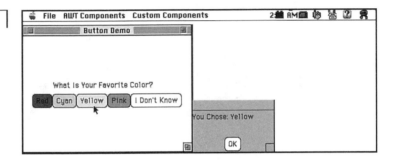

More Menuing

Human Computer Interface is a field of its own and is studied in books larger than this one. You should note, however, that the reason buttons are used when asking a user to answer a question is to present him with all options up front so he can make a fair decision.

The AWT demo has progressed to support radio buttons, check boxes, buttons, and pull-down menus. This section expands on the menuing to include support for pop-up menus. A pop-up menu is used on a frame to enable a user to make changes to some setting. For example, most word processors employ this feature to enable you to set fonts. In Java, you generate a pop-up menu by creating an instance of the Choice class and calling its addItem() method to sequentially add new options to the menu. At any time you can call the getSelectedItem() method to get the label of the currently selected option.

Although in the radio button and check box demos you are able to match the color of the option to the color of the components, it is not really possible to do with a pop-up menu. Instead, you change the color of the Frame to match the color selected by the user with the setColor() method.

AWT Basics

Listing 5.10 contains the code for the ChoiceDemo class. To add this code to the running AWT application, simply compile it, and then uncomment the code in the FileFrame method that creates a new instance of the ChoiceDemo class. Figure 5.6 shows the ChoiceDemo class in action.

Listing 5.10 The AWT Demo Application is Enhanced with the ChoiceDemo Class

```
package industrial;
import java.awt.*;
//ChoiceDemo implements a pop-up menu from which users can select
//their favorite color
public class ChoiceDemo extends FileFrame {
        //GUI components
        private      Label       text;
        private      Choice      colorPicker;

        //construcutor, creates a new Frame with the title passed
        //as a parameter
        public ChoiceDemo(String title) {
                super(title);

                //create all components
                text = new Label("What Is Your Favorite Color?");

                colorPicker = new Choice();
                colorPicker.addItem("Red");
                colorPicker.addItem("Cyan");
                colorPicker.addItem("Yellow");
                colorPicker.addItem("Pink");
                colorPicker.addItem("I Don't Know");

                //add them to the screen
                this.setLayout(new GridLayout(2, 1));
                this.add(text);
                this.add(colorPicker);
        }


        //set the background color to match the user's choice
        public void setColor(String arg) {
                if(arg.equals("Red")) {
                        setBackground(Color.red);
                }
                else if(arg.equals("Cyan")) {
                        this.setBackground(Color.cyan);
```

```
                }
        else if(arg.equals("Yellow")) {
                this.setBackground(Color.yellow);
        }
        else if(arg.equals("Pink")) {
                this.setBackground(Color.pink);
        }
}


//trap all mouse clicks
public boolean action(Event evt, Object arg) {
        //did the event occur over a button
        if(evt.target instanceof Choice) {
                this.setColor(((Choice)evt.target).getSelectedItem());
                super.doResponse("You Chose:
                ➥"+((Choice)evt.target).getSelectedItem());
                return true;
        }

        return super.action(evt, arg);
}
}
```

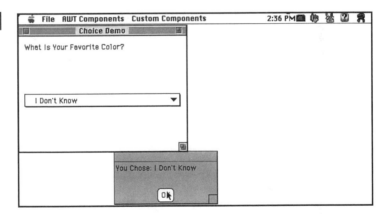

FIGURE 5.6

Adding pop-up menus to the AWT demo application.

Scrolling Lists

If you take a pop-up menu and stretch out the number of choices visible at one time, you end up with a scrolling list. A scrolling list serves two purposes:

1. It enables a user to view more than one option at a time.

2. If warranted by the application, it enables the user to select more than one item from the list.

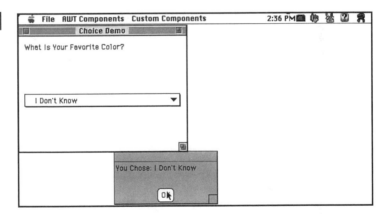

AWT Basics

You produce a new scrolling list by creating an instance of the List class. The List class's constructor takes two parameters, an int indicating the number of rows visible at any one time, and a Boolean indicating whether multiple selections are possible. Options are added to the list by calling List's addItem() method. At any time you can query the object for its currently selected options by calling either getSelectedItem() if the list supports only one selection at a time, or getSelectedItems() if the list supports selection of multiple items.

As with ChoiceDemo, the Frame's background color is set to match whatever the user selects as his favorite color. The listing for the ChoiceDemo class is contained in listing 5.11, and figure 5.7 shows the class in action.

Listing 5.11 Using the ListDemo Class to Allow a User to Choose His Favorite Color

```
package industrial;
import java.awt.*;
//ListDemo class presents the user with a scrolling list of options
public class ListDemo extends FileFrame {

        //GUI components
        private      Label       text;
        private      List        choices;

        //constructor, accepts a String to use as the title
        public ListDemo(String title) {
                super(title);

                //create the components
                text = new Label("What Is Your Favorite Color?");

                //create a new List object. With the potential to display up
                //to five options at the same time. Multiple selections
                //are disallowed by passing in a value of false
                //as the second constructor.
                choices = new List(5, false);

                //add options to the list
                choices.addItem("Red");
                choices.addItem("Cyan");
                choices.addItem("Yellow");
                choices.addItem("Pink");
                choices.addItem("I Don't Know");
```

```
                        this.setLayout(new GridLayout(2, 1));
                        this.add(text);
                        this.add(choices);
                }


                //set the background color
        public void setColor(String arg) {
                        if(arg.equals("Red")) {
                                setBackground(Color.red);
                        }
                        else if(arg.equals("Cyan")) {
                                this.setBackground(Color.cyan);
                        }
                        else if(arg.equals("Yellow")) {
                                this.setBackground(Color.yellow);
                        }
                        else if(arg.equals("Pink")) {
                                this.setBackground(Color.pink);
                        }
                }

        public boolean action(Event evt, Object arg) {
                        //did the event occur over a button
                        if(evt.target instanceof List) {
                                this.setColor(((List)evt.target).getSelectedItem());
                                super.doResponse("You Chose:
  "+((List)evt.target).getSelectedItem());
                                return true;
                        }

                        return super.action(evt, arg);
                }
        }
```

AWT Basics

FIGURE 5.7

The ListDemo class running under MacOS.

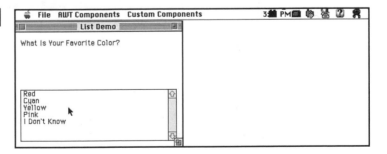

Creating Text Boxes

Different types of questions merit different types of answers. Usually, you can get user input from a pop-up menu or through radio buttons, but you often need to offer the freedom of keyboard input. It makes sense, for example, to place all fonts in a pop-up menu because you have only so many options to use; if you only have 10 fonts, it is no big deal to show them all. If you want the user to be able to answer any question at all, however, you need to use some sort of text box for her to place her answer. For example, when you log in to a computer, it wouldn't be very logical for the available passwords to be placed in a pop-up menu from which users select. A better choice is to use two text fields and let the user type the login name in one, and the password in another.

In Java, the TextField class creates a one-line text input box, and the TextArea class creates a multiline text input box. Both classes actually extend the TextComponent class and have similar methods and constructors. A TextField object is created by passing its constructor an integer representing the number of columns wide that it should be; a TextArea is created by passing along integers representing the number of columns and rows that the object should occupy on the screen. Both classes support additional constructors which also accept a String object to be displayed as the initial contents of either the TextField of TextArea object.

At any time you can call the getText() method, which returns the component's contents.

Listing 5.12 contains the code required to add a TextField demo Frame to your application, and listing 5.13 contains the code required to add a TextArea demo Frame to your application. Figure 5.8 shows the screens built by both classes.

Listing 5.12   The TextField Component Enables up to One Line of User Input

```
package industrial;
import java.awt.*;
//TextField class allows the user to answer the question "What
//is your favorite color" with any string
public class TextFieldDemo extends FileFrame {

        //GUI controls
        private        Label                    text;
        private        TextField                theTextField;
        private        Button                   answer;

        //constructor, accepts a string as a parameter and uses
        //it as the title
```

```
public TextFieldDemo(String title) {
        super(title);
        //create the componets
        text = new Label("What Is Your Favorite Color?");
        theTextField = new TextField(20);
        answer = new Button("Answer!");
        //use the GridBagLayout manager to draw the screen
        GridBagLayout myLayout = new GridBagLayout();
        GridBagConstraints constraints = new GridBagConstraints();
        this.setLayout(myLayout);

        constraints.gridx = 0;
        constraints.gridy = 0;
        constraints.gridwidth = 5;
        constraints.gridheight = 1;
        myLayout.setConstraints(text, constraints);
        this.add(text);

        constraints.gridy = 1;
        myLayout.setConstraints(theTextField, constraints);
        this.add(theTextField);
        constraints.gridx = 2;
        constraints.gridy = 3;
        constraints.gridwidth = 1;
        constraints.gridheight = 1;
        myLayout.setConstraints(answer, constraints);
        this.add(answer);
}

//trap the action generated when a user clicks on a button
public boolean action(Event evt, Object arg) {
        //did the event occur over the button
        if(evt.target instanceof Button) {
                super.doResponse("You Chose:
                ➥"+theTextField.getText());
                return true;
        }

        return super.action(evt, arg);
}
}
```

Listing 5.13 shows the code for the TextArea component, which enables mulitple lines of input.

FIGURE 5.8

*Allowing dynamic
user input with
the TextArea
and TextField
components.*

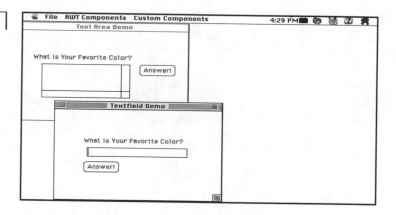

Listing 5.13   The TextArea Component Enables Multiple Lines of User Input

```java
package industrial;
import java.awt.*;
//TextAreaDemo class allows the user to answer the question "What
//is your favorite color" with any string
public class TextAreaDemo extends FileFrame {

        //GUI controls
        private       Label              text;
        private       TextArea           theTextArea;
        private       Button             answer;

        //constructor, accepts a string as a parameter and uses
        //it as the title
        public TextAreaDemo(String title) {
                super(title);

                //create the componets
                text = new Label("What Is Your Favorite Color?");
                theTextArea = new TextArea(5, 20);
                answer = new Button("Answer!");

                //use the GridBagLayout manager to draw the screen
                GridBagLayout myLayout = new GridBagLayout();
                GridBagConstraints constraints = new GridBagConstraints();
                this.setLayout(myLayout);

                constraints.gridx = 0;
                constraints.gridy = 0;
```

```
                    constraints.gridwidth = 5;
                    constraints.gridheight = 1;
                    myLayout.setConstraints(text, constraints);
                    this.add(text);

                    constraints.gridy = 1;
                    constraints.gridheight = 5;
                    myLayout.setConstraints(theTextArea, constraints);
                    this.add(theTextArea);
                    constraints.gridx = 7;
                    constraints.gridy = 1;
                    constraints.gridwidth = 1;
                    constraints.gridheight = 1;
                    myLayout.setConstraints(answer, constraints);
                    this.add(answer);
            }


            //trap the action generated when a user clicks on a button
            public boolean action(Event evt, Object arg) {
                    //did the event occur over the button
                    if(evt.target instanceof Button) {
                            super.doResponse("You Chose: "+theTextArea.getText());
                            return true;
                    }

                    return super.action(evt, arg);
            }
    }
```

Custom AWT Components

Up to this point you have created all classes that are referenced by the first pull-down menu, "AWT Components." You should now have little trouble adding a front end to any text-based application that you may have already built. Keep in mind, however, that although the premanufactured AWT components are functional, they are rarely enough to build a full GUI. Most applications require you either to piece together a bunch of AWT components to build your own more complex ones or to work from the ground up to create your own GUI controls.

As a final component to the chapter's example application, you will build a frame that scrolls an image using a few AWT classes—Frame, Canvas, Toolkit, and Scrollbar—to see how you can piece them all together to produce a class that scrolls an image in a window.

Before you dive into code for the component, you need to evaluate what you need it to do. The following steps detail the process:

1. First, you will pass it an Image object that will be displayed in the frame.
2. Next you will want to place scroll bars along the right and bottom of the Frame to enable the user to scroll through the image in the Frame.

To accomplish the previous points, the Canvas, Toolkit, and Scrollbar classes will be used with the Frame class.

The Canvas class is perfect for painting images. It has a method called "paint" that you can overload and paint any image on the Canvas.

The Toolkit class is one that you almost never want to play with because it serves as an abstract superclass to most classes in the AWT. It does, however, contain methods for obtaining and manipulating images, and you will use them to obtain the image that you are going to display. Specifically, you will use the method getImage(), which takes as a parameter a path to an image and returns this image.

Without too much guesswork, you can figure out that the Scrollbar class throws a scroll bar up on the screen. The class supports a constructor that accepts an integer indicating the orientation of the scroll bar, integers indicating the size of the slider, and the minimum and maximum values that the scroll bar can represent.

Before you begin coding the component, one last decision needs to be made—how are you going to scroll the image? Actually, scrolling an image is rather easy when you examine the drawImage() method used to put the image on screen in the first place. This method not only accepts an image to draw, but also coordinates for the top-left corner of the image. Because the top-left corner of a Frame is (0,0), you can simulate image scrolling by altering the coordinates at which the Image is drawn. To obtain the alternate coordinates, simply trap all mouse activity in the scroll bar region, set member data to equal the offset, and then call repaint(). Listings 5.14a through 5.14c contain the ScrollingFrame class and a class called PictureCanvas. Combined, these classes create the desired scrolling image effect. An example of the output is shown in figure 5.9.

Listing 5.14a contains the constructor for the ScrollingFrame class, along with various member data declarations. Here the actual screen is built.

Five: AWT Basics

Listing 5.14   Code to Scroll an Image Around a Frame

```java
package industrial;
import java.awt.*;
import java.awt.image.*;
//Class ScrollingFrame. Will display an image and allow a user to scroll
//through it.
public class ScrollingFrame extends FileFrame implements ImageObserver {

        //GUI components
        private     Image           theImage;
        private     Scrollbar       hscroll;
        private     Scrollbar       vscroll;
        private     PictureCanvas   myCanvas;


        //constructor takes a String as a parameter which is used as the
        //title of the Frame
        public ScrollingFrame(String title) {
                setTitle(title);

                //get the Image
                theImage =
                ➥Toolkit.getDefaultToolkit().getImage("shaker.gif");

                //create the components
                myCanvas = new PictureCanvas(theImage);
                hscroll = new Scrollbar(Scrollbar.HORIZONTAL, 0, 0, 0, 100);
                vscroll = new Scrollbar(Scrollbar.VERTICAL, 0, 0, 0, 100);

                //place them on the screen
                setLayout(new BorderLayout());
                add("Center", myCanvas);
                add("South", hscroll);
                add("East", vscroll);

        }
```

Listing 5.14b contains action()and handleEvent() methods. The handleEvent() method is passed an Event object and based on the value of that object sets, tells the canvas displaying the image to resize itself.

AWT Basics

Listing 5.14b   Using the action() and handleEvent() Methods

```
//catch any events which would be passed to action
public boolean action(Event evt, Object arg) {
        return super.action(evt, arg);
}


//catch scrollbar events. These would not be passed to action.
public boolean handleEvent(Event evt) {
        if(evt.target == hscroll) {
                myCanvas.setXOffset(((Integer)evt.arg).intValue());
                repaint();
                return true;
        }
        else if(evt.target == vscroll) {
                myCanvas.setYOffset(((Integer)evt.arg).intValue());
                repaint();
                return true;
        }
        return super.handleEvent(evt);
}

}
```

The PictureCanvas class in listing 5.14c is the class that displays the image. It is passed an Image object and first paints it to the screen at (0,0). When either of its offset variables are changed (through a call to setYOffset() or setXOffset()), the picture will be redrawn at the new coordinates. The code's result is shown in figure 5.9.

Listing 5.14c   Using PictureCanvass to Display an Image

```
//a canvas which displays a picture. The point at which the picture is
//drawn can be altered.
class PictureCanvas extends Canvas {
        private      int        xOffset = 0;
        private      int        yOffset = 0;
        private      Image      myImage;

        //Constructor is passed an image to display
        public PictureCanvas(Image theImage) {
                myImage = theImage;
        }
```

```
//alter the x position at which the image is drawn
public void setXOffset(int x) {
        xOffset = x;
}

//alter the y position at which the image is drawn
public void setYOffset(int y) {
        yOffset = y;
}

//paint the image, with regard to th offset variables. This gives us
//the scrolling effect.
public void paint(Graphics g) {
        g.drawImage(myImage, -xOffset, -yOffset, this);
}
```
}

FIGURE 5.9

*The ScrollingFrame
class running under
MacOS.*

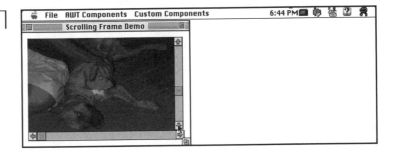

Open and Save Dialog Boxes

Stop for a second and take a breath. So far, this chapter has covered pretty much every
class in the AWT. Material was presented that demonstrated how to use components by
themselves, and other material was presented that demonstrated how to combine a series
of classes to form your own component. One other feature was previously presented that
was not covered in great detail—opening and saving documents.

Opening and saving documents is a rather tricky topic to discuss because each application
deals with the operations in unique ways. You have to make a lot of application-specific
decisions when you need to preserve the state of an the application.

Listing 5.6, which introduced the FileFrame class, covered the code implementation for
creating an Open File dialog box and a Save File dialog box.

AWT Basics

Both types of dialog boxes are actually instances of the FileDialog class where a parameter in the constructor indicates whether the dialog box should be for opening a new file or for saving the current file. In addition to passing a mode to FileDialog when you create a new instance, you also pass a dialog box title and a frame indicating the box's owner. Listing 5.15 contains a snippet of code from listing 5.7 where the Open and Save dialog boxes are actually created.

Listing 5.15   Code Used to Create Open and Save File Dialog Boxes

```
//create an open dialog
public void createOpenDialog() {
        FileDialog myDialog = new FileDialog(this, "Open File",
        ➥FileDialog.LOAD);
        myDialog.setDirectory(".");
        myDialog.setFile("openFile.txt");
        myDialog.show();
}

//create a save dialog
public void createSaveDialog() {
        FileDialog myDialog = new FileDialog(this, "Save File As",
        ➥FileDialog.SAVE);
        myDialog.setDirectory(".");
        myDialog.setFile("newFile.txt");
        myDialog.show();
}
```

You will also note the additional methods in the FileDialog class that enable you to set the default directory (setDirectory()), and suggest a file name (setFile()). Of course, because FileDialog extends Dialog, you must call its show() method to actually get the dialog box to appear.

Layout Managers

As you probably noticed during the introduction of the code for the AWT demo application, the setLayout() method was implemented. This method is passed an instance of either GridLayout, GridBagLayout, CardLayout, BorderLayout, or FlowLayout. This call tells the component in question which layout manager to use when building the screen. The layout manager in turn tells the top-level component where to place components on the screen.

Those of you who are used to building screens in terms of pixels may be a bit confused, but, as stated at the beginning of this chapter, a pixel-based layout system breaks down when component size is unknown.

The AWT presents five different layout managers that help you properly build screens; unfortunately, they leave a lot to be desired. In fact, for most situations, you will find that the GridBagLayout class is the only one that enables you to layout screens that meet your specifications 100 percent of the time. Although powerful, GridBagLayout suffers because it is often awkward and hard to learn.

The following sections begin with basic coverage of each AWT layout managers, its uses, and pros and cons. Then you will see a small application that demonstrates how each layout manger deals with the same set of widgets.

FlowLayout

For most components, FlowLayout is the default layout manager; it is also the most basic. It places components one right after another in a straight line. If it reaches the end of the line, component layout simply continues on the next line down. The only time that you will ever want to use this class is if you have a basic screen that only uses one or two components. FlowLayout supports three constructors (see listing 5.16) that enable you to specify where the components should be aligned (CENTER, LEFT, and RIGHT), and also what the default space between each should be. As with all layout managers, components are added using the add() method.

Listing 5.16   FlowLayout Constructors

```
//Default constructor, aligns components center, and uses
//a five pixel horizontal and vertical gap
public FlowLayout();

//Aligns components "align" (LEFT, RIGHT, or CENTER), and uses
//a five pixel horizontal and vertical gap
public FlowLayout(int align);

//Aligns components "align" (LEFT, RIGHT, or CENTER), and uses
//a five "hgap" horizontal gap and a "vgap" vertical gap
public FlowLayout(int align, int hgap, int vgap);
```

CardLayout

If you have ever flipped though a stack of 3×5 index cards, you will have little trouble understanding the CardLayout class. This class lets you specify a series of "cards" where only one can be viewed at a time.

You can add components to the class using the addLayoutComponent(String name, Component target) method, where the name variable is a unique identifier, and the target variable indicates where the "card" should be displayed.

To flip through the cards sequentially, call next(Component target) and previous (Component target); again, target indicates where the information should be displayed.

For nonsequential access to the cards the method show(Container target, String name) is called, where the name variable matches the unique identifier applied when the component was originally added.

The class supports the following constructors:

- CardLayout(), which creates a default card layout.
- CardLayout(int hgap, int vgap), which creates a card layout with a "hgap" horizontal gap and a "vgap" vertical gap.

BorderLayout

BorderLayout enables you to lay out components in terms of five relative screen positions: north, south, west, east, and center. Each component stretches to fill the screen; those placed east and west stretch vertically; those placed north and south stretch horizontally; the component placed in the center stretches in both directions. Components are added by calling the add() method and passing it not only the component but also one of the five screen positions. For example, add("North", new Label("North")) adds a label at the top of the screen.

Two constructors are supported, and are listed as follows:

- BorderLayout(), which creates a default border layout.
- BorderLayout(int hgap, int vgap), which creates a border layout with a "hgap" horizontal gap and a "vgap" vertical gap.

GridLayout

Although the layout managers covered already do not have much practical use, GridLayout will probably show its face from time to time in your applications. GridLayout divides the screen into a grid, and each component takes up one block on the grid. Every block in the grid must contain a component, and no support is provided either to skip over one block on the grid or to enable a component to take up more than one block.

The number of rows and columns in the "grid" is specified as parameters to one of the constructors. The class supports a default constructor (GridLayout(int rows, int cols)) that creates a grid of the specified size. An additional constructor (GridLayout(int rows, int cols, int hgap, int vgap)) enables you to specify not only a grid size, but also default spacing between each component.

Components can be added to the screen by using the add() method, where adding occurs in a left to right fashion. The block size of the grid defaults to the size of largest component and remains constant for all blocks. In many cases, components are stretched and look unappealing. For this reason, you should only stick with GridLayout when all components are the same size.

GridBagLayout

GridBagLayout is both the most flexible layout manager and the hardest to learn. It works in conjunction with the GridBagConstraints class and gives you the freedom to build screens that meet your specifications 100 percent of the time.

In contrast to GridLayout, which creates a grid with a preset number of rows and columns, GridBagLayout allocates space to the grid on the fly and is determined by GridBagConstraints's variables.

The following is the basic procedure required when building a screen using the GridBagLayout manager:

1. Create a new instance of GridBagLayout.
2. Call setLayout() with the GridBagLayout object.
3. Create a new instance of GridBagConstraints.
4. Configure GridBagConstraints's variables to properly deal with the component.
5. Apply GridBagConstraints to the component.
6. Add the component to the screen.

AWT Basics

The procedure seems relatively logical, but until you spend a lot of time working with the class, you will have great trouble with the fourth item. Basically, GridBagConstraints offers a series of variables that do things such as tell which grid block the component should take up, the number of blocks that it can occupy, and also things such as how the component is to be stretched when the screen is resized. The exact use of each variable is detailed in the following sections.

gridx, gridy

The gridx and gridy values specify the "block" on the grid that needs to be occupied by the component; gridx indicates the row, and gridy indicates the column.

gridwidth, gridheight

The gridwidth and gridheight values specify how many grid "blocks" should be taken up by the component.

weightx, weighty

The weightx and weighty values specify how a component is to be stretched when the screen is resized. A value of 0 means that it never changes size. This value is rather tricky to properly configure; set it around 100, and tweak it later.

fill and anchor

The fill value is used when the component's display size is larger than its requested size. The value determines whether (and how) to resize the component. The default value is NONE, and other values are as follows:

- HORIZONTAL. Does not change height, but stretches the component's width.
- VERTICAL. Does not change width, but stretches the component's height.
- BOTH. Stretches both the height and width of the component.

The anchor value is used when the component's display size is smaller than the grid block and specifies where in the block to place the component. The default value is CENTER, and additional valid values are NORTH, NORTHEAST, EAST, SOUTHEAST, SOUTH, SOUTHWEST, WEST, and NORTHWEST.

Implementing the Layout Managers

Now that you have a basic understanding of the potential each layout manger has, this section takes five different buttons and shows what each layout manager can do with them. You will create a small application that displays the five different buttons in one part of the screen and displays a pop-up menu that enables you to change layouts in the other part of the screen. All components are visible in the same Frame, and the only pull-down menu option enables the user to quit the application.

The Panel class, covered earlier, is a great tool for grouping together different sets of components. The following example takes advantage of the fact that each panel can have its own layout, enabling you to alter the layout of the five buttons in one Panel without affecting the layout of the Panel that displays the pop-up menu. Both panels are added to the main Frame, which has a consistent layout of GridBagLayout.

Switching Between Layout Managers

In the constructor for the panel that contains the different components, you place all five buttons on the screen using the FlowLayout() layout manager. Switching between different layout managers is easy except for GridBagLayout and BorderLayout.

If you add a series of components to a screen using one layout manager, the call setLayout() using a different layout manager, and then call layout(), the screen is properly redrawn for you. This operation will cause problems with BorderLayout and GridBagLayout because they add components in unique ways. Listing 5.17 shows the code used to add the components using the BorderLayout layout manger.

One final thing to note is that CardLayout is meant to display only one component at a time. Therefore, when this option is selected you only see one component.

Listing 5.17 Code to Add Five Buttons to a Screen Using the BorderLayout Layout Manager

```
this.removeAll();
this.setLayout(new BorderLayout());
this.add("North", button1);
this.add("South", button2);
this.add("West", button3);
this.add("East", button4);
this.add("Center", button5);
```

Notice the removeAll() method, which removes all previously added components from the screen.

Using the GridBagLayout

Because the GridBagLayout layout manager provides the flexibility to lay out components however you desire, you can build a lot of flexibility into your demo screen. In fact, nothing is stopping you from designing a demo GridBagLayout screen that looks identical to a screen created by any of the other layout managers. As a demonstration of a capability that GridBagLayout possesses over any other layout managers, you will design a screen that displays all five buttons in a staircase effect. If you read over the different values that can be set in GridBagConstraints, you will note the ones that help most are gridx and gridy; they enable you to move each successive component horizontal an interval, and also vertical that same interval. Because each button is the same size, you set gridwidth and gridheight to equal 1; weightx and weighty are best started at 100 and then tweaked. In the following listing, 100 is a suitable value. Listing 5.18 shows the code for this application.

Listing 5.18 Code to Place All Five Buttons on the Screen Using the GridBagLayout Layout Manager

```
//remove the buttons
this.removeAll();

//create the necessary objects
GridBagLayout myGB = new GridBagLayout();
GridBagConstraints myConst = new GridBagConstraints();
```

```
//set the layout
this.setLayout(myGB);

//add all componets to the screen
myConst.gridx = 0;
myConst.gridy = 0;
myConst.weightx = 100;
myConst.weighty = 100;
myConst.gridwidth = 1;
myConst.gridheight = 1;
myGB.setConstraints(button1, myConst);
this.add(button1);
myConst.gridx = 5;
myConst.gridy = 5;
myGB.setConstraints(button2, myConst);
this.add(button2);
myConst.gridx = 10;
myConst.gridy = 10;
myGB.setConstraints(button3, myConst);
this.add(button3);
myConst.gridx = 15;
myConst.gridy = 15;
myGB.setConstraints(button4, myConst);
this.add(button4);
myConst.gridx = 20;
myConst.gridy = 20;
myGB.setConstraints(button5, myConst);
this.add(button5);
```

Implementing the Application

You have pretty much covered everything new that this application has. Most of the code should be familiar to you because the basic form of the application is similar to the AWT demo developed in the beginning of this chapter. The Layout Demo application has three different classes: a Panel to display the buttons, a Panel on which the pop-up menu will be, and a Frame to house everything.

The full source for the whole application is in listing 5.19, and a screen shot containing a sample output is shown in figure 5.10.

Listing 5.19a contains member data and a constructor for the LayoutDemo class. This class builds the screen used by the application. Note how the GridBagLayout manager is used to place the components on-screen.

AWT Basics

Listing 5.19a   A Sample Application that Demonstrates All Layout Managers

```
package industrial;
import java.awt.*;
import java.awt.image.*;
import java.io.*;

//parent class to all classes developed in our application
//provides common menus, and access to common methods
public class LayoutDemo extends Frame {
        //create menu componets
        private      MenuBar        myMenuBar;
        private      Menu           fileMenu;
        private      MenuItem       fileQuit;

        //create panels
        private      LayoutPanel      theLayout;
        private      ChoicePanel      theOptions;

    //constructor, creates a new Frame with the title "LayoutMangers Demo"
    public LayoutDemo() {
            //create components
            theLayout = new LayoutPanel();
            theOptions = new ChoicePanel(theLayout);

            //draw the screen
            setBackground(Color.white);
            resize(250, 200);
            GridBagLayout myGB = new GridBagLayout();
            GridBagConstraints myConst = new GridBagConstraints();

            this.setLayout(myGB);

            myConst.gridx = 0;
            myConst.gridy = 0;
            myConst.gridwidth = 5;
            myConst.gridheight = 5;
            myGB.setConstraints(theLayout, myConst);
            this.add(theLayout);

            myConst.gridx = 0;
            myConst.gridy = 5;
            myConst.gridwidth = 1;
            myConst.gridheight = 1;
```

```
            myGB.setConstraints(theOptions, myConst);
            this.add(theOptions);

            setTitle("LayoutManagers Demo");
            this.initMenus();
            show();
    }
```

Listing 5.19b contains code to complete the look of your application. The insets() method creates a border around the screeen, and the initMenus() method places the various menus on-screen.

Listing 5.19b   Placing the Final Touches on the Application

```
        //set up a border around the Frame ... aesthetic reasons only
        public Insets insets() {
                return new Insets(10, 10, 10, 10);
        }

        //this class will create all menus and add them to the menubar
        private void initMenus() {
                //create the menus
                myMenuBar = new MenuBar();
                fileMenu = new Menu("File", true);

                //create choices for the file menu
                fileQuit = new MenuItem("Quit");

                //add choices to the file menu
                fileMenu.add(fileQuit);

                //add the file menu
                myMenuBar.add(fileMenu);

                //add the menubar to the frame
                this.setMenuBar(myMenuBar);
        }
```

Listing 5.19c contains the action() and handleEvent() methods, which manage all events that might occur in this frame. Note that events which will occur in one of the added panels are not managed here.

Listing 5.19c   Event Management with action() and handleEvent()

```
        //catch menu choices
        public boolean action(Event evt, Object arg) {
                if("Quit".equals(arg)) {
                        System.exit(0);
                 return true;
                }
                return false;
        }


        //handleEvent must be overidden to trap Event.WINDOW_DESTROY
        public boolean handleEvent(Event e) {
                if(e.id == Event.WINDOW_DESTROY) {
                        this.hide();
                        return true;
                }
                return super.handleEvent(e);
        }
}
```

Listing 5.19d contains the constructor for the class, which is the meat of our application. This class, which extends Panel, contains five buttons; all of which may be displayed using any one of the different layout managers.

Listing 5.19d   Displaying Five Components with LayoutPanel Using Five Layout Managers

```
public class LayoutPanel extends Panel {
        //GUI Components
        private          Button          button1;
        private          Button          button2;
        private          Button          button3;
        private          Button          button4;
        private          Button          button5;

        //Constructor, will draw the screen using the FlowLayout layout
        //manager
        public LayoutPanel() {
                //set the layout manager
                this.setLayout(new FlowLayout());

                //create the components
```

```
                button1 = new Button("1");
                button2 = new Button("2");
                button3 = new Button("3");
                button4 = new Button("4");
                button5 = new Button("5");
                //add the components to the Frame
                this.add(button1);
                this.add(button2);
                this.add(button3);
                this.add(button4);
                this.add(button5);
        }
```

Listing 5.19e contains the code to alter the layout manager to be one of the following:

- FlowLayout
- GridLayout
- CardLayout
- BorderLayout

Listing 5.19e   Making FlowLayout the Current Layout Manager

```
        public void setFlowLayout() {
                this.setLayout(new FlowLayout());
                layout();
        }


        //make the current layout manager GridLayout
        public void setGridLayout() {
                this.setLayout(new GridLayout(3, 2));
                layout();
        }


        //make the current layout manager CardLayout
        public void setCardLayout() {
                this.setLayout(new CardLayout());
                layout();
        }
```

continues

AWT Basics

Listing 5.19e   Continued

```
//make the current layout manager BorderLayout
public void setBorderLayout() {
        this.removeAll();
        this.setLayout(new BorderLayout());
        this.add("North", button1);
        this.add("South", button2);
        this.add("West", button3);
        this.add("East", button4);
        this.add("Center", button5);
        layout();
}
```

Listing 5.19f contains the code necessary to implement in the GridBagLayout layout manager. Note how the values given to the GridBagConstraints object affect the final screen.

Listing 5.19f   Making GridBagLayout the Current Layout Manager

```
public void setGridBagLayout() {
        //remove the buttons
        this.removeAll();

        //create the necessary objects
        GridBagLayout myGB = new GridBagLayout();
        GridBagConstraints myConst = new GridBagConstraints();

        //set the layout
        this.setLayout(myGB);

        //add all componets to the screen
        myConst.gridx = 0;
        myConst.gridy = 0;
        myConst.weightx = 100;
        myConst.weighty = 100;
        myConst.gridwidth = 1;
        myConst.gridheight = 1;
        myGB.setConstraints(button1, myConst);
        this.add(button1);

        myConst.gridx = 5;
        myConst.gridy = 5;
        myGB.setConstraints(button2, myConst);
        this.add(button2);
```

```
                myConst.gridx = 10;
                myConst.gridy = 10;
                myGB.setConstraints(button3, myConst);
                this.add(button3);

                myConst.gridx = 15;
                myConst.gridy = 15;
                myGB.setConstraints(button4, myConst);
                this.add(button4);

                myConst.gridx = 20;
                myConst.gridy = 20;
                myGB.setConstraints(button5, myConst);
                this.add(button5);
                layout();
        }
}
```

The final class in this application also extends Panel and uses a pop-up menu to allow a user to choose between any of the various pop-up menus (see listing 5.20).

Listing 5.20   Using the ChoicePanel Class to Display a Pop-Up List of All Available Layout Managers

```
// When the value of the pop-up menu is changed an associated
// LayoutPanel will be told to change its layout manager.
public class ChoicePanel extends Panel {
        //GUI components
        private        Choice                    layoutPicker;
        private        LayoutPanel                theDestination;

        //constructor, accepts a LayoutPanel obejct and tells that panel
        //when to change its layout
        public ChoicePanel(LayoutPanel destination) {
                //set the destination of our events
                theDestination = destination;

                //create pop-up menu
                layoutPicker = new Choice();

                //add the options
                layoutPicker.addItem("FlowLayout");
                layoutPicker.addItem("GridLayout");
                layoutPicker.addItem("GridBagLayout");
```

continues

AWT Basics

Listing 5.20   Continued

```
                    layoutPicker.addItem("CardLayout");
                    layoutPicker.addItem("BorderLayout");

                    //add the choice
                    this.add(layoutPicker);
            }


            //trap all events
            public boolean action(Event evt, Object arg) {
                    //did the event occur in the choice, if so find out where,
                    //and then tell the LayoutPanel to change its current
                    //layout manager.
                    if(evt.target instanceof Choice) {
                    if(((Choice)evt.target).getSelectedItem().equals("FlowLayout"))
    {
                                theDestination.setFlowLayout();
                                return true;
                        }
                        else
                        ➥if(((Choice)evt.target).getSelectedItem()
                        ➥.equals("GridLayout")) {
                                theDestination.setGridLayout();
                                return true;
                        }
                        else
                        ➥if(((Choice)evt.target).getSelectedItem()
                        ➥.equals("GridBagLayout")) {
                                theDestination.setGridBagLayout();
                                return true;
                        }
                        else
                        ➥if(((Choice)evt.target).getSelectedItem().
                        ➥equals("CardLayout")) {
                                theDestination.setCardLayout();
                                return true;
                        }
                        else if
                        ➥(((Choice)evt.target).getSelectedItem().
                        ➥equals("BorderLayout")) {
                                theDestination.setBorderLayout();
                                return true;
                        }
                    }
                    return super.action(evt, arg);
            }
    }
```

FIGURE 5.10

*The Layout Demo
Application in action.*

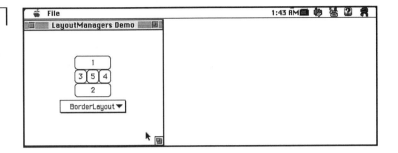

Summary

Having completed this chapter, you should have accomplished two things: gained a full grasp of the AWT, as well as a base library of reusable code. Before you move on to the next chapter on the AWT, stop and look over what you have done. In the next chapter, you will build a complete application framework that you can simply subclass to add a GUI front end onto any application.

AWT Basics

Chapter 6

Advanced AWT

In this chapter you will incorporate the skills you learned in Chapter 5, "AWT Basics," to build a flexible component-based application framework. This framework consists of a series of classes, that, when either imported or extended, enable you to build a GUI rapidly. You will find this useful for both adding a GUI to an existing text-based application and creating a new GUI application.

The Need for a GUI Framework

As you develop more applications, you spend considerable time building similar GUIs. Although these GUIs may differ in function, most applications appear similar. By encapsulating all GUI components into flexible, reusable classes, you allow yourself to concentrate on developing the "meat" of the application.

The maximization of back-end development time occurs for one major reason: User-interface code basically remains the same from one application to another. This characteristic hearkens to the 1980s when Apple Computer pioneered efforts to grant all applications a common look and feel. The company published a series of human-computer interface guidelines and asked all developers to follow them for consistency. As a result, a user can sit down at virtually any application that conforms to user interface standards and determine how to use the application in a relatively short time. By encapsulating code that is often reused into extendible classes, you separate yourself from the drudgery of implementing this code more than once.

The implications of this framework reach into many areas. To those individuals familiar with object-oriented programming, this code fulfills the object-oriented promise of creating reusable code. Individuals with a background in procedural programming also should be excited by this.

Planning for the Future

This book's goal is to teach the object-oriented application design process. This chapter begins by showing you how to design this framework and ends with the actual implementation. Many programmers become so eager to begin the application that they start coding long before they are ready. Planning ahead ensures that your code is completely reusable. Failing to plan before you begin developing often leaves you with classes that—although they might work well in the original application—are basically useless outside of that application.

This framework's design contains features required by all applications. The following sections encapsulate them into classes that don't require interaction from the programmer during the design process. The developer extends the principle class to allow the back-end methods to merge with the GUI methods. The programmer also builds into the framework a support for infinite extensibility. As you work with the framework, in fact, you will develop a library of classes that complement the framework in a manner that works best with the general appearance your applications need. As an added bonus, you can trade classes with other developers working with the framework. If you design your additional classes correctly, you can distribute them to individuals who are not working with the framework but who still need access to its functions.

Designing the Application

Brainstorm for a minute about the basic features every application must support—for example, pull-down menus, error dialogs, and standard dialog boxes. Then look closer at the features most applications support—for example, the ability to show an image in a window of an unknown size. With these features in mind, you can modify the framework to allow further customization.

An application must have support for pull-down menus. Individual applications determine the extent to which you can implement these menus, but all applications must offer File and Edit menus.

The File menu must offer support for creating a new window, closing the current window, saving the current file, and opening a previous file. Of course, the File menu also should offer the ability to quit the application.

The Edit menu must offer support for clipboard interaction (Cut, Copy, and Paste). Although additional menu support is not necessary, it is often desirable.

In addition to menu support, you must offer support for communicating with the user via dialog boxes. Use this communication for one of the following reasons:

- To relay information to the user
- To ask a question of the user

Both modal and modeless dialog boxes require support in an application.

Starting the Application Framework

Developing a framework that is both basic enough for all applications and powerful enough to make itself useful is not an easy task. If you implement features that are too specific, the framework no longer serves all applications. However, if you do not add enough features, the framework becomes essentially useless.

A modal dialog box blocks user interaction until the user dismisses the dialog box. A modeless dialog box enables the user to continue using the application before dismissing the dialog box.

All GUI applications must support menus, but the extent to which you can implement menus varies within applications.

You need not look much further than the previous chapter for strong menu code. The FileFrame class from Chapter 5 offers support for menus on a few levels, including the ever important File menu. Almost all menu classes, however, are declared private. Because you want classes that work with your framework to have the freedom to modify away, it is crucial that all variables are publicly accessible. You will therefore want to ensure that most classes in your framework are declared public.

After you determine that your menu code exists, and you identify needed modifications, you can begin writing that portion of the framework. First, note the steps required to make the transition from Chapter 5 menu code to the code used here:

1. Copy listing 5.6 into a new text window.

2. Remove all code that implemented any menu other than the File menu.

3. Add similar support for an Edit menu.

4. Ensure that all classes are declared public.

Applying these steps to the FileFrame class from Chapter 5 provides the code fragment in listing 6.1.

Listing 6.1   Code to Add File and Edit Menus to an Application

```
//menu components. we make everything public to allow for access from
//other classes, packager, etc... while the framework is great for any
//application users should be able to modify anything they desire w/o
//editing this class.
Public   MenuBar          myMenuBar;
public   Menu             fileMenu;
public   MenuItem         fileNew;
public   MenuItem         fileOpen;
public   MenuItem         fileSave;
public   MenuItem         fileQuit;
public   Menu             editMenu;
public   MenuItem         editUndo;
public   MenuItem         editCut;
public   MenuItem         editCopy;
public   MenuItem         editPaste;

//this class will create all menus and add them to the menubar
//public void initMenus() {
        //create the menus
        myMenuBar = new MenuBar();
//add the menubar to the frame
        this.setMenuBar(myMenuBar);
        fileMenu = new Menu("File", true);
        editMenu = new Menu("Edit", true);
    //create choices for the file menu
        fileNew = new MenuItem("New Frame");
        fileOpen = new MenuItem("Open...");
        fileSave = new MenuItem("Save...");
        fileQuit = new MenuItem("Quit");
```

```
        //add choices to the file menu
        fileMenu.add(fileNew);
        fileMenu.add(fileOpen);
        fileMenu.add(fileSave);
        fileMenu.addSeparator();
        fileMenu.add(fileQuit);

        //add the file menu
        myMenuBar.add(fileMenu);

        //create the choices for the edit menu
        editUndo = new MenuItem("Undo");
        editCut = new MenuItem("Cut");
        editCopy = new MenuItem("Copy");
        editPaste = new MenuItem("Paste");

        //add choices to the edit menu
        editMenu.add(editUndo);
        editMenu.addSeparator();
        editMenu.add(editCut);
        editMenu.add(editCopy);
        editMenu.add(editPaste);

        //add the component menu
        myMenuBar.add(editMenu);
}
```

Moving the Menu Code to Completion

In addition to declaring all classes public, the framework class needs one additional modification. If you allow child classes to modify the menu structure of a menu bar created within its parent class, you must refrain from calling the show() method. Chapter 5 called this method in the constructor of FileFrame after adding menus to the Frame. This process must follow that order precisely; after you call show(), you cannot easily modify the menu structure.

In the modified version of the menu code, the child classes should have the capability to fully modify the menu bar. Thus, you should refrain from calling show() and instead allow the child classes to call this method. Actually, this situation enables framework users to wait to display the frame until completing certain tasks, such as loading an image.

Event-Trapping

In addition to offering support for visually creating menus, the framework must contain built-in support for trapping the events generated when the user selects a menu option. Again, you can borrow the action() method from code developed in listing 5.6. Here, you implement basic support for the menu options and allow child classes to override the method to handle unique situations. More often than not, all significant event-trapping occurs in child classes. By implementing the action() method, however, you provide framework users with a set of guidelines for implementing their own version of the method.

Listing 6.2 illustrates the action() method, as well as helper methods called by action(). These helper methods create items such as an Open File dialog box, a Save File dialog box, or a new top-level Frame. Because the parent class traps the menu choices associated with the helper methods, you must override only the helper method itself instead of trapping the menu choice again. In addition, you can take advantage of the helper methods' ability to perform some specific tasks. With the Open File dialog helper method, for example, simply wait until the dialog box is dismissed, then call getFile() to find out the name of the selected file, and finally stream in that file. Thus, you never have to open and create the dialog box itself. (The ➽ symbol indicates a line that would fit on the previous line were this a computer screen.)

Listing 6.2   Methods to Trap Menu Selections and to Respond to Specific Helper Tasks

```
//create a new frame, a utility method called when Fill-->New is
//selected
public void createNewFrame(String title) {
        FrameWork newFrame = new FrameWork(title);
        newFrame.resize(300, 200);
        newFrame.show();
}
//create open dialog
public void createOpenDialog() {
        myOpenDialog = new FileDialog(this, "Open File",
FileDialog.LOAD);
        myOpenDialog.setDirectory(".");
        myOpenDialog.setFile("openFile.txt");
        myOpenDialog.show();
}
```

```
//create save dialog
public void createSaveDialog() {
        mySaveDialog = new FileDialog(this, "Save File As",
        ➥FileDialog.SAVE);
        mySaveDialog.setDirectory(".");
        mySaveDialog.setFile("newFile.txt");
        mySaveDialog.show();
}
//display the String arg in a modal dialog
public void doResponse(String arg) {
        ModalOK          theResponse = new ModalOK(this, arg);

        theResponse.pack();
        theResponse.show();
}
//trap menu choices
public boolean action(Event evt, Object arg) {
        if("New Frame".equals(arg)) {
                this.createNewFrame("New Frame");
        return true;
        }
        else if("Open...".equals(arg)) {
                this.createOpenDialog();
        return true;
        }
        else if("Save...".equals(arg)) {
                this.createSaveDialog();
        return true;
        }
        else if("Quit".equals(arg)) {
                System.exit(0);
        return true;
        }
        return super.action(evt, arg);
}
```

Responding to User Input

A series of flexible dialog boxes is important to the success of this application framework. An application must communicate with a user not only through menus, but via dialog boxes. With code reuse, you can modify some of the code created in Chapter 5 to serve as a dialog box repository.

This modification involves implementing a flexible, consistent means of understanding the user's answers to questions posed in the dialog boxes. You always can institute a unique manner to deal with each new dialog box, but doing so can make your code hard to read. Instead, institute a method, similar to the action() method, to be called when the dialog is dismissed. This method uses a series of if statements to determine how to process the user's answer.

If for one moment you think that this is going to be difficult to implement, realize that basically the same situation exists in the action() method. Create a method called tellResponse(), which passes both a reference to the calling object and a string representing the user's answer to the question posed in the dialog box. Processing the answer now involves testing—through a series of "if" statements—for the proper "reaction" method to call. Because the framework does not contain a vested interest in the answer to any dialog box, the version of tellResponse() in the framework itself will not contain any arguments. These are instead implemented in a child class.

The Question Class

For an illustration of exactly how this notification occurs, refer to the Question class in listing 6.3. A Question object prompts the user with a question, and the user types an answer and clicks either OK or Cancel. Of course, if the user clicks Cancel, no action is taken. If this happens, pass a reference to the Question object through tellResponse(); a null String indicates that the user clicked Cancel. Otherwise, pass not only a reference to the Question object, but also the text the user entered. This created dialog passes a reference to the object which owns it, and the tellResponse() method notifies that object when the dialog is dismissed.

Listing 6.3   Setting a Dialog Box to Prompt the User to Answer Either OK or Cancel to a Question

```
package industrial;
import java.awt.*;
//Question class allows the user to answer a user specified question
//with either OK or Cancel. In either case, the object which owns the
//class will be notified through its tellResponse() method.
public class Question extends Dialog {

        //GUI controls
        private        Label                text;
        private        TextField            theTextField;
        private        Button               okButton;
```

```
private        Button                  cancelButton;
private        String                   theAnswer = null;
private        FrameWork                theParent;
//constructor, accepts a string as a parameter and uses
//it as the question. Also accepts a reference to the object
//which owns the dialog.
public Question(FrameWork parent, String incomingText) {
    super(parent, true);
    theParent = parent;

    //create the components
    text = new Label(incomingText);
    theTextField = new TextField(20);
    okButton = new Button("OK");
    cancelButton = new Button("Cancel");
    //use the GridBagLayout manager to draw the screen
    GridBagLayout myLayout = new GridBagLayout();
    GridBagConstraints constraints = new GridBagConstraints();
    this.setLayout(myLayout);

    constraints.weightx = 100;
    constraints.weighty = 100;
    constraints.gridx = 0;
    constraints.gridy = 0;
    constraints.gridwidth = 6;
    constraints.gridheight = 1;
    myLayout.setConstraints(text, constraints);
    this.add(text);

    constraints.gridy = 1;
    myLayout.setConstraints(theTextField, constraints);
    this.add(theTextField);
    constraints.gridx = 5;
    constraints.gridy = 3;
    constraints.gridwidth = 1;
    constraints.gridheight = 1;
    myLayout.setConstraints(okButton, constraints);
    this.add(okButton);
    constraints.gridx = 3;
    myLayout.setConstraints(cancelButton, constraints);
    this.add(cancelButton);

    this.pack();
    this.show();
}
```

continues

Designing the Application

Listing 6.3   Continued

```
//place a border around the dialog
public Insets insets() {
      return new Insets(15, 15, 15, 15);
}

public String getLabel() {
      return text.getText();
}

//trap the action generated when a user clicks on a button
public boolean action(Event evt, Object arg) {
      //did the event occur over a button
      if(evt.target instanceof Button) {
            //notify the owner that the dialog has been dismissed
            if(((Button)evt.target).getLabel().equals("OK")) {
                theP    arent.tellResponse(this,theTextField.getText());
            }
            else {
                  theParent.tellResponse(this, null);
            }
            this.hide();
            return true;
      }
      return super.action(evt, arg);
}
}
```

The Question dialog box offers a dialog standard to most applications. You also should offer support dialog boxes that both pose a question to the user and allow him to click Yes or No. A third type of dialog, the ModalOK, comes from the ModalOK class, which was implemented in listing 5.2, modified to call the tellResponse() method. Finally, you should offer a dialog class that prompts the user to answer a question with OK or Cancel (see Fig. 6.1).

FIGURE 6.1

The Question dialog box posing.

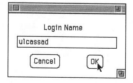

Six: Advanced AWT

The YesNo class

Listing 6.4 illustrates a class called YesNo. This class passes a string and displays that string aside two buttons: a Yes label and a No label. When a user clicks on either button, the action() method closes the dialog box and notifies the parent. As with all Dialog classes, the tellResponse() method is called when the dialog is dismissed. In this case, the YesNo class passed to tellResponse() will be a reference to the calling object and a string, which will either contain the value "Yes" or "No."

Listing 6.4   The YesNo Class Prompts the User to Answer a Question with Either Yes or No

```
package industrial;
import java.awt.*;
//YesNo class allows the user to answer a user specified question
//with either Yes or No. In either case, the object which owns the class
//will be notified through its tellResponse() method.
public class YesNo extends Dialog {

    //GUI controls
    private      Label                text;
    private         Button               okButton;
    private         Button               cancelButton;
    private         String               theChoice = null;
    private         FrameWork           theParent;

    //constructor, accepts a string as a parameter and uses
    //it as the question. Also accepts a reference to the object which
    //owns the dialog.
    public YesNo(FrameWork parent, String incomingText) {
        super(parent, true);

        //assign the parent
        theParent = parent;

        //create the components
        text = new Label(incomingText);
        okButton = new Button("Yes");
        cancelButton = new Button("No");
        //use the GridBagLayout manager to draw the screen
        GridBagLayout myLayout = new GridBagLayout();
        GridBagConstraints constraints = new GridBagConstraints();
        this.setLayout(myLayout);
```

continues

Listing 6.4   Continued

```
            constraints.weightx = 100;
            constraints.weighty = 100;
            constraints.gridx = 0;
            constraints.gridy = 0;
            constraints.gridwidth = 6;
            constraints.gridheight = 1;
            myLayout.setConstraints(text, constraints);
            this.add(text);

            constraints.gridx = 5;
            constraints.gridy = 3;
            constraints.gridwidth = 1;
            constraints.gridheight = 1;
            myLayout.setConstraints(okButton, constraints);
            this.add(okButton);
            constraints.gridx = 2;
            myLayout.setConstraints(cancelButton, constraints);
            this.add(cancelButton);

            this.pack();
            this.show();
        }


    //place a border around the dialog
    public Insets insets() {
            return new Insets(15, 15, 15, 15);
    }
    //trap the action generated when a user clicks on a button
    public boolean action(Event evt, Object arg) {
            //did the event occur over a button
            if(evt.target instanceof Button) {
              theParent.tellResponse(this,((Button)evt.target).getLabel());
                this.hide();
                return true;
            }
            return super.action(evt, arg);
    }
}
```

Figure 6.2 illustrates the YesNo dialog box prompting a user with a possible follow-up to the question posed in figure 6.1.

FIGURE 6.2

The YesNo dialog box prompting the user to continue or not.

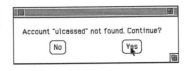

The ModalOK Class, Revisited

As previously stated, this chapter implements a modified version of the ModalOK dialog box. Instead of simply closing the dialog box, the action() method now also calls the tellResponse() method in the object that owns the dialog box. Listing 6.5 illustrates the new ModalOK class. Figure 6.3 illustrates the dialog box informing the user of a rather unfortunate situation.

Listing 6.5   Presenting the User with a Statement and Enabling Her to Click OK

```
package industrial;
import java.awt.*;
//A modal dialog enables the user to enter input and click OK.
public class ModalOK extends Dialog {
        private Button okButton;         //the button which the user will
                                         //click to dismiss the box

        private FrameWork theParent;     //reference to the dialog's owner

        public ModalOK(FrameWork parent, String theMessage) {
                super(parent, false);    //tell Dialog that we are modal

                //set up the parent reference
                theParent = parent;

                //set the layout manager
                GridBagLayout gb = new GridBagLayout();
                GridBagConstraints contraints = new GridBagConstraints();
                setLayout(gb);

                //create the widgets
                okButton = new Button("OK");
                Label message = new Label(theMessage);

                //place the widgets on the screen
                contraints.fill = GridBagConstraints.NONE;
                contraints.anchor = GridBagConstraints.CENTER;
                contraints.ipadx = 20;
```

continues

Listing 6.5   Continued

```
        contraints.ipady = 20;
        contraints.weightx = 1.0;
        contraints.weighty = 1.0;
        contraints.gridwidth = GridBagConstraints.REMAINDER;
        contraints.gridheight = GridBagConstraints.RELATIVE;

        gb.setConstraints(message, contraints);
        add(message);

        contraints.ipadx = 0;
        contraints.ipady = 0;
        contraints.weightx = 0.0;
        contraints.weighty = 0.0;
        contraints.gridwidth = 1;
        contraints.gridheight = GridBagConstraints.REMAINDER;

        gb.setConstraints(okButton, contraints);
        add(okButton);

        //force our dialog box to take minimum of space
        pack();

        //display the dialog
        show();
    }

    //trap the ok click
    public boolean action(Event evt, Object arg) {
        //if the user clicked on the OK button close the dialog box,
        //and call tellResponse()
        if(evt.target instanceof Button) {
                this.hide();
              theParent,tellResponse(this, ((Button)evt.target)
            ➥getLabel());
        }
        return true;
    }
}
```

FIGURE 6.3

The ModalOK dialog box relaying a message from the application to the user.

Three Failures To Login; Logging Out.

OK

Six: Advanced AWT

The Decision Class

A final dialog box you must implement is a slightly modified version of the previous Question class. It is common to prompt the user to answer a question, allow a free-text answer, and support OK and Cancel buttons. However, it is also common for an application to prompt the user to answer a question using only the OK and Cancel buttons. Creating this class involves little difficulty: Simply remove the TextField from the Question dialog box. You also must modify the action method to send tellResponse() OK or Cancel instead of the text in the TextField.

Listing 6.6 illustrates the Decision class. Figure 6.4 illustrates this dialog box supporting the continuing password dialog box.

Listing 6.6   The Decision Class Prompts the User with a Question

```
package industrial;
import java.awt.*;
//Decision class prompts the user for an answer to either accept or
//cancel some question. When the user answers, the parent will be notified
//through Its tellResponse() method.
public class Decision extends Dialog {

    //GUI controls
    private      Label                  text;
    private          Button                  okButton;
    private          Button                  cancelButton;
    private          String                  theChoice = null;
    private          FrameWork               theParent;

    //Decision class allows the user to answer a user specified question
    //with either OK or Cancel. In either case, the object which owns
    //the class will be notified through its tellRespose() method.
    public Decision(FrameWork parent, String incomingText) {
        super(parent, true);

        //assign the parent
        theParent = parent;

        //create the components
        text = new Label(incomingText);
        okButton = new Button("OK");
        cancelButton = new Button("Cancel");
        //use the GridBagLayout manager to draw the screen
        GridBagLayout myLayout = new GridBagLayout();
        GridBagConstraints constraints = new GridBagConstraints();
```

continues

Designing the Application

Listing 6.6   Continued

```
            this.setLayout(myLayout);

            constraints.weightx = 100;
            constraints.weighty = 100;
            constraints.gridx = 0;
            constraints.gridy = 0;
            constraints.gridwidth = 6;
            constraints.gridheight = 1;
            myLayout.setConstraints(text, constraints);
            this.add(text);

            constraints.gridx = 5;
            constraints.gridy = 3;
            constraints.gridwidth = 1;
            constraints.gridheight = 1;
            myLayout.setConstraints(okButton, constraints);
            this.add(okButton);
            constraints.gridx = 2;
            myLayout.setConstraints(cancelButton, constraints);
            this.add(cancelButton);
        this.pack();
        this.show();
    }


    //place a border around the dialog
    public Insets insets() {
        return new Insets(15, 15, 15, 15);
    }


    //trap the action generated when a user clicks on a button
    public boolean action(Event evt, Object arg) {
        //did the event occur over a button
        if(evt.target instanceof Button)
{theParent.tellResponse(this,((Button)evt.target).getLabel());
            this.hide();
            return true;
        }
        return super.action(evt, arg);
    }
}
```

Six: Advanced AWT

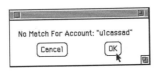

FIGURE 6.4

*The Decision class
notifying the user of
more password
trouble.*

Finishing the Application Framework

To complete this chapter, two tasks remain. First, you must integrate the various pieces of
the framework together. Then, you must develop a small proof-of-concept application with
the framework.

Finishing the Framework

Listing 6.7 provides the completed framework. Most of the framework was created during
this chapter; the rest is simply glue used to hold it together.

Listing 6.7   The Completed Application Framework

```
package industrial;
import java.awt.*;
import java.awt.image.*;
import java.io.*;
//Generic application framework. Can be subclassed by users to either
//create an instant GUI to a text-based application, or used as a
//starting point for new applications.
public class FrameWork extends Frame {

        //menu components. we make everything public to allow for access
        //from other classes, packages, etc... while the framework is
        //great for any application users should be able to modify anything
        //they desire w/o editing this class.
        public      MenuBar         myMenuBar;

        public      Menu            fileMenu;
        public      MenuItem        fileNew;
        public      MenuItem        fileOpen;
        public      MenuItem        fileSave;
        public      MenuItem        fileQuit;
        public      Menu            editMenu;
        public      MenuItem        editUndo;
        public      MenuItem        editCut;
```

continues

Listing 6.7   Continued

```
public        MenuItem      editCopy;
public        MenuItem      editPaste;


//file dialogs
public FileDialog myOpenDialog;
public FileDialog mySaveDialog;


//constructor, creates a new Frame with the title passed as a
//parameter
    public FrameWork(String title) {
      super.setBackground(Color.white);
      super.resize(300, 200);
      super.setTitle(title);
      this.initMenus();
}


//set up a border around the Frame ... asthetic reasons only
public Insets insets() {
      return new Insets(10, 10, 10, 10);
}
//this class will create all menus and add them to the menubar
public void initMenus() {
      //create the menus
      myMenuBar = new MenuBar();
      //add the menubar to the frame
      this.setMenuBar(myMenuBar);
      fileMenu = new Menu("File", true);
      editMenu = new Menu("Edit", true);

      //create choices for the file menu
      fileNew = new MenuItem("New Frame");
      fileOpen = new MenuItem("Open...");
      fileSave = new MenuItem("Save...");
      fileQuit = new MenuItem("Quit");

      //add choices to the file menu
      fileMenu.add(fileNew);
      fileMenu.add(fileOpen);
      fileMenu.add(fileSave);
      fileMenu.addSeparator();
      fileMenu.add(fileQuit);
```

```
        //add the file menu
        myMenuBar.add(fileMenu);

          //create the choices for the edit menu
            editUndo = new MenuItem("Undo");
            editCut = new MenuItem("Cut");
            editCopy = new MenuItem("Copy");
            editPaste = new MenuItem("Paste");

        //add choices to the edit menu
            editMenu.add(editUndo);
            editMenu.addSeparator();
            editMenu.add(editCut);
            editMenu.add(editCopy);
            editMenu.add(editPaste);

        //add the component menu
        myMenuBar.add(editMenu);
}


//create a new frame, a utility method called when File-->New is
//selected users may want to overload with this method or to trap
//the New selection is an action method which precedes this class.
public void createNewFrame(String title) {
        FrameWork newFrame = new FrameWork(title);
        newFrame.resize(300, 200);
        newFrame.show();
}


//create open dialog
public void createOpenDialog() {
        myOpenDialog = new FileDialog(this, "Open File",
        FileDialog.LOAD);
        myOpenDialog.setDirectory(".");
        myOpenDialog.setFile("openFile.txt");
        myOpenDialog.show();
}


//create save dialog
public void createSaveDialog() {
        mySaveDialog = new FileDialog(this, "Save File As",
        FileDialog.SAVE);
```

continues

Designing the Application

Listing 6.7   Continued

```
                mySaveDialog.setDirectory(".");
                mySaveDialog.setFile("newFile.txt");
                mySaveDialog.show();
    }


    //display the String arg in a modal dialog
    public void doResponse(String arg) {
            ModalOK         theResponse = new ModalOK(this, arg);

            theResponse.pack();
            theResponse.show();
    }


    //catch menu choices
    public boolean action(Event evt, Object arg) {
            if("New Frame".equals(arg)) {
                    this.createNewFrame("New Frame");
              return true;
            }
            else if("Open...".equals(arg)) {
                    this.createOpenDialog();
                return true;
            }
            else if("Save...".equals(arg)) {
                    this.createSaveDialog();
                return true;
            }
            else if("Quit".equals(arg)) {
                    System.exit(0);
              return true;
            }
            return super.action(evt, arg);
    }

//will be given info when a dialog is dismissed, it is up to a child
//class to override this method to actually deal with any amount
//of user interaction.
public void tellResponse(Object arg, String answer) {
}
```

```
//handleEvent must be overridden to trap Event.WINDOW_DESTROY.
//By placing this method here in the framework, child classes
//will not have to worry about catching this event.
public boolean handleEvent(Event e) {
        if(e.id == Event.WINDOW_DESTROY) {
                this.hide();
                return true;
        }
        return super.handleEvent(e);
    }
}
```

Putting the Application Framework to Use

At this point, you should have support both for standard menus and a series of dialogs. Together the classes form a flexible, reusable framework.

To demonstrate the application's functions, create a small application that extends the framework and accomplishes the following tasks: adds new menu options, creates dialog boxes, and traps dialog choices though a tellResponse() method. Additionally, the demo application uses the createOpenDialog() method in the dialog parent to draw the open file dialog. Using this method allows the application to call getFile() to identify the selected file. Simply print the file name as files stream into an application in an application-specific manner.

Listing 6.8 illustrates the demo application. Figure 6.5 shows the application in various states.

Listing 6.8   A Small Application to Demonstrate the Application Framework

```
import industrial.*;
import java.awt.*;
//Class DemoApplication, proves the funcitonality of the application
//framework.
public class DemoApplication extends FrameWork {

    //Constructor, creates a new frame with the string passed to it.
    public DemoApplication(String windowName) {
            //call the parent constructor, sets up the
            //title, and creates the File and Edit menus.
            super(windowName);
```

continues

Listing 6.8   Continued

```
            //add our application specific menus
            this.initMyMenus();

            //display the dialog
            super.show();
    }


//class initMyMenus will add a new menu to the existing File and
//Edit menus
public void initMyMenus() {
        //create menu objects
        Menu dialogMenu = new Menu("Dialogs", true);
        MenuItem dialogQuestion = new MenuItem("Question...");
        MenuItem dialogDecision = new MenuItem("Decision...");
        MenuItem dialogYesNo = new MenuItem("Yes / No...");
        MenuItem dialogModalOK = new MenuItem("ModalOK...");

        //add them together
        dialogMenu.add(dialogQuestion);
        dialogMenu.add(dialogDecision);
        dialogMenu.add(dialogYesNo);
        dialogMenu.add(dialogModalOK);

        //add our new menu to the main menubar.
        super.myMenuBar.add(dialogMenu);
    }


//class tellResponse, will trap all dialog box dismissals
public void tellResponse(Object arg, String inString) {
        if(arg instanceof Question) {
                if(inString == null) {
                        System.out.println("I created a Question, and
                        you clicked \"Cancel\"");
                }
                else {
                        System.out.println("I created a Question, and
                        you said: "+inString);
                }
        }
        else if(arg instanceof Decision) {
            System.out.println("I created a Decision, and you
            said: "+inString);
```

Six: Advanced AWT

```
        }
         else if(arg instanceof YesNo) {
              System.out.println("I created a YesNo, and you said:
              "+inString);
         }
         else if(arg instanceof ModalOK) {
              System.out.println("I created a ModalOK, and you said:
              "+inString);
         }
    }

//catch menu choices
    public boolean action(Event evt, Object arg) {
        if("Question...".equals(arg)) {
              Question myQuestion = new Question(this, "What Is Your
              Favorite Food?");
          return true;
        }
        else if("Decision...".equals(arg)) {
              Decision myDecision = new Decision(this, "Are You
              Sure, Your Favorite Food Is Fudge?");
          return true;
        }
        else if("Yes / No...".equals(arg)) {
              YesNo myYesNo = new YesNo(this, "Is Your Favorite Food
              Fudge?");
          return true;
        }
        else if("ModalOK...".equals(arg)) {
              ModalOK myModalOK = new ModalOK(this, "Your Favorite
              Food Is Fudge");
          return true;
        }
        return super.action(evt, arg);
    }

//example of how the createOpenDialog method in the FrameWork
//class
//can be used to draw the open dialog
public void createOpenDialog() {
      super.createOpenDialog();
      String myFile = myOpenDialog.getFile();
      System.out.println(myFile);
}

//main method
```

continues

Designing the Application

Listing 6.8   Continued

```
        public static void main(String args[]) {
            DemoApplication myDemo = new DemoApplication("Child");
        }
    }
```

FIGURE 6.5

*The demo applica-
tion at various points
of execution.*

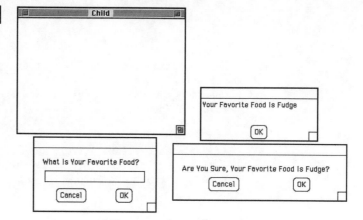

Summary

You now have created a flexible application framework to use as a tool when building
your own applications. In the future, you can add new components to the framework to
customize the look, feel, and function of an application that you develop.

Six: Advanced AWT

Chapter 7

Beginning Data Structures: Taking Advantage of java.util

I n the broadest sense, the term *data structure* applies to any means for storing and retrieving data; it is a huge area studied in many university-level courses. This chapter and Chapter 8, "Advanced Data Structures," in no way attempt to teach how to build every imaginable type of data structure, but teach you about developing data structures in Java. These chapters focus on "growable data structures" as it is an area where developers are often a bit unsure. Although most developers are familiar with the development of growable data structures, this development has probably been in a language like C++ or Pascal where growable data structures are implemented with pointers. Java does not use pointers, and building a dynamically sized data structure without pointers requires a reorganization of your thought process.

Working in a Pointer-Free Enviroment

A common belief—stemming from a heavy background in Pascal, C, or C++—is that to implement any sort of growable data structure, you must manipulate pointers. This belief could not be further from the truth, as a look at the actual purpose of pointers shows.

Listing 7.1 illustrates an example of how you might insert a new node into a linked list written in C.

Listing 7.1   The C Function to Insert a New Value onto the End of a Linked List

```
/*      Function to insert an int "toBeInserted" at the end of a list
➥whose end is pointed to be *tailPtr. */
void insertAtEnd(struct list *tailPtr, int toBeInserted) {
     newPtr = (struct list *)malloc(sizeof(struct list));
     newPtr -> info = toBeInserted;
     tailPtr -> next = newPtr;
     newPtr -> next = NULL;
}
```

It is obvious in this code that pointers are totally necessary for the management of the linked list. The real purpose served by pointers in listing 7.1 is not to allocate the memory for the list dynamically, but rather to track dynamically allocated memory. The follow-up statement is that the implementation of growable data structures requires only the capability to dynamically allocate memory and to be able to track this memory. Java provides these mechanisms without forcing a developer to deal with pointers.

The realization that pointers are not at all necessary to implement growable data structures comes as great news to anyone who has ever struggled with pointer manipulation. What comes as even greater news is that Java takes care of most memory issues for you; although garbage collection is by no means perfect, in rare cases you may want to take care of garbage collection yourself.

In addition to managing garbage collection and not requiring the use of pointers, Java provides the "java.util" package that contains classes for many basic data structures. This chapter focuses on the use of the java.util package. The focus of the next chapter shifts to the development of your own data structures from scratch.

Introducing java.util

When beginning with a new language, you spend significant time building a library of reusable code snippets. In the case of an object-oriented language like Java, a flexible class library is critical to developing any application in a reasonable amount of time. Many of these classes will not be a programming feat, but will still involve a large time commitment. Fortunately, in the design of Java, the engineers at Sun have taken care of many of these classes already. The java.util package implements a series of growable data structures that you will find indispensable.

Although you will no doubt find java.util indispensable, its usefulness is limited. This limitation with the java.util package is that the coverage, although wide, is not very deep. The data structures implemented are by no means advanced enough for large amounts of information; they are all quite flexible, however, and it is easy to use them as building blocks for larger data structures.

The Vector Class

The Vector class is basically a growable array. Where an array has a fixed upperbound position, a Vector can grow indefinitely. The existence of this class is quite exciting because any industrial strength application needs access to dynamic storage. By making this dynamic storage part of the basic API, developers are saved time as they do not have to implement it themselves.

The Vector class, however, should not be taken for granted. As with C++ or Pascal, growable data structures have significantly more overhead than those that are of fixed size. The situation is basically a catch-22. You can use statically bounded arrays and not dedicate any resources to allocation of additional memory; by doing so, however, you are forced to work within predefined boundaries. Or you can allow for indefinite growth, but deal with the overhead of on-the-fly memory allocation. The problem has been pondered for years, and the Vector class does propose a "happy medium" that is quite elegant when properly managed.

Understanding memory allocation is integral to developing fast code using the Vector class. This section begins by showing the various uses of the Vector class and then continues with a discussion of why the code executes in the manner that it does.

Listing 7.2 shows the Vector constructors as provided by the Java API. The first constructor simply creates a Vector object with a default initial size. The second and third constructors create Vector objects with different initial sizes. The third constructor, in addition to affecting initial size, creates a Vector that grows by a user-defined factor.

Listing 7.2   The Three Constructors Supported by the java.util.Vector Class

```
public Vector();
public Vector(int initialCapacity);
public Vector(int initialCapacity, int capacityIncrement);
```

Depending on your choice of Java development platforms, your actual results will vary. What you should note is not the actual times, but rather the relationship between the times.

To see how the different constructors react to the steady insertion of a series of Objects, consider a benchmarking application that times the insertion of 100,000 Integer objects into first an empty Vector, then into a Vector created to hold 100,000 Objects, and finally into a Vector created to first hold 50,000 objects, but with a capacityIncrement of 50,000.

This benchmarking application is contained in listing 7.3a through 7.3c and a test output is in listing 7.4.

All variables are set up in listing 7.3a.

Listing 7.3a   Variables Used in the VectorBenchmarks Class

```
package industrial;
import java.util.*;

public class VectorBenchmarks {
    private    final      int        MAXELEMENTS = 100000;
    private    long        begin;
    private    long        end;
    private    Vector      slowVector;
    private    Vector      midVector;
    private    Vector      fastVector;
    private    Integer[]   integerArray;
    private    Integer     myInteger;
```

The first part of the constructor for the VectorBenchmarks class is shown listing 7.3b. Here the array and vectors are initialized, and you also create an integer object that will be inserted into the objects. One final note on thecapacityIncrement parameter in the Vector constructor (the third constructor in listing 7.2 uses this parameter) should be mentioned. The variable causes the Vector to increase by capacityIncrement number of elements every time the Vector is full. If you pass in a zero, however, the Vector doubles in size every time it is full.

Listing 7.3b   Initialization of Needed Variables

```
public VectorBenchmarks() {
    //Integer object to be inserted
    myInteger = new Integer(42);

    //an array with space for MAXELEMENTS
    integerArray = new Integer[MAXELEMENTS];

    //a vector with default initial size
    slowVector = new Vector();

    //a vector with initial capacity of (1/2)*MAXELEMENTS and a
    capacityIncrement of (1/10)*MAXELEMENTS
    midVector = new Vector(MAXELEMENTS/2, MAXELEMENTS/2);

    //a vector with initial capacity of MAXELEMENTS
    fastVector = new Vector(MAXELEMENTS);
```

Listing 7.3c takes the newly initialized Vector and array objects and fills them with Integer objects. After the insertion is complete, the time needed to complete the insertion is given.

Listing 7.3c   Filling the Array and Vector Objects with Integer Objects

```
//insert MAXELEMENTS into slowVector
begin = System.currentTimeMillis();
for(int i=0; i<MAXELEMENTS; i++) {
    slowVector.addElement(myInteger);
}
end = System.currentTimeMillis();
System.out.println("Time to insert MAXELEMENTS into
slowVector: "+ (end-begin) +" milliseconds");

//insert MAXELEMENTS into integerArray
begin = System.currentTimeMillis();
for(int i=0; i<MAXELEMENTS; i++) {
    integerArray[i] = myInteger;
}
end = System.currentTimeMillis();
System.out.println("Time to insert MAXELEMENTS into
integerArray: "+ (end-begin) + "milliseconds");
//insert MAXELEMENTS into fastVector
begin = System.currentTimeMillis();
for(int i=0; i<MAXELEMENTS; i++) {
```

continues

Beginning Data Structures

Listing 7.3c   Continued

```
                    fastVector.addElement(myInteger);
        }
        end = System.currentTimeMillis();
        System.out.println("Time to insert MAXELEMENTS into
        ➥fastVector: "+ (end-begin) +" milliseconds");


        //insert MAXELEMENTS into midVector
        begin = System.currentTimeMillis();
        for(int i=0; i<MAXELEMENTS; i++) {
            midVector.addElement(myInteger);
        }
        end = System.currentTimeMillis();
        System.out.println("Time to insert MAXELEMENTS into midVector:
        ➥"+ (end-begin) +" milliseconds");
    }

    public static void main(String args[]) {
        VectorBenchmarks myVectorBenchmarks = new VectorBenchmarks();
    }
}
```

Listing 7.4 gives the output generated by the benchmarking application. As you can see, insertion into the array was fastest because are dealing with a pre-allocated memory buffer. After you begin dealing with Vectors insertion time increases, however, as you can see through proper planning, you are able to receive a fast insertion time in the fastVector example.

Listing 7.4   Output of the VectorBenchmarks Application

```
Time to insert MAXELEMENTS into slowVector: 5483 milliseconds
Time to insert MAXELEMENTS into integerArray: 1600 milliseconds
Time to insert MAXELEMENTS into fastVector: 3200 milliseconds
Time to insert MAXELEMENTS into midVector: 4216 milliseconds
```

The huge differences in insertion times for the benchmarking application above prove how important it is to calculate your space needs in advance. To properly calculate space needs, you need not only an understanding of your application, but also an understanding of the possibilities that Java presents.

One purpose of this chapter and Chapter 8 is to teach you about developing data structures in Java. In a broader sense, this book teaches not only about the Java language, but more importantly, stresses planning your application long before attempting to write even one line of code. By planning your applications ahead of time, you have a much better chance of writing memory-efficient code the first time.

Implementing Stacks Using java.util

A *Stack* is a linear data structure to which new items are always added and deleted from the same point. A stack is considered a *Last-In-First-Out* (LIFO) data structure because the first item to which you have access is the last one that you added to the stack. If stacks are a new concept to you, you might be confused about their implementation and purpose. Stacks are basically simple and quite useful, as they allow an infinite amount of objects to be manipluated in a logical manner.

Look at figure 7.1, which illustrates a stack. The numbers 1, 2, 3, and 4 (in that order) have been pushed onto this stack. The numbers 5, 6, and 7 are waiting to get pushed onto the stack.

If you think back to all the trouble you might have had learning pointer manipulation, you should be rather excited that stacks can be implemented in Java without the need for pointers. In fact, it is even possible to implement a stack in one line of code! The ease with which you can implement a stack is due to Sun's provision of a class called java.util.Stack, which does most of the work for you.

Figure 7.1

A pictorial representation of a stack.

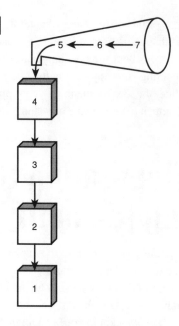

The java.util.Stack Class

Chances are many of you thought about how easy it would be to be able to implement a stack using the java.util.Vector class. Well, you are by no means alone, Stack's parent is Vector, and Sun obviously realized the same thing as you!

Note the Java API listing for java.util.Stack in listing 7.5. The method list is rather small, and you should have little trouble seeing how it is implemented.

Listing 7.5   The Java API Listing for java.util.Stack

```
public class java.util.Stack extends java.util.Vector
➥{
        public   boolean empty();
        public   Object peek();
        public   Object pop();
        public   Object push(Object item);
        public   int search(Object o);
}
```

Implementing the Stack Class

Coverage of the Stack class begins with the development of a small application that shows proper usage of the different methods in the class. You then develop a practical solution that you may need to use in an application of your own. As a side note, this section shows not only how to implement an instance of java.util.Stack (which is designed to handle objects only), but also how to manipulate Stack to work with base types also.

Programming with Types

It is a well-known fact that with few exceptions, everything in Java is an object. As a direct result , many classes in the java.util package are designed to operate on Objects. This can be very useful because it provides for incredible flexibility for the developer; there are situations, however, where it is desirable to program with types instead of with objects. In order to facilitate the usage of types in an environment where objects are expected, Java provides wrapper classes that engulf base types to enable the manipulation of types as objects.

Table 7.1 shows all Java base types along with their associated wrapper classes. Of course, before you can begin to work with wrapper classes, you need to understand how to convert from a type to a wrapper class and vice-versa. The third column of table 7.1 shows how to use a wrapper class's constructor to convert a base type into an object. The fourth column gives the method supported by the wrapper class for conversion back to its associated base type.

TABLE 7.1

Wrapper Classes and Their Associated Base Types

Base Type	Wrapper Class	Type→ Object	Object→ Type
int	java.lang.Integer	Integer newInteger = new Integer(42)	newInteger.intValue()
Boolean	java.lang.Boolean	Boolean myBoolean = new Boolean(true)	myBoolean.BooleanValue()
char	java.lang.Character	Character myCharacter = new Character('a')	myCharacter.charValue()
float	java.lang.Float	Float myFloat = new Float(3.0)	myFloat.floatValue()
double	java.lang.Double	Double myDouble = new Double(7.0)	myDouble.doubleValue()
long	java.lang.Long	Long myLong = new Long(42)	myLong.longValue()

As you can see, converting between a base type and a wrapper class is beyond easy. Listing 7.6 uses the wrapper classes as well as the concept of inheritance to create a class called IntStack that subclasses java.util.Stack to provide a Stack class that enables you to manipulate ints in an environment traditionally dominated by Objects. To accomplish this, do the following:

1. Create a class called IntStack that subclasses java.util.Stack.

2. Add a method called Push() that is used to push ints onto the stack.

3. In Push(), accept an int as a parameter, translate it to an Integer object, and pass it to IntStack's parent.

4. Create methods called Peek() and Pop(). These methods will return—as an int— the top object on the stack.

5. In Peek() and Pop(), call the respective method in IntStack's parent. Take the Object return value from this method, first convert it to an Integer, then to an int, and finally return it.

Listings 7.6a and 7.6b show the IntStack class and a driver that demonstrates the functionality of the class.

In listing 7.6a you create the IntStack class. The conversion between objects and base types is rather obvious. If you have any trouble, refer to table 7.1.

Listing 7.6a   A Traditional Stack Data Structure that Can Be Used to Manipulate ints

```
package industrial;
import java.util.*;
class IntStack extends java.util.Stack {

    public int Peek() {
        return ((Integer)super.peek()).intValue();
    }

    public int Pop() {
        return ((Integer)super.pop()).intValue();
    }

    public Object Push(int i) {
        return super.push(new Integer(i));
    }
```

```java
    public int Search(int i) {
        return super.search(new Integer(i));
    }
}
```

Listing 7.6b uses the IntStack class in a simple application. First some ints are pushed onto the stack, then you search for one specific int, and finally you remove everything on the stack.

Listing 7.6b   A Driver to Demonstrate the Functionality of the IntStack Class

```java
public class StackDemo {
    IntStack myStack;

    public StackDemo() {
        myStack = new IntStack();
        int tempInt;

        //Push 100 integers onto the stack
        for(int i=0; i<100; i++) {
            myStack.Push(i);
        }

        //Find the index of 42
        tempInt = myStack.Search(42);

        //Pop off all integers
        while(!myStack.empty()) {
            tempInt = myStack.Pop();
        }
    }

    public static void main(String args[]) {
        StackDemo myStackDemo = new StackDemo();
        System.out.println("Done");
    }
}
```

Real-World Stack Applications

It is easy to say that stacks are cool, but that is not a convincing argument for using them. Why bother with dynamically sized, sequentially assessable data structures when arrays are so much easier and faster to manipulate? It is not hard to find people willing to argue either side of the dynamically sized versus statically sized data structure controversy.

On one side of the coin, you will find proponents of static data structures. These types of data structures are easy to maintain and are very predictable. When space limitations are hardcoded into a class, however, that class often becomes one of a very single purpose. One of the joys of Object Oriented Programming is code reuse. If you develop a class that can manage an infinite data set that class will be usable

Being able to write a class that treats data sets of all sizes in the same manner is rather fantastic. Just think of how annoying it would be to have some useful code break if it had to deal with a data set larger than some fixed quantity.

The application in listing 7.7, which evaluates a post-fix expression, demonstrates how a Stack enables you to write code that deals with any amount of data. Post-fix notation is useful for representing a mathematical expression in an environment where rules of precedence are not required. To convert from infix to postfix, you basically shove all operands to the left of the equation, and all operators to the right. Then, when evaluating the expression, you scan the input until an operator is reached and applies that operator to the two previous operands.

As an example, take the expression 3 + 4 in infix, which translates to 3 4 + in postfix. To evaluate this expression by using a stack, you would push the operands 3 and 4 on the stack. After you reached the operator +, you would pop off the 3 and 4 and apply the operator and push the result back onto the stack. A slightly more complex example is that the infix expression of ((3 + 2) - 5) * (6 / (1 - 9)) translates to 3 2 + 5 - 1 9 - 6 / * in postfix. This expression can be evaluated by using the same formula used in the previous example. First, 3 and 2 would be pushed onto the stack. When the first operator is reached (+), the stack would be popped twice, and the result would be pushed back on. If you follow through with this algorithm, pushing all operands on the stack and popping when a operator is reached, you will end up with a final value of 0.

Postfix expressions are incredibly easy to evaluate with a stack because you can scan the expression left-to-right and, if the current token is an operand, push it onto the stack. If the current token is an operator, you simply have to pop the top two tokens off the stack, evaluate them using the current token, and push the result back onto the stack. After you reach the end of the expression, you simply have to pop the stack to get the answer to the expression. Listing 7.7 is the sample application that evaluates a post-fix expression passed in as a command-line argument. Note that the application assumes the existence of a method called eval, and also isOperand. eval("5," "6," "*") would return 30, and isOperand("5") would return true.

Figure 7.7 An Application that Uses a Stack to Evaluate a Post-Fix Expression

```java
package industrial;
import java.util.*;
public class CalcDemo {
    Stack calcStack;

    public CalcDemo(String postString) {
        calcStack                    = new Stack();
        StringTokenizer stin     = new StringTokenizer(postString);
        String               theNextToken;

        while(stin.hasMoreTokens()) {
            try{
                theNextToken = stin.nextToken();
                System.out.println("theNextToken: "+theNextToken);

                //the current token is an operand, simply push onto
                //the stack
                if(this.isOperand(theNextToken)) {
                    calcStack.push(theNextToken);
                }

                //the current token is an operator, pop twice and eval
                else {
                System.out.println("0: "+theNextToken);
                    calcStack.push(this.eval(calcStack.pop(),
                    ➥calcStack.pop(), theNextToken));
                }

                //is the next token, the last token on the stack?
                //if this is the last token, the it is our answer
                if(!stin.hasMoreTokens()) {
                    System.out.println("answer: "+calcStack.pop());
                }
            }
            catch(EmptyStackException ese) { System.out.println("err:
            ➥"+ ese); }
        }
    }

    public static void main(String args[]) {
        System.out.println("Post-Fix String: "+ args[0]);
        CalcDemo myCalcDemo = new CalcDemo(args[0]);
    }
}
```

Beginning Data Structures

Storing Information in a Hash Table

The way you store information in an application is rather important. You usually need to have constant access to various parts of some information set, and, as this set grows, speed becomes an important issue. You can store large information sets in many ways, but the hash table data structure is one of the more popular. A *hash table* works by dividing the large data set into small groups (hopefully of equal size). Each of these small groups is stored sequentially. Assuming you know the manner in which the data set was divided, it becomes a simple chore to find a specific part of that data set.

For example, if you store the names of many people in a hash table, you can break up the large group into smaller groups by developing categories based on the first letter of their last name. Figure 7.2 illustrates how a group of names can be categorized in this manner.

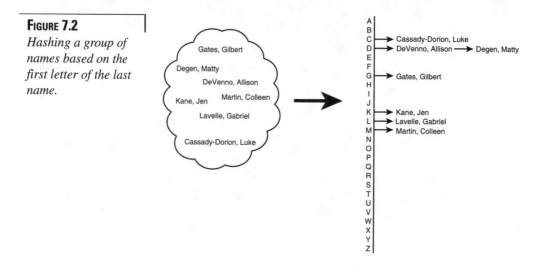

FIGURE 7.2

Hashing a group of names based on the first letter of the last name.

One thing to note about figure 7.2 is that the data seems to group around a certain area. In fact, the letter "D" has more than one name "hashed" to the same location. As you can imagine, storing a huge collection of names with this system would be rather impractical. You would end up with such large groupings around specific letters that searching would take forever!

You can achieve an optimal hash table by finding the perfect hash code. Because no data set is the same, every data set should have its own hash code. For example, the implementation in figure 7.2 is practical for a small group of names; if the names being hashed are associated with members of the same family all having the same last name, however, you would then have a less-than-optimal situation—all names in the data set would hash to the same location.

Another key attribute in finding an optimal hash code is the time it takes to derive that code from the data. Remember that you need to derive that key when you insert an item into the table, and when you search for that item later on. Although you might find an even distribution of data if you average the two's compliment of the number with 42,000 random integers, the time to derive this key would be more than is desirable.

There are trade-offs that you have to make when deciding on a hash code, and often you will have to experiment with various values. You usually find that the best manner to go about deciding on a perfect hash code is to look at the full data set and identify points where data seems to cluster. If you can minimize (and equalize) the size of all clusters, chances are you have found a good hash code.

The java.util.Hashtable Class

Those who have been following the theme developed in this chapter will realize that an implementation of a hash table coming from the java.util package will be used. In fact, listing 7.8 contains the API listing for the java.util.Hashtable class.

Among the other premiums provided by java.util.* is a class called "Hashtable." The API listing for this class is provided in listing 7.8.

Listing 7.8   The Java API Listing for java.util.Hashtable

```
public class java.util.Hashtable extends java.util.Dictionary implements
➥java.lang.Cloneable {
//Constructors
public Hashtable();
public Hashtable(int initialCapacity);
public Hashtable(int initialCapacity, float loadFactor);
//Methods
public void clear();
public Object clone();
public boolean contains(Object value);
public boolean containsKey(Object key);
```

continues

Listing 7.8   Continued

```
public Enumeration elements():
public Object get(Object key);
public boolean isEmpty();
public Enumeration keys();
public Object put(Object key, Object value);
protected void rehash();
public Object remove();
public int size();
public String toString();
}
```

Telling the Hashtable How to Do its Job

Although many classes in the Java API are very intuitive, the Hashtable class presents a question. The fact that each data set has its own hash code was established earlier in this chapter. However, there is no method in java.util.Hashtable to set or change the hash code. This obviously is not an oversight, but rather follows logically with other beliefs surrounding object-oriented programming.

Objects are meant to be self-contained "entities." If programmed properly, they should be able to function perfectly in any environment. For this reason, the Hashtable class is not required to know the objects that it will house. Instead, every object in the hash table is required to tell the hash table how to hash. The hash table object in figure 7.3 is asked to insert some new object. For this process to happen, the following steps must occur:

1. After the hash table is asked to insert a new object, the hash table asks the new object for its hash code.

2. The new object responds by sending the return value of its hashCode() method.

3. The hash table now asks the new object how to test for equivilance between other instances of the same class.

4. The new object tells the hash table about about the equals() method contained within the new object.

5. Using the new object's equals() and hashCode() methods, the hash table inserts the new object in its proper position.

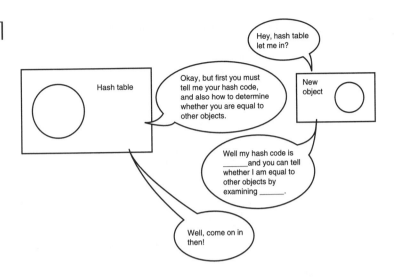

FIGURE 7.3

Before a hash table accepts a new object, the hash table needs certain information.

By now you should have a pretty good understanding of what needs to occur for an object to get inserted into a hash table, but you now need to know how this insertion is performed. This insertion is actually rather easy, and you should have little trouble implementing it in your application.

You can add the support to a class for hashing by overloading two methods in the java.lang.Object class (remember that java.lang.Object is the "universal parent"). These methods are

```
public native int hashCode()
```

and

```
public boolean equals(Object obj)
```

The key to note in the preceding paragraph is that implementing support for a hash code is easy. What is not so easy is actually deciding what that hash code should be.

When you overload hashCode(), you need to return an integer that can be used as a hash code; when you overload equals(), you need to return a Boolean that indicates whether the object passed in is equal to the current object. Listing 7.9 shows how a contact book application might design these methods. The listing obviously does not give all code for the contact book, but instead shows how support for the hashCode() and equals() methods would be implemented in a object that holds information for an individual contact. All methods that are referenced are assumed to perform a duty that is made obvious by their name.

Listing 7.9   An Object Must Know How to be Hashed and How to Tell Whether It Is Equal to Other Objects

```
//return a hash code based on the phone number
public int hashCode() {
            return Integer.parseInt(this.getPhoneNumber().substring(9,
            ➥12));
    }

//return a boolean true if the object passed in contains identical
//contact information as the current object.
public boolean equals(Object obj) {
      ContactBookEntry tempEntry = (ContactBookEntry)obj;
      boolean phoneBool =
this.getPhoneNumber().equals(tempEntry.getPhoneNumber());
      boolean faxBool = this.getFaxNumber().
      ➥equals(tempEntry.getFaxNumber());
      boolean emailBool = this.getEmail().
      ➥equals(tempEntry.getEmail());
      boolean fnameBool = this.getFname().
      ➥equals(tempEntry.getFname());
      boolean lnameBool = this.getLname().
      ➥equals(tempEntry.getLname());
      boolean mnameBool = this.getMname().
      ➥equals(tempEntry.getMname());
      boolean addressBool = this.getAddress().
      ➥equals(getAddress());
      return ((phoneBool == faxBool) == (emailBool == fnameBool)
      ➥   == (lnameBool == mnameBool) == addressBool);
    }
```

It is important to note the manner chosen to compute the hash code in listing 7.9 is by no means the only hash code that would work. Choosing to use part of the phone number as a hash code is one option; another possible idea would be to average the ASCII values of the first three letters in the person's name.

Why It Is Required That We Overload hashCode() and equals()

The beginning of this section stated that you had to implement support for the hashCode() and equals() methods; if you look at java.lang.Object, however, you will note that those methods are not abstract and in fact are implemented at that level. The manner in which

NOTE

The manner in which equals() is overloaded is quite similar to the manner that String overloads equals(). For example, if you create two string objects (string1, and string2) and both hold the word "Smalltalk," then string1.equals(string2) would return true. If you use the form string1 == string2, however, the return is false because the == comparison returns false if the two objects in question are not references to the same object.

java.lang.Object implements these methods is rarely desirable for practical purposes, and if your hash table is going to show any semblance of balancing, then you will want to overload the methods yourself. In fact, you can take this one step further and state that without overloading equals(), your hash table might not function properly. In listing 7.9 we overloaded equals() to test if the two objects being compared contain the same data. The implementation of equals() in java.lang.Object only looks to see if the two objects being compared reference the same value.

In the contact book application in listing 7.9, equals() is overloaded to return true if the two objects in question contain the same data. With the contact book application, you rarely have a situation where two references to the same object were entered. But chances are you could have a situation where someone entered the information twice. If someone creates two contact book entries for the same person, then these entries might be treated as equal.

The manner in which java.lang.Object generates a hash code is not as clear as the manner in which it decides if two objects are equal. You may find, however, that the hash code produced by java.lang.Object— although valid—is rarely practical. A valid return value means that it observes the following two rules that are defined in Javasoft's online documentation at

```
http://java.sun.com:80/products/JDK/CurrentRelease/api/
java.lang.Object.html#6130.
```

- Whenever invoked on the same object more than once during an execution of a Java application, the hashCode() method must consistently return the same integer. This integer need not remain consistent from one execution of an application to another execution of the same application.

- If two objects are equal according to the equals method, then calling the hashCode method on each of the two objects must produce the same integer result.

Working with the Hashtable Class

You spent the beginning of this section delving into what is needed when developing an optimal hash table, but you have not actually developed anything yet. You will finish this section by developing a small application that hashes the contact book objects discussed earlier. Due to space constraints, the contact book contains entries only for phone number, first name, and last name. The code contained in listings 7.10a through 7.10c is an example of the powerful prospects of hash tables, and also an example of how easy it can be to create a hash table in Java.

In listing 7.10a is the beginning class representing a single contact book entry. Here basic variables are set up, and public getXXX() and setXXX() methods are implemented to manipulate member data.

Listing 7.10a   A Sample Application that Performs Hashing on a Series of Contact Book Entries

```java
package industrial;
import java.util.*;
class ContactBookEntry  {
    private    String    phoneNumber;
    private    String    fname;
    private    String    lname;

    public ContactBookEntry() {}

    public void setPhoneNumber(String pnum) {
        phoneNumber = pnum;
    }
    public void setFname(String fnam) {
        fname = fnam;
    }

    public void setLname(String lnam) {
        lname = lnam;
    }

    public String getPhoneNumber() {
        return phoneNumber;
    }
    public String getFname() {
        return fname;
    }

    public String getLname() {
        return lname;
    }
```

In listing 7.10b you complete the class begun in 7.10a by implementing hashCode() and equals() methods.

Listing 7.10b   The hashCode() and equals() Methods

```
public int hashCode() {
    return Integer.parseInt(this.getPhoneNumber().substring(9,
    ➥12)));
}

public boolean equals(Object obj) {
    ContactBookEntry tempEntry = (ContactBookEntry)obj;
    boolean phoneBool =
    ➥this.getPhoneNumber().equals(tempEntry.getPhoneNumber());
    boolean fnameBool =
    ➥this.getFname().equals(tempEntry.getFname());
    boolean lnameBool =
    ➥this.getLname().equals(tempEntry.getLname());
    return ((phoneBool == fnameBool) == lnameBool);
}
}
```

In listing 7.10c is a small driver that creates a new hash table and adds to it a series of ContactBookEntry objects. After a few objects have been added to the hash table, you can play around with some of the other methods in java.util.Hashtable that allow you to access the data stored in the table.

Lisitng 7.10c   Using a Driver to Create a New Hash Table

```
public class HashDemo {
    public    final          int        MAXCONTACTS = 10;
    public    Hashtable             theTable;
    public    ContactBookEntry    myContactBook[];

    public HashDemo() {
        theTable =    new Hashtable();
        myContactBook = new ContactBookEntry[ MAXCONTACTS ];
        myContactBook[0] = new ContactBookEntry();
        myContactBook[0].setFname("Luke");
        myContactBook[0].setLname("Cassady-Dorion");
        myContactBook[0].setPhoneNumber("265-487-2201");
```

continues

Storing Information in a Hash Table

Listing 7.10c   Continued

```
      myContactBook[1] = new ContactBookEntry();
      myContactBook[1].setFname("Matt");
      myContactBook[1].setLname("Degen");
      myContactBook[1].setPhoneNumber("265-888-1234");
      myContactBook[2] = new ContactBookEntry();
      myContactBook[2].setFname("Gabe");
      myContactBook[2].setLname("Lavella");
      myContactBook[2].setPhoneNumber("265-367-4297");

      myContactBook[3] = new ContactBookEntry();
      myContactBook[3].setFname("Allison");
      myContactBook[3].setLname("DeYenno");
      myContactBook[3].setPhoneNumber("265-571-4498");

      for(int i=0; i<=2; i++) {
          theTable.put(myContactBook[i], myContactBook[i]);
      }

      System.out.println("Hash Table: Full");

      if(theTable.containsKey(myContactBook[2])) {
          System.out.println("Hash Table: Contains
          ➥myContactBook[2]");
      }
      else {
          System.out.println("Hash Table: Does not contain
          ➥myContactBook[2]");
      }

      if(theTable.contains(myContactBook[3])) {
          System.out.println("Hash Table: Contains
          ➥myContactBook[3]");
      }
      else {
          System.out.println("Hash Table: Does not contain
          ➥myContacBook[3]");
      }
  }

  public static void main(String args[]) {
      HashDemo myDemo = new HashDemo();
  }
}
```

Although the application in 7.10c proves that the hashtable is actually working, figure 7.4 demonstrates what the hash table would look like after the various contacts have been inserted. Note that because hashCode() returns an int, the range of the hash values is the full range of int. Due to space (and logical) constraints, only the relevant range of values that hashCode could return is displayed.

FIGURE 7.4
This is how the hash table would look after the various contacts have been inserted.

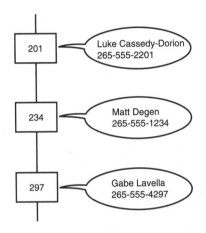

201 — Luke Cassedy-Dorion 265-555-2201

234 — Matt Degen 265-555-1234

297 — Gabe Lavella 265-555-4297

Miscellaneous Hashtable Methods

NOTE

Throughout this book, the term *growable data structure* is used alternately with the term *dynamic data structure*. Both represent the same concept, that of a data structure able to hold an infinite amount of data.

So far, inserting and searching through a hashtable has been covered. There are additional methods in the Hashtable class that you will find useful. The additional methods present in the class were not discussed because the methods are described relatively well by their signatures. The constructors, however, definitely deserve discussion. The first constructor, (Hashtable()), takes no parameters and creates a default hash table. The first constructor was used in listing 7.10a because it is sufficient for small data sets. As your data set grows, however, you will want to use the other two constructors because they enable you to fine tune the performance of the hash table.

As with any growable data structure, speed is sacrificed every time that the data structure grows. For this reason you will want to control both the initial size of the data structure and the rate at which it grows. The second constructor, (Hashtable(int initialCapacity)), in listing 7.8 enables you to pass in an initial capacity. If you know, for example, that your hash table is going to have to hold 100,000 elements, then you should use this constructor because your hash table will not have to grow while the 100,000 elements are being added.

The third constructor (Hashtable(int initialCapacity, float loadFactor)) supported by Hashtable enables you to control the time at which rehashing occurs. This constructor enables you to pass in two values, the initial size, and a number called loadFactor. *loadFactor*—which has a default setting of 0.75—is the number that affects the point at which a hash table resizes. You will want to set this number somewhere between 0.0 and 1.0. The hash table resizes whenever the number of items in the table increases to the current capacity multiplied by the load factor. The amount that the hash table resizes is not controllable by the programmer. It will be somewhere around twice the size when resizing occurs, but could be more or less.

Implementing a Queue Using Classes from java.util

Although java.util presents many useful data structures, this chapter began by stating that these data structures are rarely enough for a complete application. Chapter 8 details how to create your own growable data structures without the need to use any parts of the java.util package. Although java.util does not provide many data structures in their final form, it does provide a series of rather generic growable data structures that can be manipulated to enable the creation of more developed data structures. One such generic data structure is the Vector class. The next few pages contain information that demonstrates how the Vector class can be used to form other data structures.

In introductory data structure classes, around the same time that stacks are introduced, queues are also introduced. Basically the opposite of a stack, a *queue* enables manipulation of objects in a First-In-First-Out manner. For example, a printer queue manages an infinite number of incoming documents. As each document hits the printer queue, it is appended to the bottom of an ever growing list. As the printer finishes printing a document, it asks the printer queue for a new document to print. Because the queue provides service on a first-come-first-served basis, it sends the printer the document that is at the top of its list. The queue will then "bump-up" each document in the queue.

For some reason the Java development team decided to not include support for queues in the java.util package. They did, however, provide the java.util.Vector class, which you can subclass to create a Queue class.

Required Methods for the Queue Class

Remember that stacks and queues do basically the same thing, only in the reverse order. If you check the declaration of java.util.Stack, you will note that this class extends Vector. Logically, you can conclude that it would be rather easy to write a queue class that extends Vector also.

The methods that Queue needs to support are very similar to those required of Stack. They are:

- put() adds an object to the end of the queue
- get() removes the top object on the queue and returns it to the user.
- peek() "peeks" at the top Object and returns it without removing it from the queue.
- empty() returns a Boolean true if the queue is empty and a Boolean false if there are items in the queue.

As stated at the beginning of this section, the Queue class extends java.util.Vector and will subsequently be able to access all of Vector's methods. In fact, because the support for Queue's methods basically exists (under different names) in Vector, no method in Queue will be more than three lines long! Table 7.2 provides a side-by-side comparison of the method that Queue needs to support, and the methods in Vector that offers that support. After you look over table 7.2, look at listing 7.11 where the Queue is actually implemented.

TABLE 7.2		*Method Needed in Queue*	*Method Supported by Vector*
The Methods in Vector that Help Implement Queue	Name	get()	removeElementAt(int index)
	Purpose	Returns the top element in the Queue. Also deletes that element from the Queue	Removes the element at the specified index. You will use it to remove the 0th (or top) element.
	Name	put(Object obj)	addElement(Object obj) addElement
	Purpose	Adds a new object onto the Queue	Adds a new Object as the last item of the Vector
	Name	peek()	firstElement()

continues

TABLE 7.2		Method Needed in Queue	Method Supported by Vector
Continued	Purpose	Returns the top element without removing it from the Queue.	Removes the top element without removing it from the Vector.
	Name	empty()	isEmpty()
	Purpose	Returns a Boolean true if the Queue is empty. Otherwise, returns a Boolean false.	Returns a Boolean true if the Vector is empty. Otherwise, returns a Boolean false.

Now that we know how we are going to write the Queue class, let's go forward and code it. The class in listing 7.11 may just be the shortest Queue you have ever implemented.

Listing 7.11   Implementing a Queue in Java

```java
package industrial;
import java.util.*;

public class Queue extends java.util.Vector {
    //get() returns the top object on the queue
    public Object get() {
        Object tempObject = super.firstElement();
        super.removeElementAt(0);
        return tempObject;
    }

    //pus() adds a new element to the bottom of the queue
    public void put(Object obj) {
        super.addElement(obj);
    }

    //peek() returns the top element on the queue
    public Object peek() {
        return super.firstElement();
    }

    //empty() allows us to check if the queue contains no elements.
    public boolean empty() {
        return super.isEmpty();
    }
}
```

Furthering the java.util Advantage

The fact that you are able to implement a Queue class in about ten lines of code is a compelling reason to take advantage of jave.util. An added bonus is that not only can you create the Queue based on the Vector class, but you can also create a large variety of linear growable data-structures.

Double-Ended Linked Lists

If a queue and a stack ever got together and became one, you would have a double-ended linked list. Where queues and stacks limit the "end" at which insertion and deletion can occur, double-ended linked lists enable you to insert and delete an element at either end.

As with any data structure, the big question is: What am I ever going to use this for? It is cool to be able to lean back at a cocktail party and strike up a conversation on the benefits of double-ended versus single-ended linked lists, but will this get you anything beyond a date? Humor aside, a data structure is useless if you do not have concrete knowledge of how it can benefit a solution that you need to put into place.

An Overview of a Semi-Sorted Linked List

Although your use of double-ended linked lists is limited only by your imagination, one common use is to keep a growing data set in some order so that your worst-case search time is less than the number of elements in the list. For example, imagine a system where you are rapidly collecting data and do not have the resources to sort this information on the fly. Assuming random distribution of data, a solution for keeping tabs on the data would be to insert larger elements at the end of the list and smaller elements at the beginning of the list.

Because the terms "larger" and "smaller" are completely relative, it is important to decide what they will be relative to. As previously stated, incoming data is assumed to be totally random, so it is logical to assume that any element can be picked as a point against which all other elements are compared.

Now that you have an understanding of the manner in which the semi-sorted link list operates, it is important to discuss specifically how this operation is implemented. You must first determine what the linked list needs to do to stay sorted, and then you must learn how to create a double-ended linked list from the Vector class.

The final project involves two classes:

- DoubleEndedLinkedList, which subclasses Vector
- SortedDoubleEndedLinkedList, which subclasses DoubleEndedLinkedList

The method for keeping data sorted has the potential for failing if incoming data is already sorted. At the close of this chapter, a test of your own skills would be to write a more intelligent sorting method.

To stay sorted, the linked list first picks a point to which all greater than or less than comparisons are made. Based on the previous assertion that random data allows us to pick any element as a reference, it is a safe bet to pick the first element as the reference point. As new elements enter the list, all elements larger than the reference point are added to the end of the list. Conversely, all elements less than the reference point are added to the beginning of the list.

Knowing that the first element is less than the last element and that all elements in between are in some sort of order has great advantages when you are searching through that data later. By knowing at which end to begin searching, you are able to have an average search time of approximately the number of elements in the list divided by two.

Figure 7.5 represents the SortedDoubleEndedLinkedList class. All the class methods are somewhat obvious in nature; because this class subclasses DoubleEndedLinkedList, however, it is not yet prudent to discuss how each method is implemented. Instead, you will break from this discussion and discuss the implementation of DoubleEndedLinkedList. After you have developed the code for DoubleEndedLinkedList you will return to SortedDoubleEndedLinkedList and cover the implementation of each method required by that class. Finally, you will put both the classes together, and you will be "ret-to-go!"

FIGURE 7.5
An object diagram for SortedDouble-EndedLinkedList.

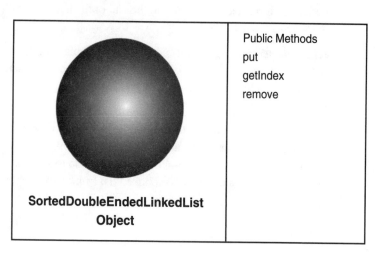

SortedDoubleEndedLinkedList
Object

Public Methods
put
getIndex
remove

The DoubleEndedLinkedList Class

The methods in DoubleEndedLinkedList are slightly altered versions of the methods in Vector (the parent class), and the study of this class is facilitated by a concrete understanding of Vector. (Now is a good time to read the beginning of this chapter if you are skipping around.) Looking at the object diagram in figure 7.6, you should note that because it is a double-ended list, it needs to enable insertion at either end.

FIGURE 7.6

An object diagram for DoubleEnded-LinkedList.

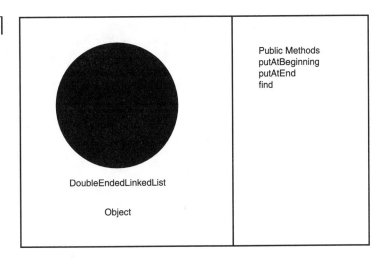

DoubleEndedLinkedList

Object

Public Methods
putAtBeginning
putAtEnd
find

Contained within the Vector class are two methods for insertion:

- addElement(). Accepts an object as a parameter and inserts it at the end of the Vector.

- insertElementAt(). Accepts as parameters both an object and an index. The object will be inserted into the Vector at the position dictated by the index.

It doesn't take Sherlock Holmes to determine that addElement() can be modified to act as the insertAtEnd() method. Also, after you know that a Vector is zero indexed, you probably won't have much trouble realizing that insertElementAt() can be passed an index of zero to insert the element at the beginning of the Vector.

According to figure 7.6, the only method that still needs a definition is find(). This method is implemented by calling Vector's indexOf() method with an identical parameter set. It is reproduced in DoubleEndedLinkedList for clarity, and everything runs fine without this method. (Of course, you would have to call indexOf() instead of find().) The source code for DoubleEndedLinkedList is contained in listing 7.12. As you can see, everything pretty much relies on Vector for execution.

Listing 7.12   DoubleEndedLinkedList

```
package industrial;
import java.util.*;
/*    class DoubleEndedLinkedList
      extends Vector to isolate certain methods that will allow for
      ↪adding at the end
      and at the beginning of a linked list
*/
class DoubleEndedLinkedList extends Vector {
      //adds to the beginning of the linked list. Used when the new
      //object is smaller than the middle object.
      protected void putAtBeginning(Object obj) {
            super.insertElementAt(obj, 0);
      }

      //adds to the end of the linked list. Used when the new object is
      //greater than the middle object.
      protected void putAtEnd(Object obj) {
            super.addElement(obj);
      }

      //returns the index of the object passed in. We also pass in a
      //starting index which will tell us whether to search the first
      //section or the second section.
      protected int find(Object obj, int startingIndex) {
            return super.indexOf(obj, startingIndex);
      }
}
```

The SortedDoubleEndedLinkedList Class

Now that you have built SortedDoubleEndedLinkedList's parent, refer back to figure 7.5 and note that the earlier assertion that much of the support in SortedDoubleEnded LinkedList comes from DoubleEndedLinkedList is completely correct.

Unlike DoubleEndedLinkedList, which had to offer support for insertion at either end, SortedDoubleEndedLinkedList needs to support only one public method for insertion. Not because that insertion is only supported from one end, but because the user is not involved with the end choice.

SortedDoubleEndedLinkedList supports a method called put() that accepts as a parameter an Integer object. The put() method then performs one of the two options listed below.

- First, put() tests to see whether any objects are currently in the linked list. If there are not, you mark this object as the center object, and insert it into the list.

- If an object is already in the list, however, test to see whether the new object belongs at the beginning or the end of the list and then call an appropriate method DoubleEndedLinkedList to insert the new object. Of course, you increment a counter that tracks the number of objects in the class.

In addition to adding a new object to the sorted list, you will want to be able to find the index of an object currently in the list. You will discover that keeping the list in some order speeds up the search for that object. Insertion is not a complicated process, and neither is searching. The necessary steps are outlined below:

- Test to see whether the object for which you are searching occurs before or after the middle object.

- Call DoubleEndedLinkedList's find() method with not only the current object as a parameter, but also with a zero or the index of the middle object. If the object you are searching for is less than the middle object, you pass in a 0. If the object you are searching for is greater than the middle object, you pass in the middle index. The integer that gets passed up acts as a starting point for your search. Thus, it is easy to see that you can usually eliminate half the number of element comparisons when doing the search!

The final method that SortedDoubleEndedLinkedList needs to support is a manner in which you can delete an object. In this method, you pass in an object to be deleted. SortedDoubleEndedLinkedList then performs the following steps.

getIndex() is called to find the index of the item for which we are searching.

Then the removeElementAt() method (implemented in Vector) is called with the newly discovered index.

Beginning Data Structures

Listings 7.13a through 7.13c documents this class rather well. Take a look at the class and then implement it in an application you are working on. You could, for example, write an application that compares search time in the class to search time in a standard linked list.

In listing 7.13a the SortedDoubleEndedLinkedList class is set up. Also implemented here is the put() method that inserts a new object into the list. Notice how comparison operators are used to deciding where the new object should be placed.

Listing 7.13a   The SortedDoubleEndedLinkedList Class

```
package industrial;
import java.util.*;
/*      class SortedDoubleEndedLinkedList
        extends DoubleEndedLinkedList to manage insertion and deletion of
        ➥items keeping
        them in a semi-sorted fashion
 */
class SortedDoubleEndedLinkedList extends DoubleEndedLinkedList {

        private int        integerCount = 0;              //count of items in
        ➥the list
        private int        middleValue;                   //the value of the
        ➥middle object
        private int        middleIndex = 0;               //index of the
        ➥middle element

        public void put(Integer theInt) {
                //do we already have objects in the linked list
                if(integerCount != 0) {
                        //should the new object go at the end of the list
                        if(theInt.intValue() >= middleValue) {
                                super.putAtEnd(theInt);
                        }
                        //else, the new object should go at the beginning of
                        //the list
                        else {
                                super.putAtBeginning(theInt);
                                //adding to the beginning moves the middle index
                                //up one, so increment
                                middleIndex++;
                        }
                }
                //else, this is the first object to hit the list
                else {
```

```
                    middleValue = theInt.intValue();
                    //note we could also call putAtEnd. Since this is the
                    //first element the result would be the same.
                    super.putAtBeginning(theInt);
            }
            //increment our object counter
            integerCount++;
    }
```

Listing 7.13b contains the getIndex() method that locates the index (in our list) of an object.

Listing 7.13b   The getIndex() Method

```
//returns the index of the object passed in. Since we have knowledge
//of the distribution, we are able to eliminate many elements where
//searching.
public int getIndex(Integer theInt) {
        //is the needed index past the midpoint?
        if(theInt.intValue() >= middleValue) {
                return super.find(theInt, middleIndex);
        }
        //else, the needed int is in the first half of the list
        return super.find(theInt, 0);
}
```

Finally, the remove() method is implemented in listing 7.13c.

Listing 7.13c   The remove() Method

```
//removes the object which is passed in. Note this is done by
//calling a method which actually resides in Vector.
public void remove(Integer theInt) {
        int fooIndex = this.getIndex(theInt);

        //if fooIndex less than the middleIndex? If so then we need
        //to decrement middleIndex before we remove the object in
        //question.
        if(fooIndex < middleIndex) {
                middleIndex—;
        }
        //else, fooIndex is greater than middleIndex. Either way we
        //remove the object in question
```

continues

Listing 7.13c   Continued

```
                        super.removeElementAt(fooIndex);
            }
}
```

Summary

This chapter began to explore the core of an application, data structures. This chapter did not, however, cover everything that you need to know to develop your own data structures in Java. This chapter simply discussed the java.util package that provides some elementary data structures. This package is great because it not only enables you to quickly implement some common data structures (java.util.Stack), but also enables you to rapidly create new data structures based on existing models. As you move on to Chapter 8, you will learn how to create any data structure from the ground up in Java!

Chapter 8

Advanced Data Structures

Chapter 7, "Beginning Data Structures: Taking Advantage of java.util," began by introducing the concept that development of data structures was not only possible in Java, but also much easier (and more enjoyable) than in languages such as C++ or Pascal. The discussion started with a basic overview of the fact that pointers are really not necessary; however this concept was not discussed in much depth. Instead of discussing the manner in which it is possible to implement data structures from scratch, the focus was on the java.util package, which contains many pre-built data structures. Chapter 8 moves from the discussion on working within the confines of what is provided by the Java API and into a discussion of what it takes to develop data structures completely from scratch.

As with all chapters, the focus is on design; everything is thoroughly planned before one line of code is written. As you finish this chapter, you will be pleasantly surprised with the code you will have developed. Code is re-used heavily from data structure to data structure, and all code is logically written and easy to understand.

Building Stacks and Queues

In Chapter 7, stacks and queues were implemented with the aid of the classes in the java.util package. Because the Stack class already existed in the java.util package, it was possible to implement a stack in a few lines of code. This section also covers stacks and queues, however, this time around we will look at the form of each data structure. In looking at the form of each data structure it will become plainly obvious that the two data structures are almost identical in form.

As was stated in Chapter 7, stacks and queues are two of the most basic data structures on the block.

As you will remember from the discussion in Chapter 7, stacks and queues are nothing more than a bunch of nodes all linked together. Each node has a link to the next (the linking is one-way), and you must access the nodes sequentially. Of course, the main benefit is that using dynamic data structures does not limit the amount of information you can store.

Stating that stacks and queues are just a bunch of nodes linked together hints that their design will be pretty much the same. This is quite true; the only real difference between the two data structures is the manner in which you add and subtract nodes. A queue is a First-In-First-Out (FIFO) data structure, and a stack is a Last-In-First-Out (LIFO) data structure.

In looking at the process by which stacks and queues will be implemented, coverage will first cover similarities and then differences.

Working on the Similarities Between Stacks and Queues

Because stacks and queues are just a combination of nodes that are enabled to link to one other node at the most, you will need some sort of node class that will be managed by the stack and queue to build both of these data structures. To further illustrate this point, look at figure 8.1, which illustrates the basic form of a stack and a queue. Note that both the stack and queue in the figure are composed on identical building blocks (or nodes). What is unique about each figure is the manner in which nodes are added and subtracted.

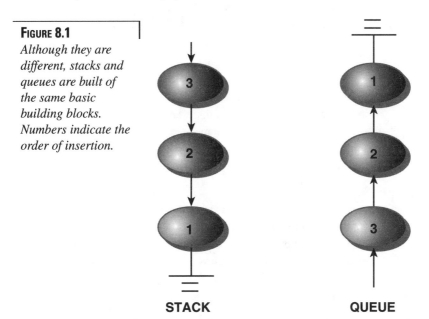

FIGURE 8.1

Although they are different, stacks and queues are built of the same basic building blocks. Numbers indicate the order of insertion.

STACK

QUEUE

To begin the venture into stacks and queues, you will look at coding the Node class. The Node class is the "basic building block" common to the form of stacks and queues. The requirements of a stack and queue have been covered in the current section. Working on the premise that the Node class will encapsulate all features common to stacks and queues, a union of both feature sets will produce the features needed of the Node class. These features are

- The capability to either link to, at most, one other Node object
- The capability to "hold" an object as its value
- The capability to return this object to anyone who requests it
- The capability to return the next node in line
- The capability to return the value of the next node in line
- The capability to change the next node in line
- The capability to change the value of the next node in line
- The capability to sense if the next node in line does or does not exist

Managing the Existence of Zero Nodes

C++ developers must be pleasantly surprised to see that the node does not have to dispose of itself after you are done with it. Ahh the joys of garbage collection.

Having a firm grasp of what is needed, you can now begin working on how to implement it. First of all, you need to understand that someone may ask for a node that does not exist. What happens, for example, when a node has only one node in the queue, and you ask that node for the next node in line? An error of this magnitude could cause some rather large problems, and the Node class will need some bullet-proof protection to keep this error from happening. This level of protection is implemented by taking advantage of one of Java's most elegant features—exceptions.

An *exception* is a class that is instantiated and "thrown" when something out-of-the-ordinary, or "exceptional," occurs. Exceptions are not meant to be used to catch general errors because it is more expensive to throw an exception than it is to check for the existence of an error condition. You will use exceptions in an application when a class has the potential to be manipulated in a manner that is not always expected and will cause undesirable (or unpredictable) output.

Listing 8.1 defines the exception used in the Node class. It will be thrown whenever a user tries to either access a nonexistent node or the value of a nonexistent node. The String passed in will be a small description of the executing method.

Listing 8.1   NoSuchNodeException Will be Thrown If and Only If a User Attempts to Access a Non-Existent Node

```
package industrial;
public class NoSuchNodeException extends Exception {
```

Eight: Advanced Data Structures

```
        public String theName;
        public Object theValue;

        public NoSuchNodeException(String name, Object value) {
            super("Exception thrown due to: "+ name);
            theName = name;
            theValue = value;
        }
    }
```

When to Use the NoSuchNodeException

Because you have determined that an exception is useless if it is not thrown whenever an error occurs, you must carefully study the design of the Node class and note all potential sources of problems. You then will note of all locations where a non-existant node might be accessed, and ensure that your code throws an exception instead of attempting to access the non-existant node.

A few pages ago in the section "Working on the Similarities," a list presented the features that the Node class will offer. The process of identifying potential sources of error begins at that list. Examine all features, and any that involve accessing a node that may or may not exist, should be noted as needing the protection of exception handling.

When dealing with a "chain" of nodes, a good chance that you could be at an "end" node and ask that node for the next node in line. Because no nodes follow an end node, any methods that look past the current node are flagged as potential problems.

The list of required features for the Node class includes four that need access to a node other than the current one. These requirements include:

- Returning either the value contained in the current node or returning the node itself.
- Altering the current node node (both the node itself and its value).

The rest of the requirements for the Node class entail management of the current node. This work is considered safe because any attempts to access the methods of a non-existent class would be caught at compile-time, and thus a run-time exception would never have an opportunity to come into play.

Diagramming the Node Class

You are almost ready to write the code for the Node class. You must, however, first diagram the methods that your Node class will need to implement to offer support for the requirements detailed at the beginning of this section. When diagramming these methods, note the methods that have potential to cause errors and be sure to build in checks to ensure that exceptions are thrown when necessary.

The Node class is illustrated in figure 8.2; all methods that can throw an exception are shaded.

FIGURE 8.2
Diagram for the Node class.

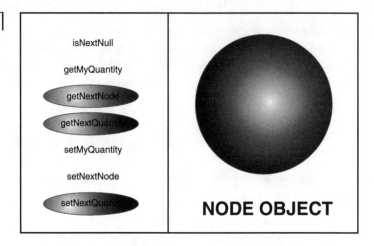

isNextNull

getMyQuantity

getNextNode

getNextQuantity

setMyQuantity

setNextNode

setNextQuantity

NODE OBJECT

Implementing the Node Class

Refer to listings 8.2a through 8.2d, which show the code for the Node class. Note that the quantity field is defined as an Object. This definition gives the Node class the flexibility to hold anything that the user desires. Remember that not only is this Node class used in the Stack and Queue classes, but you must be able to implement it in any linear linked-list data structure you use.

Listing 8.2a contains setup code for the Node class. Two private variables are used to track the quantity held by the current node, and also the Node that is referred to by the current node. These values are passed to the constructor, and therefore are setup at initialization.

Listing 8.2a   Setting up the Node Class

```
package industrial;

public class Node {

    //the next Node in line. is private due to the fact that we
    //only want to allow access through public methods.
    private      Node              myNextNode;

    //the value of our current quantity. can only be accessed through
    //public methods.
    private      Object            myQuantity;

    //only constructor, accepts a quantity and also a link to the next
    //node in line.
    //if this node is to stand-alone, pass in null for the nextNode
    //value.
    public Node(Node nextNode, Object quantity) {
        myNextNode = nextNode;
        myQuantity = quantity;
    }
```

Listing 8.2b contains the isNextNull() method. This method is rather important because it enables you to check whether the current node links to another node. It is less expensive to call this method before attempting to access a node that may or may not exist, than it is to wait until an exception is thrown while attempting to access a non-existent node.

Listing 8.2b   The isNextNull() Method

```
    //allow to find out if there is a next node ... without throwing
    //an exception.
    public boolean isNextNull() {
        return (myNextNode == null);
    }
```

In listing 8.2c are methods that return values of Node's private member data.

Listing 8.2c   Methods Used to Access Node's Private Member Data

```
            //return the current quantity which this node holds

            public Object getMyQuantity() {
                return myQuantity;
            }

            //return the next node in line
            //throws NoSuchNodeException if that node does not exist
            public Node getNextNode() throws NoSuchNodeException {
                    if(myNextNode == null){
                            throw new NoSuchNodeException("get next node", this);
                    }
                    return myNextNode;
            }

            //return the next quantity in line
            //throws NoSuchNodeException if that node does not exist
            public Node getNextQuantity() throws NoSuchNodeException {
                    if(myNextNode == null) {
                            throw new NoSuchNodeException("get next quantity",
this);
                    }
                    return myNextNode.getNextQuantity();
            }
```

In listing 8.2d are the methods that enable altering of Node's private member data.

Listing 8.2d   Methods Used to Alter Node's Private Member Data

```
            //set the value of the current node
            public void setMyQuantity(Object quantity) {
                myQuantity = quantity;
            }

            //set the value of the next node in line. note this can be used
            //to set the next node to null and effectively delete a link in the
            //chain.
            public void setNextNode(Node newNode) {
                myNextNode = newNode;
            }

            //set the value of the next quantity in line.
```

```
//throws NoSuchNodeException if there is no next node
//to "house" the quantity.
public void setNextQuantity(Object quantity) throws
➥NoSuchNodeException {
    if(myNextNode == null) {
        throw new NoSuchNodeException("set next value", this);
    }
    myNextNode.setMyQuantity(quantity);
}
}
```

Working on the Differences Between Stacks and Queues

Although the Stack and Queue classes share the same Node class, they manage that class in unique ways. This is necessary because keeping nodes in FIFO order is different from keeping nodes in LIFO order. The chapter first discusses what it takes to develop a stack and then what is required for building a queue.

Using the Node Class to Develop a Stack

Although you have not yet written one line of your Stack class, you are already on the way because you have already developed the Node class. The Node class is a building block that is manipulated by the Stack class to provide access in LIFO fashion.

The a first step in developing the Stack class is to decide on the set of features that the class needs to support. It is relatively obvious that addition and removal of nodes is required; however, additional features add to the functionality of the class. The full feature set that you will implement is as follows:

- Addition of objects to the stack (called pushing)
- Removal of items from the stack (called popping)
- Searching for a given node
- Deleting any given node
- Peeking at the value of the top node

Advanced Data Structures

It is possible that a user might ask the last node in a stack for the next node in line, the code in the Stack class must look for these situations and take cautions. In the Node class exception-handling is used to ensure that a non-existent node is never accessed. It was necessary to add this precaution into the Node class so that users of that class are protected.

Because the Stack class will become the user of the Node class and will take on users of its own, this exception handling must propagate through to the Stack class. Referring back to the feature list covered earlier in this section, four features have the capability to attempt to access a non-existent node. These features are

- Popping of the stack, which has the potential to cause an error if a user attempts to pop an empty stack

- Peeking a the top node's value, which has the potential to cause an error if a user attempts to peek at an empty stack

- Removal of a node, which has the potential to cause an error if a user attempts to remove a node which does not exist in the stack

- Searching for a node, which has the potential to cause an error if a user attempt to find a node which does not exist

Figure 8.3 diagrams the Stack class.

FIGURE 8.3
Visualizing the Stack class.

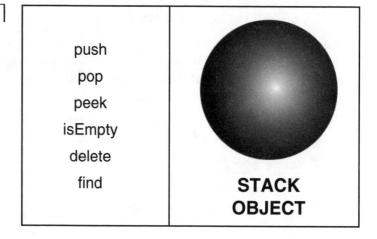

push
pop
peek
isEmpty
delete
find

STACK OBJECT

Exploring the push() Method

The purpose of the push() method is to add another node into the stack. This method does not need to know whether the stack is empty or, for example, whether it already has 42 nodes in it.

The push() method functions by looking at the current head node, and creating a new node that links to that head node. The head Node will then be told that it should reference the newly created node. This process is illustrated in figure 8.4.

FIGURE 8.4

Pushing a new node onto the stack.

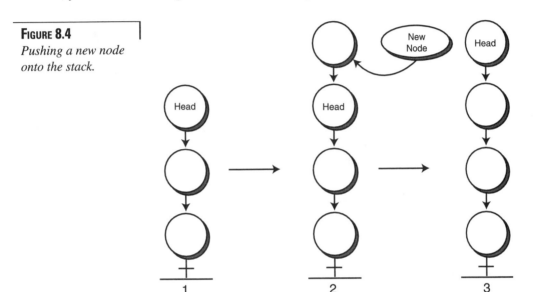

Exploring the pop() Method

Where the push() method is charged with adding nodes to the stack, the pop() method removes them from the stack. A non-existent node has the potential to be referenced (when the stack is empty), so that you will want to test for this case and throw an exception if necessary.

The method functions by setting a temporary node to reference the head, and then setting the head node equal to the next node in the stack. The temporary node is the return value of this function. The pop() method is illustrated in figure 8.5.

FIGURE 8.5

Popping a node off the stack.

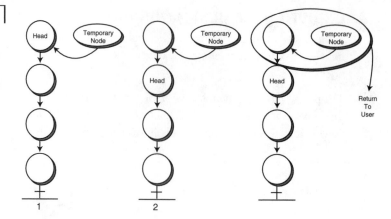

Exploring the peek() Method

A less destructive version of the pop() method is the peek() method. This method returns the value of the head node, however, it does not actually remove the node from the stack. Of course, if the head node is null, you will want to throw an exception.

Exploring the isEmpty() Method

The isEmpty() method is a utility method that users can access to determine whether the stack is empty. This method tests the head node to see if it is null. You will not want this method to throw an exception because it is in place so that users can test a stack before calling a method that could potentially throw an exception.

Each and every programmer uses different terms to refer to objects that are helpers, or extras, to the current application. My first computer science teacher used the term "dummy" to describe any such object (and most of the class). Other common terms are "foo" and "bar."

Exploring the delete() Method

The delete() method is one of the trickier methods the Stack class implements. As was stated previously, this method's inclusion violates LIFO access rules, but it is a rather helpful method.

The method functions on the basic principle that if you set the node before a node that needs to be deleted to reference the node after the node that needs to be deleted, then the node in the middle becomes inaccessible and is considered deleted (not to mention fair game for garbage collection).

You will create three *dummy nodes*, which will traverse the stack and then be used to re-create object references. Of course you will want to throw an exception if the node that you want to delete does not exist. Figure 8.6 illustrates how this deletion is actually accomplished.

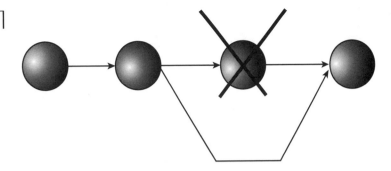

FIGURE 8.6

Deletion of a node in the stack is accomplished by "linking around" a Node.

In both the delete() and find() methods, the equals() method is used to determine whether one object equals another object. The equals() method enables objects to tell the stack how they are alike. Remember that using == only returns true if the two objects in question reference the same object.

Exploring the find() Method

The final method supported in the Stack class is a find() method. This method functions in a manner similar to the delete() method. This time, however, you will not be deleting a node; instead you will return the index (starting with 1) of the node which is passed in. If the node is not in the stack, you will throw an exception.

Implementing the Stack Class

Having discussed how all methods will be developed, you are ready to dive in and actually code them. Listings 8.3a through 8.3d contain the Stack class.

Listing 8.3a contains the constructor for the class. The constructor accepts as a parameter a quantity for the initial node to hold. A new node is created with this quantity.

Listing 8.3a   The Constructor Creates a New Node with a Query-Specified Quantity

```
package industrial;

public class Stack {
      //a reference to a head node will allow us to always know where to
      //base all insertions and deletions from.
      private Node head = null;

      //when creating a new Stack our head node will reference a Node with
      //the value in question and will have a null reference to other
      //Nodes.
```

continues

Advanced Data Structures

Listing 8.3a   Continued

```
        public Stack(Object quantity) {
            head = new Node(null, quantity);
        }
```

In listing 8.3b are the push(), pop(), and peek() methods. The push() method attaches a new node onto the stack, the pop() method removes it from the stack, and the peek() method returns the top node's quantity.

Listing 8.3b   The push() and pop() Methods of the Stack Class

```
        //when adding a new Node onto the stack we will create a new node
        //and pass the current head reference as the next Node in line. We
        //will then move the head reference up so that it now references
        //the top Node.
        public void push(Object quantity) {
            Node myNode = new Node(head, quantity);
            head = myNode;
        }

        //the pop method will return the top Node and then move the head
        //reference down in line.
        public Object pop() throws NoSuchNodeException {
            Node temp = head;
            //first test if the head is null. this indicates that the
            //stack is empty
            if(head == null) {
                throw new NoSuchNodeException("head is null", this);
            }

            //if we are this far we have been able to confirm that the
            //head reference is not null. However we still do not know
            //if there is more than one Node in the stack. If
            //there is then head will reference that node, otherwise an
            //exception will be thrown and head will be set to null.
            try{      head = head.getNextNode(); }
            catch(NoSuchNodeException nsne) { head = null; }

            return temp.getMyQuantity();
        }
```

```
//the peek method will return the value of the head node. if head
//is null then an exception will be thrown.
public Object peek() throws NoSuchNodeException {
     if(head == null) {
          throw new NoSuchNodeException("head is null", this);
     }

     return head.getMyQuantity();
}
```

In listing 8.3c are the isEmpty() and delete() methods. The isEmpty() method is a utility method that enables you to test whether the stack is empty. The delete() method removes a node from the stack.

Listing 8.3c   Testing for an Empty Stack without Throwing an Exception

```
//this method allows us to test for an empty stack without throwing
//an exception. if the head reference is to null then we know
//that the stack contains no Nodes.
  public boolean isEmpty() {
      if(head == null){
           return true;
      }
      return false;
}


//the delete method will either delete the Node which is passed
//in, or will throw an exception if that Node does not exist.
public void delete(Object deleteMe) throws NoSuchNodeException {
        Node dummyNode0 = head; //this will trail the current node
        Node dummyNode1 = head; //this will be used to track the
        //location of the current node
        Node dummyNode2 = null; //this will be used to used to
        //reference the node after the current node

        //test to see if our list is only one Node long
        try{       dummyNode2 = head.getNextNode(); }
        catch(    NoSuchNodeException nsne) { dummyNode2 = null; }
```

continues

Advanced Data Structures

Listing 8.3c   Continued

```
                //test to see if the node which needs to be deleted is the
                //first Node
                if(deleteMe.equals(head.getMyQuantity())) {
                      head = head.getNextNode();
                      return;
                }

                //loop until either dummyNode1 references the node which
                //needs to be deleted or the node after dummyNode1 is a
                //null node.
        while(!deleteMe.equals(dummyNode1.getMyQuantity()) &&
        ➥!dummyNode1.isNextNull()) {
                      dummyNode0 = dummyNode1;
                      dummyNode1 = dummyNode2;

                      //we test to see if the node which follows dummyNode2
                      //is null due to the fact that if it is then a
                      //call to getNextNode would throw an exception.
                      if(dummyNode2.isNextNull()) {

                            //the next node is null, we therefore set
                            //dummyNode2 equal to null instead of
                            //the next node in line.
                            dummyNode2 = null;

                            //test to see if dummyNode1 references the node
                            //which we want to delete if not, we throw an
                            //exception.
                            if(!deleteMe.equals(dummyNode1.getMyQuantity()))
    {
                                  throw new NoSuchNodeException("delete can
                                  ➥not happen, node DNE", this);
                            }
                      }

                      //the node which follows dummyNode2 is not null then a
                      //call to getNextNode is safe
                      else {
                            dummyNode2 = dummyNode2.getNextNode();
                      }
                }
                //"loop around" the node which we want to delete.
                dummyNode0.setNextNode(dummyNode2);
        }
```

The find() method in listing 8.3d functions in a fashion similar to the delete() method. Unlike the delete() method, however, nodes are located, not removed from the stack.

Listing 8.3d   The find() Method Returns the Number of Nodes

```
//find will return the number of nodes (starting with 1, NOT
//zero) which the node in question is from the beginning
//of the stack. If the node does not exist anywhere in the
//stack then and exception will be thrown.
public int find(Object findMe) throws NoSuchNodeException {
        int counter = 1;
        Node dummyNode = head;
        while(!findMe.equals(dummyNode.getMyQuantity())) {
                counter++;
                if(!dummyNode.isNextNull()) {
                        dummyNode = dummyNode.getNextNode();
                }
                else {
                        throw new NoSuchNodeException("find can not
                        ➥happen, node DNE", this);
                }
        }
        return counter;
    }
}
```

Before moving on to the development of a queue by using the same Node class used to develop the Stack class, proof is offered that this project actually works. Listing 8.4 is a driver that creates a new Stack, adds a series of Integer objects, deletes a few, searches for a few, and then prints the remaining Integers. Note that the delete() and find() methods will prove that they function in all cases by throwing the necessary exception when they are passed a node that does not exist in the Stack.

Listing 8.4   A Driver that Demonstrates that All Methods in the Stack Class Function Properly

```
import industrial.*;
public class Driver {
      private Stack myStack;

      public Driver() {
              //create a new Stack
```

continues

Listing 8.4   Continued

```
myStack = new Stack(new Integer(42));
//add the integers 0..10
for(int i=0; i<=10; i++) {
    System.out.println("push: "+ i);
    myStack.push(new Integer(i));
}


//delete 42
try{ System.out.println("delete 42"); myStack.delete(new
➥Integer(42)); }
catch(    NoSuchNodeException nsne) {
➥System.out.println("err:"+nsne); }
//try to delete 333
try{ System.out.println("delete 333"); myStack.delete(new
➥Integer(333)); }
catch(    NoSuchNodeException nsne) {
➥System.out.println("err:"+nsne); }
//delete 10
➥try{ System.out.println("delete 10"); myStack.delete(new
➥Integer(10)); }
catch(    NoSuchNodeException nsne) {
➥System.out.println("err:"+nsne); }
//try to find 10
try{ System.out.print("find 10: ");
    System.out.println(myStack.find(new Integer(10)));
    }
catch(    NoSuchNodeException nsne) {
➥System.out.println("err:"+nsne); }
//find  5
try{ System.out.print("find 5: ");
    System.out.println(myStack.find(new Integer(5)));
    }
catch(    NoSuchNodeException nsne) {
➥System.out.println("err:"+nsne); }
//pop the remaining integers are print to the screen
while(!myStack.isEmpty()) {
    try{
        System.out.println("pop: "+
        ➥(Integer)myStack.pop());
    }
    catch(NoSuchNodeException nsne) {
    ➥System.out.println("err: "+nsne); }
}
}
```

Eight: Advanced Data Structures

```
        public static void main(String args[]) {
            Driver myDriver = new Driver();
        }
}
```

The following shows the output generated by the application in listing 8.4.

```
push
pull
lift
tuck
wiggle
wuck

push: 0
push: 1
push: 2
push: 3
push: 4
push: 5
push: 6
push: 7
push: 8
push: 9
push: 10
delete 42
delete 333
err: industrial.NoSuchNodeException: Exception thrown due to: delete can
↦not happen, node DNE
delete 10
find 10: err: industrial.NoSuchNodeException: Exception thrown due to:
↦find can not happen, node DNE
find 5: 5
pop: 9
pop: 8
pop: 7
pop: 6
pop: 5
pop: 4
pop: 3
pop: 2
pop: 1
pop: 0
```

Using the Node Class to Form a Queue

Well congratulations, you just built your first data structure in Java! If, however, you think that you are close to finishing, you are very much mistaken. Our exploration into data structures has just begun!

The most logical data structure to begin developing after you have developed the Stack class is a queue. As was stated previously, the only manner in which a queue differs from a stack is in the way it manipulates its nodes. A stack allows LIFO access to nodes, whereas a queue allows FIFO access to nodes.

Transitioning the Stack code over to the code that the Queue class needs is not difficult; however, it does require you to look at the problem in a slightly different manner because a Stack only has to keep a reference to one side of the chain of nodes. You pushed and popped from the same end of the stack; your head reference was always to the most recently added node. Because the Queue class will need FIFO access to its nodes, you need to track both the first node that was added to the queue (the head) and the last node that was added (the tail). You will always remove from the location marked by the head and add to the queue from the position marked by the tail.

As with the Stack class, the possibility that a reference to a non-existent object will be generated is still an ever-present danger. In these cases, an exception will need to be thrown.

Designing the Queue Class

The design process for your Queue class is significantly aided because it implements a set of features similar to those features supported by the Stack class. In fact, the implementation of this class does not even require an object diagram; you will reference the one generated for the Stack class. Although you will not need an object diagram, you will need to learn how the methods will be implemented.

Eight: Advanced Data Structures

Each method in the Queue class is implemented in a manner very different than the manner in which it was implemented in the Stack class. This occurs because the empty condition is signaled in a totally different fashion, and you will need to access the nodes in a completely different order. So take a quick glimpse back to figure 8.3 and buckle down for a dive into the inner workings of a FIFO data structure!

The diagram in figure 8.7 shows three possible stages that a queue can be in while items are being added and removed. These stages are

1. The first stage indicates a queue that contains five nodes, also indicated are the head and tail nodes.

2. In the second stage, you remove one node by moving the head reference down one.

3. In the third stage, you add a node by tacking a new node on the bottom and moving the tail reference down one.

In all cases, the numbers on the nodes indicate the order in which they were inserted (from the beginning).

The insertion and deletion of nodes diagrammed in figure 8.6 are implemented with push() and pop() methods. The other methods needing support in your class are find(), isEmpty(), peek(), and delete(). As with the Stack class, inclusion of the delete() method goes against the FIFO access rules, but is provided as a convenience to users. Also identical to the methodology that was used to build the Stack class is a strong adherence to exceptions. Your Queue class will take advantage of exceptions at every opportunity.

Although little time has been spent discussing the manner in which you are going to implement the methods in the Queue class, you are almost ready to begin coding. This may come as a surprise to you readers who are familiar with this book's strong commitment to design. It is, however, the strong commitment to design that enables you to take the design developed for the Stack class and use it when writing the Queue class.

To take advantage of the design used in the Stack class you have to accept that like the Stack class, the Queue class is charged with manipulating a series of nodes kept in a linear order. Thus although similar methods names are used, each method will be implemented in a manner different from the manner in which the Stack class implemented its methods.

Now that a clear understanding of what the Queue class needs to do has been developed, it is time to figure out how the Queue class is going to operate. In listings 8.6a through 8.6d is the full code for the Queue class.

In listing 8.6a is the constructor that the Queue class will use. It creates a new node containing a quantity passed in as a parameter. Additionally the head and tail nodes are set up to refer to this new node.

Listing 8.6a   The Constructor for the Queue Class

```
package industrial;

//class to implement a FIFO queue
public class Queue {
      private Node head = null; //will reference the beginning of the
                                //queue deletions will be based on this
      private Node tail = null; //point will reference the end of the
```

```
//queue insertions will be based on this point
//generic constructor, takes a object as its parameter and
//creates a new node which contains this quantity.
//both the head and tail references are set to look at this
//node
public Queue(Object quantity) {
        head = new Node(null, quantity);
        tail = head;
}
```

In listing 8.6b is the push() method. This method functions by first testing to see if the queue is empty. If the queue is empty a new queue is created. Otherwise a new node is attached to the end of the queue, and the tail reference is moved down one node.

Listing 8.6b   The push() Method Adds a New Node to the Queue

```
//push will add a new node onto the queue. this is done by
//tacking a new node onto the queue and moving the tail
//reference down one. the special case where the queue is empty
//or where it contains one node is take care of by the first
//conditional.
public void push(Object quantity) {
        //does our queue contain one node? or is it empty?
        if(tail == head || tail == null) {
                tail = new Node(null, quantity);
                head.setNextNode(tail);
        }
        //there is more than one node in out queue
        else {
                Node myNode = new Node(tail, quantity);
                tail.setNextNode(myNode);
                tail = myNode;
        }
}
```

In listing 8.6c are the pop() and peek() methods. Both function by referring the top node on the queue, however, the pop() method additionally will delete the top node on the queue. In both methods, if the user attempts to call one on an empty queue, an exception will be generated.

Listing 8.6c   The pop() Method Removes the Top Node from the Queue

```
//pop will remove the top node from the queue by setting a
//temp node equal to the node referenced by head, setting
//the head node equal to the next node in line, and then
//returning the temp node. if the queue is empty an
//exception will be thrown.

public Object pop() throws NoSuchNodeException {
     Node temp = null;

     if(head == tail) {
             throw new NoSuchNodeException("queue empty", this);
     }
     else {
              temp = head;
              head = head.getNextNode();
     }
     return temp.getMyQuantity();
}

//peek will return the object held by the node referenced by
//head. if the queue is empty, an exception
//will be thrown
public Object peek() throws NoSuchNodeException {
     if(head == tail) {
             throw new NoSuchNodeException("queue empty", this);
     }
     return head.getMyQuantity();
}
```

Listing 8.6d begins by introducing the isEmpty() method, which returns true if the head and tail nodes reference each other. Additionally, the delete() and find() methods traverse the queue until either the node needed is found, or the end of queue is reached. If the end is reached and the desired node has not been found, the exception will be thrown. If the node is found, the delete() method will link around the found node, and the find() method will return the index of the found node.

Listing 8.6d   The isEmpty() Method Enables a User to Test Whether the Queue Contains Elements.

```
//The delete() and find() methods traverse the queue looking for a
//specific node, and they the perform a task similar to their name,
     public boolean isEmpty() {
             return (head == tail);
```

```
        }

        //delete will remove a node from the queue by "linking around"
        //that node. if the node does not exist
        //anywhere in the queue then an exception will be thrown
        public void delete(Object deleteMe) throws NoSuchNodeException {
                Node dummyNode0 = head;
                Node dummyNode1 = head;
                Node dummyNode2 = head.getNextNode();

                //are we attempting to delete the first node
                if(deleteMe.equals(head.getMyQuantity())) {
                        head = head.getNextNode();
                        return;
                }

                while(!deleteMe.equals(dummyNode1.getMyQuantity()) &&
                //(dummyNode2 != tail)) {
                        dummyNode0 = dummyNode1;
                        dummyNode1 = dummyNode2;
                        dummyNode2 = dummyNode2.getNextNode();
                }
                //does dummyNode1 reference the node which we want to delete
                if(deleteMe.equals(dummyNode1.getMyQuantity())) {
                        dummyNode0.setNextNode(dummyNode2);
                }
                //is the node which we want to delete the last node in the
                //chain
                else
                if(deleteMe.equals(dummyNode1.getNextNode()-
                .getMyQuantity())) { dummyNode1 = tail;

                }
                //if dummyNode1 does not reference the node which we want to
                //delete and the next node in the chain is not the node
                //which we want

        //to delete then our node does not exist and we should throw
        //an exception
                else {
                        throw new NoSuchNodeException("delete can not happen,
node DNE", this);
                }
        }
```

continues

Listing 8.6d   Continued

```
//find will search for a node in a manner similar to the manner
//that delete searched for the node.

//however here we will return an integer that indicates the index
//(starting with 1) of that node in our queue. If the node does
//not exist in the queue then an exception will be thrown.
public int find(Object findMe) throws NoSuchNodeException {
        int counter = 1;
        Node dummyNode = head;
        while(!findMe.equals(dummyNode.getMyQuantity())) {
                counter++;
                if(dummyNode != tail) {
                        dummyNode = dummyNode.getNextNode();
                }
                else {
                        throw new NoSuchNodeException("find can not happen,
                        ➥node DNE", this);
                }
        }
        return counter;
    }
}
```

Testing the Queue Class

By now you should have studied the class and should be ready to implement it in your
next big project. If for some reason you had trouble with the class, take a look at the driver
in listing 8.7 and the output generated by the driver given in listing 8.8. That driver is the
one used when testing the Queue class and proves that all methods work when an exception does or does not occur.

Listing 8.7   A Driver Used for the Class in Listing 8.6

```
import industrial.*;
public class Driver {
      private Queue myQueue;

      public Driver() {
            //create a new queue
            myQueue = new Queue(new Integer(42));
```

```
//push on a series of Integers
for(int i=0; i<=10; i++) {
      System.out.println("push: "+ i);
      myQueue.push(new Integer(i));
}

//try to find 12
try{      System.out.print("find 12: ");
            System.out.println(myQueue.find(new Integer(12)));
      }
catch(      NoSuchNodeException nsne)
➡{ System.out.println("err:"+nsne); }
//find 10
try{      System.out.print("find 10: ");
            System.out.println(myQueue.find(new Integer(10)));
      }
catch(      NoSuchNodeException nsne)
➡{ System.out.println("err:"+nsne); }

//try to delete 12
try{ System.out.println("delete 12"); myQueue.delete(new
➡Integer(12)); }
catch(      NoSuchNodeException nsne)
➡{ System.out.println("err:"+nsne); }
//delete 0
try{ System.out.println("delete 0"); myQueue.delete
➡(new Integer(0)); }
catch(      NoSuchNodeException nsne){System.out.println("err:
➡"+nsne); }
//delete 6
try{ System.out.println("delete 6"); myQueue.delete
➡(new Integer(6)); }
catch(      NoSuchNodeException nsne) { System.out.println("err:
➡"+nsne); }
//delete 10
try{ System.out.println("delete 10"); myQueue.delete(new
➡Integer(10)); }
catch(      NoSuchNodeException nsne) { System.out.println("err:
➡"+nsne); }
//delete 42
try{ System.out.println("delete 42"); myQueue.delete(new
➡Integer(42)); }
catch(      NoSuchNodeException nsne) { System.out.println("err:
➡"+nsne); }
//display the remaining nodes
while(!myQueue.isEmpty()) {
```

continues

Listing 8.7   Continued

```
                try{
                        System.out.println("pop: "+
                        ➥(Integer)myQueue.pop());
                }
                catch(NoSuchNodeException nsne) {
                ➥System.out.println("err: "+nsne); }
        }
    }

    public static void main(String args[]) {
        Driver myDriver = new Driver();
    }
}
```

The following is the output generated by the sample application in listing 8.7.

```
push: 0
push: 1
push: 2
push: 3
push: 4
push: 5
push: 6
push: 7
push: 8
push: 9
push: 10
find 12: err: industrial.NoSuchNodeException: Exception thrown due to: find
➥can not happen, node DNE
find 10: 12
delete 12
err: industrial.NoSuchNodeException: Exception thrown due to: delete can
➥not happen, node DNE
delete 0
delete 6
delete 10
delete 42
pop: 1
pop: 2
pop: 3
pop: 4
pop: 5
pop: 7
pop: 8
pop: 9
```

Getting a Bit More Advanced

You have now developed two different data structures in Java: the stack and the queue. These data structures were written from scratch and did not use the API for any node-tracking functions. This is all very impressive; however, the coolest part of the development was that by spending some time on the design of the Stack class, you were able to spend time on the design of the Queue class. You were also able to design a Node class, which was used without modification, in both the Stack and Queue classes.

So where to go from here? You have already done more than many college undergrads do in their first class on data structures! The next (and last) data structure this chapter helps you build is a binary search tree.

Because binary search trees are not the most advanced data structures around, you will actually use the tree to develop a rather interesting application.

The inclusion of the application in a chapter on data structures is a bit radical. Traditionally, books on data structures focus on actual code and spend little time on what can actually be done with what you build from chapter to chapter. A few books discuss what can be done with a data structure, but, again, it is rare to see one used in an application.

This "lack of inclusion" by other authors is not due to a lack of desire by writers, but rather due to space constraints. Data structures are the foundation upon which applications are built, and building an application that takes advantage of a variety of data structures can be a large undertaking. The application that you will write in this chapter presents a GUI interface to a binary search tree. The application displays a series of buttons that enable a user to manipulate the tree, and reveals a display panel that shows the contents of the tree.

This project starts with a brief introduction to binary search trees and continues with the procedures of designing the application. To help you to focus on the data structure apart from the user interface (UI), the tree itself is covered first, and then you will link it to the UI. The chapter ends the building of the application with a brief discussion of its faults and challenges you to fix them.

What is a Binary Search Tree?

In the previous sections, you built data structures that used unary nodes; those with the potential to link to at most one other node. A binary search tree is also composed of nodes that store some data, however, these nodes have the capability to link to two other nodes, hence the name "binary." By placing the nodes in the tree in a logical manner, speed to find one is increased, hence the name "search."

This "logical manner" translates to keeping the nodes in order during insertion. This explanation is discussed in greater detail as the chapter progresses.

As with anything related to computer science, a binary search tree's structure is described by many terms. Figure 8.8 shows a simple binary search tree that contains a number of unique nodes.

The node that contains the number 42 is considered the *root* of the tree. In addition to being the root, it is the parent node for the nodes that contain 10 and 43. Following along logically, 42 is the grandparent to the nodes that contain 6 and 3000. Although the nodes that contains 10 and 43 are the children of 42 they are also parent to the nodes that contain 6 and 3000 (respectively). This *family-oriented* naming convention follows down throughout the entire tree.

Even more noteworthy than the names applied to each node is the placement of each node in the tree. Every left child of a node is of a lesser value, and every right child is of a greater value. This means that insertion will take longer than in a standard linked list, but searching will take much less time. If, for example, you insert 100,000 random nodes into a linked list and then want to search for a node that happens to be last in the list, you would be forced to do about 100,000 comparisons, which is expensive and can take a long time; however, if you had placed those same 100,000 random nodes into a binary search tree, you would only need to log(2) 100,000 (around 16.9) comparisons to find this same node.

FIGURE 8.8

The general form for a binary search tree.

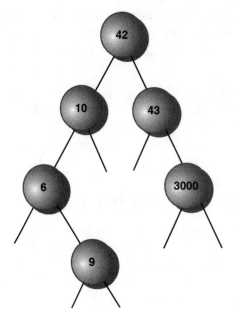

Planning the Application

As was stated previously, this application will be introduced in two parts—first the data structure and then the UI. To implement a bare-bones tree, the Node class needs only some basic features:

- It must be capable of linking to two other nodes at the most.
- It must be capable to hold a value.
- It must be capable of offering some method for determining whether it is greater than, less than, or equal to another node.
- It must be capable of knowing its height in the tree (root node is considered height 0)
- It must "know" the number of children it has.

When developing the Stack and Queue classes, the only comparison that you had to do on each node was testing for equality against another node. However, because each node of the binary tree is not only compared for equality but also for greater-than or less-than conditions, a problem arises. When only testing for equality, the equals() method (in java.lang.Object) was used, and this allowed you to let a node have a value of any object. However, java.lang.Object does not have greater-than or less-than method; all nodes will therefore have to use specially created methods. To provide for easier reading, the base type "int" is used for the value of each node.

Developing Node-by-Node

Now it's time to design the first class in this project, which will be the Node class. Note, however, that each node is actually its own "mini" binary search tree. Refer to figure 8.8 and cover the node that contains 42. See how you now have two binary trees with roots at the node, which contains 10, and also the node that contains 43? This is good because it lets you develop a single class and allow it to relate to other classes of the same type. Figure 8.9 shows the object diagram for the node class.

The methods listed in figure 8.9 should not surprise you; you may have predicted the list before you even saw it. The one method that might draw your attention is insert(). In Queue and Stack, you saw classes manipulating nodes—but here the nodes are manipulating themselves?! This occurs partly because you have empowered each node to act as an intelligent independent object. Not only does it know its height and number of descendants, but it also knows how to add a new node onto itself. Remember that not only are instances of BinaryTree nodes in a tree, but they can also be separate binary trees.

FIGURE 8.9
The object diagram for the BinaryTree class.

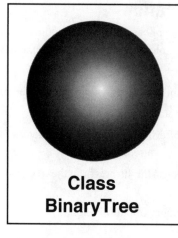

	getHeight
	setHeight
	getNumDescendents
	setNumDescendents
	getKey
	setKey
	insert
	getLeft
	setLeft
Class	getRight
BinaryTree	setRight

An oft-debated topic in binary search tree research is what to do with nodes that are equal to each other. One school says to place them to the left, and the other says to place them to the right. Although it matters little which way you go, I have chosen to reject duplicate nodes all together. This enables the application to stay neutral in the left/right child fight and enables me to do some interesting UI development when it comes to presenting error messages.

You may be wondering how a node inserts another node onto itself. The following list presents the thought processes a BinaryTree object will go through when deciding where to place a new node.

1. Compare the value of the new node to the current value.

2. If the new value is equal to the current value, present the user with an error message, as your tree will contain only unique nodes.

3. If the new value is less than the current value, look at the left node. If that node exists, tell it to deal with the new node. If the left node is null, however, you can insert the new value as the left node.

4. If the new value is less than the current value, look at the right node. If that node exists, tell it to deal with the new node. However, if the right node is null, you can insert the new value as the right node.

It is easy to see that the process will continue over and over until a null node is reached. The process is further illustrated by figure 8.10.

Before jumping into the code for the BinaryTree class, a few more features of the class must be covered. Tracking the number of children a node has is a rather elegant solution, which is based on the fact that when inserting a new node, you only visit nodes that are going to be parents of that new node. Therefore, every time you discover that the new node's value is less than or greater than the current node's value during an insertion, you tell the current node to increase its child count.

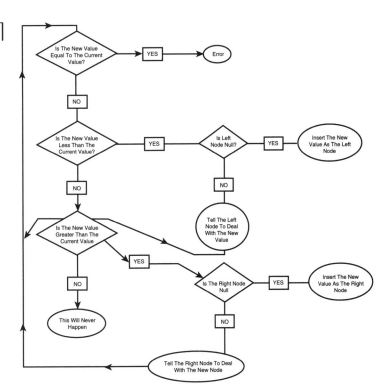

A potential point of confusion in listing 8.9c is the reference to a class called ModalOK. This class will be introduced when UI issues are covered later in the chapter and is simply a modal dialog box that displays the error message passed to it.

Although a node's children are constantly growing, the node's height is fixed when that node is inserted. Because a new node is one level below its parent, you can set the height of a node by adding one to the value of its parent's height. So after you have decided where to insert a new node, you have to find out what the height of the new node's parent is and add one to it. If the parent does not exist, you can conclude that the node is the root of the tree and has a height of 0. Take a look at the code in listings 8.9a through 8.9c where the BinaryTree class is actually written.

In listing 8.9a is the constructor that is used when creating a new BinaryTree node. It is passed an int that is used as the key for the node (or quantity, or value), and also another BinaryTree, which is the parent of this new node. Additionally the node sets its height equal to 0 if its parent is null, or 1 + the height of its parent if its parent is not null.

Listing 8.9a   The Constructor for the BinaryTree

```
package industrial;
//this is the meat of the program. the class is a node of the tree, and our
//tree will be made up of as many nodes as is necessary.
public class BinaryTree {
    //the data stored in the node
    private int key;
    //these three nodes are "pointers" to succors (or predecessors)
    private BinaryTree left;
    private BinaryTree right;
    private BinaryTree parent;
    //the height of the current node
    private int height=0;
    //the number of descendants of the current node
    private int numDescendents;
    //an error dialog which is created when necessary
    private ModalOK theError;

    //constructor, creates a new tree with the given int as its value
    public BinaryTree(int theKey, BinaryTree p) {
        key = theKey;              //set the current key
        parent = p;                //the parent (or null for the root)
        numDescendents = 0;        //the number of descendants always
                                   //zero for a new node

        //the parent is null we are at the root otherwise
        //the current height is one more than the parent's height
        if (parent != null)
            height = (parent.getHeight() + 1);
        else
            height = 0;

        //a new node has no children (yet)
        left=null;
        right=null;
    }
```

Listing 8.9b contains a series of utility methods that enable the viewing and alteration of BinaryTree's private member data.

Listing 8.9b   Utility Methods Used to Enable Access to Private Member Data

```
//returns the height of the current node
public int getHeight()
     { return height; }

//returns the number of descendants of the current node
public int getNumDescendents()
     { return numDescendents; }

//sets the height of the current node to h
private void setHeight(int h)
     { height = h; }

//sets the number of descendants of the current node to nd
private void setNumDescendents(int nd)
     { numDescendents = nd; }

//returns the current value of key
public int getKey() {
     return key;
}

//allows us to alter the value of key
private void setKey(int k) {
     key = k;
}

//set the value of the left node
public void setLeft(BinaryTree newLeft) {
     left = newLeft;
}

//set the value of the right node
public void setRight(BinaryTree newRight) {
     right = newRight;
}
//set the value of the left node
public BinaryTree getLeft() {
     return left;
}

//set the value of the right node
public BinaryTree getRight() {
     return right;
}
```

The insert() method in listing 8.9c will insert a new BinaryTree in its proper location in the tree. The method functions by performing the following steps:

1. It first checks to see whether the value that is being inserted is equal to the value of the current node. If this occurs, an error message is generated, and the method exits.

2. The insert() method next checks to see whether the new value is less than the current one. If it is, one of two things happens—if there is a left child, the left child is told to manage the node and begins at step one. If there is no left child, a new node is created as the left node with the key of the new value.

3. If condition 2 does not return true, the insert() method checks to see whether the new value is greater than the current value. If it is, one of two things will happen— if a right child exists, the right child will be commanded to manage the node, and it begins at step one. If no right child exists, a new node is created as the left node, with the key of the new value.

Listing 8.9c   The insert() Method of the BinaryTree Class

```
//inserts the new key at its correct position, also sets num
//descendents, and height
public void insert(int newKey) {
    //does the node already exist in this tree?
    if (newKey ==  key)
        ModalOK.createModalOK("Key Already Exists");
    //is the new value less than the current value? if so we
    //insert to the left
    else if (newKey <  key) {
     this.setNumDescendents(this.getNumDescendents() + 1);
        //if left is not null we have more children and pass the
        //value down
        if (left != null) {
            left.insert(newKey);
        }
        //otherwise we stick a new node on the left
        else
            left = new BinaryTree(newKey, this);
    }
    //is the new value greater than the current value? if so we
    //insert to the right

    else if (newKey >  key) {
```

```
                this.setNumDescendents(this.getNumDescendents() + 1);
            //if right is not null we have more children and pass the
            value down
            if (right != null) {
                right.insert(newKey);
            }
            //otherwise we stick a new node on the right
                else
                right = new BinaryTree(newKey, this);
        }
    }
}
```

Dealing with Problems: An Error Dialog Box

Although the code in listings 8.9a through 8.9c ensures that your data is in a manageable form, it needs some sort of interface if the user is to learn about manipulation of binary trees. You will now develop an interface that the user will use to view and manipulate data. Part of this interface is a small dialog box to display an error message that notifies the user when he does things, such as attempting to insert a duplicate node or inserting a value that is not an integer.

The class is rather simple and does not need an object diagram; in fact, it only supports two methods. Following is a list of the features the dialog box will need to support.

- The dialog box needs to stop the user from interacting with the application until he tells the dialog box that he understands the issue at hand.

- The dialog box needs to stop disallow input until the user acknowledges the issue.

- The dialog box needs to support an obvious method by which the user can let the dialog box know the user understands the issue at hand.

- The dialog box needs to display any amount of text, yet retain a uniform look.

The first bullet above can be implemented by making the dialog box modal. A button marked OK that, when clicked, dismisses the box will bring support for the second bullet. The third bullet is addressed by enabling the caller to pass in a String object and then display that String in the dialog box. This dialog box extends java.awt.Dialog and takes advantage of the pack() method, which forced the Frame to take up the minimum space required by its components. Thus, the box will always be the same size relative to the String length. Finally, use the GridBagLayout manager to keep the button size relative to the String size.

The code for the dialog box is shown in listing 8.10. In the class's constructor the screen is built; including display of the error message, and OK button. After OK is clicked, an event is sent to the action() method, and the action() method will close the dialog box.

Listing 8.10   A Modal Dialog Box That Will Display Any Text

```
package industrial;
import java.awt.*;
//the error dialog
class ModalOK extends Dialog {
        private Button okButton;                //the button which the user will
                                                //click to dismiss the box

        private static Frame createdFrame;      //the frame used to house
                                                //dialog box

    public ModalOK(Frame parent, String theMessage) {
            super(parent, true);       //tell Dialog that we are modal

            //set the layout manager
            GridBagLayout gb = new GridBagLayout();
            GridBagConstraints constraints = new GridBagConstraints();
            setLayout(gb);

            //create the widgets
            okButton = new Button("OK");
            Label message = new Label(theMessage);

            //place the widgets on the screen
            constraints.fill = GridBagConstraints.NONE;
            constraints.anchor = GridBagConstraints.CENTER;
            constraints.ipadx = 20;
            constraints.ipady = 20;
            constraints.weightx = 1.0;
            constraints.weighty = 1.0;
            constraints.gridwidth = GridBagConstraints.REMAINDER;
            constraints.gridheight = GridBagConstraints.RELATIVE;

            gb.setConstraints(message, constraints);
            add(message);
```

```
        constraints.ipadx = 0;
        constraints.ipady = 0;
        constraints.weightx = 0.0;
        constraints.weighty = 0.0;
        constraints.gridwidth = 1;
        constraints.gridheight = GridBagConstraints.REMAINDER;

        gb.setConstraints(okButton, constraints);
        add(okButton);

        //force our dialog box to take minimum of space
        pack();
    }


//trap the ok click
public boolean action(Event e, Object arg) {
        //if the user clicked on the OK button close the dialog box
        if(e.target == okButton) {
            hide();
            if(createdFrame != null)
                createdFrame.hide();
        }
        return true;
    }


public static void createModalOK(String dialogString) {
        if(createdFrame == null)
            createdFrame = new Frame("Dialog");

        //actually create the dialog
        ModalOK theModalOK = new ModalOK(createdFrame, dialogString);
        createdFrame.resize(theModalOK.size().width,
        ➥theModalOK.size().height);

        //display the dialog
        theModalOK.show();
    }
}
```

Figure 8.11 shows the what the ModalOK class looks like after it is instantiated.

FIGURE 8.11

*The sample execution
of the ModalOK
class.*

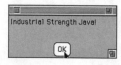

The Finishing Touches

The application is nearing completion; all that is needed is a user interface.

The interface being designed offers a split frame where information is collected in the left half and is displayed in the right.

Before you build that screen, concentrate on the options you need to present to the user. Obviously, the user needs some way to enter data for a new node. There needs to be support for creating a new tree and clearing the display screen.

Additionally, the user needs to be able to view the nodes and their attributes. He should be able to view the nodes via three standard traversals: preorder, inorder, and postorder, as follows:

■ A *preorder* traversal visits all nodes starting at the root, displaying its left children and then its right children.

■ An *inorder* traversal displays all nodes in order.

■ A *postorder* traversal displays the left-most children first, then the right-most children, and finally the root of the tree.

The last feature you will add is the capability to find the rank of any node. The rank is defined by the order in which the node would occur during an inorder traversal.

The ability to insert a new node is managed by keeping a reference to the root of the tree. Whenever you have a new node to insert, you must tell the root about it and let the root manage the insertion. If the root cannot attach it as a left or right child, it instructs one of its children to deal with the node.

The traversals are designed to be recursive in nature and to operate by drilling down the tree until a null value is hit, indicating that a specific branch has come to an end. In all cases, the traversals build an output string as each node is visited. After the traversal is finished, a string containing the node's attributes is displayed.

Finding the rank of a node also is recursive but is a bit trickier than the traversals. The process is based on the relation between a node's rank and the number of children that node has. You basically search through the tree looking for the node, incrementing a counter every time a new node is visited.

The code for the application is shown in listings 8.11a through 8.11d.

In listing 8.11a is a constructor for the BinaryTreeUI class, along with various member variables. The constructor is charged with building the screen.

Listing 8.11a   A Constructor for the BinaryTreeUI Class

```
package industrial;
import java.awt.*;
//Binary tree program
//the driver for the tree, also implements the pre,in,post-order
//traversals and the rank method
public class BinaryTreeUI extends Frame {

    //mostly gui stuff
    private TextField input = new TextField(100);
    private TextArea result = new TextArea(15, 25);
    private Button clear = new Button("Clear");
    private Button add = new Button("Add");
    private Label note = new Label("Traversals");
    private Button preorder = new Button("Preorder");
    private Button inorder = new Button("Inorder");
    private Button postorder = new Button("Postorder");
    private String sOutput = new String();
    private BinaryTree theTree;
    private Button newTree = new Button("New Tree");
    private Panel leftPanel = new Panel();
    private Panel rightPanel = new Panel();
    private Button rank = new Button("Rank");
    private ModalOK theError;

    //constructor, again all gui stuff
    public BinaryTreeUI(String title) {
        super(title);
        leftPanel.setLayout(new GridLayout(6, 2, 10, 10));
        leftPanel.add(input);
        leftPanel.add(new Label(""));
        leftPanel.add(clear);
        leftPanel.add(add);
        leftPanel.add(newTree);
        leftPanel.add(rank);
        leftPanel.add(note);
        leftPanel.add(new Label(""));
        leftPanel.add(preorder);
```

continues

Advanced Data Structures

Listing 8.11a   Continued

```
        leftPanel.add(inorder);
        leftPanel.add(postorder) ;

        rightPanel.add(result);
        this.setLayout(new GridLayout(1, 2));
        this.add(leftPanel);
        this.add(rightPanel);
    }
```

Listing 8.11b contains the rank() method. This method recursively searches through the binary tree, starting at the node passed to it for the int passed in as a parameter. If the node is not found, an error dialog box is created to tell the user that the number is not present in the tree.

Listing 8.11b   The rank() Method

```
        //the rank method. implemetnations is pretty obvious, uses recursion
        private int rank(BinaryTree t, int searchInt) {
            int tempInt = t.getKey();
            if (tempInt == searchInt) {
                if (t.getLeft() == null)
                        return 1;
                    else
                        return (t.getLeft().getNumDescendents() + 2);
            }
            else if (searchInt < tempInt)
                return (rank(t.getLeft(), searchInt));
            else if (searchInt > tempInt) {
                if (t.getLeft() == null)
                    return (1 + rank(t.getRight(), searchInt));
                else
                    return (rank(t.getRight(), searchInt) +
                    ➥t.getLeft().getNumDescendents() + 2);
            }
            if (t.getLeft() == null || t.getRight() == null)
                return (1);
            else
                { ModalOK.createModalOK("Number Not Present"); return 0;
    }
        }
```

Listing 8.11c contains the methods that will perform the inorder, preorder, and postorder traversals. Each works by recursively referencing child nodes while building an output string containing data about each node.

Listing 8.11c The Methods that Perform the Inorder, Preorder, and Postorder Traversals

```
//inorder traversal, recursive
private void inorder(BinaryTree t) {
    if (t != null) {
        inorder(t.getLeft());
        sOutput += ("height: " + t.getHeight() + " Descendents: "
        + t.getNumDescendents() + " key: " + t.getKey() + "\n");
        inorder(t.getRight());
    }
}

//preorder traversal, recursive
private void preorder(BinaryTree t) {
    if (t != null) {
        sOutput += ("height: " + t.getHeight() + " Descendents: "
        + t.getNumDescendents() + " key: " + t.getKey() + "\n");
        preorder(t.getLeft());
        preorder(t.getRight());
    }
}

//postorder traversal, recursive
private void postorder(BinaryTree t) {
    if (t != null) {
        postorder(t.getLeft());
        postorder(t.getRight());
        sOutput += ("height: " + t.getHeight() + " Descendents: "
        + t.getNumDescendents() + " key: " + t.getKey() + "\n");
    }
}
//gui
public Insets insets() {
    return new Insets (10, 10, 10, 10);
}

//gui
private void clearInput() {
```

continues

Advanced Data Structures

Listing 8.11c   Continued

```
        input.setText("");
        result.setText("");
}

//creats a new tree. note this is not called for the first tree as
//one is automatically created on launch
private void doNew() {
    theTree = null;        //we can get away with simply making the
                           //root null due to the fact that the
                           //garbage collector will free up memory
                           //allocated to the other nodes.

    firstTime = true;
}
```

Listing 8.11d contains the action() method, which waits for input from the user. After the action() method is passed an event, the method examines the event and calls an associated method. Additioanlly in this listing is the main() method that creates a new instance of the BinaryTreeUI class.

Listing 8.11d   The action() Method

```
//the action method, deals with all events
boolean firstTime = true;
public boolean action (Event evt, Object arg) {
    if ("Clear".equals(arg)) {
        this.clearInput();
        return true;
    }
    else if ("New Tree".equals(arg)) {
        this.doNew();
        return true;
    }
    else if ("Add".equals(arg)) {
        if (firstTime) {
            firstTime = false;
            try {      int myInt =
            ➥Integer.parseInt(input.getText());
                    input.setText("");
                    theTree = new BinaryTree (myInt, null);
}
```

```
                              catch (NumberFormatException nfe) {
                              ➥ModalOK.createModalOK("Not An integer"); }
                    }
                    else {
                         try {       int myInt =
                         ➥Integer.parseInt(input.getText());
                                   input.setText("");
                                   theTree.insert(myInt); }
                         catch (NumberFormatException nfe) {
                         ➥ModalOK.createModalOK("Not An Integer"); }
                    }
                    return true;
               }
          else if ("Rank".equals(arg)) {
               int sInt;
               int myInt = Integer.parseInt(input.getText());
               sInt = this.rank(theTree, myInt);
               result.setText("The Rank of " + myInt + " is " + sInt);
               return true;
          }
          else if ("Inorder".equals(arg)) {
               sOutput = "";
               this.inorder(theTree);
               result.setText(sOutput);
               return true;
          }
          else if ("Preorder".equals(arg)) {
               sOutput = "";
               this.preorder(theTree);
               result.setText(sOutput);
               return true;
          }
          else if ("Postorder".equals(arg)) {
               sOutput = "";
               this.postorder(theTree);
               result.setText(sOutput);
               return true;
          }
          else if (evt.id == Event.WINDOW_DESTROY) {
               System.exit(0);
               return true;
          }
          else
               { return false; }
     }
```

continues

Advanced Data Structures

Listing 8.11d   Continued

```
        //the main method
        public static void main(String[] args) {
            Frame f = new BinaryTreeUI("Binary Tree");
            f.pack();
            f.resize(500, 300);
            f.show();
        }

} //class binary tree driver
```

Summary

This chapter taught you how to build your own data structures from scratch and a little bit about application building along the way.

As you go on to explore other data structures, remember that writing a dynamic data structure in a pointer-free language can be a bit confusing. If you are used to managing memory for yourself, you might feel a touch constrained by the fact that Java does not permitted this. As this chapter has shown, however, data structures implemented in Java are actually a touch more elegant than in languages that use pointers. Additionally it is much easier to implement a data structure in Java than it is in a pointer-based language.

Chapter 9

Input/Output: Using Streams

All I/O in Java is handled through something called a stream. A *stream* is a one-way path along which data may travel. Most stream classes come in pairs—one for input and one for output.

One of the most attractive aspects of I/O in Java is that it is very easy to implement and maintain, due to the following features of the language:

- Separation of input and output methods into different classes
- Portability between different data sources and destinations

The separation of output methods from input methods aids I/O development in that it ensures that potential errors are flagged as compile-time and not run-time errors. As was stated previously, I/O classes exist as pairs; one half of that pair takes care of output, and the other half takes care of input. Therefore any attempt to read data from an output stream would result in a compile-time error, which is significantly easier to track down when compared to a run-time error.

The second manner in which Java facilitates I/O involves portability between one communication source or destination and another. In many languages, I/O is defined in very limited (and platform-dependent) terms. In a language where I/O is defined in such strict terms, it can be difficult to alter the source or destination of an existing I/O configuration. Not so in Java. In fact, it is amazingly easy to take a piece of code that reads in data from a remote file and make some alterations so that same piece of code reads in data from a remote database.

Visualizing Streams: Choosing the Right Stream for Your Application

Knowing the Java API inside and out is not enough if you want to develop powerful applications. It is essential that you fully understand OOP and the minute details of the Java language. Another key element is the ability to take your knowledge of OOP and Java and apply that knowledge to solve a problem. Java provides streams as an easy I/O tool, but also provides a wide variety of stream classes from which to choose. The phrase "wide variety" translates to 22, and with so many to choose from, confusion is likely.

A common problem when developing with streams is to misunderstand the stream classes and to choose a stream class that is not optimal for your situation. This does not necessarily imply that your application will produce incorrect results, but it does mean that you are not choosing the easiest manner to solve a problem.

As is implied by the previous paragraph, choosing the best stream is not always easy to do. This chapter covers the use of each class and builds an application that demonstrates their use. When you finish studying this chapter, you will have a detailed understanding of all classes and have little trouble picking the correct one for your applications.

Starting at the Top: InputStream and OutputStream

As illustrated by figure 9.1, almost all stream classes extend either of the abstract classes, InputStream and OutputStream.

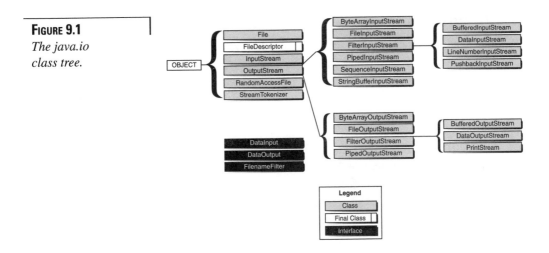

FIGURE 9.1
*The java.io
class tree.*

Note that all classes are part of the java.io package, and extend off InputStream and
OutputStream.

InputStream

The class InputStream is the abstract base class from which all input stream classes
extend. Listing 9.1 contains the API listing for the class, and full descriptions of the
methods follow.

Listing 9.1   API's java.io.InputStream

```
public class java.io.InputStream extends java.lang.Object {
    //Constructors
    public InputSream();

    //Methods
    public int available();
    public void close();
    public void mark(int readlimit);
public boolean markSupported();
    public abstract int read();
    public int read(byte b[]);
    public int read(byte b[], int off, int len);
    public void reset();
    public long skip(long n);

}
```

Input / Output: Using Streams

Reading in Data

It is relatively obvious in listing 9.1 that the three read() methods facilitate the reading in of data. Although their names make their purpose obvious, their signatures can be slightly puzzling. All read() methods read in data one byte at a time, and all have "int return value;" where the return value is –1 when the end of stream is reached. Taking this into account, the method defined as "public int read()" is rather confusing. If data is read in as a byte, then why is that byte returned as an int? Because the range of values available to bytes is 0 to 255 (inclusive), and the range of values available to ints is 2,147,483,648 to 2,147,483,647 (inclusive), int has enough "room" to contain the value of a byte. The extra space needed for an int is used to allow the end-of-stream –1 return value. Therefore it is true to state that the value of the int returned by the read() method will always be between –1 and 255 (inclusive), with the value of –1 occurring only when the stream no longer contains any data.

Reading Data One Byte at a Time

Reading in data one byte at a time is handled by the method defined as "public abstract int read()". Often this method is used in a loop to read in all data present in a stream. For example, the following code will read all data present in the stream "incoming" and append it to a String object.

```
int tempInt;
String total = new String();
while((tempInt = incoming.read()) != -1) {
    total += tempInt;
}
```

Note that while in the InputStream class, this method is abstract—any child class will provide an implementation.

Reading Data Into an Array

The read() methods defined with byte arrays in their signatures read in data directly to the array defined as b. In the case of the first method (defined as read(byte b[])), the method attempts to fill the entire array with bytes from the stream. If the end of stream is reached before the array is filled, the call only fills the array until that end is reached. The return value is the total number of bytes read into the buffer, or –1 if the end is reached prematurely. The second read method (defined as "read(byte b[], int off, int len)") reads data into the array starting at b[off] and ending at b[off+len]. If off+len is greater than b.length, len defaults to b.length-off (defined as "read(byte b[], int off, int len)").

Skipping Ahead

The skip() method is useful if you need to read in only part of a stream and want to parse out the useless data *while* reading, instead of afterward. This method skips over *n* number of bytes along the stream (where *n* is passed as a long). If *n* + the current position is greater than b.length, then *n* defaults to b.length—the current position. In all cases, the return value is the actual number of bytes actually skipped over.

Moving Back and Forth along a Stream

You will find the mark and reset methods extremely useful. Where the skip() method enables you to simply jump *n* bytes in one direction, these methods enable you to return to a specific part of the stream. Simply position yourself at a point along the stream (using the read() or skip() methods), and then call the mark() method. To return to that position, simply call the reset() method.

Where the skip() method was stated to be useful when moving past a set of unwanted data in a stream, often the data needed is not placed in the stream in a linear fashion. For this reason, the mark() and reset() methods allow you to read in parts of a stream, which are not stored in a linear fashion.

A demonstration of the mark() and reset() methods is provided in the following listing. The code here will read in data from one stream into two byte arrays. After all lines have been executed, both arrays will contain identical data. Note that InputStream is an abstract class, and the stream, in, used in this listing is understood to be an instance of a class that extends InputStream. Listing 9.2 leaves b1 and b2 with the same information.

Listing 9.2 Using the mark() and reset() Methods to Create Two Arrays with Identical Data

```
//declare two arrays to house data
byte b1[] = new byte[MAXBYTES];
byte b2[] = new byte[MAXBYTES];

//move forward along the stream
in.skip(42);

//read in data
in.mark();
in.read(b1);
in.reset();
in.read(b2, 0, MAXBYTES);
```

Checking What's Left

Just so you don't feel that it wasn't left out, coverage of the available() method is provided. As its title implies, this method returns the total number of bytes that can be read from the stream.

Returning Allocated Resources

When you create an instance of a stream object, that stream is automatically "opened." Because Java supports automatic garbage collection, a logical conclusion would be that after you are finished with the stream, the resources allocated to that stream are returned to the system. This conclusion, although logical, unfortunately is untrue. The garbage collector will at some point get around to calling a stream's finalize() method, which releases allocated system resources. However, because the garbage collector runs on a low priority thread, this "return of allocated resources" can take a very long time. To ensure rapid return of allocated resources, call a stream's close() method after you are finished with that stream.

OutputStream

The abstract class OutputStream acts as the complement to the abstract class InputStream. It is subclassed by various classes to enable the writing of data to a stream. Listing 9.3 contains the API listing for the class, and full descriptions of the methods follow.

Listing 9.3   Java API's java.io.OutputStream

```
public abstract class java.io.OutputStream extends java.lang.Object {
    //Constructors
    public OutputStream();

    //Methods
    public void close();
    public void flush();
    public void write(byte b[]);
    public void write(byte b[], int off, int len);
    public abstract void write(int b);
}
```

Writing to a Stream

Just as InputStream provides three versions of read(), OutputStream provides three methods for writing out data. Review the listing 9.3 and note that the three write() methods are used for outputting data.

Writing One Byte at a Time

All three write() methods write out data in the form of a byte; the method write(b), however, accepts b as an int. This is not a bug, but a feature. Because many byte operations render the byte an int, the method was designed this way. Of course, only the lower 8 bits of the int are passed along, and the upper 24 are discarded.

Writing Groups of Bytes

The other two versions of write() output data passed in as a byte array; write(byte b[]) outputs the entire b.length bytes to the stream; "write(byte b[], int off, int len)" enables you to be more specific about which part of the array you want to output. The method attempts to write from b[off] to b[off+len] (inclusive). If off+len is greater than b.length, then len defaults to b.length - off.

Getting Rid of Unwanted Data

The flush() method takes any bytes left in the buffer and writes them to the stream.

Returning Allocated Resources

As with InputStream, the close() method, although often neglected, is a very important method. If this method is not called on an OutputStream when you are finished with it, the used resources remain in use for a while. At some point the garbage collector will get around to freeing up those resources, but it could take a while. It is crucial when writing an application to be frugal when using memory and associated system resources. If you are not frugal, it is possible that your application will prematurely run out of memory while running. Depending on the operating system, this could either cause the application to shut down or crash the computer. Using the close() method after you are finished with a stream helps to return memory to the application.

Extending InputStream and OutputStream

Having a grasp of the methods provided by the InputStream and OutputStream classes is the key to understanding all other stream classes because most other stream classes subclass InputStream or OutputStream.

The following sections present discussions on the various stream classes that subclass InputStream and OutputStream. Each section both discusses the manner in which the child class manages the abstract methods in either InputStream or OutputStream, and also new methods introduced by the child class.

As was stated previously, many stream classes occur in pairs; one for input and one for output. In some cases only one half of that pair is provided. The following sections first present the classes that have I/O pairs, then the classes that stand alone. If you ever feel that a discussion on a class does not cover a specific method, note that the coverage is actually there, though it may be hidden. Classes often do not change the purpose of inherited methods, and thus a definition of the method can be found among that class's ancestors.

Using PipedOutputStream and PipedInputStream

Piped streams enable two threads to communicate with each other. A PipedOutputStream fills a "pipe" with some information, then a PipedInputStream reads that data back out. The term "pipe" refers to a common location in memory accessed by two different classes. Listing 9.4 provides the API listing for PipedOutputStream. Listing 9.5 provides the API listing for PipedInputStream. Each class is discussed in detail in the sections which follow it.

Listing 9.4   Java API's java.io.PipedOutputStream

```
public class java.io.PipedOutputStream extends java.io.OutputStream {
    //Constructors
    public PipedOutputStream();
    public PipedOutputStream(PipedInputStream snk);

    //Methods    public void close();
    public void connect(PipedInputStream snk);
    public void write(byte b[], int off, int len);
    public void write(int b);
}
```

Where the class in listing 9.4 allows data to be written to a stream, PipedInputStream in listing 9.5 will read it back out.

Listing 9.5   Java API's java.io.PipedInputStream

```
public class java.io.PipedInputStream extends java.io.InputStream {
    //Constructors
    public PipedInputStream ();
    public PipedInputStream (PipedOutputStream src);

    //Methods
    public void close();
    public void connect(PipedOutputStream src);
    public int read(byte b[], int off, int len);
    public int read();
}
```

Forging a Connection

Because PipedInputStream and PipedOutputStream are reading and writing from the same source, it is obvious that you need a connection between an instance of PipedInputStream and an instance of PipedOutputStream. You can make the connection in two ways:

- When instantiating the stream objects, using a constructor which accepts a stream as a parameter
- After the stream objects are instantiated, using the connect() method

Listing 9.6 shows the different ways communication between a PipedOutputStream and a PipedInputStream can be established. It should be noted that each example produces exactly the same result.

Listing 9.6 Two Ways to Establish a Connection between PipedStreams

```
//Establishing a connection using the constructors
PipedOutputStream out = new PipedOutputStream();
PipedInputStream in = new PipedInputStream(out);

//Establishing a connection using the constructors version 2
PipedInputStream in = new PipedInputStream();
PipedOutputStream out = new PipedOutputStream(in);

//Establishing a connection using the connect method
PipedInputStream in = new PipedInputStream();
PipedOutputStream out = new PipedOutputStream();
in.connect(out);

//Establishing a connection using the connect method version 2
PipedInputStream in = new PipedInputStream();
PipedOutputStream out = new PipedOutputStream();out.connect(in);
```

Communication Between the Streams

It is essential that you understand that the purpose of the PipedOutputStream and PipedInputStream classes is to facilitate communication between threads. While one thread is writing, the other is blocked from reading from that stream. With the reverse true also, the means that it is not possible for two classes to simulta-neously read and write to the same stream.

Because PipedOutputStream and PipedInputStream subclass OutputStream and InputStream (respectively), all methods made available to OutputStream and InputStream are made available to PipedOutputStream and PipedInputStream. The processes of sending and receiving data are managed by the same read and write methods that were presented in the discussion of OutputStream and InputStream. Listing 9.7 shows how you might use these methods to communicate between streams. Note that to conserve space, some code has been cut and is simply discussed in comments.

Listing 9.7   Using PipedStreams to Communicate between Threads

```
class WriteData extends Thread {
    PipedOutputStream myPOS;
    public WriteData(PipedOutputStream POS) {
        myPOS = POS;
    }

    public void start() {
        //set up the Thread
    }

    pubic void run() {
        //write data to the PipedOutputStream
    }
}
public class UsePipeStreams {
    public static void main(String[] args) {
        try{
            PipedOutputStream out = new PipedOutputStream();
            PipedInputStream in = new PipedInputStream(out);
            WriteData myWriter = new WriteData(
out);
            myWriter.start();
            int theData;
            while((theData = in.read()) != 1) {
                System.out.println((char)theData);
            }
        }
        catch(IOException ioe) { System.out.println("err: "+ioe); }
    }
}
```

Using ByteArray Streams

The ByteArrayInputStream class and the ByteArrayOutputStream class enable arrays of bytes to be used as the communication path between streams. ByteArrayOutputStream writes a byte array to a stream, and ByteArrayInputStream reads it back. As with other topics presented in the chapter, the methods present in the class are listed first, then discussed in detail.

Using the ByteArrayOutputStream Class

Listing 9.8 contains the Java API listing for the class ByteArrayOutputStream.

Listing 9.8   Java API's java.io.ByteArrayOutputStream

```
public class java.io.ByteArrayOutputStream extends java.io.OutputStream
{
    //Fields
    protected byte buf[];
    protected int count;

    //Constructors
    public ByteArrayOutputStream();
    public ByteArrayOuputStream(int size);

    //Methods
    public void reset();
    public int size();
    public byte[] toByteArray();
    public String toString();
    public String toString(int hibyte);
    public void write(byte b[], int off, int len);
    public void write(int b);
    public void writeTo(OutputStream out);
}
```

Filling a ByteArrayOutputStream

Inside a ByteArrayOutputStream object, data is stored in an array, which has the ability to grow as new data is added. However, because it takes time to grow an array, it is important that the space allocated originally for the array is close to what will be needed. Of course in some situations, the amount of space needed is unknown, and in these cases a best estimate will suffice. The initial storage capacity of a ByteArrayOutputStream object is specified as a parameter to its constructor, and a default constructor is also provided.

ByteArrayOutputStream() creates an array with room for 32 bytes; this array will grow as needed. Again, because it takes time for the array to grow, situations that need more than 32 bytes should use the second constructor, which enables you to specify the initial size of the array. The following line, for example, creates a new ByteArrayOutputStream with room for 42 bytes; of course, this array will resize if needed.

```
ByteArrayOutputStream  out = new ByteArrayOutputStream(42)
```

After you have created an instance of ByteArrayOutputStream, you can fill it with data. Not surprisingly, you can fill it with data using different versions of the write() method. Because ByteArrayOutputStream subclasses OutputStream, its write() methods are quite similar to those in OutputStream:

- write(int b) writes b as a byte to the stream.
- write(byte b[], int off, int len) writes the data in the array b[] to the stream. The parameter off specifies a start index, and the parameter len specifies the number of entries in b[] which should be written. If out+len+1 is greater than the total available bytes, only those from b[off] to b[(b.length - 1)] written out.

Retrieving Data from a ByteArrayOutputStream

You can retrieve information from a ByteArrayOutputStream with the methods toByteArray(), toString(), and writeTo(). Listing 9.9 examines the usage of all the methods discussed in the sections that follow and assumes there is a ByteArrayOutputStream named "out" that is storing some data.

Listing 9.9   Three Methods of Retrieving Data from a ByteArrayOutputStream

```
//Getting the information as a byte array
byte byteArray[] = new byte[ out.size() ];
byteArray = out.toByteArray();

//Getting the information as a String (two methods that
//produce identical results.
String myString = out.toString();
String myOtherString = out.toString(0);

//Passing the information to an output stream. Note that
//DataOutputStream will be covered later in this chapter, and
//is simply provided as an example.
DataOutputStream dos = new DataOutputStream();
out.writeTo(dos);
```

The toByteArray() Method

The toByteArray() method returns a byte array containing the contents of the current stream. The length of the array can be predetermined by referencing the size() method of ByteArrayOutputStream. The following code is an example of this:

```
int size = myByteArray.size();
byte[] myByteArray = new byte[size];
myByteArray = myByteArrayOutputStream.toByteArray();
```

The toString() Method

To retrieve the information as a String, you need to use either of the toString() methods. By itself, toString() returns the contents of the current stream without alteration. Each byte is converted to its respective character, and they are all concatenated onto the String.

Using toString(int hibyte) returns the contents of the stream as a String where each character is formed by combining the lower 8 bits of hibyte as the upper 8 bits of the new character, and the byte in question forms the remaining bits of the new character. The actual computation is performed using the following formula:

```
(char)(((hibyte & 0xff) << 8) ¦ (byte in question & 0xff))
```

From this formula, you can see that calling toString(0) has the same effect as calling toString().

The writeTo() Method

If, instead of getting the information as a byte array or String, you desire to pass the information to another OutputStream, the writeTo() method will work for you. This method takes an OutputStream as a parameter and fills it with the contents of the current stream.

Finishing with a ByteArrayOutputStream

The data is not actually discarded. Rather, an internal variable—count—which indicates the number of bytes in the stream, is set to 0, having the effect of discarding the data. Space allocated to the buffer, however, remains intact.

As with all child classes of OutputStream, you will want to call the close() method when you are finished with the stream, as it forces the return of allocated system resources. If you will need a Byte-ArrayOutputStream later in your application, however, you may want to hold off on letting the system have its resources back. Due to the fact that allocating resources takes time, by using already allocated resources, your application places less of a strain on the computer. Calling the reset() method contained in ByteArrayOutputStream effectively discards all stored data, yet does not force you to reallocate system resources when a ByteArrayOutputStream is again needed.

The advantage of not "closing" the stream is that all system resources allocated to the stream remain allocated. Because this includes memory allocated to the buffer, you will find that recycling the current space and not discarding the current object saves a great deal of time.

Using the ByteArrayInputStream Class

The ByteArrayInputStream class proves most useful when your application needs to read in an existing data set in the form of a stream. This data set, in the form of an array of bytes, is passed to the ByteArrayInputStream constructor and acts as a constant source of input for the stream, as in listing 9.10.

Listing 9.10   The API listing for java.io.ByteArrayInputStream

```
public class java.io.ByteArrayInputStream extends java.io.InputStream {
    //Fields
    protected byte buf[];
    protected int count;
    protected int pos;

    //Constructors
    public ByteArrayInputStream(byte buf[]);
    public ByteArrayInputStream(byte buf[], int offset, int length);

    //Methods
    public int available();
    public int read();
    public int read(byte b[], int off, int len);
    public void reset();
    public long skip(long n);
}
```

Reading from a ByteArrayInputStream

The read() methods present in the ByteArrayInputStream class are similar to those supplied by its parent (InputStream) and read either one byte (read()) or a series of bytes directly into a byte array (read(byte b[],int off, int len)), where off indicates the starting index that data is read into, and len indicates the maximum number of values that should be read into the array.

Filling a ByteArrayInputStream

Filling a ByteArrayInputStream is an interesting concept. When you create an instance of the object, you pass it a byte array; however, the contents of the array are not copied. Rather, the array is set up as a constant source of data for the stream. The stream is considered full when b contains data from b[0] to b[b.length - 1].

Moving Around the Stream

If, while reading in data from the stream, you decide that you don't need sequential access to the data, the skip(n) method enables you to skip over n bytes. If you attempt to skip over more bytes than are available, you will skip directly to the last byte in the stream.

Finishing with the Stream

As with ByteArrayOutputStream, ByteArrayInputStream supports both the close() and reset() methods. The close() method will close the stream, and return any resources allocated to it. However if this stream will be needed at some later point, simply calling the reset() method is potentially a better idea. Remember that allocating resources takes time, and that if a stream can be reused, the application's efficiency increases.

Writing to and from Files: FileInputStream and FileOutputStream

One of the most popular types of I/O that an application may need to perform is file I/O. Files are used to store created documents, preference files, and just about any other type of data imaginable. Java provides a variety of classes for file I/O; FileInputStream and FileOutputStream are two of these classes.

Later in this chapter, you will find a discussion of the RandomAccessFile class, which can also be used for file I/O. Because file I/O is one of the first things that you usually learn in a new language, you no doubt have had experience dealing with file I/O in other languages. As you learn about these classes, think about how much easier file I/O in Java is when compared to some other languages. As with all the discussions on streams, API listings are provided ahead of time to enable you to get acquainted with the class. Take a minute to study listings 9.11 and 9.12 and get ready to dive into file I/O!

Listing 9.11   The FileOutputStream Class

```java
public class java.io.FileOutputStream extends java.io.OutputStream {
    //Constructors
    public FileOutputStream(File file);
    public FileOutputStream(FileDescriptor fd);
    public FileOutputStream(String name);

    //Methods
    public void close();
    protected void finalize();
    public final FileDescriptor getFD();
    public void write(byte b[]);
    public void write(byte b[], int off, int len);
    public void write(int b);
}
```

Listing 9.12   The API Code for java.io.FileInputStream

```java
public class java.io.FileInputStream extends java.io.InputStream {
    //Constructors
    public FileInputStream(File file);
    public FileInputStream(FileDescriptor fd);
    public FileInputStream(String name);

    //Methods
    public int available();
    public close();
    protected void finalize();
    public final FileDescriptor getFD();
    public int read();
    public int read(byte b[]);
    public int read(byte b[]);
    public long skip(long n);
}
```

Sending Information to a File

When instantiated, the FileOutputStream class opens an output stream to a file; where the file is passed as a parameter. The constructors accept either an instance of a File or FileDescriptor object, or a String representing a system-dependent file path.

To note about running applications that use FileOutputStreams, is that if the user running the application does not have write privileges for a particular file, a SecurityException will be thrown. Good code will test for this situation and display an error message if the exception is thrown.

After you have an instance of a FileOutputStream object, you are ready to begin sending data. Assuming that you have been reading this chapter in a linear fashion, you will have no trouble understanding the write() methods used by FileOutputStream; as they are identical to those used in OutputStream. If you are looking for a recap, the methods are as follows:

- write(byte b[]), which writes the entire byte array to the file
- write(byte b[], int off, int len), which writes from b[off] to b[off+len} to the stream
- write(int b), which writes b as a byte to the stream

Retrieving Information from a File

Because you need to read the information back from a file after you have written it to that file, the FileInputStream class provides the necessary methods. As with FileOutputStream, a new instance of FileOutputStream is created with either a File or FileDescriptor object, or with a String representing a system-dependent file path.

An instance of FileInputStream enables information to be read using the methods defined in FileInputStream's parent class, InputStream. Again, if you have not been reading this chapter in a linear fashion, a review of the read() methods defined in InputStream are reviewed here:

- read() which reads in one byte of information from the stream. This method returns an int with the value of –1 if the stream is empty, or an int with the value of the total number of bytes read if the stream is not empty.
- read(byte b[]) which will read data into b[] until the entire array is full. The return value for this method is identical to the return value for read() listed above.
- read(byte b[], int off, int len) which will read data into b[] from b[off] to b[len]. If off+len is less than b.length, then len will default to b.length-1-off.

Finishing Up with File I/O

Both FileInputStream and FileOutputStream support the close() method. The close() method functions in a fashion similar to the other close() methods discussed in this chapter, releasing allocated system resources.

Implementing File I/O Methods

Knowledge of FileInputStream and FileOutputStream is extremely important. Your applications now have the capability not only to create data, but also to store that data. It is hard to develop any form of powerful application without the aid of files.

In conclusion to the section on FileInputStreams and FileOutputStreams, you will build a text editor application. The application will make use of the application frame work developed in Chapter 6, and will support the following features:

- Creation of new files
- Saving of files
- Opening saved files
- Editing of an active file

When the application loads, it prompts the user with an empty text area, along with File and Edit menus. At that point, the user can opt to either begin writing in the current text area, open a saved text area, create a new blank text area, or quit the application.

Examining the Feature Set

When the user wants to open a saved file, the following steps occur:

1. The user selects Open from the File menu.
2. An Open File dialog box asks the user to select a file for opening.
3. The user selects a file and clicks the OK button in the Open File dialog box.
4. A new FileInputStream object is created with a reference to the selected file.
5. The FileInputStream object streams in the contents of the file.
6. The FileInputStream object takes the file's contents and uses it to create a new editor window.

When the user wants to save the current file, the following steps occur:

1. The user selects Save from the File menu.
2. A Save File dialog box asks the user to select a file name and path to be used when saving the current editor.
3. The user enters a file name, chooses the correct path, and clicks the OK button in the Save File dialog box.

4. A new FileOutputStream object is created with a reference to the selected file.

5. The FileOutputStream object streams the contents of the current editor to the new file.

When the user wants to create a new editor window, the following steps occur:

1. The user selects New Frame from the File menu.

2. A new instance of the editor class is created and displayed.

Due to the fact that you will be taking advantage of the application frame work developed in Chapter 6, many aspects related to the application have already been developed. These aspects include:

- The menu structure
- Methods for creating Open and Save dialog boxes
- Event handling methods

Deciding on the Class Structure

Having covered the features present in the application, and also the manner in which those features are implemented, let's take a look at the classes that will be developed.

A class called TextEditor extends the FrameWork class developed in Chapter 6, and adds functionality to complete the user interface (UI), and stream to and from the disk.

A class called IndustrialEditor simply contains a main() method, and in that method creates a new instance of the TextEditor class.

In addition to the two new classes developed for this application, the FrameWork and ModalOK classes are used. These classes are part of the application frame work developed in Chapter 6, and are not reprinted in this chapter.

Implementing the TextEditor Class

Listings 9.13a through 9.13n contain the code for the TextEditor class. Note how you benefit from the FrameWork call in that little work is spent on the UI and event handling.

The code present in listing 9.13a contains the two constructors supported by the TextEditor class. Both accept a title to be displayed in the title bar of the new editor, and the second accepts an additional parameter to be used as initial text for the editor. This second constructor is used when opening a new file, and is passed the complete file as String object.

Listing 9.13a   Building a Basic Text Editor in Java

```java
package industrial;

import java.awt.*;
import java.io.*;


//Class TextEditor a basic text editor which knows how to write itself
//to disk and also how to create a new instance of itself with data
//loaded from disk.
public class TextEditor extends FrameWork {
    //the TextArea where information will be entered
    private     TextArea        theArea;

    //Constructor creates a new empty TextEditor, with title "title".
    public TextEditor(String title) {
        super(title);

        //create the text area
        theArea = new TextArea(30, 55);

        //build the screen
        this.setLayout(new BorderLayout());
        this.add("Center", theArea);

        //display the screen
        this.pack();
        this.show();
    }


    //Constructor creates a new TextEditor with contents initialText
    //(usually read from disk). And tittle matching the file path
    //(title).
    public TextEditor(String title, String initialText) {
        super(title);

        //create the text area
        theArea = new TextArea(initialText, 30, 55);

        //build the screen
        this.setLayout(new BorderLayout());
        this.add("Center", theArea);
```

continues

Listing 9.13a   Continued

```
        //display the screen
        this.pack();
        this.show();
    }
```

Listing 9.13b contains three methods—createNewFrame(), createSaveDialog(), and createOpenDialog()—all of which override associated methods in the FrameWork class, and are called when the user chooses either New Frame, Save, or Open from the File menu.

Listing 9.13b   createNewFrame(), createSaveDialog(), and createOpenDialog()

```
//createNewFrame() overrides createNewFrame() in FrameWork
public void createNewFrame(String title) {
    System.out.println("does this ever get called\n");
    TextEditor myNewTextEditor = new TextEditor("Untitled");
}


//createSaveDialog() overrides createSaveDialog() in FrameWork,
//however that method is still called via a super.xxx
//reference. In FrameWork the is still called via a super.xxx
//Here we take the selected file, create a full path to the file
//and pass that path to saveTo() where the file is
//actually streamed out.
public void createSaveDialog() {
    super.createSaveDialog();
    String pathName = mySaveDialog.getDirectory();
    pathName +=  System.getProperty("file.separator");
    pathName += mySaveDialog.getFile();
    this.saveTo(pathName);
}


//createOpenDialog() overrides createOpenDialog() in FrameWork,
//however that method is still called via a super.xxx reference.
//In FrameWork the actual open dialog is created. Here we take the
//selected file, create a full path to the file and pass that
//path to openNew() where the file is actually streamed in.
```

```
public void createOpenDialog() {
    super.createOpenDialog();
    String pathName = myOpenDialog.getDirectory();
    pathName += System.getProperty("file.separator");
    pathName += myOpenDialog.getFile();
    this.openNew(pathName);
}
```

Listing 9.13c contains two private helper methods called by createSaveDialog(), or createOpenDialog(). The openNew() method (called by createOpenDialog()) is passed as a parameter a file path and creates a new editor which displays the contents of the file located at the file path passed as a parameter. The saveTo() method (called by createSaveDialog()) is passed as a parameter a file path, and saves the contents of the current editor to that file. (Note that the ➡ symbol indicates the line normally fits on the previous line.)

Listing 9.13c   Two Private Helper Methods Called by createSaveDialog() or createOpenDialog()

```
//is called by createSaveDialog(), and is passed a file path as a
//parameter. The file path is used to create a new
//FileOutputStream and the contents of the current editor are
//written to the file
private void openNew(String pathName) {
    try{      FileInputStream myFileStream = new
    ➡FileInputStream(pathName);
                DataInputStream myStream = new
                ➡DataInputStream(myFileStream);

                String newString = new String();
                while(myStream.available() > 0) {
                    newString += myStream.readLine();
                    newString += "\n";
                }

                TextEditor newTextEditor = new TextEditor
                ➡(pathName,newString);
                myStream.close();
                myFileStream.close();
            }
        catch(IOException ioe) {
            ModalOK theModalOK = new ModalOK(this, "Error, could
```

continues

Writing To and From Files: FileInputStream and FileOutputStream

Listing 9.13c   Continued

```
                            not create new file");
            }
      }
      //is called by createOpenDialog(), and is passed a file path as a
      //parameter. The file path is used to create a new FileInputStream
      //and from that stream the contents of the file are read in and
      //used to create a new editor.
      private void saveTo(String pathName) {
            try{      FileOutputStream myFileStream = new
            ➥FileOutputStream(pathName);
                        DataOutputStream myStream = new
                        ➥DataOutputStream(myFileStream);

                        myStream.writeChars(theArea.getText());
                        myStream.close();
                        myFileStream.close();
                  }
            catch(IOException ioe) {
                  ModalOK theModalOK = new ModalOK(this, "Error, could
                  ➥not create new file");
            }
      }
}
```

Implementing the IndustrialEditor Class

At this point you have already developed most of the application. All that is left to do is write the IndustrialEditor class. This class simply contains a main method and creates a new instance of the TextEditor class. The class is listed in listing 9.14.

Listing 9.14   A Driver for the IndustrialEditor Application

```
import industrial.TextEditor;

public class IndustrialEditor {

      public static void main(String[] args) {
            TextEditor myTextEditor = new TextEditor("Untitled");
      }
}
```

Filtering Streams

Recall the statement from the beginning of the chapter that you often will want to use more than one stream class to achieve optimal results. This section introduces two stream classes, FilterInputStream and FilterOutputStream, that effectively sit on top of an existing stream to enhance functionality. What occurs when a *filter stream* (a child class of either FilterInputStream or FilterOutputStream) is used, is that the filter stream manipulates the data heading towards the underlying stream. For example, the filter stream LineNumberInputStream sits on top of any InputStream, and allows access to the data in the underlying InputStream one line at a time.

FilterInputStream and FilterOutputStream introduce little functionality themselves, however seven child classes implement extensive functionality. The following child classes are fully discussed in this section:

- BufferedInputStream and BufferedOutputStream
- DataInputStream and DataOutputStream
- LineNumberInputStream
- PushBackInputStream
- PrintStream

First, however, FilterInputStream and FilterOutputStream are covered.

If you take a look at the API listings in listings 9.15 and 9.16 for FilterInputStream and FilterOutputStream, you will see the methods and constructors made available by these classes. Of special note are not the methods (as nothing new is really provided) but the constructors that accept a stream as a parameter. By providing a constructor which accepts a stream as a parameter, that stream passed in becomes the underlying stream which has its data manipulated by the filter stream.

Listing 9.15   The Java API Listing for java.io.FilterOutputStream

```
public class java.io.FilterOutputStream extends java.io.OutputStream {
    //Fields
    protected OutputStream out;

    //Constructors
    public FilterOutputStream(OutputStream out);
```

continues

Listing 9.15   Continued

```
    //Methods
    public void close();
    public void flush();
    public void write(byte b[]);
    public void write(byte b[], int off, int len);
    public void write(int b);
}
```

Moving on to listing 9.16 is the class FilterInputStream which will filter any child class of InputStream.

Listing 9.16   The Java API Listing for java.io.FilterInputStream

```
public class java.io.FilterInputStream extends java.io.InputStream {
    //Fields
    protected InputStream in;

    //Constructors
    protected FilterInputStream(InputStream in);

    //Methods
    public int available();
    public void close();
    public void mark(int readlimit);
    public boolean markSupported();
    public int read();
    public int read(byte b[]);
    public int read(byte b[], int off, int len);
    public void reset();
    public long skip(long n);
}
```

After looking over listings 9.15 and 9.16, and by reading the introduction to filter stream, you should have a tight grasp on this powerful concept. In your development you will rarely use either FilterInputStream or FilterOutputStream by itself, due to the few enhancements made at this level. Rather, you will use either one of its child classes, or subclass it yourself to create a stream needed in an application you are building.

Because the power of filter streams becomes obvious when studying child classes of FilterInputStream and FilterOutputStream, detailed discussion is limited to these child classes.

Using the DataOutputStream and DataInputStream Classes

Looking at the child classes of the filter streams reveals two very interesting streams. Looking back through this chapter, you will note that all previously discussed streams read and write data byte by byte. While it is functional to read and write data as a byte, often your source or destination data will be in a different form. If you want to write a series of long integers (long data type) to a stream, for example, you would have to do this byte by byte, which is time consuming. The process would be much easier if there were some way by which you could read and write those long integers directly as long integers.

DataOutputStream and DataInputStream move away from the other stream classes that can only read and write bytes to a stream, and add methods which read and write all primitive types, along with String objects. Take a look at the listing for DataOutputStream in listing 9.17 and listing 9.18 for DataInputStream. The listings are interesting as the problem of reading and writing primitive types is solved.

Listing 9.17   The Java API Listing for java.io.DataOutputStream

```
public class java.io.DataOutputStream extends java.io.FilterOutputStream
➥implements java.io.DataOutput {
    //Fields
    protected int written;

    //Constructors
    public DataOutputStream(OutputStream out);

    //Methods
    public void flush();
    public final int size();
    public void write(byte b[], int off, int len);
    public void write(int b);
    public final void writeBoolean(boolean b);
    public final void writeByte(int v);
    public final void writeBytes(String s);
    public final void writeChar(int v);
    public final void writeChars(String s);
    public final void writeDouble(double v);
    public final void writeFloat(float f);
```

continues

Listing 9.17   Continued

```
    public final void writeInt(int v);
    public final void writeLong(long l 0);
public final void writeShort(int v);
    public final void writeUTF(String s);
}
```

Where the DataOutputStream class provides methods for writing primitive types, the DataInputStream provides methods for reading primitive types. DataInputStream is listed in listing 9.18.

Listing 9.18   The Java API Listing for java.io.DataInputStream

```
public class java.io.DataInputStream extends java.io.FilterInputStream
➥implements java.io.DataInput {
    //Constructors
    public DataInputStream(InputStream in);

    //Methods
    public final int read(byte b[]);
    public final int read(byte b[], int off, int len);
    public final boolean readBoolean();
    public final byte readByte();
    public final char readChar();
    public final double readDouble();
    public final float readFloat();
    public final void readFully(byte b[]);
    public final void readFully(byte b[], int off, int len);
    public final int readInt();
    public final String readLine();
    public final long readLong();
    public final short readShort();
    public final int readUnsignedByte();
    public final int readUnsignedShort();
    public final String readUTF();
    public final static String readUTF(DataInput in);
    public final int skipBytes(int n);
}
```

Looking over listings 9.17 and 9.18, you should understand the potential that these classes bring. In the following sections, you will learn how to use each method present in Data-InputStream and DataOutputStream.

Reading and Writing Bytes

As stated previously, the purpose of DataInputStream and DataOutputStream is to read and write Java's primitive data types. In this section, you will learn about reading and writing of bytes using DataOutputStream and DataInputStream. It should be noted that even though most streams which will be "filtered" by either of these Data streams provide support for reading or writing of bytes, this support was added to DataOutputStream and DataInputStream as a matter of convenience. The methods used for writing bytes are

- write(int b), which writes v as a byte to the stream
- write(byte b[], int off, int len), which writes from b[off] to b[len] to the stream
- writeByte(int v), which writes b as a byte to the stream
- writeBytes(String s), which writes the string s to the stream, discarding the upper eight bits

The methods used from reading bytes back from the stream are

- read(byte b[]), which fills b[] with data from the stream
- read(byte b[], int off, int len), which fills b[] from b[off] to b[len] with data from the stream
- readByte(), which reads the next byte from the stream and uses that byte as its return value

When studying the writeBytes() method, which writes a String object to the underlying stream, it is important to note two additional methods used for reading that String object back, as follows:

- readLine(), which reads in the first line and returns it as a String object. To note here is that a line is defined as a series of characters terminated by a carriage return, newline character, or a carriage return and a newline character. This method was used to read in saved files in the text editor application developed earlier in this chapter.
- readFully(byte b[], int off, int len), which reads data into b[] from b[off] to b[off+len]

Reading and Writing Chars

Reading and writing of the primitive type char is facilitated with the following methods:

- readChar(), which reads the next char in the stream and returns it
- writeChar(int v), which writes v to the underlying stream
- writeChars(String s), which writes the String s to the underlying stream

Reading and Writing Booleans

The Boolean primitive type can have a value of either true or false, allowing applications to perform logical computations. Reading and writing of Booleans using the DataOutputStream and DataInputStream classes is handled by the following methods:

- readBoolean(), which reads a Boolean from the stream and uses that value as its return value
- writeBoolean(Boolean v), which writes v to the stream

Reading and Writing the short, int, and long Primitive Types

The reading and writing of signed 2-byte short integers (short data type) is facilitated by the following methods:

- readShort(), which reads in the next short and returns it as the method return value
- writeShort(short s), which writes s to the underlying stream

The reading and writing of signed 32-bit integers (int data type) is facilitated by the following methods:

- readInt(), which reads the next int in the stream and returns this int as the method's return value
- writeInt(int n), which writes n to the underlying stream

The reading and writing of signed 64-bit long integers (long data type) is facilitated by the following methods:

- readLong(), which reads the next long in the stream and returns this int as the method's return value
- writeLong(long n), which writes n to the underlying stream

Reading and Writing Floats and Doubles

The reading and writing of the float data type is handled by the following methods:

- readFloat() which reads the next float in the stream and returns that float as the method return value
- writeFloat(float f) which writes f to the underlying stream.

The reading and writing of double precision floating point numbers handled by the following methods:

- readDouble() which reads the next double in the stream and returns that double as the method return value
- writeDouble(double d) which writes d to the underlying stream

Reading and Writing Data in Unicode Transmission Format

The Unicode Transmission Format (UTF) is a standard for encoding 16-bit Unicode characters in 8-bit bytes. Even though the Unicode characters are represented with 16-bits inside the Virtual Machine, many Operating Systems do not allow for 16-bits storage. For this reason, the UTF is often used to make Unicode data more portable.

Reading and writing of data using the UTF is managed with the following methods:

- readUTF(DataInput r) which reads data from r, and returns it as a String object.
- writeUTF(String w) which writes w to the underlying stream in UTF.

Putting I/O Classes to Work

Having covered the DataInputStream and DataOutputStream, it is time to use the material in an actual application. Actually, if you remember the text editor application developed in listings 9.13 and 9.14, you will remember that although not discussed, these classes were used in conjunction with FileInputStream and FileOutputStream.

Listing 9.19 contains a small application that opens a file, writes an int to it, reads that int back in, adds one to the int, and prints the result. In this application the readInt() and writeInt() methods are used to access the ints.

Listing 9.19   An Application that Demonstrates Filter Streams

```java
import java.io.*;

public class filterDemo {

    public static void main(String args[]) throws IOException {
        try{
            FileInputStream      fin        = new
            ↦FileInputStream("data.txt");
            FileOutputStream     fout       = new
            ↦FileOutputStream("data.txt");

            DataInputStream      din        = new
            ↦DataInputStream(fin);
            DataOutputStream     dout       = new
            ↦DataOutputStream(fout);

            int                  myInt      = 41;
            int                  tempInt    = 0;

            dout.writeInt(myInt);
            tempInt = din.readInt();
            tempInt++;

            System.out.println("The meaning of life is: "+
            ↦tempInt);
        }
        catch(FileNotFoundException fnf)
        ↦{ System.out.println("err:"+ fnf); }
    }
}
```

Using Buffered Streams

Two additional filter streams are BufferedInputStream and BufferedOutputStream which
work to help improve I/O efficiency. Often used with File streams, these streams were
designed as a work-around for slow read and write methods. They function by filling a
"buffer" with your data and by only reading or writing when that buffer is full. Your data
reaches its destination eventually, but only in big chunks rather than of byte by byte. This
is done because it is, for example, much faster to read and write 512 bytes at once than it
is 1 byte 512 times.

As with all stream discussions, first you will have a moment to look over the API listing for BufferedInputStream and BufferedOutputStream, then the manner in which the class used is discussed. Listing 9.20 contains the Java API listing for BufferedOutputStream.

Listing 9.20 The Java API Listing for java.io.BufferedOutputStream

```
public class java.io.BufferedOutputStream extends
➥java.io.FilterOutputStream {
    //Fields
    protected byte buf[];
    protected int count;

    //Constructors
    public BufferedOutputStream(OutputStream out);
    public BufferedOutputStream(OutputStream out, int size);

    //Methods
    public void flush();
    public void write(byte b[], int off, int len);
    public void write(int b);
}
```

Listing 9.21 contains the API listing for the class BufferedInputStream. This class allows for data to be read in as one large "chunk" instead of byte by byte.

Listing 9.21 The Java API Listing for java.io. BufferedInputStream

```
public class java.io.BufferedInputStream extends
➥java.io.FilterInputStream{
    //Fields
    protected byte buf[];
    protected int count;
    protected int marklimit;
    protected int markpos;
    protected int pos;

    //Constructors
    public BufferedInputStream(InputStream in);
    public BufferedInputStream(InputStream in, int size);

    //Methods
    public int available();
    public boolean markSupported();
```

continues

Using Buffered Streams

Listing 9.21   Continued

```
    public int read();
    public int read(byte b[], int off, int len);
    public void reset();
    public long skip(long n);
}
```

In learning about the BufferedInputStream and BufferedOutputStream classes, you will have little difficulty getting to know these classes well because of the level of parallelism employed between these classes and other classes, as is discussed in the chapter.

Working with BufferedInputStream and BufferedOutputStream

BufferedInputStream and BufferedOutputStream are nice because they're so easy to learn. Although data is read in slightly differently when compared to other streams covered in this chapter, the method signatures are quite familiar, which means that just like InputStream and OutputStream themselves, data is manipulated using the standard read() and write() methods. The only difference between the API for BufferedInputStream/BufferedOutputStream and InputStream/OutputStream exists in their constructors. Being the smart reader you are, you have just guessed that it is in the constructors for BufferedInputStream and BufferedOutputStream that the size of the internal data buffer is set.

The following constructors are used by BufferedInputStream and BufferedOutputStream.

- BufferedInputStream(InputStream in), BufferedOutputStream(OutputStream out)
- BufferedInputStream(InputStream in, int size),
  BufferedOutputStream(OutputStream out, int size)

Using the constructor for either class, which takes only one parameter, will allocate a buffer to hold 512 bytes. However you desire to change the buffer size, simply use the second constructor which accepts as an additional parameter, an int, and uses the value of this int to allocate the buffer size.

To demonstrate the difference between file access with a BufferedOutputStream, you will develop an application which benchmarks writing to a file with simply a FileOutputStream, and then with a BufferedOutputStream working with a FileOutput-

Stream. This application, contained in listing 9.22, performs the following steps:

1. Fills a byte array with 10,000 bytes.

2. Records the time necessary to write those 10,000 bytes to a file using only a FileOutputStream. This time is then printed to the screen.

3. Records the time necessary to write those same 10,000 bytes to a file using a BufferedOutputStream (with buffer size 5,000) on top of a FileOutputStream. This time is then printed to the screen.

4. Records the time necessary to write those same 10,000 bytes to a file using a BufferedOutputStream (with buffer size 10,000) on top of a FileOutputStream. This time is then printed to the screen.

Listing 9.22 The Buffered Stream Benchmark Test

```
import java.io.*;

public class BufferTest {

    public static void main(String args[]) throws IOException {
        FileOutputStream        fout       = new
        ➥FileOutputStream("data.txt");
        BufferedOutputStream    bout1      = new
        ➥BufferedOutputStream(fout, 5000);
        BufferedOutputStream    bout2      = new
        ➥BufferedOutputStream(fout, 10000);
        byte[]                  myArray    = new byte[ 10000 ];
        long                    begin      = 0l;
        long                    end        = 0l;

        for(int i=0; i<10000; i++) {
            myArray[i] = (byte)i;
        }

        begin = System.currentTimeMillis();
        for(int i=0; i<10000; i++) {
            fout.write(myArray[i]);
        }
        end = System.currentTimeMillis();
        System.out.println("FileOutputStream: "+ (end-begin));

        begin = System.currentTimeMillis();
```

continues

Using Buffered Streams

Listing 9.22   Continued

```
        for(int i=0; i<10000; i++) {
                bout1.write(myArray[i]);
        }
        end = System.currentTimeMillis();
        System.out.println("BufferedOutputStream1: "+ (end-begin));

        begin = System.currentTimeMillis();
        for(int i=0; i<10000; i++) {
                bout2.write(myArray[i]);
        }
        end = System.currentTimeMillis();
        System.out.println("BufferedOutputStream2: "+ (end-begin));
    }
}
```

Obviously, timing results vary from machine to machine. When examining the output for this application, do not concentrate on actual times but rather on how the times compare to each other.

Listing 9.23 contains the output generated by the application in listing 9.22. What is impressive to note about this output is that when using a BufferedOutputStream with a buffer of size 5,000, output is almost 60 times faster than the FileOutputStream by itself. When a BufferedOutputStream of size 10,000 is used, this speed gap jumps to almost 73 times faster than the standard FileOutputStream. Although it may not seem too important to worry about a few thousand milliseconds, it is important to note that in the above data set, the data used is very small. Just image the time your applications would save if they used BufferedOutputStreams to save 50 MB files!

Listing 9.23   Output for the Benchmark Test

```
    FileOutputStream: 10883
    BufferedOutputStream1: 183
    BufferedOutputStream2: 150
```

Using the PrintStream Class

If you have ever written an application that uses the line System.out.println(), you have already used the class PrintStream. The PrintStream class is compromised—for the most part—of a series of overloaded print() and println() methods, each of which accepts a parameter and prints out the parameter accepted.

Listing 9.24   The Java API Listing for java.io.PrintStream

```
public class java.io.PrintStream extends java.io.FilterOutputStream {
    //Constructors
    public PrintStream(OuputStream out);
    public PrintStream(OutputStream out, boolean autoFlush);

    //Methods
    public boolean checkError();
    public void close();
    public void flush();
    public void print(boolean b);
    public void print(char c);
    public void print(char s[]);
    public void print(double d);
    public void print(float f);
    public void print(int i);
    public void print(long l);
    public void print(Object obj);
    public void print(String s);
    public void println();
    public void println(boolean b);
    public void println(char c);
    public void println(char s[]);
    public void println(double d);
    public void println(float f);
    public void println(int i);
    public void println(long l);
    public void println(Object obj);
    public void println(String s);
    public void write(byte b[], int off, int len);
    public void write(int b);
}
```

Following the pattern set forth by the previous sections in this book, you probably expect to see detailed notes on each method. This is unneccessary because a method in this class can take only one of two actions:

- Any method with the write() signature will write its parameter to the underlying stream.

- Any method with the writeln() signature will write its parameter plus a newline to the underlying stream.

Finally, it is important to discuss the two constructors supported by the PrintStream class:

- PrintStream(OutputStream out) will simply print data to the stream out.
- PrintStream(OutputStream out, Boolean autoflush) will print data to the stream out. Additionally if autoflush is true all buffered bytes will be forced to out every time a newline is encountered. If autoflush is false, then buffered bytes will not be forced to out.

The PrintStream class has no InputStream counterpart.

Using the LineNumberInputStream Class

When dealing with large quantities of data, you will often want to manage that data one line at a time. For example, often when importing data into a database, newline characters act as row deliminators. If you were writing code to take data from a stream and import it into a database, you would want to read it in one line at a time. The LineNumber-InputStream class sits on top of any InputStream, enabling you to read-in data from that InputStream while keeping track of lines.

The methods defined by LineNumberInputStream pretty much speak for themselves. Look at listing 9.25.

Listing 9.25   The Java API Listing for java.io.LineNumberInputStream

```
public class java.io.LineNumberInputStream extends
➥java.io.FilterInputStream {
    //Constructors
    public LineNumberInputStream(InputStream in);

    //Methods
    public int available();
    public int getLineNumber();
    public void mark(int readLimit);
    public int read();
    public int read(byte b[], int off, int len);
    public void reset();
    public void setLineNumber(int lineNumber);
    public long skip(long n);
}
```

LineNumberInputStream Overview

The methods in LineNumberInputStream bring many enhancements to a standard InputStream. These methods include standard read() methods which read in data one byte at a time, and also the following helpful methods:

- getLineNumber() which returns an int representing the current line number
- setLineNumber(int destination) which sets the current line number in the file to destination
- skip(long n) which skips over *n* bytes of data in the stream

You will use these methods when the part of a stream which contains the desired data set is nonlinear. Meaning that you need only bits and pieces of a stream, and those bits and pieces are not located next to each other.

As an example of the capabilities of the LineNumberInputStream class, take a look at listing 9.26, which shows a sample application jump around a file using the methods discussed previously.

Listing 9.26 A Demonstration of LineNumberInputStream

```
import java.io.*;

public class LineNumberTest {

    public static void main(String args[]) throws IOException {
        try{        FileInputStream            fin = new
        ➥FileInputStream("data.txt");
                    LineNumberInputStream      lin = new
                    ➥LineNumberInputStream(fin);

                    //print the current line
                    System.out.println("Current Line: " +
                    ➥lin.getLineNumber());

                    //move ahead five lines
                    lin.setLineNumber(5);

                    //print the current line
```

continues

Listing 9.26   Continued

```
                           System.out.println("Current Line: " +
                         ➥lin.getLineNumber());
              }
           catch(FileNotFoundException fnfe) { System.out.println("err:"
    ➥+fnfe); }

       }
}
```

Listing 9.27 contains the output generated by the application in listing 9.26.

Listing 9.27   The LineNumberTest Application Output

```
Current Line: 0
Current Line: 5
```

Using the PushBackInputStream Class

The last filter class to get coverage is the PushBackInputStream class. This class enables you to "peek" at a byte before you actually read it. This feature is helpful if (for example) the desired set of data is marked by a particular identifying byte which precedes the data set. Listing 9.28 shows the methods supported by this class.

Listing 9.28   Java API's java.io.PushBackInputStream

```
public class java.io.PushBackInputStream extends
java.io.FilterInputStream
  {
     //Fields
     protected int pushBack;

     //Constructors
     public PushBackInputStream();
```

```
//Methods
public int available();
public boolean markSupported();
public int read();
public int read(byte b[], int off, int len);
public void unread(int n);
}
```

Although all methods in the class PushBackInputStream are useful, the method which makes this class stand out is unread(). unread() provides PushBackInputStream with the ability to return a byte after deciding that the byte is not needed. For example, the following code fragment will leave back the PushBackInputStream object, with the same data it started with:

```
byte myByte = (byte)back.read();
back.unread(myByte);
```

Using the SequenceInputStream Class

Just as there are children of FilterInputStream that have no output counterparts, there are children of InputStream that have no output counterparts, including SequenceInputStream and StringBufferInputStream. As is the case with other streams not part of an I/O pair, as the discussion below shows, the nature of the stream does not call for it to be part of an I/O pair. This section discussed SequenceInputStream, and the following section discusses StringBufferInputStream.

SequenceInputStream enables you to "chain" together a series of InputStreams, thus taking a disjoined set of input sources and combining them into one. Look at the Java API listing for SequenceInputStream in listing 9.29. Notice that the two constructors accept a series of InputStreams as parameters.

Listing 9.29   Java API's java.io.SequenceInputStream

```
public class java.io.SequenceInputStream extends java.io.InputStream {
    //Constructors
    public SequenceInputStream(Enumeration e);
    public SequenceInputStream(InputStream is1, InputStream is2);
```

continues

Listing 9.29   Continued

```
//Methods
public void close();
public void read();
public void read(byte b[], int pos, int len);
}
```

As stated above, it is the constructors that make this class so useful. As shown below, the constructors allow InputStream to be chained together.

- SequenceInputStream(Enumeration e) accepts an Enumeration object, and chains together all InputStreams contained within that object. The Enumeration class—contained in the java.util package—enables you to group together an infinite number of objects.

- SequenceInputStream(InputStream is1, InputStream is2) chains together is1 and is2.

Regardless of the constructor you choose, the streams are still dealt with in a similar manner. Each stream is taken in the order of input and concatenated onto the preceding stream. When you finish reading from one stream, the read() method automatically begins reading from the next stream, all seamless to the user. Look at the code in listing 9.30, where two FileInputStreams have been concatenated. The read() method in SequenceInputStream begins reading file1 and continues reading until it reaches the end of file2.

Listing 9.30   The Concatenation of Two FileInputStreams Using One SequenceInputStream

```
FileInputStream file1 = new FileInputStream("file1.txt");
FileInputStream file2 = new FileInputStream("file2.txt");
SequenceInputStream allFiles = new SequenceInputStream(file1, file2);
```

It is obvious that the SequenceInputStream class can make the creation of your application easier. Instead of managing multiple input streams and constantly checking for an end of stream, you can leave it up to the streams to manage themselves. Although listing 9.30 uses two FileInputStreams to create the SequenceInputStream, you can use any combination of streams that subclass InputStream when creating a SequenceInputStream.

Using the StringBufferInputStream Class

The StringBufferInputStream class is the only class that subclasses InputStream, which has yet to be discussed in this chapter. This class is quite similar to ByteArrayInput-Stream, but uses a String object to create the stream instead of a byte array. In fact, that level of similarity can be taken further to correctly state that the underlying stream produced by both classes is identical. Your usage of one over the other will depend on the need shown by your application. If you need to work with a byte array, use ByteArray-InputStream, however, if you need to work with a String object use StringBufferInput-Stream. The Java API listing for StringBufferInputStream is contained in listing 9.31.

Listing 9.31   Java API's java.io.StringBufferInputStream

```
public class java.io.StringBufferInputStream extends java.io.InputStream
{
    //Fields
    protected String buffer;
    protected int count;
    protected int pos;

    //Constructors
    public StringBufferInputStream(String s);

    //Methods
    public int available();
    public int read();
    public int read(byte b[], int off, int len);
    public void reset();
    public void skip(long n);
}
```

As with ByteArrayInputStream, this class's biggest feature is accessed through its constructor. The constructor—StringBufferInputStream(String s)—is passed a String object, and that String object becomes the data source for the stream.

The RandomAccessFile Class

From this chapter, you should be familiar with the following two statements:

1. All stream classes extend either java.io.InputStream or java.io.OutputStream.

2. There is an exception to every rule.

The RandomAccessFile class is the exception to rule 1. This class directly subclasses java.lang.Object. It is contained in the java.io package and implements both the DataOutput and DataInput interfaces. This class allows read and write access to a file. What also should be noted is that the access need not be sequential. You can easily adjust your position within the file. Note in listing 9.32 the number of methods supported by this class. These methods enable RandomAccessFile to be very versatile; not only can it act as an InputStream, but it can also act as an OutputStream.

Listing 9.32   Java API's java.io.RandomAccessFile

```
public class java.io.RandomAccessFile extends java.lang.Object implements
 java.io.DataOutput,
 java.io.DataInput {
    //Constructors
    public RandomAccessFile(File file, String mode);
    public RandomAccessFile(String name, String mode);

    //Methods
    public void close();
    public final FileDescriptor getFD();
    public long getFilePointer();
    public long length();
    public final int read(byte b[]);
    public final int read(byte b[], int off, int len);
    public final boolean readBoolean();
    public final byte readByte();
    public final char readChar();
    public final double readDouble();
    public final float readFloat();
    public final void readFully(byte b[]);
    public final void readFully(byte b[], int off, int len);
    public final int readInt();
    public final String readLine();
    public final long readLong();
    public final short readShort();
```

```
        public final int readUnsignedByte();
        public final int readUnsignedShort();
        public final String readUTF();
        public void seek(long pos);
        public int skipBytes(int n);
        public void write(int b);
        public final void writeBoolean(boolean b);
        public final void writeByte(int v);
        public final void writeBytes(String s);
        public final void writeChar(int v);
        public final void writeChars(String s);
        public final void writeDouble(double v);
        public final void writeFloat(float f);
        public final void writeInt(int v);
        public final void writeLong(long l 0);
        public final void writeShort(int v);
        public final void writeUTF(String s);
}
```

Looking Inside RandomAccessFile

The sheer number of methods supported by this class can make it rather intimidating. On the other hand, having so many methods at your disposal can be exciting. Most of the methods contained in RandomAccessFile should be familiar to you from the DataOutput-Stream and DataInputStream classes. What does need to be studied is the manner in which one stream can provide read and write access, and the manner in which you can change your position in a string.

Those of you who are familiar with C will probably relate RandomAccessFile to the manner in which C deals with I/O.

When you create a new RandomAccessFile object you pass it to either a File object or a String object representing a system-dependent file path, and a String object representing the mode with which the file is to be opened. If this mode String object has a value of "r," the stream will have read only permission to the file. However, if the mode String object has a value of "rw," the stream will have read/write access to the stream.

The name RandomAccessFile stems from the fact that you can randomly jump around the file when reading or writing. The getFilePointer() method returns the current position in bytes of the file pointer from the beginning of the file. This position can be altered using the seek() method; seek() is passed a long integer that represents the position at which the next read should start. This position begins at the start, where the first byte is zero indexed.

Summary

This chapter covered a lot of ground. It is not assumed that you know all the methods in the java.io class, but you should leave this chapter with an understanding of all classes in this package. If you are a little shaky, reread specific parts of the chapter to better understand the information provided. After you feel that you understand all the methods, take some time to experiment with the different stream classes. Any large application that you may develop will rely heavily on I/O, and you will benefit greatly from an understanding of the classes covered in this chapter.

Chapter 10

Introducing Networking

One of the most exciting aspects of Java is programming for a network. Experienced network programmers are familiar with the headaches caused by trying to convince different hardware and operating systems to communicate in anything but the most primitive ways. The java.net package includes classes that enable the programmer to easily pass data across networks. When this factor is combined with Java's platform independence, network programming becomes as simple as coding for the stand-alone computer.

In this chapter and the next, you will learn how to use Java to pass information between programs running on separate machines. Java will do much of the work for you; however, you first must become familiar with several concepts. Because many programmers with years of experience are just now becoming familiar with the technical details of the Internet, the first section of this chapter introduces the necessary concepts to learn network programming. The topics covered in this chapter follow:

- Network concepts
- java.net: an introduction
- Applets versus applications
- Implementing your first server
- Implementing your first clients
- Implementing your first applet
- Multithreaded chat applets

Programming for Networks

The java.net package was designed to transfer data across TCP/IP networks. Although there is no reason the classes cannot be extended to deal with other protocols, the examples provided throughout this chapter deal with TCP/IP.

When your computer sends data to another machine, it must deal with a handful of variables. What type of machine will receive the data? What types of wires will actually carry the data? With the immense size and complexity of the Internet, rarely does one know the answer. Even if one did, it would be poor style for the programmer to assume a certain set of conditions would always hold true. However, one is not expected to write programs that detect different types of networks and behave differently. Instead, the network is divided into layers. Each layer handles a piece of the task. The result is that the big picture can easily be divided into distinct tasks and jobs.

Layers

When you execute a simple network program, such as a telnet session, the data you transfer passes through seven distinct network layers. The uppermost layer is represented by the application you are running, and the lowermost layer is represented by the actual network connection (wire) plugged into your machine. When you send information, another header is appended to the data each time the data is passed to a lower level. When the information is returned, each layer strips off one header. The seven layers, in descending order, are shown and described in table 10.1:

	Number	Name	Description
TABLE 10.1	7	Application	Provides an interface to end-user processes
Network Layers	6	Presentation	Specifies architecture-independent formats, encodes/decodes data, encrypts/decrypts data
	5	Session	Handles sockets
	4	Transport	Manages user connections, ensures reliability
	3	Network	Addresses and routes packets
	2	Logical Link	Frames packets, defines physical data flow
	1	Physical	Defines electrical and mechanical properties

Of these seven layers, application, transport, network, and physical can be considered the "primary" layers, while you are learning networking. To make things even simpler, the code you will write deals with either the application or the transport layer. The following mini-table associates these layers with concrete examples:

HTTP, TCP, IP (Application, Transport, and Network) can all be referred to as protocols. The physical layer refers to topologies. It would not be too "wrong" to simplify this and refer to all examples as protocols.

Layer	Example(s)
Application	HTTP, FTP, SMTP, Telnet
Transport	TCP, UDP
Network	IP
Physical	Ethernet, Fiber Optic, Token Ring

The classes of java.net deal with either the application layer or the transport layer. An example of the application layer is an URL; an example of the transport layer is a socket. If you feel competent with the information presented so far, great. If not, you will understand it better as you see how java.net implements the concepts.

URLs

A Uniform Resource Locator (URL) is the fully qualified address of an object on the Internet. It specifies the protocol, host, port, and file to be accessed. A generic URL format follows:

```
[protocol]://[full.host.address]:{Port}/[file/path]
```

The port is optional and does not need to be specified if you are accessing the default port for the protocol. Here are two examples:

```
http://www.xyz.org:8080/letters/g.html
```

```
ftp://ftp.xyz.org/letters/english/h.txt
```

Ports, Protocols, and Connections

A *port* is not a physical opening in your computer or some network control box. Rather, it is a number that allows a system to maintain multiple network connections simultaneously. A protocol is another way of saying a rule. *Protocols* are the standards that govern the Internet. Finally, a *connection* is just what you would imagine it to be. You will see how it applies to network programming.

A single machine accepts data from a variety of network connections simultaneously through the use of ports. Many common services have a dedicated port. Because some ports are reserved for common services ("common" is a misnomer—many common services are rare proprietary standards that are seldom used these days), the programmer cannot use any port (see table 10.2). Ports numbered under 1024 are often referred to as *reserved ports*, many of which are reserved for a specific program. None of these ports are available to standard users on Unix computer systems. If your program is designed for all types of users, not just administrators, it is important that you only attempt to use ports over number 1024.

	Port Number	Service
TABLE 10.2		
Well-Known Services and Their Reserved Ports	21	FTP
	23	Telnet
	25	SMTP (mail)
	80	HTTP (web)
	119	NNTP (news)

Although you will find the services mentioned in the table running on their default port on most machines, the services may also be running on a second port. A simple way to have two web servers on one machine is for the second to run on a non-standard port. The URL http://my-.machine.name:8080 specifies that a web server is running on port 8080.

The Internet and all networks are governed by a series of protocols. Each protocol is a group of rules that specify how applications that conform to the protocol behave. TCP, IP, UDP, HTTP, SMTP, and most of the acronyms that are associated for the Internet are protocols. Protocols define every detail of how a message is sent from the header format to the "end" command. Luckily, with Java, the developer does not need to understand all the intimate details of each protocol, only their general properties and behavior.

Network programming has two general types: connection and connectionless. *Connection*-oriented programming is exactly what the term implies—the client and server have a communication link that is open and active from the time the application is executed until it is closed. Using Internet jargon, the Transmission Control Protocol (TCP) is a connection-oriented protocol. It is a reliable connection—packets are guaranteed to arrive in the order they are sent. A familiar example of a connection-oriented network is the phone system.

In *connectionless* programming, each instance that packets are sent, they are transmitted individually. No link to the receiver is maintained after the packets arrive. The Internet equivalent is the User Datagram Protocol (UDP). Connectionless communication is not reliable—not all packets may arrive at the destination, and they might arrive out of order. A familiar example here is the United States Postal Service.

If you are curious about the details of the protocols discussed, you can read the Requests For Comments (RFCs) for each protocol. Internet protocols are governed by RFCs. If you want, you can find a complete listing of RFCs at the following URL:

```
http://ds.internic.net/ds/rfc-index.html.
```

The RFCs shown in table 10.3 govern the most popular and common protocols.

	RFC	Protocol
TABLE 10.3		
Protocols and	768	UDP
Their RFCs	791	IP
	793	TCP
	821	SMTP
	822	Text Message Protocol
	854	Telnet
	1034	DNS
	1157	SNMP
	1171	PPP
	1350	TFTP
	1602	The Internet Standards Process

Client-Server Programming

The most common model of network programming is referred to as *client-server* programming. The concept is simple: A client machine makes a request for information or sends a command to a server; in return, the server passes back the data or results of the command. Most often, the server only responds to clients; it does not initiate communication.

A good client-server architecture distributes the processor load between both machines. Routines that access data on the server should be executed on the server, whereas the client should be able to parse the returned data and interpret user commands instead of simply passing them to the server.

Networking Terminology Wrap-Up

It is important that you are familiar with the terminology discussed so far. If it is still a little fuzzy, don't worry. The terminology becomes clearer as you read the chapter. To paraphrase Sun's slogan, the network is the computer; programming for it is no different than programming for a single machine.

The best advice to remember throughout the chapter is that the java.net package does the work for you. Although it is good to be familiar with the details of the network, you do not have to deal with them. If you don't think what you have laid out will work, try it before redesigning your code or giving up.

With Java, the network can be as simple or complex as you need. If you want to pass a command and response between two machines over TCP/IP, it takes only a few lines of code; however, you can also extend java.net to transfer objects across any network protocol.

The java.net Package

Unlike most other popular languages, everything you need to begin is included in the Java Development Kit. The java.net package provides the tools necessary to transmit and receive information reliably and easily over the Internet or intranets. You can think of java.net as consisting of four distinct "subpackages":

This chapter focuses on the first three divisions. The last category consists of classes that are the foundations for the other classes. They provide java.net with a great deal of flexibility for the advanced network programmer. Normal applications never need to use or implement these interfaces.

- **URLs.** An address on the internet
- **Sockets.** A connection to another machine
- **Datagrams.** A packet to be sent across the network
- **Low-level.** The average programmer does not deal with these

URLs

The simplest interface to networking is provided by java.net.URL. It is used to access the entire contents of a given URL. Three URL classes are covered in this section:

- java.net.URL
- java.net.URLConnection
- java.net.URLEncoder

Uniform Resource Locator

An URL is an object that is used to refer to or access an object on the Internet. (The ➡ symbol indicates a line that would normally fit on the previous line.)

Listing 10.1   The Java API Listing for java.net.URL

```
public final class java.net.URL extends Object{
//Constructors
public URL(String protocol, String host, int port,
➡String File) throws MalformedURLException;
public URL(String protocol, String host, String File)
 throws MalformedURLException;
public URL(String spec) throws MalformedURLException;
public URL(URL context, String spec)
 throws MalformedURLException;
//Methods
public boolean equals(Object obj);
public final Object getContent() throws IOException;
public String getFile();
public String getHost();
public int getPort();
public String getProtocol();
public String getRef();
public int hashCode();
public URLConnection openConnection() throws IOException;
public final InputStream openStream() throws IOException;
public boolean sameFile(URL other);
public String toExternalForm();
public String toString();
protected void set(String protocol, String host, int port,
➡String file, String ref);
}
```

An URL can be constructed with a single string or with individual specifications for the protocol, host, port, and file. URLs can also be specified relative to another URL. The getFile(), getHost(), getPort(), getProtocol(), and getRef() methods all return a portion of the URL specified by the URL object.

The data specified by the URL object can be accessed in three ways:

- The getContent() method returns the contents.
- The openConnection() method returns the information through an URLConnection.
- The openStream() method returns the information through an InputStream.

Listing 10.2 shows the simplest possible use of the URL class. It defines a class that is passed an address, and returns the contents of the object at that address. It is important to note that the Java Development Kit only provides content handlers for a few data types: text, HTML, and simple image types. Although you can write your own content handlers, you can, in most cases, simply write code to parse the data that is returned.

Listing 10.2   returnText.java

```
package industrial;

import java.net.*;
import java.io.*;

//  This class is designed only to return data
//  encoded as text/plain. Because it is designed as a
//  simple example, exceptions are not caught.

public class returnText
{
    //  call returnText and display results on STDOUT
    public static void main(String[] args)
    throws MalformedURLException, IOException
    {
        System.out.println(returnText(args[0]);
    }

//  gets the contents of an URL and returns it
    public static String returnText(String address)
    throws MalformedURLException, IOException
    {
        URL returnURL = new URL(address);
        return (String) returnURL.getContent();
    }
}
```

The following example shows the output of listing 10.2. The URL in the example is a text/plain file that contains the string "test text."

Listing 10.3   returnText Sample Run

```
%java returnText http://studsys.mscs.mu.edu/~brumbaug/text
test text
%
```

URLConnection

The URL class is limited in what information can be downloaded. You have access to much more information by using java.net.URLConnection. Data such as size, content type, and when the file was last modified are accessible. The details of the class are listed below.

Listing 10.4   java.net.URLConnection

```
public abstract class java.net.URLConnection extends Object{
//Constructors
protected URLConnection(URL url);
//Variables
protected boolean allowUserInteraction;
protected boolean connected;
protected boolean doInput;
protected boolean doOutput;
protected long ifModifiedSince;
protected URL url;
protected boolean useCaches;
//Methods
public static boolean getDefaultAllowUSerInteraction();
public static String getDefaultRequestProperty(String key);
protected static String guessContentTypeFromName(String fname);
protected static String guessContentTypeFromStream
  (InputStream is) throws IOException;
public static synchronized void setContentHandlerFactory
  (ContentHandlerFactory fac) throws Error;
public static void setDefaultAllowUserInteraction
  (boolean defaultallowuserinteraction);
public static void setDefaultRequestProperty
  (String key, String value);
public abstract void connect() throws IOException;
public boolean getAllowUserInteraction();
public Object getContent()
  throws IOException, UnknownServiceException;
public String getContentEncoding();
public int getContentLength();
public long getData();
public boolean getDefaultUseCaches();
public boolean getDoInput();
public boolean getDoOutput();
public long getExpiration();
public String getHeaderField(String name);
public String getHeaderField(int n);
```

continues

Introducing Networking

Listing 10.4   Continued

```
public long getHeaderFieldDate(String name, long Default);
public int getHeaderFieldInt(String name, int Default);
public String getHeaderFieldKey(int n);
public long getIfModifiedSince();
public InputStream getInputStream()
  throws IOException, UnknownServiceException;
public long getLastModified();
public OutputStream getOutputStream
  throws IOException, UnknownServiceException;
public String getRequestProperty(String key);
public URL getURL();
public boolean getUseCaches();
public void setAllowUserInteraction(boolean allowuserinteraction);
public void setDefaultUseCaches(boolean defaultusecaches);
public void setDoInput(boolean doinput);
public void setDoOutput(boolean doouput);
public void setIfModifiedSince(long ifmodifiedsince);
public void setRequestProperty(String key, String value);
public void setUseCaches(boolean usecaches);
public String toString();
}
```

URLConnection provides an assortment of methods. Some of them are rarely used; however, you will want to be familiar with several key methods.

The connect() method performs the actual network connection; it is called by methods that depend on being connected.

The getContent() method is similar to the method of the same name in URL, but it returns an Object instead of an URL.

The getContentLength(), getContentType(), getContentEncoding(), getDate(), getLastModified(), and getExpiration() methods return information about the object specified by the URL, if it can be determined. If you are using HTTP, you can access more data by using the getHeaderField(), getHeaderFieldInt(), and getHeaderFieldDate() methods.

Finally, you can use different methods to specify how the instance behaves. You can find the current status by using the get methods and change the current status with the set methods; getDoInput() and getDoOutput() determine whether the connection is read/write or read-only; getUseCaches() specifies whether the URL can be loaded from memory, if available, or whether the Object should be reread from the disk; getIfModifiedSince() can be used to prevent an URL from being accessed if it has not been recently changed; and getAllowUserInteraction() is used to determine whether the data transfer depends on user-interaction. An example of such a transfer is typing a password.

Table 10.5 shows the default values of the most commonly used URLConnection variables.

TABLE 10.5	Property	Default Value
Default values of URLConnection properties	DoInput	True
	DoOutput	False
	UseCaches	True
	IfModifiedSince	True
	AllowUserInteraction	False

Listing 10.5 shows you how to access the wealth of information that getURLConnection() provides. The getsetData() method displays and modifies some of that information.

For simplicitiy's sake, exceptions are not caught in this example. In larger programs, especially any program written and tested by more than one person, handling exceptions is very important. Your attention here, however, should be focused on the networking aspects of this example. Exception handling is dealt with in Chapter 12, "Distributed Computing with Java."

Listing 10.5   getsetData.java

```
package industrial;

import java.net.*;
import java.io.*;

//   This class is designed to print out a variety of
//   information about a given URLConnection. It also
//   changes some of the properties.

public class getsetData
{

  public static void main(String[] args)
  throws MalformedURLException, IOException
  {
```

Introducing Networking

continues

The java.net Package   333

Listing 10.5   Continued

```
   //  first we need to create the URLConnection
   URL u = new URL(args[0]);
   URLConnection uc = u.openConnection();

   //  now we can access the information
   System.out.println(args[0]);
   System.out.println("Content Type: " + uc.getContentType());
   System.out.println("Was last modified: " + uc.getLastModified());
   System.out.println("Size: " + uc.getContentLength());
   System.out.println("Can we use cache? " + uc.getUseCaches());

   //  now alter UseCaches property
   uc.setUseCaches(true);

   //  now show change
   System.out.println("Now can we use cache? " + uc.getUseCaches());
  }
}
```

Listing 10.6 displays the output from executing this program. In the first example, the user does not have permsission to change the UseCaches property because it is a remote file. In the second, the property can be changed. However, because you are looking at a text file on your hard drive, much of the data is unknown.

Listing 10.6   getsetData sample run

```
%java getsetData http://studsys.mscs.mu.edu/~brumbaug
http://studsys.mscs.mu.edu/~brumbaug
Content Type: text/html
Was last modified:
Size:
Can we use cache? Yes
java.lang.IllegalAccessError:
    at java.net.URLConnection.setUseCaches(URLConnection.java 279)
    at getsetData.main(getsetData.java:26)
%

c:>java getsetData file://autoexec.bat
file://autoexec.bat
Content Type: text/plain
Was last modifed: 0
Size: -1
```

Ten: Introducing Networking

```
Can we use cache? Yes
Now can we use cache? No
c:>
```

URLEncoder

A final class deserves mention during a discussion about URLs—java.net.URLEncoder.
URLs are not transmitted as ASCII or Unicode strings. The spaces in an URL are converted to plus signs, and non-alphanumeric characters are transmitted with their hex codes.
URLs are thus enabled to use only characters from a portable subset of ASCII, so that
computers using a variety of character sets can use identical URLs. The API specification
for URLEncoder is shown in listing 10.7.

Listing 10.7   java.net.URLEncoder

```
public class URLEncoder extends Object {
  //no constructors
  //methods
  public static String encode(String s);
}
```

Listing 10.8 is a sample program that prints an URL before and after encoding. The goal
is to demonstrate how URL data is actually transmitted. It is easier to show with a sample
program than with description.

Listing 10.8   encode.java

```
package industrial;

import java.net.*;
import java.io.*;

//This class will print a URL before and after
//it is encoded by java.net.URLEncoder

public class encode
{
  public static void main(String[] args)
  {
    String s = new String(args[0]);
    // s = args[0]
```

continues

Listing 10.8   Continued

```
        System.out.println("before: " + s);
        s = URLEncoder.encode(s);
        System.out.println("after: " + s);
    }
}
```

As you can see in the sample run in listing 10.9, all non-alphanumeric characters were converted by the encode() method.

Listing 10.9   encode sample run

```
%java encode http://www.millikin.edu
before: http://www.millikin.edu
after: http:%3a%2f%2fwww%2emillikin%2eedu
%
```

URL and URLConnection enable the programmer to access information through a variety of standard Internet services; however, you usually need a server designed to fit a specific project's requirements. URL and URLConnection fall short in that aspect; they were designed to provide an easy interface to standard network services and are limited to standard services. To implement a server or access data you wrote on a server, you need to become familiar with sockets and datagrams.

Sockets

The classes java.net.Socket and java.net.ServerSocket are the heart of Java networking. They enable two or more processes to reliably communicate over the network. Although the Socket class can be used to transmit datagrams, it is usually used to implement a connection-oriented stream protocol. ServerSocket listens for clients requesting connections on a specified port, usually infinitely, but a time-out can be specified. After a connection is made, the server program creates a Socket so that it can pass information back to the client (see fig. 10.1).

Before discussing the constructors and methods of Socket and ServerSocket, the class InetAddress must be mentioned. An InetAddress represents the actual number, not the name or IP address of a computer. The name studsys.mscs.mu.edu is never used by your program; instead it uses the corresponding address, 134.48.4.25. The class itself is fairly simple, as listing 10.10 shows.

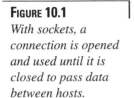

FIGURE 10.1

With sockets, a connection is opened and used until it is closed to pass data between hosts.

Listing 10.10   java.net.InetAddress

```
public final class InetAddress extends Object {
  //No Constructors
  //Methods
  public static syncrhonized InetAddress[] getAllByName
    (String host) throws UnknownHostException;
  public static syncrhonized InetAddress getByName
    (String host) throws UnknownHostException;
  public static InetAddress getLocalHost()
    throws UnknownHostException;
  public boolean equals(Object obj);
  public byte[] getAddress();
  public String getHostName();
  public int hashCode();
  public String toString();
```

InetAddress has no constructors. Instead, it provides three methods that return an InetAddress. The getHostName()method returns a String containing the host's name. An array of bytes representing an IP address is returned by getAddress(). Lastly, getAllByName() returns an array of InetAddresses containing all the available addresses for a host. (A single computer can be assigned multiple IP addresses.)

Listing 10.11   java.net.Socket

```
public final class Socket extends Object {
  //Constructors
  public Socket(String host, int port)
    throws UnknownHostException, IOException;
  public Socket(String host, int port, boolean stream)
    throws UnknownHostException, IOException;
```

Introducing Networking

continues

Listing 10.11   Continued

```
    public Socket(InetAddress address, int port)
      throws IOException;
    public Socket(InetAddress address, int port, boolean stream)
      throws IOException;
    //Methods
    public static synchronized void setSocketImplFactory
      (SocketImplFactory fac) throws IOException, SocketException;
    public synchronized void close() throws IOException;
    public InetAddress getInetAddress();
    public InputStream getInputStream();
    public int getLocalPort();
    public OutputStream getOutputStream() throws IOException;
    public int getPort();
    public String toString();
}
```

Socket provides the programmer with four constructors. The address of the server may be
specified as a String or an InetAddress. In each case, an optional Boolean parameter
implements a connectionless socket if set to false. After the socket is created,
getInetAddress and getPort provide information about the server, whereas getLocalPort
provides information about the machine on which the Socket was created. The methods
getInputStream and getOutputStream provide access to the InputStream and
OutputStream, which are used for the actual communication.

Listing 10.12   java.net.ServerSocket

```
public final class ServerSocket extends Object {
  //Constructors
  public ServerSocket(int port) throws IOException;
  public ServerSocket(int port, int count) throws IOException;
  //Methods
  public static synchronized void setSocketFactory
    (SocketImplyFactory fac) throws IOException, SocketException;
  public Socket accept() throws IOException;
  public void close() throws IOException;
  public InetAddress getInetAddress();
  public int getLocalPort();
  public String toString();
}
```

ServerSocket provides two constructors:

- The port number to listen on must be specified
- Count, an optional parameter, specifies how long the ServerSocket should listen

By default, the ServerSocket listens indefinitely or until it is closed. After a connection is made, getInetAddress() returns the client's address. The accept() method returns a Socket that is connected to the client.

Datagrams

Although Socket and ServerSocket are most often used to implement client/server programs, datagrams offer a faster alternative. *Datagrams* are used to implement a connectionless protocol, such as UDP. One machine sends packets, each with a destination address attached, and then forgets about it (see fig. 10.2). The packets are not guaranteed to arrive, and, if they all arrive, their order of arrival is not necessarily the order they were sent. Datagrams are not reliable, but the lack of reliability means less overhead, making the connection faster. A UDP packet contains a header of only 8 bytes, whereas a TCP header occupies 20 bytes.

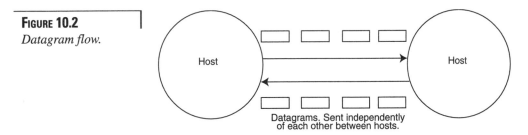

Datagrams. Sent independently of each other between hosts.

Datagrams may seem useless if they are not reliable. However, their speed is often needed. Many game servers, which are programs that communicate with several clients constantly sending small pieces of information, rely on datagrams. The program will not fail if a command to increment the scores does not reach the client. A real-world example of datagrams is Domain Name Service (DNS). Each time you type an Internet address, it must be converted to its numeric equivalent. This uses DNS, which relies on UDP or datagrams. Without the low overhead of datagrams, every single name lookup would take longer, and the Internet would have even more traffic on it.

Two classes are used to implement datagrams in Java:java.net.DatagramPacket and java.net.DatagramSocket. DatagramPacket is the actual packet of information, an array of bytes, that is transmitted over the network. DatagramSocket is a socket that sends and

Introducing Networking

receives DatagramPackets across the network. You can think of a DatagramPacket as a letter and a DatagramSocket as the mailbox that the mailcarrier uses to pick up and drop off your letters.

DatagramPacket

A DatagramPacket is an object that can be transferred through DatagramSockets (see table 10.13). It is much like an envelope; it holds data.

Listing 10.13   java.net.DatagramPacket

```
public final class DatagramPacket extends Object {
  //Constructors
  public DatagramPacket(byte[] ibuf, int ilength);
  public DatagramPacket(byte[] ibuf, int ilength,
    InetAddress iaddr, int iport);
  //Methods
  public InetAddress getAddress();
  public byte[] getData();
  public int getLength();
  public int getPort();
}
```

The DatagramPacket class provides the programmer with two constructors. The first is used for DatagramPackets that receive information. This constructor needs to be provided with an array to store the data and the amount of data to receive. The second is used to create DatagramPackets that send data. The constructor needs the same two pieces of information, plus the destination address and port. The methods are fairly self-explanatory. The data itself or variables of the DatagramPacket can be accessed using the get methods.

DatagramSocket

DatagramSockets are the mechanisms which will send and receive DatagramPackets (see table 10.14). They are the mailboxes in which you drop off and pick up the letters you are transferring.

Listing 10.14   java.net.DatagramSocket

```
public final class DatagramSocket extends Object {
  //Constructors
  public DatagramSocket() throws SocketException;
  public DatagramSocket(int port) throws SocketException;
  //Methods
  public synchronized void close();
  public int getLocalPort();
```

```
    public synchronized void receive(DatagramPacket p)
      throws IOException;
    public void send(DatagramPacket p) throws IOException;
    protected synchronized void finalize();
}
```

Again, two constructors are provided by the class DatagramSocket. The programmer can specify a port to use or allow the system to randomly assign one. The getLocalPort() method can be used to determine the port if you allow the system to choose. Because DatagramPackets contain a destination address, the DatagramSocket class does not need to know where it is sending the packets. Continuing the previous analogy, your mailbox does not need to be aware of where letters that are placed in it are supposed to be sent. The receive() method waits for DatagramPackets to arrive and stores them. After you are done using the socket, you should call the close() method to free the port. The finalize() method is used to force the system to perform garbage collection.

Implementing Datagrams

Datagrams are faster than streams-oriented network connections because there is no overhead from error correction. In order to ensure reliability, however, sockets must be used. Two examples of when datagrams might prove to be the best option are for small, one-time messages sent across the network or for a game where the client and server are frequently exchanging data. If a message fails to arrive, however, no serious consequences arise. Table 10.6 shows what each class can do and how it does it:

TABLE 10.6	Class	Direction	Protocol
Sending Information Across the Network	Socket	Sends data	TCP (connection-based)
	ServerSocket	Receives data	TCP (connection-based)
	DatagramSocket	Sends and receives data	UDP (connectionless)
	DatagramPacket	Sent and received by DatagramSocket	UDP (connectionless)

Low-Level java.net Classes

All of the major classes provided by java.net have now been introduced; however, several classes remain that are called by the Java VM to do the dirty work. Most applications never need to implement the interfaces provided by these classes. One of the major classes is java.net.SocketImpl. It is called by java.net.Socket and java.net.ServerSocket to implement the socket connection (see table 10.7). Although Java was designed with the Internet and the TCP/IP protocol suite in mind, it is not limited to those protocols.

Subclasses of SocketImpl can implement sockets as needed by different network environments. These classes could be utilized in code that was developed to run only behind a firewall or on a network that was not running TCP/IP.

	Class	Description
TABLE 10.7	URL	Uniform Resource Locator
java.net Classes	URLConnection	Downloads content from an URL object
	URLEncoder	Translates from text to x-www-form-urlencoded
	InetAddress	Host name and corresponding IP address
	Socket	TCP socket for transmitting data
	ServerSocket	TCP socket for listening for data
	DatagramPacket	Data to be sent via a DatagramSocket
	DatagramSocket	UDP socket for two-way communication

Many of these low-level classes contain Factory in their name. Classes such as java.net-.SocketImplFactory, java.net.URLStreamHandlerFactory, and java.net.ContentHandler-Factory are used to create the actual object referred to in their name. Again, normal applications do not need to use the interfaces provided by these classes.

Applets versus Applications

The java.net classes provide access to remote machines; when combined with the fact that web browsers often download and execute Java bytecode without the user being aware of what is being executed, or the fact that a foreign program is running on her machine, security issues arise. Applets are limited in what they can do because of these factors. Applets can only open network connections to the machine from which they were downloaded. Though all clients are not applets, applets are only used to create client programs; servers must be implemented as applications. Although web browsers provide an easy medium for enabling users to download an up-to-date client, clients can also be implemented as applications.

java.net Wrap Up

The java.net package provides the programmer with a variety of methods for sending and retrieving information across the network. The Java VM takes care of the extremely low-level network access, enabling you to focus on writing a good application without worrying about network inconveniences. Everything required to implement client and server applications is provided by the Java Development Kit. Client/Server programming across networks that run on the TCP/IP protocol suite is not much more complicated than developing applications that are designed to be executed on one machine. In the next section, you will learn how to implement basic clients and servers. The examples cover both TCP and UDP (sockets and datagrams).

"First-Time" java.net Programmer Examples

Client-Server applications today are nearly synonomous with networked applications. The client and server in almost all cases split the work load in some fashion. When writing client/server code, the first question asked is usually, "Where do I begin?" The first step is to define how your client and server will communicate. Yes, you need to write your own protocol for how your program will transmit data. After your protocol is defined, you are free to develop either side. If you are working in a team, the two can be developed simultaneously. As long as you follow the protocol you defined, the client and server can be developed independently of each other.

Developing the Server Side

You will first learn how to implement a basic server application. The server, when executed, waits for a connection on port 1976. After a client connects, the server prints the IP address of the client and shuts down. No communication flows back to the client. It does not get any more basic than this.

You begin the server like any other Java application. You need to import the java.net.* in order to use Socket and ServerSocket (see listing 10.15). The package java.io.* is not actually used. It is a good idea to get used to including java.io when you use java.net, however, because most real networking uses streams. The main() method simply creates an instance of firstServ, which does the actual work for the server.

Listing 10.15 socketServer.java

```
package industrial;

import java.net.*;
import java.io.*;
```

continues

Listing 10.15   Continued

```
public class socketServer
{
  public static void main(String args[])
  {
    // main creates an instance of firstServ
    firstServ fs = new firstServ(1976);
  }
}
```

The firstServ class contains only two variables, the ServerSocket itself and the Socket, that could be used to communicate with the client (return information). Refer to listing 10.16, which has only one possible constructor and no methods that are part of this class. When an instance of firstServ is constructed, it waits for a client, prints the IP address, and shuts down.

Listing 10.16   firstServ.java

```
class firstServ
{
  ServerSocket ss;
  Socket s;

  firstServ(int port)
  {
  try
  {
   // initialize the ServerSocket
    ss = new ServerSocket(port);
    System.out.println("Server started on port: " + port);
   // wait for a connection, this blocks the current thread
    s = ss.accept();
  }
  catch(Exception e)       //print error message
  {
    System.out.println("could not create sockets");
    System.out.println(e);
  }
    //print client's InetAddress
    System.out.println("connection from " + s.getInetAddress());
    System.out.println("shutting down the server");
    try
```

```
    {
    //shut down server, release port
    ss.close();
    }
    catch(Exception e)
    {
      System.out.println("could not close server socket");
      System.out.println(e);
    }
  }
}
```

The easiest way to test a server is to use a telnet program that enables you to specify the port to which you want to connect. If you are on a Unix machine, you can leave a space after the IP address and then type the port number. Most telnet programs designed for personal computers also enable you to specify the port. Listing 10.17 is an example of a connection; the left-hand column represents the server, whereas the right represents the client. The relative times of the events are displayed from top to bottom (that is, what is higher up occurs first).

Listing 10.17   firstServ Sample Run

```
%java socketServer
Server started on port: 1976
                                        %telnet 134.48.4.25 1976
                                        %

connection from 169.207.8.123
shutting down the server
%
```

Although this server is almost useless, you should now understand the basic steps taken to implement a server. Whatever processing the server has to do before it returns data is the same as any other code. You will learn about using streams to pass data back and forth and how to deal with multiple clients at the same time later in this chapter's chat example. The next example deals with a simple client/server program that is implemented using datagrams.

Listing 10.18 demonstrates a slightly more complex server that uses datagrams instead of sockets. It is an *echo server*. After a connection is made, it echoes back whatever is sent by the client instead of simply hanging up the connection. It is more complex because it has to listen to the client and then repeat what the client says.

Introducing Networking

The block of code in listing 10.18 is simple. The necessary variables are declared, and the DatagramSocket is initialized. Two final variables are also declared—the port on which the server is to run, and the maximum size of the message to be passed to the server and then back to the client.

Listing 10.18   echoServer.java First of Two2

```
package industrial;

import java.net.*;
import java.io.*;

public class echoServer
{
  static final int serverPort = 1976;
  static final int packetsize = 1024;

  public static void main (String[] args)
    throws SocketException
  {
    DatagramPacket packet;
    DatagramSocket socket;
    byte[] data;
    int clientPort;
    InetAddress address;
    String str;
     socket = new DatagramSocket(serverPort);
```

Listing 10.19 contains an infinite loop. The server runs forever, listening for an incoming packet on port 1976, echoing the packet back to the client, and then waiting again. This does not imply that the server can handle multiple packets coming in at the same time. After a packet is received, the server stops listening until the entire loop has been executed and the blocking DatagramSocket.receive() method is called again.

Listing 10.19   echoServer.java Second of Two

```
    for(;;)
    {
      data = new byte[packetsize];
      packet = new DatagramPacket(data, packetsize);
      try
      { // wait infinitely for a packet to arrive
        socket.receive(packet);
      }
```

```
catch(IOException e)
{
  System.out.println("DatagramSocket could not receive a
  ➥packet");
  System.out.println(e);
  System.exit(0);
}

//get data about client in order to echo data back
address = packet.getAddress();
clientPort = packet.getPort();

//print string that was received on server's console
str = new String(data, 0, 0, packet.getLength());
System.out.println("String: " + str);
System.out.println("From: " + address);

//echo data back to client
packet = new DatagramPacket(data, packetsize, address,
➥clientPort);
try
  {
  socket.send(packet);
}
catch(IOException e)
{
  System.out.println("DatagramSocket could not return the
  ➥packet");
  System.out.println(e);
  System.exit(0);
}
}
}
}
```

The server-side of this example is now complete. Unlike when writing a server that uses sockets, there is no simple tool, such as telnet, for testing a server that uses datagrams. Writing the client-side of this application, however, is as simple as the server-side implementation.

Developing the Client Side

The client-side networking code actually looks very similar to the server-side networking code. This is true with many applications that use datagrams because the java.net.DatagramSocket class is used to both send and receive DatagramPackets.

In the following code, listing 10.20, the needed variables are declared. As in the server code, the port number of the server and the maximum packet size are hard-coded. In addition, this piece of code checks to make sure that two command-line arguments are passed; if not, it exits the code and displays usage instructions.

Listing 10.20 echoClient.java First of Three

```java
package industrial;

import java.net.*;
import java.io.*;

public class echoClient
{
  static final int serverPort = 1976;     // the port number to connect
  static final int packetsize = 1024;     // at a common packet size

  public static void main(String args[])
    throws SocketException, UnknownHostException //not handling exceptions
  {
    DatagramSocket socket;          // how we send it
    DatagramPacket packet;          // what we send it in
    InetAddress address;            // where it is going
    String messageSend;             // what is sent
    String messageReturn;           // what we get back
    byte[] data;

    if (args.length != 2)           // make sure command line parameters
                                    // correct
    {
      System.out.println("usage: java echoClient <server name>
      ➥<message>");
      System.exit(0);
    }
```

Listing 10.21 deals with initializing the variables. The command line parameters are parsed, and the needed variables are set so that enough information is available to create a DatagramPacket. You might want to review the method java.lang.String.getBytes() if you are unfamiliar with it. It is used often when dealing with datagrams because they transfer data as arrays of bytes and not strings.

Listing 10.21   echoClient.java Second of Three

```
address = InetAddress.getByName(args[0]);
socket = new DatagramSocket();
data = new byte[packetsize];
messageSend = new String(args[1]);
messageSend.getBytes(0, messageSend.length(), data, 0);
//remember datagrams hold bytes
packet = new DatagramPacket(data, data.length, address, serverPort);
```

In the final section of code, shown in listing 10.22, the network connection occurs. The client sends the DatagramPacket to the server. The DatagramPacket is then reinitialized and used to receive the packet that is returned from the server. Finally, the data in the returned packet is displayed on the screen.

Listing 10.22   echoClient.java Third of Three

```
try
{
  socket.send(packet);
}
catch(IOException e)        // do catch exceptions here
                           // since error is possible due to
                           // non-code (network) problems

{
  System.out.println("could not send packet");
  System.out.println(e);
  System.exit(0);
}

// packet is reinitialized because it will be
// used for receiving instead of sending
packet = new DatagramPacket(data, data.length);

try
{
  socket.receive(packet);
}
catch(IOException e)
{
  System.out.println("could not receive a packet");
  System.out.println(e);
  System.exit(0);
}
```

Introducing Networking

continues

Listing 10.4   Continued

```
        //display the returned data on the client console
        messageReturn = new String(packet.getData(), 0);
        System.out.println(messageReturn + " returned from server");
    }
}
```

The term "dynamically resize" refers to the ability to increment or decrement the size of the array while the code is executing. Each packet could be "just the right size." For efficiency reasons, this is often necessary.

Listing 10.23 shows the server running on a machine named studsys.mscs.mu.edu, whereas the client is running on matt.brumbaugh.com. As you can see at the end of the example, the server is still running, waiting for another connection, while the execution of the client has halted. This is normal; when you shut down a client connection, such as your web browser, you do not expect the server to stop running.

In the following two lists, the code on the left corresponds to the server's screen, whereas the code on the right corresponds to the client screen.

Listing 10.23   The Server Running on studsys.mscs.mu.edu: The Client Running on matt.brumbaugh.com

```
%java serverEcho          %java clientEcho studsys.mscs.mu.edu test
String: test              %Returned from server: test
From: matt.brumbaugh.com  %
```

Listing 10.24   echoClient and echoServer Sample Run

```
%java serverEcho
                          %java clientEcho studsys.mscs.mu.edu test
String: test
From: matt.brumbaugh.com
                          %Returned from server: test
                          %
```

The formatting in this example works nicely. The text is displayed cleanly on the screen. Simple alterations of the echo program, however, may not appear as cleanly because the data is always passed over the network as an array of bytes that holds 1024 bytes. To keep things simple, the example did not dynamically resize the array. If extra characters at the end of a string will affect your application, however, you will need to make sure that each DatagramPacket contains an array of bytes without extra characters.

UDP versus TCP

You should now be comfortable using java.net.DatagramSocket and java.net.Data-gramPacket to transfer information across the network using UDP. Reliability was not very important in listing 10.23; nor did the code repeatedly send data to the same destination, making the echo service a prime example of when datagrams are used. In fact, all standard Unix machines run an echo service on port 7. You are probably curious about when else an unreliable network protocol might be the best method of implementing a network application. The following is a listing of common network applications that run on top of—that is they use—TCP.

TCP Network Services

Telnet

File Transfer Protocol

Simple Mail Transfer Protocol

Network News Transfer Protocol

In a likewise manner, the following services, and the programs that take advantage of them, rely on UDP.

UDP Network Services

Domain Name Services

Trivial File Transfer Protocol

Network File System

Ping

daytime server (Unix)

echo (Unix)

talk (Unix)

UDP is most desirable when information is either sent or requested frequently from a variety of sources. Some applications, such as telnet, demand a dedicated connection, or socket. Other applications, such as SMTP, need a guarantee that the entire message arrived and that it arrived in the correct order. Datagrams, however, should not be dismissed as impractical. Every time your machine searches by host name for another machine on the Internet, UDP is used. Although most of your applications (and most of the remainder of this chapter) focus on TCP and sockets, a good developer always considers whether sockets or datagrams would be better suited for the task at hand.

Client Applets

So far, this chapter's examples have been applications. Everything that you have done could be repeated in other programming languages, only with more difficulty. One of the major advantages of using Java is your ability to create programs that are loaded by a common browser and then executed on the client machine. The programs, or *applets*, are ideal for writing client code.

The fact that users do not have to download or install a client program on their machine has two key advantages:

■ The server can be accessed by anybody with access to a Java-enabled web browser, not just those who purchase or download the client application.

■ The client program can be changed on a frequent basis, even daily, and the end users do not have to reinstall the program or download patches—a major advantage for administrators of corporate intranets.

Java applets are often thought of as nifty web-based animations or flashing, multicolored text. Yes, many applets are not much more than glitz; however, the java.applet package can be used to implement powerful client applications that can be used to play games, access a database, or communicate with a mainframe.

Applet Restrictions

The user interfaces in the examples in this chapter have been deliberately kept simple. This chapter does not address the user interface issue. If you have any questions, however, you should refer to the chapter on java.awt (Chapters 4 and 5).

As was mentioned previously, applets are limited in what they can do because the user does not necessarily choose to execute applet code. These limitations affect how you may use the java.net classes. Java applets can only create network connections to the host from which they came. That is, if an applet is on a home page at a machine named matt.brumbaugh.com, it can only open connections to matt.brumbaugh.com. The security policy that restricts applets is part of the browser the user is running, not part of Java itself. Also, code exists that will bypass some security policies set by different browsers. These facts should not be interpreted to mean that the security restrictions are merely recommendations. Any code written to get around security issues can become out-of-date with a new browser version or a tighter security policy. Also, bypassing security policies can potentially violate the trust of the user. As a Java programmer, you should treat the fact that you can execute your code on somebody else's machine as a privilege and not a right. In order to be sure all users can run your program, it is best to write code that works with security limitations that at times seem burdensome and oversecure.

java.net Limitations

The next example was chosen to illustrate a limitation of the java.net package. Experienced network programmers are probably aware that the ping command, often used to test whether a machine is alive, uses a protocol known as Internet Control Message Protocol. ICMP sits on top of IP; however, it is not a fully functional network layer protocol like TCP. The current Java Development Kit provides access to TCP and UDP; however, no classes are available to make calls to IP directly or to ICMP. Without using native methods, the ping command, as it is specified in the RFC, could not be simulated in Java.

The example acts much like a ping command, although it does not use ICMP commands. It sends a DatagramPacket to the echo server on the host machine, which resides on port 7. It measures and displays the amount of time, in milliseconds, before the packet is returned, just as the ping command does. A true ping utility accepts the host name of the machine to try to connect to as a parameter; however, applets can only open connections to the machine from which they were downloaded. This applet shows two limitations of java.net: one deals with applet security, and the other deals with the actual protocols that java.net cannot handle.

NetSpeed.java

The first section of code, shown in listing 10.25, contains standard applet methods including init(), start(), and stop(). When the applet is loaded, it attempts to get the host name of the machine from which it was loaded. The search may fail if you load the applet from your hard drive using the file:// tag unless your machine has a registered domain name. If the init() method does not print the host name to the standard output, it could not get the host name. Chances are, the applet would not work on a machine without a host name because the machine is probably not running an echo server on port 7. The init() method also creates an instance of the NetTest class, which does the actual simulated pinging. Finally, init() creates the user interface; start() only calls super.start(); stop() calls super.stop() and the stop() method of the NetTest class.

Listing 10.25   NetSpeed.java First of Two

```
import java.net.*;
import java.awt.*;
import java.lang.*;
import java.applet.*;

public class NetSpeed extends Applet
{
```

continues

Listing 10.25   Continued

```
NetTest nt;
    //separate class to handle the network connection
TextArea display;
String host;
    //must be address where applet was downloaded from
Button tryAgain;

public void init()
{
  try
  {
    //get address wher applet came from
    //we much connect back to this host
    host = this.getCodeBase().getHost();
    //for debugging purposes
    System.out.println(host);

    nt = new NetTest(InetAddress.getByName(host));
    display = new TextArea("Click on the button\n");
    //intialize GUI components
    display.setEditable(false);
    tryAgain = new Button("Send Packet");
    tryAgain.resize(20,40);

    this.setLayout(new BorderLayout()); // layout GUI components
    this.add("South", tryAgain);
    this.add("Center", display);
  }
  catch (Exception e)
  {
    System.out.println(e);
  }
}

public void start() //a generic start method
{
  super.start();
}

public void stop() //calls default stop along with NetTest's stop method
{
  super.stop();
  nt.stop();
}
```

Ten: Introducing Networking

In the next section of code in listing 10.26, the class netSpeed, which extends java.applet. Applet, is concluded. The action() method, which handles events, comes first. The only valid event is if the "tryAgain" button is pressed, which simply calls the calltest() method. The calltest() method serves two purposes:

- It invokes the test() method of the NetTest class. This method actually sends a packet to the echo server on the machine from which the applet was downloaded.
- It displays the results in the TextArea.

The appendText() method is used so that users can compare results from multiple tests. If the value –1 was returned, calltest() notifies the user that the host could not be contacted. This could be due to a network error or the fact that the machine is not running an echo server.

Listing 10.26 netSpeed.java Second of Two

```java
// When send button pressed, rerun and update display
public boolean action(Event e, Object what)
{
  if(e.target == tryAgain)
  {
    calltest();
    return(true);
  }
  return(false);
}

void calltest()
{
  display.appendText("Sending packet to " + host +"\n");
  long returnTime = nt.test();
  if(returnTime >0 )
    {
      display.appendText("To reach " + host + " took "
        + Long.toString(returnTime) + " ms.\n");
    }
  else
    display.appendText(host + " could not be reached.\n");
}
}
```

Introducing Networking

NetTest.java

The next section of code, shown in listing 10.27, begins the NetTest class. NetTest handles the actual network connections and keeps track of the amount of time between when the packet was sent and when it was returned. NetTest implements Runnable—the first example in this chapter to use threads. As you will see in the remaining listings, threads are necessary in network programming to enable multiple users. In this situation, however, the thread is used mainly to keep track of time.

Three final variables are declared:

- echoPort is set to 7 because it is the standard port for the echo service.
- maxTime is set to 2,500, under the assumption that any packet that does not return within 2.5 seconds (2,500 milliseconds) is lost.
- interval is set to 50, the number of milliseconds the thread sleeps when nothing is occurring.

The constructor needs to know the InetAddress of the host from which the applet was downloaded. Everything else in listing 10.27 should be self-explanatory.

Listing 10.27   NetTest.java First of Three

```
class NetTest implements Runnable
{
    static final int echoPort = 7;
    static final int maxTime = 2500;
    static final int interval = 50;

    DatagramSocket dgsock;
    InetAddress ia;
    long timesent;
    long time;
    Thread timeOut;
    Thread listen;
    byte number = 0;

    //constructor is passed address applet originated at
    public NetTest(InetAddress ia)
    {
        this.ia = ia;
    }
```

Listing 10.28 consists of the test() method, which is called whenever the user presses the button to send a packet. Test creates the DatagramSocket to send and receive packets and a DatagramPacket to be sent. It uses a thread to keep track of the amount of time between when the packet was sent and returned. It returns this value to the piece of code that called it.

Listing 10.28   NetTest.java Second of Three

```java
public long test()
{
  byte[] b = new byte[1];
  b[0] = ++number;
  time = -1;

  try
  {
    dgsock = new DatagramSocket();
  }
  catch (Exception e)
  {
    System.out.println("Could not create DatagramSocket");
    System.out.println(e);
  }

  if (listen == null)
  {
    listen = new Thread(this);
    listen.start();
  }

  DatagramPacket packet = new DatagramPacket(b, b.length, ia,echoPort);
  timesent = System.currentTimeMillis();
  long dieTime = timesent + maxTime;

  try
  {
    dgsock.send(packet);
    while (System.currentTimeMillis() < dieTime)
    {
      Thread.sleep(interval);
      if(time != -1)
        return(time);
    }
```

continues

Listing 10.28   Continued

```
    }
    catch (Exception e)
    {
        System.out.println("Error sending packet.");
       System.out.println(e);
    }
    //return what is probably -1, error handling
    //is in actual applet code
    return(time);
  }
```

Listing 10.29 consists of the run() and stop() methods. The run() method is used to listen for incoming (returned) DatagramPackets. The stop() method simply kills the listen thread and then closes the DatagramSocket, returning the port to the system.

Listing 10.29   NetTest.java Third of Three

```
  // Run method for the listen thread
  public void run()
  {
    byte[] b2 = new byte[1];
    DatagramPacket packet = new DatagramPacket(b2, b2.length);

    try
    {
      while (true)
        {
          dgsock.receive(packet);
          if(b2[0] == number)
          {
            time = System.currentTimeMillis() - timesent;
            listen = null;
            return;
          }
        }
    }
    catch (Exception e)
    {
      System.out.println("Could not receive packet");
       System.out.println(e);
      listen = null;
      return;
    }
  }
```

```
    // make sure thread dies and the socket is closed
  public void stop()
  {
    if (listen != null)
      {
        listen.stop();
      }
    dgsock.close();
  }
}
```

NetSpeed and NetTest Wrap-Up

The NetSpeed program enables the user to see how long it takes to bounce a packet back and forth between his machine and the machine on which the applet resides. From this example you should have become familiar with using the java.net package in the applet environment, and you should have a basic understanding of how the limitations of java.net affect your programming.

Listing 10.30 shows a bare-bones HTML file that you can modify to place the applet on your page.

Listing 10.30   netspeed.html

```
<!DOCTYPE HTML PUBLIC "-//IETF//DTD HTML//EN">
<HTML>
<HEAD>
<TITLE>
NetSpeed test page
</TITLE>
</HEAD>

<BODY>
The applet should be below this line
<HR>
<P>

<APPLET code = "NetSpeed.class" width=400 height=200>
</APPLET>

<HR>
The applet should be above this line
<P>

</BODY>
</HTML>
```

Chatting and Sockets

If you are an experienced network programmer, or a fast learner, you probably are growing tired of trivial examples. To conclude this chapter, you will learn how to write a chat applet and server—a popular example for learning because it requires threads for multiuser support and an understanding of how to write to and read from sockets using the java.io classes. Many fancy chat applets can be found on the web; this one is fairly vanilla. The goal in the remainder of the chapter is to introduce you to multithreaded network code. Threads are a necessity if a server is going to support more than one client at a time (see Chapter 13, "Thinking in Terms of Threads"). The client also uses threads to listen for messages from the server while receiving input and sending messages.

As you look over the code, notice that it has been intentionally broken up into more classes and methods than are necessary for an application of this complexity. AppletServer and ChatApplet have been designed as examples for you to experiment with and expand. To quote Professor Doug Harris, "Programming is not a spectator sport." The best thing for you to do when you finish this chapter is to tinker with and build onto these classes.

The Chat Server

This section initiates the development of the server. It consists of three classes:

- **AppletServer.** Contains the constructors for the server as well as the main() method. It also receives the initial connection from the client.

- **ClientConnect.** Constructed for each client connection, ClientConnect handles all further communication between the client and server. It welcomes new clients and then waits for messages to be received. It returns each message received to each client, including the sender.

- **Watcher.** Loops infinitely checking to see whether the client that created each instance of ClientConnect is still connected. If not, it updates the AppletServer's display and closes the socket.

The server is presented in three sections, one for each class. The first class presented is AppletServer. The main() method simply invokes one of three constructors. If the server is launched with the command "java AppletServer," the default port, 1976, is used. An optional flag, -f, calls the second constructor, causing the server to pop up a frame that displays a list of each client. The list displays the ID of each client, as well as the host of the client. Finally, the server may be launched using both the -f flag and a specified port number, "java AppletServer -f <port_#>."

The AppletServer Class

Each constructor creates the thread in which the server runs and initializes a ServerSocket. If the user specifies at the command line, a Frame with a List is created and displayed. The run() method causes the ServerSocket to listen for and accept connections. When a connection is made, an instance of ClientConnect is created, and the new client is added to the list displayed on the screen if applicable (see listing 10.31).

Listing 10.31   AppletServer.java

```java
import java.net.*;
import java.io.*;
import java.util.*;
import java.awt.*;
import java.lang.*;

public class AppletServer extends Thread
{
  protected final static int defaultPort = 1976;
  protected int paramPort;
  protected ServerSocket server;
  protected ThreadGroup tg;
  protected List clientList;
  protected Vector clientVector;
  protected Watcher watcher;

  public static void main(String[] args)
  {
    int port = -1;
    boolean background = true;

    if (args.length == 0)
      new AppletServer();
    else if (args.length == 1)
    {
      if (args[0].equals("-f"))
      {
        background = false;
        new AppletServer(background);
      }
      else
      {
        try
        {
```

continues

Introducing Networking

Listing 10.31   Continued

```
        port = Integer.parseInt(args[0]);
        new AppletServer(port, background);
      }
      catch(NumberFormatException e)
      {
        System.out.print("not a valid port number");
        System.out.println("use an integer over 1024");
        System.out.println(e);
        System.out.println();
        System.out.println("Starting server on " + defaultPort);
        new AppletServer();
      }
    }
  }
  else if ((args.length == 2)  && args[0] == "-f")
  {
    background = false;
    try
    {
      port = Integer.parseInt(args[0]);
      new AppletServer(port, background);
    }
    catch(NumberFormatException e)
    {
      System.out.print("not a valid port number");
      System.out.println("use an integer over 1024");
      System.out.println(e);
      System.out.println();
      System.out.println("Starting server on " + defaultPort);
      new AppletServer(defaultPort, background);
    }
  }
  else
    System.out.println("usage: java AppletServer [-f] [<port_#>]");
}

public AppletServer()
{
  super();          //create thread

  try
  {
    server = new ServerSocket(defaultPort);
  }
  catch(IOException e)
```

Ten: Introducing Networking

```
      {
        System.out.println("could not create ServerSocket");
        System.out.println(e);
        System.exit(1);
      }

      tg = new ThreadGroup("Connections");
      clientList = new List();
      clientVector = new Vector();
      watcher = new Watcher(this);

      this.start();
    }

    public AppletServer(boolean background)
    {
      super();          //create thread

      try
      {
        server = new ServerSocket(defaultPort);
      }
      catch(IOException e)
      {
        System.out.println("could not create ServerSocket");
        System.out.println(e);
        System.exit(1);
      }

      tg = new ThreadGroup("Connections");
      clientList = new List();
      clientVector = new Vector();
      watcher = new Watcher(this);

      Frame f = new Frame("AppletServer Monitor");
      f.add("Center", clientList);
      f.resize(400, 300);
      f.show();

      this.start();
    }

    public AppletServer(int port, boolean background)
    {
        super();          //create thread

      try
```

continues

Introducing Networking

Listing 10.31   Continued

```
  {
    server = new ServerSocket(port);
  }
  catch(IOException e)
  {
    System.out.println("could not create ServerSocket");
    System.out.println(e);
    System.exit(1);
  }

  tg = new ThreadGroup("Connections");
  clientList = new List();
  clientVector = new Vector();
  watcher = new Watcher(this);

  Frame f = new Frame("AppletServer Monitor");
  f.add("Center", clientList);
  f.resize(400, 300);
  f.show();

  this.start();
}

public void run()
{
  try
  {
    for(;;)
    {
      Socket client = server.accept();
      ClientConnect cc = new ClientConnect(this, client, tg, watcher);

      synchronized(clientVector)
      {
        clientVector.addElement(cc);
        clientList.addItem(cc.toString());
      }
    }
  }
  catch(IOException e)
  {
    System.out.println("error accepting connections");
    System.out.println(e);
```

```
        System.exit(1);
      }
    }
  }
}
```

The ClientConnect Class

ClientConnect handles the communication between the server and clients. The constructor is passed the instances of Socket and ThreadGroup to which the client belongs. It also receives the AppletServer and Watcher variables; one instance of these covers all client connections. The constructor then opens the DataInputStream and PrintStream, which are used to listen for and send data to the server. The final action of the constructor is to start the thread that handles communication.

You may be wondering why sendtoone() and sendtoall() are not integrated into one method. In this example, it is unnecessary, but the design allows for extensions to the code to enable multiple chat channels or private messages.

The run() method initially welcomes the client. It then enters a loop in which it reads lines of input sent by the client. If the input line is not null or empty, the sendtoall() method is invoked. Notice that in the IOException thrown by java.io.DataInputStream.readLine(), no error message is displayed. This exception is thrown if the user leaves the page without pressing the disconnect button, thus calling the stop() method to avoid excess messages on the screen. Finally, the run() method closes the socket and streams, and stops the thread, as well.

ClientConnect also contains two additional methods. The sendtoone() method actually sends messages received by the server back to the client via the PrintStream. The sendtoall() method loops through each client in the clientVector calling sendtoone() to actually send the information across the network.

Listing 10.32 contains the source for the ClientConnect class.

Listing 10.32   ClientConnect.java

```
class ClientConnect extends Thread
{
  protected static int ID = -1;
  protected String name;
  protected Socket socket;
  protected DataInputStream dis;
  protected PrintStream ps;
```

continues

Listing 10.32   Continued

```
protected AppletServer gas;
protected Watcher watcher;

public ClientConnect(AppletServer gas, Socket socket,
  ThreadGroup tg, Watcher watcher)
{
  super(tg, "Client #" + ++ID);

  this.gas = gas;
  this.socket = socket;
  this.watcher = watcher;
  name = "default";

  try
  {
    dis = new DataInputStream(socket.getInputStream());
    ps = new PrintStream(socket.getOutputStream());
  }
  catch(IOException e)
  {
    System.out.println("error opening streams");
    System.out.println(e);
  }

  this.start();
}

public void run()
{
  String str;
  int length;

  ps.println("Welcome to the chat room\n");

  try
  {
    for(;;)
    {
      str = dis.readLine();
      if ((str != null) || (str != ""))
        sendtoall(str);
      else
        break;
    }
  }
```

```
    catch(IOException e)
    {
            //No output here because an IOException will
            //be thrown if somebody leaves the chat room
            //without disconnecting. However, this does
            //not effect execution of the program.
        }

    finally
    {
      try
      {
        dis.close();
        ps.close();
        socket.close();
      }
      catch(IOException e)
      {
        System.out.println("error closing socket");
        System.out.println(e);
      }
      synchronized(watcher)
      {
        watcher.notify();
      }
    }
  }

  public void sendtoone(String s)
  {
    ps.println(s);
    ps.flush();
  }

  public void sendtoall(String s)
  {
    int clientNumber;
    clientNumber = gas.clientVector.size();
    for (int i = 0; i < clientNumber; i++)
    {
      ClientConnect cc =
        (ClientConnect)gas.clientVector.elementAt(i);
      cc.sendtoone(s);
    }
  }
}
```

The Watcher Class

Watcher is the final class that is part of the AppletServer application. It monitors the clients to see whether they are connected and deletes records of disconnected clients from the Vector in which they are stored, as well as the list that is displayed on the console of the server. The constructor is passed the instance of AppletServer. It then starts the thread, which does all of the work.

The run() method consists of one loop. The thread pauses for 2.5 seconds each time through the loop and then goes through the clientVector, which contains information about clients, to see whether their threads are alive. If the thread is dead, it removes all references to it. The source code is shown in listing 10.33.

Listing 10.33   Watcher.java

```
class Watcher extends Thread
{
 AppletServer gas;
 int clientNumber;

 Watcher(AppletServer gas)
 {
  super(gas.tg, "Connection Monitor");
  this.gas = gas;
  this.start();
 }

 public synchronized void run()
 {
  for(;;)
  {
   try
   {
    this.wait(2500);
   }
   catch(InterruptedException e)
   {
    System.out.println(e);
   }

   synchronized(gas.clientVector)
   {
    clientNumber = gas.clientVector.size();
    for (int i = 0; i < clientNumber; i++)
    {
```

```
      ClientConnect cc =
        (ClientConnect)gas.clientVector.elementAt(i);
      if (cc.isAlive() == false)
      {
       gas.clientVector.removeElementAt(i);
       gas.clientList.delItem(i);
            clientNumber--;
       i--;
      }
     }
    }
   }
  }
 }
```

The Chat Client

AppletServer is fairly simple. It passes data received back to all clients and is designed to be easily modified and extended. The client side of the program, ChatApplet, is similar. It sends all input to the server and displays all responses (see listing 10.34). All the code here is in one class; however, the code is discussed in three sections. The first section covers the init(), start(), and stop() methods. The next section discusses the run() method. The last section covers event handling and several other methods.

The init() method serves two functions; it lays out the screen and reads a parameter from the HTML file. The port number must be specified in the HTML file. If it reads a number less than 1024, it defaults to port 1976. The rest of the method is devoted to laying out the GUI. Basically, three panels are used, each being laid out with the BorderLayout. One panel contains the connect, send, and disconnect Buttons. Another only holds the TextArea where the conversation is displayed. The final panel holds a TextField where the user enters input.

Listing 10.34   ChatApplet.java First of Three

```
import java.net.*;
import java.io.*;
import java.lang.*;
import java.awt.*;
import java.applet.*;

public class ChatApplet extends Applet implements Runnable
{
```

continues

Listing 10.34   Continued

```
int port;
Socket socket;
DataInputStream dis;
PrintStream ps;
String name;
boolean connected;
boolean newbie = true;
Thread thread;
int reconTries = 0;

TextField writemsg;
TextArea msgs;
Button connect;
Button send;
Button disconnect;

public void init()
{
 String p = new String(this.getParameter("port"));
 port = Integer.parseInt(p);
 if (port < 1024)
 {
   System.out.println("defaulting to port 1976");
   port = 1976;
 }

 writemsg = new TextField();
 msgs = new TextArea();
 connect = new Button("Connect");
 send = new Button("Send");
 disconnect = new Button("Disconnect");

 Panel p1 = new Panel();
 p1.setLayout(new BorderLayout());
 p1.add("Center", msgs);

 Panel p2 = new Panel();
 p2.setLayout(new BorderLayout());
 p2.add("Center", writemsg);

 Panel p3 = new Panel();
 p3.setLayout(new GridLayout(1, 3));
 p3.add(connect);
 p3.add(send);
 p3.add(disconnect);
```

```
   this.setBackground(Color.white);
   this.setForeground(Color.black);
   this.setLayout(new BorderLayout());
   this.add("South", p2);
   this.add("North", p3);
   this.add("Center", p1);
   this.show();
}

public void start()
{
  msgs.setText("Please enter your name before");
  msgs.appendText("pressing connect.\n");
}

public void stop()
{
  try
  {
   send(name + " has left the chat room");
   dis.close();
   ps.close();
   socket.close();
  }
  catch(IOException e)
  {
   System.out.println("error shutting down connection");
   System.out.println(e);
  }

  if ((thread != null) && thread.isAlive())
  {
   thread.stop();
   thread = null;
  }
}
```

Listing 10.35 consists solely of the run() method. The run() method loops endlessly (until disconnection), listening for data from the server. Each time a string is read via the DataInputStream, it is appended to the conversation unless it is an empty string. If the string is empty, the client assumes there is an error. It tries to reconnect to the server. After three failures, the applet gives up, notifies the user, and shuts down. Listing 10.35 shows the run() method.

Listing 10.35   ChatApplet.java Second of Three

```
public void run()
{
 String str;
 try
 {
  for(;;)
  {
   try
   {
    thread.sleep(1000);
   }
   catch(InterruptedException e)
   {}
   str = dis.readLine();

   if(str != null)
   {
    msgs.appendText(str + "\n");
   }
   else
   {
       if (reconTries <= 2)
       {
    msgs.appendText("Connection Lost\n");
    msgs.appendText("Attempting to restore connection\n");
       reconTries++;
    reconnect();
       }
       else
       {
        msgs.appendText("Tried to reconnect 3 times.\n");
        msgs.appendText("Giving up, the server is down.\n");
        try
        {
         dis.close();
         ps.close();
         socket.close();
        }
        catch(IOException e)
        {
          System.out.println("error closing connection");
          System.out.println(e);
        }
         thread.stop();
```

Ten: Introducing Networking

```
                thread = null;
            }
        }
    }
}
catch(IOException e)
{
  System.out.println("error communicating with server");
  System.out.println(e);
}
}
```

The final section of ChatApplet handles events and contains several methods used for communication purposes (see listing 10.36). The action() method determines whether the user is trying to send data, connect, or disconnect. If the user wants to send data, the applet first checks to make sure the user has connected to the server. Likewise, if the user is trying to connect, the client ensures that she has not already connected. The disconnect button calls the stop() method and resets the display if the user wants to reconnect.

The connect() method is called when the user enters her name and presses the Connect button. It opens the Socket, DataInputStream, and PrintStream and starts the thread. The reconnect() method calls the connect() method if the connection is lost. Lastly, the send() method sends messages out over the PrintStream. The rest of the code follows:

Listing 10.36   ChatApplet.java Third of Three

```
public boolean action(Event e, Object o)
{
 if ((e.target == send) && (e.arg != ""))
 {
  if (newbie == true)
  {
   msgs.appendText("You must first connect to the server.\n");
    msgs.appendText("Please type your name and press connect.\n");
     writemsg.requestFocus();
  }
  else
  {
   send(writemsg.getText());
   writemsg.setText("");
     writemsg.requestFocus();
   return true;
  }
```

continues

Introducing Networking

Listing 10.36   Continued

```
  }
  else if (e.target == connect)
  {
    if (newbie == true)
     {
    connect();
      newbie = false;
      name = writemsg.getText();
      writemsg.setText("");
      writemsg.requestFocus();
      msgs.setText("Begin chatting\n");
     }
   else
    msgs.appendText("already connected!\n");
   return true;
  }
  else if (e.target == disconnect)
  {
   stop();
   newbie = true;
     msgs.setText("enter your name and press connect\n");
     writemsg.requestFocus();
   return true;
  }
  return false;
  }

public boolean connect()
{
 boolean con = true;

 try
 {
    socket = new Socket(this.getCodeBase().getHost(), port);
    dis = new DataInputStream(socket.getInputStream());
    ps = new PrintStream(socket.getOutputStream());
      thread = new Thread(this);
      thread.start();
 }
 catch(IOException e)
 {
  con = false;
  System.out.println("connection failed");
  System.out.println(e);
```

```
    }
    return con;
}

public boolean reconnect()
{
 boolean recon;

 recon = connect();
 if (recon)
 {
  recon = true;
 }
 else
 {
  recon = false;
 }
 return recon;
}

public void send(String str)
{
 ps.println(name + ": " + str);
}
}
```

Chat Wrap-Up

Overall, ChatApplet is fairly simple. It sends whatever the user types to a server and displays everything it is sent. Possible additions include a display window showing who is connected, private messages, or even multiple chat channels. All these require code that is no more complex than what has been covered. For your convenience, an HTML file that loads ChatApplet is shown in listing 10.37.

Listing 10.37   chat.html

```
<!DOCTYPE HTML PUBLIC "-//IETF//DTD HTML//EN">
<html> <head>
<title>Annoying Chat</title>
</head>

<body>
Below is an Chat applet.
```

continues

Introducing Networking

Chatting and Sockets

Listing 10.37   Continued

```
<p>

<center>
<APPLET CODE="ChatApplet" WIDTH=500 HEIGHT=300>
  <PARAM name="port" value="1976">
  </PARAM>
</APPLET>
</center>

</body>
</html>
```

Summary

By now you should be comfortable sitting down and writing network code at the same speed as you write Java code in general. In fact, you should experiment with the examples provided in this chapter and write some of your own code before continuing. The next chapter deals with advanced networking techniques and presents implementations of several common servers, including SMTP and HTTP.

Most readers probably fall into one of two categories: programmers with a network background or programmers unfamiliar with the network. If you are in the first group, you understand by now how much the java.net package provides that has not previously been integrated into a popular language. Also, you realize that programming with the classes in java.net.* is much simpler than using TLI or other network extensions. If you are in the second group and thought to yourself, "What was all the fuss about network programming being so tricky," be glad that you have Java as a tool so that programming for the network is more accessible than ever.

The java.net package contains all the classes that are necessary in order to program for the Internet. From the simple downloading of data via a URLConnection to writing complex client-server applets using multiple threads and sockets, it is all built into the Java Development Kit. Java is network-aware. For the programmer, this means guaranteed compatibility across platforms and versions. As more and more users demand applications that are "network-ready," Java and the java.net package promise to be at the forefront of development technologies.

Chapter 11

Advanced Networking

This chapter builds upon your basic networking knowledge to help you create complex client/server applications. Servers are simply network applications that provide a service to client applications or applets. You build servers using many of the same techniques used for any Java application. Servers also pose their own unique problems, however: They potentially handle many different clients concurrently and thus must run for long periods of time. Most servers start when the host computer starts and run until the host computer shuts down.

Java is a natural language for building servers. In addition to the many benefits Java provides to any application writer, several language features help you build robust servers. Automatic garbage collection, for example, helps eliminate memory leaks (storage that is allocated but never released). Servers contain the inherent ability of multitasking, which requires threads and synchronization support. In addition, the exception mechanism ensures that errors are detected and handled before crashing the server. Although it is certainly possible to build reliable servers using other languages, Java's clean integration of these features makes it a natural choice for this task.

As you progress through this chapter, you will develop a set of classes ready to use in creating your own internet or intranet clients and servers. Your goal in this chapter is to build an e-mail application, but you can use the illustrated techniques to build servers and clients for other TCP-based applications, such as network news, chat, file transfer, remote login, and custom web servers.

The Application—An E-Mail Client/Server

Assume that your company wants you to create a LAN-based e-mail solution. This application would require the following characteristics:

- Integrates easily with the Internet
- Is accessible from a variety of different user platforms, such as Mac, PC, and Unix
- Supports a variety of information types
- Enables users to turn their computers off at night
- Enables users to search the corporate information database to find the e-mail address assigned to any individual

Although many other requirements might exist, these characteristics are key for this development project.

Client/Server Protocol Issues

You must first translate these high-level requirements into a selection of the protocols used in your e-mail application. Network protocols define in detail the interactions and exchanges allowed between a client and a server. A protocol must specify the following:

- The set of messages to be sent and received. A protocol could have USERNAME and PASSWORD messages, for example.
- The exact format of each message, even down to the bit level. USERNAME, for example, is message code 4.
- The sequence of messages allowed. PASSWORD must follow a USERNAME message, for example.
- The actions to take when sending or receiving a specific message. In this example, the protocol must check the user's password.

Many different client-server protocols currently exist in common use; you likely make frequent use of such protocols as NNTP (network news), HTTP (web access), SMTP and POP (e-mail), NFS (file service), telnet (remote login), and FTP (file transfer). All of these protocols can be divided into broad categories based on the type of connection between the client and server, and the amount of information, known as state, kept by the server.

Connection or Connectionless Servers

The first major distinction among different groups of client-server protocols is operation over a connection-oriented or connectionless service. For Java, that means TCP (Transmission Control Protocol) or UDP (User Datagram Protocol). Connection-oriented protocols depend on TCP's reliable delivery service; the sender either receives transmitted data in an error-free manner, or the protocol notifies the sender of the failure. Because it is connectionless, UDP provides no guarantees of service; it instead relies only upon the best efforts of the underlying transport networks. UDP packets can be inadvertently lost, reordered or even duplicated during their transmission through the Internet, so your client and server application must be able to handle these occurrences.

Java 1.0 does not provide a standard means of accessing IP-level services. For example, you cannot implement PING in Java without using native methods. Likewise, you cannot implement any new transport protocol that runs directly over IP.

Unlike UDP, TCP's extra service is an added overhead cost. Before you send your application data over TCP, a two-packet exchange usually appears to set up the connection—this is called a *three-way handshake*, but the third packet can often carry user data. Another two or three packets are exchanged when you close the connection. Sending your simple query and gaining a response, therefore, can entail exchanging seven or more packets between the client and server computers. Different TCP implementations vary in their effectiveness in piggy-backing TCP control packets with user data packets. Figure 11.1 shows the packet exchanges for a request/response transaction using TCP and using UDP.

FIGURE 11.1

Packet exchanges for TCP versus UDP.

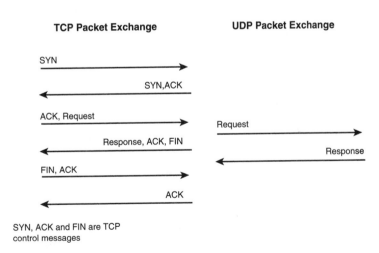

SYN, ACK and FIN are TCP control messages

With UDP, you simply format a request packet and send it to the server. This action returns a response packet, unless the network discards the request or the response packet. If you decide to use UDP, you must code the reliability mechanisms built into TCP into your client and server programs. For most applications, the added implementation effort is not worth the performance gains of using UDP. With general mechanisms, TCP may not be as efficient as a protocol tailored for a specific application, but only the most performance-critical protocols, such as network file service, justify the added effort. Because most client/server protocols are based on connections, your focus in this chapter is to build servers using TCP sockets.

Stateless Servers

The second major distinction among different client-server protocols is the amount of state information the server remembers.

Extensions to HTTP, particularly those that maintain state in the client and pass it to the server, complicate HTTP's stateless model. HTTP uses a technique called *cookies* to save state information related to a specific server. Browsers that support cookies add the saved state information to the HTTP request header.

Assume that you want to build an *elapsed time* server. In one approach, your client opens a TCP connection to your server. The server remembers the time the connection opens (the "state"), computes, and returns the elapsed time on command (a newline character). Your client periodically processes a println() to send a newline character and then reads and displays the time spent waiting. When the expected event occurs, your client processes a println(), reads the final elapsed time computed by the server (ignoring the transmission delay between the client and server computers), and closes the TCP connection. The server absorbs most of the burden of keeping state information (in this case, the start time). The client deals simply with maintaining the TCP connection and sending commands to the server. Each command can implicitly or explicitly reference state information stored by the server. Of course, in this example, maintaining the TCP connection demands much more work than locally computing the elapsed time.

In a stateless approach, one in which your server keeps no state information, the client opens a TCP connection to the server, sends a request to obtain a start-time, stores the returned 64-bit value, and closes the connection. This model of open-request-response-close is the same approach used by HTTP. When your client needs to compute the elapsed time, the client opens a connection to the server and writes the 64-bit value. Your server reads the value, computes, and returns the elapsed time as text. The server then closes the connection to indicate that the transaction is complete.

NOTE

Internet protocols are documented in Requests For Comment (RFCs). RFCs have been used since the beginning of Internet development as a permanent record to document information exchanges between researchers and implementers. The first RFC was issued in 1969; now, over 2,000 exist. Not every RFC specifies an Internet protocol standard, however. In the last few years, the author classifies every new RFC as informational, experimental, preliminary standard, draft standard, or Internet standard. Unlike many other standards, you can easily download RFCs from http://ds. internet.net/ds. In addition, the file rfc-index.html contains a list of all RFCs in reverse numerical order, beginning with the most recent.

In both of these cases, your server computes the elapsed time. In the stateless approach, the client supplies all the information the server needs to perform its task (that is, the start-time value). If your network contains several elapsed time servers (with synchronized clocks), your client can open the connection to a different server each time and still obtain an accurate computation of the elapsed time (again ignoring network delays). Any server can compute the elapsed time because the client maintains the complete state information and sends it with every request. (Note that this stateless example uses TCP. If based on UDP, the client/server protocol would be complicated by adding retransmission and sequencing techniques to ensure reliable delivery.)

Picking Your Protocols

If necessary, you can use several different protocols to accomplish the varied tasks required by the application. You can design a new client/server protocol from scratch, but why bother? The Internet protocol family has benefited from many hundreds of thousands of hours of design work, as well as testing by several thousand contributors. If a defined Internet client/server protocol suits your task, use it. Select a protocol by scanning the list of Internet RFCs for a match in function. The effort you spend looking for a predefined protocol will more than compensate you by avoiding protocol design problems that emerge later when the client/server application is deployed. Among other issues, client/server protocol design must consider race conditions, failure modes, and the transmission characteristics of the Internet environment. Figure 11.2 lists the most commonly used Internet protocols.

By using a standard protocol, you often can obtain the client-side application commercially. Many application situations exist to allow you to use standard client software and tailor the server to meet your needs. For example, you will use a web browser client for server status monitoring in a later example.

The Simple Message Transport Protocol (SMTP) is the Internet standard for carrying mail between mail servers. Although not explicitly mentioned in the specification, the SMTP also can send e-mail from a client to a server. Post Office Protocol version 3 (POP3) is one standard approach for a client to retrieve mail from a server-based mail storage area, and many commercially available e-mail client packages support the popular SMTP/POP protocol combination. Although a variety of database access protocols exist, ranging in complexity from simple to full-featured query languages, you decide on an HTTP/CGI query approach to access the name/address database. These three protocols—SMTP, POP, and HTTP—form the foundation of your e-mail server application.

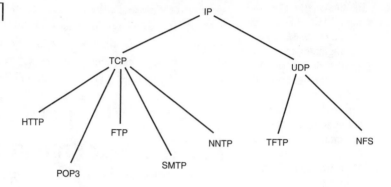

Figure 11.2
Commonly used Internet protocols.

HTTP - HyperText Transfer Protocol
POP3 - Post Office Protocol version 3
FTP - File Transfer Protocol
SMTP - Simple Message Transfer Protocol
NNTP - Network News Transfer Protocol
TFTP - Trivial File Transfer Protocol
NFS - Network File System

Server-Specific Issues

Servers are different from ordinary applications or applets in a variety of ways. For applet developers or user-interface intensive applications, Java provides standard toolkits, such as AWT, to simplify development. Java 1.0 provides more support than most systems for client-side network communications, but the language still lacks many facilities for server development. Next, you will develop classes tailored for constructing servers in the same way that the core Java packages provide applet support.

In designing these classes, consider how a typical network server application differs from a regular Java application:

- The Internet standard for date/time format differs from that used by standard Java.
- The end-of-line sequence for Java (\n) differs from the Internet standard (\r\n).
- Efficient use of network resources ranks as an important consideration.
- Client activity monitoring protects against disconnected clients.

Although these issues are often ignored in client development, you must develop a server application framework to assist in coding servers. This should include classes for Internet date, output stream, and command input.

InetDate Class

Unfortunately, the Java date/time class does not produce the exact Internet standard date/time format. RFCs 822 and 1123 specify the preferred time format as a three-letter abbreviated day of the week, followed by the date, a four-digit year, and the GMT time. An example of the standard date/time format follows:

Sun, 06 Nov 1994 08:49:37 GMT

JavaSoft is developing a server support package called Jeeves, which provides support for writing general-purpose servers, as well as special HTTP-based servlets. The classes you develop in this chapter are similar to, but different from, those in Jeeves. Because Jeeves exists only in alpha release at the time of publication, detailed API comparisons with JavaSoft's package are not possible. However, this book notes significant design and philosophy similarities when applicable.

The InetDate class is a subclass of the standard Java Date class that provides the correct format. The extra constructors that deal with the many ways to create a Date object have been removed from the sample code, but you should define them in your package. The InetDate class overrides the toString() method of Date to add the day of the week abbreviation to the string and produce a fixed two-character date field, as shown in the following code.

```
class InetDate extends Date {
    public InetDate () {
    super();
    }

    public InetDate (String date) {
    super(date);
    }

    private final static String dayOfWeek[] = {
    "Sun, ", "Mon, ", "Tue, ", "Wed, ", "Thu, ", "Fri,
    ➥", "Sat, "
    };

    public String toString() {
    if (this.getDate() < 10)
      return (dayOfWeek[this.getDay()] + "0" +
      ➥this.toGMTString());
    else
      return (dayOfWeek[this.getDay()] +
      ➥this.toGMTString());
    }

}
```

The Java.io. PrintStream implementation for println() illustrates a common issue in object-oriented design: the tradeoff between performance, and flexibility or strict adherence to OO design principles. The code for "println(int i);" could have been implemented as "print(b); println();" to localize the knowledge of the end-of-line termination sequence to the println() method.

Instead, the Java implementers used "print(a); write('\r');" to spreading the knowledge of the end-of-line terminator into all println() methods. In this case, that approach is reasonable, because most programs use '\r' to end each line. The extra effort spent rewriting the affected methods to adhere to the Internet standard is also minimal: separate String. valueOf() methods handle the real implementation effort, conversion of the different data types to print form.

Note that the InetDate class does not attempt to correct any of the perceived deficiencies of the basic Java Date class.

InetOutputStream Class

Servers have unique requirements relating to end-of-line termination and efficient use of network resources. You can solve any server-specific output problems with a single InetOutputStream class. This class implements OutputStream and deals with the end-of-line and buffering issues.

Problems with PrintStream

Although most TCP-based client/server protocols exchange information encoded in ASCII characters rather than straight binary, you should not use a PrintStream for output. Java uses the Unix convention of \n as the end-of-line character. When you generate a println("text"), a \n character automatically attaches to the end of the string. Single end-of-line characters do not conform to the Internet standard, though. True to its roots and the days of mechanical output devices, the Internet standard remains the two-character sequence of \r and \n, or carriage-return and linefeed.

Depending on your TCP implementation, you may notice that the characters arrive individually or in small clumps, even though you used a println() statement to output a complete line. PrintStream converts the characters in the string from Unicode to ASCII and writes to the output stream one character at a time. Because the OutputStream classes pass individual characters to TCP but IP expects packets from TCP, the TCP implementation must convert this stream of characters into packets for transmission across the Internet.

Most implementations of TCP buffer characters wait a few hundred milliseconds for additional characters to be written to the stream before they actually build and transmit the next data packet. This delay compensates for the character-at-a-time nature of streams.

Eleven: Advanced Networking

Other TCP implementations use only a short delay, if any, which requires that your application properly bundles individual characters together into a single write. Because this aspect of TCP behavior is not yet standardized for Java, you must buffer characters for better efficiency.

Figure 11.3 shows the characters of a println() being processed and sent over a TCP connection. Because TCP is a stream protocol, only the sequence of characters is preserved and not any record boundaries. The characters from one print() may be read by multiple read() calls or one read() call can return chacaters from multiple print() calls.

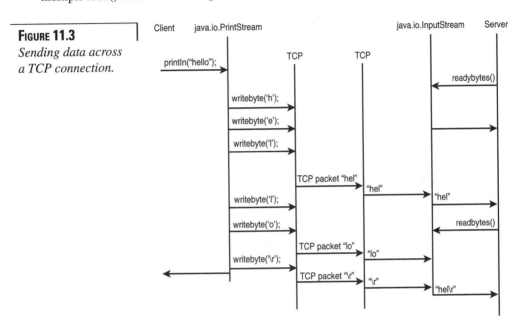

FIGURE 11.3

Sending data across a TCP connection.

Implementing InetOutputStream

The constructor for InetOutputStream automatically creates a BufferedOutputStream, if necessary, and allows you to control whether a flush() occurs at every end of line or under program control. The InetOutputStream extends the FilterOutputStream function and defines the methods available from a PrintStream, as shown in the following.

```
public class InetOutputStream extends FilterOutputStream {
    private boolean linemode;

    public InetOutputStream(OutputStream out) {
    this(out, true);
    }

    public InetOutputStream(OutputStream out, boolean linemode) {
    super((out instanceof BufferedOutputStream) ? out : new
    ➥BufferedOutputStream(out));
    this.linemode = linemode;
    }

    OutputStream getOutputStream() {
    return out;
    }

    void setLinemode(boolean flag) {
    linemode = flag;
    }
```

Propagating IOExceptions

Unlike Printstream, the InetOutputStream also propagates all IOExceptions to your application. In most cases, an IOException is a signal indicating that the connection to the client has broken and that the server must abort processing. Do not ignore these exceptions. The write() method looks for the linefeed character and generates any needed buffer flushing to implement the buffer mode currently active, as shown in the following listing.

```
public void write(int i) throws IOException {
    out.write(i);
    if (linemode && (i == '\n'))
      out.flush();
    }
```

Adding Overloaded print() Methods

You must add overloaded methods of print() for all basic data types. The following example illustrates only a few of the different overloaded versions of print().

```
public void print(Object obj) throws IOException {
    print(String.valueOf(obj));
    }
```

```
synchronized public void print(String str) throws IOException {
int length = str.length();
for (int i = 0 ; i < length ; i++) {
  write(str.charAt(i));
}
}

public void print(char chr) throws IOException {
print(String.valueOf(chr));
}

public void print(int i) throws IOException {
print(String.valueOf(i));
}
```

Changing Line-Termination Characters

To change the line termination from a single newline character, override the println()
method to terminate each line with a carriage-return and linefeed. The following code
shows how to declare the various types of println() as synchronized to prevent random
interleaving of individual output characters when more than one thread writes to a single
stream.

```
synchronized public void println() throws IOException {
write('\r');
write('\n');
}
```

Overriding println() Methods

Now override the println() methods for the various argument types to print the data and
output the new line termination characters. The following code illustrates only the
methods for a few argument types.

```
synchronized public void println(Object obj) throws IOException {
print(obj);
println();
}

synchronized public void println(String str) throws IOException {
print(str);
println();
}
```

continues

```
    synchronized public void println(char chr) throws IOException {
    print(chr);
    println();
    }

    synchronized public void println(int i) throws IOException {
    print(i);
    println();
    }

  }
```

The InetOutputStream class provides a network-efficient and standards compliant OutputStream wrapper for TCP connections.

TimeoutInputStream Class

What if a client establishes a connection to your port but never sends any commands? What if the client crashes or is disconnected from the network in the middle of the request/response exchange? In many cases, your server will become blocked while waiting for input that never arrives. The TimeoutInputStream wraps a timeout mechanism around any InputStream to detect these situations. If your server is blocked while waiting for input and the timeout expires, an exception is generated allowing your server to clean-up and handle other clients.

TCP automatically detects a communication failure only if information has been sent but not acknowledged as received. TCP retransmits unacknowledged information periodically and throws an exception if it is unsuccessful after a number of attempts. When TCP completes sending, however, it waits for packets from the remote host; the failure detection mechanisms do not activate, and the connection can remain alive indefinitely. If the client leaves and this set of circumstances occurs when your server is generating a read() on an ordinary InputStream, the read() will not complete, and TCP will not throw an Exception.

Normally, this problem will not occur to a client. Most TCP implementations refrain from sending the acknowledgment in order to give the server application time to process the request and return a response. If the response returns quickly enough, TCP can piggy-back both the response and acknowledgment into a single packet. Thus, the server likely will not crash in the middle of a client-originated transaction that cannot detect the failure. Even if this unlikely event happens, however, a user often supervises the operation of the client and eventually can abort the connection.

These situations are shown in figure 11.4. In (a), the client crashes (or communication is broken) during a transaction and the server's TCP detects the failure and eventually aborts the connection. In (b), the failure is transactional after the server has sent the response and is waiting for the next request. In this case, the server waits forever for the next request.

FIGURE 11.4
Connection failure modes.

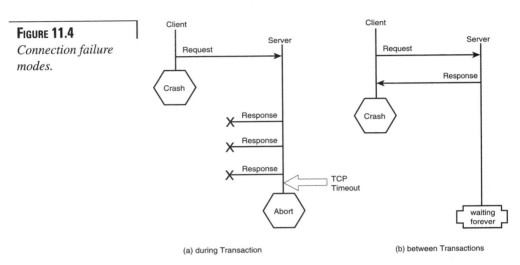

(a) during Transaction   (b) between Transactions

Implementing TimeoutInputStream

During the creation of a new TimeoutInputStream instance, the system remembers the current thread as the *owner* of the stream. Only the owner of the stream blocks waiting for input, and you interrupt this thread when the timeout expires. You can add this new stream instance to the static list of instances maintained by the class. Your TimeoutInputStream subclasses InputStream, as illustrated in this code:

```
public class TimeoutInputStream extends InputStream {
    static Vector instanceList = new Vector();

    InputStream in;
    long lastActive;
    Thread owner;

    public TimeoutInputStream(InputStream in) {
    this.in = in;
```

continues

TimeoutInputStream Class   389

```
    lastActive = 0;
    owner = Thread.currentThread();
    instanceList.addElement(this);
    }
```

You provide methods to read and change the lastActive variable, as shown in the following listing.

```
protected void setLastActive(long time) {
    lastActive = time;
    }

    protected long getLastActive() {
    return lastActive;
    }
```

Resetting Timeout

Override all data handling methods to clear the lastActive variable and reset the timeout mechanism when a read operation successfully completes, as shown here:

```
    public int read() throws IOException {
    int rtn = in.read();
    lastActive = 0;
    return rtn;
    }

    public int read(byte b[], int off, int len) throws IOException {
    int rtn = in.read(b, off, len);
    lastActive = 0;
    return rtn;
    }

    public long skip(long n) throws IOException {
    long rtn = in.skip(n);
    lastActive = 0;
    return rtn;
    }
```

Providing Access to Non-data Handling Methods

You also provide pass-through methods that make the various non-data handling methods of the encapsulated stream available, as shown in the following listing.

```
public int available() throws IOException {
return in.available();
}

public synchronized void mark(int readlimit) {
in.mark(readlimit);
}

public synchronized void reset() throws IOException {
in.reset();
}

public boolean markSupported() {
return in.markSupported();
}
```

Closing the TimeoutInputStream

When closing the stream, you remove it from the list of streams monitored for activity:

```
public void close() throws IOException {
  in.close();
  lastActive = 0;
  owner = null;
  instanceList.removeElement(this);
  }
```

Interrupting the Blocked Thread

Finally, you provide an abort() method, which is called when the system detects a timeout. Because Java 1.0 does not implement thread interrupt, the only other option for interrupting a thread blocked on input is to kill the thread and close the stream. This releases any allocated operating system resources:

```
protected void abort() {
  try {
    if (owner != null) {
      owner.stop();
      close();
    }
  }
  catch (Exception e) {
  }
  }

}
```

If your handler must perform some clean-up, you can catch ThreadDeath; remember to throw it again, or the thread will never really die.

Implementing the StreamMonitor

In addition to the mechanism built into TimeoutInputStream to detect input inactivity, you must add a separate thread to actually monitor the streams. A StreamMonitor accomplishes this task.

Create the StreamMonitor instance in a high-level thread, generally the Main thread, to monitor the TimeoutInputStream instances. Specifically, to have permission to interrupt the blocked thread, the StreamMonitor thread must be a member of the ThreadGroup of the thread blocked for input. It also can be a member of any parent ThreadGroup. If you create the StreamMonitor either in the main() routine or inside the Server, the StreamMonitor always has permission to do its job.

StreamMonitor subclasses Thread; its default behavior runs every 60 seconds and aborts any stream idle for more than about 5 minutes. These values are representative of those useful for most TCP-based services:

```
class StreamMonitor extends Thread {
  static long timeout = 5*60*1000;
  final static long runInterval = 60*1000;
```

Initializing the StreamMonitor

Because the StreamMonitor operates as a background support thread, you must indicate that it is a daemon thread and set its priority below normal client handling. You automatically start it in its constructor:

```
public StreamMonitor() {
 super("StreamMonitor");
 setPriority(Thread.NORM_PRIORITY - 1);
 setDaemon(true);
 this.start();
 }
```

Determining Timeout Intervals

StreamMonitor processing is simple: The monitor sleeps most of the time and wakes periodically to scan the list of instances maintained by TimeoutInputStream as a static class variable. If a stream's lastActive value is 0, recent activity has occurred— set lastActive to the current time. If the lastActive is non-zero, compute the elapsed time and decide whether the timeout interval has expired. When the timeout interval expires, call abort() on the stream:

```
public void run() {
while (true) {
  try {
    Enumeration enum = null;
    sleep(runInterval);
    long currTime = System.currentTimeMillis();
    enum = TimeoutInputStream.instanceList.elements();
    while (enum.hasMoreElements()) {
      TimeoutInputStream stream =
      ➥(TimeoutInputStream)(enum.nextElement());
      long lastActive = stream.getLastActive();
      if (lastActive == 0)
        stream.setLastActive(currTime);
      else if ((currTime - lastActive) > timeout)
        stream.abort();
    }
  }
  catch (InterruptedException e) {
    System.out.println(e);
  }
}
}
```

Note that calling abort() produces a call to close(). This removes the stream from the TimeoutInputStream instance list. The standard Java enumerators do not handle the case of removing elements from the underlying list correctly: The enumerator skips over the next element. Time outs should be infrequent occurrences, however, so you can ignore this situation and not implement a Vector enumerator.

CommandInputStream

A significant part of the effort in coding a server relates to parsing commands and their arguments. The CommandInputStream works like a tokenizer. Its only difference is that instead of returning strings, CommandInputStream returns integer values that represent the command strings. When you create a CommandInputStream, you assign it either a pre-built keyword table or an ordered list of keyword strings. When CommandInputStream recognizes a keyword, it returns the index into this list. As usual, negative values indicate situations such as end-of-line and end-of-file:

```
class CommandInputStream {
    DataInputStream in;
    StringTokenizer st;
    KeywordTable keywordTable;
    String keyword;
    String standardDelimiters;

    public static final int TT_EOF = -1;
    public static final int TT_EOL = -2;
    public static final int TT_OTHER = -3;

    public CommandInputStream(InputStream input, String list[]) {
    this(input, list, " \t\r\n");
    }

    public CommandInputStream(InputStream input, String list[], String
    ➥delimiters) {
    this(input, new KeywordTable(list), delimiters);
    }

    public CommandInputStream(InputStream input, KeywordTable table,
    ➥String delimiters) {
    in = (input instanceof DataInputStream) ? (DataInputStream)input :
    ➥new DataInputStream(input);
    standardDelimiters = delimiters;
    st = new StringTokenizer("");
    keywordTable = table;
    }
```

Saving Keyword Tables as Static Variables

Although you can recreate the keyword table each time you create a new
CommandInputStream, you might consider creating the table once and saving it as a static
variable in the handler class. The createKeywordTable() method provides a convenient
way to obtain this table for later reference:

```
public static KeywordTable createKeywordTable(String list[]) {
return new KeywordTable(list);
}
```

Converting Tokens to Command Indexes

Commands generally occupy one line apiece in most TCP-based protocols. Your handler
calls nextCommand() to read a new line and obtain the first token. You can obtain the

actual token text by calling getCommandString(). Convert this token into a command index by finding the token in the keyword table:

```java
int nextCommand() throws IOException {
try {
  String nxt = in.readLine();
  st = new StringTokenizer(nxt, standardDelimiters);

  keyword = st.nextToken();
  int index = keywordTable.tokenFor(keyword);
  if (index >= 0)
    return index;
  return TT_OTHER;
}
catch (EOFException e) {
  return TT_EOF;
}
catch (NoSuchElementException e) {
  return TT_EOL;
}
}

String getCommandString() {
return keyword;
}
```

Getting Arguments of the Command

As with a StringTokenizer, calling hasMoreArgs() and nextArg() accesses additional arguments on the command line. In nextArg(), however, the system throws an exception if more arguments are not available. Because a StringTokenizer parses each command line, you can switch delimiter sets on each call to nextArg():

```java
boolean hasMoreArgs() {
return st.hasMoreTokens();
}

String nextArg() {
return st.nextToken();
}

String nextArg(String delimiters) {
return st.nextToken(delimiters);
}
```

Accessing the Input Stream

You can provide methods to read lines directly from the encapsulated input stream and to propagate a close():

```
String readLine() throws IOException {
String nxt = in.readLine();
return nxt;
}

void close() throws IOException {
in.close();
}

}
```

Although you developed them independently, you can merge the functions of CommandInputStream and TimeoutInputStream into one class by using CommandInputStream in all of your servers.

Command KeywordTable

The CommandInputStream uses a helper class, KeywordTable, to search the keyword table and return the index of the word in the keyword list. For the following examples, which involve only a few keywords, use a simple linear search to perform a case-insensitive comparison:

```
class KeywordTable {
  String stringTable[];

  public KeywordTable(String table[]) {
  stringTable = table;
  }

  int tokenFor(String key) {
  int length = stringTable.length;
  for (int i = 0; i < length; i++) {
    if (key.equalsIgnoreCase(stringTable[i]))
      return i;
    }
  return -1;
  }
}
```

For protocols with many more commands, you can replace the linear search with a hash table lookup. In this case, the hash key is the command string and the object returned from get() is an Integer object whose value is the index in the keyword list. For added performance, you can tailor the hash function and the size of the table to guarantee a fast lookup with no collisions.

Server, ClientHandler, and ClientHandlerFactory

In your server framework, three abstract classes exist: a Server, which manages network sockets; a ClientHandlerFactory, which creates the correct ClientHandler object; and the ClientHandler, which actually provides the service. Although creating these three classes might appear to be overkill, several operations are common across the many types of servers. You benefit from code reuse as you build more complex servers.

This approach of producing a class or method simply to create object instances is formally known as the *factory class/method*. A factory encapsulates the knowledge you need to produce a specific instance. Java uses factory classes in several different places. For example, you use a factory method to create enumeration objects.

Server Class

The Server abstract class defines the functions for the concrete classes that manage ServerSockets, accept new connections from clients, and match the clients to service handlers. The Server class implements Runnable so that you can run it from either a separate thread or from the main thread. The base class maintains a static list of its instances so that status and control tasks can monitor or communicate with all servers. This list of server instances is available through the usual enumeration approach. You create the Server object with a reference to your factory object:

```
abstract class Server implements Runnable {
  protected static Vector serverList = new Vector();
  protected ServerSocket listener;
  protected ClientHandlerFactory clientFactory;
  protected boolean running;
```

continues

```
static Enumeration elements() {
return serverList.elements();
}


protected Server(ClientHandlerFactory factory) {
clientFactory = factory;
synchronized (serverList) {
  serverList.addElement(this);
}
}


}
```

TCP and UDP use *ports* to determine the service that handles a packet. Two ports exist in each packet: a source port and a destination port. These ports are 16-bit numbers—ports 0 through 1023 apply to standard servers and are well-known ports. For example, HTTP is assigned to well-known port 80. The networking code for client sockets automatically selects an unused source port, but server code must provide the port number. Well-known port assignments (along with other assigned numbers) are defined in the "Internet Assigned Numbers" RFC1700. Figure 11.5 shows multiple clients communicating through the well-known ports on the server. TCP port 7 is distinct from UDP port 7; although, by convention, a given service uses the same port for both TCP and UDP if the service is available over either transport.

ClientHandlerFactory Class

The ClientHandlerFactory abstract class encapsulates all the knowledge and policy you need to link a new client connection to a handler. For example, you call the ClientHandlerFactory to determine the well-known TCP port and service name, and to create the actual client handlers:

```
public abstract class ClientHandlerFactory {
   protected int port;
   abstract String getName();
   int serverPort() {
   return port;
   }
   abstract ClientHandler createClientHandler(Socket
   ➥connection);
   }
```

The policy for the exact type of client handler is generated totally within createClientHandler(). Depending on the connection's origin, you can create one of several different handlers with different security restrictions. For example, you can create a full-featured handler to serve clients on the same network as the server, or within the same naming domain. You can create a restricted handler for general client access, or you can create a status or control handler only for clients on the same machine as the server, or for specific network management hosts—simply return null for any connection you do not want to service. In addition, instead of creating a new handler for each request, you can build a factory that manages a set of precreated objects. All these differences in creating client handlers are invisible to the Server.

Eleven: Advanced Networking

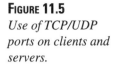
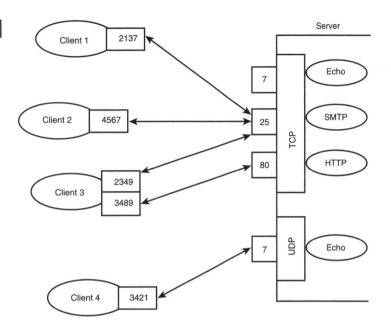

FIGURE 11.5
*Use of TCP/UDP
ports on clients and
servers.*

ClientHandler Class

The ClientHandler abstract class works as the base for all classes that implement server functions. ClientHandler implements Runnable to allow your handlers to run as separate threads. Among other functions, the abstract class maintains a reference to the connection. The definition of ClientHandler follows:

```
abstract public class ClientHandler implements Runnable {
  Socket connection;

  public ClientHandler(Socket connection) {
  this.connection = connection;
  }

  abstract public void run();
}
```

SimpleServer and ThreadedServer

You construct two subclasses of Server: a simple version that serves only one client at a time, and a multithread, multiclient version.

SimpleServer

The first subclass of Server is a SimpleServer loop that handles one client at a time. This limited function is appropriate for infrequently used services, quickly responding services, or services that are inherently single-tasking because of limitations in the underlying system. For example, a server that accesses a single-user database package or single-user physical devices must prevent multiple threads from making concurrent requests. The easiest way to prevent concurrent access is to handle one client at a time. As with all Servers, the SimpleServer instance contains a reference to a specific type of factory:

```
class SimpleServer extends Server {
   public SimpleServer(ClientHandlerFactory factory)
{
   super(factory);
   }
```

Using the ServerSocket

Your run() method contains the code to both create the ServerSocket and to wait for a connection from the client. After the connection occurs, call the clientFactory to create the handler object. ClientHandlers implement Runnable() so that you can call their run() method to service the client. After the handling is complete, loop back and wait for another connection:

```
public void run() {
ClientHandler handler;
running = true;
try {
  listener = new ServerSocket(clientFactory.serverPort());
  while (running) {
    Socket connection = listener.accept();
    if (!running)
```

```
      return;
    if (connection == null)
      continue;
    handler = clientFactory.createClientHandler(connection);
    if (handler == null) {
      connection.close();
      continue;
      }
    handler.run();
  }
}
```

Catching and Logging Exceptions

Of course, you should catch and log all exceptions. The "finally" clause guarantees that the ServerSocket closes if the server exits for any reason:

```
catch (Exception e) {
  System.out.println(e);
}
finally {
  try {
    listener.close();
  }
  catch (IOException e) {
  }
}
}

}
```

A SimpleServer can handle only one client at a time. If other clients attempt to connect to the service when it is in use, the system queues or refuses the connection requests.

Serving Multiple Concurrent Clients

The other subclass of Server is a multithreaded version that can handle multiple concurrent requests. This subclass creates a thread to run the handler for each new connection. Multithreading works well in building applications and applets, but it is essential in building servers. The SimpleServer approach suffices for some simple, quick services, but general servers must be prepared to provide service concurrently to clients throughout the Internet.

To limit the load placed on the system, and to ensure satisfactory service for all clients, servers generally impose a limit on the number of simultaneous connections allowed. Create a ThreadedServer with a factory and the maximum number of allowed threads, as follows:

```
public class ThreadedServer extends Server {
  ThreadGroup group;
  int maxThreads;
  int activeEstimate;

  public ThreadedServer(ClientHandlerFactory factory) {
  this(factory, 10);
  }

  public ThreadedServer(ClientHandlerFactory factory, int maxThreads)
{
  super(factory);
  this.maxThreads = maxThreads;
  }
```

Monitoring Thread Activity

Use a ThreadGroup to keep track of the threads created to handle clients. Call activeCount() to determine how many threads are currently active as defined by the system:

```
int activeCount() {
if (group != null) {
  activeEstimate = group.activeCount();
  return activeEstimate;
}
else
  return 0;
}
```

Handling New Connections

As with all servers, a ServerSocket waits for clients to connect. When a client connects, check to see whether you are already handling the maximum number of allowed connections. Instead of tracking the actual number of active threads at any given time, the estimate counts thread creation, not death. You should correct your estimate when you reach the maximum threshold. If you have not reached the maximum thread limit, you can create a new handler and a new thread to run the handler code:

```
public void run() {
group = new ThreadGroup(Thread.currentThread().getName());
activeEstimate = 0;
running = true;
try {
  listener = new ServerSocket(clientFactory.serverPort());
  while (running) {
    Socket connection = listener.accept();
    if (!running)
      return;
    if (connection == null)
      continue;
    if (activeEstimate >= maxThreads) {
      activeEstimate = group.activeCount();
      if (activeEstimate >= maxThreads) {
        connection.close();
        continue;
      }
    }
    ClientHandler clientHandler =
    ➥clientFactory.createClientHandler(connection);
    if (clientHandler == null) {
      connection.close();
      continue;
    }
```

Creating Client-Handling Threads

To determine the thread that handles each client, use the string representation of the connection as the name of the thread. Because you assign all handler threads into a group and define a meaningful name for each thread, use the most general Thread constructor:

```
    Thread t = new Thread(group, clientHandler,
    ➥connection.toString());
    activeEstimate++;
    t.start();
    connection = null;
    clientHandler = null;
    t = null;
  }
}
catch (Exception e) {
  System.out.println(e);
}
```

Closing ServerSockets

As before, make sure to close the ServerSocket before exiting:

```
finally {
  try {
    listener.close();
  }
  catch (IOException e) {
  }
}
}

}
```

Note that your application still services only one client between the time the ServerSocket.accept() returns (indicating that a connection has been established) and the time it calls accept() again. Although most TCP implementations temporarily queue connection requests in order to give the server code time to call accept() again, you should do as little processing as possible in this loop to prevent unnecessarily rejected connections. The code creating the input and output streams, for example, belongs in the first few lines of the ClientHandler's run() method and executes on the new thread.

HTTPHandler Class

Because of its general nature and wide-spread browser support, HTTP is a good base client/server protocol for many customized applications. These custom servers are based on the generic HTTPHandler class, which provides basic HTTP operation. Later in this chapter, you will build two custom HTTP servers as part of the overall e-mail server.

Basic HTTP processing is very simple: You read a multiline request header terminated by a blank line. The first line of the request starts with a command keyword (GET, HEAD, POST, etc.), followed by a URL and HTTP version information. Subsequent lines provide additional information related to the request.

After processing the command, send a response header and response data back to the client. The response header begins with a line consisting of a protocol identifier ("HTTP/1.0"), a numeric response code, and explanatory text. Additional response information lines follow this response status line, and as with the request, the response header terminates in a blank line. A response code of 200 (following the "HTTP/1.0") indicates that the request was successful. The server closes the TCP connection after returning the response.

Eleven: Advanced Networking

Both the request and the response headers can contain modifiers or additional information fields. The format involves keyword/value pairs, one per line, with the keyword separated from the value information by a colon.

The HTTP protocol handler is an abstract subclass of ClientHandler. This handler supports only the three most common commands: GET, HEAD, and POST.

```
abstract class HTTPHandler extends ClientHandler {
  CommandInputStream in;
  InetOutputStream out;

  private final static String keywordList[] = {
  "GET", "POST", "HEAD"
  };

  static KeywordTable keywordTable =
  ➥CommandInputStream.createKeywordTable(keywordList);

  private final static int CMD_GET = 0;
  private final static int CMD_POST = 1;
  private final static int CMD_HEAD = 2;

  private final static String delimiters = "
  ➥\t\r\n";

  public HTTPHandler(Socket connection) {
  super(connection);
  }
```

Servicing HTTP Connections

Create the command input and output streams, and then read the HTTP request. For this simple HTTP server, ignore the other attributes of the request and call a handler method specific to each of the supported commands:

```
public void run() {
try {
  in = new CommandInputStream(connection.getInputStream(),
  ➥keywordTable, delimiters);
  out = new InetOutputStream(connection.getOutputStream(), false);
  int cmd = in.nextCommand();
```

continues

```
      String arg = in.nextArg();
      switch (cmd) {
        case CMD_GET:  handleGET(arg);
                       break;
        case CMD_POST: handlePOST(arg);
                       break;
        case CMD_HEAD: handleHEAD(arg);
                       break;
        default:       handleOther();
      }
    }
    catch (Exception e) {
      ServerLog.out.println(e);
    }
    finally {
      try {
        out.close();
      }
      catch (IOException e) {
      }
    }
  }
}
```

Handling HTTP Requests

If your subclass does not override a particular command method, the system returns a standard "not implemented" response. Because you normally expect multiline responses, the InetOutputStream appears in multiline mode that requires you to flush() the output:

```
void handleGET(String arg) throws IOException {
out.println("HTTP/1.0 501 method not implemented");
out.println();
out.flush();
}

void handleHEAD(String arg) throws IOException {
out.println("HTTP/1.0 501 method not implemented");
out.println();
out.flush();
}

void handlePOST(String arg) throws IOException {
out.println("HTTP/1.0 501 method not implemented");
out.println();
```

```
        out.flush();
        }

        void handleOther() throws IOException {
        out.println("HTTP/1.0 400 Bad request");
        out.println();
        out.flush();
        }

    }
```

Mail Storage Abstractions

Storage of e-mail ranks as a key component of your server. Two separate servers, SMTP and POP, interact with the e-mail store, so you must produce a common abstraction to isolate both services from the details of mail storage. The top-level class, MailDomain, produces abstract mail interactions for a community of users. You create a Maildrop class to manage the temporary storage on the mail server for a given user. (Maildrop distinguishes the temporary server storage of mail from the permanent storage in mail boxes on the client computers.)

MailDomain Class

The highest level abstraction, MailDomain, has both a name (its SMTP host name) and a set of users. Your SMTP and POP servers call the MailDomain object to validate recipient addresses, check passwords, and access a user's Maildrops. Information about users, such as their password, must be persistent. The Properties class provides both the persistent and quick access using hashing techniques, so you can implement the MailDomain by using a Properties object.

Mail Domain Properties File

Use the user name as the key to the Properties table; the return value string contains the user's password, Maildrop file name, and any other necessary information. A "|" character separates the fields. Meanwhile, the special user name DOMAIN.NAME stores the DNS name of the host. A sample MailDomain file follows:

```
DOMAIN.NAME=yourhost.com
Joe=bluesky¦/etc/mb/joe
Sue=redwood¦/etc/mb/sue
```

In this example, Joe's password is "bluesky," and Sue's mail is stored in "/etc/mb/sue."

In a complete production system, you must include ways to add a new user, delete a user, and change a user's password. For added security, you can store a one-way cipher of the password rather than plain text. In future Java releases, you also can use the new built-in security services to authenticate users. For this example, the operator must manually edit the Properties file.

Implementing the MailDomain Class

You create a new MailDomain instance with the file name of its properties file. The constructor loads the properties table from the file and determines the domain name:

```
public class MailDomain {
  Properties p;
  String domainName;

  MailDomain(String fname) throws IOException {
  p = new Properties();
  p.load(new FileInputStream(fname));
  domainName = p.getProperty("DOMAIN.NAME");
  if (domainName == null)
    throw new IOException("domain name property missing");
  System.out.println("Domain name is " + domainName);
  }

  String domainName() {
  return domainName;
  }
```

For larger systems, when it is not practical to load all user information into memory, you can change the implementation to access user information stored as a file. To provide this flexibility in implementation, MailDomain includes a Properties object rather than subclassing from Properties.

Validating the User

The MailDomain provides methods to validate a user for receipt of mail, to check a user's password for login, and to create the Maildrop object that provides access to the user's temporary mail store. To validate a mailbox name, first check the domain name and then verify the user:

```
boolean validateUser(String rcpt) {
if (rcpt.endsWith("@" + domainName)) {
  String user = rcpt.substring(0, rcpt.length() -
domainName.length() -1);
  return p.getProperty(user) != null;
  }
return false;
}
```

Verifying User Password

The "|" characters separate items in the user's properties string. The user's password appears as the first item in the list:

```
boolean checkPassword(String user, String passwd) {
String userInfo = p.getProperty(user);
return (userInfo != null) ? userInfo.startsWith(passwd + "|") :
false;
}
```

Opening the MailDrop File

Mail handling software calls getMaildrop()for the mail store abstraction for the indicated user. The domain properties file retrieves Information about the user's mail drop to create the Maildrop:

```
Maildrop getMaildrop(String user) throws IOException {
String userInfo = p.getProperty(user);
String mdfile = userInfo.substring(userInfo.indexOf('|') + 1,
userInfo.length());
return Maildrop.getMaildrop(mdfile);
}
```

Writing E-Mail to Maildrops

Finally, the MailDomain manages the process of writing a received message to the user's Maildrop. For each recipient, extract the local maildrop name, obtain its Maildrop object, and deliver the message. You can catch all exceptions and return false on any error. An additional try/finally block appears around md.deliverMsg() to guarantee Maildrop release-*

```
  boolean deliverMsg(String msg, Vector recipients) {
  try {
    Enumeration enum = recipients.elements();
    while (enum.hasMoreElements()) {
      String recp = (String)(enum.nextElement());
      String user = recp.substring(0, recp.lastIndexOf('@'));
      Maildrop md = getMaildrop(user);
      try {
        md.deliverMsg(msg);
      }
      finally {
        md.release();
      }
    }
    return true;
  }
  catch (Exception e) {
    ServerLog.out.println(e);
    return false;
  }
  }

}
```

Maildrop Class

Maildrop objects shield the mail handling servers and the MailDomain class from the implementation details of mail storage. You can store the actual mail messages in several ways. The most common ways are storing one message per file within a directory dedicated to a user, or storing all messages for a user within a single file. The first method is more processor-efficient for temporary storage of a few messages, while the second method offers more space efficiency for longer-term storage. In addition, you can use database facilities for mail stores. For the following exercise, store messages one per file in a directory for each user.

Maildrop directories contain only message-related files created and managed by a Maildrop object. To maintain reception order, message files receive numeric names in an ascending order. That is, the first message stored in a file earns the name "1," while a second message becomes "2."

Creating Maildrop Objects

Create a Maildrop object by passing it the name of the user's mail directory:

```
public class Maildrop {
  static Hashtable maildropList = new Hashtable();
  int useCounter;
  String fname;
  String prefix;
  boolean locked;
  int msgID[];
  boolean msgDeleted[];
  int msgLength[];

  Maildrop(String fname) throws IOException {
  locked = false;
  this.fname = fname;
  prefix = fname + File.separator;
  }
```

Synchronization issues are critical for Maildrop objects. One or more threads may attempt to deliver a new message into a mailbox at the same time another thread retrieves messages. To support both concurrent SMTP and POP access, you can allow multiple SMTP threads to deliver new mail but only one POP client to control the maildrop.

Accessing Mail Directories

Your handler calls getMaildrop() to access the mail directory, and then release() when finished. If a Maildrop object for the indicated user is already allocated, the system returns that object; otherwise, it creates a new instance. A useCounter keeps track of the number of handlers using a given Maildrop object. Because you call it to obtain a Maildrop instance, getMaildrop() must be a class method:

```
static Maildrop getMaildrop(String fname) throws IOException {
Maildrop md;
synchronized (maildropList) {
  md = (Maildrop)(maildropList.get(fname));
  if (md == null)
    md = new Maildrop(fname);
  md.useCounter++;
}
return md;
}
```

Releasing Mail Directories

Remove the Maildrop object from the instance list when all handlers have released it:

```
synchronized void release() {
useCounter—;
if (useCounter == 0)
  maildropList.remove(this);
}
```

Scanning Mail Directories

A directory stores messages as files. You can obtain a list of messages by scanning the contents of the mail drop directory:

```
String[] listMailfolder() throws IOException {
File md = new File(fname);
if (!md.exists() ¦¦ !md.canRead() ¦¦ !md.isDirectory())
  throw new FileNotFoundException("not a maildrop");
String files[] = md.list();
return files;
}
```

Delivering Mail Messages

Delivery is relatively easy with one message per file. Simply scan the directory to determine the highest file name, increase this value by 1, create a new file, and write your message. Because you rescan the directory within this method, you can allow multiple threads to deliver messages by using the synchronized modifier:

```
synchronized void deliverMsg(String msg) throws IOException {
int maxID = 0;
String files[] = listMailfolder();
for (int i = 0; i < files.length; i++) {
  int id = Integer.parseInt(files[i]);
  if (id > maxID)
    maxID = id;
}
maxID++;
RandomAccessFile fs = new RandomAccessFile(prefix + maxID, "rw");
fs.writeBytes(msg);
fs.close();
}
```

Retrieving Mail Messages

Retrieving messages from the maildrop is much more complicated than adding them. Three arrays capture the state of the maildrop. Because the file names are numeric text strings, you can convert these file names back into numbers for easy sorting and manipulation. The msgID[] stores and lists these message ID values or file names as ints. These IDs appear in an increasing order to reflect the order of delivery into the maildrop.

Marking Messages for Deletion

The msgDeleted[] provides a flag for each message to indicate that the message is marked for deletion. The third array surveys the length of each message. You build this information each time you call refresh():

```
void refresh() throws IOException {
String files[] = listMailfolder();
msgID = new int[files.length];
for (int i = 0; i < files.length; i++) {
  int id = Integer.parseInt(files[i]);
  int j = 0;
  while ((j < i) && (id > msgID[j]))
    j++;
  System.arraycopy(msgID, j, msgID, j+1, i-j);
  msgID[j] = id;
}
msgDeleted = new boolean[msgID.length];
msgLength = new int[msgID.length];
for (int i = 0; i < msgID.length; i++) {
  msgDeleted[i] = false;
  msgLength[i] = computeLength(i);
}
}
```

Restricting Multiple Maildrop Logins

To prevent multiple POP e-mail clients from manipulating the same Maildrop, you can define a locking mechanism. This ensures only one maildrop login at a time. When you lock the Maildrop, you also build the list of messages in the mail drop by calling refresh(). Likewise, when you unlock the maildrop, you clear its message information and must provide a subsequent lock() before you can manipulate messages. This locking mechanism is implemented as follows:

```
synchronized boolean lock() {
if (locked)
  return false;
try {
  refresh();
  locked = true;
  return true;
}
catch (IOException e) {
  ServerLog.out.println(e);
  return false;
}
}

boolean isLocked() {
return locked;
}

void unlock() {
msgID = null;
msgDeleted = null;
msgLength = null;
locked = false;
}
```

Counting Maildrop Messages

You also can provide methods that count the number of messages in the mail drop,
compute the length of each message, and compute the total mail drop length. POP requires
these functions. Because SMTP stores messages with the required two-character end-of-
line sequence ("\r\n"), you can use the file length as the POP message length:

```
int count() {
return msgID.length;
}

int messageLength(int id) {
return msgLength[id];
}

int maildropLength() {
int total = 0;
for (int i = 0; i < msgLength.length; i++)
```

```
    total += msgLength[i];
  return total;
  }

  protected int computeLength(int id) throws IOException {
  File f = new File(prefix + msgID[id]);
  return (int) f.length();
  }
```

Accessing Message Content

To make the contents of a message available as an InputStream, open the file that holds the message and return a FileInputStream object:

```
InputStream getMessage(int id) throws IOException {
  return new FileInputStream(prefix + msgID[id]);
  }
```

Resetting Message Deletion Flag

To support deleting messages and subsequent undeletion before committing changes, you must maintain an array of flags that indicate whether a given message is marked for deletion. You must also provide a reset() method that resets the deletion flags:

```
void delete(int id) {
  msgDeleted[id] = true;
  }

void reset() {
  for (int i = 0; i < msgDeleted.length; i++)
    msgDeleted[i] = false;
  }
```

Updating the Maildrop

After the POP session, either unlock() the maildrop or update() it with changes made during the POP session. When you update the maildrop, the system deletes any messages so marked and unlocks the maildrop:

```
void update() {
  for (int i = 0; i < msgDeleted.length; i++) {
    if (msgDeleted[i]) {
```

continues

```
            File f = new File(prefix + Integer.toString(msgID[i]));
            f.delete();
        }
    }
    unlock();
    }


}
```

Simple Message Transport Protocol (SMTP)

Originally, e-mail transmission was a function handled by the file transfer protocol (FTP). When the networking community migrated to TCP/IP, the e-mail functions separated into a separate protocol based on FTP. This link appears in the command syntax and response code formats. Commands from the client to the servers are four-letter commands followed by a space. Responses from the server to the client start with a three-digit response code, followed by a user-readable text message.

The Simple Message Transport Protocol (SMTP) is specified in RFC821. Initiate the SMTP session by sending a HELO command, and terminate the session with a QUIT command. Sending a message in SMTP involves a three-step process:

1. Initiate the sequence and identify the sender of the message with a MAIL FROM: command.

2. Specify the recipients using one or more RECP TO: commands.

3. Transmit the message by issuing a DATA command, writing the message to the server, and ending it with a line containing only a "." character.

Responses from the server to the client appear in a special format designed for easy processing. Single-line responses, or the last line of a multiline response, begin with the 3-digit code, followed by a space character. Each line except the last in a multiline response starts with the three-digit code, followed by the "-" character; the last line starts with the three-digit code, followed by a space. The system expects the same three-digit code in all lines of a multiline response. The response codes are designed for automated processing without regard to the text:

■ A first digit of 2 indicates success.

■ A first digit of 3 indicates success in a multi-command sequence.

- A first digit of 4 indicates temporary failure.
- A first digit of 5 indicates permanent failure.

The second digit involves additional categories. In practice, each SMTP command defines a specific set of expected three-digit response codes. Servers should use one of the defined codes to ensure maximum operability with clients.

Sending Mail Using SMTP

After constructing your toolkit and basic classes, you can shift your attention to building the client and servers applications. The first application is sending e-mail. As previously identified, mail moves from the client to the server through SMTP.

Figure 11.6 shows the packet exchanges between the client and server when sending one message.

FIGURE 11.6

SMTP packet exchanges to send a message to User1 and User2.

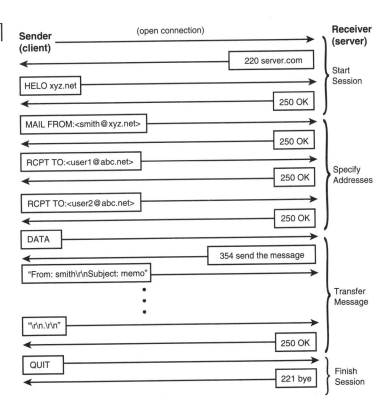

An SMTP Client

Before building the server, construct a client to become familiar with SMTP operation. Because SMTP operates on e-mail messages, model your object design around the message rather than the e-mail protocol.

The SMTPMessage class contains String variables for the relay host name, the sender and recipient's mail addresses, the subject or header, and the body. As an extension to the example in this section, you can add a Vector of parts for a multimedia version.

Creating SMTPMessage Objects

Create an SMTPMessage object by specifying the name of your e-mail relay host. For applets, the standard security manager restricts the relay host to the same as the document's codeBase. The default SMTP port 25 applies if you do not specify otherwise:

```java
public class SMTPMessage {
  protected String smtpServer;
  protected String from;
  protected String to;
  protected String subject;
  protected String header;
  protected String body;
  protected int smtpPort;

  protected DataInputStream in;
  protected InetOutputStream out;

  private final static int defaultPort = 25;

  private SMTPMessage() {
  }

  public SMTPMessage(String server) {
  this(server, defaultPort);
  }

  public SMTPMessage(String server, int port) {
  smtpServer = server;
  smtpPort = port;
  }
```

Setting Message Header Fields

Provide the following accessor methods to set the various String variables that hold information about the message:

```java
public void setFrom(String from) {
this.from = from;
}

public void setTo(String to) {
this.to = to;
}

public void setSubject(String sub) {
subject = sub;
}

public void setHeader(String hdr) {
header = hdr;
}

public void setBody(String body) {
this.body = body;
}
```

Sending the Message

The submit() method performs the actual protocol processing. After you verify the parameters, open a connection to the SMTP relay host and create the input and output streams. The server sends a "220" response with its official host name as an argument. You respond with a HELO command with your host name:

```java
public void submit() throws IOException {
    if ((from == null) || (to == null))
      throw new IllegalArgumentException("missing parameters");
    Socket s = new Socket(smtpServer, smtpPort);
    try {
      in = new DataInputStream(s.getInputStream());
      out = new InetOutputStream(s.getOutputStream(), true);
      checkResponse("220", "");
      out.println("HELO there.com");
      checkResponse("250", "HELO: ");
```

Sending Message Content

After sending the HELO, enter the mail mode by sending a MAIL FROM: command with the sender's mail address. In SMTP, < and > brackets surround mail addresses, as in the example, <smith@xyz.com>. Next, send the recipient's addresses, followed by the actual message content. After receiving the complete message, the server returns its response. Finish the transfer by sending a QUIT command:

```
      out.println("MAIL FROM:<" + from + ">");
      checkResponse("250", "MAIL FROM: ");

      sendRecipients();
      sendData();
      out.println("QUIT");
      checkResponse("221", "QUIT ");
      out.close();
    }
    catch (IOException e) {
      s.close();
      throw e;
    }
    }
  }
```

Verifying Response Codes

Use checkResponse() to verify the reception to the expected three-digit reply code. This method also handles the multi-line response format. If the response does not match, the system throws an exception:

```
    protected void checkResponse(String resp, String msg) throws
    ➡IOException {
    String str = in.readLine();
    if (!str.startsWith(resp)) {
      throw new SMTPErrorException(msg + str);
      }
    while (str.startsWith(resp + '-'))
      str = in.readLine();
    }
```

Addressing E-mail Recipients

SMTPMessage accepts a comma-separated list of recipient e-mail addresses. Two address forms are accepted: the specific "user@host.net" and the personalized form with a text string (usually the user's name), followed by the actual Internet address in angle brackets. Extract each Internet mail address from the string, and send it to the server, one per RCPT command. Follow this format: RCPT TO:<someone@xxx.org>. The server acknowledges each recipient individually, so you loop until the complete string is processed:

```java
protected void sendRecipients() throws IOException {
int currIndex = 0;
try {
  while (to.length() > currIndex) {
    String rcpt;
    int endIndex = to.indexOf(',', currIndex);
    if (endIndex == -1)
      endIndex = to.length();
    rcpt = to.substring(currIndex, endIndex);
    currIndex = endIndex + 1;
    int start = rcpt.indexOf('<');
    if (start >= 0)
      rcpt = rcpt.substring(start + 1, rcpt.indexOf('>'));
    rcpt = rcpt.trim();
    out.println("RCPT TO:<" + rcpt + ">");
    checkResponse("250", "RCPT TO: ");
  }
}
catch (SMTPErrorException e) {
  System.out.println(e);
  throw new UnknownUserException();
}
}
```

Formatting and Sending SMTP Messages

After identifying all the recipients, send the DATA command. You assemble the message header from its component fields for such information as date, from, and to, and separate the header from the message body with a blank line. RFC822 defines the detailed syntax of Internet mail messages. If a text body is supplied, add an extra "." to the start of any line that begins with a "." to prevent a false end-of-message indication. Finally, mark the end of the message with a line that contains only a ".", which is the string ".\r\n". After the server reads the sequence "\r\n.\r\n", it delivers the message to the indicated maildrops and returns a response code. The method to format and send an SMTP message follows:

```java
protected void sendData() throws IOException {
  out.println("DATA");
  checkResponse("354", "DATA: ");
  out.setLinemode(false);
  out.println("Date: " + new InetDate());
  out.println("From: " + from);
  out.println("To: " + to);
  if (subject != null)
    out.println("Subject: " + subject);
  if (header != null)
    out.println(header);
  out.println();

  if (body != null) {
    StringBuffer buf = new StringBuffer(body.length());
    int first = 0;
    int last;
    while ((last = body.indexOf("\n.", first)) != -1) {
      buf.append(body.substring(first, last) + "\n..");
      first = last + 2;
    }
    if (first > 0) {
      buf.append(body.substring(first));
      out.print(buf.toString());
    }
    else
      out.print(body);
  }
  out.println();
  out.println(".");
  out.flush();
  checkResponse("250", "message: ");
  out.setLinemode(true);
}
```

Defining Exceptions

Define the following two new exceptions that relate directly to SMTP processing:

```java
class UnknownUserException extends IOException {
  UnknownUserException() {
  }

  UnknownUserException(String msg) {
```

```
  super(msg);
  }
}

class SMTPErrorException extends IOException {
  SMTPErrorException() {
  }

  SMTPErrorException(String msg) {
  super(msg);
  }
}
```

SMTP Applet Client

You can use SMTPMessage for several aspects of your web page. Here, you build an
applet that sends comments back to you through e-mail. To use this applet, you must
define the recipient address in your code or web page. Replace the string "me@there.com"
with your actual e-mail address:

```
public class SMTPApplet extends Applet {
  TextField fromLine;
  TextField toLine;
  TextArea body;

  public static final String MAILBOX = "me@there.com";
```

Basic Interface Layout

In init(), you create a simple BorderLayout panel with a text line asking for user comments, a TextArea to accept typing, and a "Send" button. Figure 11.7 shows the results of
the code.

```
  public void init() {
  setLayout(new BorderLayout());
  add("North", new Label("Please enter your comments:"));
  body = new TextArea(15, 40);
  add("Center", body);
  Panel p = new Panel();
  p.setLayout(new BorderLayout());
  p.add("East", new Button("Send"));
  add("South",p);
  show();
  }
```

Figure 11.7

The resultant dialog box.

Handling Message Submission

You provide a standard action() method to handle the button press. When the user clicks on "Send," you create a new SMTPMessage, set its to/from fields, and call submit(). Because sending the message can demand some time, you should consider creating a new thread solely to call submit() and allow the main user interface thread to continue. The basic action() method follows:

```
public boolean action(Event e, Object arg) {
if (e.target instanceof Button) {
  String what = (String)arg;
  if (what.equals("Send")) {
    try {
      SMTPMessage msg = new SMTPMessage(getCodeBase().getHost());
      msg.setFrom("applet@thishost.net");
      msg.setTo(MAILBOX);
      msg.setBody(body.getText());
      msg.submit();
    }
    catch (Exception ex) {
      System.out.println(ex);
    }
    return true;
  }
}
return super.action(e, arg);
}
}
```

SMTPHandler

Now build the SMTP server side, starting with its factory object. Because the SMTP handlers must access the MailDomain, the MailDomain object is passed into the factory and stored for use when creating handler objects. This factory definition assigns SMTP to port 25 by default:

```
public class SMTPFactory extends ClientHandlerFactory
{
    MailDomain domain;

    public SMTPFactory(MailDomain domain, int port) {
    this.domain = domain;
    this.port = port;
    }

    public SMTPFactory(MailDomain domain) {
    this(domain, 25);
    }

    String getName() {
    return "SMTP";
    }

    ClientHandler createClientHandler(Socket
    ➥connection) {
    return new SMTPHandler(connection, domain);
    }
}
```

> **NOTE**
>
> If your computer runs an SMTP server on port 25, the call to create the ServerSocket fails. Only one program can access a server socket at a time. If you use a Unix computer, you also might not have privileges to use a well-known socket—multiuser operating systems generally protect the well-known sockets in order to keep users from replacing a standard server with their own version. In either case, you can test your server by changing the factory to use a different port number outside the protected range. Generally, this port number is greater than 1024.

Creating Command Keyword Tables

The SMTP handler itself subclasses from ClientHandler and contains a static command keyword table:

```
class SMTPHandler extends ClientHandler {
  MailDomain domain;
  CommandInputStream in = null;
  InetOutputStream out;

  private final static String keywordList[] = {
  "RCPT", "MAIL", "DATA", "HELO", "QUIT", "RSET","NOOP"
  };
```

continues

```
static KeywordTable keywordTable =
➥CommandInputStream.createKeywordTable(keywordList);

    private final static int CMD_RCPT = 0;
    private final static int CMD_MAIL = 1;
    private final static int CMD_DATA = 2;
    private final static int CMD_HELO = 3;
    private final static int CMD_QUIT = 4;
    private final static int CMD_RSET = 5;
    private final static int CMD_NOOP = 6;

    private final static String delimiters = " \t\r\n";

    public SMTPHandler(Socket connection, MailDomain domain) {
    super(connection);
    this.domain = domain;
    }
```

Responding to Connection Openings

The protocol processing occurs inside your run() method. After creating the input and output streams, start the client exchange by sending a reply code of "220" and your domain name. Essentially, you respond to the connection opening. The first command you receive should be a HELO, which supplies the clients's name:

```
public void run() {
try {
  InputStream inStream = new
  ➥TimeoutInputStream(connection.getInputStream());
  in = new CommandInputStream(inStream, keywordTable, delimiters);
  out = new InetOutputStream(connection.getOutputStream(), true);
  String cmdLine;

  out.println("220 " + domain.domainName() + " ready");
  if (in.nextCommand() != CMD_HELO) {
    out.println("503 Bad sequence of commands");
    return;
  }
  if (in.hasMoreArgs()) {
    System.out.println("connected to " + in.nextArg("\r\n"));
  }
  out.println("250 " + domain.domainName());
```

Handling E-Mail Commands

After responding, enter a loop of collecting keywords and performing protocol processing. You support the minimum required set of commands for exchanging e-mail:

- MAIL: Command to initiate a message transfer
- RSET: Command to reset the protocol state
- NOOP: No operation command
- QUIT: Command to terminate the session

Receiving any other command indicates an error. MAIL is a complex operation, so you provide a separate function to perform this operation. For RSET and NOOP, simply respond "OK"; for QUIT, exit. Again, the "finally" clause ensures proper closing of the connection. The basic command loop follows:

```
      while (true) {
        int cmd = in.nextCommand();
        switch (cmd) {
          case CMD_MAIL:
            receiveMAIL();
            break;

          case CMD_RSET:
          case CMD_NOOP:
            out.println("250 OK");
            break;

          case CMD_QUIT:
            out.println("221 bye");
            return;

          case CommandInputStream.TT_OTHER:
System.out.println("unknown command - " + in.getCommandString());

          default:
            out.println("503 Bad command sequence");
            return;
        }
      }
    }
    catch (Exception e) {
      System.out.println(e);
    }
    finally {
```

continues

```
    try {
      out.close();
    }
    catch (IOException e) {
      System.out.println(e);
    }
  }
}
```

As you learned in coding the SMTP client, the MAIL command initiates a sequence of additional commands that lead to the transmission of the message. You will receive the following:

- The MAIL FROM command, which identifies the sender of the message
- One or more RECP TO: commands, which identifies the recipients of the message
- A DATA command, which indicates the start of the message transmission
- The actual message, which ends with a line containing only a "." character

Getting Sender's E-Mail Address

In SMTP, < and > brackets surround all e-mail addresses. You can switch delimiter sets to extract the next argument, which is the sender's mail address:

```
void receiveMAIL() throws IOException {
String arg = in.nextArg(" <\r\n");
if (!"FROM:".equalsIgnoreCase(arg)) {
  out.println("503 Bad command sequence");
  throw new BadCmdSequence("MAIL " + arg);
}
out.println("250 OK");
String sender = in.nextArg(" <>\r\n");
```

Collecting E-mail Recipient Addresses

Allocate a Vector to hold the list of recipient addresses. Each address is specified in its own RCPT TO: command. For each address, you validate your ability to accept mail for that user, and you continue to collect recipients until receiving the DATA command:

```
Vector recipients = new Vector();
boolean done = false;
while (!done) {
  switch (in.nextCommand()) {
    case CMD_RCPT:
```

```
              arg = in.nextArg(" <\r\n");
              if (!"TO:".equalsIgnoreCase(arg)) {
                out.println("503 Bad command sequence");
                throw new BadCmdSequence("RCPT " + arg);
              }
              String recp = in.nextArg(" <>\r\n");
              if (domain.validateUser(recp)) {
                recipients.addElement(recp);
                out.println("250 OK");
              }
              else
                out.println("550 invalid user");
              break;
            case CMD_DATA:
              done = true;
              break;
            case CMD_NOOP:
              continue;
            case CMD_RSET:
              return;
            case CMD_QUIT:
              out.println("221 bye");
              throw new IOException("aborted");
            default:
              out.println("503 Bad command sequence");
              throw new BadCmdSequence(in.getCommandString());
          }
        }
        out.println("354 send message");
```

Collecting the Message Text

The message is transmitted as a sequence of lines terminated by a line containing only a
".". To prevent false indication of end-of-message if the message contains lines with only a
".", the client adds an extra "." to any line starting with a ".". You must reverse this process
and strip the first "." from any line of more than one character. After collecting the
complete message, deliver the message to the recipients and return the appropriate
response code. Note that the MailDomain class hides all the details of mail storage from
the SMTP server:

```
    StringBuffer msg = new StringBuffer();
    while (true) {
      String str = in.readLine();
```

continues

```
     if ((str.length() > 0) && (str.charAt(0) == '.')) {
       if (str.length() == 1)
         break;
       str = str.substring(1, str.length());
     }
     msg.append(str);
     msg.append("\r\n");
   }
   if (domain.deliverMsg(msg.toString(), recipients))
     out.println("250 OK");
   else
     out.println("450 failure");
   }
 }
```

Indicating SMTP Command-Processing Errors

Define the following new exception to indicate an error in SMTP command processing:

```
class BadCmdSequence extends IOException {
  public BadCmdSequence() {
  super("Bad command sequence");
  }

  public BadCmdSequence(String what) {
  super("Bad command sequence: " + what);
  }
}
```

Receiving Mail Using POP

POP, or the Post Office Protocol, provides a means for a client to retrieve mail held on a server. POP is designed for personal computers that, unlike large servers, only periodically connect to the Internet. With SMTP, the sender controls delivery of a message. When a message is sent through SMTP, the server usually tries to connect to the destination immediately. If the destination is not available, the server periodically retries until it returns the message as undeliverable; the sender defines the timing of the retries. With POP, the message remains on a server until the client connects to retrieve it. POP makes it practical to send e-mail to a subscriber attached to the Internet via a dial-up connection.

The POP command/response procedures are similar to but simpler than SMTP procedures. A "+OK" indicates positive responses, whereas an "-ERR" indicates negative responses.

In a typical scenario, the client follows these steps:

1. Log in to the server by sending a USER and PASS commands.
2. Determine the number of waiting messages by using the STAT command.
3. Retrieve each message using RETR and then mark the message for deletion using DELE.
4. Exit and delete the message by using the QUIT command.

A typical POP session is shown in figure 11.8 where the user logs in and retrieves one message.

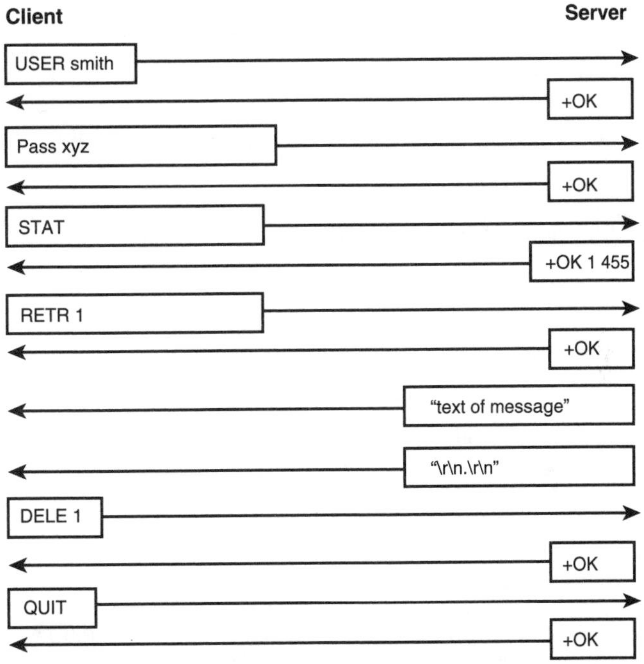

FIGURE 11.8
POP3 packet exchanges to retrieve and delete one message.

POP3HandlerFactory Class

You provide the usual factory to create the POP handler on the standard well-known port of 110. For an intranet server, modify the factory to place additional restrictions on the client. For example, you can allow access to your POP server only from your own networks. This factory accepts connections from any clients and depends on the password facility to keep mail private:

```
public class POP3HandlerFactory extends ClientHandlerFactory {
  MailDomain domain;

  public POP3HandlerFactory(MailDomain domain) {
  this.domain = domain;
  }

  int serverPort() {
  return 110;
  }

  String getName() {
  return "POP";
  }

  ClientHandler createClientHandler(Socket connection) {
  return new POP3Handler(connection, domain);
  }
}
```

POP3Handler Class

Your POP3 handler supports only the minimum required commands for a POP server. The handler does not support the use of the server as a semi-permanent mailbox. The POP3 handler subclasses ClientHandler and initializes its static keyword table for command parsing:

```
class POP3Handler extends ClientHandler {
  CommandInputStream in;
  InetOutputStream out;
  MailDomain domain;
  Maildrop md;

  private final static String keywordList[] = {
  "STAT", "LIST", "RETR", "DELE", "QUIT", "RSET", "NOOP", "USER",
  ➥"PASS"
  };

  static KeywordTable keywordTable =
  ➥CommandInputStream.createKeywordTable(keywordList);

  private final static int CMD_STAT = 0;
  private final static int CMD_LIST = 1;
```

```
private final static int CMD_RETR = 2;
private final static int CMD_DELE = 3;
private final static int CMD_QUIT = 4;
private final static int CMD_RSET = 5;
private final static int CMD_NOOP = 6;
private final static int CMD_USER = 7;
private final static int CMD_PASS = 8;

private final static String delimiters = " \t\r\n";

public POP3Handler(Socket connection, MailDomain domain) {
super(connection);
this.domain = domain;
}
```

Opening POP3 Session

In your run() method, you create your input and output streams and then send a "+OK"
response to the client. The client responds with USER and PASS commands to authenticate access to the maildrop:

```
public void run() {
try {
  in = new CommandInputStream(connection.getInputStream(),
  ➥keywordTable, delimiters);
  out = new InetOutputStream(connection.getOutputStream(), true);

  out.println("+OK ready");
  if (in.nextCommand() != CMD_USER) {
    out.println("-ERR");
    return;
  }
  String user = in.nextArg();
  out.println("+OK");
  if (in.nextCommand() != CMD_PASS) {
    out.println("-ERR must enter password");
    return;
  }
  String passwd = in.hasMoreArgs() ? in.nextArg() : "";
  if (!domain.checkPassword(user, passwd)) {
    out.println("-ERR invalid login");
    return;
  }
```

Providing Maildrop Access

After checking the password, obtain the user's Maildrop and lock it. If the Maildrop is involved in another POP session, the lock() call returns false, and you respond with "mailbox busy." After the user logs onto the POP3 server, call handleCommands() to provide access to the maildrop. Use the "finally" clause to ensure that you release the maildrop if you terminate abnormally:

```
    md = domain.getMaildrop(user);
    if (!md.lock()) {
      out.println("-ERR mailbox busy");
      return;
    }
    out.println("+OK");

    handleCommands();
  }
  catch (Exception e) {
    System.out.println(e);
  }
  finally {
    if (md != null)
      md.release();
    try {
      out.close();
    }
    catch (IOException e) {
    }
  }
}
```

Handling POP Commands

After the user logs onto the POP3 server, you can read a command, execute it and loop until the user issues a QUIT command. Call handler methods for all non-trivial command processing:

```
  void handleCommands() throws Exception {
  try {
    boolean done = false;
    while (!done) {
      int cmd = in.nextCommand();
      switch (cmd) {
        case CMD_STAT:
          handleSTAT();
          break;
```

```
        case CMD_LIST:
            handleLIST();
            break;

        case CMD_RETR:
            handleRETR();
            break;

        case CMD_DELE:
            handleDELE();
            break;

        case CMD_RSET:
            md.reset();
            break;

        case CMD_NOOP:
            out.println("+OK");
            break;

        case CMD_QUIT:
            done = true;
            break;

        default:
            out.println("-ERR bad command");
        }
    }
    out.println("+OK");
    md.update();
}
catch (Exception e) {
    md.unlock();
    throw e;
}
}
```

Determining Maildrop Information

In response to the STAT command, return the number of messages waiting in the maildrop and the total number of characters in those messages:

```
void handleSTAT() throws IOException {
out.println("+OK " + md.count() + " " + md.maildropLength());
}
```

Determining Message Length

The client uses the LIST command to obtain the length of a given message, or a message-by-message indication of the size of each message in the maildrop. You only include those messages not marked for deletion. In POP, multiline responses are terminated by a line containing only a ".". Because the other lines of the response never start with a ".", it is not necessary to check for doubling of an initial ".":

```
void handleLIST() throws IOException {
int count = md.count();
if (in.hasMoreArgs()) {
  int id = Integer.parseInt(in.nextArg());
  if ((id <= count) && md.msgDeleted[id - 1]) {
    out.println("+OK");
    out.println("" + id + " " + md.messageLength(id - 1));
    out.println(".");
  }
  else
    out.println("-ERR invalid msg number");
}
else {
  out.println("+OK");
  for (int i = 0; i < count; i++) {
    if (!md.msgDeleted[i])
      out.println("" + (i+1) + " " +  md.messageLength(i));
  }
  out.println(".");
}
}
```

Retrieving Messages

In response to a RETR command, return the indicated message. POP numbers messages waiting in the maildrop starting from 1. Because you expect the message to constitute many, switch the output steam to manual flush. Afterwards, restore the output to line mode. As with SMTP, you must insert an extra "." in front of any line that starts with a ".". This code appears similar to that found in SMTPMessage:

```
void handleRETR() throws IOException {
int cnt;
int i = Integer.parseInt(in.nextArg()) - 1;
out.setLinemode(false);
out.println("+OK");
InputStream in = md.getMessage(i);
byte buf[] = new byte[1024];
while ((cnt = in.read(buf)) > 0) {
```

```
     out.write(buf, 0, cnt);
   }
   in.close();
   out.println(".");
   out.flush();
   out.setLinemode(true);
 }
```

Deleting Messages

In response to a DELE command, mark the indicated message for deletion:

```
void handleDELE() throws IOException {
if (in.hasMoreArgs()) {
  md.delete(Integer.parseInt(in.nextArg()) - 1);
  out.println("+OK");
}
else
  out.println("-ERR msg number needed");
}

}
```

NOTE

When implementing the same approach using Jeeves, define a servlet rather than a completely different HTTP service. Servlets are the server-side equivalents of applets; that is, Java programs designed to execute in an environment provided by an HTTP server and intended as a Java-style replacement for Common Gateway Interface (CGI) programs. The servlet queries the name database and returns the answer to the client.

You do not actually delete the message until the POP session has been closed.

Querying the Name/ Address Database

You might decide to forgo complex query protocols for the simplicity of a CGI-style query using HTTP. HTTP defines two different approaches for sending a query to the server: GET and POST. Using GET, you include the query information as part of the URL, which is separated from the CGI information with a "?". Using POST, you send the query information as a content body appended to the request. Because of the simple nature of the name queries, you use the much simpler ISINDEX form of GET. To retrieve a user's e-mail address, your client sends a "GET" request to the server with a URL of "/address", followed by a "?" and the user's name.

Implementing the NameQueryFactory

Because you want the query server to run concurrently with other normal HTTP servers, you cannot use the standard port 80. Instead, assign it port 1234 in your factory class. The factory class for the NameQuery server follows:

```java
public class NameQueryFactory extends ClientHandlerFactory {
    public NameQueryFactory() {
    this(1234);
    }

    public NameQueryFactory(int port) {
    this.port = port;
    }

    String getName() {
    return "NameQuery";
    }

    ClientHandler createClientHandler(Socket connection) {
    return new NameQueryHandler(connection);
    }
}
```

Implementing the NameQueryHandler

Your NameQueryHandler simply subclasses the basic HTTPHandler:

```java
class NameQueryHandler extends HTTPHandler {

    public NameQueryHandler(Socket connection) {
    super(connection);
    }
```

Override handleGet() to parse the URL of the query, look up the answer, and then return it as plain text. The "content-type" field tells the browser how to handle the data in the response. "Text/plain" indicates that the data is text, instead of sound or some other information type, and preformatted ASCII, instead of HTML. By using the content-type information, web browsers display the information you send as if it was printed to the Java console. Any substantial user database is stored on disk as a file or database. The following example provides an outline to which you can add your specific database access code:

```
    void handleGET(String arg) throws IOException {
    StringTokenizer st = new StringTokenizer(arg, " ?\n\r");
    if ("/address".equalsIgnoreCase(st.nextToken())) {
      if (st.hasMoreTokens()) {
        String user = st.nextToken();
        out.println("HTTP/1.0 200 OK");
        out.println("server: ISJhttpd/1.0");
        out.println("content-type: text/plain");
        out.println();

        // lookup and output user's information

        out.flush();
      }
      else {
        out.println("HTTP/1.0 200 OK");
        out.println("server: ISJhttpd/1.0");
        out.println("content-type: text/plain");
        out.println();

        // lookup and output everything in database

        out.flush();
      }
    }
    else {
      out.println("HTTP/1.0 404 not found");
      out.println();
      out.flush();
    }
    }
}
```

The Complete E-Mail Server

After completing the implementation of the protocol-specific server code, you can proceed to put the pieces together to form the complete e-mail server application. First, however, you must deal with the non-network protocol problems of operating and maintaining a practical server environment. These functions include monitoring server status, logging of events, and configuring the server.

Monitoring

Network management and monitoring is a complex subject with its own suite of protocols, such as SNMP or CMIP, and specialized client software. Instead of writing another complex server, however, you can reuse existing server code and client applications to provide some simple status-monitoring functions. Use HTTP instead of a network management protocol to turn any web browser into a status display console. Follow the same approach as the NameQueryServer, and subclass HTTPHandler.

Implementing the same approach using Jeeves, define a servlet instead of a completely different HTTP service. The servlet computes the status information and returns it to the client. As a separate HTTP server, the status service can run at a different (and probably lower) thread priority than other HTTP-based services.

By default, your factory places the StatusServer on port 1235 to avoid conflict with normal HTTP or the NameQuery server:

```
public class ServerStatusFactory extends
ClientHandlerFactory {
  public ServerStatusFactory() {
  this(1235);
  }

  public ServerStatusFactory(int port) {
  this.port = port;
  }

  String getName() {
  return "Status";
  }

  ClientHandler createClientHandler(Socket connection) {
  return new ServerStatusHandler(connection);
  }
}
```

This sample server supports two URLs or commands:

- View server-specific status
- View general runtime status.

For server-specific status, obtain the list of servers maintained as a Server class variable, and go through the list getting infomation about each service. The exact information is server-specific and not defined in this example.

The runtime status response uses a client-pull technique to periodically update the display. The "refresh:" attribute of the response instructs your browser to automatically reload the page after the indicated interval. In this case, ask for reloads every 30 seconds. The "content-type: text/plain" indicates that preformatted ASCII is returned. The code for the server follows:

```
class ServerStatusHandler extends HTTPHandler {

  public ServerStatusHandler(Socket connection) {
  super(connection);
  }

  void handleGET(String arg) throws IOException {
  if ("/status".equalsIgnoreCase(arg)) {
    out.println("HTTP/1.0 200 OK");
    out.println("server: ISJhttpd/1.0");
    out.println("content-type: text/plain");
    out.println();
    Enumeration enum = Server.elements();
    while (enum.hasMoreElements()) {
      Server s = (Server)(enum.nextElement());

      // compute and format status information

    }
    out.flush();
  }
  else {
    out.println("HTTP/1.0 200 OK");
    out.println("server: ISJhttpd/1.0");
    out.println("content-type: text/plain");
    out.println("refresh: 0");
    out.println();
    Runtime r = Runtime.getRuntime();
    out.println(new InetDate());
    out.println("free memory: " + r.freeMemory());
    out.println("total memory: " + r.totalMemory());
    out.flush();
    }
  }
}
```

Using HTTP, it is simple to define additional commands. You can extend the "/status" URL to an ISINDEX query with the name of a specific server, or you can add additional URLs for other types of status information.

Logging Messages

In the previous examples, you print status and error messages to System.out. Although useful for debugging, you want to log status and error messages to a file for later analysis when dealing with an operating server. Writing to a file can result in delays in servicing clients as the log message writes to disk. To avoid this added delay, perform the actual file output in a thread separate from those handling clients. Client handlers communicate with the logging thread using a PipedOutputStream / PipedInputStream pair, which provides an in-memory buffer that appears to the client handler as a PrintSteam and to the logging thread as an InputStream. To mimic the System class, define a static variable out in the ServerLog class that can always output messages. This variable is initialized as System.out; output is not redirected to a file until a ServerLog instance is created. ServerLog is a subclass of Thread:

```
public class ServerLog extends Thread {
  PrintStream logFile;
  PipedInputStream inputPipe;
  LogPrintStream logStream;
  static PrintStream out = System.out;

  public ServerLog(String filename) throws IOException {
  this(new PrintStream(new FileOutputStream(filename)));
  }

  public ServerLog(PrintStream logFile) throws IOException {
  this.logFile = logFile;
  inputPipe = new PipedInputStream();
  logStream = new LogPrintStream(inputPipe);
  setDaemon(true);
  start();
  if (out == System.out)
    out = logStream;
  }

  PrintStream getOutputStream() {
  return logStream;
  }
}
```

Writing to the Log File

Because you handle the conversion from Unicode to ASCII in the LogPrintStream object, the ServerLog thread must only read from the PipedInputStream and write to the FileOutputStream without performing any conversions. The run() method is a simple loop:

```
public void run() {
  try {
    DataInputStream in = new DataInputStream(inputPipe);
    String line;
    while ((line = in.readLine()) != null) {
      logFile.println(line);
    }
  }
  catch (Exception e) {
  }
  }
}
```

Logging Server Information

The LogPrintStream class is a subclass of PrintStream designed for logging server information. You create a new LogPrintStream with a reference to a PipedInputStream:

```
class LogPrintStream extends PrintStream {
  Date timestamp;

  public LogPrintStream(PipedInputStream in) throws IOException {
  super(new PipedOutputStream(in));
  timestamp = new Date();
  }
```

Naming and TimeStamping Log Messages

You override the regular println(String) method to prepend a date/time stamp and the name of the current thread to any messages you write to the log. Because you name threads after the connection they handle, each log message is tagged with the identity of the remote client:

```
synchronized public void println(String s) {
  timestamp.setTime(System.currentTimeMillis());
  super.println(timestamp.toString() + " " +
  ➥Thread.currentThread().getName() + ": " + s);
  }
}
```

Putting It All Together

With all the protocol and server support classes defined, you are ready to put together the complete application. In the main() method of your server, you create:

- A LogServer
- A StreamMonitor
- A ThreadedServer-based SMTP server
- A ThreadedServer-based POP server
- A SimpleServer-based NameQuery server.
- A SimpleServer-based ServerStatus server

Almost every server requires some amount of configuration information. For this server, you must specify the name of the log file, the file name of the domain properties file, and the maximum number of threads for each type of ThreadedServer. Pass the name of the properties file that holds this configuration information as the first argument to main():

```
class EmailServer {

  public static void main(String[] args) {
  try {
    Properties params = new Properties();
    params.load(new FileInputStream(args[0]));
    int maxThreads;
```

Creating the ThreadGroup

Create a ThreadGroup for all Server threads, the ServerLog, the StreamMonitor, and the MailDomain object:

```
ThreadGroup allServers = new ThreadGroup("servers");
ServerLog ld = new ServerLog(params.getProperty("log.filename"));
new StreamMonitor();
MailDomain domain = new
➥MailDomain(params.getProperty("mail.domain"));
```

Creating SMTP Server

Next, create each working server that directly supports the e-mail clients. To handle multiple concurrent clients, use a ThreadedServer for SMTP and POP, and create a Thread to run each instance of ThreadedServer. Select 5 as the default number of SMTP connections:

```
maxThreads =Integer.parseInt(params.getProperty("smtp.maxthreads",
➥"5"));
Server smtpServer = new ThreadedServer(new SMTPFactory(domain),
➥maxThreads);
new Thread(allServers, smtpServer, "SMTP").start();
```

Creating POP Server

Then create the POP server. Because the average POP client session lasts much longer than SMTP, set the default maximum number of connections to 20:

```
maxThreads = Integer.parseInt(params.getProperty("pop.maxthreads",
➥"20"));
Server popServer = new ThreadedServer(new
➥POP3HandlerFactory(domain) 20);
new Thread(allServers, popServer, "POP").start();
```

Creating the NameQueryServer

Create the last client service server, the NameQueryServer. Because HTTP operates under quick turnaround, and because the corporate database might exist as a single-user system, create a SimpleServer and a thread to run the server:

```
Server lookupServer = new SimpleServer(new NameQueryFactory());
new Thread(allServers, lookupServer, "NameQuery").start();
```

Creating the Status Server

Next, create the status server. It is unlikely that multiple clients access this server, so you can use only the SimpleServer and a server thread:

```
Server status = new SimpleServer(new ServerStatusFactory());
new Thread(allServers, status, "ServerStatus").start();
}
catch (Exception e) {
ServerLog.out.println(e);
}
}

}
```

Summary

You have now completed the e-mail server application and have a set of classes to help you build other network servers. You can use the framework classes of Server, InetOutputStream, InetDate, CommandInputStream and LogPrintStream to implement servers for various other protocols and services.

You can adapt the SMTP, POP and HTTP classes to solve a variety of problems. For example, add code to the SMTP server to perform automatic mail responder functions when command messages are sent to specific mail addresses. You can use this function to automate mailing list maintenance, return requested documents, and other automated reply functions.

Examples of how to customize an HTTP server are provided by the name query and status monitoring servers. As an alternative to completely customizing the HTTP server, Chapter 17 describes how to create servlets that tailor the behavior of the Jeeves HTTP server.

Chapter **12**

Distributed Computing with Java

Widespread enthusiasm for Java is due in large part to the perception that it is a "network-aware" language with special Internet capabilities. However, its real strength in this domain is its portability. By virtualizing a processor and environment, it provides for platform-independent programs, able to execute anywhere within a heterogeneous network. Prior to the release of version 1.1 of the Java Developer Kit (JDK), Java itself did not address the wider issues of distributed computing, particularly those related to communication between objects residing on different networked machines. These are the issues covered in this chapter.

Be forewarned, this chapter does not of necessity have quite the same pragmatic approach as the previous ones; most of the discussion is focused on the "bleeding edge" of Java technology, which—although now officially released—will still evolve as it is adopted by mainstream developers and as any remaining shortcomings are exposed.

However, despite its immaturity, Java support for true distributed computing is extremely important. Distributed computing, with an emphasis on distributed objects, may well become the dominant development paradigm in the near future. Current applications, written with the assumption that they will always run within the confines of a single machine, are always limited by the computing power available on a single machine and do not scale well. By contrast, a distributed application can run on a single machine, or several as appropriate, and so can take advantage of the increasing ubiquity of networked computers to increase both performance and capacity.

Distributed computing is not a new development and is based on more than a decade of research and development. This chapter aims to acquaint you with the associated mindset and the fundamental issues faced when moving from a single processor environment, placing these in a historical context. It then discusses in some detail the two main approaches supported by the JDK: the Java-specific Remote Method Invocation (RMI) and the more heterogeneous Java/IDL CORBA support.

Such support, coupled with Java's inherent portability, almost guarantees it a preeminent role in this rapidly expanding field.

Distributed Computing

Computing involves bringing computer hardware and software resources to bear on a set of information in order to solve problems for people. Taking a broad view, distributed computing is not a niche area, but rather encompasses the whole of computing. The case of a single computer running a program on some local data files and providing results to a user is one end of a spectrum, which stretches out at the other extreme to multiple users, networked machines, and information spread around the globe.

It is a complex field, with a large number of forces and constraints making a one-size-fits-all solution impractical. Each problem to be solved involves differently distributed information, groups of people, and machines. Each situation has different forces at work; economics is a major factor, but geography, performance requirements, integrity, resilience, and availability also greatly affect the solution space.

What's more, these forces change over time, often quite rapidly. Not only must a distributed system meet initial requirements, it must be able to evolve gracefully to meet future, often unpredictable, demands.

Thirty years ago, computers were multimillion dollar resources, and the demand for their services by researchers was rising. Rather than try to duplicate the expensive machinery, the U.S. Information Processing Techniques Office (IPTO) decided it would be more cost effective to create a data network linking the machines and their users. The research and development that ensued lead directly to today's Internet (Salus 1995).

At that time, there were fewer choices; it simply was not economically feasible to provide dedicated computers to everyone who could use one.

The model of a centralized processor and storage with remote users connected via terminals is still common today. It has advantages—having a single copy of information held centrally avoids issues of inconsistency. The hardware and software maintenance expertise can be centralized, and access to the information closely controlled.

However, the approach has as many disadvantages. It doesn't scale well. As more users require access, the central site has to become more and more powerful. A limit is reached at some point, and the system cannot grow any further. Another major problem is that of resilience; if the central node fails, the whole system is unable to function at all. If the system happens to be central to a large corporation, the effect of such a failure could be devastating.

With the increasing availability of cheaper computing, first as minicomputers and then microcomputers, the possibilities changed. It became feasible to connect a network of machines together to spread the load, achieving higher levels of performance and resilience than could be achieved with a single monolithic machine.

First came the classic "client/server" pattern where data stored on a central server is accessed and processed by remote client applications. This reduces the processing bottleneck, but increases the demands on the network because all data has to be transferred back and forth between client and server.

Next came the "peer" pattern where, as far as possible, the data resides on the machines where it is to be processed, and the distinction between clients and servers diminishes. This brought new problems related to data consistency. Although some data is only relevant to a single user or program, other data must be shared and appear consistent to all users wherever it is stored. Changes made on one system must be reflected to other systems, and some form of synchronization put in place to exclude the possibility of two or more systems making incompatible changes to the same data. Having multiple copies of the data increases its availability, but it also increases the complexity of ensuring its consistency.

Although distributing computing resources decreases the impact of any system failing, the additional links and machines actually increase the number of places where a system can fail. Even if data is distributed, if the node fails where the data you want is located, then it is just as inaccessible as if it had been on a single system.

It would be reasonable at this point to give a couple of examples, which should be familiar to most Internet users. Large repositories of files on the Internet are accessed using File Transfer Protocol (FTP) (colloquially known as FTP sites). These take the centralized approach and, despite having high bandwidth links (multiple 45 Mbps T3) and lots of disk storage (about 100 GB) and memory (about 512 MB), they are still only able to serve on the order of a few thousand users simultaneously. Many tackle this limit by setting up mirror sites, but this still puts the onus on the user to select an appropriate site. By contrast, the "USEnet" network news service is inherently distributed, with millions of users accessing the feeds via their local servers. The data is not "mission critical," so missed and duplicated news items are not the problem they would be for a financial corporation.

The point of this discussion is that there is no single optimum arrangement of processing, storage, and networking links to suit every situation. It is up to the designer to make a reasonable guess at the usage patterns and choose the best mix and deployment of resources.

The Need For Transparency

One design principle that helps you plan a successful system is to design for flexibility. If the components of the system can be rearranged, even after the system has been deployed, then you can compensate for even major miscalculations in the analysis/design phase. The key to achieving this flexibility is transparency. A good working definition of *transparency* is "the concealment from the user and the application programmer of the separation of components in a distributed system so that the system is perceived as a whole rather than a collection of independent components" (Coulouris, Dollimore, Kindberg 1994).

The ISO Reference Model for Open Distributed Processing identifies eight forms of transparency as cited in CDK 1994:

- **Access transparency.** Identical operations are used to access remote and local data.

- **Location transparency.** Data is accessed without clients knowing its location.

- **Concurrency transparency.** Multiple processes are able to access data without concern for each others' existence.

- **Replication transparency.** Multiple copies of data can be created to increase availability and performance while presenting the appearance of a single copy to clients.

- **Failure transparency.** Parts of the implementation can fail while allowing clients to continue their processing undisturbed.

- **Migration transparency.** Data can move between and around the system without clients being aware of the location change.

- **Performance transparency.** The system configuration can change to accommodate changing loads without affecting clients.

- **Scaling transparency.** The system can expand in capacity and scale without requiring structural changes to itself or its clients.

Transparency at various levels is an attempt at controlling the complexity of distributed software systems and making them resilient in the face of change. By separating concerns, designers can concentrate on each facet of operation without worrying about how it might affect other aspects of the system.

By now you might have realized that transparency in another guise is also a cornerstone of object-oriented programming (OOP), where it is known as encapsulation.

Distributed Object Computing

Object orientation is currently the prevailing paradigm for new software development. It offers several advantages over the structured approaches it builds upon, not the least of which is *encapsulation*—the hiding of implementation details from users of objects. With distributed objects, even the geographical location of the implementation is hidden. Object orientation makes a crucial distinction between an object's interface (what the object does) and its implementation (how it does it). Users of an object see only the interface, and all dialog with the object is performed via this interface.

A real-world analogy might be where a modern small business uses an office service. In this case the interface will be one or more telephone and facsimile numbers. To potential clients, it appears as if the business has dedicated reception staff and all the amenities. The real implementation is that the staff is serving dozens of other similar businesses. As the business becomes established, it can afford to employ its own staff, and so the implementation changes. Now the phone numbers connect to different people in a different place, but this has no effect on the clients, who may remain completely unaware of the shift. The interface remains constant, so even business stationery need not be reprinted.

The fundamental support for encapsulation within object-oriented languages makes them good tools for achieving the transparency required for successful distributed systems.

What Java Brings to the Party

The examples developed in Chapter 11, "Advanced Networking," illustrate Java's advantages over C or C++ in a networked environment.

A particularly noteworthy asset of Java is that its standard library code supports common Internet protocols, encapsulated within its java.net.URL and java.net.URLConnection classes, as well as the lower level socket's interface.

Although interpreted Java code may execute more slowly than its compiled C++ counterpart, network overhead is likely to be more significant in determining application performance (especially if the link is a low-speed connection to the Internet). In many cases, the user of the application would notice little if any difference in responsiveness between a C++ and a Java implementation.

Java is especially powerful because a client machine may be running any operating system that supports the Java environment. This requires only a single version of the program. With a C++ implementation, a recompilation is necessary for each type of client platform. Furthermore, incompatibilities between environments can require extensive recoding—a potentially very expensive proposition, given today's heterogeneous networks. In a word, Java's edge is portability.

What Java Lacks

In a distributed application, it is the designer's responsibility to select the protocol used to move data between client and server. Sometimes a well-known and supported protocol may be available, such as FTP for transferring files. More often, with a custom database application, for example, no such protocol exists, and it is necessary to both design and build an application-specific protocol to connect both parts of the program.

In this situation, Java itself offers no advantage over other languages. If performance bottlenecks are discovered when the system is deployed, functionality will have to migrate to rectify the problem. The protocol between client and server must change, and so must the code which implements the protocol; in fact, it has to change for each different arrangement, making empirical tuning an expensive business. In other words, Java lacks support for location transparency.

A Glimmer of Light

So, what is to be done? How can Java be used to construct successful distributed systems that are able to evolve to meet the changing demands placed upon them? The transparency requirement is common to most distributed applications; creating a common reusable architectural framework to support it should greatly aid the design and implementation process.

Do such frameworks and interoperability standards exist? The answer is a qualified 'yes'— the qualification being that much of what is available is still in its early stages of development, and where standards are mature, their adaptation to Java is still undergoing refinement. The two main initiatives covered in this chapter are the Java Remote Method Invocation (RMI) services from JavaSoft and the Common Object Request Broker Architecture (CORBA) standard from the Object Management Group (OMG).

As a prelude to understanding these initiatives, it is worthwhile to look at the fundamentals on which these systems are built, particularly the Remote Procedure Call (RPC) abstraction.

Distributed Computing Fundamentals

For basic TCP/IP network programming, C/C++ and Java programmers have an interface provided by the libraries. The interface originated with Berkeley Unix (as did TCP/IP) and is called the "socket." *Sockets* are quite flexible and provide the functionality needed for communicating between machines.

However, as an abstraction, sockets are still very low-level constructs. Usually, when programmers want to execute another section of code, they simply call it, passing arguments and receiving a returned result. The question arises as to why it is so much harder to call code that resides on another machine than code on the local machine. Certainly there is more work to be done but it is the sort of work that should be automated and carried out under the covers. This was the thought of some of the pioneers working on distributed computing more than a decade ago; that it should be possible to provide a more natural abstraction to the programmer. The result is known as the Remote Procedure Call, where code on another machine can be called the same way as local code.

A Suitable Abstraction—The RPC

It is instructive to examine how a local procedure call works before generalizing to cover RPCs. A procedure call is considered *local* when the calling code and the called procedure both reside in the same process.

In this case the data required by the procedure being called is passed as a number of arguments. These arguments are placed in memory, usually on a stack, along with the return address where execution will resume on completion of the call. The thread of execution passes to the called procedure by jumping to its location in memory.

The called procedure retrieves the return address from the stack and makes a note of it. It then gets the arguments off the stack and uses them to perform its computations, before storing the results back onto the stack. Finally it returns to the calling procedure by jumping to the return address; the caller reads the results and continues with its execution.

From this description, you can see that calling a local procedure relies heavily on both calling and called procedures sharing an address space. Both had to agree on locations to jump to for controlling the flow of execution. Both required read/write access to shared memory in order to pass arguments and return results. To implement an RPC mechanism, the memory address-based approach must be replaced with one better suited to a networked environment.

Implementing Transparency

A primary aim of RPC (and indeed distributed computing in general) is to provide transparency; to reduce or eliminate the differences between local and remote calls from the programmer's perspective.

However, the fact that the two *are* different in a number of ways is somewhat inescapable; it is up to the designer of the RPCs implementation to decide just how visible those differences should be.

There is a constant tension between providing transparency and providing sufficient control to the programmer.

Exception handling is one important area where this tension is apparent. Local calls are extremely reliable, whereas networks are far less so. Packets may be lost, servers may not be available, or may "go down" part way through an exchange. Calls may fail because the caller had insufficient privileges to perform the operation. A reasonable compromise is to provide sufficient transparency to hide the details of message passing and data formatting, but to expose failure conditions, giving control over how to handle them to the user.

Another area of difficulty is addressing: In the local model, the piece of code to be called was specified by a memory address. The RPC has to provide a way of specifying both the host machine on which the code resides, and which copy of the code to call, as there may conceivably be several versions.

There is no easy solution to all the issues that arise, and each implementation makes compromises appropriate to its design goals.

The steps that might be taken by an RPC implementation to map a local call to an exchange of messages over a connection are shown in figure 12.1.

There are three main tasks that must be accomplished by an RPC implementation:

- **Binding.** Finding the location of the remote procedure or service
- **Communications.** Providing a reliable network connection that enables the transmission of requests and responses
- **Interface to user code.** Converting the procedure call to a block of data, which can travel across the connection, and reassembling it at the other end

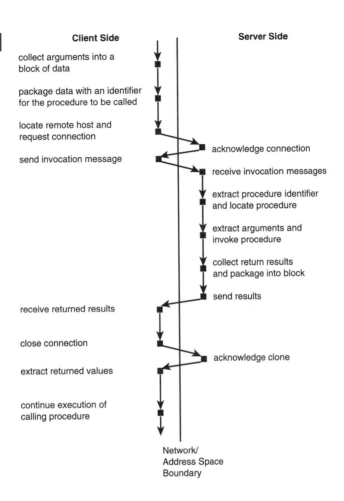

FIGURE 12.1

The outline of a possible RPC implementation.

Client Side

collect arguments into a block of data

package data with an identifier for the procedure to be called

locate remote host and request connection

send invocation message

receive returned results

close connection

extract returned values

continue execution of calling procedure

Server Side

acknowledge connection

receive invocation messages

extract procedure identifier and locate procedure

extract arguments and invoke procedure

collect return results and package into block

send results

acknowledge clone

Network/
Address Space
Boundary

Binding

With distributed systems, it would be very unusual for the location of the remote portion of the code to be known when the code was written. The eventual users will expect to be able to move server code between machines to suit their particular network. This makes it necessary for clients to have a way to discover the location of the server portion of the routines, preferably at run-time.

A similar problem occurs on the Internet, where web servers may move between hosts with different Internet protocol (IP) numbers, yet hotlists in browsers are not automatically changed. Here it is solved by mechanisms such as the Domain Name Service (DNS), which maps the host name part of the URL into an IP number.

For small intranets, it is possible to individually enter details of the server locations into each client. For large systems, such as the Internet, such a static approach is not tenable. A complete distributed naming service becomes necessary. Servers contact this service and provide their details; clients contact the service and perform queries to find the addresses of the servers that they need.

Communications

After the host with the server code has been found, the code responsible for communication has to support a "circuit" between client and server. Of course, in a packet-based network, the circuit doesn't really exist, but it is a useful abstraction to insulate the rest of the code from the realities of imperfect networks—transparency at work once again. In real networks, packets may travel across different routes and may get corrupted or even lost.

The code implementing the virtual circuit must perform operations such as packet retransmission and reordering to compensate.

Interface To User Code—Stubs and Skeletons

Code is necessary at both the local and remote ends of the connection to maintain the transparency perceived by users of the RPC. At the local end, a *stub* procedure acts as a proxy for the remote procedure. It has the same signature (name, arguments, return type) as the remote procedure, but its job is to package the arguments as a message and pass the message on to the communications code. On completion of the remote call, the message containing the results emerges from the communications code, and the stub extracts the return value before passing it back to the caller.

The counterpart of the stub, located on the server side, is termed a *skeleton*. It converts incoming messages into arguments and calls the procedure's implementation. When the code has finished executing, it converts the return value to a message and passes it on to the communications code for return to the calling stub.

Marshaling the Arguments

The stub collects together the arguments into a block for sending to the remote machine. This packaging is known as *marshaling* the arguments. The converse operation, of extracting individual data items, is called *unmarshaling*.

For arguments passed by value such as integers or Booleans it is a straightforward operation to bundle them together. An issue arises, however, when an argument is a reference to data rather than the data itself. The data referenced is in the local machine, and if it is to be accessed or modified by the remote procedure, it also has to be copied across and the reference seen by the remote code adjusted to reference the copy.

Some implementations force the programmer to marshal reference arguments, but provide library code to help. Others automatically marshal reference types they know about, but limit the programmer to using only those types.

Remote Dispatch

A mechanism is needed to determine the procedure to execute on the remote machine. One approach is simply to number the procedures and to use these numbers to index the implementations on the server. A more general solution is to generate a signature for the procedure that is based on the name, argument types, and return types. The latter makes it possible to perform typesafe calls.

Interface Definition

Requiring the programmer to manually create the stub and skeleton code would be counterproductive. Instead, tools are used to generate both the client-side stubs and the server-side skeletons. The interface between the client and server is defined in one of two ways:

- In the same language as the implementation
- In a specialized Interface Definition Language (IDL) specifically designed for the task

Because IDLs are translated into the actual implementation language, they enable the calling code and the remote procedure to be implemented in different languages. They can also have a cleaner declarative syntax because they are specialized to the task of interface definition. A disadvantage is that they present yet another language for the developer to learn.

RPC in the Real World

Remote Procedure Calls provided the foundation for many previous distributed systems. Their history dates back over 10 years to work at Xerox in the early eighties. Sun's involvement with RPC mechanisms is also significant; they originated what is probably the most widespread application based on RPCs, the Network File System (NFS). One reason for the success of NFS is that it uses a standard "wire"-level format (called XDR for External Data Representation) for data traveling across the network. By following the standard, machines with different byte orderings can interoperate and cross mount file systems.

RPCs are also the fundamental building block of the Open Software Foundation's (OSF) Distributed Computing Environment (DCE), which is a currently available, multiplatform, commercially distributed system. DCE has many similar aims to the CORBA initiative, but is based on the procedural rather than object-oriented paradigm. To aid implementation of distributed systems, it provided a Distributed File Service (DFS), a Distributed Time Service, a Distributed Security Service (DSS), threads, and the Distributed Directory Service for naming.

As useful as it is, the RPC abstraction is based on the procedural programming paradigm. With the increasing popularity of objects, the RPC has been evolved to handle interactions between objects. Coverage of two such architectures form the remainder of this chapter.

- JavaSoft's Remote Method Invocation is designed from the outset to be Java specific. It is, therefore, very well integrated with the Java language.

- OMG's Common Object Request Broker Architecture (CORBA) is designed to be language independent, allowing objects written in a variety of languages, running on a range of machines, to interoperate seamlessly.

The types of applications you are writing determine which architecture you choose. Both schemes have their costs and benefits. Although it is difficult to do justice to either approach in these few pages, the following information should provide a foundation for future exploration.

Looking further ahead, it is quite possible that the differences between the two approaches will become much less relevant for application programmers as improved tools become available. When component-level technologies, such as Java Beans, begin to mature, the glue connecting the components may become largely invisible.

An interesting introductory paper on distributed computing from Sun Microsystems can be obtained from

```
http://www.sunlabs.com/technical-reports/1994/abstract-29.html
```

It argues that complete location transparency can be disastrous. Failing to distinguish between local and remote objects can produce detrimental results.

Java Remote Method Invocation

To provide a distributed object facility for Java applications and applets, the JavaSoft division of Sun has released the Java Remote Method Invocation (RMI) package with version 1.1 of the JDK.

Along with Java Database Connectivity (JDBC) and the Java Interface Definition Language, RMI forms part of the so-called Java Enterprise API. Although it doesn't address all the issues of deploying objects in a heterogeneous environment, it provides the facilities needed by a wide range of distributed Java applications.

By compromising on some generality, RMI has been designed to retain the semantics of the Java object model and provide close integration with the rest of the Java system. It allows objects in one Java Virtual Machine (VM) to call methods on objects residing in other Java VMs, with very little change in either the local or remote code. The main difference from the user's perspective is the need to handle the additional exceptions that may be generated by a remote object, mostly related to issues of communication.

The Design of RMI

The aim of the RMI designers was to provide a "native" solution to the area of distributed Java objects. As such they restricted their scope to objects implemented in Java, rather than create a universal solution to allow communication with any object across any protocol.

The design objectives were as follows:

- To make the process of invoking remote objects as similar as possible to that of invoking local objects to clients of those objects
- To partially reveal the location of objects, allowing client code to treat them differently where appropriate
- To maintain the type safety and security of the native Java environment
- To be extensible, so future enhancements such as replicated objects fit neatly into the overall architecture

The RMI implementation of JDK 1.1 has largely achieved these goals. How well they have been achieved will become apparent as the Java development community gains more experience with them.

Converting into a Distributed Application: An Example

Rather than discuss the way RMI is implemented and then develop an example, this section takes the opposite approach of presenting the example first. From an initial version of the example, which is purely local, you will see how it is converted into a distributed application, with part running on a server machine and part locally. Seeing RMI in action should provide a strong basis for the more detailed discussion which follows.

The Client Interface

The example program is a simple address book. A simple GUI client allows Address objects to be added, edited, viewed, and removed from the AddressBook. The GUI code is trivial; the main panel displays a list of the names whose addresses are stored in the address book. The list is used to select an address, and four buttons are used to select the action to be performed:

- **Add.** Displays an empty address dialog box, allowing a new entry to be created.
- **Edit.** Brings up an address dialog box containing the address corresponding to the name selected in the list. Fields may be modified, and the resulting address may be saved or discarded.
- **View.** Brings up an address dialog box containing the address corresponding to the name selected in the list.
- **Remove.** Deletes the address entry for the selected name.

The classes that implement the Address and AddressBook are shown in listing 12.1.

Listing 12.1 Implementation of the Local Version of the Address Book

```
import java.util.*;

class Address {
    public Address( String iName
                  , String iStreet
                  , String iCity
                  , String iState
                  , String iPhone) {
        name   = iName;
        street = iStreet;
        city   = iCity;
        state  = iState;
        phone  = iPhone;
    }

    public String getName()  {return name;}
    public String getStreet(){return street;}
```

```
        public String getCity()  {return city;}
        public String getState() {return state;}
        public String getPhone() {return phone;}

    private String name;
    private String street;
    private String city;
    private String state;
    private String phone;
}

class AddressBook {

    public AddressBook(){}

    public void add(Address iAddress) {
        addresses.put(iAddress.getName(), iAddress);
    }

    public Address getAddress(String name) {
        return (Address)addresses.get(name);
    }

    public void delete(String iName) {
        addresses.remove(iName);
    }

    public String [] getNames() {
        int i = 0;
        String [] array = new String[addresses.size()];

        Enumeration e = addresses.keys();
        while (e.hasMoreElements()) {
            array[i] = (String)e.nextElement();
            i++;
        }
        return array;
    }

    private Hashtable addresses = new Hashtable();
}
```

The essentials of the AddressBook interface are the calls to add and remove entries…

```
void add(Address iAddress);
void delete(String iName);
```

...plus the calls to enumerate the names stored, and to retrieve a particular address, given the name, as follows.

```
String [] getNames();
Address getAddress(String name);
```

The AddressBook class is essentially a wrapper for the Hashtable class. The choice of a single call to retrieve the list of names rather than an enumeration style call was made because the object was destined to become remote. Making a call for each name could become quite expensive over a slow network connection. By moving the enumeration to the server code, the overhead is avoided (at the expense of a possible reduction in generality). There is no Name class because names are simply stored as strings. The structure of the application is shown in figure 12.2.

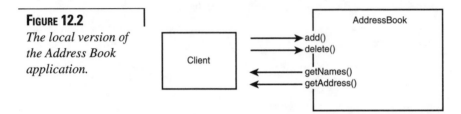

FIGURE 12.2
The local version of the Address Book application.

As with many first attempts at a solution, the structure of the preceding code is not ideal. An improvement would be to formalize the expectations of the GUI client with respect to the AddressBook class by introducing an abstract interface. Any class that implements the interface can then be used with the same GUI. Although not strictly necessary for a purely local application, this does improve the structure. Only the operations relevant to the client are exposed in the interface. The refined structure is shown in figure 12.3.

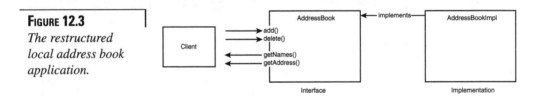

FIGURE 12.3
The restructured local address book application.

Moving AddressBookImpl to the Server

RMI provides much of its support for distribution via inheritance. The classes that are to be situated on a remote platform inherit from base classes in the RMI package.

The AddressBook interface seen by the client is known as a *Remote Interface*. As such, it must extend java.rmi.Remote, which is itself an interface without any methods. The remote AddressBook interface is declared in listing 12.2.

Listing 12.2　The AddressBook Remote Interface

```
public interface AddressBook extends java.rmi.Remote {
    void     add (Address iAddress)     throws java.rmi.RemoteException;
    void     delete (String iName)      throws java.rmi.RemoteException;
    Address  getAddress (String name)   throws java.rmi.RemoteException;
    String[] getNames ()                throws java.rmi.RemoteException;
    }
```

The main change to note is the addition of the "throws remoteException" clauses to each of the methods. Users of this interface must handle remote exceptions, or declare that they pass them on, so this is one place where the client code requires modification. Note that the interface must be public, or the client will be unable to access the remote implementation.

Next, the implementation class containing the code has to derive from an RMI class which supplies server functionality. We derive from the UnicastRemoteObject class, whose resulting structure is shown in figure 12.4.

FIGURE 12.4
The resultant structure of the UnicastRemoteObject class.

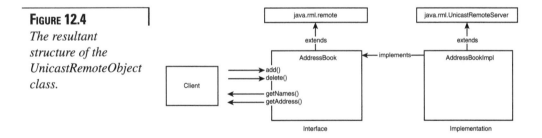

By simply changing the derivation of the AddressBook interface and AddressBookImpl implementation, much of the server-side work has been done. The remaining server side modifications are to add exception clauses methods and to add a main() routine to the AddressBookImpl class.

Modification to Remote Methods

The remotely invoked methods must be declared with "throws java.rmi.RemoteException" clauses to match the interface. Not so obviously, the constructor must also have such a clause, even though the body is empty in the case of the AddressBookImpl class! This situation occurs because there is an implicit call to the constructor of the UnicastRemoteObject super class (remember that super classes are created first), and this might throw the exception.

Adding a main() Routine

The remote version of the address book differs from the original in that the AddressBookImpl class is running as a separate process and so must have its own main() routine (see listing 12.3). This class is responsible for the following:

- Creating and installing a security manager. The security manager controls class loading and must be present for RMI to allow even local classes to be loaded. AddressBookImpl uses the default RMISecurityManager class.

- Creating an instance of the AddressBookImpl class. When the AddressBookImpl instance is created, the UnicastRemoteServer super class starts listening for requests to the object on an anonymous TCP port.

- Binding the instance to a name. The Naming class binds the instance to a name, making it possible for remote clients to obtain a reference to the object in order to call its methods. The name is stored in a registry on the server.

Listing 12.3   The New main() Method

```
public static void main(String args[]) {
    System.setSecurityManager(new RMISecurityManager());
    try {
        AddressBookImpl impl = new AddressBookImpl();
        System.out.println("Binding AddressBook1");
        Naming.rebind("rmi://servername/AddressBook1", impl);
        System.out.println("AddressBook1 available ...");
    }
    catch (Exception e){
        System.out.println("AddressBookImpl.main: exception!:"
                            + e.getMessage());
        e.printStackTrace();
    }
}
```

The server is compiled with javac. The final step before running the server is to generate the underlying code that supports the remote AddressBook interface. The *rmic* tool performs this function. It is similar to the IDL compiler which is used by RPC to generate its stubs, but in this case there is no separate IDL, and the compiler works directly at the level of the compiled classes.

Client-Side Modifications

Two areas in the client code require changes. They are related to the following:

- Binding to a remote object
- Handling of remote exceptions

In the local case, the client could simply refer to the AddressBook object because it obtained a reference to it when it constructed it. In the remote case, this situation changes because getting a reference to the AddressBook requires knowing the name of the instance of AddressBook (there could be many of them); the code must handle the situation where one doesn't exist (see listing 12.4).

Listing 12.4   The Client-Side Method to Obtain Reference to Remote AddressBook

```
public void getAddressBook(String where) {
    try {
        String name = "//servername/AddressBook1";
        Remote obj = Naming.lookup(name);

        if (obj instanceof AddressBook) {
            book = (AddressBook)obj;
            System.out.println("Found AddressBook: " + name);
        }
        else {
            System.out.println(name + " is not an AddressBook");
            reportStatus(name + " is not an AddressBook");
            }
        System.out.flush();
        }

    catch (RemoteException ex) {
        ex.printStackTrace();
        reportStatus("RemoteException during lookup.");
        }
    }
```

For simplicity the example uses a single name which is known at compilation time to both client and server sides—"AddressBook1." To get a reference to the remote object, the Naming class is used to access the registry on the server. The Naming.lookup() method returns a reference to the remote AddressBookImpl object, which allows its methods to be called, just as they would be on a local object.

There is a slight difference. Because the object is remote, there are many more ways in which method invocations can fail. As a result, the client has to add handlers for the remote exceptions that may occur. In the example, these simply report that such an exception occurred, but in a real application they would be tied in to a recovery procedure.

An Elegant Solution

It should be evident by now that RMI provides an elegant way for objects on different machines to communicate. In return for relatively minor modifications to the code, RMI provides great flexibility regarding where objects are located. The following sections provide a more detailed explanation of the key issues, expanding on several themes that were glossed over in the presentation of the example. For the complete story, see the reference documentation and samples in the JDK.

The Layered RMI Architecture

RMI can be visualized as a three-layer architecture, as shown in figure 12.5, each layer providing services to the layer above.

- Stubs and skeletons layer
- Remote reference layer
- Transport layer

The application code which uses RMI resides above the top layer.

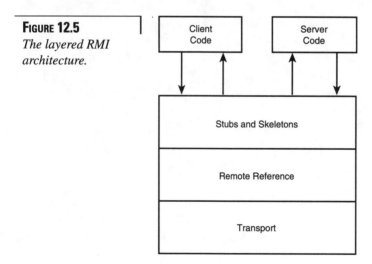

FIGURE 12.5
The layered RMI architecture.

When a client invokes a remote method, the call flows down through the layers, being transformed as it goes, thus creating a data stream that travels across the transport. It is then reconstituted as it moves up through the layers on the server side and emerges as a call to the remote method. The results of the invocation make the reverse journey, with control finally returning to the calling code in the client.

Figure 12.6 shows the flow of a method invocation.

FIGURE 12.6

A remote method invocation.

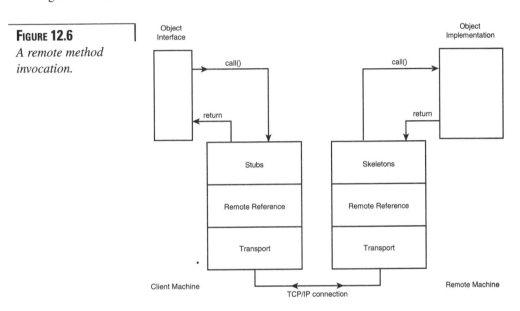

Each layer has different responsibilities as described in the sections that follow:

Stubs and Skeletons Layer

Stubs and skeletons perform complementary functions. They form the interface between the RMI services and the code that calls and implements remote objects. They are responsible for marshaling the arguments and unmarshaling return values. To do this, they use the Object Serialization service, a set of APIs new to JDK 1.1, which converts objects to a stream representation and back again. The serialization is what allows objects to be moved transparently between processes. Object Serialization is usable (and useful) even if no remote objects are involved, as shown later when it is used to add persistence to the address book. In this case, the Reference Layer provides the marshaling streams to the stubs and skeletons. Both stubs and skeletons are specific to the types of remote objects. For this reason, they must be generated from the application supplied code, hence the need for the rmic compiler.

Remote Reference Layer

The remote reference layer provides a constant interface to the stubs and skeletons mentioned above. To accomplish this it has to mask the differences between different server protocol implementations. For instance,

- Servers may support only point-to-point invocations, where a single client interacts with only a single object.
- Servers may also support replication, where a number of replicated remote objects must be kept in synchronization whenever one instance is modified.
- Remote objects may not be continually active and might only be loaded from disk when a client invokes one of their methods.

The code at this layer can be selected by the user by choosing (or implementing) a suitable base class, which is extended by the remote object's implementation.

Transport Layer

The transport layer handles the connection details and provides a channel between the Java Virtual Machines (VMs), which execute the client and host code. At this level, object identifiers are used to specify remote objects, and endpoints denote specific Java VMs. The *wire* transport protocol, including the network data representation, is fully documented in the RMI specification.

The Packages

The RMI API is contained in four packages, java.rmi, java.rmi.server, java.rmi.registry, and java.rmi.dgc. The following list shows only the classes and interfaces, and omits the various exceptions which may occur. RMI exceptions extend java.rmi.RemoteException, which itself extends java.io.IOException. Although there appear to be many classes to learn about, those marked with an asterisk are used internally by the generated stubs and skeletons or distributed garbage collector, and are irrelevant to mainstream RMI users.

- java.rmi

    interface Remote

    class Naming

    class RMISecurityManager

- java.rmi.server

  interface LoadHandler

  interface RMIFailureHandler

  interface RemoteCall *

  interface RemoteRef *

  interface ServerRef *

  interface Skeleton *

  class LogStream

  class Operation *

  class ObjID *

  class RMIClassLoader

  class RMISocketFactory

  class RemoteObject

  class RemoteServer

  class RemoteStub *

  class UID *

  class UnicastRemoteObject

- java.rmi.registry

  interface Registry

  interface RegistryHandler

  class LocateRegistry

- java.rmi.dgc

  interface DGC *

  class Lease *

  class VMID *

Name Binding and the Registry

To call methods on an object, a reference to that object is needed. For local objects, this is simply returned from the "new" operator when the object is created. Remote objects are different in that they already exist elsewhere, and a mechanism is needed to obtain a reference so they can be used.

RMI provides the registries for this purpose. Objects in a server process each have names that are simply strings chosen by their developers to identify them. Using a registry on the server, clients can identify by name the objects they wish to call and obtain references to them.

A *registry* is a remote object that implements the java.rmi.registry.Registry interface. Registries act as name servers, maintaining a mapping between objects on a host and the names with which they were registered. A single registry can hold all name bindings for a host, or multiple registries may be created—one per server process.

Typically, the server process will instantiate an object of the java.rmi.registry. LocateRegistry class and call its createRegistry() method to create a registry on a specified port. The remote objects then call the bind() or rebind() methods of the registry to associate themselves with a name.

As its name suggests, the LocateRegistry class is also used to locate registries. A client wishing to use a remote object first calls a getRegistry() method of the LocateRegistry class to obtain a reference to a registry. It then calls the lookup() method on the registry, passing the name of the remote object it wishes to use. If the registry contains the name, it returns a reference to the object it identifies. The reference is returned as the RemoteObject superclass and is cast to the actual class of the remote object before use.

The java.rmi.Namimg class implements the java.rmi.registry.Registry interface and provides a Uniform Resource Locator syntax for naming the objects. An URL such as the following would identify an object on the host "mycelium.com" on port 7867 called "Address1."

```
rmi://mycelium.com:7867/Address1
```

Remote Objects

Remote objects on the server extend the interface they expose to clients by including methods for creation and exporting. All objects to be accessed remotely using RMI must implement the java.rmi.Remote interface. This is usually achieved by inheriting from the java.rmi.server.RemoteObject class or one of its descendents, as follows.

```
java.lang.Object
    |
    +——java.rmi.server.RemoteObject
            |
            +——java.rmi.server.RemoteServer
                    |
                    +——java.rmi.server.UnicastRemoteObject
```

The RemoteObject class implements the java.lang.Object behavior for remote and provides the remote semantics of Object by implementing methods for hashCode, equals, and toString.

The java.rmi.server.RemoteServer class extends RemoteObject and adds methods to create and export remote objects. It is not used directly, but acts as an abstract superclass. Concrete subclasses then determine the semantics of the remote reference, as was discussed in the previous section about the remote reference layer.

The only concrete subclass provided in the current RMI implementation is the one used in the address book example, namely the UnicastRemoteObject class, which defines a single (nonreplicated) remote object whose references are valid only while the server process is running. It uses TCP streams to provide support for point-to-point active object references (invocations, parameters, and results).

Mechanisms and Techniques

RMI employs a number of interesting mechanisms to implement distributed objects, a few of which are mentioned in this section.

Dynamic Loading of Classes

Conventional Remote Procedure Calls require stub code to be linked in with the client code when the application is built. In contrast, RMI can take advantage of Java's bytecode mechanisms to download such code from the server as it is needed if it is not available locally. It can download not only the remote interfaces and stub code, but also the classes needed for parameters and return calls, or even the entire client code base. This is known as *dynamic class loading*.

The mechanism to achieve this magic uses a class loader, such as RMIClassLoader, and a security manager, such as RMISecurityManager, to ensure that classes are downloaded only if they are not available locally, and that they are only obtained from a trusted source. The rules governing which class loader is used depend on whether the client is an applet or an application, and are covered in depth in the published documentation.

Argument Passing

Variable types passed to or from a remote object can be any Java type—user defined classes or primitives. If the class is not available locally, it must be loaded from the remote site.

When a local object is passed as a parameter to a remote object, the object is copied. Similarly, objects "returned" from the remote call are created in the local VM.

When a remote object is passed as an argument, the stub is copied, so only remote interfaces are available for that object (even if it actually implements non-remote methods and exists on the same remote VM).

Distributed Garbage Collection

RMI supports distributed garbage collection of remote objects. A count is kept on the server end of both local and remote references to remote objects. The garbage collector reaps the object only when there are no references left.

Object Serialization Services

When methods are invoked on remote objects, data flows across the connecting link in both directions. Argument data passed to the method must be transferred across to the remote object, and the result data must be transferred back to the local caller.

As part of the JDK 1.1 release of Java, JavaSoft has extended the java.io package to support writing arbitrary objects to a stream, along with enough structural information so that they may be reconstructed perfectly when read back. These extensions are known as the *Object Serialization Services*. In addition to handling the data transfer needs of RMI, they form a basis for adding persistence to Java objects.

The following sections describe the design issues addressed by the services and the new classes and interfaces they introduce. It also shows how the services are useful in their own right, by using them to add persistence to the address book sample.

Serializing Objects

The serialization services take a data structure as input (such as an object or group of objects) and produce an encoded stream of bytes as output. This serial stream can then be written across a network or modem connection, or to storage media, such as a hard drive. The services also perform the converse operation of taking an encoded stream of bytes and producing the original set of data items that produced them.

This process is a fairly straightforward operation for primitive types, such as integers that have a single value of fixed size. To be generally useful, however, the mechanism must handle arbitrarily complex types, including classes defined by the user, and must ensure that references to other objects also remain valid. All of this must be achieved without special attention from the programmer. Remember that achieving transparency means making remote calls almost indistinguishable from local ones.

Referential Integrity

Consider what it means to pass a collection object to a remote method call, such as the Hashtable of Address objects in the address book example. Not only must the Hashtable object be transferred over, but so must all the Address objects it contains, even though they are probably scattered across memory and not in a neat contiguous block. Otherwise, it will fail as soon as the remote object tries to use an address in the Hashtable. Ensuring that references remain valid is known as maintaining *referential integrity*.

In some ways it is a similar situation to a hypertext document on the web. A graphical web page is not stored as a single file at the server, but rather as a set of files, some textual and some binary. The relationships between these files is stored in the HTML text as a set of references. When a web browser downloads the page, it must read the page as it is being transferred and watch for embedded image references. As these references are encountered, the browser must make additional requests to the server to retrieve the images, a process that is largely transparent to the browser user who sees only the final rendering of the page. It becomes noticeable when the page is saved locally for later viewing. Because most browsers save only the HTML document, the images will no longer be accessible and are rendered instead as broken icons—referential integrity was not preserved.

The Object Serialization Services maintain referential integrity by flattening the structure formed by the objects and their references into a stream. Visualizing the structure as a graph, with the objects holding data as the nodes and the references between them as the arcs or lines, the stream writer traverses the graph, writing the contents of each node to the stream. Effectively, each reference is recursively replaced by the contents of the object it refers to. If there are multiple references to the same object, the services employ a reference sharing mechanism so the object's data is only written once.

Versioning of Streams

An interesting challenge tackled by the serialization services occurs when the class being reconstituted from the stream is a different version from the class that was written to the stream. For example, what if the services were used to stream a copy of the address book to disk, and then you chose to change the Address class to include a zip code field? How should the updated application behave when the previously saved addresses are read in? No single answer will be "right" in every case, but the services provide default behavior that is useful in most cases, along with a capability to tailor for specific requirements.

Because the names of fields are embedded in the stream along with the data values, each of the fields in the new version of the object will be matched with its value in the old version, even if these are in a different order. New fields will not have a corresponding value and so will take on default values.

Along with the name of an objects class, a 64-bit Stream Unique Identifier (SUID) formed from the hash of the class is placed in the stream. Later versions of the class trying to reconstitute themselves from the stream must declare that they are compatible with the SUID encoded in the stream. A tool called *serialver* is supplied with the JDK, which determines the SUID for a class. The SUID may then be pasted into later versions of the class that are compatible. An example might look like the following:

```
static final long SerialVersionUID = 3487495895819393L;
```

This scheme avoids the possibility of a different class with the same name being accidentally reconstituted with incompatible data.

Some changes cannot be compensated for, such as if the class is moved in the inheritance hierarchy. A comprehensive list of compatible and incompatible forms of type evolution is provided in the JDK documentation.

Security and Serialization

Serialization is often performed on data when it is leaving the Java VM, and deserialization when it is entering. It is reasonable to ask whether the data might be tampered with while it is outside the VM, causing a security breach when read back in.

Some fields, such as those containing open file handles, might be vulnerable, and these should be declared with the "transient" keyword. Transient fields are not serialized. It is also worth noting that items reconstituted from a stream are copies of the original objects; new memory is allocated as they are created, so they will never overwrite existing objects. Finally, classes may be loaded as objects read in from the stream, but they are subject to the same standard security management as any other class.

Private fields are serialized as well as public fields. Thus, if any data in a class is sensitive, you will have to decide how best to deal with it. If it is important that it is transferred as part of the stream, an option may be to encrypt it as part of the serialization process. This could be done by defining your own serialization routines or by passing the unencrypted stream through a separate filter.

Java Support for Serialization

The Object Serialization Services build upon the classes and interfaces already present in the JDK 1.0.2 release of the java.io package. Interfaces are added that must be implemented by objects using the services, and new stream classes and interfaces extend existing streams to handle objects. These new additions are detailed in the following sections.

Making Your Objects Serializable

To make use of the serialization services, objects to be streamed must implement either the Serializable or Externalizable interfaces, which are defined in listing 12.5.

Listing 12.5   The Serializable and Externalizable Interfaces

```
package java.io;

public interface Serializable();

public interface Externalizable extends Serializable {
    public void writeExternal(ObjectOutput out) throws IOException;
    public void readExternal(ObjectInput in) throws IOException,
                                    ClassNotFoundException;

}
```

To be used by RMI, the classes of all arguments and return values used by a remote object must therefore implement one of these interfaces. The RemoteObject class itself implements the Serializable interface.

Classes implementing Serializable specify which of their members are not to be written to the stream by preceding them with the "transient" keyword. They may optionally declare readObject() and writeObject() methods for their own processing of the streaming, but for most applications the default processing will be quite sufficient.

Classes implementing Externalizable, however, take full responsibility for their external representation. They must implement both readExternal() and writeExternal() methods to read and write their contents from the stream, as well as coordinate with their superclass to handle its contents.

The Enhanced Streams

Two new interfaces, ObjectInput and ObjectOutput, define the abstract interfaces for the new stream classes.

```
public interface ObjectOutput extends DataOutput
public interface ObjectInput extends DataInput
```

The existing DataOutput and DataInput interfaces declare methods for streaming the primitive Java types—bytes, longs, floats, and the like. ObjectOutput and ObjectInput extend them to handle objects (classes derived from java.lang.Object), arrays, and Strings.

These interfaces are implemented by the two new stream classes:

```
public class ObjectOutputStream extends OutputStream
                                implements ObjectOutput,
                                           ObjectStreamContents

public class ObjectInputStream extends InputStream
                               implements ObjectInput,
                                          ObjectStreamContents
```

The classes are complementary. Items written to ObjectOutputStream are reconstituted from the stream by ObjectInputStream in the order in which they were written.

The constructors of both classes take an existing stream as an argument, which allows great flexibility in the way the classes are used. The passed stream may be a TCP/IP connection to a remote VM, allowing the transfer of the streamed object's state to another host. Alternatively, the stream might be a disk-based file, providing persistence by storing and retrieving the streamed object's state.

The ObjectOutputStream class introduces the writeObject() method to write objects to the stream, declared as follows:

```
public final void writeObject(Object obj) throws IOException
```

This is complemented by readObject() in the ObjectInputStream class, declared as follows:

```
public final Object readObject() throws OptionalDataException,
                                        ClassNotFoundException,
                                        IOException
```

Deserializing an object is equivalent to creating a new object of the same class with its default (no arguments) constructor. The fields are then set from the values in the stream, starting with those of any superclasses and finishing with those of the most derived class.

Other methods are provided to allow most aspects of the streaming process to be customized. For most applications, however, such as the following example, the default behavior is quite sufficient. The JDK 1.1 documentation provides the full definitions of the classes and interfaces so it is not duplicated here.

An Example of Persistence

As was mentioned previously, the Object Serialization Services have been packaged separately from the RMI services because they are useful in other contexts, such as the implementation of object persistence. To demonstrate this aspect of the new streams, this

Twelve: Distributed Computing with Java

section adds persistence to the address book example so that when the server process is stopped and restarted, the address data is still available.

Two methods, write() and read(), are added to the AddressBookImpl class to implement persistence (see listing 12.6). Notice that the names do not appear in the AddressBook interface. This means they can be called only from methods running in the same Java VM as the AddressBookImpl object (that is, on the server) and not from your AddressClient object across the network. They are part of the local interface of AddressBookImpl only, not its remote interface.

Listing 12.6   The AddressBookImpl write() Method

```java
public void write(String filename){
    try {
        FileOutputStream   f = new FileOutputStream(filename);
        ObjectOutputStream s = new ObjectOutputStream(f);
        s.writeObject(addresses);
        s.flush();
    }

    catch (IOException e){
        System.out.println("Exception while Writing");
        return;
    }
}
```

Individual Address entries are stored in the Hashtable "addresses," which is a private field of the AddressBook class (see listing 12.7). The AddressBook.write() method first creates a FileOutputStream with the passed file name, and then it passes the stream to the constructor of the ObjectOutputStream. With one call to s.writeObject() the entire contents of the Hashtable are written to the file, neatly preserving its structure. This is significantly easier than iterating through an enumeration of the Hashtable and Addresses and explicitly writing each field.

Listing 12.7   The AddressBookImpl read() Method

```java
public void read(String filename)
    {
    try {
        FileInputStream in = new FileInputStream(filename);
        ObjectInputStream s = new ObjectInputStream(in);
        addresses = (Hashtable)s.readObject();
```

continues

Distributed Computing with Java

Listing 12.7   Continued

```
        }

    catch (FileNotFoundException e){
        addresses = new Hashtable();
        System.out.println("No input file found; Creating a new
        ➥one...");
        return;
    }
    catch (IOException e){
        System.out.println("Exception while Reading");
        return;
    }
    catch (ClassNotFoundException e){
        System.out.println("ClassNotFoundException while Reading");
        return;
    }
}
```

The AddressBook.read() method is very similar to the write() method, except that read() uses the ObjectInputStream, and the readObject() method is used to create an instance of the Hashtable containing the addresses. The FileNotFoundException is thrown when an existing set of addresses doesn't exist or cannot be found.

The corresponding catch clause handles the situation by creating an empty Hashtable.

The constructor, previously empty, now contains a call to read(). Thus when an AddressBookImpl is created, it tries to initialize itself with any previously entered addresses. Similarly, the calls that may modify the stored addresses now invoke the write() methods, ensuring that any changes are immediately saved to disk (see listing 12.8).

Listing 12.8   The Modified AddressBookImpl Methods

```
public AddressBookImpl() {
    read("address.dat");
}

public void add(Address iAddress) {
    addresses.put(iAddress.getName(), iAddress);
    write("address.dat");
}

public void delete(String iName) {
    addresses.remove(iName);
    write("address.dat");
}
```

Obviously this is a simpleminded approach; the "hard-coded" file name would be out of place in anything but a pedagogical example, and for higher volumes of data it would probably be inefficient to write to disk after each modification. Nonetheless, this example illustrates that persistence has been added to Java by the Object Serialization Services in a very elegant and natural way.

RMI Conclusion

The addition of Remote Method Invocation and Object Serialization Services to Java has seriously strengthened its claim to being the preeminent network programming language. The original innovation of downloadable, portable byte code has been complemented by the new capability to seamlessly transfer data in a similar manner (the Object Serialization Services) and to transparently communicate with the objects once transferred (RMI).

Perhaps for the first time, programmers have been given distributed object support as part of a standard language distribution. How soon it takes them to explore the possibilities and develop a new generation of applications to take advantage of them remains to be seen. It is certainly true that the introduction of these services comes at an appropriate time, given the rapidly growing popularity of the Internet.

In the past, distributed computing was of interest to a small number of programmers, mostly those working on in-house systems for larger corporations with large networks. With low-cost Internet connections becoming common, even domestic computers have access to huge networked resources. RMI is likely to fuel the development of the first generation of "personal" distributed computing software, with a potential market of millions of copies.

By placing RMI in the core component of the JDK from version 1.1 onwards, JavaSoft obviously intends for all conforming Java implementations to support it, and for developers to be able to rely on its availability. At the time of this writing, Win32 and Solaris versions were available, with others such as OS/2 and Linux set to follow.

If RMI has an Achilles' heel, it is a lack of interoperability with existing systems and other languages. To achieve such a clean, easy-to-use set of services, JavaSoft started with a clean slate and created a very Java-specific solution. For personal software, this is not much of an issue. Inside corporate enterprises and for large systems, it is likely to meet with stiff competition from Java/IDL CORBA based solutions, for reasons which will become clear in the next section.

Java and CORBA

Even before work started on the language which was to become Java, the issue of creating interoperable distributed objects was a challenge facing the computer industry. A key requirement was the creation of suitably open standards. In a rare show of unity, several major industry players, Sun among them, came together to create such standards, and in 1989 the Object Management Group (OMG) was born. In 1991 the group produced the Common Object Request Broker Architecture (CORBA) specification and in the years since has been working continuously to both refine the specification and develop a comprehensive distributed object architecture with CORBA as its cornerstone. Currently the OMG's 600-plus membership reads like a "Who's Who" of the computer industry, including IBM, HP, Novell, Apple, Oracle, CERN and Netscape. Given this level of support, CORBA can be truly considered an industry standard.

Sun has been developing the Java IDL tools, in parallel with RMI, to allow Java objects and applications to interoperate with CORBA-compliant distributed objects. Java IDL (a key aspect of CORBA) has not been shipped with JDK 1.1 because it is still undergoing standardization by the OMG. However, like RMI, Java IDL is part of the Java Enterprise API; it forms part of the core library API, which means developers can assume it will be present on all Java implementations.

The following sections provide some background on the OMG, a roadmap to the comprehensive architecture they have defined, and some details on Java IDL itself, mainly the proposed mapping between the IDL and Java languages.

The Object Management Group: Building a Standard

When the OMG was formed, a perceived weakness in the standards organizations of the time, particularly those in the fields of telecommunications and computer languages, was the length of time needed for a standard to be processed. In areas of rapid development, standards tended to lag behind current technological capabilities. This caused proprietary extensions to be adopted in the interim, resulting in a great waste of time and money. Familiar examples are V34 modems and ANSI C where manufacturers were forced to improvise until suitable standards emerged.

Thus, the risk of a slow standardization process is the formation of de facto standards, such as NetScape's influence on HTML. For a new standard to be adopted, it generally has to be backward compatible with existing practice, which often means taking on the "baggage" of previous de facto standards.

Conversely, rapid standardization may be risky. Standards may be incapable of meeting the needs of their audience because they were rushed out with insufficient thought and consultation. Standards authoring is a most demanding activity; it is important to involve as many interested parties with as much industry experience, intellectual firepower, and political clout as possible. Meanwhile, the groups developing the specifications must be organized so communication between authors is productive and efficient.

To tackle these problems, the OMG aimed to "fast-track" standards, working in cycles much shorter than those of existing organizations. To facilitate this, adoption of existing approaches and standards was given priority.

"Fast tracking" is relative of course; standardization is still measured in terms of years. However, the OMG has been active for eight years and by drawing on the extraordinarily wide pool of industry experience of its member organizations, their creation, the Object Management Architecture (OMA), is the most technically credible vision for distributed object computing currently available. The OMA is based on the following key principles:

- Openness
- Heterogeneity
- Portability
- Interoperability

All of these are important for its widespread acceptance. Being open means that no single company can manipulate the market place. Modern networked environments are internally diverse, so a "universal solution" to which the OMG aspires must be applicable to different communications protocols, with a range of implementation languages across different operating systems, running on a range of hardware.

The standard must also be sufficiently detailed so that different parts of a system created by different parties can be seamlessly integrated.

An interesting insight into the OMG's standardization process is provided by Roger Sessions. As the coauthor of the Object Persistence Services, his 1996 book, *Object Persistence—Beyond Object Oriented Databases*, describes not only the resulting standard but the personal aspects and political wrangling leading to its adoption.

The Competition

Only one major software company of note has so far refused to involve itself with the OMG—Microsoft. Given its track record and corporate culture of competition over cooperation, this is perhaps understandable. Microsoft has positioned its ActiveX and Distributed Component Object Model (DCOM) "standards" in opposition to CORBA.

As a strategy for general distributed object computing, ActiveX/DCOM is technically weak. It is based on Microsoft's GUI desktop technology "OLE" and is neither platform nor language independent. The effect it might have on the field is a subject of hot debate: Its parentage is to be weighed against its more proprietary and Windows-centric architecture.

Currently DCOM is in its early stages. Only limited descriptions of how it might interwork with Java objects are available so it won't be further discussed here. The proposed DCOM "standard" is available on the Internet at

```
http://ds1.internic.net/internet-drafts/draft-brown-dcom-v1-spec-01.txt
```

A comparison between CORBA and ActiveX/DCOM is available at

```
http://www.omg.org/activex.htm
```

The Object Management Architecture (OMA)

Although CORBA is the best-known portion of the OMG's architecture, it is only the bottom layer or core. CORBA provides the underpinnings for all the higher level services and facilities which are necessary for complex software systems. By providing strong guidelines on how software can be structured, the OMA forms the basis of a new generation of reusable software components and systems.

The Reference Model

The Reference Model acts as a "road map" for the OMA. It describes the major components of the OMA and how they work together. It can be described approximately with a layered model, with the most application-specific concerns (roughly corresponding to the concept of componentware) at the top, and most general areas (such as object communication) at the bottom. Table 12.1 illustrates the layered OMA Reference Model.

TABLE 12.1	Layer	Description
The OMA Reference Model Layers	Application Objects (AO)	Corresponds roughly to traditional application programs.
	Common Facilities (CF)	Corresponds to the level of abstraction of application frameworks, such as the AWT component of Java.
	Common Services (CS)	Provides system level services; includes functionality such as persistence and concurrency, which are useful to a whole range of object types.
	Object Request Broker (ORB)	Provides the "plumbing," a bus to carry messages between objects, on a single machine or across a network.

Late in 1995, the OMG extended the architecture slightly at the Common Facilities level to account for the development of domain specific objects and frameworks. Realizing the orthogonal nature of industry specific concerns, the architecture has a notion of vertical divisions for different types of industry.

The architecture is thus much more comprehensive than either of the approaches so far considered: RPCs fall entirely within the bottom ORB layer, with RMI additionally providing a minimal subset of the Common Services functionality.

The Standards

Using the OMA for guidance, the OMG has been developing the standards in a bottom-up manner. The Application Objects layer has no standards yet, though several industry groups are actively discussing them. Sectors represented include business object management, financial and accounting, medical and healthcare, and telecommunications.

Likewise, the Common Facilities standards are still being developed; the areas covered are user interfaces, information management, system management, and task management.

The Common Services specifications, together known as CORBAservices, have been adopted and published. The services are Naming, Event Management, Persistent Objects, Lifecycle, Concurrency, Externalization, Relationships, Transactions, Query, Licensing, Property, Security, and Time.

As you can see, the range is very comprehensive. The base CORBA specification itself is very mature. The first version was released in 1991, with the second major version, CORBA 2.0, arriving in 1994. As a result there are many commercial implementations. The CORBA specification makes a distinction between its core, which covers its architecture and the syntax and semantics of its Interface Definition Language, and the language bindings, which determine its "APIs" for various languages. To be CORBA-compliant, an implementation must support the core specification and at least one language binding. Bindings currently exist for C, C++, Smalltalk, and Ada'95. The Java binding is currently being standardized (along with the COBOL binding) with a final version expected mid 1997.

The OMG recently made the full set of its adopted specifications available online via the web. They are well-written and can be downloaded in Postscript (PS) or Portable Document Format (PDF) from

```
http://www.omg.org/specindx.htm
```

The Object Model

The Object Model is common to all OMG-compliant technologies. The Object Model defines common object semantics, allowing objects to be represented in a form independent of implementation. It concentrates on interfaces and forms a "frame of reference" for all the other groups working under the OMG banner.

To provide for extensibility, a Core Object Model is defined which must be supported in any compliant system. Extensions are handled as "extensions," which are not required to be supported. Extensions are grouped into "Profiles." Profiles will usually support a particular area of application, such as Object Oriented Databases.

CORBA Terminology

Although the concepts of object orientation are well understood, the paradigm has been developed independently by many different groups, leading to a proliferation of names for these concepts. Java and CORBA have different backgrounds and use different terms for the same entities. The following discussion uses the OMG's terms, with references to equivalent concepts in the Java world. The OMG terminology is shown in an italicized typeface as it is introduced.

Groups of objects, known as *object systems*, work together to provide *services* to *clients*. Clients use services by issuing *requests*. Objects are identified through their lifetime by object identifiers.

A request consists of an *operation* (analogous to a Java method), a set of *parameters* (Java arguments), and an optional request context (no Java equivalent).

In the CORBA model, a strong distinction is made between *interfaces* and *implementations*. An object's interface lists the operations it can perform and its *attributes* (the equivalent of Java's fields). Confusingly, the code that implements the operation is termed a *method*. There is no notion of private or protected operations in an interface. Interfaces may be composed using multiple inheritance as in Java.

Each operation is characterized by a *signature*, consisting of its *identifier* (name), the names and types of its parameters, a returned *result*, and *exceptions* it can throw (like exceptions in Java). Parameters have *modes*, which specify whether they are used for input, output, or both.

Attributes may be read/write or read-only. They are logically equivalent to a pair of Get() and Set() operations (or just a Get() operation in the case of read-only attributes).

Not everything is an object, however. As in Java, there are *basic types,* such as Booleans and integers, and *constructed types,* such as sequences and arrays. Also, the CORBA documentation often mentions *pseudo-objects*. These are not full objects, but are a convenient way of representing composite data such as one might find in a request to an object. In fact, the Object Request Broker (ORB) itself is considered a pseudo object.

Object References

CORBA Objects are manipulated using Object references, whereas Java objects are passed by value. This was a conscious design decision by the Java designers, as referencing and dereferencing (implemented with pointers in C, Java's ancestor) were seen to be hard to learn and one of the biggest sources of programming errors. Although there are references in Java, they are hidden from the programmer. This is perhaps the most fundamental difference between the Java Object Model and the CORBA one, as will become apparent when the proposed Java language binding is discussed later.

An Object Reference is created when an object is created and may be used to identify an object for the purpose of requesting services during its lifetime. Object references themselves are not portable across ORBs, which are at liberty to implement them in the most convenient manner for the language/environment in which they will be used. Instead, they may be *stringized*—converted to a string and made persistent. The stringized representation may be transmitted to other ORBs, then reconstituted into an Object Reference which is valid for that ORB.

Object Request Brokers (ORBs)

The Common Object Request Broker Architecture is, as its name states, an architecture. It has a number of components that act together to enable objects to communicate. This collection is known as an Object Request Broker. ORBs may be implemented in a number of ways, yet still remain fully CORBA-compliant because CORBA defines interfaces to be provided rather than specifying implementation details. A flow chart of an ORB is shown in figure 12.7.

FIGURE 12.7

Representation of an ORB.

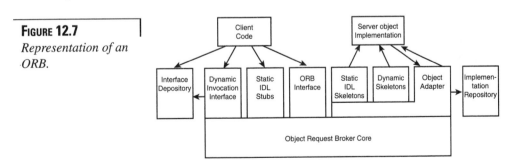

In a generally heterogenous CORBA system, an ORB will exist on each machine. This situation is not strictly necessary if the architecture is an asymmetrical client-server, where there are either no objects on the client or they are never accessed remotely. In this case, a simpler layer of code that is able to forward requests to servers will suffice.

Clients issue a request that identifies the target object, the operation, and a number (this may be zero) of parameters. This request is processed by the local ORB and forwarded to the appropriate implementation. If the object implementation is on a remote host, the ORB communicates with its counterpart on that host to effect the call. If the call is synchronous, the caller will wait for completion of the remote call and any resulting data to be returned. Failure of the call causes an exception, which is handled by the caller. If the call is asynchronous, the caller does not wait for completion.

Interfaces

Objects Interfaces are defined using OMGs Interface Definition Language. As in the RPC model examined earlier, these are used to generate stubs and skeletons in the implementation languages. For instance, if an object were implemented in the Ada language, and the client program were written in C, the client stubs generated from the IDL would be in C and the implementation skeletons would be in Ada.

In addition to stubs/skeletons, the IDL interface definitions are compiled to a queryable form and stored in an *interface repository*, providing a store of "meta-data" for use by the ORB (see fig. 12.8).

FIGURE 12.8
Use of an interface repository.

IDL	Interface Definitions

IDL Compiler

Interface Repository

Stubs

Skeletons

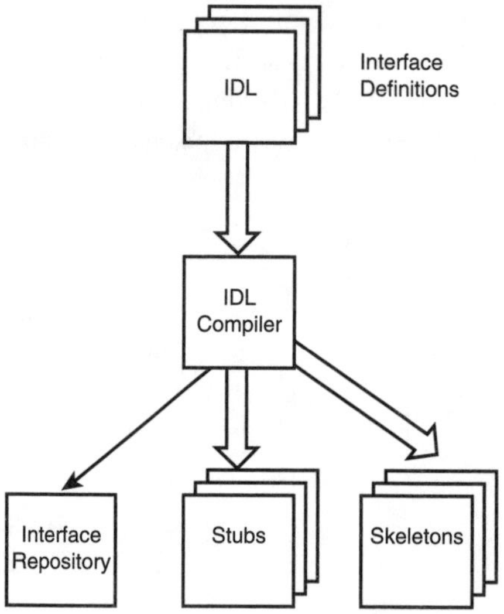

Client-Side Invocation

Two approaches to invoking operations on objects are supported by the ORB. One is the conventional static approach, where the client uses compiled stubs, which are linked into the client code. The second approach is dynamic where the entire call is constructed at run-time. The dynamic interface is the same for all ORBs/objects, whereas the static stubs will be specific to the interfaces of the objects being called.

Static Invocation

Static binding is the approach used by both RPC and RMI. It is well-suited to the traditional corporate intranet style of application development, where all aspects of the applications, including the way their objects are distributed, are under the control of one project or department. The IDL compiler generates the proxy stubs for the remote objects, and skeletons for their implementations.

Several advantages accrue from having all the information available at compile time:

- Static type checking is possible, so programs are robust.
- Performance is also good because operations are requested with a single API call.
- A familiar model is presented to developers, hopefully leading to good productivity and more readable code.

Dynamic Invocation

The alternative to static stubs and skeletons is to build the entire call dynamically. This makes possible a whole range of applications which are difficult to build using only static interfaces; applications such as Network Management tools and Application Builders, which cannot have build time knowledge of all the objects they will be applied to.

CORBA provides full support for a dynamic style of interface with its Dynamic Invocation Interface (DII). The DII provides the same interface regardless of the program objects it is accessing, unlike the static stubs, which are specific to a particular class.

To discover the interface details so that a request can be built, the Interface Repository (IR) provides a source of meta-data about objects. IR definitions are usually generated from the IDL interfaces by similar tools to those that generate the stubs, although, in keeping with the dynamic approach, the IR API includes calls to dynamically create interface definitions, too. IRs are implemented as a set of persistent objects, which hold the data that describes the interfaces. They are arranged in a containment hierarchy, which is navigated by name.

Server-Side Function and Object Adapters

The dynamic invocation approach is unique to CORBA across the systems discussed in this chapter and is not currently supported by RMI. However, the new Java Beans model for component software (from Sun) implies the need for such "reflection" about the components of a system, prompting the development and inclusion of the Java Reflection APIs in JDK v1.1. Likewise, the principal procedural distributed framework, DCE (mentioned earlier), has no similar facilities.

Objects Adapters provide the bulk of server-side functionality. They manage the server-side equivalent of Interface Repositories, known as Implementation Repositories (and sadly both have identical acronyms), which hold details of the object implementations the server can use.

New object implementations are installed on the server by the Object Adapter, which registers their details in the Implementation Repository.

One type of Object Adapter is mandated for all CORBA compliant ORBs—the Basic Object Adapter (BOA). It is intended to be able to handle most "regular" object implementations, but may be replaced for special cases, such as where objects are being served from an object-oriented database.

Object Adapters have a number of responsibilities, including the following:

- Generation and interpretation of object references
- Activation and deactivation of object implementations
- Invocation of methods, using skeletons
- Advertising available services to the outside world

When requests arrive at the Object Adapter, they look identical whether they were the result of a static invocation or built using DII.

Object Activation/Deactivation

Activation is the process of readying objects to perform operations, and deactivation is the converse process. When a request is made to an object's interface by a client, that object may not be able to process the request immediately because it is not in memory at the time; for instance, it may be a persistent object in a database, or its operation code may be part of a dynamically linked library that is not currently loaded. It is the responsibility of the BOA to load all necessary parts so the call may proceed.

Dynamic Skeleton Interface (DSI)

An interesting server-side interface is the *Dynamic Skeleton Interface* (DSI), which enables object implementations to be built without knowledge of the object type they will implement. Its main practical use is for creating *bridges* to non-CORBA environments, such as Microsoft's ActiveX (formerly known as Object Linking and Embedding—OLE) or the Common Lisp Object System (CLOS). The code using the interface interprets the requests and maps them to a form compatible with the foreign object system.

Interoperability and Inter-ORB Protocols

Although the ORB model is useful for visualizing its operation from a programmer's perspective, it is apparent that its functionality is actually distributed between address spaces, and usually across machines. The client and server components of the ORB must somehow be able to communicate. In the general case where an ORB exists on each machine, the ORBs must be able to communicate with a common protocol. In the original CORBA 1.x standard, exactly how this was to be achieved was never specified.

To work in an open environment, it became apparent that not only must ORBs facilitate communication between objects, but that different ORB implementations must be able to interoperate. Without this capability, client objects would be restricted to hosting on only one vendor's product. CORBA 2.0 specifies a set of common message formats and data representations to enable communication between ORBs, called the General Inter-ORB Protocol (GIOP). IDL data types are mapped into a Common Network Representation (CNR) for transmission, taking into account byte ordering and alignment issues. CNR plays the same role as Sun's XDR, which was mentioned previously in connection with NFS.

GIOP itself doesn't specify the communications protocol used to transfer its messages. Instead, it uses a specific protocol appropriate to its application. One communications protocol is mandated by the CORBA 2.0 standard: It is the Internet Inter-ORB Protocol (IIOP), which uses TCP/IP as its transport. Other protocols may be implemented by a particular ORB for GIOP messaging, and these are referred to as Environment-Specific Inter-ORB Protocols (ESIOPs). A prominent example is the Distributed Computing Environment Common Inter-ORB Protocol DCE-CIOP, which allows for interworking with existing DCE systems.

The Interface Definition Language (IDL)

IDL is a cornerstone of the whole OMG strategy. Because the various specifications concentrate on specifying interfaces rather than prescribing implementations, the language that expresses these interfaces is of primary importance.

Compared with most languages, the structure of IDL is very straightforward. It doesn't have to specify implementation, so it avoids control structures and the like, giving it an entirely declarative style. Its syntax is much like Java's, with additional keywords introduced to handle the additional semantics of distributed objects.

IDL, of course, is not directly encountered by the programmers who use the objects that it describes. Instead, all the constructs are mapped to a target programming language by an IDL compiler before being used. Despite its C/Java-like syntax, IDL is designed to be effectively neutral with respect to its target languages, and it largely succeeds. Currently, standard mappings exist not only to C and C++, but also to rather different languages, such as Ada and Smalltalk. Mappings to Java and COBOL are currently passing through the adoption process.

The following discussion uses the OMG's terminology, which is different in places to that used by a Java programmer. The following chart provides an approximate guide.

IDL Term	Java Term
Module	Package
Attribute	Field
Operation	Method
Derived class	Subclass
Base class	Superclass

Rather than providing a complete reference for IDL, the following sections concentrate on where it differs from Java or C, particularly in its structure and the new keywords it adds. The aim is to present enough information to allow you to read IDL files. The full reference for IDL is presented in Chapter 3 of the CORBA 2.0 specification.

The Preprocessor

If you are familiar with C or C++ programming, you will have encountered the *C preprocessor*. Its role is to handle issues that are not really part of the language but are instead related to the development environment. Specifically, it performs tasks such as including the contents of one file in another, hiding sections of code if certain conditions are true (for example, hiding debug code for a release build), and textually replacing symbols with other symbols (macro substitution). The preprocessor, as its name suggests, processes the code before it is seen by the compiler or other tools.

IDL uses the same preprocessing scheme as C/C++ to handle environmental issues. Preprocessor directives (commands) appear in IDL source files preceded by a # symbol. For example, the directive #include "codex.idl" would be replaced with the contents of the codex.idl file before compilation. The directives supported by IDL are fully compatible with the ANSI C/C++ preprocessor. In practice, there will unlikely be a separate preprocessor tool, but instead its function will be implemented as the first pass of an IDL compiler, as it is in many modern C/C++ environments.

The Structure of IDL

The main entities contained in an IDL file (alongside their closest Java counterparts) are listed in the following chart.

IDL Term	Java Term
Modules	Packages
Interfaces	Interfaces
Attributes	Fields
Operations	Methods
Constants	Constants
Typedefs	Aliases for types—no Java equivalent
Exceptions	Exceptions

At the risk of over-simplifying, IDL consists of a number of module definitions, each of which contains interface definitions. Constants, typedefs, and exceptions may appear almost anywhere, whereas operations and attributes are always part of an interface definition. A pseudocode outline is shown in listing 12.9.

Listing 12.9   IDL Pseudocode to Illustrate Structure

```
module marsupial {
    constants       // module specific
    typedefs
    exceptions

    interface kangaroo {
        constants   // interface specific
        typedefs
        exceptions

        attributes
        operations
    }

    interface platypus {
        ...
    }
}
```

Modules, Naming, and Scoping

Modules in IDL have a similar function to the package mechanism of Java. They don't have any effect on the code, but instead they are used to control the name space (scope) of various other entities. Placing names in a scope means they will not conflict with others in the system. Although only a short form of the name is specified, each named entity has a full "scoped" name, allowing it to be referred to unambiguously when necessary. As in Java, modules can be nested to form a naming hierarchy.

Modules are not the only constructs that create a new scope; scopes are also created by:

- Interfaces
- Structures
- Unions
- Operations
- Exceptions

Modules are different because they are solely concerned with naming issues, whereas the other constructs imply additional semantics.

The algorithm used to determine scoped names is simple. As the file containing the IDL is read, a new scope is created whenever one of the above mentioned constructs is encountered. The scoped name is generated by taking the name of the scope (module name, interface name, and so on), appending the double colon (::) and prepending it to the item being named. Items may appear at file scope, where there is no scope name defined. In this case, only the "::" is prepended as shown in listing 12.10.

Listing 12.10   An Example of Scoping

```
const short K = 3;

module wombat {
    const short K = 4;

    interface ears {
        const short K = 5;

        // at this point you have three definitions of K
        // just referencing K yields 5
        // whereas ::K is 3 and ::wombat::K is 4

    ...

    };
};
```

Parameter lists also open a scope, so their names will not conflict with others. Items that can have a scoped name follow:

- Types
- Constants
- Enumeration values
- Exceptions
- Interfaces
- Attributes
- Operations

Names are case insensitive. For example Fox and FOX are considered the same name, so cannot be used by different items in the same scope. However, references to a name must use the same case as the definition.

All names defined by CORBA are treated as if they appear in the module CORBA, thus their scoped name is preceded by "CORBA::".

Interfaces and Inheritance

IDL interfaces are very similar to their Java counterparts. As with Java, they can inherit from other interfaces. The terminology used by the OMG follows the C++ path: Rather than super and sub classes, the terms are base and derived. Thus the interface from which another interface is derived is called its base interface.

IDL interfaces support multiple inheritance, though with slightly different semantics than the Java interfaces. When discussing multiple inheritance, a diamond-shaped graph is often used. Figure 12.9 shows four interfaces, A, B, C, and D, with the links between them signifying inheritance.

In IDL, this arrangement would be specified as follows:

```
interface A         {...}
interface B : A     {...}
interface C : A     {...}
interface D : B, C {...}
```

The derived class is separated from its base class (or classes) by a single colon, whereas multiple base classes are separated by commas.

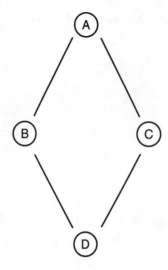

FIGURE 12.9

The diamond-shaped representation of multiple inheritance.

A is the base interface: It is a direct base of B and C, and it is an indirect base interface of D. In OMG IDL it is illegal to inherit from two interfaces that have the same name for an operation or attribute. It is also illegal to redefine operations or attributes in derived interfaces. However, it is legal to redefine constants, types, and exceptions. Where there is a conflict, the scoped name is used to eliminate ambiguity.

In contrast, Java enables B and C to have methods (operations) with the same name. If the signatures differ, then they are considered to be two different methods (the name is overloaded). If they have identical signatures, then they can have only one implementation. The problem of conflicting attributes does not arise because Java does not allow attributes to be specified in its interfaces.

In IDL, operations must all have distinct names within a scope (not just distinct signatures), as they are used at runtime. There is no provision for Java/C++ style overloading of method names.

IDL Data Types

Basic data types in IDL correspond to the primitive types in Java and have a single value of fixed size. Most of the basic types are very similar to their Java counterparts, but a few details are different. IDL also has a set of composite types called *constructed types,* which hold many values.

Basic Types

There is no "int" keyword in IDL to denote integers, but instead, the two sizes of integers are denoted by "short" (a 16-bit value) and "long" (a 32 bit value). Like C, and unlike Java, IDL has the notion of signedness and unsignedness. *Unsigned* values may take only positive values, that makes them useful for array indexes and the like, but liabilities when it comes to arithmetic operations. The only advantage to unsigned values is that they can represent numbers that are twice as large. Both shorts and longs in IDL can be made unsigned by preceding them with the "unsigned" keyword.

Floating point numbers in IDL (float, double) are the same as their Java namesakes, as defined by the IEEE 754-1985 specification.

Booleans are similar in IDL, with uppercased keywords used for "TRUE" and "FALSE" values.

Characters, denoted by the "char" keyword in IDL, are 8-bit quantities, in contrast to the 16 bits used by Java. Thus they do not support Unicode. The value of characters may be modified during transmission as long as their meaning stays the same, such as when international character sets are used to replace the base ISO Latin-1 8859.1 character set.

Octets, denoted by the "octet" keyword, are simply 8-bit values, and their contents are guaranteed not to change during transmission.

One type introduced by IDL is not so much a type, but it acts as a placeholder for a type. Denoted by the "any" keyword, it can refer to any IDL defined type.

Enumerations are ordered lists of identifiers, introduced by the "enum" keyword. Their purpose is to act as named constants. Enumerations are part of C and C++ but not Java.

Constructed Types

Structures are records, introduced by the keyword "struct"; they are structured collections of fields without any associated behavior. In other words, they are classes without methods.

Unions are variant records denoted by the "union" keyword. They are a name for a collection of superimposed structure types. If a union is declared as type A or type B, then the union could at any time hold data corresponding to type A OR to type B, but not both at the same time. Unions in IDL are *discriminated* unions, which means that they must contain a field that determines which of the possible structures they actually represent. Syntax here is similar to a Java switch statement, with the "switch" keyword determining the discriminator, and a number of "case" keywords separating the possible structure definitions.

Template Types

A *sequence* is a one-dimensional array of objects with a size often fixed at compile time and a length determined at run-time. Syntax is similar to the C++ approach to declaring templates, using left and right angle brackets to enclose the type argument.

```
// a sequence of 32 bit values, maximum 10 values
sequence<long,10>
// a sequence of 32 bit values
sequence<long>
```

Mapping this to a real language, the size determines the size of a buffer able to hold items of this type. The length determines how many items are actually held in the sequence; and thus in a call, how many of the items were to be transferred. Sequences can be nested as in the following snippet.

```
sequence<sequence<long> >
```

Strings are a special case of sequences: They are sequences of type char, but are acknowledged as a separate type because many languages, including Java, have good support built in to handle character strings. All 8-bit characters are allowed, except null.

IDL supports multidimensional, fixed size arrays. When arrays are passed to a call, the whole array is passed.

Exceptions

Exceptions serve a similar purpose in both Java and IDL. In IDL they are not objects, but separate types that can be declared to have structured data members. They are introduced with the "exception" keyword.

Attributes

The equivalent of Java's fields are IDL's attributes. However, Java does not permit fields to appear in interfaces. In fact, exposing data members is a practice often frowned upon by the object-oriented community, largely because it implies a dependency on a certain implementation, and also because it is hard to ensure that the attribute is updated in a controlled way.

The confusion arises because in languages such as Java and C++, the implementation and interfaces are specified in the same language. For example, consider the following:

```
attribute short length;
```

In a single language this implies that length is implemented as a short integer, which restricts derived interfaces. With IDL, an attribute definition is almost always mapped into the implementation language as a pair of methods or operations, one to get the value and another to set it; using the attribute keyword is considered a shorthand representation for this pair of methods. IDL also allows you to specify that attributes cannot be set explicitly, by specifying the "readonly" keyword:

```
readonly attribute short length;
```

In this case, only the get() method is defined for this attribute in the implementation language.

Operations

Operations encapsulate the behavior of objects and are probably the most complex items to declare. This complexity is especially true because they must also specify the additional semantics that arise from being distributed. Two examples of operations are

```
string Fooey( in long inVal, out long outVal) raises (FooEx);
```

and

```
oneway void Foo( in string Thingy);
```

The syntax is similar to a Java method call with a few additions. Not only are the names and types of parameters specified, but also their semantics (modes), using one of the keywords "in," "out," or "inout." These are used to specify which direction the parameter is passed, as described in the following list

- **in.** Parameter passes from client to server
- **out.** Parameter passes from server to client
- **inout.** Parameter passes in both directions

The exceptions which may occur as a result of performing the operation are specified as a comma delimited list after the "raises" keyword.

The "oneway" keyword specifies the semantics of the whole operation. It is optional and its use implies best-effort semantics. In other words, there is no guarantee of delivery. Otherwise, operations use at-most-once semantics. No exceptions are defined for oneway operations, although they might raise standard exceptions.

The Pros and Cons of IDL

The preceding sections covered most of what you'll need to know in order to read IDL interface definitions. The syntax is quite similar to both Java and C, so any culture shock should be minimal.

Being designed specifically for interface definition has allowed IDL to remain simple yet powerful enough to represent object interface semantics, even in a fully distributed system.

Describing interfaces in IDL ensures that they are "clean" and not reliant on a particular implementation. From an IDL specification, all the language-specific code can be generated by tools (except of course for the implementation!). Clients of objects with IDL interfaces can be coded in any supported language, as can the implementations. Furthermore, objects can take advantage of the wealth of functionality provided by CORBA and the CORBAservices.

Of course, having a separate language does increase the complexity of a development environment somewhat. It's another language with which developers must become familiar, and extra steps are required for the conversion between IDL and Java sources. However, these are relatively minor disadvantages in the case of larger development projects, where they will be greatly outweighed by the flexibility gained.

The JAVA IDL System and Tools

At the time of writing, Sun's support for Java IDL was at a fairly early stage of development, and the toolkit was designated as an alpha release. Supplied as part of the package were an IDL compiler, a portable ORB core, and a copy of the proposed mapping between IDL and Java (along with a few samples and a little documentation).

Objects to be accessed remotely supply their interfaces as IDL definitions. The compiler, "idlgen," compiles these IDL interfaces into Java client stubs and server skeletons. Java applets and applications then use the stubs to call methods on the remote objects. The stubs call the portable ORB core, which communicates with the remote ORB via an available protocol.

The alpha toolkit release did not support the standard IIOP protocol, but instead used a lightweight proprietary protocol called the "Door ORB" protocol to communicate with other Java based servers. IIOP is scheduled for delivery when Java IDL is officially released. Also to be delivered is a module to connect Java IDL directly to SunSoft's NEO range of CORBA products.

The Rear Mirror View

Hopefully, the preceding sections gave you a fair overview of the two main approaches to distributed object support for Java. It is not entirely clear why Sun/JavaSoft have provided two solutions to the same problem. Although it is true that RMI and Java IDL are aimed at different market sectors, it seems that Sun is suffering from the same ailment that plagues many other large fragmented corporations, such as IBM. Different divisions, each required to be a "profit center," have to look after their own interests ahead of those of other groups within the company.

Sun has been a long-time supporter of the OMG, with an existing range of CORBA-based products. However, the Java developers were not closely allied with the CORBA groups and, buoyed by the burgeoning success of Java technologies, obviously felt they could provide a more elegant solution by making it Java specific. It's certainly true that Java developers greatly outnumber their CORBA-experienced counterparts. It's also true that RMI is an elegant solution, unhindered by any approval process by an external body. However, CORBA has many undeniable advantages, and by focusing resources on one approach, Sun could have provided a CORBA-based solution with most of the advantages of RMI. Providing an ORB as part of the Java VM is just one possibility.

There is no clear division between the RMI and CORBA approaches, with considerable overlap in their areas of potential application. It seems that RMI is perhaps best suited to smaller scale "personal" applications, especially those that use the Internet to some extent. CORBA is probably better suited to heterogeneous corporate intranet environments, where its capability to integrate with other languages and legacy systems is important.

Java in a Corporate Setting

Java IDL-based CORBA solutions will be of most interest to corporate developers building so-called mission critical, enterprise applications. The term "middleware" is common in these environments, where it applies to software "glue," such as CORBA and DCE. To date, most CORBA products have been sold into corporate environments, where multithousand dollar price tags and "per seat" run-time licenses are common.

The forces that act to form the corporate computing environment are quite different from those experienced in small offices and the home environment. A small saving in hardware costs becomes significant when applied to thousands of user workstations. Even relatively simple operations, such as installing software updates, become a major issue with large numbers of machines.

Consequently, corporations find the *thin client* model—where a central, relatively costly resource is leveraged across the whole user base—very appealing. They perceive the new dedicated Java machines, without local storage, as a direct replacement for the systems of dumb terminals and mainframes currently deployed. Software is automatically downloaded from a central source, making it easy to update. User data is stored centrally, facilitating backups.

At least initially, Java and CORBA solutions will fit this traditional client-server model. Remote objects on the server will do most of the processing, whereas local objects will present good-looking graphical user interfaces to the applications. Lightweight Java ORBs can be downloaded with application software to perform the communication functions; full ORBs are unnecessary because clients do not need to communicate directly. Objects at the server end can be coded in an appropriate language, such as C or COBOL. Legacy applications and databases can be given object-oriented interfaces, implemented as bridges using CORBAS Dynamic Server Interface.

This is the model best supported by the first wave of Java/CORBA tools (such as OrbixWeb from Iona and JOE from Sun). As the tools mature, it is likely that greater support for peer-to-peer arrangements of objects will be provided. Groupware and workflow applications benefit most from these arrangements.

Standardization of the IDL bindings for the Java language by the OMG is a critical next step. It must happen before CORBA becomes a viable distributed computing framework for Java, with strong third-party support. The standard is currently receiving a lot of attention, with an expected end point around the second or third quarter of 1997. It is likely that the final standard will be close to the one submitted by Sun Microsystems, as supplied in the Java IDL distribution, and in online form on their web page at

```
http://splash.javasoft.com/JavaIDL/pages/IDLtoJava.html
```

As much of an advance as it is, inter-object communication may still be at too low a level of abstraction or granularity for tomorrow's applications. Distributed objects are just one facet (albeit a major one) of component-oriented paradigms. To close out this chapter, the next section covers Sun's proposal for a software component model, which subsumes concerns over RMI or IDL by allowing either or both within its architecture.

Java IDL or RMI: The Java Beans Initiative

Java Beans is Sun's proposal for a component-level model for Java. Software components address the granularity of software packaging. Traditionally, software has either been sold as complete, monolithic applications or as low-level libraries for developers. Components offer a higher level of functionality than most libraries, but lower than that of applications, such as word processors. Such granularity is expected to promote reuse, while making it easier to develop applications tailored to the needs of users (rather than the one-size-fits-all approach of current application software).

The Java Beans model is similar to existing models such as OLE/ActiveX and OpenDoc. The model is based on containers and components, called Beans. Java Beans does not itself address the distributed objects issue, but subsumes it by integrating the RMI and Java/IDL approaches within its framework. Beans are not automatically turned into distributed objects because this would impose inappropriate overhead in many cases. Instead they are easily made into distributed objects using the appropriate services. Likewise, existing APIs are used to support the following services:

- Persistence using Java Object Serialization
- Reflection using the Java Core Reflection API
- Packaging using the JAR file format

Beans have both run-time and design-time parts. At design time, the Bean provides code to enable its handling in an application builder. Using the Reflection APIs (which perform a similar function to the CORBA Interface Repository), the builder can discover all the information it requires about the bean to support its integration into the application being built. Complex Beans may provide their own editors as part of the design-time code.

Many Beans will have a GUI component based on the AWT, though some (especially those that run on servers) may be completely non-visual.

Beans can even determine their context at run-time and exhibit visual or non-visual behavior as appropriate. It is expected that most Beans will be small- to medium-sized components, from buttons to more complex controls such as grids and text editors.

For more information, visit the Java Beans web page at

```
http://splash.javasoft.com/beans/
```

Several companies, such as IBM, have also announced support for the Java Beans model, integrating it with their existing OpenDoc technology.

References and Further Reading

References to resources on the Internet have a habit of going out of date, even before they are published in paper form, which is particularly true with the rapidly evolving field of distributed objects. To help you explore the field beyond the overview given in this chapter, a web page has been set up at

```
http://www.mycelium.com/published/isj/
```

It contains links to interesting documents and sites on the web related to distributed object technology.

Summary

Networking is intrinsic to most visions of future computing. The technologies behind distributed computing aim to hide the presence of the network, enabling developers to create software without regard for where its objects will be eventually located. In use, the objects are geographically distributed for best efficiency, while interoperating seamlessly to give an illusion of locality to the user.

Sun has provided two choices of distribution mechanism for Java objects. Remote Method Invocation is an elegant, Java specific approach introduced with JDK 1.1. The alternative Java IDL mechanism is based on the open CORBA2 standard from the Object Management Group and caters to larger heterogeneous systems. Either can be used to provide the underlying distribution capabilities to support the JavaBeans software component model.

References

Salus, Peter H., *Casting the Net*, Addison Wesley 1995, ISBN 0-201-87674-4

Coulouris, George; Dollimore, Jean; Kindberg, Tim, *Distributed Systems: Concept and Design, Second Edition,* Addison Wesley 1994, ISBN 0-201-62433-8

Sessions, Roger, *Object Persistence: Beyond Object Oriented Databases,* Prentice Hall 1996, ISBN 0-13-192436-2

Harkey, Dan; Edwards, Jeri; Orfali, Robert; Wiley John, *Distributed Object Survival Guide,* 1995, ISBN 0471129933

Chapter 13

Thinking in Terms of Threads

The use of multiple threads is a low-level technique that enables a program to perform more than one job at a time. Effective application of multiple threads requires a strong conceptual understanding of these mechanisms provided by Java. This chapter, therefore, includes detailed discussions of the underlying concepts that support these powerful techniques.

The Thread Model

A *thread* (or "thread of control") is often defined as "a single sequential flow of control within a program." Every Java program contains at least one thread that performs the operations denoted by code in the expected order. Consider the simple "Hello World" program in listing 13.1.

Listing 13.1   A Simple "Hello World" Program

```
public class HelloWorld {
public static void main(String[] args) {
        System.out.println("Hello World");
}
}
```

When this program is run, the Java VM creates an initial thread of control. This thread enters main(), enters the System.out.println() method, and then proceeds to perform the necessary operations to make "Hello World" appear on the console. Finally, after returning from println(), the thread exits from main(), and the program terminates. Figure 13.1 shows the progress of the thread through main() and println().

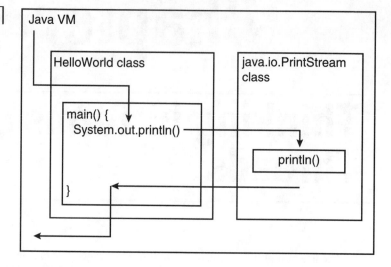

FIGURE 13.1
Flow of control through the Hello World program.

Single-threaded applications, such as the previous example, only perform one operation at a time. Multithreaded applications (or multithreaded applets) enable simultaneous execution of multiple operations in *parallel*.

Applications of Threads

Threads are often used when a program needs to do more than one task at a time, such as when a GUI must respond to the user while the program simultaneously transfers a file or prints data. Creating separate threads of control to handle these jobs is preferable to constructing a complex loop that attempts to transfer the next block of a file, print some data, and check for user actions that require a response.

Threads are also appropriate when an activity needs to be performed on a regular basis. Although it's possible, for example, to have an application perform animation by regularly checking whether it's time to display the next image (as well as responding to the user, processing data, and so on), it's much easier to create a separate thread of control that is devoted to handling the animation.

Finally, threading can also enable a program (such as the server application of a client/server system) to respond according to demand. For example, by creating a separate thread to handle requests as they arrive from multiple clients, the server design is simplified (because each thread considers only one request), and the load on the server platform becomes proportional to the number of client requests; in other words, the server responds to the demands of the clients by creating threads to handle their requests. Indeed, unless a program is multithreaded, there is no easy way to take advantage of the extra processing power of a multiprocessor system.

Threads in Design

To demonstrate some possible applications of threads, consider the simple object hierarchy example in listings 13.2a and 13.2b.

Listing 13.2a   Abstract Worker Class

```
public abstract class Worker {
//Do the processing required for this task
public void doTask(Task task);
}
```

Listing 13.2b   Abstract Supervisor Class

```
public class Supervisor {
public void getWorkDone(Task[] tasks) {
        for(int t=0; t<tasks.length; t++) {
                //create a new Worker to do the job
                Worker w = new Worker();
                //give that worker the job to do
                w.doTask(tasks[t]);
        }
}
}
```

The Supervisor class is able to create Worker objects on demand to do Tasks. Although this seems ideal for completing many Tasks, there's a flaw. The single thread of control in getWorkDone() creates a new Worker and then enters doTask(), but the thread is then occupied with that Task. Only after completing the Task does the thread of control return to getWorkDone() (see fig. 13.2). The thread then circles the for loop to create another Worker to do the next Task. In fact, getWorkDone() would operate just as quickly by creating only one Worker to process all the Tasks in *series*.

Figure 13.2

*Flow of control
between Supervisor
and Worker.*

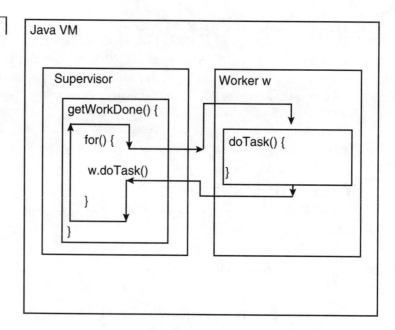

Having a separate Task object for each task to be performed may simplify the design and
the code of the program, but it doesn't allow the code to process Tasks in parallel unless
multiple threads are also used.

Processing Tasks in Parallel

If doTask() is capable of creating a new, separate thread to perform the processing of a
Task, then the initial thread of control can return immediately to getWorkDone() and
create another Worker while the separate thread continues to execute doTask(). For each
Task, a new Worker object (and thread) is created, which all process in parallel.

In fact, most real-world objects implement parallel activity. A human supervisor allocating
tasks to human (or mechanical) workers doesn't need to wait for each worker to complete
an assigned task before proceeding; workers perform various tasks while the supervisor
and other workers handle other business.

Several Java API classes that you may already have used create separate threads of
control. Loading an image via java.applet.getImage() is handled by a separate image-
loading thread that builds the image as the data is received. A class that implements
java.applet.AudioClip to reproduce sound may also create a separate thread to handle the
playing and looping of the audio.

Candidates for Threading

Here are some examples of cases where a multithreaded design can work well:

- Packaging complex, time-consuming operations that can proceed independently upon starting.

- Providing services, particularly those that don't return results, such as the case of an object that sends log messages to a slow printer while ignoring printing errors. Services that return no results are often appropriate for threading because code invoking them has no need to wait for them to complete and could continue to do other work while the service is provided.

- Performing autonomous tasks. For example, a GUI object that displays a date/time clock.

- Responding to external and possibly asynchronous events. For example, when receiving data via a network connection or serial port.

- Modeling the real world behavior of a set of autonomous systems. For example, an industrial-control system that monitors results from several asynchronous output sources and generates multiple control values.

It's appropriate to consider the use of separate threads wherever one object can usefully carry out work independently of other objects.

When Not to Use Threads

Creating separate threads of control burdens system resources. Furthermore, some systems support a limited number of threads. Only a limited number of threads can actually run concurrently. The mechanisms that Java provides to enable variables to be shared among threads impose an overhead that restricts the access to those variables. Arranging for complex interaction or communication between many threads can be error-prone. Potential defects may be caused by *race conditions*, which occur where the behavior of the system is affected by very subtle shifts in the timing of actions that are performed by multiple threads.

In short, threads are not the universal solution to all programming problems; they should be used when concurrent activity is appropriate and when they contribute to elegant system design.

A Candidate Class for Threading

Listing 13.3 presents a simple (and rather artificial) example to consider: an object that generates a checksum of all the bytes in a file. This might be used as a quick check for data file corruption, for instance. The checksum calculated is a number generated by adding the values of all the bytes in the file (ignoring overflows).

Listing 13.3   The unthreaded FileChecksum Class

```java
import java.io.*;

//A simple file checksum object
public class FileChecksum {

//object variables
private long length;        //of the File
private long sum;

//constructor
public FileChecksum(File f)
        throws FileNotFoundException {
        //get the length of the file
        length = f.length();

        //initialize the sum to 0
        sum = 0;

        //Open a FileInputStream for this file
        FileInputStream fis = new FileInputStream(f);

        //Loop through all of the bytes in the file
        //and generate a checksum.
        try {
                for(int i=0; i<length; i++)
                        sum += (long)fis.read();
        }

        catch(IOException e) { }

        finally {
                try {
                        fis.close();
```

```
        }
            catch(IOException e) { }
        }
}

//object methods
public long getChecksum() {
    return sum;
}
}
```

In order to calculate the checksum, the constructor must read every byte from the file. With a large file, this method could take quite some time to execute. Much of that time might be spent waiting for the next block of the file to be read from disk; this time could be used to perform other processing. What is required is a way to enable the checksum operation to run in parallel with other operations. The section entitled "A Threaded FileChecksum" specifies how to extend the FileChecksum class to use a separate thread of control.

Threads in Java

In some languages that include support for threads, almost any set of statements can be run in parallel by simply bracketing them with specific keywords, as in the fragment of a sorting algorithm in Concurrent Pascal shown in listing 13.4.

Listing 13.4   A Concurrent Pascal Cobegin/end Block

```
begin { sort block }
  cobegin { do the following statements concurrently }
    sort(1, n);
    sort(n+1, limit);
  coend    { end of concurrent stuff }
  merge(1, n+1, limit);
end. {the program }
```

In Java's object-oriented environment, however, separate threads, like anything else, are represented as objects. Parallel processing is accomplished by creating objects that use threads to perform their own processing.

The Thread Object and the Runnable Interface

In Java, the creation and control of threads is performed via the java.lang.Thread class. Just to be clear, the capitalized term, "Thread," or "Thread object," refers only to the java.lang.Thread class and its instances; "thread" refers to a thread of control. Every thread of control in a Java Virtual Machine (VM) is associated with a Thread object. Creating a Thread object is the only way to create a separate thread of control. A newly created Thread object can't perform any parallel processing unless the code that is to be run in parallel is indicated to the object. This is accomplished by passing the Thread constructor an object that implements the java.lang.Runnable interface.

An initial Thread object is created when an application starts. This thread then calls main() (or in the case of an applet, init()). Additional Thread objects can be created wherever an object needs to perform processing in parallel with other threads. Each new thread calls the run() method of the associated Runnable object. Listing 13.5 shows the definition of the Runnable interface.

Listing 13.5   The Java API Definition of java.lang.Runnable

```
public abstract interface Runnable {
        //Any Runnable object provides this
        //method.  A new thread will call this
        //method.
        public abstract void run();
}
```

Understanding which run() method is called by a new thread is complicated because the Thread class itself provides a run() method and implements the Runnable interface. The two possible situations are

1. A new object is created that is of the Thread class (or a subclass). It is not passed any Runnable object when it is constructed. The new thread will call the run() method of the new Thread object.

2. A new Thread object is created and passed an existing Runnable object. The new thread will call the run() method of that Runnable object.

The run() method contains the code executed by the new thread which can contain calls to methods of "this" or any other object. A run() method indicates where a newly created Thread enters a Java program in the same way that main() is indicative of where the initial thread starts.

Constructing New Threads

The Thread class provides the following constructors:

Listing 13.6   The Constructors for java.lang.Thread

```
//Construct a new Thread.
public Thread()

//Construct a new Thread and pass it an object that
//implements the Runnable interface.
public Thread(Runnable target)

//Construct a new Thread as a member of the given
//ThreadGroup to run the given Runnable object.
public Thread(ThreadGroup group, Runnable target)

//Construct a new Thread with the given name.
public Thread(String name)

//Construct a new Thread in the given ThreadGroup
//with the given name.
public Thread(ThreadGroup group, String name)

//Construct a new Thread with the given name
//to run the given Runnable object.
public Thread(Runnable target, String name)

//Construct a new Thread as a member of the given
//ThreadGroup, with the given name,
//to run the given Runnable object.
public Thread(ThreadGroup group,
              Runnable target,
              String name)
```

ThreadGroups are discussed later, in the section about Thread Grouping; a ThreadGroup is an object that associates a set of Threads into a group.

Every Thread object has an associated name; the name may be passed when the Thread object is created; it can be changed and read with setName() and getName(), defined in listing 13.7.

Listing 13.7   Methods Operating on a Thread's Name

```
//Set the Thread's name to the given String which
//may not be null.
public final void setName(String name);

//Return the Thread's current name.
public final String getName();
```

If a name is not specified, the Thread constructors generate one. Names do not need to be unique and are mainly useful in debugging. Thread's toString() method incorporates the name in the returned String.

Java has no limit to the number of Threads that may be created, although different VM implementations might impose their own limits according to the limitations of the underlying operating system on which they run. If the Java VM is a single operating system process, for example, and each java thread requires an equivalent operating system thread, then the maximum number of Java threads is limited to the maximum permitted by the operating system. In practice any such limit is not likely to be a problem, except in very large applications with hundreds of threads.

A Threaded FileChecksum

To demonstrate the use of a thread, the FileChecksum class can be extended as in listing 13.8 so that the checksum calculation is run as a separate thread. This enables the program to proceed with other work while the checksum is calculated.

Listing 13.8   A Threaded FileChecksum Class

```
import java.io.*;

//File checksum object which uses a Thread to calculate the
//checksum in parallel with other processing.
public class FileChecksum implements Runnable {

//object variables
private long              length;        //of the File
private long              sum;

private boolean           finished;
public  Thread            thread;
private FileInputStream   fis;
```

```
//constructor
public FileChecksum(File f)
        throws FileNotFoundException {
        //get the length of the file
        length = f.length();

        //initialize the sum to 0
        sum = 0;

        //clear the finished flag
        finished = false;

        //Open a FileInputStream for this file
        fis = new FileInputStream(f);

        //Create a Thread object that will run our
        //processing for us.  Pass the filename as
        //the name of the Thread.  Pass this as the
        //object to be run by the new Thread.
        thread = new Thread(this, f.getName());

        //Start the new thread running.
        thread.start();

} //end of constructor

//The run() method that the Runnable interfaces requires
//us to declare.  This is the method that the new thread
//of control will call.
public void run() {
        //Loop through all of the bytes in the file
        //and generate a checksum.
        try {
                for(int i=0; i<length; i++)
                        sum += (long)fis.read();
        }

        catch(IOException e) { }

        finally {
                finished = true;
                try {
                        fis.close();
                }
                catch(IOException e) { }
```

continues

Listing 13.8   Continued

```
        }

            //Leaving the run() method will stop the
            //thread.
    }

    //object methods

    //getChecksum will return -1 if we haven't finished
    //calculating the checksum yet.
    public long getChecksum() {
            if(finished)
                    return sum;
            else
                    return -1;
    }
    }       //end of FileChecksum
```

In the new FileChecksum constructor, this is passed as the Runnable. When the new thread is started by calling the start() method of the new Thread object, the following occurs:

1. The new thread of control enters the run() method of the Runnable supplied, the FileChecksum object itself.

2. When the run() method exits, the thread of control finishes and dies. The FileChecksum object is unaffected by this.

A thread finishes when run() returns just like a Java program finishes when the initial thread returns from main().

Providing a run() Method to a Thread

There are two ways of associating a run() method with a Thread object:

- By passing a Runnable to the Thread constructor
- By subclassing Thread and providing a run() method in the new class (because the Thread class implements Runnable).

The default Thread.run() method does nothing, so it must be overridden to do any useful work. Listing 13.9 shows how FileChecksum might be implemented as a subclass of Thread:

Listing 13.9 The Threaded FileChecksum Class as a Subclass of Thread

```
import java.io.*;

//File checksum object which uses a Thread to calculate the
//checksum in parallel with other processing.
public class FileChecksumThread extends Thread {

//object variables
private long              length;        //of the File
private long              sum;

private boolean           finished;
private FileInputStream   fis;

//constructor
public FileChecksumThread(File f)
        throws FileNotFoundException {

        //Call a Thread constructor with the name of the
        //file as the Thread name.
        super(f.getName());

        //get the length of the file
        length = f.length();

        //initialize the sum to 0
        sum = 0;

        //clear the finished flag
        finished = false;

        //Open a FileInputStream for this file
        fis = new FileInputStream(f);

        //Start the thread going.
        this.start();

} //end of constructor

//This run() method overrides the one in Thread.
public void run() {

        //Loop through all of the bytes in the file
        //and generate a checksum.
        try {
```

continues

Listing 13.9   Continued

```
                    for(int i=0; i<length; i++)
                            sum += (long)fis.read();
        }

        catch(IOException e) { }

        finally {
                finished = true;
                try {
                        fis.close();
                }
                catch(IOException e) { }
        }
    }

//object methods

//getChecksum will return -1 if we haven't finished
//calculating the checksum yet.
public long getChecksum() {
        if(finished)
                return sum;
        else
                return -1;
}
}        //end of FileChecksum
```

After a thread has been created, the start() method must be called to start the separate thread of control. After start() returns, assume that the new Thread executes in parallel with all other threads in the system. Exactly when the various threads in the system execute is determined by the Java VM scheduler, which is discussed later in the section about Thread Scheduling.

The Thread.start() method shouldn't be confused with the Applet.start() method. Thread.start() is called to start a separate thread of execution running. Applet.start() is called when an applet object should start processing.

Getting a Result from FileChecksum

A good design goal is to ensure that any code that previously used the FileChecksum class should be able to use the new version with minimal changes. However, consider the following code in listing 13.10:

Listing 13.10   Code that Uses a FileChecksum Object

```
//Create a file checksum object and get the
//checksum.
FileChecksum fc = new FileChecksum("a.tmp");
int sum = fc.getChecksum();
```

This code isn't aware that FileChecksum now does its work in parallel. The call to getChecksum() comes immediately following the creation of the FileChecksum object, when it's unlikely that the FileChecksum thread has completed reading the file. Though getChecksum() has been changed to check whether the calculation has finished and, if not, to return a value of –1 to indicate that the checksum isn't yet available, all the code that uses a FileChecksum still needs to be changed to check for the –1 return value, as in figure 13.3. Ideally, getChecksum() should wait until the checksum is available before returning. Java supports language mechanisms to enable this, and they're discussed later in the section on Concurrent Thread Interaction. For the moment, think of the "finished" flag as a simple way for the thread that calculates the checksum to communicate with any threads that want to obtain the result of that calculation.

FIGURE 13.3

A less than ideal way of checking whether the checksum is available.

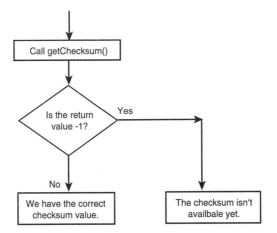

Understanding Multithreaded Code

When reading multithreaded code, it's important to be clear about which thread executes what code. A method of a Runnable object can be called by any thread, not just threads that are calling its run() method. Thus, as in the FileChecksum example in listing 13.10, any thread could call getChecksum().

A Thread object merely represents a thread and provides methods to control that thread; Runnable objects actually perform the work in parallel. Each Thread calls run() for one and only one Runnable object, and although it's possible to have the run() method of a single Runnable object being executed by several Threads at once, a single Runnable object is usually associated with a only a single Thread object.

The Thread Lifecycle

A Thread object, after initial creation, must be started. Starting the Thread object causes the new, separate thread of control to call a run() method. The Thread object stays in this "running" state until it's stopped, although it may be suspended and then restarted for a number of reasons (refer to the later sections about Mutual Exclusion, Wait, and Notify). A Thread object can be in one of the following states (these state names are not part of the Java API; they're used only for explanation):

- **Created.** A Thread object is in this state when it is first created. The only methods that can be called while a thread is in this state are start(), which changes the Thread object to the Running state, or stop(), which changes it to Dead. Any other methods called throw a java.lang.IllegalThreadStateException.

- **Running.** A Thread object in this state is available for execution along with all other Running Threads. The Java VM Scheduler decides which threads are actually executing at any one time, following rules explained later in the section about scheduling and priority. While in this state, the Thread can be suspended by suspend() or killed (state becomes dead) by stop(). Exiting the run() method (either by design or because of an uncaught exception) also changes the Thread state to dead.

- **Suspended.** A suspended Thread object is not executed by the scheduler and remains suspended until either the resume() method is called, which changes the Thread object back to the Running state, or the stop() method is called. A thread can suspend itself for a period of time by calling the sleep() method, although resume() cannot be used to waken a sleeping Thread object. Calling sleep(), which is a class method, always affects the *current* thread.

  Threads may also be suspended when performing I/O, or they may be suspended through the use of synchronization primitives.

- **Dead.** A dead Thread cannot be restarted and is eligible for garbage collection under the same conditions as any other object.

Methods that Change Thread State

The methods that change or test the Thread object state are shown in listing 13.11. Figure 13.4 shows the methods for each Thread state that may be called to change that state and what effect they have.

Listing 13.11   java.lang.Thread Methods Affecting a Thread's State

```
//Make a newly created Thread eligible for execution.
public synchronized void start();

//Stop thread by throwing ThreadDeath
public final void stop();

//Stop thread by throwing an Exception or Error.
//Normal code should just use stop().
public final synchronized void stop(Throwable o);

//Returns true if the Thread is in the Running or Suspended
//states.
public final boolean isAlive();

//Put the current Thread to sleep for the specified
//time. Note that this is a static method and always
//operates on the current Thread.
public static void sleep(long millis)
        throws InterruptedException;

//As sleep(long millis), but allows more precise
//specification of time.
public static void sleep(long millis,
                              int nanos)
        throws InterruptedException;

//Suspend a Thread. The Thread will become eligible for
//execution again when resume() is called.
public final void suspend();

//Resume a Thread that has been suspended by a call to
//suspend(). If the Thread has not been suspended this
//way resume() will have no effect.
public final void resume();
```

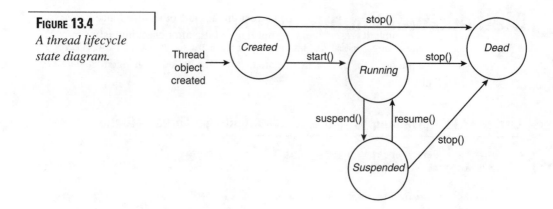

Figure 13.4

A thread lifecycle state diagram.

Thread Lifecycle

For many applications of threading, it's not necessary to change the thread state other than to call start() to start the new thread running. Because a thread exits on return from the run() method of the target Runnable, calling stop() is usually unnecessary.

The sleep() calls might be used in a thread that starts and monitors some potentially time-consuming operation, such as sending data over a network link, to cause the thread to sleep for a period of time and then wake up to check the progress of the operation.

Suspending and resuming threads can be useful where one thread controls the operation of one or more other threads. In a real implementation of the Worker/Supervisor classes given earlier in the section on Threads in Design, for example, the Supervisor might suspend some Worker threads to allow others more processor time.

Testing Thread States

The Thread class provides a single method for testing the Thread object state. The isAlive() method returns true if the Thread object has been started but not yet stopped (that is, the Thread object is in either the Running or Suspended state). A return of false indicates that the Thread has either not yet been started or has completed and is now Dead.

Signaling a thread to stop running by setting a flag is a common requirement, and the Java API defines three methods to support this. The Thread.interrupt() method can be called, for any thread, to set a Thread internal Boolean flag to true. Two other methods, Thread.isInterrupted() and Thread.interrupted(), return the state of this flag—true if interrupt() has been called for the Thread, false if not. Thread.interrupted() is a static method that always checks the flag for the current thread. The other difference between the two is that interrupted() resets the interrupt flag to false after checking; isInterrupted() does not.

With these methods it's easy for a loop in a run() method to be stopped in a controlled fashion by interrupting the Thread object running it, as shown in listing 13.12, which also defines the methods that handle Thread interrupts.

Listing 13.12   A run() Method that Checks for Interrupts

```
//Send an interrupt to a Thread.

public void run() {

    //loop until this thread is interrupted
    do {
        //do some operation
        doSomeWork();
    while(!interrupted());
}
```

The run() method continues to loop until interrupt() is called for the Thread object which is running it. The next time that interrupted() is called, it returns true to indicate that an interrupt has been requested, and the loop will terminate.

Stopping Threads

There are three events that can stop a running thread:

- An exception is thrown and not caught
- The thread returns from the run() method of the Runnable object
- The Thread object is destroyed

Throwing an Exception

Any uncaught exception stops a thread. The run() method cannot throw exceptions (none are listed in its definition in the java.lang.Runnable interface), so any uncaught exceptions that occur within a thread can't be caught by any other thread. An uncaught exception in run() causes that thread to stop running after all clauses have been executed and the uncaughtException() method has been invoked for the ThreadGroup, of which the Thread object is a member.

The Thread.stop() method operates by throwing a ThreadDeath object. java.lang. ThreadDeath is not a subclass of Exception but rather of java.lang.Error. ThreadDeath is a special case of Throwable that generates no error message or stack trace, if it is not caught. ThreadDeath can be caught in a run() method, though this isn't usually necessary. If caught, it must be rethrown after handling to ensure that the thread is properly stopped.

When a run() method exits a try because of a ThreadDeath (or any other exception), any applicable "finally" blocks are executed. Throwing a ThreadDeath via stop() is therefore a safe and preferred way to stop a thread. For example, when an application quits, it may use stop() on all its running threads. Placing cleanup code in "finally" blocks enables a threaded object to exit cleanly because the Thread is stopped or because of any other Exception. Listing 13.13 shows a code outline that catches ThreadDeath and allows some cleanup to occur before the thread exits.

Listing 13.13   Catching ThreadDeath in a run() Method

```
public void run() {
        try {
                //do work
        }
        catch(ThreadDeath td) {
                //clean up
                throw td; //re-throw ThreadDeath
        }
}
```

Exiting run()

Instead of explicitly calling stop() to stop a thread, a variable can be used as a flag (a variable set by some code to indicate to any other code that a particular condition is true) to request that the run() method should exit at the next convenient point. For example, a run() method containing a loop might check the flag at the end of each iteration and jump out of the loop if the flag is set true. The run() method of FileChecksum can easily be modified to operate this way, as shown in listing 13.14.

```
private boolean stopFlag = false;

public void stopThread() {
        stopFlag = true;
}

public void run() {

        //Loop through all of the bytes in the file
        //and generate a checksum.
        try {
                for(int i=0; i<length; i++) {
                        //if the flag is set, exit the
                        //loop (and the run() method).
                        if(stopFlag)
                                break;
                        sum += (long)fis.read();
                }
        }

        catch(IOException e) { }

        finally {
                finished = true;
                try {
                        fis.close();
                }
                catch(IOException e) { }
        }
}
```

Destroying a Thread

One final way to completely stop a thread remains. The destroy() method, defined in listing
13.15, kills a thread in a non-catchable manner. This is not a safe or usual way to stop a
thread, and it should be used as a last resort. For example, a large Java application with many
threads, one of which detects an irrevocable error, might need to kill off all threads in the
system before halting the Java VM. If some threads catch ThreadDeath and refuse to respond
to stop() calls, the only way to kill those threads is through the destroy() call.

Listing 13.15   The java.lang.Thread destroy() Method

```
//Destroy a thread, without any cleanup. A last resort.
public void destroy();
```

In the java.lang.Thread class, this method just throws java.lang.NoSuchMethodError. Subclasses of Thread might override destroy() to handle special cases. For example, a thread that handles a low-level interface to a device driver or allocates native resources might implement a destroy() method. This ensures a graceful exit for however the thread is stopped.

Waiting for Threads to Die

The Thread.join() method is useful when one thread is required to stop() another and wait until the stop is complete. This method has three forms, as shown in listing 13.16:

The System.exit() call deserves attention here. When exit() is called, all running threads are killed and the Java VM exits. This does not guarantee to call stop() or destroy() or even to finalize Threads. The bottom line here is that exit() should only be called in response to a fatal error of some kind. Even then, it's often preferable to invoke stop() to stop the entire ThreadGroup hierarchy (see the later section on Thread Grouping). This enables Threads to clean up and exit gracefully.

Listing 13.16   The java.lang.Thread Join Methods

```
//wait forever for thread to die
public final void join() throws InterruptedException

//millis is number of milliseconds to wait
public final synchronized void join(long millis)
        throws InterruptedException;

//millis is number of whole milliseconds to wait
//nanos is more precise specification of time.
public final synchronized void join(long millis,
                                        int nanos)
        throws InterruptedException;
```

It's often necessary for one thread to wait for another to complete. In the case of the FileChecksum example, for instance, a thread might want to wait until the checksum calculation has completed, which could be done by calling isAlive() for the other thread, sleeping if it returns true and then checking again, and repeating this until isAlive() returns false, indicating that the thread has died. However, Java provides the join() method to simplify this.

The join() method for a Thread object suspends the current thread until that Thread object dies (isAlive() returns false). For example, because the thread used in FileChecksum is public, it's easy to use the stopFlag mechanism and wait for the thread to die, as shown in listing 13.17:

Listing 13.17   Calling join() on a Thread

```
FileChecksum fc = new FileChecksum(ourFile);

//...

//stop the checksum
fc.stopThread();
fc.thread.join();        //wait for thread to die
```

Thread Scheduling and Priority

The Java VM scheduler can choose any thread in the Running state for execution; however there are a few simple constraints. When a processor is available to run a thread, the scheduler chooses one for execution ("schedules" a thread) from among the eligible Threads, based on their *priority*.

A Thread's priority is defined by an integer value between Thread.MIN_PRIORITY and Thread.MAX_PRIORITY. Threads are prioritized by calling the setPriority() method and are read with getPriority(). A newly created thread inherits the priority from the Thread object of its creator thread. Thread.NORM_PRIORITY is the default priority level.

You would set a thread's priority to be larger than NORM_PRIORITY if you intended that thread to be given more processor time than others. For example, in a word-processing application that performs background spell checking, a thread that handles user keystrokes would be given a higher priority than the thread that performs checking so that the application responds quickly to text being typed and only checks spelling when the user pauses.

Also, the Java VM garbage collector is sometimes implemented as a Thread with a lower-than-normal priority. This is intended to prevent the garbage collector from slowing the response of the system by taking up processor time at the expense of threads running at normal priority.

Setting and Checking Thread Priority

A Thread object's priority is set and checked via these methods:

Listing 13.18   java.lang.Thread Methods that Operate on a Thread's Priority

```
//Set a Thread's priority.  If the newPriority is
//not between MIN_PRIORITY and MAX_PRIORITY (inclusive)
//then throw the exception.
```

continues

Thinking in Terms of Threads

Listing 13.18   Continued

```
public final void setPriority(int newPriority)
        throws IllegalArgumentException;

//Return a Thread's current priority.
public final int getPriority();
```

Scheduling Threads

The scheduler is not required to choose the thread with the highest priority for execution, but it usually does. When several Threads have the same (highest) priority, the scheduler chooses one at random. If the chosen Thread is implementation-dependent, then the scheduler is not required to allocate processor time fairly among competing Threads. In general, processor-intensive Threads with higher priorities should call yield() frequently (discussed later in the section on preemptive scheduling). This method causes a thread to give up the processor and allows the scheduler to consider giving lower-priority Threads a share of processor time.

In some cases, the scheduler may choose lower-priority Threads for execution if higher-priority Threads have had exclusive use of the processor for too long. Thread priority can therefore be used only to bias the scheduler to favor some Threads and cannot guarantee a certain order of execution. However, a Java implementation isn't required to do this and so, conversely, unless higher-priority threads spend some time suspended, lower-priority threads may get no processor time at all.

Preemptive Scheduling

Calling setPriority() for another Thread object can have another unexpected effect. If the new priority is greater than that of the currently executing thread, then the current thread stops executing (is "de-scheduled"), and the thread, which now has the higher priority, is scheduled. This is called *preemptive* scheduling (the higher-priority thread "preempts" the lower-priority one).

Priority setting is often used with a preemptive scheduler to improve response times to asynchronous events. For example, if an application contains a thread to perform lengthy computation-intensive work and contains another thread to handle GUI interaction with a user, the computation thread is normally set at a lower priority than the GUI thread. This enables the GUI thread to respond quickly to user actions by preempting the computation thread.

Five events might cause the scheduler to deschedule the current thread and schedule another thread:

- ■ The current thread reaches the dead state (stop() is called or run() exits).

- The current thread becomes suspended, possibly because it calls suspend(), sleep(), or another method that suspends the thread. It's likely, for example, that many of the methods in the java.io classes will suspend a thread while I/O is being performed.

- Another thread with a higher priority becomes eligible (preempted) because it just had its priority increased, was suspended, and has now re-entered the running state, or has just been started.

- The thread calls the yield() method, which requests the scheduler to deschedule the current thread and schedule another. This method is often used in computation-intensive code to ensure a fairer allocation of processor time. If no other thread is eligible for execution, the current thread is rescheduled.

- In some implementations, the time allotted to the thread expires. On such time-slicing systems, a thread is forcibly descheduled by the scheduler in favor of another when a certain time limit is reached.

Yielding

The yield() method is defined in listing 13.19. Note that it's static, so Thread.yield() can be called from any code, not just from within a run() method. As was stated previously in the section on scheduling threads, calling yield() causes a currently executing thread to relinquish the processor and allows the scheduler to consider other threads for execution. On a non-time-sliced system, threads that perform no sleep() calls and are not suspended by any other operations should periodically call yield() to ensure that the scheduler has an opportunity to share the processor time between all eligible threads.

Listing 13.19   The java.lang.Thread yield() Method

```
//Relinquish execution to other eligible threads.
public static void yield();
```

You should always remember that your classes might be used in many different situations. Assuming a class contains a processor-intensive method that might tie up the CPU for a long time, you should include yield() calls in that code so that if the class is used in a multithreaded Java program, the method won't hog the processor.

The Java Language Specification does not *require* that time-slicing is implemented. Most run() methods that contain long loops should therefore contain yield() calls, so that non-time-slicing implementations ultimately share time more effectively. The loop in the run() method of FileChecksum might therefore be as it is in listing 13.20.

Thinking in Terms of Threads

Listing 13.20   The FileChecksum run() Method Incorporating yield()

```
//Loop through all of the bytes in the file
//and generate a checksum.
try {
        for(int i=0; i<length; i++) {
                //if the flag is set, exit the
                //loop (and the run() method).
                if(stopFlag)
                        break;
                sum += (long)fis.read();
                //yield every 256 bytes.
                if(i % 256)
                        thread.yield();
        }
}
```

Even non-multithreaded applications may benefit from calling yield(). The Java VM garbage collector (gc) is sometimes run as a low-priority Thread, thus using any spare time (when all other threads are suspended) for garbage collection. In a single-threaded application that never calls yield() and creates many temporary objects, the gc thread might not be scheduled until the VM runs out of memory and forces the garbage collector to free up space. In such a situation, memory usage increases throughout the run time of the application, which may cause excessive paging and slow the whole system. When garbage collection is eventually forced to occur, the application may appear to freeze for a while as many objects are discarded and the memory is reorganized.

It's good programming practice to assume that your objects will be used as part of a multithreaded application. Insert calls to yield() in time-consuming loops or other operations.

Most of the threading examples discussed so far have covered threads that start, perform some processing, and then stop when complete. However, it's sometimes necessary to create threads that aren't intended ever to stop. Java provides support for this with daemon threads, discussed next.

Daemons

With a simple single-threaded application, it's easy to determine when the Java VM exits—when main() is complete. However, if main() creates and starts one or more Thread objects and then exits, other threads will continue running. The Java VM will not exit until all those threads have also stopped.

TIP

A trick that is sometimes used to encourage garbage collection is to place a call to System.gc() (or Runtime.gc(); both are methods that call the VM garbage-collection code) at the end of run() methods. These calls enable a thread that is about to finish to use the last of its runtime operations to perform garbage collection. Note that a call to gc() doesn't guarantee garbage collection. You should also know that finalize() methods can be called by your thread from inside gc().

A *daemon* Thread object controls a thread that may not be intended to stop running. The Java VM treats daemon threads differently in one way—it continues running until all non-daemon threads have been stopped and then automatically kills all daemon Threads before exiting.

Examples of threads that might run "forever" include the Java VM garbage collector or a "watchdog" thread that monitors the system for deadlock. These are often implemented as low-priority threads. The Java VM should ignore threads such as these when determining if the system should terminate via the exit() method and so these threads are marked as daemons.

Also, consider a threaded object that provides an onscreen clock. This thread updates the display every second and sleeps between updates. To stop this thread when the application quits, some object could be responsible for monitoring the Thread and calling stop() on it appropriately. A more elegant design results if the thread doesn't need to be stopped but is left to die when the JVM exits. This design requires the JVM to be capable of distinguishing between self-terminating threads and daemon threads that can simply be killed.

The methods defined in listing 13.21 enable setting and checking of the daemon status of a Thread object.

Listing 13.21 java.lang.Thread Methods Operating on a Thread's Daemon Flag

```
//Set on to true to mark this thread as
//a daemon.  This method must be called
//before start() or the exception is thrown.
public final void setDaemon(boolean on)
        throws IllegalThreadStateException;

//Returns the daemon flag of the Thread.
public final boolean isDaemon();
```

A Thread object created by a daemon thread is marked automatically as a daemon; Threads created by non-daemon threads aren't. The daemon status of a Thread object can be changed at any time by calling setDaemon() and passing true to make the thread a daemon or false to make it non-daemon.

Thread Grouping

Complex applications can contain many threads performing many separate tasks. Sometimes these tasks are distinct as in a spreadsheet application where one thread manages a GUI and another performs calculations. In this case, there's only one thread to control if the user asks to suspend the calculation; however, if many spreadsheets are open, it's likely that a good design would assign one thread to each sheet (specifically, each object representing a spreadsheet would implement its own thread). Being able to handle all threads as a single "group" would be convenient, such as when the need to suspend all the calculating threads at once occurs. The java.lang.ThreadGroup class enables this with a ThreadGroup object controlling a set of Threads.

Threads and ThreadGroups

Every Thread object in the JVM is a member of one ThreadGroup (known as its "parent" ThreadGroup). Just as an initial thread is created when an application starts, a default ThreadGroup (called "main") is also created (in fact there might be several initial Threads and ThreadGroups; see the later section on Debugging for more details). Further ThreadGroups can be created as required. ThreadGroup provides the constructors shown in listing 13.22.

Listing 13.22   java.lang.ThreadGroup Constructors

```
//Create a new ThreadGroup as a member of the
//same ThreadGroup as the current Thread, with
//the given name.
public ThreadGroup(String name);

//Create a new ThreadGroup as a member of the
//given ThreadGroup with the given name.  The
//parent ThreadGroup may not be null.
public ThreadGroup(ThreadGroup parent,
                   String name)
```

The parent ThreadGroup of any Thread object can be obtained by calling the Thread.getThreadGroup() method. Thus, use this method to get the default ThreadGroup from within the main() method, which runs under the initial thread, as shown in listing 13.23.

Listing 13.23   Getting the Current Thread and ThreadGroup in main()

```
public void main(String[] args) {
        //get the current Thread
        Thread ct = Thread.currentThread();

        //get the default ThreadGroup
        ThreadGroup tg = ct.getThreadGroup();
```

A newly created Thread object is placed in the same ThreadGroup as its creator unless another ThreadGroup is specified to the constructor. After specifying the ThreadGroup of a new Thread object, Threads cannot be moved from one ThreadGroup to another. Threads are automatically removed from their ThreadGroup when they die.

Operations on ThreadGroups

As well as allowing a name to be passed to the constructor, the ThreadGroup class also provides setName() and getname(), which are direct equivalents of the Thread methods of the same names . As with a Thread object's name, the name of a ThreadGroup is mainly useful in debugging.

As the second ThreadGroup constructor implies, ThreadGroups can also contain other ThreadGroups as well as Threads. Operations on any ThreadGroup apply to all the Threads in that group, plus all the ThreadGroups in that group, plus all the Threads in those ThreadGroups, and so on. Operations continue down this hierarchy of Threads and groups.

Reconsider the previous spreadsheet example. The application might be capable to support multiple documents, with each document containing multiple spreadsheets. It would then be useful to have a hierarchy of threads and groups, as shown in figure 13.5.

Document1 contains one sheet and Document2 contains two sheets. Suspending all calculation by the Sheet threads is accomplished by suspending the Document's ThreadGroup. Suspending the processing in Document2 is accomplished by suspending only Document2's ThreadGroup.

The ThreadGroup class supports the operations on descendants of a ThreadGroup as shown in listing 13.24.

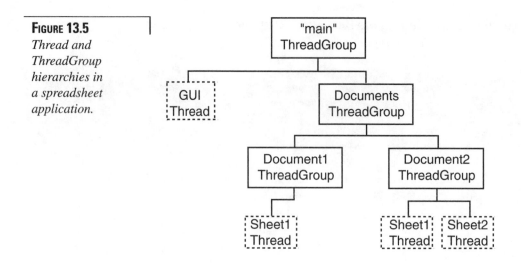

FIGURE 13.5
Thread and ThreadGroup hierarchies in a spreadsheet application.

Listing 13.24   java.lang.ThreadGroup Method Operating on All Threads and Subgroups

```
//Call suspend() on all Threads in this group and
//subgroups.
public final void suspend();

//Call resume() on all Threads in this group and
//subgroups.
public final void resume();

//Stop all Threads in this group and subgroups.
public final void stop();

//Set the maximum priority for all Threads in this
//group and all subgroups. Does not change the current
//priority of existing Threads.
public final void setMaxPriority(int pri);

//Get the maximum priority value for this group.
public final int getMaxPriority();
```

Setting the maximum priority does not affect threads already in the group that have higher priorities than the new maximum—it just "caps" any priority values in future calls to Thread.setpriority() in that ThreadGroup. You might use this in the spreadsheet example to set the maximum priority for the Document's ThreadGroup at startup to NORM_PRIORITY -1. Thus, any calculation threads subsequently created would have a priority lower than normal, biasing the scheduler to favor the GUI thread. This would improve the application's response to the user and prevent the application from appearing to lock up when many sheets require complex, time-consuming recalculations.

Handling Empty ThreadGroups

Threads are removed from their ThreadGroup when they die, and it's therefore possible for a ThreadGroup to become empty. It's sometimes convenient to delete a ThreadGroup object when it becomes empty. In the Spreadsheet example, it might be useful to delete a Document's ThreadGroup when all Sheet threads exit. Java provides a "daemon" flag for ThreadGroups that enables their deletion that is set and checked by the methods shown in listing 13.25.

Listing 13.25   java.lang.ThreadGroup Method Operating on Priorities

```
//Set the daemon flag for this ThreadGroup.
public final void setDaemon(boolean daemon);

//Get the daemon flag for this ThreadGroup.
public final boolean isDaemon();
```

ThreadGroups, like Threads, can also be marked as daemons and inherit the daemon status of their parent ThreadGroups. A daemon ThreadGroup can contain both daemon and non-daemon Threads. Marking a ThreadGroup as a daemon does not affect the daemon status of the Threads in that group.

In fact, all the daemon flag means for ThreadGroups is that they are automatically destroyed when all the Threads in it have completed and all the ThreadGroups in it have been destroyed—when it becomes empty. The daemon name is a little misleading because the daemon status of a ThreadGroup is not related to the daemon status of any Threads in that group and does not affect how the JVM behaves when exiting.

The ThreadGroup Hierarchy

At any time, there is only one hierarchy of ThreadGroups that contains all the Threads and ThreadGroups in the Java VM system. The getParent() method returns, for any ThreadGroup, the ThreadGroup object of which it is a member and the parentOf() method enables checking of whether one ThreadGroup is the ancestor of another.

The ThreadGroup class also contains a number of methods that enable the monitoring and display of the current Thread and ThreadGroup hierarchy as shown in listing 13.26.

```
//Return the parent group of this ThreadGroup
//or null if this is the top-level system ThreadGroup.
public final ThreadGroup getParent();

//Return true if this ThreadGroup is a parent of
//g, or anywhere in g's ancestors.
public final boolean parentOf(ThreadGroup g);

//List the ThreadGroup.  Prints a tree display of the
//entire hierarchy of ThreadGroups and Threads below
//and including this ThreadGroup on System.out.
//Useful for debugging.
public void list();

//Returns an estimate of the number of active Threads in
//this Thread group and all subgroups.
public int activeCount();

//Returns an estimate of the number of active ThreadGroups
//in this Thread group and all subgroups.
public int activeGroupCount()

//Copies, into the specified array, references to every
//active Thread in this Thread group and all active
//subgroups. Use the activeCount() method to get an
//estimate of how big the array should be.  Returns the
//number of Threads put into the array.
public int enumerate(Thread list[]);

//As enumerate(Thread[]), but if recurse is false only
//enumerates Threads for this ThreadGroup, not any
//subgroups.
public int enumerate(Thread list[],
                     boolean recurse);
```

The activeCount() and activeGroupCount() methods both return an estimate. An estimated count is possible only because Threads might be added, removed, or die in the ThreadGroup hierarchy during processing (for example, between calling activeCount() to obtain an estimate of the number of threads in the group and creating an array of that size to pass to enumerate() the contents of the ThreadGroup might change). The only way to traverse the hierarchy of Threads and ThreadGroups and know that the results are complete is to subclass ThreadGroup and perform the traversal in a method of that class.

Because all the methods of ThreadGroup that affect the hierarchy are *synchronized* (refer to the section on synchronization), a synchronized method of a subclass of ThreadGroup can safely traverse the Threads in that group without the risk of the contents of the ThreadGroup changing during the traversal.

For example, suppose a server application has threads of two classes and needs to return counts of the number of threads of each class as seen in listing 13.27.

Listing 13.27   Example of Subclassing ThreadGroup

```java
public class ThreadTypeA extends Thread {
        //some subclass of Thread...
}

public class ThreadTypeB extends Thread {
        //some other subclass of Thread...
}

public class CountingThreadGroup extends ThreadGroup {

//Default constructor
public CountingThreadGroup() {
        super(Thread.currentThread().getThreadGroup(), "NoName");
}

//Enumerate all the Threads in this group
//and all subgroups into an array.
private Thread[] enumerateAll() {
        int count = this.activeCount();
        Thread[] t = new Thread[count];
        this.enumerate(t);
        return t;
}

//Count only threads of class c.
public synchronized int countType(Class c) {
        Thread[] t = enumerateAll();
        int count = 0;
        for(int i=0; i<t.length; i++)
                if(t[i].getClass() == c)
                        count++;
        return count;
}

}
```

The countType() method can safely check all the Threads that are members of the CountingThreadGroup without the risk that threads will die or be added to the group during the counting because it is a synchronized method. The later section on synchronization explains this, but for now you can assume that while a thread is in this synchronized method, no other thread can call another synchronized method of the CountingThreadGroup object.

ThreadGroups and Exceptions

An exception occurring in any thread is thrown to the outermost catch that applies. If no catch to handle the "this" subclass of Throwable is found, the thread is killed (after all applicable "finally" blocks have been executed.) The last action of a dying thread is to call its ThreadGroup's uncaughtException() method.

Listing 13.28   java.lang.ThreadGroup uncaughtException Method

```
public void uncaughtException(Thread t,
                             Throwable e);
```

The default java.lang.ThreadGroup implementation of uncaughtException() passes Thread object and Throwable to the uncaughtException() method of the ThreadGroup's parent, thus propagating the call up the hierarchy of ThreadGroups. If there is no parent—that is, the ThreadGroup is the top of the hierarchy—Throwable's printStackTrace() method is called. The printStackTrace() method outputs to System.out a trace of all the methods that have been called on the way to where the exception occurred. It's the method that prints the stack trace that's seen when any uncaught Exception occurs in a Java application.

The uncaughtException() method is not final and can be overridden by subclasses of ThreadGroup to perform clean-up operations. When called, uncaughtException() cannot prevent the thread from dying.

Thread Security

A running Java VM can contain classes from a variety of packages. This is especially true in a web browser where there may be applets loaded from many different web sites. Therefore, it's important that security mechanisms exist to control and monitor Threads, so that Java code from any package cannot arbitrarily interfere with the operation of threads in other packages. Without any security, for example, an applet could be written that could interfere with the threads running the web browser itself, stopping them and crashing the browser.

Both the Thread and ThreadGroup classes provide checkAccess() methods (shown in listing 13.29) that determines if the current thread is allowed to perform certain actions on that Thread object or ThreadGroup. If access is not permitted, checkAccess() throws a java.lang.SecurityException.

Listing 13.29   java.lang.Thread and java.lang.ThreadGroup checkAccess Methods

```
//Thread class checkAccess().  Throws SecurityException
//if access to this thread is not permitted.
public void checkAccess();

//ThreadGroup class checkAccess().  Throws SecurityException
//if access to this group is not permitted.
public final void checkAccess();
```

Several Thread and ThreadGroup methods call checkAccess() before they proceed, as shown in the following lists.

In ThreadGroup:

- ThreadGroup(ThreadGroup parent, String name)
- setMaxPriority(int maxPriority)
- destroy()

In Thread:

- All constructors that pass a ThreadGroup
- setPriority(int newPriority)
- setName(String name)

In both:

- stop()
- suspend()
- resume()
- setDaemon(Boolean on)

In non-applet Java VMs, a SecurityManager may not exist, and hence access is permitted to all Threads and ThreadGroups. However, the Thread class checkAccess() is not final and therefore may be overridden to provide security even when no SecurityManager is present, as in listing 13.30.

Listing 13.30   A SecureThread Class Implementing checkAccess()

```
public class SecureThread extends Thread {

//Only threads in the allowed group or any of
//the group's descendants may access us.
private ThreadGroup allowedGroup;

//Constructors
public SecureThread(Runnable r) {
        super(r);
        //The allowed group is the group the
        //current thread is in.
        allowedGroup = this.getThreadGroup();
}

public SecureThread(ThreadGroup g, Runnable r) {
        //Create this as a member of group g,
        //which is then the allowed group.
        super(g, r);
        allowedGroup = g;
}

public void setAllowedGroup(ThreadGroup tg) {
        if(tg != null) {
                //should we allow this change?
                checkAccess();
                allowedGroup = tg;
        }
}

//Overrides Thread.checkAccess.
public void checkAccess() {
        //If there's a security manager, let it check
        //first.  If it disallows, it'll throw the
        //SecurityException.
        SecurityManager sm = System.getSecurityManager();
        if(sm != null)
                sm.checkAccess(this);

        //If there's no allowed group, then access
        //is allowed, otherwise check.
        if(allowedGroup == null)
                return;

        //Check to see if the current thread is
        //in the allowed group.  First, find the
        //ThreadGroup g for the current thread.
```

```
        ThreadGroup g;
        g = Thread.currentThread().getThreadGroup();

        //If g is the allowed group, then access is allowed.
        if(g == allowedGroup)
                return;

        //Check if the allowed group is an ancestor
        //of g.  If not, throw an exception.
        if(!allowedGroup.parentOf(g))
                throw new SecurityException();
}
}
```

The checkAccess() method implements greater security than any SecurityManager, enabling control only from Threads in a specified group.

To use a SecureThread, call setAllowedGroup() to establish what set of groups can access this SecureThread. This class might be useful in a package that contains multiple threads to prevent other packages from inadvertently affecting its operation.

Concurrent Thread Interaction

So far, all the examples of threaded objects in this chapter have been self contained. Each object contains its own data, which is private to that object and the thread calling run(). The exception is the stopFlag that FileChecksum uses to determine whether run() should exit. This variable is checked by the FileChecksum run() method and set by stopThread(). However, stopThread() may be called from methods of any other object and, therefore, by any thread in the system. It's therefore possible that more than one thread may try to access stopFlag at the same time; one calling stopThread() and a FileChecksum thread testing stopFlag.

In the case of FileChecksum, this isn't a real problem because stopFlag is only changed from false to true. Java guarantees that the reading or writing of a Boolean, char, byte, short, int, or float variable is *atomic* (once started by one thread, a write or read must complete before any other thread can affect that variable). After the stopFlag is set true by stopThread(), it will be read as true when it is next checked by run().

When interactions become more complex than simply setting and testing binary flags, further problems can occur. Consider the method in listing 13.31.

Listing 13.31   Incrementing a Shared Variable

```
private int theCount=0;

//This method counts the number of times it has been
//called.
public int howManyTimes() {
        theCount += 1;  //increment the counter
        return theCount;
}
```

If two threads, A and B, running under a time-sliced scheduler, call howManyTimes(), the following might occur:

1. A enters the method, reads theCount (which holds 0), increments its copy of it, and returns 1.

2. B is scheduled, enters the method, reads theCount (which still holds 0), increments its copy, and returns 1.

3. B writes the value 1 back into theCount and returns 1.

4. A is rescheduled, writes back its copy (value 1) into theCount, and returns 1.

As a result, theCount's value is 1 and both threads receive a return value of 1 from howManyTimes() despite the fact that the method is called twice. This situation is sometimes called a coherency problem, or a race condition. The term "race" comes from the fact that the two threads are in a so-called race to update the variable.

Synchronized Methods

To solve this coherency problem, howManyTimes() can be marked as "synchronized," as shown in listing 13.32.

Listing 13.32   Synchronized Incrementing of a Shared Variable

```
public synchronized int howManyTimes() {
        theCount += 1;  //increment the counter
        return theCount;
}
```

A thread calling a synchronized method *locks* the "this" object when the method is entered and *unlocks* this just before returning. Only one thread may have a lock on an object at any one time. As a result, only one thread can execute the body of the method at once. For the synchronized version of the method, the following happens:

1. A enters the method, locks this, reads theCount (which holds 0), increments its copy of theCount, and returns 1.

2. B is scheduled, enters the method and attempts to lock this. Because A already has it locked, B is suspended.

3. A is re-scheduled and writes back its copy (value 1) into theCount, unlocks this, and returns 1. Unlocking this makes B eligible for execution again.

4. B is re-scheduled, gets a lock on this, reads 1 from theCount, increments it to 2, writes 2 back, unlocks this, and returns 2.

Mutual Exclusion

Locking out multiple threads so that only one can enter a method at one time is called *mutual exclusion* because threads exclude each other from the body of a synchronized method. Any block of code protected from access by multiple threads is called a *monitor* in concurrent programming terminology.

If a class is designed only for single-threaded use, this should be clearly stated in its documentation as a restriction.

When an object or class variable is accessed by more than one method, synchronization should always be used to ensure that reading and writing don't overlap. In fact, every method of every class should be considered as a possible candidate for synchronization. This applies even in classes that are non-threaded because other threaded objects might create and share objects of any class. Synchronization has its share of overhead, but this is usually outweighed by the benefits of a multithreaded application.

Listing 13.33 presents some example code using synchronized methods that will be discussed in the following sections to explain uses of mutual exclusion.

Listing 13.33   Synchronized Methods Protecting Shared Variables

```
private Vector v;

public synchronized void push(Object o) {
        //insert this element as the last in the Vector
```

continues

Concurrent Thread Interaction

Listing 13.33 Continued

```
        int s = v.size();
        v.insertElementAt(o, s);
}
public synchronized Object pop() {
        //remove the last element in the Vector
        //and return it.
        Object o = v.lastElement();
        int s = v.size();
        v.removeElementAt(s-1);
}
```

A thread entering push() or pop() locks "this" and therefore excludes other threads from entering either method.

Locks and Synchronized Blocks

The *synchronized* keyword can also be used to lock and unlock an object around a block of code instead of using an entire method. This is useful in the following situations:

- Synchronizing the entire method is likely to lock the object for an inconvenient length of time.

- The method doesn't return (for example, the run() method of a Thread).

When synchronizing a block, Java requires that you specify the object to be locked. The version of push() in listing 13.34 is equivalent to the version in listing 13.33, which synchronized the entire method by declaring it synchronized:

Listing 13.34 The push() Method Implemented with a Synchronized Block

```
public void push(Object o) {
        synchronized(this) {
                //insert this element as the last
                //in the Vector
                int s = v.size();
                v.insertElementAt(o, s);
        }
}
```

Every Java object contains a lock; it's part of the java.lang.Object class. It often makes sense to lock an object other than this. For example, push() and pop() could lock the Vector object to protect it from access by multiple threads, as in listing 13.35:

Listing 13.35   Synchronization on an Object

```
public void push(Object o) {
        synchronized(v) {
                //insert this element as the last
                //in the Vector
                int s = v.size();
                v.insertElementAt(o, s);
        }
}
public synchronized Object pop() {
        synchronized(v) {
                //remove the last element in the Vector
                //and return it.
                Object o = v.lastElement();
                int s = v.size();
                v.removeElementAt(s-1);
        }
}
```

The API for the java.util.Vector class shows that many of its methods are synchronized already (including insertElementAt(), removeElementAt(), and lastElement()). These methods lock the Vector object when called. The push() and pop() methods in listing 13.35 also now lock the Vector object; however, if a thread attempts to lock an object that it has already locked, that lock is always granted; a thread can't lock itself out. Thus a synchronized block, such as push() or pop(), can freely call another block or method synchronized on the same object.

To summarize, a thread that synchronizes an object locks out other threads from also synchronizing that object. It does not lock itself out.

Synchronized Class Methods

Class methods can also be synchronized; however, because no object is available, they lock the java.lang.Class object for that class. If an object method requires access to a class variable, synchronize on the Class object, as in listing 13.36.

Listing 13.36   Synchronization on the Class Object

```
private static
    Vector classVector;
//Get the size of the classVector.  Synchronized to prevent mutual
//access to class variables.
```

continues

Listing 13.36   Continued

```
public static synchronized void getSize() {
        return classVector.size();
}

public synchronized void addObject() {
        //access the classVector.
        synchronized(this.getClass()) {
                classVector.insertElementAt(this,
                        classVector.size());
                classVector.trimToSize();
        }
}
```

As addObject() demonstrates, a thread can have locks on a number of objects at the same time. The addObject() method itself is synchronized, so this will be locked. The addObject() method also contains a block synchronized on this.getClass(), so the Class object will also be locked. The synchronizing on the Class object is necessary because addObject() accesses the static classVector variable, and it's possible that another thread might call the class method getSize() at the same time.

Synchronization and Overriding Methods

The *synchronized* keyword is not considered by Java when determining whether a method in a subclass overrides a method in the superclass. In other words, you can override a method that is synchronized with one that isn't (and vice versa), but this should be done with caution.

For example, the java.lang.StringBuffer class provides a synchronized method to append a String to the end of the buffer. Listing 13.37 demonstrates a method that uses a StringBuffer.

Listing 13.37   Relying on a Method's Synchronization

```
public void addStringToBuffer(String s, StringBuffer sb) {
        //Add the string to the buffer. It doesn't
        //matter if several threads all try to append
        //at once because StringBuffer.append() is
        //synchronized.
        sb.append(s);
}
```

If a subclass of StringBuffer overrides append() with an unsynchronized version and that subclass is passed to addStringToBuffer(), then no synchronization protects the call to append(). Because two threads need to call addStringToBuffer() simultaneously for problems to occur, the bug might remain hidden for a long time before surfacing. The ensuing section about deadlock also demonstrates problems that can occur when it's not obvious whether a method is synchronized.

Suspending Threads

If thread A needs to stop and wait for thread B to reach a certain point, it appears that the best way to achieve this is to call suspend() on A and have B later call resume() on it. However, calling suspend() can suspend a thread at any point, even if it's executing a synchronized block. Any locks held by the thread will still be held while the thread is suspended. This makes suspend() and resume() unsuitable for controlling the execution of a thread that needs to stop and wait for some condition. Instead, Java provides the wait() and notify() methods as described in the next section.

Wait and Notify

Locks are sometimes called *condition variables* in concurrent programming terminology because they can be used to make a thread wait until some condition is true. To do this, locks can be manipulated directly via the wait() and notify() methods of the java.lang.Object class, as shown in listing 13.38.

Listing 13.38 java.lang.Thread wait() and notify() Methods

```
//Wait on this object until notified.
public final void wait()
        throws InterruptedException;

//Wait until notified or the specified time has elapsed.
public final void wait(long millis)
        throws InterruptedException;

//Wait until notified or the specified time has elapsed.
public final void wait(long millis,
                      int nanos)
        throws InterruptedException;

//Notify a single thread waiting on this object.
```

continues

Listing 13.38   java.lang.Thread wait() and notify() Methods

```
public final void notify();

//Notify all threads waiting on this object.
public final void notifyAll();
```

A thread calling an object's wait() is suspended until either of two situations occurs:

1. Another thread calls that same object's notify() or notifyAll().
2. The wait() is interrupted, which throws an InterruptedException.

When no thread is waiting, invoking notify() or notifyAll() does nothing.

Both wait() and notify() are object methods and share this restriction; they must be called from within a method or block that is synchronized on the object being waited on or notified. For instance, if code calls myObject.wait() or myObject.notify() on an object called myObject, such a call must be made from inside a block synchronized on myObject. This guarantees that only one thread can call wait(), notify(), or notifyAll() on an object at any one time. If the object isn't locked, a java.lang.IllegalMonitor StateException is thrown, as in listing 13.39.

Listing 13.39   Legal and Illegal Calls to notify()

```
public void notifyThis(){
        notify();        //ILLEGAL, isn't synchronized
}

public synchronized void notifyThis() {
        notify();        //LEGAL, synchronized on "this"
}

public void notifyThis() {
        synchronized(this) {
                notify();        //LEGAL, synchronized
                                 //on "this"
        }
}

public void notifyObject(Object obj) {
        synchronized(obj) {
                obj.notify();    //LEGAL, synchronized
                                 //on "obj"
        }
}
```

Uses of Condition Variables

Condition variables can be used to handle situations where mere synchronized methods won't suffice. Consider a simple producer/consumer example, as shown in listing 13.40. In this class, produce() is called to supply a String of data, and consume() is called to return the most recent data. Note that if consume() is called and there is no data, a consuming thread must wait until data exists before returning.

Listing 13.40   A Simple Producer/Consumer Class

```
public class ProduceConsume {
private String data;

public synchronized String consume() {
        String result;

        //If there is no data, wait.
        if(data == null)
                this.wait();

        //There is data.  Consume it.
        result = data;
        data = null;

        return result;
}

//Produce some data.
public synchronized void produce(String s) {
        //We don't care, in this example, if there is
        //already data there; we replace it with the
        //latest up-to-date information.
        data = s;
        this.notify();
}
}
```

The synchronization ensures that only one thread reads or writes data at any one time. The call to wait() means that a thread calling consume() when there's no data is suspended in a wait().

A thread that calls produce() places the data in the shared variable and calls notify() in case any consumer threads are waiting. If a thread is waiting, notify() makes it eligible for scheduling again. When more than one thread is waiting, one is randomly chosen (by the scheduler) to be notified. A consumer thread that's woken by the notify will return from wait() and consume the data.

When looked at closely, this example appears to present a problem. If wait() is called from within the synchronized consume() method, how can any thread then enter produce() (which is also synchronized) to call notify()? The answer is that a thread releases the lock on entry to wait() before suspension. When eventually rescheduled after being notified, the thread obtains the lock again (waiting, if necessary, until no other thread has the lock) before returning from wait(). Figure 13.6 illustrates these concepts.

FIGURE 13.6

*Two threads calling
ProduceConsume
methods.*

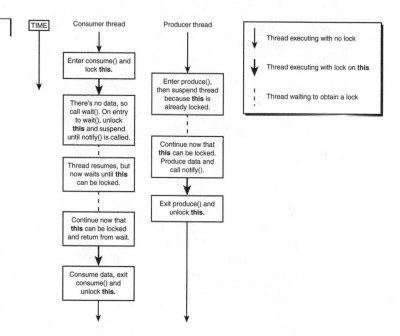

FileChecksum Using wait() and notify()

Earlier, the FileChecksum class was rewritten to use a separate thread to do the processing, with getChecksum() modified to return −1 if the processing is incomplete. Listing 13.41 shows FileChecksum modified to enable getChecksum() to wait until the calculation finishes.

Listing 13.41   A Threaded FileChecksum Class

```java
import java.io.*;

//File checksum object which uses a Thread to calculate the
//checksum in parallel with other processing.
public class FileChecksum implements Runnable {

//object variables
private long            length;          //of the File
private long            sum;

private boolean         finished;
public  Thread          thread;
private FileInputStream fis;

//constructor
public FileChecksum(File f)
        throws FileNotFoundException {
        //get the length of the file
        length = f.length();

        //initialize the sum to 0
        sum = 0;

        //clear the finished flag
        finished = false;

        //Open a FileInputStream for this file
        fis = new FileInputStream(f);

        //Create a Thread object that will run our
        //processing for us.  Pass the filename as
        //the name of the Thread.  Pass this as the
        //object to be run by the new Thread.
        thread = new Thread(this, f.getName());

        //Start the new thread running.
        thread.start();

} //end of constructor

//The run() method that the Runnable interfaces requires
//us to declare.  This is the method that the new thread
//of control will call.
public void run() {
```

continues

Listing 13.41 Continued

```
        //Loop through all of the bytes in the file
        //and generate a checksum.
        try {
                for(int i=0; i<length; i++)
                        sum += (long)fis.read();
        }

        catch(IOException e) { }

        finally {
                synchronized(this) {
                        finished = true;
                        //notify any threads waiting.
                        this.notifyAll();
                }
                try {
                        fis.close();
                }
                catch(IOException e) { }
        }
    }

    //object methods

    //getChecksum will wait if we haven't finished
    //calculating the checksum yet, unless interrupted.
    public synchronized long getChecksum() {
        if(!finished) {
                try {
                        this.wait();
                }

                catch(InterruptedException e) {
                        return -1;
                }
        }
        return sum;
    }
}           //end of FileChecksum
```

A thread that calls getChecksum() before the checksum is available will be suspended by
the wait() until the checksum calculation completes and notifyAll() is called by run().

More Complex Interaction via Condition Variables

Imagine a class that controls access to a printer. Only one thread may send data to the printer at any one time. Assume that the printer also supports several different paper sizes, but switching between paper trays is inefficient; so it would be preferable to send together print jobs that require the same paper size, to minimize tray changes. An initial attempt is shown in listing 13.42.

Listing 13.42 SimplePrinterAccess Class

```
public class SimplePrinterAccess {
//paper sizes
public static final int LETTER=0,
        LEGAL=1, A4=2;

private Printer thePrinter;

public synchronized void printJob(String data, int paperSize) {
        //set up the right paper size
        thePrinter.changePaperTray(paperSize);

        //print the job
        thePrinter.printTheJob(data);
    }
}
```

NOTE

The notifyAll() method is equivalent to calling notify() for every waiting thread. All waiting threads become eligible for execution. The order in which they are rescheduled is not guaranteed.

As defined by the SimplePrinterAccess class, while any thread is in the synchronized printJob() method, threads trying to enter are locked out, so the requirement that only one thread can be printing at any one time is satisfied. Now assume that three threads, A, B, and C, call printJob() in that order. Threads A and C request LETTER size paper, and B requests the A4 paper size. Because A enters printJob() first, the printer prepares LETTER size paper, and then A starts printing. Meanwhile, B and C both try to enter and become suspended. When A completes, either B or C gains entry to printJob(). The most efficient job to print next would be C because that too requires LETTER size paper and this would avoid having to change the paper tray. However, because there's no guarantee which thread, B or C, gets the lock and enters printJob(), there's no guarantee which job will print next.

Listing 13.43 demonstrates a second version of the class that uses condition variables and attempts to ensure that the most appropriate job is printed next.

Listing 13.43   EfficientPrinterAccess Class

```
public class EfficientPrinterAccess {
//paper sizes
public static final int LETTER=0,
        LEGAL=1, A4=2,
        //The number of different paper sizes
        PAPER_SIZES=3,
        //A value to indicate no size yet chosen
        UNKNOWN=-1;

//There are as many elements in these
//arrays as there are paper sizes and
//the paper size values above are used
//to index it.
private Object flag[];

//Accesses to this array are synchronized on "this."
//This array counts the number of jobs of each paper
//size waiting to print (on the flag[] element of the
//same array index).  The paper size values are
//used to index this array.
private int    count[];

//Keep track of which paper size is
//in use.  Initially, we don't know
//what size is set up.
private int currentPaperSize=UNKNOWN;

//This flag is true while some thread is printing.
private boolean printing;

private Printer thePrinter;

//Constructor
public EfficientPrinterAccess() {
        //Create an Object for each paper size
        //to use as a condition variable.
        this.flag = new Object[PAPER_SIZES];
        for(int i=0; i<=this.flag.length; i++)
                this.flag[i] = new Object();

        //Use an integer for each paper size to
        //count the number of jobs waiting.
        //They're all initialized to zero.
        this.count = new int[PAPER_SIZES];
}
```

```
private void waitOnQueue(int paperSize) throws InterruptedException {
        synchronized(flag[paperSize]) {
                flag[paperSize].wait();
        }
}

private void wakeUpQueue(int paperSize) {
        synchronized(flag[paperSize]) {
                flag[paperSize].notify();
        }
}

public void printJob(String data, int paperSize)
throws InterruptedException {
boolean needToWait;

        //Is there anyone printing?
        synchronized(this) {
                needToWait = printing;
                printing = true;

                //If we're going to wait, increment
                //the count of jobs waiting now so that
                //we can be sure whichever thread is
                //printing will notice we're waiting.
                if(needToWait)
                        count[paperSize]++;
        }

        if(needToWait) {
                //wait on the appropriate queue
                waitOnQueue(paperSize);
        }

        //set up the right paper size
        if(currentPaperSize != paperSize)
                thePrinter.changePaperTray(paperSize);

        //print the job
        thePrinter.printTheJob(data);

        synchronized(this) {
                //now wake any suspended thread that wants to
                //use the same paper size as we just did.  If
                //there's no job using the same size, then just
                //find any suspended thread and start it.
```

continues

Listing 13.43   Continued

```
                    boolean wokeSomebody = false;

                    if(count[paperSize] > 0) {
                            wakeUpQueue(paperSize);
                            wokeSomebody = true;
                            count[paperSize] -= 1;
                    }
                    else
                    {
                            for(int i=0; i<count.length; i++) {
                                if((i != paperSize)
                                && (count[i] > 0)) {
                                        wakeUpQueue(i);
                                        wokeSomebody = true;
                                        count[i] -= 1;
                                        break;
                                }
                            }
                    }

                    //Finally, clear the printing flag if
                    //we're done (that is, unless we woke
                    //some other thread to print).
                    if(!wokeSomebody)
                            printing = false;
            }
    }
}
```

The first point to note about this example is that it's considerably more complex than SimplePrinterAccess, which hid all the synchronization by giving this responsibility to the Java VM.

The printJob() method is not synchronized because more than one thread must be allowed to execute it at once. The first thread to enter printJob() is allowed to print; if other threads enter while that first thread is printing, they are suspended via wait() (in waitOnQueue()) until the printing thread is done.

To understand the operation of EfficientPrinterAccess, consider the "flag" array of Objects and the "count" array as associated. The flag array elements are used as condition variables to implement a set of queues, one for each paper size supported. The count array records the number of threads waiting in each queue.

The following list details the operation of EfficientPrinterAccess when threads A, B, and C call it as described earlier:

1. The first thread, A, on entering printJob(), tests the "printing" flag to determine whether any other thread is currently using the printer. Because this flag is shared between threads, this test is placed inside a synchronized block. If printing is false, then A doesn't need to wait, and "printing" may be set to true. Thread A continues, sets up the paper size if necessary, and calls printTheJob().

2. Now the second thread, B, enters printJob(). It also tests printing, but because it's now true, B must wait. B can't call wait() from inside the block that is synchronized on this because of the deadlock problem discussed earlier. Instead, B leaves the synchronized block and calls waitOnQueue() to suspend itself on the appropriate condition variable.

3. Thread A now completes printing. It enters the second synchronized block and examines the count array to determine whether any of the queues have threads waiting for the printer. It tests the queue holding jobs for the same paper size first. Finding that one queue has thread B suspended, thread A calls wakeUpQueue() to notify B. Thread A then exits printJob(). B is rescheduled, sets up the paper tray, and prints.

4. If thread C enters printJob() before A is done, it too ends up waiting on a queue. But because A first checks the queue for jobs requiring the same paper size as itself, it schedules C next and avoids changing the paper tray.

Unfortunately, this attempt contains a subtle bug. Imagine that thread B enters printJob(), checks printing, and must wait. B increments the appropriate count and leaves the first synchronized block. At that point, however, B is descheduled before calling waitOnQueue() (maybe because the time-slice has expired, or somewhere else in the system a higher priority thread has become runnable, preempting B). The next thread to be scheduled is A, which completes printing and then checks the queue counts. Because one of the counts is nonzero, A calls wakeUpQueue(). But thread B was descheduled before calling wait(), so there is no thread to respond to the the notify() call. B, when eventually rescheduled, calls wait(), and waits possibly forever, having missed the notify() call.

This type of defect (similar to the problem shown with listing 13.31 in the section on Concurrent Thread Interaction) is often called a *race condition* because it only appears if the timing of thread scheduling is exactly right (or exactly wrong, depending on your point of view). To overcome this particular problem, a condition variable is required to "remember" notify() calls. Such a variable is called a semaphore.

Semaphores

If you're familiar with concurrent programming in other languages, you may have noticed that Java condition variables are similar (although not identical) to Dijkstra's *semaphore* construct: wait() corresponds to waiting on a semaphore and notify() corresponds to signaling. The major difference is that a semaphore may be signaled before any process or thread waits, but when no thread is waiting invoking notify() has no effect.

Semaphores are like condition variables that don't forget notify() calls if no thread is waiting but save them until the next wait(). The behavior of a semaphore is defined in listing 13.44.

Listing 13.44   Definition of a Semaphore

```
wait(s):
    when s > 0 then
        s = s - 1
        continue

signal(s):
    s = s + 1
```

The definition of waiting on a semaphore implies that a process finding s at zero will wait until s becomes non-zero, but if s is already non-zero (because the semaphore was signaled earlier), the thread can continue without being suspended. Listing 13.45 shows how simple it is to implement a semaphore in Java.

Listing 13.45   The Semaphore Class

```
package industrial;

public class Semaphore {

//S is the "signal" variable.
private int s = 0;

//C counts the number of threads waiting on this
//semaphore, because it's often useful to know whether
//anything is waiting.
private int c = 0;
```

```
//Return true if any thread is waiting on this semaphore.
public synchronized boolean isWaiting() {
        return (c > 0);
}


//Wait on the semaphore.  If the wait is interruped,
//abandon the wait and throw the exception.
public synchronized void sWait() throws InterruptedException {
        //If the semaphore has been signaled, then
        //we may continue and decrement s,
        //otherwise we must wait.
        if(s == 0) {
                //Increment the count of threads waiting.
                c++;
                try {
                        this.wait();
                }
                finally {
                        //Decrement the count of threads
                        //waiting.
                        c--;
                }
        }
        //If the wait is interrupted, this line will
        //not be executed.
        s -= 1;
}

public synchronized void sSignal() {
        //increment the signal count
        s += 1;

        //notify anyone waiting.  This will
        //notify only one thread if
        //there are several waiting.  If no thread
        //is waiting, then the call has no effect.
        this.notify();
}
}
```

This is a complete Semaphore class that can be used in any application. The sWait() and sSignal() methods are equivalents to wait() and notify(). The names come from the operations defined for Dijkstra's semaphore construct. The isWaiting() method provides a quick check (returns true) if any threads are waiting on the semaphore.

The sWait() and sSignal() methods are exactly like wait() and notify() except for the following:

1. There's no need to call them from inside a synchronized block because they're already synchronized.

2. If there's no thread waiting, a call to sSignal() will remember the signal and the next thread that calls Wait() won't be suspended. Remember that a call to notify() when there's no thread waiting does nothing; the call isn't remembered.

Listing 13.46 shows the printer access class, rewritten to use the Semaphore class.

Listing 13.46   SemaphorePrinterAccess Class

```
import industrial.Semaphore;

public class SemaphorePrinterAccess {
//paper sizes
public static final int LETTER=0,
        LEGAL=1, A4=2,
        //The number of different paper sizes
        PAPER_SIZES=3,
        //A value to indicate no size yet chosen
        UNKNOWN=-1;

//There are as many elements in this
//array as there are paper sizes, so there
//is one semaphore per paper size.
private Semaphore sems[];

//This array of ints keeps track of jobs
//waiting on the semaphores.
private int count[];

//Keep track of which paper size is
//in use.  Initially, we don't know
//what size is set up.
private int currentPaperSize=UNKNOWN;

//Flag is true if some thread is printing.
private boolean printing;

private Printer thePrinter;
```

```
//Constructor
public SemaphorePrinterAccess() {
        //Create a Semaphore for each paper size
        //to use as a condition variable.
        sems = new Semaphore[PAPER_SIZES];
        count = new int[PAPER_SIZES];
        for(int i=0; i<=sems.length; i++) {
                sems[i] = new Semaphore();
                count[i] = 0;
        }
}

public void printJob(String data, int paperSize)
throws InterruptedException {
boolean needToWait;

        //Is there anyone printing?
        synchronized(this) {
                needToWait = printing;
                printing = true;

                //Increment the count so the thread
                //currently printing knows to signal
                //us when it's done.
                if(needToWait)
                        count[paperSize]++;
        }

        if(needToWait)
                sems[paperSize].sWait();

        //set up the right paper size
        if(currentPaperSize != paperSize)
                thePrinter.changePaperTray(paperSize);

        //print the job
        thePrinter.printTheJob(data);

        synchronized(this) {
                //now wake any suspended thread that wants to
                //use the same paper size as we just did.  If
                //there's no job using the same size, then just
                //find any suspended thread and start it.
                boolean wokeSomebody = false;

                if(count[paperSize] > 0) {
```

continues

Listing 13.46   Continued

```
                              sems[paperSize].sSignal();
                              wokeSomebody = true;
            }
            else
            {
                for(int i=0; i<sems.length; i++) {
                        if((i != paperSize)
                        && (count[i] > 0)) {
                                sems[i].sSignal();
                                wokeSomebody = true;
                                break;
                        }
                }
            }

            //Finally, clear the printing flag if we're
            //done and nobody else is about to print.
            if(!wokeSomebody)
                    printing = false;
        }
    }
}
```

There's now one Semaphore for each paper size queue; each used as a condition variable. Calling sSignal() on a Semaphore means that any existing or future sWait() call is "notified"; thus the race condition that affects EfficientPrinterAccess won't occur.

The count array is incremented when any thread intends to suspend itself on a Semaphore. If the count array isn't used, another race condition may occur. For example, suppose thread B detects a need to wait, but is descheduled immediately before calling sWait(). Because no thread is waiting when A checks, none of the semaphores are signaled, and B waits "forever" again. The use of the count array ensures that A always signals an appropriate semaphore, regardless of scheduling order.

Synchronizing on Semaphores

A synchronized method or block enforces the restriction that only one thread may execute inside that block at any one time. However, there are situations when this form of synchronization can't be used, such as the following examples:

- An object requires mutual exclusion between the execution of several methods, not just while a thread is within one method.

- More than one thread (but not an unlimited number) is permitted to execute code at any one time.

The first of these conditions might be appropriate when an object provides access to some resource, but operations on the resource are provided by multiple methods. For example, consider a class that provides access to a log file. Only one thread may access the logfile at any one time, but while a thread is accessing the file, it may need to call several different methods. Listing 13.47 shows such a class.

Listing 13.47 Mutual Exclusion over Several Methods

```
import industrial.Semaphore;
import java.io.*;

public class LogFile {

private File            logFile;
private FileOutputStream logFOS;
private PrintStream     logPS;
private Semaphore       logSem;

//Constructor
public LogFile(String fileName) throws IOException {
        logFile = new File(fileName);
        logFOS = new FileOutputStream(logFile);
        logPS = new PrintStream(logFOS);
        logSem = new Semaphore();
        logSem.sSignal();
}

//Gain exclusive access to the logfile
public void allocate() throws InterruptedException {
        logSem.sWait();
}

//Release the logfile
public void deallocate() {
        logSem.sSignal();
}

//Send a string to the logfile
public void log(String s) {
        logPS.println(s);
}
}
```

Whenever the semaphore logSem is signaled, the log file isn't allocated to any thread. When the object is constructed, the semaphore is initially signaled once, so the first thread to call allocate() is permitted to proceed. Other threads calling allocate() are suspended on logSem. When the first thread is done and calls deallocate(), the semaphore is resignaled and one of the suspended threads (chosen at random by the scheduler) then has exclusive access to the log file.

Throttling

Enabling a limited number of threads to execute within a block, often called *throttling*, is another application of semaphores. Suppose, for example, that to limit disk I/O, a class must permit no more than four threads to write to files at any one time, as shown in listing 13.48.

Listing 13.48   Using a Semaphore to Limit the Number of Processes in a Monitor

```
import industrial.Semaphore;
import java.io.*;

public class FileDump {

//This int is the maximum number of threads that may
//be dumping to FileDumps at any one time.
private final static int MAX_DUMPS=4;
private static Semaphore throttle;

//static initializer code
static {
        throttle = new Semaphore();
        for(int i=0; i<MAX_DUMPS; i++)
                throttle.sSignal();
}

private File f;
private FileOutputStream fos;

//Constructor
public FileDump(String fileName) throws IOException {
        f = new File(fileName);
        fos = new FileOutputStream(f);
}

//dump byte array to file
public void dump(byte[] b)
```

```
        throws InterruptedException, IOException {

                //Enter the throttled section
                throttle.sWait();

                //dump the data
                fos.write(b);

                //Leave the throttled section
                throttle.sSignal();
        }

        //close the file
        public void close() throws IOException {
                fos.close();
                fos = null;

                f = null;
        }

}
```

Here the semaphore is a class variable. Any threads calling the dump() method of any FileDump object will attempt to wait on the semaphore. Because the semaphore is initially signaled MAX_DUMPS times, up to MAX_DUMPS threads can dump data at the same time. As each thread exits dump(), it resignals the semaphore to let in another thread.

Wait and Notify on Threads

Because java.lang.Thread is a subclass of java.lang.Object, threads can call wait() and notify() on their own Thread objects. This is how the join() methods work; they call wait() on the Thread object. When a thread dies, notifyAll() is called on the Thread object so that any waiting join() calls will complete. Any other threads in wait() calls on the dying thread are, of course, also notified.

Timed Waits

A common requirement, especially in real-time systems, is for some operation to occur at regular intervals. This is an obvious application for threading; a thread can be created to perform the operation, sleeping until the next interval arrives. For example, the code in listing 13.49 is supposed to call tick() every 1,000 milliseconds (this might be to implement an on-screen clock, for example).

Listing 13.49   A run() Method to Wake up at Regular Intervals

```
public void run() {
        //Loop, waking up every second
        while(true) {
                try {
                        //Sleep for 1000 mS
                        Thread.sleep(1000);
                }
                catch(InterruptedException e) {}

                //Another second has elapsed.
                tick();
        }
}
```

This approach has a couple of problems. First of all, after the sleep() method is done, the Java VM scheduler might not start executing this thread immediately, depending on the other threads currently in the system. This can be partly overcome by setting the thread priority to Thread.MAX_PRIORITY, so that this thread is likely to preempt all others when it returns from sleep().

The second problem is that of lag. The call to tick() takes some time; for example, assume it takes 75 milliseconds. After tick() returns, the thread continues around the loop and calls sleep() again. Because that extra 75 milliseconds has elapsed, the interval between the last call to sleep() and this call is actually 1,075 milliseconds. Every iteration around the loop slips by 75 milliseconds.

To solve the lag problem, two threads can be used. The first thread operates in a loop. In each iteration, it sleeps for a specified period (the cycle time) and, on waking, notifies the other thread. It then returns to the sleep, having adjusted the time of the sleep to compensate for the time the Java VM took to schedule it after it returned from sleep(). It does this by using the System.currentTimeMillis() function, which returns the value of a timer that's incremented every millisecond.

The second thread need not be concerned with details of keeping time. It simply calls wait() and is notified by the first thread when it's time to call tick() again. Thus the first thread is unaffected by the length of time tick() takes to execute.

Here's the class that the first thread implements:

Listing 13.50   The Ticker Class

```
package industrial;

/**
The Ticker class will notify any threads waiting on it
at the specified time interval.
*/
public class Ticker extends Thread {

//Object variables

//The cycle time in milliseconds
private long cycle;

//Constructor
public Ticker(long cycleTime) {
        //Set a name for this Ticker thread
        super("Ticker at "+cycleTime+" mS");
        cycle = cycleTime;
        //set our priority to maximum so that
        //we get scheduled soon after waking.
        this.setPriority(MAX_PRIORITY);
        //mark this Thread as a daemon
        this.setDaemon(true);
        this.start();
}


//run method, overrides Thread run().
public void run() {
long    next;

        //Set the next waking to occur at "now" plus
        //the cycle time.
        next = System.currentTimeMillis() + cycle;

        try {
                while(true) {
                        //sleep till the next tick.  That
                        //will be the "next" time, so we
                        //need to sleep for the number of
```

Thinking in Terms of Threads

continues

Listing 13.50   Continued

```
                            //milliseconds until then.
                            long period = next
                            - System.currentTimeMillis();

                            if(period > 0)
                                    Thread.sleep(period);
                            else
                                    yield();

                            //wake our clients
                            synchronized(this) {
                                    this.notifyAll();
                            }

                            next += cycle;
                    }
            }

            //InterruptedExceptions will stop the ticker
            //running.
            catch(InterruptedException e) { }

            finally {
                    //If we're stopped, or a really bad
                    //Exception is thrown, we need to make
                    //sure all our clients are notified.
                    synchronized(this) {
                            this.notifyAll();
                    }
            }
    }

    //wait for a tick.  A wrapper method for wait() that
    //catches InterruptedExceptions and ignores them.
    public synchronized void waitForTick() {
            do {
                    try {
                            wait();
                            //A normal (non-interrupted)
                            //return from wait() will break
                            //from the loop.
                            //InterruptedException will cause
                            //the loop to iterate again (and
                            //re-enter the wait()).
                            break;
                    }
```

Thirteen: Thinking in Terms of Threads

```
                  catch(InterruptedException e) {}
        } while(true);
    }
}
```

The Ticker thread avoids lag partly because it doesn't do any work itself; it just notifies other threads that wait on the Ticker object. The other part of the solution is the way the duration of the sleep() call is calculated. Once during each iteration, the value of next is set to the system time at which the next tick should occur. The duration passed to sleep() is always the number of milliseconds to wait until the next tick, regardless of how long the notifyAll() call takes to operate. Actually, the calculation of period is designed to cope with the extreme situation when the time required to notify waiting threads is longer than the cycle time; in this case the call to sleep() isn't made, and lag might occur.

The class shown in listing 13.51 uses the Ticker class to call tick() every 1,000 milliseconds.

Listing 13.51   Code that Uses a Ticker

```
//Create a Ticker to fire every 1000mS
Ticker t = new Ticker(1000);

//loop that calls doWork() every tick
while(true) {
        t.waitForTick();
        tick();
}
```

In this example, if doWork() takes an excessive amount of time (more than 1,000 milliseconds, for example), this code might miss a tick (if the thread isn't waiting when Ticker calls notifyAll(), it won't be woken), but the next tick will come at the right time interval.

The Ticker thread sets its priority to MAX_PRIORITY to try to preempt any thread executing when sleep() is done. This is acceptable because the Ticker does so little work between periods of sleep, and so it won't take unreasonable amounts of CPU time.

Deadlock and Starvation

Although the problem with lag that the Ticker class solves might happen in both multi- and single-threaded programs, some programming problems are unique to concurrent programming. As well as the race conditions that were discussed earlier, starvation and deadlock may also occur in multithreaded systems.

Starvation occurs whenever a thread in an application can't proceed because it cannot gain access to a particular resource. For example, if most threads in an application spend most of their time waiting to write to a shared log file that's protected by synchronized methods, it's true to say that the system is starved.

Semaphores can be used to help identify starvation. Because a semaphore can record the number of waiting threads, a version of the Semaphore class can be written that tracks the maximum number of threads waiting. When a semaphore is used to protect access to a resource (as in the LogFile class shown earlier), the sWait() and sSignal() methods can be modified to measure the maximum amount of time for which the resource is allocated.

Starvation can also occur when eligible threads can't run because other threads don't call yield() at appropriate points, or when a waiting thread could logically continue, but program design doesn't allow for it to be notified yet. Both of these are examples of processor-time starvation.

Deadlock occurs when two or more threads all wait for some condition that is never satisfied. The classic example of this occurs when all the threads wait for each other. Because all are suspended, none can ever call notify(), and they all remain suspended indefinitely. Deadlock can be seen as an extreme (infinite) case of starvation. Consider the class in listing 13.52 which provides synchronized protection for access to an Object (which might, for example, be an Integer or String).

Listing 13.52   A Class that may Deadlock

```
public class ProtectedValue {

private Object theValue;

//Get the current value
public synchronized Object getValue() {
       return theValue;
}

//Set the current value to an object
public synchronized void setValue(Object newValue) {
       theValue = newValue;
}

//Compare this ProtectedValue to another
public synchronized boolean equalTo(ProtectedValue p) {
       return theValue.equals(p.getValue());
}

//Assigns one ProtectedValue to another
```

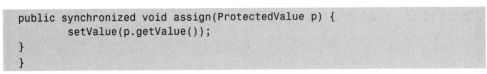

```
public synchronized void assign(ProtectedValue p) {
        setValue(p.getValue());
}
}
```

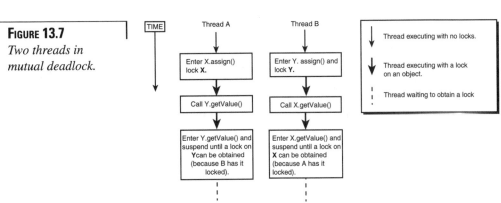

FIGURE 13.7
Two threads in mutual deadlock.

Consider two threads, A and B. Thread A has a ProtectedValue X and B has another, Y. Thread A calls X.assign(Y) to copy the value of Y at the same time that B calls Y.equalTo(X) to compare X and Y. Thread A, entering assign(), gains a lock on X. Thread B, entering equalTo(), gains a lock on Y. A then calls getValue() for Y and is suspended because B has Y locked. B calls getValue() for X and is suspended because A has X locked. The two threads are deadlocked, each waiting for the other. This is shown in figure 13.7.

This problem of *nested* synchronization usually occurs when methods synchronize on objects other than "this." This synchronization might not be explicit, but can be implied by the calling of a synchronized method (as in the previous example). It's important to be aware of class methods that are synchronized so that potential problems like those discussed in the preceding example can be identified. It's also important to consider synchronization as early as possible in class design so that appropriate methods are synchronized from version 1. Introducing synchronization to methods of a new version of a class already in use might create deadlock problems where there were previously none.

Another potential source of problems occurs when a subclass overrides a synchronized method with an unsynchronized one (or vice versa). This was illustrated earlier in the section on synchronization and overriding methods.

Synchronization should always be explicit in the class API. For example, consider a subclass of java.util.HashTable that overrides the existing synchronized put() method, as shown in listing 13.53.

Listing 13.53   Hidden Synchronization

```
public Object put(Object key, Object value) {
        //so some extra stuff that
        //doesn't need to be synchronized.
        extraStuff(key, value);
        return super.put(key, value);
}
```

The call to super.put() will be synchronized, but this subclass method declaration shows put() as unsynchronized. Any synchronization in a method should be considered as a side-effect of that method and should be at least clearly noted in the documentation. In this example, put() would probably have been better left synchronized.

Recovering from Deadlock

Prevention is far better than a cure when deadlock is concerned, but it's always possible that, for example, a thread may generate an exception and die, thus leaving other threads waiting potentially forever. In this situation, the wait() methods that take parameters are useful.

Wait() can be called with a maximum time value, specified either as milliseconds, or as milliseconds and nanoseconds. The call will then return from wait()when notify() has been called or when the specified time has expired (whichever occurs first).

Techniques for performing a detailed analysis of multithreaded program behavior to avoid deadlock are beyond the scope of this book; however, following these rules can help identify potential deadlock conditions:

- Assume that any code that is not explicitly synchronized can be executed by all possible threads at the same time. In other words, assume there are as many CPUs as available threads.

- Assume that, at any point in executing code, a thread can be descheduled enabling other threads to run for a relatively long time. In other words, assume a time-sliced preemptive scheduler.

- Remember that synchronized blocks don't enforce queueing or "fair shares" of execution time on threads.

Listing 13.54, for example, shows a loop containing a synchronized block.

Listing 13.54   Loop Containing a Synchronized Block

```
//Loop containing a synchronized block
while(someCondition) {
        synchronized(myFlag) {
                counter++;
        }
        //some other work
        doWork();
}
```

Three threads, A, B, and C, all execute the loop at once. Thread A increments counter to 1 and proceeds to call doWork(). Before A can enter the synchronized block again, threads B and C are both scheduled several times, incrementing counter. When A enters the synchronized block again, counter may be much larger than 1.

Similarly, in the code in listing 13.55, there's no guarantee that the value placed in alpha by thread A in the first synchronized block will be present in the second because other threads may intervene during the time period that thread A executes the two blocks.

Listing 13.55   Loop Containing a Synchronized Block

```
public void myMethod(int value) {
        synchronized(this) {
                alpha = value;
        }

        //some other work
        doWork();

        synchronized(this) {
                useValue(alpha);
        }
}
```

In summary, seriously consider at the very beginning of design whether to multithread your application. Also, Java is an inherently multithreaded language, and truly reusable classes must be designed to be used in multithreaded systems even if they are not threaded themselves.

Threads and Caching

The Java Language Specification enables the Java VM a considerable degree of freedom when caching variable values. Each thread has its own local working memory and values can be stored in this memory space to optimize processing. When a variable is accessed by multiple threads, it's possible, on some implementations of the Java VM, that two or more different threads can hold different values in their respective working copies of the same variable.

The rules governing the exact way that values can be cached are complex, but the essential rule to remember is that the Java VM, on entry to any synchronized block or method, must flush all unwritten cached values from thread working storage (so that new values must be read from main memory). Similarly, on leaving a synchronized block or method, the VM must write any unwritten cached values back to main memory.

In short, this means that any variables accessed within synchronized code are guaranteed to be consistent across multiple threads. Any shared variables should therefore be accessed only by synchronized code. If you refer back to the first threaded version of FileChecksum (refer to listing 13.8), you can see that the code accessing "finished" isn't synchronized, and this should be considered as a potential bug.

Volatile Variables

Another way of controlling the caching of variables is by marking them volatile (with the Java keyword "volatile"). A thread must reconcile its local copy of a volatile variable with the copy in main memory every time it accesses that variable. This ensures that multiple threads can safely access individual volatile variables, but only for Boolean, byte, char, int, short or float types. The language specification enables long and double types (which are 64 bits long) to be updated in two 32-bit chunks, and therefore one thread may read a value that another thread is halfway through updating.

A case for using volatile variables is where one thread updates a value (for example, a timer) that is read by many other threads, all of which need to be sure that they always read the latest value. Because one thread writes to the value, and all others read, the overhead of synchronizing access to the variable can be avoided by marking it as volatile so that all the reading threads will reload the value every time they access it. If, however, the value is a *long* or *double*, then, because of the possible update problem noted in the previous paragraph, access to the variable would need to be synchronized to be safe.

Debugging Threads

Debugging multithreaded applications can be complex. Race conditions and other timing-related interactions among threads can disappear or be radically altered when a program is single-stepped or has breakpoints inserted. It's often easier to add code to the program to try to trap bug conditions and to display information about the state of the program. It sometimes can be useful to add a thread to an application that monitors the other threads, watching for conditions such as deadlock, or a thread that seems to have died in an incorrect state (such a monitoring thread is known as a *watchdog*).

The Thread class provides a number of methods, shown in listing 13.56, that are sometimes useful in this approach to debugging multithreaded applications:

Listing 13.56   Thread Class Debugging Methods

```
//Count the number of stack frames for this Thread.  The
//Thread must be suspended when this method is called.
public int countStackFrames();

//Print a stack trace for the current thread.
public static void dumpStack();

//Generate a string describing this Thread.
public String toString();
```

Stack Traces

The countStackFrames() method checks how many nested method calls have been made by a thread. Each time a method is called, another stack frame is counted; each time a

If you want to try to ensure that Throwable won't be caught, so that a complete stacktrace is printed (for example, when stopping a thread that seems to be locked up), the best method is to call stop() with an instance of Throwable rather than any subclass. Most code only catches objects of the Exception class and its subclasses.

method returns, a stack frame is discarded. A stack frame is a Java VM internal structure that records information about a call to a method. You should only call this method for a suspended thread. If you suspect a recursive method is not unwinding, suspending the thread running it and calling countStackFrames() may provide a clue as to whether too many nested method calls have been made.

You can also use dumpStack() to generate a complete stack trace of all methods called for the current thread (The trace generated is the same as that provided by java.lang.Exception.printStackTrace()). The only way to cause another thread to generate a stack trace is to use the stop(Throwable t) method to generate an exception.

In fact, dumpStack() operates by creating an Exception and printing its stack trace. To generate a stack trace to a particular PrintStream rather than System.out, use code like that shown in listing 13.57.

Listing 13.57   Generating a Stack Trace to a PrintStream

```
//Generate a stack trace, for the current Thread, on
//PrintStream p.
Exception e = new Exception("Stack Trace");
e.printStackTrace(p);
```

Tracing ThreadGroup Hierarchies

The Thread.toString() method provides a String that contains the Thread object's name, priority value, and the name of the ThreadGroup to which it belongs. The ThreadGroup.list() method uses this information to describe each thread in the hierarchy. It's a good idea always to provide the Thread object with a descriptive name so that the output of list() is meaningful. The ThreadGroup class toString() method generates a similar String with the ThreadGroup's name and maximum priority.

To generate a listing that displays all the Threads and groups in the system, use code like that shown in listing 13.58.

Listing 13.58   Listing all Threads and ThreadGroups

```
//First, get the current ThreadGroup.
ThreadGroup g;
g = Thread.currentThread().getThreadGroup();

//Now move up the hierarchy of ThreadGroups until
//we reach the top.
while(g.getParent() != null) {
        g = g.getParent();
}

//Now generate a list for the entire hierarchy.
g.list();
```

Running the code in listing 13.58 from a main() on a Win32 JVM generates output, like that shown in listing 13.59.

Listing 13.59 Thread Hierarchy of a Simple Application

```
java.lang.ThreadGroup[name=system,maxpri=10]
    Thread[Finalizer thread,1,system]
    java.lang.ThreadGroup[name=main,maxpri=10]
        Thread[main,5,main]
```

The "system" ThreadGroup is the parent of all other Threads and ThreadGroups. The "main" ThreadGroup contains the "main" initial Thread that calls main(). "Finalizer" is the thread that runs the garbage collector. It's priority is low, set to 1.

Running the same code in an applet (under Netscape 3.0) provides output like that shown in listing 13.60.

Listing 13.60 Thread Hierarchy of a Simple Applet

```
java.lang.ThreadGroup[name=system,maxpri=10]
    Thread[Finalizer thread,1,system]
    java.lang.ThreadGroup[name=main,maxpri=10]
        Thread[main,5,main]
        Thread[AWT-Windows,5,main]
        Thread[AWT-Callback,5,main]
        Thread[ScreenUpdater,4,main]
        Thread[Image Fetcher 0,8,main]
        Thread[Image Fetcher 1,8,main]
        Thread[Image Fetcher 2,8,main]
        Thread[Image Fetcher 3,8,main]
        netscape.applet.AppletThreadGroup[name=applet-
myapplet.class,maxpri=6]
            Thread[Thread-2,5,applet-myapplet.class]
```

Again the Finalizer garbage-collector thread is running, but you can also see that the AWT package contains a number of Threads to handle screen updates, callbacks, and asynchronous loading of Images. The Image Fetcher threads all have a higher priority than the applet thread so that image loading takes priority over applet processing.

Netscape also uses a separate ThreadGroup for each applet; this could be for security reasons or perhaps to make it easier to control applet behavior as the user moves from page to page.

A Threaded Client/Server Application

To complete the chapter, an example of threading a simple server class for a networked client/server system is provided. The server handles requests from multiple clients for files as follows:

1. Each client connects to the server port and sends the name of a file down the socket.

2. The server responds by opening the file and sending its contents back via the same socket.

Client Class

Listing 13.61 shows the client class that makes requests from the server. The class contains a main() and can be run as a Java application. Multiple instances of this client can be run at once to present the server application (in later listings) with multiple requests at once.

Listing 13.61   Simple File Transfer Client

```
package industrial;

import java.io.*;
import java.net.*;

public class Client {
public static void main(String[] args) {
    //check arguments.
    if(args.length < 2)
        System.out.println("Usage: java Client "+
        "servername <filename>");
    else {
        int size, len, total=0;

        Socket s = null;

        System.out.println(args[1]);
        try {
            //open a socket to the
            //server
            s = new Socket(args[0],
```

```
                ThreadedServer.SERVER_PORT);

            //get streams to talk to
            //the server.
            DataOutputStream dos =
            new DataOutputStream(s.getOutputStream());
            DataInputStream dis =
            new DataInputStream(s.getInputStream());

            //send filename as UTF.
            dos.writeUTF(args[1]);

            //get data back from server.  First, get
            //file size, sent as an int.
            size = dis.readInt();
            byte[] b = new byte[size];

            do {
                len = dis.read(b);
                if(len > 0) {
                System.out.println("received "
                    +len+" bytes");
                total += len;
                }
            }
            while((len >= 0) && (total < size));

            String status = "client received "
                +total+" bytes";
            System.out.println(status);

            //Send the status string back.
            dos.writeUTF(status);
        }

        catch(IOException e) {
            e.printStackTrace();
        }

        finally {
            if(s != null) {
                try { s.close(); }
                catch(IOException e) {}
            }
        }    //end of finally block
    }    //end of else clause
    }    //end of main
}    //end of class
```

ThreadedServer Class

Listing 13.62 shows the threaded Server application. It's all contained within one ThreadedServer class that provides a main() so that a Server can be run as a Java application.

Listing 13.62   Corresponding Server Class

```
package industrial;

import java.io.*;
import java.net.*;

//A Server which can service multiple clients at once by
//creating Threads.
public class ThreadedServer implements Runnable {
//Class constants.  The port number on which the
//server listens for clients.
public static final int SERVER_PORT=6543;

//Class variables.  A count of server threads that
//we have created.
private static int serverThreads = 0;

//Class variable methods
//Increment the count of server threads running.
private static synchronized void incThreadCount() {
    serverThreads++;
}

//Decrement the thread count and return the new
//value.
private static synchronized int decThreadCount() {
    return (—serverThreads);
}

//Object variables.  The socket we use to communicate
//with the client.
private Socket s;

//Constructor
public ThreadedServer(Socket s) {
    this.s = s;
}

//Given a socket s, service a client's request on that
```

```
//socket.  This isn't the most efficient way to handle
//socket IO or file IO; it's kept simple because this
//is just an example.
public void run() {
FileInputStream      fis = null;
DataInputStream      dis = null;
DataOutputStream     dos = null;

    //The server now has a new thread.
    incThreadCount();

    try {
        //Get streams to listen to and talk to the client.
        dis = new DataInputStream(s.getInputStream());
        dos = new DataOutputStream(s.getOutputStream());

        //Read a filename from the client as a UTF
        //String.
        String fName = dis.readUTF();

        System.out.println("Client requested file \""
            +fName+"\"");

        //Open that file.
        File f = new File(fName);
        fis = new FileInputStream(f);

        //Read the file and send it.  First, allocate a
        //byte array as a buffer.
        int len = (int)f.length();
        byte[] b = new byte[1024];

        //Send the length to the client as a single int
        System.out.println(fName+": is "+len+" bytes");
        dos.writeInt(len);

        //Send the file to the client.
        int offset=0;
        do {
            //Read a block into the array.
            int blockLen = fis.read(b, 0, b.length);

            dos.write(b, offset, blockLen);
            len -= blockLen;

            //Yield to let other server threads get
```

continues

Thinking in Terms of Threads

Listing 13.62   Continued

```
                    //some time.
                    Thread.currentThread().yield();
                }
            while(len > 0);

            dos.flush();

            //wait for a confirmation from the client.
            System.out.println(fName+": delivered");
            String status = dis.readUTF();
            System.out.println(status);
        }

        catch(IOException e) {
            e.printStackTrace();
        }

        //This may be thrown by FileInputStream(File) in some
        //versions of the JDK.
/*
        catch(FileNotFoundException e) {
        }
*/

        finally {
            //finished.
            try {
                s.close();
                if(dis != null)    dis.close();
                if(fis != null)    fis.close();
                if(dos != null)    dos.close();
            }
            catch(IOException e) {
                e.printStackTrace();
            }

            //decrement the server thread
            //count, then if it has reached
            //zero (i.e., we're the last
            //thread) call the garbage
            //collector.
            if(decThreadCount() == 0) {
                System.gc();
```

```
            }
        }
    }

//class methods
private static boolean serviceClient(Socket s) {
    //Create a ThreadedServer object.
    ThreadedServer ts = new ThreadedServer(s);

    //Create a Thread and pass it the ThreadedServer
    //object as the Runnable.
    Thread t = new Thread(ts);

    //Start the thread.
    t.start();

    return true;
}

//main
public static void main(String[] args) {
    boolean         looping = true;
    ServerSocket    sock;

    try {
        //create our socket
        sock = new ServerSocket(SERVER_PORT);
    }
    catch(IOException e) {
        e.printStackTrace();
        return;
    }

    System.out.println("Accepting requests...");

    //loop accepting requests.
    do {
        try {
            //accept a connection from a client.
            Socket s = sock.accept();

            //service that request
            System.out.println("Servicing request...");
            looping = serviceClient(s);
        }
```

continues

Thinking in Terms of Threads

Listing 13.62 Continued

```
        catch(Exception e) {
            e.printStackTrace();
            looping = false;
        }
    }
    while(looping);
    }
}
```

The server application operates as follows:

1. When the application starts, the main() method enters the do loop and starts waiting for connect requests from clients by calling the accept() method of Socket. The initial thread thus spends most of its time suspended in accept().

2. When a connection is made, main() calls serviceClient() to handle the request. After returning from serviceClient(), the initial thread returns and then waits in accept(). The main() code has no knowledge (nor interest) of how serviceClient() deals with the connection.

3. The serviceClient() method deals with each request by creating a new Server object to serve that client. The Server is passed the Socket when created.

4. A Thread object is then created and passed the new Server object as the Runnable that it should execute.

5. Finally, the thread is started by calling it's Thread object's start() and serviceClient() returns.

The handling of the client request is all accomplished in the run() method that is called by the newly started thread. Most of the code in run()is fairly straightforward (and not very sophisticated) file and socket I/O. The main points to note are

■ The main loop that sends the file contents down the socket to the client includes a yield() call after each block is sent. This ensures that all the Server objects processing at the same time share the available processor time.

■ The Server class maintains a count of the number of threads running Server objects at any one time. If this count reaches zero at the end of the "finally" block in run(), a call to System.gc() is made. This means that whenever a Server finishes and is the only one left running, the last thread allocates some time to garbage collection.

Improvements to the Server

The ThreadedServer class creates as many threads as there are simultaneous client requests. On some platforms this might overload the CPU with too many eligible threads or too much simultaneous file I/O. The ThreadedServer2 class shown in listing 13.64 limits the number of threads and recycles existing threaded objects instead of creating them on demand.

The ServerTask class

To simplify listing 13.63, the code that serves the client is placed in a separate class, the ServerTask.

Listing 13.63   The ServerTask Class

```
package industrial;
import java.io.*;
import java.net.*;

public class ServerTask implements Runnable {
//object variables
//The socket used to communicate with the client
//(null when ServerTask isn't busy).
private Socket s;

//The thread that runs the ServerTask object.
private Thread t;

//Flag set true while this object is busy serving
//a client.
private boolean busy;

//Condition variable notified when a ServerTask
//completed service and becomes non-busy.
private Object flag;

//object methods

public synchronized boolean isBusy() {
        return busy;
}

//serviceRequest is called with the socket for a client
```

continues

Thinking in Terms of Threads

Listing 13.63   Continued

```
        //connection to kick an existing ThreadedServer
        //object into handling that request.
        public synchronized void serviceRequest(Socket s) {
                //make a note of the socket
                this.s = s;

                //wake the thread
                this.notify();
        }

        //Constructor
        public ServerTask(Socket s, Object flag) {
                //create a Thread, passing this as the
                //Runnable.
                this.t = new Thread(this);

                this.s = s;
                this.flag = flag;

                //Set the busy flag to true now.
                this.busy = true;

                //Start the thread;
                t.start();

                //Yield to let the task start
                Thread.yield();
        }

        public void run() {
                do {
                        //Handle one request.  If busy is false
                        //then the wait() must have been
                        //interrupted, so just repeat the loop.
                        if(busy)
                                doRequest();

                        //Mark ourselves as free and
                        //wait for some work
                        synchronized(this) {
                                //Notify any interested objects
                                //that we're now free.
                                if(flag != null) {
                                        synchronized(flag) {
```

```
                                        flag.notify();
                        }
                }
                this.busy = false;
                try {
                        this.wait();
                        this.busy = true;
                }
                catch(InterruptedException e) {}
        }
    } while(true);
}

//Given a socket s, service a client's request on that
//socket.  This isn't the most efficient way to handle
//socket IO or file IO; it's kept simple because this
//is just an example.
private void doRequest() {
FileInputStream        fis = null;
DataInputStream        dis = null;
DataOutputStream       dos = null;

        try {
                //get streams to listen to and talk to
                //the client.
                InputStream ins = s.getInputStream();
                dis = new DataInputStream(ins);
                OutputStream os = s.getOutputStream();
                dos = new DataOutputStream(os);

                //read a filename from the client.
                String fName = dis.readUTF();

                //read that file and send it back.
                File f = new File(fName);
                fis = new FileInputStream(f);

                //read the file and send it.
                //First, allocate a byte array the size
                //of the file.
                int len = (int)f.length();
                byte[] b = new byte[len];

                //now read the file into the array.
                len = fis.read(b, 0, len);
```

continues

A Threaded Client/Server Application   585

Listing 13.63   Continued

```
                    //send the length to the client as a
                    //single int
                    System.out.println(fName+": sending "+len
                            +" bytes");
                    dos.writeInt(len);

                    //send those bytes to the client in
                    //chunks of up to 256 bytes at a time.
                    int offset=0;
                    do {
                            int lenToSend
                                    = (len < 256) ? len : 256;
                            dos.write(b, offset, lenToSend);
                            len -= lenToSend;
                            Thread.currentThread().yield();
                    }
                    while(len > 0);

                    dos.flush();

                    //wait for a confirmation from the client.
                    System.out.println(fName+": delivered");
                    String status = dis.readUTF();
                    System.out.println(status);
            }

            catch(IOException e) {
                    e.printStackTrace();
            }

            //This may be thrown by FileInputStream(File) in some
            //versions of the JDK.
    /*
            catch(FileNotFoundException e) {
            }
    */

            finally {
                    //finished.
                    try {
                            s.close();
                            s = null;
                            if(dis != null)        dis.close();
```

```
                              if(fis != null)      fis.close();
                              if(dos != null)      dos.close();
                    }
               catch(IOException e) {
                         e.printStackTrace();
               }
         }
    }
}
```

ServerTask objects are created to service a client and pass a Socket and an Object (flag) that is used as a condition variable. When a ServerTask is done servicing a particular request, it clears its busy status, performs a notify() on "flag," and calls wait() on itself. The serviceRequest() method can then be called with another Socket to wake the ServerTask and service another client request. In other words, a ServerTask, once created, can be reused to service new client requests.

The main() method and associated code for the server application are defined in the ThreadedServer2 class (see listing 13.64).

Listing 13.64   The ThreadedServer2 Class

```
package industrial;

import java.io.*;
import java.net.*;

//The threaded server rewritten to service multiple clients
//at once by creating or re-using existing Servers up to
//a limit).
public class ThreadedServer2 {
//class constants
public static final int        SERVER_PORT=6543,
      THREAD_MAX=4;

//class variables
//Pool of servers available to serve requests.
private static ServerTask pool[];

//Condition variable used to wait for a free server
private static Object flag;

static {
```

continues

Listing 13.64   Continued

```
        pool = new ServerTask[THREAD_MAX];
        flag = new Object();
}

private static void serviceClient(Socket s) {
        boolean served = false;

        //The loop is synchronized on the flag condition
        //variable to avoid race conditions.
        synchronized(flag) {
                do {
                        //Try to find an available server
                        //from the pool.
                        int i;
                        for(i = 0; i<THREAD_MAX; i++) {
                                //A null entry in the array
                                //means there are no more
                                //entries.
                                if(pool[i] == null)
                                        break;

                                //see if this server is free
                                if(pool[i].isBusy())
                                        continue;
                                pool[i].serviceRequest(s);
                                served = true;
                                break;
                        }

                        //If we found no free server, is
                        //there room to create one?
                        //If so, i will be less than
                        //THREAD_MAX.
                        if((!served) && (i < THREAD_MAX)) {
                                pool[i]=new ServerTask(s,flag);
                                served = true;
                        }

                        if(!served) {
                                //There are no free servers
                                //nor slots in which to
                                //create a new server. Wait
                                //for a free server.
```

```
                                    try {
                                            flag.wait();
                                    }
                                    catch(InterruptedException e) {
                                    }
                            }
                    } while(!served);
            }       //end of synchronized block on flag.
}

//main
public static void main(String[] args) {
boolean                         looping = true;
ServerSocket            sock;

        try {
                //create our socket
                sock = new ServerSocket(SERVER_PORT);
        }
        catch(IOException e) {
                e.printStackTrace();
                return;
        }

        System.out.println("Accepting requests...");

        //loop accepting requests.
        do {
                try {
                        //accept a connection from a client.
                        Socket s = sock.accept();

                        //service that request
                        serviceClient(s);
                }

                catch(Exception e) {
                        e.printStackTrace();
                        looping = false;
                }
        }
        while(looping);
    }
}
```

A Threaded Client/Server Application

The serviceClient() method has been changed to use a pool of ServerTasks in the pool array. When a client request is received, the main thread calls serviceClient(), which checks the pool for a free ServerTask. If a free ServerTask is found, serviceRequest() is called to pass the client socket, and serviceClient() returns.

If no free ServerTask is available, and there's room in the pool for a new one, serviceClient() creates one and returns.

If all the possible ServerTasks are busy, serviceClient() waits for one to become free. To do this, the flag Object is used as a simple condition variable. The thread calling serviceClient() waits on the flag (see fig. 13.8).

The entire do loop is nested within a block synchronized on "flag." This helps to avoid a possible race condition that could occur in the following situations:

- The main thread checks the "busy" status of the ServerTasks and finds them all busy. No free slots in the "pool" array exist, so no new ServerTasks can be created.
- The main thread is descheduled in favor of one of the ServerTasks threads. This ServerTask finishes a request, calls notify() on flag, and calls wait() on this, consequently suspending its thread until a new client request is available.
- The other busy ServerTasks are scheduled next and all complete in the same way.
- The main thread is rescheduled and proceeds to wait() on flag. Because all the free ServerTasks are now in wait(), the main thread has missed its notify() call and won't be notified.

Any ServerTasks that finish servicing their clients while the main thread is executing in serviceClient() must wait until the thread running main() has called wait() before calling notify(). This wait is required because both the do loop in ThreadedServer2.serviceClient() and the notify() in ServerTask.run() are synchronized on the same flag Object.

The ThreadedServer2 class limits the number of threads to 4, so that it's easy to observe the behavior of the application during testing. Most systems should comfortably handle hundreds of threads before exhibiting problems.

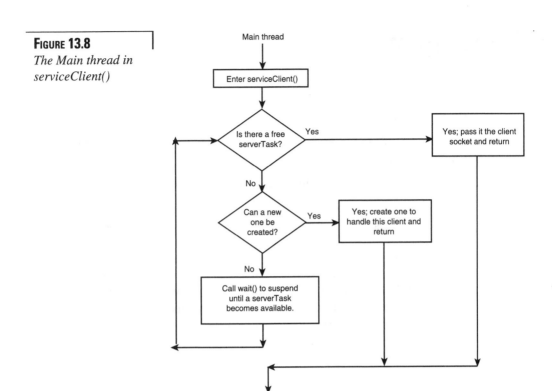

FIGURE 13.8

The Main thread in serviceClient()

Further Reading

The design and implementation of concurrent systems is a complex field in computer science. This chapter attempts to cover the basics of multithreaded programming as it's supported in Java. For further reading on these and related subjects refer to the following texts:

Lea, Doug, *Concurrent Programming in Java: Design Principles and Patterns*, Addison-Wesley, 1996 (ISBN 0-201-69581-2)

Ben-Ari, M., *Principles of Concurrent and Distributed Programming*, Prentice-Hall, 1990 (ISBN 0-13-701078-8)

Summary

This chapter introduced the idea of multithreading Java classes to produce objects that can carry out work in parallel with the code that creates them. You should be familiar with the Java Thread and ThreadGroup classes and understand how they are used.

You should have learned some basic concepts of concurrent programming, including the following:

- The technique of mutual exclusion and how Java implements this using synchronized methods and blocks.
- Communicating between threads using condition variables, wait() and notify().

Some of the common problems encountered with concurrently executing threads were covered, with examples developed through several versions to demonstrate approaches to coding that will help you to avoid or correct these problems. Working through the various versions of the printer access classes pointed out common situations in which race conditions occur and how the Semaphore class might be used to avoid them.

Chapter 14

Interfacing C/C++ and Java

Native methods are used to link C code to Java. C code is sometimes necessary because cross-platform environments may offer features that are unavailable to standard Java programs. C code is also necessary to integrate Java with legacy code. Java is designed to access native machines with the native interface and library. This chapter covers the basics of interfacing between C or C++ and the Java environment.

Also covered in this chapter is an alternative way to link C and Java code, achieved by using native processes and the exec() method. Examples provided in this chapter show how a Java program can run and control system programs and utilities.

This chapter also discusses how to make native code easy to port to another environment. The method described is similar to the peer interfacing methods used by the Java AWT to isolate platform specific code.

Native Code Necessities

Although Java is generally a very capable language, it is sometimes necessary to access the native environment. Here is a quick reference list to help you identify the most common reasons:

- Hardware access and control

- Use of commercial software and system services

- Reuse of legacy software that has not or cannot be ported to Java

- Augmenting C programs with a Java GUI

- Using native code to perform time-critical tasks

All these are perfectly legitimate reasons for interfacing with the native environment. They are not, however, reasons to abandon writing pure Java applications. The following list provides some reasons why you should not use the native methods:

- Applications are not guaranteed portable to other Java VM environments.

- Native code cannot be used by applets.

- Native code must be maintained by programmers who understand the C or C++ language.

- Native code is not secure.

- Native code is not pointer-safe.

- Proficiency in more than one programming language must be maintained.

- Versions of native code for multiple platforms are hard to maintain.

- Native access to system services and commercial libraries must be verified every time a new release becomes available.

Combating Java Limitations with Native Code

Because it is cross platform, Java is limited to what is generic to all machines. Specific hardware and system services are not included so as many machines as possible can run identical Java programs. Unfortunately cross-platform capability is a limitation for many programs that require access to hardware, system services, or old code. Java runs programs within the Java Virtual Machine.

The Virtual Machine is a simulation of a computer's CPU and memory. The Java VM does not have access to hardware or system services. The only way to gain access to hardware and system services is to use the native method API. The native method API is used to bridge the gap between Java and machine-specific libraries. This limits machine-specific information to classes other than the Java VM. Because it only needs to implement the native interface API, the Java VM is much more portable. The native method API also is a gateway for developers to write software that uses legacy software or to access machine-specific software or services.

Taking Advantage of System Services and Commercial C Libraries

Thousands of commercial libraries have been written for the C language. Every platform includes them; whether you use Windows 95, Macintosh, or Unix, a wealth of standard libraries are available. If you already depend on such libraries, using the Java native interface is required for applications that have no Java equivalent.

Legacy Software

Legacy software is any software that is currently in use and must be maintained. Legacy software is characterized as business-specific code that has a long life span (sometimes many years). Because of the advanced age of legacy software, it is rare that it is still fully understood by the company's current programming staff. If you or your company has invested in legacy software and you are migrating to a completely Java application, it may be wise to reuse as much of this code as possible in early versions. A rewrite of all legacy software to Java may not fit the schedule or budget. In some applications where the code is moving from C or C++, Java may only be used for the user interface, whereas native legacy code is used for all other processing.

A legacy application for customer order entry, for example, may have been written for OS/2 machines, but the company is moving to Windows 95 machines in the near future. The company determines that the new software should be able to run on the old OS/2 machines and new Windows 95 platforms that will slowly replace OS/2 hardware. Unfortunately, the new Windows 95 machines will begin to arrive in the next few months. The original software initially took over two years to develop and has had small changes made to it over the past year. Redesigning and rewriting the system is seen as impossible. The only machine-specific code is associated with the user interface. By writing Java code utilizing the AWT and integrating non platform-specific code via the native method API, the project can be completed before the required deadline.

It should be noted that such combinations of Java and legacy code are difficult to maintain. The staff that supports the application will need to stay proficient in the older technology, as well as Java. Any application migrated to be 100 percent Java will be much easier to maintain. In addition, the security and safety features inherent in Java will cover the entire program instead of just part of it. Conversion to 100 percent Java will eliminate many of the memory problems in C and C++. Another benefit, especially if you are moving from C++, is the simplification of programs. Java has far fewer language features than C++. A simpler language such as Java can reduce the cost of legacy code maintenance because programmers will be able to understand the code more quickly and be able to make changes sooner.

Enhancing C and C++ Code with a Java GUI

Existing C and C++ applications can take advantage of the Java environment by calling Java methods. This can be accomplished by first creating a Java application that calls the main routine of a C/C++ application. The C/C++ program could then instantiate Java objects and call their public functions.

Accessing C and C++ for Speed Reasons

Java becomes more efficient and faster as new techniques for optimization mature. Now there are improved Java VMs, JIT compilers, and compilers that create 100 percent-native executables. There may still be times when all these improvements are still not as fast as native executables developed in machine language or produced by C compilers. Due to the inherent safety and portability of Java, like array bounds checking, Java may cause some tasks to execute more slowly than the same code compiled in C or C++. Speed degradation comes in many forms. The following list demonstrates a few forms that can cause slow execution.

- Standard Java VM implementations are interpreted. Interpretation means that twice the processing power is required. Java VM instructions must be read and converted to instructions for the local CPU.

- The Java Just In Time compiler (JIT) may not be as efficient as a native program compiled with optimization.

- The computer platform may have more than one CPU. Java VM and JIT may be written to work with only one CPU.

- Garbage collection may occur too often or at critical times where speed is paramount.

- Standard Java API packages may not be efficiently written.

- Java API packages may not access environment-specific libraries that are optimally efficient. They may be either 100 percent Java or only minimally access the local environment.

- Java validates every array access to validate that the array is accessed within its bounds. Through optimization, compilers and JIT compilers reduce the number of checks, but optimizations do not eliminate all checks.

The first step of optimization is to prove that the current version is slow. Sometimes this may only require a simple comparison of a Java implementation to a native application that does a similar task. Comparing Java to native applications is only valid when running the Java application with a good JIT or as a compiled Java application. Unless the code is very similar between Java and native applications, it may be a hard comparison to make. Compare only function to function. Sometimes the order of execution is changed when converting between C or C++ to Java. For instance, reading a file may be done at the beginning of an application and then processing is performed, whereas the Java version may read a file while processing each item from a file. In the Java application, the processing appears to take longer because file I/O is included.

Speed problems may be caused by poor design and not Java. Try to isolate specific functions for speed comparison. Avoid believing that Java is taking too long unless you have a valid benchmark for the same task written in native code. It is very easy to mistakenly believe that a task that takes several minutes might be slow because of Java. In fact, a task may take several minutes when written in any language.

The most important rule of optimization is to worry about it only after the first version has been written. The wisdom in this statement is like the wisdom of not counting your chickens before they hatch. Some functions may not work as intended or be used as often as expected. Like eggs that may not produce chickens, functions may not execute as many times as expected, if they run at all. The design effort optimizing functions should be proportional to the number of times that a function or code segment runs. For instance, a function that runs hundreds of times is a better candidate for optimization than a function that runs once.

A lot of work can be done during design to increase speed, but the increase may not be worth the time invested. Optimization is a subjective quantity until it can be compared to a definitive benchmark. Do not waste time optimizing a function that has never been run to see how fast or slow the initially designed version is.

When choosing which functions to optimize with native functions, be aware of the $^{90}/_{10}$ rule. This rule states that 90 percent of execution time is spent in only 10 percent (or less) of the code. Benchmark the code until you find the 10 percent that requires the most optimization. When replacing Java with C, benchmarking is important because it is safer to keep as much of the code written in Java as possible.

Easy Native Access: Using Runtime.exec()

When mixing Java with the native environment, first consider having native applications controlled by Java. This solution does not require any direct Java to C linkage or Java instrumented native libraries. All that is needed is a native executable that performs the required functions. The native executable can communicate to the Java application in various ways. Java and native applications can use the native executable's standard I/O or read and write files that are also manipulated by the Java application.

System programs have the capability to perform various native tasks, some of which are inaccessible to Java, such as starting database servers or launching editors to view files. Java can control these applications through standard I/O by accessing the Standard In, Standard Out, and Standard Error I/O streams. If you can encapsulate all the native actions into an executable, you would have an easy method to access native tasks. This also is a simple way of launching other programs, such as Netscape, or retrieving the results of DOS commands, such as dir and attrib. Programs that accept standard I/O and std out can be used to process data within Java applications. For instance, Unix utilities such as troff (a text formatting utility) can be fed information through Standard In, whereas the results can be piped to a printer or read back into Java for further processing.

The exec() method in the Runtime class launches the native executables. This method is similar to the exec() or fork() functions found in many C libraries. The return value of exec() is a Process object. The Process object is used to access standard I/O of the application and to monitor completion status.

Accessing the Studio Streams

The Runtime class can be used to start Netscape or text editors. This is a simple method of displaying and printing a Java application's results.

Two functions in the Runtime class can be used to start native applications. The first, shown in listing 14.1, accepts a String that contains the command to be run and its options.

Listing 14.1   The exec() Method

```
Process exec(commandArray) throws Ioexception;
```

The command is simple and can be used as it is in listing 14.2 to get a DOS directory of text files:

Listing 14.2   Executing a Directory Command with exec

```
try{
     Process dosProcess = Runtime.getRuntime().exec("dir *.txt");
}catch(IOException ex){
     System.err.println("Command failed with IO Exception.");
}
```

The second version of exec() accepts an array of String variables. In this form, the command is in the zero index of the array, whereas the arguments are placed separately in the remaining array indexes. This version is slightly faster than the first because it does not need to parse the command string.

Listing 14.3   The exec() Method that Accepts a Command Array

```
Process exec(commandArray) throws Ioexception;
```

Here is the same DOS directory example using the command array version of exec().

Listing 14.4   Using a Command Array Version of exec() to Execute a DOS Directory Command

```
String dosCommand[] = new String[2];
dosCommand[0] = "dir";
dosCommand[1] = "*.txt";
try{
     Process dosDirProcess = Runtime.getRuntime().exec(dosCommand);
}catch(IOException ex){
     System.err.println("Command failed with IO Exception.");
}
```

Waiting for Programs to Complete

In this example, the Windows notepad application is started. The application waits until the user closes the notepad application and pops up a dialog box to acknowledge the fact.

The result of an exec() method is a Process object. Because the Process class implements the Runnable interface, call waitFor() to cause the current Java thread to block execution until the editor process terminates. Blocking execution is very useful when the results of running a native application will not be available until the native application terminates. In listing 14.5, you might be waiting for the user to modify the temp.txt file.

Listing 14.5   Starting a Text Editor and Waiting for It to Be Terminated

```
Process winNotepad;
try{
    // Start the windows notepad application.
    winNotepad = Runtime.getRuntime().exec("notepad temp.txt");
}catch(IOException ex){
    System.err.println("Command failed with IO Exception.");
}
try{
    // Wait until the user has exited the notepad application.
    winNotepad.waitFor();
    .
    .           // Process temp.txt
    .
}catch(InterruptedException ex){
    System.err.println("Command failed with Interrupted Exception.");
}
```

Figure 14.1 shows a flowchart of a non-blocking use of exec(). The figure shows that exec() starts a new thread that is running the notepad.exe program. Immediately after starting the thread, execution continues. A non-blocking program could use this, for example, to display a native program to the user that is a reference or file utility that has no affect on the current program.

FIGURE 14.1

A state diagram of the runtime.exec() method executing a native application and continuing the Java program's thread of execution.

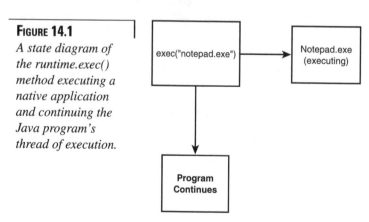

The state diagram in figure 14.2 shows the use of the runtime.waitFor() method as it is used in listing 14.5. The Java program is shown creating a thread that is running the native application notepad.exe. Immediately after the exec() call, the Java program calls the waitFor() method in the process object that represents notepad.exe. By using waitFor(), the program will cease execution (that is, block) until notepad.exe terminates.

FIGURE 14.2

The runtime.exec() method executing a native application followed by a call to runtime.wairFor().

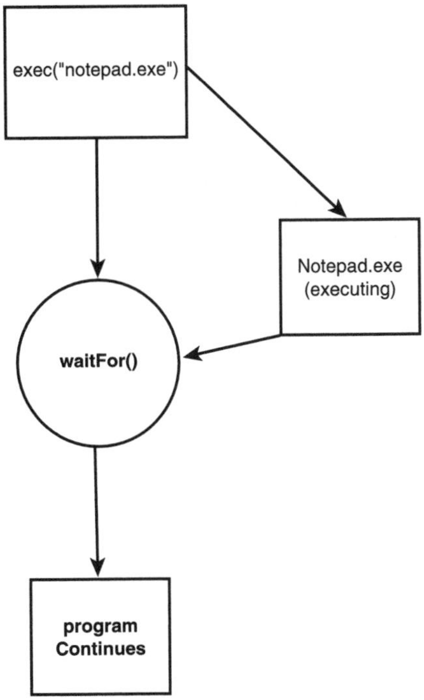

The Native Interface

To understand the native interface, an assumption about the designer's motives must be made. The designers were attempting to make a native interface that was as portable as possible. Given this assumption, it is easy to understand the mapping between Java types and C types. An interesting observation from table 14.1 is that Java promotes almost everything to a bigger word size. The only data types that survive at the same size are float and double because these are usually the same between different hardware architectures. C types like char, int, byte, and long could vary depending on the word size defined by the native compiler, so they are all promoted as high as the designers expected them to go. This means most types are promoted to 32 bits except long, which is doubled to 64 bits.

TABLE 14.1	Java Type	C/C++ Type
Java to C Type Mapping	Boolean	long
	byte	long
	char	long
	short	long
	int	long
	long	int64
	float	float
	double	double

This mapping may fool a programmer into writing native C software with the types that are required to interface with Java. On some machines this may not be speedy or memory efficient. Keep to the most efficient types required by your application and only promote or demote when interfacing with Java.

Building Java Applications that Use C/C++

The following five steps are required to build a combined Java and C/C++ application:

- Create Java files that define native methods.
- Use javah to create C header files and stub files.
- Write C code that is called by stub functions.
- Compile C code to a loadable library.
- In Java code, before native methods are called, add loadLibrary() method to link loadable library to Java.

Each of these steps is covered in detail in the following sections.

Using Native Methods in Java Classes

The following classes use the native methods that were defined in the TestObject class.

Testing Native Functions: Class GoNative

The class in listing 14.6 contains the main() for the following classes. The main() method creates a Native Test object and calls testNative(), which tests different ways to access C code. The main() method also traps IOException as well as verifies that the results of the test are accurate.

Listing 14.6 Creating a Native Test Object and Calling testNative()

```
import java.awt.*;
import java.io.IOException;
import NativeTest;
public class GoNative {
    public static void main(String args[]) {
        System.out.println("simple console application");
        System.out.println("");
        NativeTest test = new NativeTest();
        if (test.testNative()){
            System.out.println("Native methods completed OK.");
            System.out.println("HAL = "+test.nativeInt(2000));
        }else{
            System.out.println("Native methods FAILED.");
        }
        System.out.println("");
        System.out.println("(press Enter to exit)");
        try {
            System.in.read();
        } catch (IOException e) {
            return;
        }
    }
}
```

Calling Native Java Methods: Class NativeTest

This class calls the native methods of the TestObject class. Native test is also accessed from C code to prove that class data (statics), object data, and methods can be manipulated.

The first section of code in listing 14.7a contains a static initializer block. The static block calls System.loadLibrary("NativeTest"). The loadLibrary() method loads the NativeTest.dll, which contains the C implementation.

Listing 14.7a   Imports and Static Initializer Block

```
import TestObject;
public class NativeTest{
    // Static block is used to init
    // the dynamic library.
    static{
        // Load the dynamic library
        System.loadLibrary("NativeTest");
    }
    NativeTest(){
    }
```

The next method of the NativeTest class is the class constructor, shown in listing 14.7b. The constructor is used to call all the native methods that are in the class. Remember that because the NativeTest.dll library has been loaded in the static block, the library is active, so native C functions within it now exist. The only processing that occurs is that data is passed to the native method, and the results returned are compared to what was passed in. (The ➥ symbol denotes a line that would normally fit on the preceding line, were this a computer screen.)

Listing 14.7b   Class Constructor Calling Native Methods

```
boolean  testNative(){
    // Dealing with atoms
    if (nativeInt(1)!=2)return false;
    if (nativeChar((char)1)!=(char)2)return false;
    if (nativeShort((short)1)!=(short)2)return false;
    if (nativeFloat((float)1.0)!=(float)2.0)return false;
    if (nativeDouble(1.0)!=2.0)return false;
    if (nativeBoolean(true)!=false)return false;
    // Dealing with arrays
    int arraySize = 10;
    // Test int array
    int inputIntArray[] = new int[arraySize];
    for (int i = 0; i < inputIntArray.length; i++){
        inputIntArray[i] = 1;
    }
    int[] outputIntArray = nativeIntArray(inputIntArray);
    for (int i = 0; i < outputIntArray.length; i++){
        if (inputIntArray[i] != outputIntArray[i]) return(false);
    }
    // Test char array
```

```
char inputCharArray[] = new char[arraySize];
for (int i = 0; i < inputIntArray.length; i++){
    inputCharArray[i] = 1;
}
char[] outputCharArray = nativeCharArray(inputCharArray);
for (int i = 0; i < inputIntArray.length; i++){
    if (inputCharArray[i] != outputCharArray[i]) return(false);
}
// Test short array
short inputShortArray[] = new short[arraySize];
for (int i = 0; i < inputShortArray.length; i++){
    inputShortArray[i] = 1;
}
short[] outputShortArray = nativeShortArray(inputShortArray);
for (int i = 0; i < inputShortArray.length; i++){
    if(inputShortArray[i] != outputShortArray[i]) return(false);
}
// Test float array
float inputFloatArray[] = new float[arraySize];
for (int i = 0; i < inputFloatArray.length; i++){
    inputFloatArray[i] = 1;
}
float[] outputFloatArray = nativeFloatArray(inputFloatArray);
// Test double array
double inputDoubleArray[] = new double[arraySize];
for (int i = 0; i < inputIntArray.length; i++){
    inputDoubleArray[i] = 1;
}
double[] outputDoubleArray =
➥nativeDoubleArray(inputDoubleArray);
for (int i = 0; i < inputIntArray.length; i++){
    if (inputDoubleArray[i] != outputDoubleArray[i])
    ➥return(false);
}
// Test boolean array
boolean inputBooleanArray[] = new boolean[arraySize];
for (int i = 0; i < inputIntArray.length; i++){
    inputBooleanArray[i] = true;
}
boolean[] outputBooleanArray =
➥nativeBooleanArray(inputBooleanArray);
for (int i = 0; i < inputIntArray.length; i++){
    if (inputBooleanArray[i] != outputBooleanArray[i])
    ➥return(false);
}
```

continues

Interfacing C/C++ and Java

Listing 14.7b   Continued

```
// Object passing (casting for clarity).
TestObject inputObject = new TestObject( true
    ,(byte)1
    ,(short)1
    ,(int)1
    ,(long)1
    ,(float)1.0
    ,(double)1.0
    ,(char)'1'
    ,(String)"One");
TestObject outputObject = nativeObject(inputObject);
// Arrays of Objects passing
TestObject inputObjectArray[] = new TestObject[arraySize];
for (int i = 0; i < inputObjectArray.length; i++){
    inputObjectArray[i] = new
    TestObject(true,(byte)1,(short)1,(int)1,(long)1,(float)1.0,
    ➥(double)1.0,(char)'1',(String)"One");;
    }
TestObject[] outputObjectArray =
➥nativeObjectArray(inputObjectArray);
//for (int i = 0; i < inputObjectArray.length; i++){
//if(!inputObjectArray[i].isEqual(outputObjectArray[i]))
//return(false);}
callJava();
testException3();
testExceptions(1);
testExceptions(2);
// if we got here then it all worked!
return true;
}
```

The next section of code simply declares native methods of the TestObject class.

Listing 14.7c   Simple Native Method Declarations

```
// ----------
// Dealing with atoms
// ----------
native int nativeInt(int anInt);
native char nativeChar(char aChar);
native short nativeShort(short aShort);
native float nativeFloat(float aFloat);
```

```
native double nativeDouble(double aDouble);
native boolean nativeBoolean(boolean aBoolean);
// ----------
// Dealing with arrays
// ----------
native int[] nativeIntArray(int anInt[]);
native char[] nativeCharArray(char aChar[]);
native short[] nativeShortArray(short aShort[]);
native float[] nativeFloatArray(float aFloat[]);
native double[] nativeDoubleArray(double aDouble[]);
native boolean[] nativeBooleanArray(boolean aBoolean[]);
```

Listing 14.7d defines native methods used to pass Objects and Object arrays between Java and C code.

Listing 14.7d   Native Methods Used to Pass Objects and Object Arrays

```
// ----------
// Objective passing
// ----------
native TestObject nativeObject(TestObject anObject);
native TestObject[] nativeObjectArray(TestObject anObject[]);
```

Listing 14.7e   Native Method that Will Call Java from C

```
// ----------
// Calling Java from C
// ----------
native void callJava();
```

Listing 14.7f   Native Method that Generate Exceptions when Called

```
// ----------
// Generating exceptions
// ----------
native void doExceptions(int type) throws java.io.IOException,
 ➥ArithmeticException ;
```

Listing 14.7g shows the method used to call the functions in listing 14.7f.

Listing 14.7g   Java Method Used to Call Native Functions that Throw Exceptions

```
void testExceptions(int type){
    try{
        doExceptions(type);
    }
    catch (java.io.IOException ioe){
        System.out.println("Native code generated a
        ➥java.io.IOException.");
        System.out.println();
    }
    catch (ArithmeticException ae){
        System.out.println("Native code generated an
        ➥ArithmeticException.");
        System.out.println();
    }
}
```

The next section of this class defines a field used by the native testException2() method to pass information just before an exception is thrown. The last method of this class, testException3(), calls testException2, which sets the myErrorValue field and then throws an IOException. This example is provided because the native interface is unable to generate an exception other than IOException. By passing information in special class fields, the equivalent functionality can be simulated. Use this pattern of setting exception information fields and then throwing the IOException any time where a specialized exception would be required. For instance, if native code were controlling a serial port, the data returned in a specialized variable might be an I/O error number. For the implementation of the testException2() method, refer to listing 14.7h.

Listing 14.7h   TestObject Class: A Native Method that Throws an Exception and Passes Data

```
// Getting error data from exceptions
/**
 * Field used to pass error data.
 */
int myErrorValue;
/**
 * Always generates an IOException.
 * Modifies the value of myErrorValue
 * to designate errorinformation.
```

```
    */
    native void testException2() throws java.io.IOException;
    /**
     * Tests that data can be pased and used after
     * an exception is thrown.
     */
    void testException3(){
        try{
            // clear the error value
            myErrorValue = 0;
                //call native.
                testException2();
        }catch(java.io.IOException ioe){
                    System.out.println("exception
                    ➥information:"+myErrorValue);
        }
    }
} //End of class TestObject
```

Accessing Classes and Objects from C: TestObject.Java

The next class in the example is used to demonstrate several more capabilities of the native API. The TestObject.Java class helps to exercise access from C to Java methods and to access or create user defined objects. This class contains no native methods. Native code in the testStatic() method directly accesses the static class field. It will be necessary to run javah on this class so that the method structure can be imported to C code.

The TestObject class in listing 14.1a begins with two fields. The first field, testStaticInt, is to be accessed by native C from the class reference. The next is an object variable that will also be accessed, but after an object is created. Refer to listing 14.8a to see the C code that accesses these fields.

Listing 14.8a   TestObject Class: Variables

```
public class TestObject{
    static int testStaticInt = 0;
    int testObjectField;
```

The static method of listing 14.8b is called to prove that static methods can be accessed through a class reference.

Listing 14.8b   TestObject Class: The testStatic() Method

```
static int testStatic(){
    return(++testStaticInt);
}
```

The class constructor for the TestObject class is shown in listing 14.8c. The constructor has a parameter for each of the standard types and one of String class. These parameters are printed to the standard output so that the creation of an object can be verified.

Listing 14.8c   TestObject class: The Class Constructor

```
TestObject(boolean tBoolean,byte tByte,short tShort, int tInt,
➥long tLong,float tFloat,double tDouble,char tChar,String tString){
    testObjectField= 100;
    testStatic();
    System.out.println("TestObject()");
    System.out.println("tBoolean:  " + tBoolean);
    System.out.println("tByte:     " + tByte);
    System.out.println("tShort:    " + tShort);
    System.out.println("tInt:      " + tInt);
    System.out.println("tLong:     " + tLong);
    System.out.println("tFloat:    " + tFloat);
    System.out.println("tDouble:   " + tDouble);
    System.out.println("tChar:     " + tChar);
    System.out.println("tString:   " + tString);
    System.out.println("");
}
```

The next method in the TestObject class, testArrays(), shown in listing 14.8d, is used to validate that native C can call a method in an object it has created. Arrays in testArrays() are passed as parameters. Like the parameters in the constructor, the parameters are printed to validate that the method was called correctly.

Listing 14.8d   TestObject class: The testArray() Method

```
void testArrays(boolean tBooleans[],byte tBytes[],short tShorts[], int
➥tInts[],long tLongs[],float tFloats[],double tDoubles[],char
➥tChars[],String tStrings[]){
        System.out.println("testArrays()");/*
```

```
        System.out.println("tBooleans[]:   " + tBooleans);
        System.out.println("tBytes[]:      " + tBytes);
        System.out.println("tShorts[]:     " + tShorts);
        System.out.println("tInts[]:       " + tInts);
        System.out.println("tLongs[]:      " + tLongs);
        System.out.println("tFloats[]:     " + tFloats);
        System.out.println("tDoubles[]:    " + tDoubles);
        System.out.println("tChars[]:      " + tChars);
        System.out.println("tStrings[]:    " + tStrings);*/
        System.out.println("");
    }//End of testArrays() method
}// End of TestObject class
```

javah: The Header and Stub Generator

The javah utility is used to generate header files and stub files are used by native programs to interface to Java. The javah utility must be run twice for each Java class that accesses or contains native methods, first to create C header files and then with the "-stubs" parameter to create a stub file. In each example in this chapter, a BAT file is used to call javah for each native class. The batch file also copies the header and C files to their proper C development directories. A shell or BAT file should be used in this way because batch files automate the process, thus reducing errors. Listing 14.9 is the do_javah.bat file for the examples discussed so far.

Listing 14.9 do_java.bat file: Used to Generate Header and Stub Files for the Native Method Test

```
javah -classpath %CLASSPATH% -v NativeTest
javah -classpath %CLASSPATH% -v -stubs NativeTest
javah -classpath %CLASSPATH% -v TestObject
javah -classpath %CLASSPATH% -v -stubs TestObject
move *.c NativeTestDLL
move *.h NativeTestDLL
```

Files Generated by javah

The files output by javah have a wealth of information about how C can access Java. The first file to be examined is the header file for the TestObject class.

Header Files Generated by javah

The TestObject class does not define any native methods, but it does define two fields, testStaticInt and testObjectField. The Note javah has made is a comment that testStaticInt is a static variable and is not accessible. Static variables cannot be accessed directly, but they can be accessed via class methods. The reason static variables cannot be accessed is that static variables cannot be made a part of C structures (remember the native API is for C, not C++; C++ can have statics in classes, not C). The structure for the class only represents fields that are part of objects. The second field, testObjectField, in which Java was declared as an int, here is declared long. After an object has been created of this class, this field is available for access by C.

The most striking attribute of this header is that it does not contain any references to the methods in the TestObject class because all method calls are done by name, as is covered later (see listing 14.10).

Listing 14.10   javah Output: The C Header File for TestObject Class

```
/* DO NOT EDIT THIS FILE - it is machine generated */
#include <native.h>
/* Header for class TestObject */
#ifndef _Included_TestObject
#define _Included_TestObject
typedef struct ClassTestObject {
/* Inaccessible static: testStaticInt */
    long testObjectField;
} ClassTestObject;
HandleTo(TestObject);
#ifdef __cplusplus
extern "C" {
#endif
#ifdef __cplusplus
}
#endif
#endif
```

The header file produced by javah for the TestObject class has a lot more information. It contains a structure that represents the accessible data in the object, which for TestObject is myErrorValue. Following the structure definition are external definitions for each of the C methods that are to be called from the stubs file. Use these definitions to create your C functions, as shown in listing 14.11.

The first parameter of each of these methods is "struct HNativeTest *", which is the equivalent of the "this" pointer to the object.

An important observation to make of the methods that deal with arrays is that arrays are converted to object handles. An array of int, for example, is converted to HArrayOfInt because arrays are objects in Java.

Listing 14.11 javah Output: The C Header File for TestObject Class

```
/* DO NOT EDIT THIS FILE - it is machine generated */
#include <native.h>
/* Header for class NativeTest */
#ifndef _Included_NativeTest
#define _Included_NativeTest
typedef struct ClassNativeTest {
    long myErrorValue;
} ClassNativeTest;
HandleTo(NativeTest);
#ifdef __cplusplus
extern "C" {
#endif
extern long NativeTest_nativeInt(struct HNativeTest *,long);
extern unicode NativeTest_nativeChar(struct HNativeTest *,unicode);
extern short NativeTest_nativeShort(struct HNativeTest *,short);
extern float NativeTest_nativeFloat(struct HNativeTest *,float);
extern double NativeTest_nativeDouble(struct HNativeTest *,double);
extern /*boolean*/ long NativeTest_nativeBoolean(struct HNativeTest *,/
➥*boolean*/ long);
extern HArrayOfInt *NativeTest_nativeIntArray(struct HNativeTest
➥*,HArrayOfInt *);
extern HArrayOfChar *NativeTest_nativeCharArray(struct HNativeTest
➥*,HArrayOfChar *);
extern HArrayOfShort *NativeTest_nativeShortArray(struct HNativeTest
➥*,HArrayOfShort *);
extern HArrayOfFloat *NativeTest_nativeFloatArray(struct HNativeTest
➥*,HArrayOfFloat *);
extern HArrayOfDouble *NativeTest_nativeDoubleArray(struct HNativeTest
➥*,HArrayOfDouble *);
extern /*boolean*/ HArrayOfInt *NativeTest_nativeBooleanArray(struct
➥HNativeTest *,HArrayOfInt *);
```

continues

Interfacing C/C++ and Java

Listing 14.11   Continued

```
struct HTestObject;
extern struct HTestObject *NativeTest_nativeObject(struct HNativeTest
➡*,struct HTestObject *);
extern HArrayOfObject *NativeTest_nativeObjectArray(struct HNativeTest
➡*,HArrayOfObject *);
extern void NativeTest_callJava(struct HNativeTest *);
extern void NativeTest_doExceptions(struct HNativeTest *,long);
extern void NativeTest_testException2(struct HNativeTest *);
#ifdef __cplusplus
}
#endif
#endif
```

Stub Files Generated by javah

The following code shows the C stubs file generated for the NativeTest class. A stub file contains all of the Java-to-C translation. Java creates the names of methods based on the class name, the method name, and the return value of the C function that is returned. Because this file is generated by javah, it is important that this file not be used as a repository of implementations for the stubs. The drawback to keeping the implementations and stubs separate is that cut and paste operations are required after changes to the Java code.

The code in listing 14.12 shows the C stub file generated by javah for the TestObject class. Stubs are methods that are in a format that can be understood by Java. The stub method calls a C function that is closer to a human readable format. Note that this file contains nothing important because TestObject.Java does not have any native methods for which to create stubs. This file is not necessary for creating the loadable library, but is included here for completeness.

Listing 14.12   The Stub File for the TestObject Class

```
/* DO NOT EDIT THIS FILE - it is machine generated */
#include <StubPreamble.h>
/* Stubs for class TestObject */
```

Listing 14.13 contains a typical stub. The particular stub is for NativeTest.nativeInt() method and was extracted from listing 14.14 which contains the complete stub file for the NativeTest class.

Listing 14.13   Stub for the NativeTest,nativeInt() Method

```
/* SYMBOL: "NativeTest/nativeInt(I)I", Java_NativeTest_nativeInt_stub */
__declspec(dllexport) stack_item
➥*Java_NativeTest_nativeInt_stub(stack_item *_P_,struct execenv *_EE_) {
    extern long NativeTest_nativeInt(void *,long);
    _P_[0].i = NativeTest_nativeInt(P_[0].p,((P_[1].i)));
    return _P_ + 1;
}
```

The function that is defined in this stub was written in NativeTest class as int nativeInt(int anInt);. There obviously is a lot involved in going from Java to C and back again. Each stub contains six lines, defined as follows:

- The first line describes how Java stores the signature of the method. The signature is a string that can be parsed by Java.

- The second line is the stub function called by Java. All stubs pass because the first argument, P, is a pointer to the current program stack. The second parameter is a pointer to the execution environment execution environment.

- The third line is a function prototype of the implementation for this method.

- The fourth line is the C function to be called. The stack pointer P is used as an array to select arguments from the stack.

- The fifth line also uses P as a place to return the C function results back onto Java's program stack.

- The sixth line is the curly bracket that closes the stub function.

Listing 14.14   The Complete Stub File for the NativeTest Class

```
/* DO NOT EDIT THIS FILE - it is machine generated */
#include <StubPreamble.h>
/* Stubs for class NativeTest */
/* SYMBOL: "NativeTest/nativeInt(I)I", Java_NativeTest_nativeInt_stub */
  declspec(dllexport) stack_item
➥*Java_NativeTest_nativeInt_stub(stack_item *_P_,struct execenv *_EE_) {
    extern long NativeTest_nativeInt(void *,long);
    _P_[0].i = NativeTest_nativeInt(_P_[0].p,((_P_[1].i)));
    return _P_ + 1;
}
/* SYMBOL: "NativeTest/nativeChar(C)C", Java_NativeTest_nativeChar_stub */
  declspec(dllexport) stack_item
```

continues

Interfacing C/C++ and Java

Listing 14.14   Continued

```
➡*Java_NativeTest_nativeChar_stub(stack_item *_P_,struct execenv *_EE_)
{
      extern long NativeTest_nativeChar(void *,long);
      _P_[0].i = NativeTest_nativeChar(_P_[0].p,((_P_[1].i)));
      return _P_ + 1;
}
 /* SYMBOL: "NativeTest/nativeShort(S)S",Java_NativeTest_nativeShort_stub */
 declspec(dllexport) stack_item *Java_NativeTest_nativeShort_stub
 ➡(stack_item *_P_,struct execenv *_EE_){
      extern long NativeTest_nativeShort(void *,long);
      _P_[0].i = NativeTest_nativeShort(_P_[0].p,((_P_[1].i)));
      return _P_ + 1;
}
/* SYMBOL: "NativeTest/nativeFloat(F)F",
➡Java_NativeTest_nativeFloat_stub */
 declspec(dllexport) stack_item
➡*Java_NativeTest_nativeFloat_stub(stack_item *_P_,struct execenv *_EE_){
      extern float NativeTest_nativeFloat(void *,float);
      _P_[0].f = NativeTest_nativeFloat(_P_[0].p,((_P_[1].f)));
      return _P_ + 1;
}
/* SYMBOL: "NativeTest/nativeDouble(D)D",
➡Java_NativeTest_nativeDouble_stub */
 declspec(dllexport) stack_item
➡*Java_NativeTest_nativeDouble_stub(stack_item *_P_,struct execenv *_EE_){
      Java8 _tval;
      Java8 _t1;
      extern double NativeTest_nativeDouble(void *,double);
      SET_DOUBLE(_tval, _P_,
➡NativeTest_nativeDouble(_P_[0].p,GET_DOUBLE(_t1, _P_+1)));
      return _P_ + 2;
}
/* SYMBOL: "NativeTest/nativeBoolean(Z)Z",
➡Java_NativeTest_nativeBoolean_stub */
 declspec(dllexport) stack_item
➡*Java_NativeTest_nativeBoolean_stub(stack_item *_P_,struct execenv
➡*_EE_) {
      extern long NativeTest_nativeBoolean(void *,long);
      _P_[0].i = (NativeTest_nativeBoolean(_P_[0].p,((_P_[1].i))) ?
➡TRUE : FALSE);
      return _P_ + 1;
}
/* SYMBOL: "NativeTest/nativeIntArray([I)[I",
➡Java_NativeTest_nativeIntArray_stub */
```

```
  declspec(dllexport) stack_item
 *Java_NativeTest_nativeIntArray_stub(stack_item *_P_,struct execenv
➡*_EE_) {
      extern void* NativeTest_nativeIntArray(void *,void *);
      _P_[0].p = NativeTest_nativeIntArray(_P_[0].p,((_P_[1].p)));
      return _P_ + 1;
}
/* SYMBOL: "NativeTest/nativeCharArray([C)[C",
➡Java_NativeTest_nativeCharArray_stub */
  declspec(dllexport) stack_item
➡*Java_NativeTest_nativeCharArray_stub(stack_item *_P_,struct execenv
➡*_EE_) {
      extern void* NativeTest_nativeCharArray(void *,void *);
      _P_[0].p = NativeTest_nativeCharArray(_P_[0].p,((_P_[1].p)));
      return _P_ + 1;
}
/* SYMBOL: "NativeTest/nativeShortArray([S)[S",
➡Java_NativeTest_nativeShortArray_stub */
  declspec(dllexport) stack_item
➡*Java_NativeTest_nativeShortArray_stub(stack_item *_P_,struct execenv
➡*_EE_) {
      extern void* NativeTest_nativeShortArray(void *,void *);
      _P_[0].p = NativeTest_nativeShortArray(_P_[0].p,((_P_[1].p)));
      return _P_ + 1;
}
/* SYMBOL: "NativeTest/nativeFloatArray([F)[F",
 ➡Java_NativeTest_nativeFloatArray_stub */
  declspec(dllexport) stack_item
➡*Java_NativeTest_nativeFloatArray_stub(stack_item *_P_,struct execenv
➡*_EE_) {
      extern void* NativeTest_nativeFloatArray(void *,void *);
      _P_[0].p = NativeTest_nativeFloatArray(_P_[0].p,((_P_[1].p)));
      return _P_ + 1;
}
/* SYMBOL: "NativeTest/nativeDoubleArray([D)[D",
 ➡Java_NativeTest_nativeDoubleArray_stub */
  declspec(dllexport) stack_item
➡*Java_NativeTest_nativeDoubleArray_stub(stack_item *_P_,struct execenv
➡*_EE_) {
      extern void* NativeTest_nativeDoubleArray(void *,void *);
      _P_[0].p = NativeTest_nativeDoubleArray(_P_[0].p,((_P_[1].p)));
      return _P_ + 1;
}
/* SYMBOL: "NativeTest/nativeBooleanArray([Z)[Z",
 ➡Java_NativeTest_nativeBooleanArray_stub */
  declspec(dllexport) stack_item
```

continues

Interfacing C/C++ and Java

Listing 14.14   Continued

```
➡*Java_NativeTest_nativeBooleanArray_stub(stack_item *_P_,struct execenv
➡*_EE_ ) {
     extern void* NativeTest_nativeBooleanArray(void *,void *);
     _P_[0].p = NativeTest_nativeBooleanArray(_P_[0].p,((_P_[1].p)));
     return _P_ + 1;
}
/* SYMBOL: "NativeTest/nativeObject(LTestObject;)LTestObject;",
➡Java_NativeTest_nativeObject_stub */
 declspec(dllexport) stack_item
➡*Java_NativeTest_nativeObject_stub(stack_item *_P_,struct execenv
➡*_EE_ ) {
     extern void* NativeTest_nativeObject(void *,void *);
     _P_[0].p = NativeTest_nativeObject(_P_[0].p,((_P_[1].p)));
     return _P_ + 1;
}
/* SYMBOL: "NativeTest/nativeObjectArray([LTestObject;)[LTestObject;",
➡Java_NativeTest_nativeObjectArray_stub */
 declspec(dllexport) stack_item
➡*Java_NativeTest_nativeObjectArray_stub(stack_item *_P_,struct execenv
➡*_EE_ ) {
     extern void* NativeTest_nativeObjectArray(void *,void *);
     _P_[0].p = NativeTest_nativeObjectArray(_P_[0].p,((_P_[1].p)));
     return _P_ + 1;
}
/* SYMBOL: "NativeTest/callJava()V", Java_NativeTest_callJava_stub */
 declspec(dllexport) stack_item
➡*Java_NativeTest_callJava_stub(stack_item *_P_,struct execenv *_EE_ ) {
     extern void NativeTest_callJava(void *);
     (void) NativeTest_callJava(_P_[0].p);
     return _P_;
}
/* SYMBOL: "NativeTest/doExceptions(I)V",
➡Java_NativeTest_doExceptions_stub */
 declspec(dllexport) stack_item
➡*Java_NativeTest_doExceptions_stub(stack_item *_P_,struct execenv
➡*_EE_ ) {
     extern void NativeTest_doExceptions(void *,long);
     (void) NativeTest_doExceptions(_P_[0].p,((_P_[1].i)));
     return _P_;
}
/* SYMBOL: "NativeTest/testException2()V",
➡Java_NativeTest_testException2_stub */
 declspec(dllexport) stack_item
```

```
➥*Java_NativeTest_testException2_stub(stack_item *_P_,struct execenv
➥*_EE_) {
        extern void NativeTest_testException2(void *);
        (void) NativeTest_testException2(_P_[0].p);
        return _P_;
}
```

The C Implementation of Java Native Methods

The next step to integrating C/C++ to Java is the creation of C functions that are called by the stub functions. The functions are identical to the functions defined in the C header file produced by javah. Each C function defines as its first parameter a pointer to the object that contains the Java method. This pointer is used to access the data contained in the object. The object pointer is used in the same way as "this." Because any object is derived from the Object class, the actual data is not available by directly dereferencing the pointer. A special C macro is used to access the contents of the structure representing the class. The macro "unhand" is discussed in the section "Accessing Object Data."

This C file in listings 14.15a through 14.15f implements each of the native methods as was described by the stubs file in listing 14.14.

Listing 14.15a contains each of the simple functions that accept a single standard type and increments and returns the value. As you can see, there is little differenece from the usage of a normal C function. Only the second parameter is used. The object variable nativeTest is not used in any of these functions.

Listing 14.15a   C Implementation of the nativeTest Class

```
# include "NativeTest.h"
// Native Atoms
long NativeTest_nativeInt(struct HNativeTest *nativeTest,long
➥nativeInt){
        return (++nativeInt);
}
unicode NativeTest_nativeChar(struct HNativeTest *nativeTest,unicode
➥nativeChar){
```

continues

Listing 14.15a   Continued

```
       return(++nativeChar);
}
short NativeTest_nativeShort(struct HNativeTest *nativeTest,short
➥nativeShort){
       return(++nativeShort);
}
float NativeTest_nativeFloat(struct HNativeTest *nativeTest,float
➥nativeFloat){
       return(++nativeFloat);
}
double NativeTest_nativeDouble(struct HNativeTest *nativeTest,double
➥nativeDouble){
       return(++nativeDouble);
}
long NativeTest_nativeBoolean(struct HNativeTest *nativeTest,long
➥nativeBoolean){
       return(!nativeBoolean);
}
```

Listing 14.15b is similar to 14.15c except arrays of standard types are passed into C from Java. No processing is done on these arrays. The arrays are simply returned back to the Java environment. Array usage is discused in more detail through listing 14.15.

Listing 14.15b   C Implementation of the nativeTest Class

```
// Native Arrays
HArrayOfInt* NativeTest_nativeIntArray(struct HNativeTest
➥*nativeTest,HArrayOfInt *nativeIntArray){
       return(nativeIntArray);
}
HArrayOfChar* NativeTest_nativeCharArray(struct HNativeTest
➥*nativeTest,HArrayOfChar *nativeCharArray){
       return(nativeCharArray);
}
HArrayOfShort* NativeTest_nativeShortArray(struct HNativeTest
➥*nativeTest,HArrayOfShort *nativeShortArray){
       return(nativeShortArray);
}
HArrayOfFloat* NativeTest_nativeFloatArray(struct HNativeTest
➥*nativeTest,HArrayOfFloat *nativeFloatArray){
       return(nativeFloatArray);
}
```

```
HArrayOfDouble* NativeTest_nativeDoubleArray(struct HNativeTest
➥*nativeTest,HArrayOfDouble *nativeDoubleArray){
     return(nativeDoubleArray);
}
HArrayOfInt* NativeTest_nativeBooleanArray(struct HNativeTest
➥*nativeTest,HArrayOfInt *nativeBooleanArray){
     return(nativeBooleanArray);
}
```

The code in listing 14.15c show two functions. The first function, nativeObject(), accepts as its second parameter an object of the TestObject class. The object is returned back to the Java environment. The second C function, nativeObjectArray(), takes an array of objects and returns them back to Java.

Listing 14.15c   C Implementation of the nativeTest Class

```
// Objects
struct HTestObject* NativeTest_nativeObject(struct HNativeTest
➥*nativeTest,struct HTestObject *anObject){
     return(anObject);
}
HArrayOfObject* NativeTest_nativeObjectArray(struct HNativeTest
➥*nativeTest,HArrayOfObject *anObjectArray){
     return(anObjectArray);
}
```

The C function callJava(), described in listing 14.15d, does much more processing than any of the functions described to this point. The function's purpose is to accomplish the following (line numbers are included for clarity):

- Define a pointer to a class (line 2).
- Define a pointer to an object of TestObject class (line 3).
- Declare array pointers of primitive types (lines 4 through 11).
- Declare a pointer to an array of String (line 12).
- Populate the class pointer testClass with a "look up" of the TestObject class (line 15). The function FindClass() accomplishes this by passing in the current context (obtained by calling EE()) and specifying the name of the class to be found. Lines 16 through 21 validate whether the FindClass() was successful
- The statement in lines 23 through 36 calls to the constructor of the TestObject class. Constructors are called with the execute_java_constructor() function.

The execute_java_constructor() function has four required parameters. The first, on line 24, is the current context derived by calling the EE() function.

The second required parameter is the name of the class from which this object is to be derived.

The third is the class pointer that was obtained on line 15.

The fourth parameter in the execute_java_constructor() function is a text signature of the constructor. This signature is required by Java to look up the correct constructor for the object. Following the required arguments are the parameters that are to be passed to the constructor as defined by the signature defined by the fourth parameter (line 27).

- Lines 37 through 39 are used to validate that an object of TestObject class was created.

- Arrays are created next to be used in a function call (lines 42 through 50). Arrays are allocated with the ArrayAlloc() function. The ArrayAlloc() takes a constant that defines the type of primitive to be allocated, followed by the number of entries to be allocated. In the example, five of each type are allocated.

- Next, arrays are filled with values. Arrays are accessed by dereferencing the pointer and accessing the array index of the "body" member.

- Lines 76 through 87 call a member of the TestObject class with the arrays you have created in this function. Like the execute_java_constructor() function, the execute_java_dynamic_method() function has four required parameters.

The first on line 76 is the current context derived by calling the EE() function.

The second required parameter pointer to the object that has the method to be called.

The third parameter is the name of the method to be executed.

The final required parameter in the execute_java_dynamic_method() function is a text signature of the method. This signature is required by Java to look up the correct method for the object. Following the required arguments are the parameters to be passed to the constructor, as defined by the signature defined by the fourth parameter (line 79).

Listing 14.15d   C Implementation of nativeTest Class

```
1:void NativeTest_callJava(struct HNativeTest *nativeTest){
2:     ClassClass * testClass;
3:     struct HTestObject *testObject;
4:     ArrayOfInt *tBooleans;// Note: booleans are int!
```

```
5:      ArrayOfByte *tBytes;
6:      ArrayOfShort *tShorts;
7:      ArrayOfInt  *tInts;
8:      ArrayOfLong *tLongs;
9:      ArrayOfFloat *tFloats;
10:      ArrayOfDouble *tDoubles;
11:      ArrayOfChar *tChars;
12:      ArrayOfObject *tStrings;
13:      int i;
14:      printf("Locate the TestObject class.\n");
15:     testClass = FindClass(EE(),"TestObject",TRUE);
16:     if (testClass != 0){
17:         printf("Call TestObject static method.\n");
18:     execute_java_static_method(EE(),testClass,"testStatic","()V");
19:     }else{
20:         printf("failed to find TestObject class.\n");
21:     }
22:      printf("Create a test object\n");
23:     testObject = (struct HTestObject *)
24:                     execute_java_constructor(EE(),
25:                                         "TestObject",
26:                                         testClass,
27:                                         "(ZBSIJFDCLjava/lang/
                                            �íString;)",
28:                                         TRUE,
29:                                         1,
30:                                         (char)'A',
31:                                         1L,
32:                                         (byte)1,
33:                                         (float)1.0,
34:                                         (short)1,
35:                                         (double)1.0,
36:     makeJavaString("One",strlen("One")));
37:     if (testObject == 0){
38:         printf("failed to create TestObject object.\n");
39:     }
40:
41:      printf("Create test arrays.\n");
42:     tBooleans = (ArrayOfInt*)ArrayAlloc(T_BOOLEAN,5);
43:     tBytes = (ArrayOfByte*)ArrayAlloc(T_BYTE,5);
44:     tShorts = (ArrayOfShort*)ArrayAlloc(T_SHORT,5);
45:     tInts = (ArrayOfInt*)ArrayAlloc(T_INT,5);
46:     tLongs = (ArrayOfLong*)ArrayAlloc(T_LONG,5);
47:     tFloats = (ArrayOfFloat*)ArrayAlloc(T_FLOAT,5);
48:     tDoubles = (ArrayOfDouble*)ArrayAlloc(T_DOUBLE,5);
49:     tChars = (ArrayOfChar*)ArrayAlloc(T_CHAR,5);
```

continues

Interfacing C/C++ and Java

The C Implementation of Java Native Methods

623

Listing 14.15d   Continued

```
50:     tStrings =(ArrayOfObject *)ArrayAlloc(T_CLASS,5);
51:      printf("Initialize arrays to 1.\n");
52:      for(i=0;i<5;i++){
53:            printf("step =%d.\n",i);
54:            tBooleans->body[i] = (long)TRUE;
55:            printf("made bool\n");
56:            tBytes->body[i] = 1;
57:                printf("made bytes\n");
58:            tShorts->body[i] = 1;
59:            printf("made body\n");
60:            tInts->body[i] = 1;
61:            printf("made int\n");
62:            tLongs->body[i] = 1;
63:            printf("made long\n");
64:            tFloats->body[i] = (float)1.0;
65:            printf("made float\n");
66:            tDoubles->body[i] = 1.0;
67:            printf("made double\n");
68:            tChars->body[i] = '1';
69:            printf("making string\n");
70:            tStrings->body[i] =
                ➡(HObject*)makeJavaString("One",strlen("One")+1);
71:            if (tStrings->body[i] == 0){
72:                printf("ERROR making string\n");
73:            }
74:      }// end for
75:      printf("Pass all arrays to Java method.\n");
76:      execute_java_dynamic_method(EE(),
77:                                  (struct Hjava_lang_Object
                                     ➡*)testObject,
78:                                  "testArrays",
79:                                  "([Z[B[S[I[J[F[D[C[Ljava/lang/
                                     ➡String;)V",
80:                                  tBooleans,
81:                                  tBytes,
82:                                  tShorts,
83:                                  tInts,
84:                                  tLongs,
85:                                  tFloats,
86:                                  tDoubles,
87:                                  tChars,
88:                                  tStrings);
89:}// end of function callJava()
```

The next method implemented as a C function is doExceptions(), shown in listing 14.15e. This function throws IOException or ArithmeticException, depending on the type of exception that is requested via the type parameter. The function SignalError accomplishes the mechanics of setting up the throw back to Java. Note that the throw does not happen immediately. The throw will not occur until a function is exited. If there is any code after the SignalError function, the code will be executed.

Listing 14.15e   C Implementation of the nativeTest Class

```
void NativeTest_doExceptions(struct HNativeTest *nativeTest,long type){
    switch (type){
    case 1:
        SignalError(EE(),"java/io/IOException","test
        ➡error=IOException");
        break;
    case 2:
        SignalError(EE(),"java/lang/ArithmeticException","test
        ➡error=ArithmeticException");
        break;
    }
    return;
}
```

The function in listing 14.15f also throws an exception, except this function first accesses the current object to set a field in the object. The purpose of such behavior is to show that information about an exception can be returned back to the object via the object field, which is required in cases where the standard exceptions are inadequate, and a user-defined exception would be preferred. Because user-defined exceptions cannot be created and thrown from native code using SignalError(), the additional information must be passed via another method.

Listing 14.15f   C Implementation of the nativeTest Class

```
void NativeTest_testException2(struct HNativeTest *nativeTest){
    // Set a value to be used when an exception occures.
    unhand(nativeTest)->myErrorValue = 100;
    // Set up to throw the exception.
    SignalError(EE(),"java/io/IOException","test
    ➡error=ArithmeticException");
    // Return so that Java can throw the exception.
    return;
}
```

The C Implementation of Java Native Methods

Compiling and Linking Native Libraries

The next thing you need to do to create a combined Java and native C code application is to compile the C code into a loadable library. A loadable library, such as data link libraries in Microsoft Windows and NT, is required because linking between Java and C can take place only at runtime. Linking at runtime is the normal way Java links classes. All classes are treated as loadable libraries that are loaded only as they are used. Behind the scenes in the JVM, links to the classes, their fields, and methods are accomplished via the same names and signatures that have been seen so far in the native C code calls into Java to create objects and call methods. As was mentioned in the section "Stub Files Generated by javah," stubs are used so that javah can call a method marked as native. Native method marking enables the Java VM to call the function loaded in the library after the library has been loaded.

Take special care to ensure that the Java code, stub files, header files, and C code are kept synchronized with all interrelated changes. Incompatibility problems between native libraries and Java code may often be attributed to compiling and linking different versions of classes and functions. When a Java program hard crashes with a native library, most likely, the problem was caused at compile- or link-time. The following paragraphs cover many of the problems involved with these processes.

When compiling the code generated by Java, the search path for include files must have JAVAHOME/ include in the path. In the Windows 95 and NT versions, the include path also requires JAVAHOME/ include/win32.

Compiling

The compiling of native functions is identical to the process in C. The only requirement is to include the header files generated by javah into the implementation file.

Be very careful to keep the stub and header files accurate. The code may compile, but when a library is accessed by the Java code, differences can cause hard crashes that may be difficult to trace. If possible, use a make file that causes the generation of stub and header files, every time Java classes are updated.

Linking Debug and Release Versions of Your Libraries

In order to use the native C code, the code objects must be linked into dynamically loadable libraries. On Windows 95, Warp, and the Macintosh, these have the file extension .dll, and on some Unix platforms, these are called "so" libraries. Please refer to your particular platform's documentation for specific instructions.

You will need to create a debug and a release version of your library if you will be running under the Java debugger. The debug version is to be linked to Javai_g.lib, whereas the release version is linked to javai.lib. If you use MSVC++ the javai_g.lib_coff and javai.lib_coff libraries are used instead. The debug and release libraries have very different contents to support debug or release functionality.

The debug version has a different extension tacked onto the name of the loadable library so that the Java debugger can distinguish which version is to be loaded. In the case of a library called MyNative.dll, the debug version would be MyNative_g.dll. The "g" version is loaded by java_g and appletviewer_g, while the normal version is loaded by java and javaw.

If there is no "_g" version in the path, the javag interpreter generates a "library not found" exception. Also, the proper javah native library must be linked with the native implementation. So the MyNative.dll must be linked with Java_g.lib, while the MyNative_g.dll must be linked with MyNative_g.dll.

Improper creation of these debug and release versions can be very dangerous! For instance, if you run an application on Windows NT, java.exe loads and uses javai.dll. A native .dll created for debug loads and uses javai_g.dll. Objects used specifically for debug will not be initialized in the javai_g.dll, and this eventually causes Java to crash. Unfortunately, the crash may not occur until after the program has been running for some time.

It is important to remember that the difference between debug and release versions has nothing to do with the debug setting being turned on when compiling Java or C code! "Debug" simply means that the native library is linked with a debug library used by the debug version of the Java VM (Java_g, javaw_g, and appletviewer_g). Released versions are also simply linked with the release version of the native tool library, so that they can be run on the release Java VM (Java, javaw, and appletviewer).

Accessing Java from C

When developing Java programs with native methods, C code may be required to call Java. There are three main reasons to do this:

- Data access
- Creating objects
- Callbacks

For data access, C can call methods to retrieve class data without breaking the integrity of objects by accessing the fields directly, which sometimes is the only way to access a class's data. For instance, the Hashtable class can only be accessed through its method interface.

Sometimes native functions need to create and manipulate Java objects. Often it is easier to pass data through these new objects instead of directly manipulating existing objects. To do this, objects that represent a collection of data are passed back to the caller for processing. For instance, a native method for reading a digital camera's picture creates an image object to pass the data to the caller instead of manipulating each bit in the caller's object space.

Another possibly useful programming technique when C calls Java is to use a callback. Callbacks enable one part of the program to asynchronously initiate another process. A thread can be started so that the native code can wait or monitor events that are inaccessible to normal Java. After the event occurs, a method can be called to register the event with the Java program. This frees the main program from the task of monitoring events when the thread of control is not conducive to making these periodical checks. For instance, a native function that monitors a game port can call a Java method when the firing button is pressed, freeing the main program to concentrate on complex drawing functions.

Accessing Object Data

Every call to a native method contains a handle to the current instance of the class. With this handle, the current object's data can be accessed. The unhand macro is used to dereference the object pointer so that the object's fields can be accessed. Only normal object fields can be dereferenced. Static fields are not available directly from the objects handle (see execute_java_static_method()).

With the unhand() macro, an object's primitive types are accessed like fields in a structure. For instance, listing 14.16 shows a Java class with its native function that accesses the parent object's data field. The two integer fields, a and b, will be read by the native print() method and incremented by the native increment() method.

Listing 14.16   Example Java Class to Be Accessed from C

```
/ Java class
class Foo{
      int a;
      int b;
```

```
    Foo(){
        a = 1;
        b = 1;
    }
    native print();
    native increment();
}
```

The listing of 14.17 contains the implementation of the print() method specified in listing 14.16. The function uses the pointer to the HFoo structure, which is the "this" pointer for the object. The unhand macro is called on the pointer to dereference the pointer to point to the structure that points to the objects data. The a and b fields are accessed by pointer dereference of the unhand() results, followed by the field identifier.

Listing 14.17   The C Implementation of the Native print() Method

```
// C native functions accessing back to foo
void Foo_print(struct HFoo * this){
    printf("this objects contents: %d,%d\n",unhand(this)-
    ➡>a,unhand(this)->b);
}
```

Listing 14.18 uses the same dereference technique to access the object fields for modification. The increment() method is used to increment the a and b fields. Note in this example that the object is being accessed directly. Accessing the objects field directly is much more efficient than calling an accessor method written in Java because it requires a costly call back into the Java VM to perform the function. An accessor is not required here because the native function is actually part of the same class; it is accessing its own data and not breaking any class encapsulation guidelines.

Listing 14.18   The C Implementation of the Native increment() Method

```
void Foo_increment(struct HFoo * this){
    unhand(this)->a = unhand(this)->a + 1;
    unhand(this)->b = unhand(this)->b + 1;
}
```

The procedure for accessing Java object fields from native code is often required when data in the object is manipulated. Because there is no way to pass data by reference into native C code, the only alternative to passing data is to return it in the method call. Such a technique is okay with only a single value, but it is not possible if the native code causes multiple changes. Also, a return value is not always possible. The variable, for example, might be a private field and should not be visible to any other object.

Method Signatures and Passing Data to Java Methods

Before learning the ways to call Java functions, you need to become familiar with the signature parameter that all Java functions have in common. The signature parameter is used by the Java VM to locate a specific method. Java cannot look up a method just by its name. It must also know the types of parameters and the return value. Armed with this information, Java can properly locate and call the method.

The method signature for constructors and methods that take no data is simply "()." Alternatively, the same dynamic or static method signature could be expressed as "()V" where the V translates as the void type.

Designating Primitive Types

Signatures of constructors that take arguments are built by inserting a special translation of the primitive and object types. Table 14.2 lists the primitive types and their equivalent signature types. Primitive signatures are single letters that are used to distinguish the type to be used in arguments or as return types.

TABLE 14.2	*Java Type*	*Signature Type*
Primitive Type Signatures	Boolean	Z
	byte	B
	char	C
	short	S
	int	I
	long	J
	float	F
	double	D

These single characters are placed inside the parentheses to signify parameters, and are placed after the parentheses to specify the type the method returns. Do not use spaces or commas because they are not allowed; spaces cause interpretation of the signature to fail. For the Java method shown in listing 14.19, the equivalent signature that is required to access it is "(ZBSIJFDC)I."

Listing 14.19   Method Specification Matching the "(ZBSIJFDC)I" Method Signature

```
int foo(boolean tBoolean,byte tByte,short tShort, int tInt,long
➥tLong,float tFloat,
➥double tDouble,char tChar,String tString);
```

Designating Arrays of Primitive Types

When an array is passed into or returned from a method, the class signature is different. For arrays, a bracket ([) character is fixed to the type character. The signature, "([Z[B[S[I-[J[F[D[C)V," is used to designate the method in listing 14.20. Arrays need to be passed into native methods whenever the Java program uses them and needs to pass the data to native C code. Alternativly, a C program may create arrays that are returned.

Listing 14.20   Method Specification Matching the "([Z[B[S[I[J[F[D[C)V" Method Signature

```
void testArrays(boolean tBooleans[],byte tBytes[],short tShorts[], int
➥tInts[],long tLongs[],
➥float tFloats[],double tDoubles[],char tChars[]);
```

For multidimensional arrays, simply add a [for each extra dimension. For instance, an array defined as having two dimensions, such as "int point[][];", would require [[I to designate a two-dimensional integer array.

Designating Objects

Objects signatures are similar to class signatures except that the L is prefixed and the ";" character is appended to the end of the class signature. For instance, the String class would be formatted as "Ljava/lang/String;". A user-defined class, TestObject, would be defined as "LTestObject;". These signature definitions are placed into the signature string just like primitives, but without spaces or commas.

Class signatures are used any time a Java method is to be called from native C code. This use also is true for constructors that need method signatures to locate the correct version of a constructor that matches the parameters listed in the signature.

The following code shows an example of a Java method that returns an object and mixes primitive types, a primitive array, and object types. The equivalent signature for this method is "(I[JLTestObject;Ljava/lang/String;)Ljava/util/Vector."

The C Implementation of Java Native Methods

Listing 14.21 Matching the "(I[JLTestObject;Ljava/lang/String;)Ljava/util/ Vector" Method Signature

```
Vector foo(int anInt,long longArray[],TestObject obj[], String str);
```

If you are ever unsure about how to format a signature, create a native function that is equivalent to the Java function, and then run javah with the -stubs option. The C file that is created will have the proper formatting of the signature for the method in a comment block just above the stub call.

Accessing Java Classes and Objects

Four types of functions are used to access the Java environment. These enable class look-up, object instantiation, and execution of static or dynamic functions. Accessing Java from C is important because native methods are parts of classes and require access to methods just like all other methods have access. Also, native methods need to be able to create objects because a native method may be called to build objects that will be used later. A native method in an image processing system may, for example, need to call other methods to get setting information and may create objects that represent images that it processes.

Table 14.3 lists the functions that can be used to access Java classes and methods. They are described in detail in the following sections.

TABLE 14.3

Java to C Access Functions

Access Function	Purpose
FindClass()	Used to load a class for access or to create objects.
Execute_java_static_method()	Used to access a class static method.
execute_java_constructor()	Used to create new Java objects.
Execute_java_dynamic_method()	Used to execute methods of an object.

FindClass() Method

FindClass is the C equivalent of the loadClass() method in the ClassLoader class. The definition and implementation of this method are quite simple.

Listing 14.22 FindClass Function Definition

```
ClassClass *FindClass(ExeEnv *ee, char *class_name, bool_t resolve);
```

The ee parameter is the execution environment; class_name is the C string signature of the requested class. Class signatures are created by using the same package and class name that is normally used with all "." characters substituted with the "/" character. For instance, java.lang.Vector would become java/lang/Vector.

The code of listing 14.23 loads a class named TestObject.

Listing 14.23   Example of FindClass: Creating a Class Reference to the TestObject Class

```
ClassClass * testClass;
testClass = FindClass(EE(),"TestObject",TRUE);
```

Find class is used to access information about a Java class. The return value is used in the Execute_java_static_method() to resolve the class that the static method executed. FindClass also is used in the execute_java_constructor() method to access the constructor method for the class.

execute_java_static_method()

After a class has been found, any static function may be called by using the execute_java_static_method() function. Here is the definition of this function:

Listing 14.24   The execute_java_static_method() Function Definition

```
long execute_java_static_method(  ExeEnv *ee
                                , ClassClass *classHandle
                                , char *methodName
                                , char *signature
                                ,…);
```

Here, the classHandle field contains the handle to a Java class, and methodName is the name of a static function within the referenced class. If execute_java_static_method() does not locate the method name, then the function returns 0, otherwise it returns 1. Listing 14.25 looks up a class and calls its static method.

Listing 14.25 Example of the execute_java_static_method() Function

```
testClass = FindClass(EE(),"TestObject",TRUE);
    if (testClass != 0){
            printf("Call TestObject static method.\n");
        execute_java_static_method(EE(),testClass,"testStatic","()V");
        }else{
            printf("failed to find TestObject class.\n");
        }
```

execute_java_constructor()

Whenever a Java object needs to be created by native code, execute_java_constructor() is used. The execute_java_constructor() function creates Java objects of a specific class, using a specific class constructor. If this function succeeds, it returns a handle to an object. If it fails, it returns zero.

The execute_java_constructor() function has four required parameters:

- The first is the current context. The context can be derived by calling the EE() function.

- The second required parameter is the name of the class that this object is to be derived from.

- The third parameter is the class pointer that was obtained by calling the FindClass() function.

- The fourth and final required parameter in the execute_java_constructor() function is a text signature of the constructor. This signature is required by Java to lookup the correct constructor for the object.

Following the required arguments are the parameters that are to be passed to the constructor (see listing 14.26).

Listing 14.26 Definition of the execute_java_constructor_method() Function

```
HObject *execute_java_constructor_method(  ExeEnv *ee
                                , ClassClass *classHandle
                                , char *methodName
                                , char *signature
                                ,…);
```

Listing 14.27 creates an object from a user-defined object.

Listing 14.27   An Example of the execute_java_constructor_method() Function

```
testClass = FindClass(EE(),"TestObject",TRUE);
if (testClass != 0){
    printf("failed to find TestObject class.\n");
}
testObject =  (struct HTestObject *)execute_java_constructor(EE()
            ,"TestObject"
            ,testClass
            ,"(ZBSIJFDCLjava/lang/String;)"
            ,TRUE,1,(char)'A',1L,(byte)1,(float)1.0,(short)1,
            ➥(double)1.0,makeJavaString("One",strlen("One")));
if (testObject == 0){
    printf("failed to create TestObject object.\n");
}
```

execute_java_dynamic_method()

After a Java object is available, its non-static methods may be called. In other words, the normal methods of the object can now be called. This is accomplished with the execute_java_dynamic_method() function.

The execute_java_dynamic_method() function has four required parameters.

- The first is the current execution context.
- The second required parameter is pointer to the object that has the method to be called.
- The third is the name of the method to be executed.
- The fourth required parameter in the execute_java_dynamic_method() function is a text signature of the method. This signature is required by Java to lookup the correct method for the object.

Following the required arguments are the parameters that are to be passed to the constructor as defined by the signature defined by the fourth parameter, as in listing 14.28.

Listing 14.28   The Definition of the execute_java_dynamic_method() Function

```
long execute_java_dynamic_method(  ExeEnv *ee
                                 , HObject *objHandle
                                 , char *methodName
                                 , char *signature
                                 ,…);
```

The example in listing 14.29 calls a Java method defined as void testBoolean(Boolean);. Note that the handle to the object must be cast to HObject in order to prevent the compiler from generating warnings.

Listing 14.29   Example of the execute_java_dynamic_method() Function

```
execute_java_dynamic_method(EE(),
                            (struct Hjava_lang_Object *)testObject,
                            "testBoolean",
                            "(Z)V",
                            true);
```

Passing Exceptions from Native Code to Java

Just like Java methods, it is sometimes necessary to generate exceptions from native code. For instance a native function that reads a file might throw an IOException when an IO error occurs. Only common Java exceptions are supported because the current native exception system does not enable user-defined exceptions. The following sections describe how the exception passing mechanism works.

Throwing Exceptions from C to Java: SignalError()

Throwing exceptions is more limited in C than it is in the Java model. In order for a native method to throw an exception, its definition needs to declare that the exception can be thrown. For example, the following native function can throw an IOException or an ArithmeticException.

Listing 14.30   Throwing an IOException of ArithmeticException

```
native void doExceptions(int type) throws java.io.IOException,
➥ArithmeticException ;
```

From C, currently only simple exceptions can be thrown. In other words, when constructing exceptions, remember that they take only one argument, the reason string. Listing 14.31 shows the definition of the SignalError() function.

Listing 14.31   Definition of the SignalError() Function

```
void SignalError(ExecEnv *env, char *type, char *reason);
```

The type is the full class name with the "." replaced with the "/". The reason string contains the text to be displayed that describes the error.

SignalError() is simple to use. In the Java class, declare the native method as capable of throwing one or more exceptions by using the code in listing 14.32.

Listing 14.32   Example of a Java Native Method that Throws Two Types of Exception

```
native someFunction(int type) throws IOException, ArithmeticException ;
```

Next, in the C implementation where the error is trapped, call SignalError() and return. Listing 14.33 shows the implementation of someFunction(), which always generates an exception based on the type requested:

Listing 14.33   A Sample C Implementation of a Function that Throws Two Types of Exception

```
void NativeTest_someFunction(struct HNativeTest *nativeTest){
    .
    .
    if(IOError){
        SignalError(EE(),"java/io/IOException","test
        ➥error=IOException");
        return;
    }
    .
    .
    if(mathError){
        SignalError(EE(),"java/lang/ArithmeticException","test
        ➥error=ArithmeticException");
        return;
    }
```

continues

Interfacing C/C++ and Java

Listing 14.33   Continued

```
        .
        .
        return;
}
```

Catching Java Exceptions: exceptionOccurred()

When calling Java methods, there is the possibility that an exception might occur. In the case of some methods, exceptions may be the only way of knowing that an error has occurred. To test for exceptions, call the exceptionOccurred() function. If it returns true then you should handle the error or generate an exception back to the Java environment.

The definition of the function is as follows:

Listing 14.33a   Definition of the exceptionOccurred() Function

```
int exceptionOccurred(ExecEnv * env);
```

To use it, just check the result after a method call.

Strings

Java strings are considered objects when in native C code; however, because they are likely to be used often, Sun has supplied several utility routines for their creation and translation in C. Be careful to use only the correct sizes of strings. Be especially aware that none of these functions depend on the null terminator, used by C. Java writes it when copying, but it does not recognize it when reading C strings.

Table 14.4 lists the string utility function that can be used by native C code. Each of these functions is discussed in more detail in the following sections.

TABLE 14.4	*Function*	*Purpose*
String Functions	javaStringLength()	Returns the length of a Java String.
	AllocCString()	Creates a C string copy of a Java String.
	javaString2Cstring()	Copies a Java String to a C character buffer.

Function	Purpose
makeCString()	Creates a C string buffer that is garbage collected by Java.
makeJavaString()	Create a Java String object.
javaString2unicode()	Copies Java Sting to a unicode buffer.

Length of a Java String: javaStringLength()

The javaStringLength() function, defined in listing 14.33b, simply returns the length of a Java String. This length is the actual size, not including any terminating character. This function is used in conjunction with many other of the String functions.

Listing 14.33b   Definition of javaStringLength() Function

```
int javaStringLength(Hjava_lang_String *string);
```

The javaStringLength() function is used whenever the length of a Java string is required. When, for example, a copy of a Java string is needed, the javaStringLength() function is called to determine the buffer size.

Java to C with alloc(): allocCString()

This function, defined in listing 14.34, automates the copy of a Java string into a preallocated C string. The pointer returned from allocCString() must be freed with C's free() function. The disadvantage of this function is that the C string is exactly the same size as the Java string. The only copied parameter is the Java string object. The function returns a pointer to a newly allocated buffer with the contents of the Java string. The size of the buffer is equal to the size of the Java string plus one.

Listing 14.34   Definition of the allocCString() Function

```
char *allocCString(Hjava_lang_String *string);
```

The return value of allocCString() is a pointer to the buffer that has been allocated. Remember to free this pointer when it is no longer needed.

The reason to use allocCString() is to create C strings that are allocated on the C heap. The *C heap* is memory that will not disappear after a function terminates. The persistence of a string is important when the string is meant to survive longer than the lifetime of the function. Another reason to use allocCString() is when passing strings to other C or C++ functions. Some functions may not be aware of Java types, so converting from Java String to C string bridges the gap and makes them compatible.

Java String to C Character Buffer: javaString2Cstring()

The function javaString2Cstring(), defined in listing 14.35, is the equivalent of allocCString() except that there must be a preallocated C string buffer. Controlling the size of the buffer may be preferable to allocCString() controlling allocation because the size of the buffer might be larger than the Java string, making it possible to later append more characters. The parameters sent to this function are the Java string object to copy, a pointer to the C character buffer, and the number of bytes to copy. The size of C string must be one larger than the amount being copied. This function returns the original address of the C buffer.

Listing 14.35   Definition of the javaString2CString() Function

```
char *javaString2CString(Hjava_lang_String *string, char *cString, int
➥amountToCopy);
```

As was mentioned previously, the specific purpose of javaString2Cstring() is to separate the memory allocation from the conversion of the Java String to the C string. This would be useful, for example, when the C string is to be modified by appending extra text to the original. First, a buffer is created by preallocating a buffer that is large enough to hold the original Java sting, plus the length of the appended text. The javaString2Cstring() function is then used to copy the Java String to the C string buffer. From this point, normal C string functions can be used to manipulate the string.

Java String to a Garbage Collected C String: makeCString()

In contrast to allocCString(), makeCString(), defined in listing 14.36, creates the C character buffer in Java memory space. This means that the buffer is garbage collected when there is no longer any reference to it. The makeCString() method returns an allocated array of characters containing a copy of the Java string, plus a null terminating character.

Listing 14.36   Definition of the makeCString() Function

```
char *makeCString(Hjava_lang_String *s);
```

The makeCString() function is useful when a C string is required that will be allocated on the local stack, and thus garbage collected when the variable on the stack goes out of scope. By using the makeCString() function, there is no reason to deallocate the C string buffer.

C String to Garbage Collected Java String: makeJavaString()

The function makeJavaString(), defined in listing 14.37, is the only way to create a new Java String object. Memory is allocated in the Java memory space and is garbage collected when no more references to it are found. This function takes an array of characters and the number of characters to copy. The number of characters to copy does not include the null terminator. This function returns a Java string object that is the length that was to be copied. This object is garbage collected when there are no more references to it.

Listing 14.37   Definition of the makeJavaString() Function

```
Hjava_lang_String *makeJavaString(char *cString, int amountToCopy);
```

The makeJavaString() function is only used to create a Java String to be used in a Java method or to set a String field in a Java object. A good example of when a String object must be created is when a text message needs to be sent from a native C function and back to Java.

Java String to Unicode: javaString2unicode()

The function javaString2unicode(), defined in listing 14.38, copies a Java string to an array of Unicodes. No allocation occurs. The C definition of a Unicode is an unsigned short. The function assumes the amount to copy is less than or equal to the length of the string, and that the buffer size is at least equal to the length to copy plus one Unicode. In other words, the amount to copy must never be larger than the Java string and the buffer must be large enough to hold the length to copy plus a null character. The original Unicode buffer's address is returned.

Interfacing C/C++ and Java

Listing 14.38   Definition of the javaString2unicode() Function

```
municode *javaString2unicode(Hjava_lang_String *string, unicode
*buffer,int amountToCopy);
```

The javaString2unicode() function is used to extend Java's unicode capability to native C because there are times when the unicode character set is used in C functions. This is true of applications whose functions already use unicode for language internalization reasons. By using javaString2unicode(), the language-specific characters can be passed from Java into C and C++ functions.

Thread Synchronization

It is sometimes necessary either to execute native code in its own thread or to ensure that native code blocks other threads from running. The native environment includes several callable functions that interface with the Java thread environment, as shown in table 14.5.

TABLE 14.5	Function	Purpose
Thread Synchroniza-tion Functions	monitorWait()	Native code will block until another thread calls notify on the current thread or a notifyAll().
	monitorNotify()	Notifies threads that have called wait().
	monitorNotifyAll()	All Java threads that have called wait() and native code that has called monitorWait() are notified.

Each function is covered in more detail below.

monitorWait()

The monitorWait() function is used the same way that wait() is used in Java. The execution of the native code will block until another thread calls notify on the current thread or a notifyAll() occurs.

monitorNotify()

The monitorNotify() function notifies threads that have called wait() that the caller has completed its task. This function is the same as the Java's notify() method.

monitorNotifyAll()

The monitorNotifyAll() function is similar to monitorNotify() except that all Java threads that have called wait() and native code that has called monitorWait() are notified. Like notifyAll() in Java threads, monitorNotifyAll() only can be called from within a synchronized method.

Native Code and Garbage Collection

One of the deadlier problems affecting native code is the Java Garbage Collector (gc). The gc can delete (or worse, move) objects that may be referenced by native methods. The only way to stop the gc from deleting or moving a referenced object is to store the reference of the object on the C stack.

The easiest way to avoid gc problems is to never store object references between calls. The following sections discuss a few techniques that enable native methods to access Java objects.

Passing Objects

Keep objects that would normally be global at the C level in the Java environment. Pass the objects into the native environment each time they are needed.

If an object is often required from the Java environment, such as a vector of values for example, an incorrect assumption is that by copying a reference to the native C code, you would save time because the vector remains accessible on the native side. The reference to the vector becomes invalid the moment the original subroutine terminates. The vector must be passed each time it is used; otherwise, the vector may be moved in memory by the garbage collector. If moved, the cashed vector reference will no longer point to the correct memory location, causing unpredictable results.

Reference Data and Methods and Other Objects from the Native Object Pointer

By using the object that is passed with every native function call, accessing methods and fields is safe until the function returns because the object is passed on the C stack. The gc will not destroy the object while it remains there. If the function does not return (because it is a thread), the objects can be copied to a global reference for use by all functions.

Build Your Own Objects

Note that objects built in C must be allocated on the stack! Do not use the heap (beware of calloc(), alloc(), malloc(), and the C++ new operator). After an object is built, it remains in effect until the handle to the object is cleared.

Using Native Methods: A Serial Port Library

To demonstrate how peer classes are used, the following sections describe how to implement a package that can be used to access serial ports on the PC (Windows 95 or Windows NT). The example shows how to isolate machine-dependent native code from machine-independent Java code by using the Peer pattern.

The SerialDevice package is not a part of any of the Java libraries or a commercial-quality API. It is useful enough to use for simple serial I/O and can be extended by the user for more complex tasks.

Isolating Native Functions: The Peer Pattern

Software *patterns* are guides that act as software cookbooks that map a particular problem or task to established implementation techniques and guidelines. Software patterns are similar to reusable components, but they are only concerned with reusing the steps to get from problems to solutions. An example of a pattern that may seem familiar is "Model View," which is used to isolate a program's function and state (the model) and the GUI that represents the model (the View). In Java, the Model View pattern is accomplished with the Observer and Observable, as discussed in Chapter 3.

Another pattern, Peer, is discussed in this section. The Peer pattern solves the problem of mixing nongeneric parts with generic ones. An example of how the Peer pattern works is demonstrated by the Java AWT.

The AWT uses the Peer pattern to hide implementation details of specific platforms (nongeneric) from cross-platform behavior (generic). This method of nongeneric hiding provides a reasonably stable way to increase the number of platforms without changing the multiplatform characteristics of a library. This hiding is accomplished by having a class that represents the multiplatform access, a class that implements platform-specific details, and an interface that is used by the multiplatform class to access the platform-specific code. In this way, by simply changing the instance of the platform-specific class, the multiplatform class can access multiple platforms.

The SerialDevice package implements the Peer pattern. The problem the Peer pattern tries to solve is to isolate machine-dependent features in Microsoft Windows 95 and NT serial device drivers. The isolation is required so that any Java program can use the SerialDevice API on any machine that implements the machine-dependent functions hidden below the public interface.

The state diagram in figure 14.3 shows how the Peer pattern is put together. The interface SerialPeer is used to represent functions that generic to serial devices. The class SerialDevice is the class that users will instantiate and use as an object that controls the serial port. The class Win32sSerial is a class with the native method calls to Windows 95 and to Windows NT. The SerialDevice class is assigned an Object of type Win32sSerial that has been cast to the SerialPeer interface type. The SerialDevice can now control serial ports by calling SerialPeer methods, which are now redirected to the Win32sSerial implementation. The Win32sSerial class can be replaced with another implementation for another machine without affecting the operation of the SerialDevice class.

Overview of the Serial Port Library

The implementation of this program is broken into eight classes and one interface inside a package named SerialDevice. NativeSerial is an example application that uses the SerialDevice package to read and write to a serial port.

The SerialDevices package holds all the classes that are required to access the native code and includes utility functions that aid in writing serial access programs. The following list shows the breakdown of the SerialDevices package used by NativeSerial.

- **SerialPeer.** This interface class isolates specific implementations of the serial device access. It is used by the SerialDevice class to access the peer for the specific platform.
- **Win32sSerialPeer.** This class is the specific implementation for NT and Windows 95. Use this class as a model for implementing SerialPeer on other operating systems.
- **SerialDevice.** This is the class that enables client classes to access the main serial functions.

FIGURE 14.3

*The classes used to
implement the Peer
pattern.*

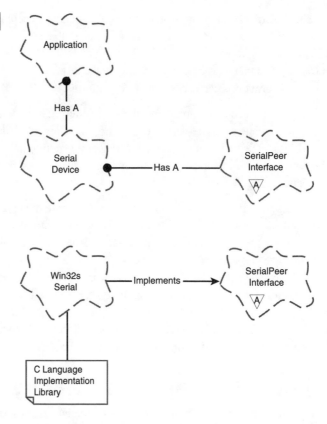

- **WaitForTokens.** This utility class is called by the serial port monitor when the serial port receives data. It can be used to wait for token events such as CON-NECT, which is returned when a modem connects.

- **Action.** This class is used by the WaitForTokens class to execute a specified function depending on the specified token.

- **SerialPortMonitor.** This class monitors the serial port and calls observers when data is received.

- **SerialData.** The SerialData class is used by SerialPortMonitor to pass serial port data and any serial event information.

The following sections describe the classes in the native serial port example.

Accessing the Serial Port: NativeSerial.Java

The steps required to use a serial device are quite simple. You start serial access by opening a serial device and configuring the device to support the hardware that is connected. The client can now read or write to the serial port. The serial device can wait on certain signals, such as Data Ready, that can be used to suspend operations on the serial port until they occur.

The following listing is an example of how the SerialDevices package is used. It enables a user to open a serial port number via a pull-down menu. After the port is open, the user may type data into an input window and monitor the serial port through the output window. The WaitForTokens class monitors the serial port for connect strings and the OK acknowledgment from a modem.

The basic GUI functionality is created in listing 14.39a. An input window is created to capture keystrokes, and an output window is created to capture input characters from the mode. A field is used to specify the serial port, as well as open and close port buttons.

Listing 14.39a   Class NativeSerial: GUI Initialization

```
import SerialDevices.*;
import java.awt.*;
import java.util.Observer;
import java.util.Observable;
public class NativeSerial extends Frame implements Observer, Action{

    public static void main(String args[]) {
        new NativeSerial();
    }// End of main()

    public NativeSerial() {
        super("NativeSerial window");
        // INIT_CONTROLS
        setLayout(null);
        addNotify();
        resize(insets().left + insets().right + 405, insets().top +
        ➥insets().bottom + 349);
        label1=new Label("Read Window", Label.CENTER);
        add(label1);
        label1.reshape(insets().left + 47,insets().top + 150,306,13);
        label2=new Label("Write Window", Label.CENTER);
        add(label2);
        label2.reshape(insets().left + 47,insets().top + 23,306,13);
```

continues

Listing 14.39a   Continued

```
        outputWindow=new TextArea(5,36);
        add(outputWindow);
        outputWindow.reshape(insets().left + 47,insets().top +
        ➥47,304,91);
        inputWindow=new TextArea(5,36);
        inputWindow.disable();
        add(inputWindow);
        inputWindow.reshape(insets().left + 47,insets().top +
        ➥172,304,91);
        openPort=new Button("Open Port");
        add(openPort);
        openPort.reshape(insets().left + 228,insets().top +
        ➥293,78,26);
        closePort=new Button("Close Port");
        add(closePort);
        closePort.reshape(insets().left + 312,insets().top +
        ➥293,78,26);
        portNumber=new TextField(7);
        add(portNumber);
        portNumber.reshape(insets().left + 150,insets().top +
        ➥293,60,26);
        label3=new Label("Port Number", Label.RIGHT);
        add(label3);
        label3.reshape(insets().left + 18,insets().top + 297,126,22);
        // Set up the serial port functions
     portNumber.setText("2");
        show();
}//End of NativeSerial() Constructor

public synchronized void show() {
   move(50, 50);
   super.show();
}//End of show()
```

Listing 14.39b shows the event handling for the class. This code is where the button events and keystroke events are monitored.

Listing 14.39b   Class NativeSerial: GUI Event Handling

```
public boolean handleEvent(Event event) {
    if (event.id == Event.ACTION_EVENT && event.target ==
    ➥openPort) {
```

```
                    clickedOpenPort();
                    return true;
        }
        else
        if (event.id == Event.ACTION_EVENT && event.target ==
        ➡closePort) {
                    clickedClosePort();
                    return true;
        }
        else
        if (event.id == Event.KEY_PRESS && event.target ==
        ➡outputWindow) {
                keyPressOutputWindow(event);
                return false;
        }
        else

        if (event.id == Event.WINDOW_DESTROY) {
            if (monitor != null){
                monitor.stop();
            }
        hide();              // hide the Frame
        dispose();           // tell windowing system to free resources
            System.exit(0); // exit
            return true;
        }
        return super.handleEvent(event);
} //End of handleEvent()
```

The next section of code is where the serial port is opened. As a precaution, the first thing done is to call clickedClosePort() to ensure that the port monitor thread is stopped and the serial port is closed. The actual SerialDevice is created next. After that, the peer is created for the specific machine and used to set up the serial device to run.

Listing 14.39c   Class NativeSerial: clickedOpenPort()

```
public void clickedOpenPort() {
    // Kill the monitor thread if it is running
    clickedClosePort();
    // Create a new SerialDevice
    serial = new SerialDevice();
    // Create the Win32 Peer
    Win32sSerialPeer nativeSerial = new Win32sSerialPeer();
    // Attach the Win32 Peer
```

continues

Interfacing C/C++ and Java

Listing 14.39c Continued

```java
serial.setSerialPeer((SerialPeer)nativeSerial);

if(serial.openSerialPort((new
➥Integer(portNumber.getText())).intValue() )){
    monitor = new
➥SerialPortMonitor(this,serial,SerialPortMonitor.INPUT);
}else{
    System.out.println("Error opening the port");
}
```

The second half of clickedOpenPort() sets up the communication between the SerialPort object and this class. The communication is accomplished with the Observer Observable pattern. Additionally, a second observer is added to parse modem tokens and send events if they occur.

Listing 14.39d Class NativeSerial: clickedOpenPort()

```java
// Create a monitor to capture input.
// Use this class as the default observer interested in input.
monitor = new
➥SerialPortMonitor(this,serial,SerialPortMonitor.INPUT);
//Create an input tokenizer and add modem commands to it.
toker = new WaitForTokens();
toker.addKeyAction("OK",this,0);
toker.addKeyAction("CONNECT",this,1);
toker.addKeyAction("CARRIER",this,2);
toker.addKeyAction("NO",this,3);
// Add tokenizer to the monitor.
monitor.addObserver(toker);

} //End of clickedOpenPort()
```

The next method, clickedOpenPort(), in listing 14.39e, is used to stop the serial port monitor and close the serial port. This method is called either when the close port button is pressed or when clickedOpenPort() is called.

Listing 14.39e Class NativeSerial: clickedOpenPort()

```java
public void clickedClosePort() {
    if (monitor != null){
```

```
            monitor.stop();
        serial.closeSerialPort();
    }
} //End of clickedClosePort()
```

The keyPressOutputWindow() method is used to capture key presses coming from the input window, as shown in listing 14.39f. Note the special handling to convert the \n character to \r so that most modems will understand that a carriage return has been hit. After the conversion is complete, the key pressed is written to the serial port via the portOut() method.

Listing 14.39f   Class NativeSerial: keyPressOutputWindow()

```
public void keyPressOutputWindow(Event ev) {
    byte [] buffer = new byte [1];
    // Translate \n to \r for modem
    // AT commands will not work without it
    if (ev.key == '\n'){
        buffer[0] = '\r';
    }else{
        buffer[0] = (byte)ev.key;
    }
    System.out.print(ev.key);
    if(serial.portOut(buffer,1)==1){
        System.out.println("Write to port OK");
    }else{
        System.out.println("failed to write to port");
    }
} //End of keyPressOutputWindow(Event ev)
```

The update() method is the implementation of the observer interface (see listing 14.39g). This function is called by the serial port monitor every time an event or character is read from the serial port. The update() method appends any character to the output window. If the character is \r, it is converted to \n before the character is appended to the output window.

Listing 14.39g   Class NativeSerial: The update() Method

```
//Observer implementation
public void update(Observable o, Object arg){
    if (o == monitor){
        String input =new String(((SerialData)arg).buffer,0);
```

continues

Interfacing C/C++ and Java

Listing 14.39g   Continued

```
        // Look for \r echoed back from modem.
        // Replace it with a \n so display looks ok.
        int test = input.indexOf('\r');
        if (test != -1){
            input = input.replace('\r','\n');
        }
        inputWindow.appendText(input);
    }
} //End of update()
```

Listing 14.39h shows the final method, action(). The action() method is the implementation of the Action interface, which is a specialized observer that accepts an index that specifies that a token has been received from the serial port. This particular implementation prints out status to the standard whenever common modem commands are received.

Listing 14.39h   Class NativeSerial: The action() Method

```
// Implementation for Action Interface
public void action(int ID){
    switch(ID){
        case 0: //OK
            System.out.println("Saw OK");
            break;
        case 1: //CONNECT
            System.out.println("Saw Connect");
            break;
        case 2: //NO CARRIER
            System.out.println("Saw CARRIER");
            break;
        case 3: //NO CARRIER
            System.out.println("Saw NO");
            break;
    }
} //End of action()
Label label1;
Label label2;
TextArea outputWindow;
TextArea inputWindow;
Button openPort;
Button closePort;
TextField portNumber;
Label label3;
```

```
        private SerialDevice serial;
        private SerialPortMonitor monitor;
        private WaitForTokens toker;
}// End of class NativeSerial
```

SerialDevice Class

The SerialDevice class is the public interface to the SerialDevices package. It connects the SerialPeer interface to the actual platform-specific native implementation.

The full listing that starts with 14.40a is the main class of the SerialDevices package. The class controls access to the serial port interface and the functions that are supported.

Listing 14.40a   Class SerialDevice: Class Constructor

```
package SerialDevices;
import SerialDevices.SerialPeer;
public class SerialDevice{
    private SerialPeer serialPeer;
    private long port;
    public SerialDevice(){
        //Determine the System type and get the correct peer
    }
```

The most important method in this class is setSerialPeer(), which is used to set the peer object to be used to access machine-specific functions.

Listing 14.40b   Class SerialDevice: setSerialPeer()

```
public void setSerialPeer(SerialPeer peer){
    serialPeer = peer;
}
```

After the peer has been set, all of the functions in the SerialPeer interface can be accessed. Nothing is done in listing 14.40c except call the peer method.

Listing 14.40c   Class SerialDevice: Serial Port Access Functions

```
public boolean openSerialPort(int portID){
    port = serialPeer.openSerialPort(portID);
    return(port != 0);
```

continues

Interfacing C/C++ and Java

Listing 14.40c   Continued

```
        }
    public boolean closeSerialPort(){
          return(serialPeer.closeSerialPort(port));
    }
    public boolean setBaudRate(int baudRate){
          return(serialPeer.setBaudRate(port,baudRate));
    }
    public boolean setStopBits(int stopBits){
          return(serialPeer.setStopBits(port,stopBits));
    }
    public boolean setParity(int parity){
          return(serialPeer.setParity(port,parity));
    }
    public boolean setDataBits(int dataBits){
          return(serialPeer.setDataBits(port,dataBits));
    }
    boolean setWaitMask(long mask){
          return(serialPeer.setWaitMask(port,mask));
    }
    long commWait(){
          return(serialPeer.commWait(port));
    }
    /**
     * @param buffer Character buffer for results size must be >=
     ➥numberOfBytesToRead
     * @param numberOfBytesToRead Number of bytes to attempt reading.
     * @returns bytes read from port.
     */
    public int portIn(byte [] buffer, int numberOfBytesToRead){
         return(serialPeer.portIn(port,buffer,numberOfBytesToRead));
    }
    /**
     * @param buffer Character buffer to Send.
     * Size must be >= numberOfBytesToRead
     * @param numberOfBytesToWrite Number of bytes to attempt sending.
     * @returns bytes written to port.
     */
    public int portOut(byte [] buffer, int numberOfBytesToWrite){
         return(serialPeer.portOut(port,buffer,numberOfBytesToWrite));
    }
```

The last method in the SerialDevice class is write(). The write() method is slightly
different from the others because it converts a Java String to an array of bytes suitable for

output to the serial device. After the byte array has been created, the portOut() is called to access the serial peer device.

Listing 14.40d   Class SerialDevice: The write() Method

```
/**
 * @param buffer String to Send.
 * @returns bytes writen to port.
 */
public int write(String buffer){
    int numberOfBytesToWrite = buffer.length();
    byte [] byteBuffer =  new byte[numberOfBytesToWrite];
    buffer.getBytes(0, numberOfBytesToWrite, byteBuffer, 0);
    System.out.println(new String(byteBuffer,0));
    return(serialPeer.portOut(port,byteBuffer,numberOfBytesToWrite));
}
}
```

SerialPeer Interface

The SerialPeer interface is used by SerialDevice to abstract calls to predetermined platform-specific implementations of the serial device. Note in the listing that it contains constants that are used later in the C code to abstract the mask bits from the platform-specific mask (see listing 14.41a).

Listing 14.41a   Interface SerialPeer: final Constants

```
package SerialDevices;
public interface SerialPeer{
    // Wait mask flags. Logical or these flags to build wait mask.
    final long BREAK   = 1;   // A break was detected on input.
    final long CTS     = 2;   // The CTS (clear-to-send) signal changed
                              //state.
    final long DSR     = 4;   // The DSR (data-set-ready) signal changed
                              //state.
    final long ERR     = 8;   // A line-status error occurred. Line-
                              //status
                              // errors are CE_FRAME, CE_OVERRUN, and
                              // CE_RXPARITY.
    final long RING    = 16;  // A ring indicator was detected.
    final long RLSD    = 32;  // The RLSD (receive-line-signal-detect)
                              //signal
```

continues

Interfacing C/C++ and Java

Listing 14.41a   Continued

```
                            // changed state.
    final long RXCHAR  = 64;  // A character was received and placed in
                            // the input buffer.
    final long RXFLAG  = 128; // The event character was received and
                            // placed in the input buffer.
                            // The event character is specified in the
                            // device's DCB structure, which is
                            //  applied to a serial port by using
                            // the SetCommState function.
    final long TXEMPTY = 256; // The last character in the output buffer
                            // was sent.
```

The second half of the SerialPeer class has the definitions for serial device access. When each of these methods is implemented by a client class such as the Win32sSerialPeer class, another class can access the functions to control a serial port.

Listing 14.41b   Interface SerialPeer: Serial Port Methods

```
    public long openSerialPort(int portID);
    public boolean closeSerialPort(long port);
    public boolean setBaudRate(long port,int baudRate);
    public boolean setStopBits(long port,int stopBits);
    public boolean setParity(long port,int parity);
    public boolean setDataBits(long port,int dataBits);
    public boolean setWaitMask(long port,long mask);
    public long commWait(long port);
        public int portIn(long port,byte [] buffer, int
        ➥numberOfBytesToRead);
        public int portOut(long port,byte [] buffer,int
        ➥numberOfBytesToWrite);
}
```

The Win32sSerialPeer Class

The Win32sSerialPeer class is the Win32s platform-specific implementation for the SerialPeer class.

An important aspect of this class is that SerialPeer is solely implemented by native functions. Having all of the SerialPeer implementations as native may not be the case for all platforms. For instance, portIn() and portOut() may need to perform special operations before the actual data is read or written. It is possible that the class could have no native methods if the functions that access the serial port are part of another Java package.

In the first listing of the Win32sSerialPeer class, a static initializer block is used to load the DLL library containing the implementations for the native methods. By using the static block, the methods are ensured that the library will exist in memory before any of the native methods can be called. If the library is not loaded successfuly when the class is loaded, an exception is thrown.

Listing 14.42a   The Class Win32sSerialPeer: Definition of a Static Initializer Block

```
package SerialDevices;
import SerialDevices.SerialPeer;
public class Win32sSerialPeer implements SerialPeer{
// Static block is used to init
    // the dynamic library.
    static{
        // Load the dynamic library
        System.loadLibrary("serialDLL/debug/serial");
    }
```

Listing 14.42b of the Win32sSerialPeer class defines each of the native methods that is to be implemented in C code. These definitions are used by javah to create header and stub files.

Listing 14.42b   The Class Win32sSerialPeer

```
native public long openSerialPort(int portID);
    native public boolean closeSerialPort(long port);
    native public boolean setBaudRate(long port,int baudRate);
    native public boolean setStopBits(long port,int stopBits);
    native public boolean setParity(long port,int parity);
    native public boolean setDataBits(long port,int dataBits);
    native public boolean setWaitMask(long port,long mask);
    native public long commWait(long port);
    native public int portIn( long port
                            , byte [] buffer, int numberOfBytesToRead);
    native public int portOut( long port
                            , byte [] buffer,int
                                ➥nNumberOfBytesToWrite);
}
```

Utility Classes in the SerialDevices Package

Three particular utility classes and one interface make using serial ports easier.

- The SerialPortMonitor class is used to echo output from the serial input stream to interested classes that implement the Observable interface. SerialPortMonitor uses the SerialData class to pass data.

- The second is the WaitForTokens class, which is used to signal events to classes that implement the Action interface. The events that the WaitForTokens waits for are tokens or, more explicitly, string patterns. When a pattern is found, WaitForToken calls the action() method of registered classes with the ID of the token encountered. WaitForToken is useful for tasks such as waiting for modem messages, such as CONNECT, OK, ERROR, and so on.

- Figure 14.4 shows how all of the classes communicate with the third class, NativeSerial. The data coming in from the serial port is read by the Serial-PortMonitor, which resends a copy of the stream to both the observer in Native-Serial, which echoes it to a TextArea box and to the WaitForToken object, which parses the stream. The WaitForToken object, when it sees a token, class the action() method of the NativeSerial object, which prints status information to the console.

The following utility classes used by the package make the serial device a little easier to use. They do not define any native methods and are not used to explicitly control the serial port. The classes do enable an application to use the serial port without as much coding because similar functions would need to be created to take their place. The main purpose of these utilities is to disseminate information coming from the serial port to objects and methods that need to be notified of serial input.

Class SerialPortMonitor

This class is a thread that extends Observable in order to pass incoming serial data to classes that implement the Observer interface.

The SerialPortMonitor waits for the serial port to send data. As each data item arrives, the SerialPortMonitor disseminates a copy of the data to each interested function. In listing 14.39g, the update() method (the implementation for the Observer interface) is called each time data is read from the serial port. The SerialPortMonitor also is used by the WaitForTokens class, which is discussed in the next section.

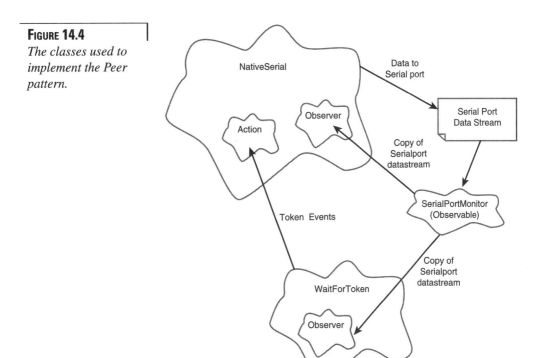

FIGURE 14.4
The classes used to implement the Peer pattern.

In listing 14.43a, the class constructor is used to create the SerialPortMonitor object that is to inform a designated Observer that information is passing through the serial interface. The direction of interest, input or output, is specified by static final variables that are passed into the constructor and compared later in the run() method. This example is limited to monitoring serial input only, but extending it should not be difficult.

Listing 14.43a   Class SerialPortMonitor: Definition and Class Constructor

```
package SerialDevices;
import java.util.Observable;
import java.util.Observer;
import SerialDevices.SerialData;
import SerialDevices.SerialDevice;
import SerialDevices.SerialPeer;
public class SerialPortMonitor extends Observable implements Runnable{
    private Thread thread;
    public static final int INPUT  = 1;
```

Listing 14.43a   Continued

```
public static final int OUTPUT = 2;
private SerialDevice targetPort;
private int direction;
public SerialPortMonitor( Observer observer
                        , SerialDevice targetPort, int direction){
    this.targetPort = targetPort;
    this.direction = direction;
    addObserver(observer);
    thread = new Thread(this);
    thread.start();
}
```

The stop() method in the SerialPortMonitor class is part of the implementation of the Runnable interface. Once called, the current object stops concurrent execution.

Listing 14.43b   Class SerialPortMonitor: The stop() Method

```
public void stop(){
    System.out.println("KilledThread!!!!!!!!");
    thread.stop();
}
```

The run() method is the other half of the Runnable interface implementation. The run() method is a never-ending loop that constantly checks the state of the serial port for incoming data. When data is found, the method notifies observers by first calling setChanged() and then notifyObservers(). (Both setChanged() and notifyObservers() are methods that were inhereted from the Observable class.) This method continues to run until the classes stop() method is called (see listing 14.43c).

Listing 14.43c   Class SerialPortMonitor: The run() Method

```
public void run(){
    System.out.println("Entered run method");
    if (direction == INPUT){
        for(;;){
            long mask = targetPort.commWait();
            //long mask = 0;
```

```
            if ((mask & SerialPeer.ERR) == SerialPeer.ERR){
                System.out.println("Got error!!!!!!!!");
                return;
            }else{
                int amountRead = 1;
                while(amountRead != 0){
                    byte [] buffer = new byte [1];
                    amountRead = targetPort.portIn(buffer,1);
                    System.out.println("Got data");
                    setChanged();
                    notifyObservers( new SerialData(
                                    buffer,amountRead,mask));
                }
            }
        }
    }
}
```

Class WaitForTokens

The class WaitForTokens is a standard observer to be used with the SerialPortMonitor class. WaitForTokens is used to catch and report instances when specific tokens are read from the serial port.

This class may be difficult to understand. The class essentially is a token parser that must also deal with Data Terminal Equipment (DTE) characters, which are used to insert data into serial streams without affecting the normal interpretation of data. DTE data often is used in voice modems to distinguish voice input from other signals, such as the tones from a telephone touch pad.

This class is similar to an Observable class, except that this method lets the user specify a trigger and a trigger value to be sent to a specific observer when the token appears, which can be very important because some devices controlled via serial communication may be quite complex. A voice modem, for example, has dozens of tokens that it may return to specify status, data, errors, or progress. Without a class such as this, the alternative amount of code could be much greater. You would, for example, require a tokenizer, a string-to-token converter, and a mechanism to call methods to replace this class. With this class, you need to write only methods that implement the Action interface, as in listing 14.44a.

Listing 14.44a   The Class WaitForTokens: Initialization and Class Constructor

```java
package SerialDevices;
import SerialDevices.Action;
import SerialDevices.SerialData;
import java.util.Observer;
import java.util.Observable;
import java.util.Vector;
public class WaitForTokens implements Observer{
    private Vector keys;
    private Vector actions;
    private Vector IDs;
    private int minWhite=' ';
    private int maxWhite=' ';
    private int minKeyLength = 100;
    private int maxKeyLength =  0;
    private StringBuffer stateBuffer= new StringBuffer(1);
    private boolean eolIsSignificant=true;
public WaitForTokens(){
        keys = new Vector();
        actions = new Vector();
        IDs = new Vector();
    }
```

The method eolIsSignificant() enables the user to configure end-of-lines as white space or to ignored them, which is important if tokens have embedded EOL characters.

Listing 14.44b   The Class WaitForTokens: Method eolIsSignificant()

```java
public void eolIsSignificant(boolean eolIsSignificant){
        this.eolIsSignificant = eolIsSignificant;
    }
```

The method whitespaceChars() is used to set the ASCII range of characters that is to be considered white space between tokens.

Listing 14.44c   Class WaitForTokens: Method whitespaceChars()

```java
public void whitespaceChars(int minWhite, int maxWhite)  {
        this.minWhite = minWhite;
        this.maxWhite = maxWhite;
    }
```

The addKeyAction() method is used to add a key, action handler and the action ID to be trapped. This function is similar to an addObserver() method, except that this method lets the user specify a trigger and a trigger value to be sent to a specific observer when the token appears.

Listing 14.44d   Class WaitForTokens: Method addKeyAction()

```
public void addKeyAction(String newKey, Action action, int ID){
        if (newKey.length() > stateBuffer.length()){
            stateBuffer= new StringBuffer(newKey.length());
        }
        minKeyLength = newKey.length() < minKeyLength
                        ? newKey.length() : minKeyLength;
        maxKeyLength = newKey.length() > maxKeyLength
                        ? newKey.length() : maxKeyLength;
        keys.addElement(newKey);
        actions.addElement(action);
        IDs.addElement(new Integer(ID));
    }
```

The update()method is the Observer implementation. Update() gathers data from the modem and monitors the data stream for keys to be matched. This function is meant to be called by the SerialPortMonitor class.

Listing 14.44e   class WaitForTokens:The update() Method

```
public void update(Observable o, Object arg){
        String input =new String(((SerialData)arg).buffer,0);
        // Look for \r echoed back from modem.
        if (input.length() == 1){
            if ((input.charAt(0) >= minWhite &&
                 input.charAt(0) <= maxWhite)
                || input.charAt(0) == '\r'
                || input.charAt(0) == '\n'){
            stateBuffer.setLength(0);
        }else{
            // Update the buffer
            stateBuffer.append(input);
            if (stateBuffer.length() >= minKeyLength){
// Look for the key in the vector
                    int location = keys.indexOf(new
                    ➡String(stateBuffer));
```

continues

Interfacing C/C++ and Java

Listing 14.44e   Continued

```
                    if (location != -1){
                        ((Action)actions.elementAt(location)).action(
                            ((Integer)IDs.elementAt(location)).intValue()
);
                        stateBuffer.setLength(0);
                        return;
                    }
                }
                if (stateBuffer.length() == maxKeyLength){
                    stateBuffer.setLength(0);
                }
            }
        }
    }
```

The method checkForShieldedDTE() is used to look for modem messages that may come inside the normal data stream (see listing 14.44f). These modem messages are preceded by the DTE (Hexadecimal 10) character. The buffer parameter is the current state of the data read from the modem. The shieldStat parameter is either null (DTE pending) or the shielded DTE code

Listing 14.44f   The Class WaitForTokens: The checkForShieldedDTE() Method

```
void checkForShieldedDTE(char buffer[],char shieldStat[])
    {
        int i;
        // If the test string has been completed then return true else
        // false Also returns the number of characters that have
        // matched so far, just in case the testString is
        // split between two buffers.
            for (i=0;i<buffer.length;i++){
            if (shieldStat[0] == 0x10){
                shieldStat[0] = buffer[i];
            }else{
                if (buffer[i] == 0x10){
                    shieldStat[0] = 0x10;
                }else{
                    shieldStat[0] = 0x00;
                }
            }
        }
        // By getting to here we have proven that the whole test
        // string is not in the buffer.

    }
```

The checkThis()method is used to test the current state of a token, as shown in listing 14.44g. If a token is being read, more of its constituent parts are added each time it is passed through this function. If the token is complete, the buffer is cleared, and the caller is signaled that the token has been read. If a token is partially recognized, but a delimiter is encountered, the token workspace is cleared. The parameter buffer is the current state of the data read from the modem. The parameter token is the work that is being waited on.

Listing 14.44g   class WaitForTokens - Method checkThis()

```
int checkThis(char buffer[],char token[])
    {
        int i;
        // If the test string has been completed then return true else
        // false Also returns the number of characters that have
        // matched so far, just in case the testString
        // is split between two buffers.
        for (i=0;i<buffer.length;i++){
        if (buffer[i] == token.tokenStr[token->currentPosition]){
                if (++token->currentPosition >= token->stringLength){
                token->currentPosition=0;// reset to keep us out of
                ➡trouble.
                             return(1);
                }
            }else{
                token->currentPosition=0;
            }
        }
        // By getting to here we have proven that the whole test
        // string is not in the buffer.
        return(0);
    }
*/
}
```

Class SerialData

The SerialData class is used as a container to pass serial data that also includes the state of the wait mask (see listing 14.45). When passing a single object, functions using the information provided by the container can retrieve the reason for data or handle signals that do not have data. The SerialData class was written to avoid having to write separate read tasks at the native interface level.

Listing 14.45   The SerialData Class

```
package SerialDevices;
public class SerialData{
    public byte [] buffer;
    public int dataLength;
    public long mask;
    public SerialData(byte [] buffer,int dataLength, long mask){
        this.buffer = buffer;
        this.dataLength = dataLength;
        this.mask = mask;
    }
}
```

Class Action

The Action interface is used by the WaitForTokens class to inform classes that implement the interface that a token has been found. The action()method accepts one parameter that is the token ID. An example of how this interface is used is shown in listing 14.46.

Listing 14.46   The Action Class

```
package SerialDevices;
public interface Action{
    void action(int ID);
}
```

SerialDevice C Code

The following sections describe C implementations for the Java native methods shown in listing 14.42.

Closing the Serial Port

The closeSerialPort() function closes a specified serial port.

Listing 14.47   The closeSerialPort() Method

```
long SerialDevices_Win32sSerialPeer_closeSerialPort(struct
➡HWin32sSerialPeer *nativeSerial,int64_t port){
    return(CloseHandle(port));
}
```

Opening the Serial Port

The openSerialPort() function opens a specified serial port by number. The function returns a handle to the port that is to be used by the Java application when accessing the same serial port.

Listing 14.48   The openSerialPort Method

```
int64_t SerialDevices_Win32sSerialPeer_openSerialPort(struct
➥HWin32sSerialPeer *nativeSerial,long port){
    char* portName;
    char test[255];
    int bytesWritten;
    HANDLE aPort;
    COMMTIMEOUTS  CommTimeOuts ;

    // convert port number to port name
    switch (port){
    case 1: portName = "COM1";break;
    case 2: portName = "COM2";break;
    case 3: portName = "COM3";break;
    case 4: portName = "COM4";break;
    case 5: portName = "COM5";break;
    case 6: portName = "COM6";break;
    case 7: portName = "COM7";break;
    case 8: portName = "COM8";break;
    default:portName = "COM1";break;
    }
    aPort = CreateFile(portName,GENERIC_READ|GENERIC_WRITE,0,NULL
                      ,OPEN_EXISTING
                      ,FILE_ATTRIBUTE_NORMAL/* |
➥FILE_FLAG_OVERLAPPED*/,0);
    if (aPort == INVALID_HANDLE_VALUE){
        return(0);
    }else{
        EscapeCommFunction(aPort, CLRDTR ) ;
        EscapeCommFunction(aPort, SETDTR ) ;

    // get any early notifications
    SetCommMask(aPort, EV_RXCHAR ) ;
    // setup device buffers
    SetupComm(aPort, 4096, 4096 ) ;
    // purge any information in the buffer
    PurgeComm(aPort, PURGE_TXABORT | PURGE_RXABORT |
```

continues

Interfacing C/C++ and Java

Listing 14.48   Continued

```
                                      PURGE_TXCLEAR ¦ PURGE_RXCLEAR ) ;
    CommTimeOuts.ReadIntervalTimeout = 0xFFFFFFFF ;
    CommTimeOuts.ReadTotalTimeoutMultiplier = 0 ;
    CommTimeOuts.ReadTotalTimeoutConstant = 1000 ;
    CommTimeOuts.WriteTotalTimeoutMultiplier = 0 ;
    CommTimeOuts.WriteTotalTimeoutConstant = 1000 ;
    SetCommTimeouts(aPort, &CommTimeOuts ) ;
    setDefaults(aPort);

    EscapeCommFunction(aPort, SETBREAK ) ;
    ClearCommBreak(aPort);
    return((int64_t)aPort);
}
```

Isolating the C Wait Mask from the Java Wait Mask

Wait masks are used by hardware devices to specify interest in specific events generated by a device. For serial ports on the PC, for instance, the mask is usually set to RXCHAR, which translates to telling the serial port to notify the program whenever a character was received and placed in the serial port's input buffer.

Another common mask is RING, which is used to notify a program that the modem is being called. Masks are used to keep overhead low by enlisting hardware to wait for events rather than having a program always checking to see whether an event has occurred. A program normally will start another thread of execution that will wait for the event while the main program continues in another thread.

The wait mask of different types of hardware are different, unfortunately. To combat this problem, the SerialDevice package uses a transposition table that maps SerialDevice masks to the specific hardware mask.

The constants in listing 14.49 are used to isolate the actual bit positions that are used by the native system. By using these constants, a developer only needs to modify the setWaitMask() and commWait() functions in this module for the signal constants supported by a particular operating system and hardware configuration.

Listing 14.46.49 Java Signal Mask Constants

```
final long JAVA_BREAK   = 1;   // A break was detected on input.
final long JAVA_CTS     = 2;   // The CTS (clear-to-send) signal
                               // changed state.
final long JAVA_DSR     = 4;   // The DSR (data-set-ready) signal
                               //changed state. A line-status
final long JAVA_ERR     = 8;   // error occurred.
                               // Line-status errors are CE_FRAME,
                               // CE_OVERRUN, and CE_RXPARITY.
final long JAVA_RING    = 16;  // A ring indicator was detected.
final long JAVA_RLSD    = 32;  // The RLSD (receive-line-signal-
                               // detect) signal changed state.
final long JAVA_RXCHAR  = 64;  // A character was received and placed
                               // in the input buffer.
final long JAVA_RXFLAG  = 128; // The event character was received
                               // and placed in the input buffer.
                               // The event character is specified
                               // in the device's DCB structure,
                               // which is applied to a serial
                               // port by using the SetCommState
                               // function. The last character
final long JAVA_TXEMPTY = 256; // in the output buffer was sent.
```

The C implementation of the function setWaitMask() sets the wait mask (see listing 14.50). The mask bits are converted from the Java mask to the Windows mask. This function looks for a Java mask in the desired mask. If a match is found, the PC mask is added to the serial port mask. When the mask is complete, the Windows SetCommMask() function is called.

Listing 14.50 The C Implementation of setWaitMask()

```
long SerialDevices_Win32sSerialPeer_setWaitMask(struct HWin32sSerialPeer
 *nativeSerial,
➥int64_t aPort,int64_t mask){
   //Convert Java flags to Microsoft flags
   long windowsMask = 0;
   if (mask & JAVA_BREAK   == JAVA_BREAK)   windowsMask |= EV_BREAK;
   if (mask & JAVA_CTS     == JAVA_CTS)     windowsMask |= EV_CTS;
   if (mask & JAVA_DSR     == JAVA_DSR)     windowsMask |= EV_DSR;
   if (mask & JAVA_ERR     == JAVA_ERR)     windowsMask |= EV_ERR;
   if (mask & JAVA_RING    == JAVA_RING)    windowsMask |= EV_RING;
   if (mask & JAVA_RLSD    == JAVA_RLSD)    windowsMask |= EV_RLSD;
```

continues

Interfacing C/C++ and Java

Using Native Methods: A Serial Port Library

669

Listing 14.50   Continued

```
   if (mask & JAVA_RXCHAR  == JAVA_RXCHAR)  windowsMask |= EV_RXCHAR;
   if (mask & JAVA_RXFLAG  == JAVA_RXFLAG)  windowsMask |= EV_RXFLAG;
   if (mask & JAVA_TXEMPTY == JAVA_TXEMPTY) windowsMask |= EV_TXEMPTY;

   return(SetCommMask(aPort,windowsMask));
}
```

Waiting for Serial Port Events

The function commWait() waits for an event specified by SetCommMask(). When the wait returns, the resulting mask contains the events that caused the event. This function then converts the PC event to the Java events and adds them to the total mask.

It is important to note that the Windows WaitCommEvent() function blocks execution until an event occurs or the wait times out. Any thread that calls the function also ceases to execute. Java applications calling commWait() should call this function from a secondary thread so that the program will continue to run while it waits on the serial port. Refer to listing 14.51.

Listing 14.51   The C Implementation of commWait()

```
int64_t SerialDevices_Win32sSerialPeer_commWait(struct HWin32sSerialPeer
  *nativeSerial,int64_t port){
    unsigned long mask;
    BOOL result = WaitCommEvent(port,&mask,NULL);
    // Convert windows event to Java event
    long javaMask = 0;
    if (mask & EV_BREAK)   javaMask |= JAVA_BREAK;
    if (mask & EV_CTS)     javaMask |= JAVA_CTS;
    if (mask & EV_DSR)     javaMask |= JAVA_DSR;
    if (mask & EV_ERR)     javaMask |= JAVA_ERR;
    if (mask & EV_RING)    javaMask |= JAVA_RING;
    if (mask & EV_RLSD)    javaMask |= JAVA_RLSD;
    if (mask & EV_RXCHAR)  javaMask |= JAVA_RXCHAR;
    if (mask & EV_RXFLAG)  javaMask |= JAVA_RXFLAG;
    if (mask & EV_TXEMPTY) javaMask |= JAVA_TXEMPTY;
    return (javaMask);
}
```

Reading Data from an Open Serial Port

The portIn() function reads data from an open serial port, as demonstrated in listing 14.52. It accepts two arguments: one is an array of bytes to use as an input buffer, and the other is a count of the maximum number of bytes to read. The function returns the actual number of bytes read from the port.

Listing 14.52   The C Implementation of portIn()

```
long SerialDevices_Win32sSerialPeer_portIn(struct HWin32sSerialPeer
*nativeSerial, int64_t aPort,HArrayOfByte *buffer,long bytesToRead){
int bytesRead;
   BOOL result;
   COMSTAT     ComStat ;
   DWORD       dwErrorFlags;
   char *data;
   int length;
   data = unhand(buffer)->body;
   // only try to read number of bytes in queue.
   ClearCommError( aPort, &dwErrorFlags, &ComStat ) ;
   length = min( (DWORD)bytesToRead, ComStat.cbInQue ) ;
   if (length == 0)return(0);
   result     = ReadFile( aPort,       // handle of file to read.
                          data,         // address of buffer that
                                        // receives data. number
                          bytesToRead,// of bytes to read. address
                          &bytesRead,   // of number of bytes read.
                                        // address of structure for
                          NULL);        // data.
      return(bytesRead);
}
```

Writing Data to the Serial Port

The portOut() function writes data to an open serial port. It accepts an array of bytes to write and a count of the number of bytes to write. The function returns the actual number of bytes written to the port.

Listing 14.53　The C Implemetation for portOut()

```
long SerialDevices_Win32sSerialPeer_portOut(struct HWin32sSerialPeer
 *nativeSerial, int64_t aPort,HArrayOfByte *buffer,long bytesToWrite){
   DWORD bytesWritten;
   BOOL result;
   char charBuffer[2];
   //int i;
   char *data;
   data = unhand(buffer)->body;
   result = WriteFile( aPort,          // handle to file to write to
                       data,           // pointer to data to write to
                                       // file number of bytes to
                       bytesToWrite,   // write pointer to number
                       &bytesWritten,  // of bytes written pointer to
                                       // structure needed for
                       NULL);          // overlapped I/O

   return(bytesWritten);
}
```

Serial Port Defaults

The setDefaults() function is used to set initial parameters of a serial port device. It has no equivalent native Java method—the closest is a utility function that initially defines the serial port and is only callable from the C library.

The defaults shown in listing 14.54 are used to put the serial device into a known state. It is possible that a program that used the serial port could have left these settings in a state that is impossible to use. By using default values as a starting point, further settings will work as expected.

Listing 14.54　The C Implementation for setDefaults()

```
void setDefaults(HANDLE aPort){
   DCB portState;
   portState.DCBlength = sizeof( DCB ) ;
   GetCommState(aPort,&portState);
   portState.DCBlength=    28;
   portState.BaudRate=     14400;
   portState.fBinary=   1;
   portState.fParity=   1;
   portState.fOutxCtsFlow=  0;
```

```
        portState.fOutxDsrFlow=   1;
        portState.fDtrControl=    2;
        portState.fDsrSensitivity=    0;
        portState.fTXContinueOnXoff=  0;
        portState.fOutX=          0;
        portState.fInX=           0;
        portState.fErrorChar=     0;
        portState.fNull=          0;
        portState.fRtsControl=    1;
        portState.fAbortOnError= 0;
        //portState.fDummy2=      0;
        //portState.wReserved=    0;
        portState.XonLim=         100;
        portState.XoffLim=        100;
        portState.ByteSize=    8;  // '.'
        portState.Parity=      0;  // '\x00'
        portState.StopBits=    0;  // '\x00'
        portState.XonChar=    17;  // '.'
        portState.XoffChar=   19;  // '.'
        portState.ErrorChar=   0;  // '\x00'
        portState.EofChar=     0;  // '\x00'
        portState.EvtChar=      0;// '\x00'
        //portState.wReserved1=  0;
        SetCommState(aPort,&portState);

}
```

Changing Serial Port Settings

The functions in table 14.6 are used to set specific port options.

TABLE 14.6	*Function*	*Purpose*
Serial Port Configura-tion Functions	setBaudRate()	Set a specific baud speed.
	setStopBits()	Sets the number of stop bits.
	setParity()	Sets the parity checking style.
	setDataBits()	Sets the width of the data word.

These four functions are the most popular settings that a programmer sets. They are also the most common settings configurable for a wide range of computer hardware. Listings 14.55 show the C implementations for these functions. The first function is setBaudRate(), which sets the specific baud at which the serial device will communicate.

Listing 14.5   The C Implementation of setBaudRate()

```
long SerialDevices_Win32sSerialPeer_setBaudRate(struct HWin32sSerialPeer
➥*nativeSerial, int64_t aPort,long baudRate){
    DCB portState;
    if(GetCommState(aPort,&portState)){
        if(portState.BaudRate != (DWORD)baudRate){
            portState.BaudRate = (DWORD)baudRate;
            return(SetCommState(aPort,&portState));
        }else{
            return(TRUE);
        }
    }else{
        return(FALSE);
    }
}
```

The setStopBits()function sets the number of stop bits. *Stop bits* are used to frame serial data and can be set to 1, 2, or 3, corresponding to 1, 1.5, and 2 stop bits, respectively.

Listing 14.56   The C Implementation of setStopBits()

```
long SerialDevices_Win32sSerialPeer_setStopBits(struct HWin32sSerialPeer
➥*nativeSerial, int64_t aPort,long stopBits){
    DCB portState;
    if(GetCommState(aPort,&portState)){
        if(portState.StopBits != (BYTE)stopBits){
            portState.StopBits = (BYTE)stopBits;
            return(SetCommState(aPort,&portState));
        }else{
            return(TRUE);
        }
    }else{
        return(FALSE);
    }
}
```

The function setParity() controls the parity checking style. *Parity checking* is the process of validating that the data transferred is correct. The default parity is 0 (none). Other parity values are 1 for odd parity and 2 for even parity.

Listing 14.57   The C Implementation of setParity()

```
long SerialDevices_Win32sSerialPeer_setParity(struct HWin32sSerialPeer
➥*nativeSerial, int64_t aPort,long parity){
    DCB portState;
    if(GetCommState(aPort,&portState)){
        if(portState.Parity != (BYTE)parity){
            portState.Parity = (BYTE)parity;
            return(SetCommState(aPort,&portState));
        }else{
            return(TRUE);
        }
    }else{
        return(FALSE);
    }
}
```

Listing 14.58 shows the C implementation for the setDataBits() function. SetDataBits() controls the width of the data word. The size selected is usually 7 or 8 bits. The default is 8 data bits. The data width can be set from 4 to 8 bits.

Listing 14.58   The C Implementation of setDataBits()

```
long SerialDevices_Win32sSerialPeer_setDataBits(struct HWin32sSerialPeer
➥*nativeSerial, int64_t aPort,long dataBits){
    DCB portState;
    if(GetCommState(aPort,&portState)){
        if(portState.ByteSize != (BYTE)dataBits){
            portState.ByteSize = (BYTE)dataBits;
            return(SetCommState(aPort,&portState));
        }else{
            return(TRUE);
        }
    }else{
        return(FALSE);
    }
}
```

Interfacing C/C++ and Java

Summary

The native code interface is useful for accessing legacy code, system service functions, and hardware. With the Runtime.getRuntime().exec() method and the Process class that it returns, Java applications can run and control executable applications with effortless programming. Also, another compiler is not required.

This chapter covered the native interface environment and used it to access serial ports. The peer method described can be used as a model for creating Java and C code that is portable to other operating systems.

Use native code wisely. Be careful to avoid corrupting the Java environment by passing bad objects or string buffers to native functions. And retain as much Java code as possible.

Chapter 15

Java Beans

Undoubtedly, the computer industry is among the most quickly evolving industries. Consider the explosion of new languages and ideas appearing every day. These new approaches seem to change even faster than the latest fashions. Today, one of the biggest trends is the component movement. As such, the Java programming language is jumping on that bandwagon with Java Beans component architecture. This chapter covers the following topics to help you understand what Java Beans is and what it does.

- What is a component?
- Java Beans component architecture
- Java Beans basics
- Developing AWT Beans
- Java 1.1 as it affects Java Beans

Using Components

In an attempt to simplify programming and reduce the average size of applications, developers are moving toward component development. A *component* is a chunk of code that has the capability to function both independently and interactively by working with other components. By conforming to an agreed standard, developers can reuse components that were produced by other developers at different points in time and in different places in the world.

End users also benefit by combining only the components that they require. For example, suppose Microsoft Word were component-based; users requiring only basic word processing functionality could simply install those components. Additionally, in cases where the user requirements change (suppose that a user needs Word's collaborative document functionality), then these components may be easily incorporated into the Word directory.

Benefits to the Developer

To a developer, components may be the best thing since sliced bread. Today's companies release new versions of their software almost monthly, due in part to large development teams; however, reuse of code is largely responsible for this rapid release of updated versions. Object-oriented programming (OOP) contributes to code reuse. Unfortunately, the unique coding styles of each developer pose difficulties. It is rare that one developer's code is easily reused by another developer.

The standardization of component architecture enables the reuse of components among a theoretically infinite number of developers. By being able to take advantage of a multitude of pre-existing components, development time shrinks dramatically. For example, a small e-mail application that normally requires a set of classes for SMTP communication could efficiently reuse existing SMTP components.

Benefits to the Consumer

Software purchases are some of the largest costs to any shop. One thousand licenses of a typical software product can be very expensive—and they might be required by everyone in your shop. And to make the cost worse, a shop often purchases a product that contains superfluous features that the shop doesn't even need.

For example, a basic calculator with five functions (+, -, *, /, square root) can be purchased for $5. For around $80, you can buy a complex graphing calculator, which contains many unnecessary features. Consumers wanting only a couple of advanced functions (such as the sine and cosine functions) are forced to purchase the more expensive product. A component-based product solves this problem by enabling the client to purchase a customized application with only the desired components.

Returning to the example of Microsoft Word, most licenses of Word are used for basic word processing. In fact the most advanced feature used by most people is the spell checker. Although there are some "power" users of Word—people who use many of the more complex and obscure features—they are rare compared to your average user. Unfortunately, because there is only one application, everyone has to buy the same product.

Fifteen: Java Beans

The Java Beans Component Architecture

This chapter uses "Beans" as a singular noun. The name "Java Beans" refers to the component architecture, which is singular. Therefore, it is grammatically correct to say "A Java Beans architecture helps reduce development time."

Although it is a big help that components are based on standards, it is too much to hope for that there would be only one standard. The focus of this chapter is one of JavaSoft's component architecture for Java; the Java Beans component architecture.

Java Beans is part of Java 1.1 and takes advantage of many of its new features, including the following:

- Communication via a delegation-based event model
- Introspection
- Serialization
- The JAR file format

It is easy to become overwhelmed when you look over the concepts listed. What is imporant to remember is that although those features are required of advanced Bean development, mastery is not a prerequesite to general Bean development. A basic understanding of the delegation based event model is, in fact, all that is needed to begin developing your first Bean.

The Java 1.1 Delegation-Based Event Model

One of the most radical changes to Java 1.1 is the delegation-based event model, which is much different from a the one used in Java 1.0.

Events in Java 1.0 communicate in a "hierarchical" event model. If an event occurs in a given component, that event travels up the component hierarchy originating at the component that generates it. The event continues up until it reaches an action() or handleEvent() method that returns true.

This event model becomes very cumbersome for the following reasons:

- If your application needs to respond to an event that occurs in a given component, it is usually necessary to subclass the component. This can generate an unwieldy sea of class files.

Java Beans

- Communication between components at different levels of the component hierarchy involves unnatural, messy coding.

- Embedding the event handling so deep within the application results in an application that is tightly integrated with its GUI. Making changes to the GUI, therefore, means a lot of code rework.

- Because locating the event source is usually based on comparisons to a string passed as a parameter, localization becomes a lengthy process.

In the delegation-based event model in Java 1.1, an object designates itself as a "listener" to another object. When an event occurs in that "other" object, the event is broadcast to all listeners. This correctly implies that an event propagates directly from the source to its listeners. Refer to figure 15.1 for an illustration of this.

FIGURE 15.1

Comparing the Java 1 and Java 1.1 Event Models.

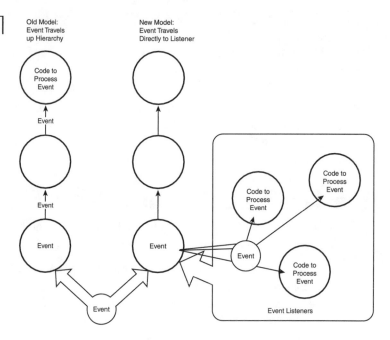

In the figure, an event travels through a system using the Java 1.0 event model (left) and the Java 1.1 event model (right). It is important to note that although both models embody an object hierarchy, only the Java 1.0 model propagates events up the hierarchy.

Implementing Java 1.1 Event Services

Java 1.0 implements all events as instances of the class java.awt.Event and differentiates them by a numeric ID. With Java 1.1, all events are instances of a childclass of java.util.EventObject; each event is represented by a unique class. There is a minor exception to this—a few events that are similar are represented by a single class and differentiated by a numeric ID. An example of this is java.util.MouseEvent which represents mouse up, mouse down, mouse drag, and mouse move events.

As indicated in figure 15.1, events propagate from a source object to a listener object. Source objects have the following characteristics:

- They broadcast events.
- They broadcast events to registered objects.
- Object properties are modified with getProperty() and setProperty() methods.

Listener objects have the following characteristics:

- They implement a specific interface that defines which methods may be invoked by the source. This interface is a childclass of java.util.EventListener.
- They must register themselves as listeners of source objects.

It is good programming practice for Java Beans developers to assume that their Beans will be used in a multithreaded environment. To ensure proper execution in multithreaded environments, at least synchronize all methods.

Figure 15.2 expands on the right half of figure 15.1 to demonstrate the step-by-step process that occurs between an event source and an event listener. This process is fully expanded with a complete example of a Java Bean in the section, "Developing Your First Java Bean."

The Importance of the Java 1.1 Event Model to Beans Developers

A message-passing medium is required for Java Beans to properly communicate with each other. A medium based on hierarchy is obviously not suitable to Java Beans; therefore, the Java 1.1 delegation-based event model was adopted.

Step 1: Event Listener registers itself with the event source.

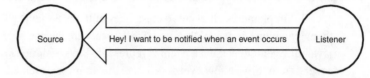

Step 2: Source Registers an incoming event

Step 3: Source Notifies Listener of event

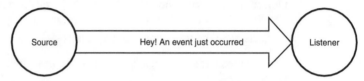

Java Beans Basics

This section explores the different forms that a Bean may take. Beans with a visual state are compared to those without a visual state. Finally, this information is used to develop an example Bean. The Java Bean developed in this section is rather basic, but more advanced demonstrations appear later in the chapter.

Java Beans with a Visual Representation

Java Beans can be placed into two distinct categories:

- Those with a visual representation
- Those without a visual representation

Java Beans with a visual representation are more common than those without one. When a component has a visual representation, it can draw itself on the screen. Examples of this would be a slider, grid, or button component.

Java Beans without a Visual Representation

Not all Java Beans require visual representations. Java Beans are ideal for various processing and communicating tasks, which any application needs to support. Examples of Beans that would not have a visual representation are those that sort objects, send e-mail, or retrieve a file by using FTP.

Developing Your First Java Bean

In this section, you will develop two tightly coupled Beans. One is a button that, when clicked, generates a pseudorandom number and tells the second Bean to display that number.

The Event Source

When referring to components, *coupling* describes the dependency of one component on another.

The event source in this application appears on-screen as a standard button. When that button is clicked, an event is sent to the listener, and then the listener displays the appropriate number. This section focuses on the formation of the event source.

All standard GUI widgets are already event sources. In the case of java.awt.Button, a listener class simply has to register itself as a listener of the Button class to enable the notification of a button click. This application uses java.awt.Button. Button is subclassed, and methods specifically designed to notify listeners are placed in that subclass.

FIGURE 15.3

Propagation of the button click from the event source to the event listener.

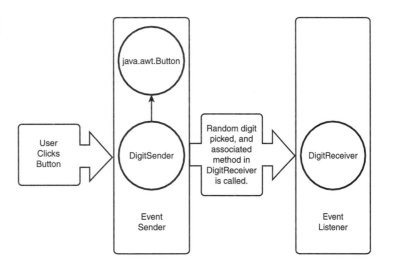

Figure 15.3 illustrates the communication link between the source and listener.

Your event source object (DigitReceiver) must do the following to facilitate this communication:

- Subclass java.awt.Button
- Support methods that enable event listeners to register and unregister themselves as listeners
- Provide facilities to track each listener
- Implement logic to generate and analyze a random number, and call the method associated with that number in each listener

Subclassing java.awt.Button

By subclassing java.awt.Button, events that are generated by user clicks first pass through the subclass, DigitReceiver. This allows DigitReceiver to sense the button click and then communicate properly with all its listeners.

Do not confuse this setup with the Java 1.0 event model. The fact that the subclass receives the event does not imply that an event hierarchy exists. The event is passed to DigitReceiver, but DigitReceiver will not pass that event to any parent classes.

Enabling Listener Registration and Tracking

Because an event source needs to track an infinite number of listeners, some growable data structure needs to be used to track those listeners. The class java.util.Vector is such a class, and it is used in your event source to track and reference listeners. Listing 15.1 contains a code that is used to add and remove listener objects from the Vector object maintained by the event source.

Listing 15.1   Methods for Maintaining the Pool of Reference Objects

```
// Register an Event Listener.
public synchronized void addDigitListener(DigitListener dl) {
    listeners.addElement(dl);
}


// Remove an Event Listener.
public synchronized void removeDigitListener(DigitListener dl) {
    listeners.removeElement(dl);
}
```

In the addDigitListener() and removeDigitListener() methods, "listeners" is an instance of the java.util.Vector class. It is extremely important that these methods employ the "synchronized" modifier. In a multithreaded environment, it permits only one object at a time to use the method marked "synchronized."

Notice the data type of the parameters accepted by the methods in listing 15.1. DigitListener is an interface implemented by all listener objects. This interface identifies the methods that are called by the event source.

Listing 15.2 contains the DigitListener interface. Any class that implements DigitListener is responsible for ensuring that each method (when called) properly displays the number referenced in its signature. To keep this example simple, only numbers greater than or equal to zero and less than or equal to five are considered.

Listing 15.2 The DigitListener Interface Defines the Methods Required of a Listener Object

```
//interface which defines the methods required of a listener object
public interface DigitListener extends java.awt.event.ActionListener {

    //each method will draw to the screen some form
    //of the digit referenced in its signature.

    public void showOne(DigitEvent e);
    public void showTwo(DigitEvent e);
    public void showThree(DigitEvent e);
    public void showFour(DigitEvent e);
    public void showFive(DigitEvent e);
    public void showZero(DigitEvent e);

}
```

Notifying Listener Objects

When a button click occurs, the event source first generates a new random number, and then it notifies each registered listener object of that new number. This registration is accomplished by calling the method in the listener object that is associated with the new random number.

The implementation details of the methods involved with notification follow.

Listings 15.3a through 15.3d define processEvent(). The processEvent() method is similar to handleEvent() in the Java 1.0 event model; they distribute an event sent to a component. However, unlike Java 1.0, processEvent() does not pass an unused event up a hierarchy.

Perhaps the most important piece of the processEvent() method is seen in listing 15.3a. It creates a clone of Vector containing the listener objects. This clone is referenced for the duration of the method. Unexpected results can occur if a clone is not used because it sets a boundary on when objects wishing to be event listeners must register. Without a clone, it is possible that the contents of Vector could change while the processEvent() method executes.

Listing 15.3a   Creating a Clone of Vector Containing the Listener Objects

```
protected void processEvent(AWTEvent evt) {
    Vector          l;
    DigitEvent      e = new DigitEvent(this);

    //create a copy of the listener vector
    synchronized(this) {
        l = (Vector)listeners.clone();
    }
```

Listing 15.3b calls the getNextRandom() method, which generates a new random number and then sets the value of the private member variable, randomInt, equal to the new random number.

Listing 15.3b   Calling the getNextRandom() Method

```
getNewRandom(); //create a new random int
```

Listing 15.3c contains the logic that examines the randomInt variable and calls the method in each listener object that is associated with the variable.

Listing 15.3c   Examining the randomInt Variable

```
if(randomInt == 0) {
    for (int i = 0; i < l.size(); i++) {
        DigitListener dl = (DigitListener)l.elementAt(i);
        dl.showZero(e);
    }
}
```

```
    else if(randomInt == 1) {
        for (int i = 0; i < l.size(); i++) {
            DigitListener dl = (DigitListener)l.elementAt(i);
                dl.showOne(e);
            }
    }
    else if(randomInt == 2) {
        for (int i = 0; i < l.size(); i++) {
            DigitListener dl = (DigitListener)l.elementAt(i);
                dl.showTwo(e);
            }
    }
    else if(randomInt == 3) {
        for (int i = 0; i < l.size(); i++) {
            DigitListener dl = (DigitListener)l.elementAt(i);
                dl.showThree(e);
            }
    }
    else if(randomInt == 4) {
        for (int i = 0; i < l.size(); i++) {
            DigitListener dl = (DigitListener)l.elementAt(i);
                dl.showFour(e);
            }
    }
    else if(randomInt == 5) {
        for (int i = 0; i < l.size(); i++) {
            DigitListener dl = (DigitListener)l.elementAt(i);
                dl.showFive(e);
            }
    }
```

When subclassing a GUI component, always pass the event up to its parent. This ensures critical processing associated with the event occurs. In the subclass of button, for example, you do take action on the button press; however, you do not draw the button in different states—that is managed in the Button class itself.

Listing 15.3d   super.processEvent

```
    return super.processEvent(evt);
}
```

Listing 15.4 contains the complete Java code for the DigitSender class. Other than the processEvent() method discussed in listing 15.3, the following is quite trivial and straight-forward.

Listing 15.4   The DigitSender Bean

```
import java.util.*;
import java.awt.*;

//The DigitSender class is a Java Bean which will send a random int
//between 0 and 5 (inclusive) to each of its listeners each time its
//GUI (a button) is clicked.
public class DigitSender extends Button implements ActionListener{
        private Random          myRandom;            //used to generate the
                                                     //random int
        private int             randomInt;           //the current random
                                                     //int
        private Vector          listeners;           //listener pool


        //constructor, creates GUI and instantiates member data
        public DigitSender() {
                super("Create New Random");
                myRandom = new Random();
                listeners = new Vector();
                myButton.addActionListener(this);
                resize(50, 50);
                setLayout(new FlowLayout());
                add(myButton);
        }


        // Register an Event Listener.
        public synchronized void addDigitListener(DigitListener dl) {
                listeners.addElement(dl);
        }


        // Remove an Event Listener.
        public synchronized void removeDigitListener(DigitListener dl) {
                listeners.removeElement(dl);
        }


        //generate a new random int
        private synchronized void getNewRandom() {
                randomInt = myRandom.nextInt()%6;
                randomInt = (int)Math.abs(randomInt);
        }
```

```
//processEvent method will call the proper method in each listener
protected void processEvent(AWTEvent evt) {
    Vector              l;
    DigitEvent          e = new DigitEvent(this);

    //create a copy of the listener vector
        synchronized(this) {
        l = (Vector)listeners.clone();
    }

    getNewRandom(); //create a new random int

    if(randomInt == 0) {
        for (int i = 0; i < l.size(); i++) {
            DigitListener dl = (DigitListener)l.elementAt(i);
            dl.showZero(e);
        }
    }
    else if(randomInt == 1) {
        for (int i = 0; i < l.size(); i++) {
            DigitListener dl = (DigitListener)l.elementAt(i);
            dl.showOne(e);
        }
    }
    else if(randomInt == 2) {
        for (int i = 0; i < l.size(); i++) {
            DigitListener dl = (DigitListener)l.elementAt(i);
            dl.showTwo(e);
        }
    }
    else if(randomInt == 3) {
        for (int i = 0; i < l.size(); i++) {
            DigitListener dl = (DigitListener)l.elementAt(i);
            dl.showThree(e);
        }
    }
    else if(randomInt == 4) {
        for (int i = 0; i < l.size(); i++) {
            DigitListener dl = (DigitListener)l.elementAt(i);
            dl.showFour(e);
        }
    }
    else if(randomInt == 5) {
        for (int i = 0; i < l.size(); i++) {
            DigitListener dl = (DigitListener)l.elementAt(i);
            dl.showFive(e);
```

continues

Java Beans

Listing 15.4   Continued

```
                    }
            }

                //always send the event to the parent of an extended GUI
                //component.
                return super.processEvent(evt);
        }
}
```

The DigitEvent class in listing 15.4 (specifically in the processEvent() method) has not yet been covered. This class represents the actual event that travels from the event source to each of its listeners. It is possible to simply transfer the event that is passed to process-Event(); however code becomes much more readable if a specific event class is used.

Our example of the DigitEvent class extends java.awt.EventSource. DigitEvent offers a constructor that accepts a reference to a Component object, and then passes that reference up to its parent. No additional functionality is added to this class because none is needed. The DigitEvent class is demonstrated in listing 15.5.

Listing 15.5   The DigitEvent class

```
public class DigitEvent extends java.awt.EventObject {
    public DigitEvent(java.awt.Component source) {
        super(source);
    }
}
```

The Event Listener

When you designed the event source class (DigitSender) and the interface DigitListener, you laid out many of the methods the event source class implements. In fact, in addition to implementing all method in the DigitListener interface, all the event listener class does is implement a few methods, which work on the class's GUI.

It is important to note that this section contains only one possible implementation of the listener: the DigitReceiver class designed in this section implements DigitListener and uses the drawString() method to draw the requested number in a Panel. Another implementation could implement DigitListener and display the number the System.out-.println() method. The DigitSender class does not care how the methods are actually implemented, it only requires that they exist.

Recall that the DigitReceiver class extends Panel and draws within itself each digit that is requested by the DigitSender class. Listings 15.6a through 15.6c contain the DigitReceiver class.

Listing 15.6a is the constructor for the class. Here, a default font and initial display character are set. Because the class extends Panel after the constuctor executes, control is passed to the paint() method.

Listing 15.6a The Constructor for the DigitReceiver Class Performs Setup

```
import java.awt.*;


//The DigitReceiver class implements DigitListener and will display any
//of the digits 0-5 when asked to.
public class DigitReceiver extends Panel implements DigitListener {
    private char currentChar;        //the current character to display


    //Constructor, sets the default size, and font. Also sets the
    //initial display character to ?
    public DigitReceiver() {
        Stefan(new Font("Helvetica", Font.BOLD, 24));
        currentChar = '?';
        resize(50, 50);
    }
```

Every time a screen redraw is necessary, the paint() method is called. This method takes the current value of currentChar and draws it on-screen using the drawString() method.

Listing 15.6b The paint() Method Draws the Value of currentChar On-Screen

```
    //the paint method get called every time the currentChar variable
    //changes value here that variable is drawn to the screen.
    public void paint(Graphics g) {
            g.drawString(String.valueOf(currentChar), 40, 25);
    }
```

As instructed by its interface, listing 15.6c contains a series of showXXX() methods. Each method alters the value of currentChar to match its constructor, and then it forces a redraw by calling the repaint() method.

Listing 15.6c The showXXX() Methods Are Called by the Event Source

```
//The following showXXX() methods are implemented as a requirement
//of the interface each changes the value of the currentChar
//variable and then causes the screen to be redrawn.

public void showZero(DigitEvent e) {
    currentChar = '0';
    repaint();
}


public void showOne(DigitEvent e) {
    currentChar = '1';
    repaint();
}


public void showTwo(DigitEvent e){
    currentChar = '2';
    repaint();
}


public void showThree(DigitEvent e){
    currentChar = '3';
    repaint();
}


public void showFour(DigitEvent e){
    currentChar = '4';
    repaint();
}


public void showFive(DigitEvent e){
    currentChar = '5';
    repaint();
}
}
```

Linking Beans

So far, two interfaces and two classes have been developed. An event sender Bean and an event listener Bean are combined with a utility class called DigitDriver.

The class in listing 15.7 extends java.awt.Frame and places the DigitSender and DigitReceiver Beans on screen. The driver class registers the DigitReceiver Bean as a listener of DigitSender's events. In addition, the class supports a main() method, which is called by the Java VM when the class is instantiated.

Listing 15.7   A Driver Class for the Digit Beans

```java
import java.awt.*;


//Class DigitDriver is a driver which links together the
//sender and listener Beans.
public class DigitDriver extends Frame{
     DigitReceiver        theListener;      //the event listener
     DigitSender          theSender;        //the event source


     //Constructor, instantiates the objects, adds them
     //to the screen, and links them together.
     public DigitDriver() {
           theListener = new DigitReceiver();
           theSender = new DigitSender();
           theSender.addDigitListener(theListener);

           setLayout(new GridLayout(1, 2));

           add(theSender);
           add(theListener);

           pack();
           show();
     }


     public static void main(String args[]) {
           DigitDriver myDriver = new DigitDriver();
     }
}
```

Java Beans

Developing AWT Beans

Chapter 6 developed a GUI application framework. This framework is a traditional class library based on the Java 1.0 event model. In this section you will convert that framework into a series of Java Beans based on the Java 1.1 event model.

In the framework in Chapter 6, basic GUI application functions are implemented by the class FrameWork. This class creates a series of GUI components that facilitate communication between the application and the user. When a GUI component is dismissed, the owner is notified by a method invocation.

When a new instance of the Decision class is created, for example, it displays in a new window a user-defined string, along with two buttons (OK and Cancel). When one of these buttons is clicked, the Decision object notifies the calling object by calling its tellResponse() method. If these classes are Beans, the owner of the Dialog class would register itself as a listener of Dialog's actions, and when either the OK or Cancel button is clicked, the Dialog class sends an event to all registered listeners.

To make the application framework Bean-based, make the following changes:

- Modify each GUI component to act as a proper event source.
- Modify the FrameWork class to act as an event listener.

Modifying GUI Components

While introducing Java 1.1 event sources during the beginning of this chapter, a series of properties were defined that must be supported by any event source. As you modify the Chapter 6 framework to make it a set of Java Beans, you must ensure that each of the event source properties is present where needed. To refresh your memory, the properties that all event sources need to support are

- The event source must offer a unique event class that can propagate from the event source to each listener.
- The event source must enable the registration and unregistration of listener objects.
- Facilities must be provided to track the pool of listener objects.
- Based on a specified input, the event source sends an event to all registered listeners.
- The event source must be designed for multithreaded environments.

Notifying Listeners

Event passing under the Java 1.0 event model is pretty cut and dry. There is one event class, and the value of one of its ID variables indicates the event source. With Java 1.1 bringing a new event model, it also brings a series of event classes, all of which are unique to their source. Because there are many different event classes, it is not always obvious which of the event classes should be used when defining communication between two Java Beans. In deciding on the event class to be used in the application framework, there are basically three options:

- The event object passed to DigitSender when a button is clicked is passed directly to each listener.
- A unique event object is written for each GUI Bean.
- A unique event object is written for the framework and reused in each Bean.

There are obvious pros and cons to each of these choices. The first needs further research to properly verify its viability. Recall in listing 15.3a that an event generated by the user clicking the button is passed to the method processEvent() as an instance of the class AWTEvent. The implementation of processEvent() in listing 15.3a creates a new instance of an event called DigitEvent, and then processEvent() passes the DigitEvent instance to each listener. It seems that creation of the extra event is not really needed, and that it would simply be easier to pass along the AWTEvent object passed to processEvent().

Although passing AWTEvent is simple, it has its disadvantages. This approach makes it difficult for listeners to ensure that the event is coming from the proper location because AWTEvent is used by almost all GUI components. Another disadvantage is that interclass dependence (coupling) is decreased. For the most part, it is nice to have tightly coupled classes because it helps preserve the integrity of your component. The rare situation when low level coupling is desired is usually for a class that needs to respond to many different inputs by using one method invocation.

Finally, the primary disadvantage is that because a generic event class is used, it makes it impossible for event listeners to verify the source of an event.

The second option uses a unique event object for each GUI Bean, which is nice because it facilitates identification of the event source, resolving the question of whether the event was generated by the framework or by another object. However, this requires managing a multitude of unique situations. It becomes difficult to track all objects in the framework, especially as the size of the framework grows.

Java Beans

The last option is a very practical solution. An event object that is unique to the framework is reused by each GUI component. The obvious concern is that that it is not possible to determine the source of the event because the event object sent by each event source would be an instantiation of one class. Decision objects and Question objects, for example, send instances of the same class as an event. There is, however, a simple solution to this problem. First look at listing 15.8, which contains a class called FrameWorkEvent.

Listing 15.8 An Instance of the FrameWorkEvent Class is Passed from Event Source to Each Listener

```
public class FrameWorkEvent extends java.awt.EventObject {
    private       String        information;

    public FrameWorkEvent(java.awt.Component source, String
 theInformation) {
        super(source);
        information = theInformation;
    }

    public String getInformation() {
        return information;
    }
}
```

Note in listing 15.8 the parameters passed to the constructor. The first is a reference to the object that created the event (the event source), and the second is an instance of a String object. By taking advantage of the getSource() method in java.awt.EventObject it is possible to retrieve a reference to the object that created the event. Additionally, use the getInformation() method in the FrameWorkEvent class to retrieve the value of the parameter string. This string can be used to pass data between the event source and listener; for example, use it to determine whether the user dismissed a dialog box by pressing OK or Cancel.

Tracking Listeners

The first example of a Java Bean in the beginning of this chapter illustrates the necessity for the source object to track an infinite number of listeners. This project uses an implementation similar to the first example.

Unlike the first example, which only processes the event generated by one button, this application considers a few situations. For example, users operating the Decision class may click either the OK or Cancel buttons to exit the dialog box. The following sections explain how to convert the Decision class to a Java Bean.

First define a class called OkCancel. OkCancel tracks each listener and is responsible for broadcasting an event to all listeners. OkCancel is registered as a listener of an instance of java.awt.Button; thus, when the button is clicked, the event travels from the button to OkCancel to all listeners. Figure 15.4 shows an event propagating from the user to the OK button to the OkCancel object, and finally to each of Decision's listeners.

FIGURE 15.4

Event propagation in the Decision class.

FIGURE 15.4

Event propagation in the Decision class.

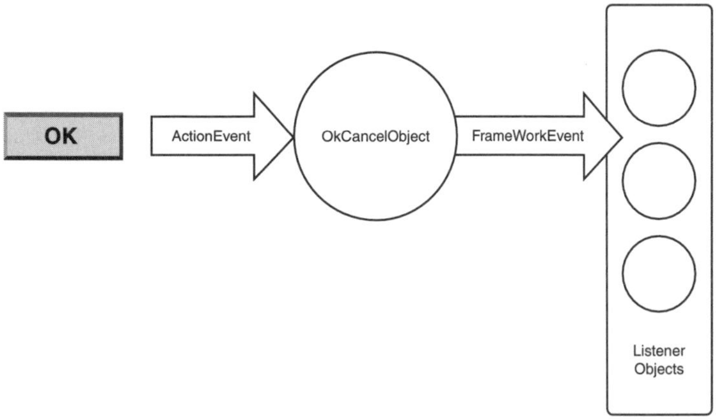

In windows that display two buttons (for example an OK and Cancel buttons), OkCancel is instantiated twice; one instance "listens" to the OK button, and one instance "listens" to the Cancel button. Listings 15.9a through 15.9n cover this class.

Listing 15.9a includes the constructor for the class. These perform two important actions:

- A Vector object is instantiated to hold references to all listeners.
- An ID field is set to either OK or Cancel to indicate the type of button "listened" to by the constructor.

Listing 15.9a   OKCancel Class Constructors

```
import java.awt.*;
import java.util.*;

public class OkCancel implements ActionListener {
    private static final int OK = 0;
```

continues

Listing 15.9a   Continued

```
        private static final int CANCEL = 1;

        private int        myID;
        private Vector     listeners;

        public OkCancel(int theID) {
            //create the listener object
            listeners = new Vector();

            //assign the id
            myID = theID;
        }
```

Listing 15.9b contains the methods that register and unregister a listener. By making these methods synchronized, survival in a multithreaded environment is ensured. References to all current listeners are contained in a Vector object called "listeners."

Listing 15.9b   Methods that Register and Unregister a Listener

```
        //add an event listener
        public synchronized void addFWEListener(FWEListener fwe) {
            listeners.addElement(fwe);
        }


        //remove an event listener
        public synchronized void removeFWEListener(FWEListener fwe) {
            listeners.removeElement(fwe);
        }
```

Listing 15.9c contains the actionPerformed() method. This method, which is called when a button is clicked, notifies all listeners of the Decision class that the dialog box has been dismissed.

Notice how the variable myID is used when creating the event. When the object is instantiated, myID is set to either OK or Cancel. In creating the FrameWorkEvent object, the extra information field in that object is set to either OK or Cancel (depending on the value of myID). This gives recipients of the event the necessary information to determine which button was clicked by the user.

Fifteen: Java Beans

Listing 15.9c   The actionPerformed() Method Dispenses an Event to All Listeners

```
//dispatch the events
public void actionPerformed(ActionEvent evt) {
      Vector              l;
      FrameWorkEvent      myEvent;

      if(myID == OK) {
             new FrameWorkEvent(this, "OK");
      }
      else {
             new FrameWorkEvent(this, "Cancel");
      }

      synchronized(this) {
             l = (Vector)listeners.clone();
      }

      for(int i=0; i<l.size(); i++) {
             FWEListner newFWE = (FWEListener)l.elementAt(i);
             newFWE.dialogDismissed(myEvent);
      }
   }
}
```

At this point you have written two classes:

- **FrameWorkEvent.** This is the actual event class.
- **OkCancel.** This class monitors the instances of java.awt.Button.

These classes provide the proper functionality to track and notify listeners of the event. The event itself has also been defined. The Bean still requires code to perform the following functions:

- Building the screen
- Linking all code together

Building the GUI

OkCancel and FrameWorkEvent are sufficiently generic to function with all the GUI Beans developed in this chapter. Each Bean provides a unique class that manages the building of the screen. This class also ensures that proper instances of OkCancel are created and that all listener objects are tracked.

Due to space constraints, this section is limited to converting the Decision class to a Java Beans and does not convert all of the GUI classes created for the framework classes. As you will learn during this conversion, however, the process used for the Decision class can be applied to any class developed in the Chapter 6 application framework.

When instantiated, the Decision class draws a user-defined string in a new modal dialog box and presents two buttons, OK and Cancel. The dialog box dismisses itself when either of these buttons is clicked.

The FWEListener interface is defined to be implemented by the Decision class. This interface is implemented by all listeners of the Bean and defines the method to be called when the dialog box is dismissed. This method accepts a FrameWorkEvent object generated by the OkCancel class as a parameter. Listing 15.10 includes the FWEListener interface.

Listing 15.10   The FWEListener Interface is Implemented by all Listeners

```
public interface FWEListener extends java.awt.event.ActionListener {

    //defines a method to be called when the
    //associated GUI Bean needs to send an event

    public void dialogDismissed(FrameWorkEvent evt);

}
```

The only remaining issue is to define the Decision class itself. This class offers the following functionality:

- Draws on-screen the user defined string (passed as a parameter to the constructor)
- Draws on-screen a button labeled "OK"
- Draws on-screen a button labeled "Cancel"
- Creates two instances of OkCancel (one to monitor each button)
- Provides mechanisms enabling listeners to register as listeners of both buttons
- Provides mechanisms to close the dialog box when a button is clicked

How the dialog box closes should be explained. Because the class that builds the screen uses two instances of OkCancel to monitor the buttons, it cannot discern when a button is clicked. A solution is to have the GUI building class register itself as a listener of each OkCancel class; therefore it properly terminates the window when notified of a button click.

The class is contained in listings 15.11a through 15.11f; discussion of each section is provided before the section is introduced.

Listing 15.11a contains declarations of private member data and the class signature. Note how implementing the FWEListener interface enables this class to register itself as a listener of an OkCancel object.

Listing 15.11a   Declarations of Private Member Data and Class Signature

```
import java.awt.*;

//Decision class prompts the user for an answer to either accept or
 cancel
//some question.
public class Decision extends Dialog implements FWEListener{
        //GUI controls
        private       Label           text;
        private       Button          okButton;
        private       Button          cancelButton;
        private       OkCancel        ok;
        private       OkCancel        cancel;
```

Listing 15.11b contains the beginning of the constructor. In this method necessary classes are instantiated. Note that when the ok and cancel objects are instantiated, a parameter is passed that informs these objects of the type of button being monitored.

Listing 15.11b   The Decision Constructor

```
//Decision class allows the user to answer a user specified question
//with either OK or Cancel.
public Decision(Frame parent, String incommingText) {
        super(parent, true);

        //create the compotes
        text = new Label(incommingText);
```

continues

Listing 15.11b   Continued

```
                    //event sources
                    okButton = new Button("OK");
                    cancelButton = new Button("Cancel");

                    //create the event listeners
                    ok = new OkCancel(OkCancel.OK);
                    cancel = new OkCancel(OkCancel.CANCEL);
```

Listing 15.11c contains the code that actually registers each listener. First, the OkCancel objects are registered as listeners of the buttons, and then the Decision object is registered as a listener of the OkCancel classes.

Listing 15.11c   Registration of All Listeners

```
//register the listeners of the buttons
                    okButton.addActionListener(ok);
                    cancelButton.addActionListener(cancel);

                    //register ourself as listeners of the OkCancel classes
                    ok.addFWEListener(this);
                    cancel.addFWEListener(this);
```

Listing 15.11d contains the code that actually draws the screen. The GridBagLayout layout manager is used to provide maximum functionality. Also in this listing, the insets() method provides a border on all sides of the dialog box.

Listing 15.11d   Drawing the Screen

```
                    //use the GridBagLayout manager to draw the screen
                    GridBagLayout myLayout = new GridBagLayout();
                    GridBagConstraints constraints = new GridBagConstraints();
                    this.setLayout(myLayout);

                    constraints.weightx = 100;
                    constraints.weighty = 100;
                    constraints.gridx = 0;
                    constraints.gridy = 0;
                    constraints.gridwidth = 6;
                    constraints.gridheight = 1;
```

```
                myLayout.setConstraints(text, constraints);
                this.add(text);

                constraints.gridx = 5;
                constraints.gridy = 3;
                constraints.gridwidth = 1;
                constraints.gridheight = 1;
                myLayout.setConstraints(okButton, constraints);
                this.add(okButton);

                constraints.gridx = 2;
                myLayout.setConstraints(cancelButton, constraints);
                this.add(cancelButton);

                this.pack();
                this.show();
        }


        //place a border around the dialog
        public Insets insets() {
                return new Insets(15, 15, 15, 15);
        }


        //called when either the OK or Cancel button is clicked.
        //closes the dialog.
        public void dialogDismissed(FrameWorkEvent evt) {
                this.hide();
        }
```

Listing 15.11e contains a method to add new listeners and a method to remove current listeners. These methods act as dispatchers and pass along any requests for registration or unregisteration to all instantiated OkCancel objects.

Listing 15.11e   Methods to Manage Registration and Unregisteration of Event Listeners

```
        //add an event listener.
        //since listeners need to be notified of both the OK button
        //clicks and the Cancel button clicks, this method
        //registers the listener with both sources.
        public synchronized void addFWEListener(FWEListener fwe) {
                ok.addElement(fwe);
```

continues

Listing 15.11e   Continued

```
                    cancel.addElement(fwe);
        }


    //remove an event listener
    //since listeners need to be notified of both the OK button
    //clicks and the Cancel button clicks, this method
    //registers the listener with both sources.
    public synchronized void removeFWEListener(FWEListener fwe) {
            ok.removeElement(fwe);
            cancel.removeElement(fwe);
        }
```

Listing 15.11f contains the dialogDismissed() method which is called when either of the buttons is clicked. This method closes the current dialog box.

Listing 15.11f   Closing the Dialog Box when Either Button is Clicked

```
    //called when either the OK or Cancel button is clicked.
    //closed the dialog
    public void dialogDismissed(FrameWorkEvent evt){
            this.hide();
        }
    }
```

At this point, GUI components and the Decision class have been converted to Beans. With a little additional effort, you can now convert all the GUI components developed in Chapter 6 to Java Beans. Concluding this section, the FrameWork class is converted to a Java Bean that works as a listener of all the GUI controls.

Converting the FrameWork Class

Making the FrameWork class a listener of the Beans that replace the GUI components requires the following two changes:

- The FrameWork class must implement the FWEListener interface.
- The dialogDismissed() method must be implemented with proper support to "listen" to each Java Bean.

Implementing FWEListener is accomplished by adding "implements FWEListener" to the class signature. A little additional work is required to properly implement dialogDismissed(). Listing 15.12 contains an implementation of the method supporting the Decision class.

Listing 15.12   Implementing the dialogDismissed() Method in the FrameWork Class

```
//as specified by the interface, this method is called when
//a button on a created dialog is clicked.
public void dialogDismissed(FrameWorkEvent evt) {
     if(evt.getSource() instanceof Decision) {
          if(evt.getInformation.equals("OK")) {
               //do ok action
          }
          else {
               //do cancel action
          }
     }
}
```

The Need For Two Frameworks

In this book you have developed two different application frameworks. One based on the Java 1.0 event model, and another compromised of Java Beans (based on the Java 1.1 event model). Having developed both frameworks, the following question arises: Why develop the same product based upon two different models?

Although developing components as Beans is definitely part of the long-term future, the truth of the matter is that developers have spent thousands of hours developing code as class libraries based on the Java 1.0 event model. Although the Java 1.1 event model, and the Java Bean specification in general, may be a more advanced event model, much code will become legacy and will never be converted. For this reason it is important that developers become familiar with both models.

It is important to note at this point that Java VMs supporting the Java 1.1 specification will be fully backward compatible. However, although this may be the case, mixing of event models in one application should never be done.

Java 1.1 as It Affects Java

This chapter now discusses some other features of Java Beans, especially how they relate to the new features in Java 1.1. Finally, there is a discussion on the differences between Java Beans and class libraries. In addition to the delegation-based event model, this section offers information on the following features new to Java 1.1:

- Serialization
- JAR files
- Introspection

Serialization

Serialization in Java provides object persistence, which usually involves writing an object's state to a file or database. The real beauty of serialization is deserialization—reconstructing objects from their serialized form.

Serialization is managed by a set of new classes in the java.io package; most notable is the ObjectOutput class. When serialized to a file, a Java Bean is given the .ser extension. Through the use of a class loader, Java code can reconstruct an object from its serialized form. The code in listing 15.13 serializes a Decision object to a file.

Listing 15.13   Serializing a Decision Object

```
//Serialize an instance of the Decision class developed above.
FileOutputStream          fop = new FileOutputStream("decision.ser");
ObjectOutput              oo  = new ObjectOutput(fop);
oo.writeObject(myDecision);
oo.flush()
```

Listing 15.14 provides code to deserialize the object serialized in listing 15.13.

Listing 15.14   Deserializing the Object Serialized in Listing 15.13.

```
ClassLoader    cl =
Class.forName("industrial.Decision").getClassLoader();
Decision      myDecision = Beans.instantiate(cl, "/home_u/ulcassad/
➥decision.ser");
```

JAR Files

Java ARchive (JAR) files are the standard deliverable form of a Java Bean. A JAR file is a mechanism that stores any number of the following in a single file:

- .class files
- Image files
- Sound files
- Serialized object files (.ser extension)
- Other JAR files
- Any other resources used by an application

The JAR format handles the large number of files associated with a Java application by placing these files in a manageable format.

Given any JAR file, it is possible to both determine the names of Java Beans in that file and possibly to instantiate any of these Beans.

Introspection

Introspection is a process that enables users of a Java Bean to determine the public methods of a class. Here "user" is defined as either another object at run-time or as a builder application. By providing a standard mechanism that supports introspection, a user may easily manipulate an unknown Java Bean.

This standard mechanism, introspection, is managed in two ways:

- Through analysis of common design patterns
- Through explicit specification

A design pattern is a standard mechanism used when writing code. The most obvious of these are the getXXX() and setXXX() methods, which are used to manipulate class properties. Through analysis of design patterns, users performing introspection can develop a clear representation of the Java Bean.

When analysis of design patterns does not give a clear enough picture of a Java Bean, a developer can use explicit specification functionality by writing a class that implements the BeanInfo interface. This interface (defined in listing 15.15) enables a Java Bean to specify information about the data and data manipulation supported by the Java Bean. All methods in listing 15.15 defined by the interface are abstract. This means that their implementation in a given class is optional.

Listing 15.15   The BeanInfo Interface Allows a Java Bean to Explicitly Specify Its Properties

```
public interface java.Beans.BeanInfo {
    public abstract BeanInfo[] getAdditionalBeanInfo();
    public abstract int getDefaultEventIndex();
    public abstract int getDefaultPropertyIndex();
    public abstract EventSetDescriptor() getEventSetDescriptors();
    public abstract MethodDescriptor() getMethodDescriptors();
    public abstract PropertyDescriptor[] getPropertyDescriptors();
}
```

Summary

Components are changing the face of computing. Within a few years, all development and deployment of applications will be based around different component frameworks. Ultimately, components from totally different developers will be capable of working together in perfect harmony.

This chapter covered significant ground, and by now you should be an expert on Java Beans development. Learning the details of Java Beans development will make you much more marketable. Before you move on to other material, sit down and convert some of your old class libraries into Java Beans. After you have done this, write some Java Beans from scratch.

Chapter 16

Jeeves and Java Servlets

This chapter covers the newest aspect of Java networking—servlets. Servlets are the server-side equivalents of applets. They are Java programs designed to execute in an environment provided by an HTTP server. Intended as a Java-style replacement for Common Gateway Interface (CGI) programs, servlets are supported as an extension package to JDK 1.1 and use a Java-based HTTP server that implements the newly defined Servlet API. Like applets, servlets can be automatically downloaded to the server, and untrusted servlets run in a secured environment. Unlike applets, servlets have no user interface and do not use the AWT classes. Servlets and applets are compared in table 16.1. In this chapter, you are introduced to the basic features of the Jeeves HTTP server and learn how to construct your own servlets.

TABLE 16.1	*Servlet*	*Applet*
Comparison of Servlets and Applets	Subclass of GenericServlet	Subclass of Applet
	Runs in a server	Runs in a browser
	Must be multithreaded or thread safe	Generally single thread per applet
	No direct user interface	Uses AWT for user interface
	If downloaded to server, controlled access to files and network	If downloaded to browser, no access to files and network access back only to serving host
	If local to server, full access to files and network	n/a

Introduction to Servlets

The obvious question since the introduction of Java and the HotJava browser with its client-side applets has been this: What can Java do for the server side? Java applets facilitate the addition of specialized functions, such as intelligent forms, to a web page; developers may add custom processing functions to the server with the new Servlet API definitions, which extend Java web server functionality.

Deficiencies of CGI

Most HTTP servers support the Common Gateway Interface (CGI) to connect to external programs. This interface enables you to add custom processing functions to an HTTP server. With CGI, HTTP servers can return not only static documents, but they can supply dynamic contents generated by CGI-compatible programs written in C, Perl, shell script, or many other languages. HTML forms information that is generally processed on the server using a CGI program. CGI programs can also process tasks, such as updating server-based files, which are not possible or practical using client-side techniques such as Java applets or JavaScript. CGI programs receive information about the task by means of environment variables or by reading input from the program's standard input stream (stdin on Unix). They write results to their standard output stream (stdout on Unix) which is returned to the web client by the server.

NOTE

Because Jeeves is being released after JDK 1.1, this chapter covers Jeeves and the Servlet API at the time of the JDK 1.1 interface freeze and concentrates on the essentials of Servlet programs and the features expected in the final product. Each new release of Jeeves has brought changes to the Servlet API and added functionality to the provided HTTP server. Because the examples are based on the Jeeves Alpha 2 release API, some examples may need minor corrections to work with the final Jeeves release. The latest information on Jeeves and the Servlet API can be found at http://java.sun.com/products/java-server/.

Although CGI is an important first step in the generation of dynamic web content and HTML-controlled processing, it suffers in two areas:

- Performance
- Security

Initiating a new operating system process is necessary to execute the CGI program referenced in the HTTP request. This leads to performance problems. Despite the proposal of various other schemes—such as FastCGI, which does more intelligent process management, and server-specific APIs developed by Netscape and other HTTP server vendors—CGI is still the most common approach.

Undoubtedly the biggest weakness of CGI (and similar techniques) is a lack of formal security mechanisms. Without a secure runtime system, web masters must closely inspect CGI programs for programming flaws and security loopholes that could be exploited to disrupt operations or obtain sensitive information. Through experience, a list of defensive programming techniques have been compiled for CGI programs to prevent known security problems. (For example, always limit user-entered data to the standard printing character set to prevent entry of special shell command escape characters.) Despite these counter-measures, many shared-user web hosts restrict the use of CGI programs. Dynamic content may often be limited to forms processing; to go beyond this, a safe and secure environment is required for creating dynamic content. A Java-based solution can provide the needed security.

Servlet API Goals

The Servlet API is designed to replace CGI as the standard interface between HTTP servers and HTML-processing programs, although implementation is initially limited mostly to the JavaSoft-developed Jeeves HTTP server. Java programs implementing the Servlet API are called *servlets*—the server-side equivalent of applets. Servlets execute in a special environment provided by a web server that supports the new Servlet API. This environment supplies all the resources needed for servlets to run and enforces the security model to maintain system integrity. This approach is similar to the controlled execution environment provided by web browsers for applets. The Servlet API has the following attributes:

- **Ease of use and understanding.** The Servlet API is similar to CGI in terms of HTTP information available, making the conversion of existing CGI programs to servlets feasible.

- **High performance.** The Servlet API eliminates the overhead of starting an external program to serve each request; it enables servlets to practically perform all server operations, including basic file serving.

- **Platform independence.** Like applets, servlets run on any server platform that provides a Java Virtual Machine supporting the Servlet API.

- **Transport independence.** The Servlet API has base classes that are independent of the transport protocol used to carry web content and subclasses that are specific to HTTP. Specific versions of the Servlet API can be developed for future web transport protocols.

- **Secure and safe.** Untrusted servlets run in a secured environment, as described in the "Security" section later in the chapter, that protects access to the network and other local resources. Trusted servlets have full access to local resources.

Java's Servlet API has a significant advantage over CGI in terms of performance, transport independence, and security. The differences between servlets and CGI are highlighted in table 16.2. The use of servlets for all web server operations makes a very powerful and flexible web platform. For example, server administrators can easily augment the file serving servlet to collect statistics on files requested or track user information, or augment the error response servlet to specialized error messages.

TABLE 16.2		*Servlet*	*CGI*
Comparison of Servlet API and CGI	Language	Java	Any programming language
	Invocation	Direct method call	Run program
	Parameters	ServletRequest methods	Environment variables
	Runtime Checks	Java Virtual Machine	Language specific
	Security	Java Security Manager	Operating system specific

Servlet API Overview

Briefly, the Java Servlet API is comprised of three packages that define high-level functionality, HTTP-specific support, and dynamic HTML creation support. You can assume these packages are available on any server platform supporting servlets.

The java.servlet package contains classes that define the high-level servlet functionality independent from the details of using HTTP for transport. These classes are as follows:

- Servlet
- GenericServlet
- ServletContext
- ServletInputStream
- ServletOutputStream
- ServletRequest
- ServletResponse

The java.servlet.http package contains subclasses of the generic classes in java.servlet and an HTTP-specific utilities class. You use these classes in building servlets that specifically support HTTP. These classes are as follows:

- HttpServlet
- HttpServletRequest

- HttpServletResponse
- FormServlet
- HttpUtils

The java.servlet.html package contains 13 HTML support classes that provide operations for assembling HTML elements such as tables, imagemaps, and forms. These classes are as follows:

- HtmlApplet
- HtmlChoice
- HtmlContainer
- HtmlDefinitionList
- HtmlElement
- HtmlForm
- HtmlFrameset
- HtmlImageMap
- HtmlList
- HtmlPage
- HtmlRow
- HtmlTable
- HtmlText

Together, these three packages define the Servlet API and form the basis for building servlets. These packages are covered in more detail in "The Servlet API," later in this chapter. Of course, web servers that support servlets are likely to offer vendor-specific classes in addition to these standard ones. The HTTP server included in the Jeeves package has its own set of JavaSoft-specific classes (such as the sun.server.* and sun.security.* packages). These vendor-specific packages provide additional support for implementing servlets beyond the basic API. The JavaSoft classes provide support for additional security mechanisms, regular expression parsing, and cache file handling, among others.

Jeeves at Your Service

JavaSoft supports the Servlet API as part of its Jeeves server development package. Designed to simplify the construction of network services software, Jeeves has three main elements:

- A set of JavaSoft-specific classes for building servers and advanced servlets. This extensive set of classes (most are not externally documented) are found in the sun.server and sun.security packages.

- A complete HTTP server written in Java that extensively uses the JavaSoft-specific packages. The server provides a first implementation of the Servlet API and demonstrates the practicality of using built-in servlets for all server functions.

- A set of classes for implementing servlets that utilize HTTP. These classes are in the java.servlet packages and define the Servlet API.

Server Construction Toolkit

To enable the construction of high-performance servers using Java, Jeeves defines a server framework that manages multiple network connections, service threads, and client handlers. This framework is used to build connection-oriented (TCP-based) servers that use multiple threads to handle concurrent client connections. These server construction classes are part of the sun.server package and include Server, ServerHandler, and ServerParameters. Jeeves only supports TCP as the transport protocol; no support is provided in Jeeves for implementing UDP-based servers.

A Jeeves-based server has a main thread that accepts incoming connections on a ServerSocket, deploys the actual service processing to a handler thread, and loops back to accept additional connections. The handler threads are allocated from a pool of service threads to reduce the overhead of thread allocation for each request. By using a different thread to handle each connection, the server can service several clients concurrently. Server connection processing and request handling is shown in figure 16.1. The framework classes have been optimized to reuse objects and thus avoid object creation and garbage collection overhead.

FIGURE 16.1
Server request handling.

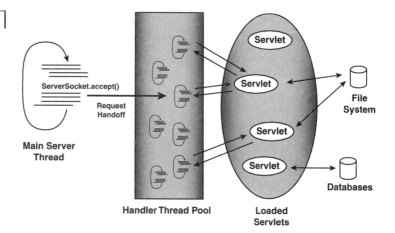

ServerSocket.accept()

Request
Handoff

Main Server
Thread

Servlet

Servlet

File
System

Servlet

Servlet

Databases

Handler Thread Pool

Loaded
Servlets

Jeeves HTTP Server Overview

The Jeeves HTTP server uses the server construction toolkit. A main thread listens on an administrator-configured TCP port for incoming HTTP requests. Each request is dispatched to a separate service thread to process the request. To handle a request, the HTTP server carries out the following:

1. Creates an HttpServletRequest object from the information in the HTTP request header.

2. Applies the path translation rules from the rules.properties file to convert the URL into the name of the appropriate servlet. All URLs are converted into a servlet name; the longest matching rule is used to perform the translation.

3. Verifies access permission to the resource according to the information in the acl.properties file.

4. Translates the servlet name according to the information in the servlet.properties file into a full pathname, such as URL, codebase, or class name information which specifies how to load the servlet.

5. Loads and, if necessary, initializes the servlet. Every HTTP request either invokes a servlet or returns an error.

6. Creates an HttpServletResponse object with basic response information such as the server identification and current time.

7. Calls the servlet's service() method passing the request and response objects as arguments.

8. Completes the transaction by ensuring that the response is sent and, if appropriate, that the connection is closed.

Because servlets can be identified by a full URL, servlets can be downloaded from the network, similar to applets, and executed on the server. These steps are described in the following sections.

Creating the HttpServletRequest

The server creates an HttpServletRequest object to store all the information about the HTTP request. This object's methods provide access to all the fields in the HTTP header and supply information about the TCP connection. The HttpServletRequest object performs the same functions as the environment variables used to communicate request information to CGI programs.

Translating the URL to Servlet Name

In Jeeves, all URL requests either implicitly or explicitly refer to a servlet. The mapping of URL to servlet name is determined by using a translation table defined by the rules.properties file. This file contains entries such as

```
/=file
/servlet/special=myservlet
/servlet=invoker
/admin/adminservlet=admin
```

The string to the left of the equals sign (=) is matched against the requested URL; the longest match starting from the left of the request URL is used in the translation. The string to the right of the = is the name of the servlet that handles the request; this name is subsequently mapped into the servlet's codebase and class name. The string "/" to the left specifies the default mapping as "file," which provides the usual HTTP file service.

Explicitly invoke a servlet by using an URL such as /servlet/counter. This URL is actually mapped to a reference to the invoker servlet (matching the "/servlet" translation rule) that takes the rest of the URL as the name of the servlet to execute. In this example, the URL /servlet/special is mapped to myservlet rather than invoker. This mapping of file names or directory paths to servlets is the basis for dynamic content.

Checking Access

If the access checking entry (enable.acls) is enabled in the httpd.properties file, the server determines the resource being accessed and checks access permissions. Resources are characterized as follows:

- Files and directories for access via the FileServlet, which serves files
- Servlets for access via the InvokerServlet, which executes arbitrary servlets
- The welcome file for directory access

If your file service and invocation servlets do not use the standard names "file" and "invoker," they will need to implement their own access checking. The mechanics of access checking is described in more detail in the "Security" section later in the chapter.

Servlet Loading

If the named servlet is not already loaded, the name must be converted into the information needed to load the servlet. A servlet is loaded from an URL or codebase and class name as defined in the servlet.properties file. Only one instance of any servlet is created, and this instance is reused to handle subsequent requests. Initialization parameters for each servlet can be specified in the servlet.properties file; these parameters are passed to the init() method after the servlet is loaded but before the service() method is called. This process is shown in figure 16.2.

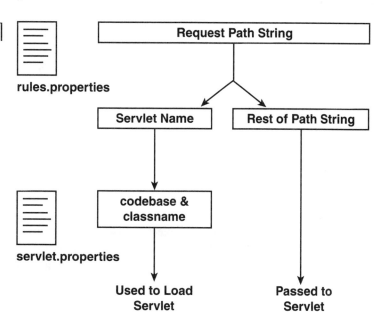

FIGURE 16.2
The servlet loading process.

Completing the Request

To complete the HTTP request, a ServletResponse object is created to build the response header, and then the servlet's service() method is called. Servlets are generally structured to contain the service() and sendResponse() methods. The service() method verifies the HTTP request and calls the sendResponse() method to actually perform the requested operation. The servlet writes its output to an output stream retrieved from the ServletResponse. After the HTTP requested is handled, the server usually closes the connection.

Security

As web servers expand their roles from simply providing access to publicly available documents to becoming the center of workgroup and enterprise computing, security becomes increasingly important. Not all files, directories, or servlets should be accessible to anyone that knows the URL. For example, Jeeves has a built-in administration applet/servlet pair that lets an administrator reconfigure the server; obviously access to this servlet must be controlled. You may want to control access to web pages in the same manner that file servers provide read-access controls for files. The security model of web servers in general, and Jeeves specifically, resembles the security measures found on traditional file servers or shared computers.

Jeeves' security model is designed to block the most common and serious threats or attacks to your server:

- **Theft or alteration of data.** By providing the usual identity-based access controls, Jeeves enables server administrators to control access. Protected information often includes server's web pages and administrative data.

- **Malicious code attacks.** By restricting untrusted servlet code to a secured environment, potentially malicious, destructive code can be downloaded and run without fear.

- **Eavesdropping.** Users of your site may be concerned about protecting their financial or other sensitive data from being intercepted and read from your server.

Jeeves offers a variety of security and protection mechanisms for your server. These are based on HTTP's security features, the Secure Sockets Layer (SSL), and the security mechanisms inherent in Java's protected Virtual Machine environment. Security features derived from the Java Virtual Machine, secure administration, and the security sandbox are inherent in the Jeeves server. Others, such as the various authentication mechanisms, are specified on an individual file or servlet basis. The security mechansisms presented in the following sections are supported by Jeeves.

Basic Authentication

Basic authentication supported by HTTP permits user access to restricted areas of a web page by validating an entered user name and password. Based on the user's identity, access is granted according to an access control list. Place basic password authentication protection on a given file or servlet by using the AdminServlet or editing the acl.properties file. However, this standard HTTP mechanism has two well-known problems:

- Passwords are sent on the Internet in a form (known as cleartext) that any eavesdropper can read.
- The server needs to store the passwords in a cleartext form that anyone with access to the server can read.

The security provided by the HTTP basic mode is not sufficient to prevent a determined attack to your server.

Digest Authentication

Improper access is more difficult to achieve if digest authentication is used; the password, as entered by the user, is used to cipher some randomly generated text that is sent by the server. The resulting cipher is sent back to the server. This system is more secure than basic authentication because the user's password is never transmitted on the Internet. The server, knowing the user's password, calculates what the correct cipher should be and compares it to the coded message sent by the client. Enable digest authentication protection on a given file or servlet by using the AdminServlet or by editing the acl.properties file.

SSL Server Authentication

Users not only need to identify and authenticate themselves to their server; in addition, users need a way to identify and authenticate the server to which they are sending information. The process for an eavesdropper to secretly redirect your connection to a different server is straight-forward. Secure Socket Layer (SSL) server authentication is usually accomplished with the assistance of a third-party "Certificate Authority," which provides a high level of assurance that the server's identity is what it claims to be. Third-party authentication reduces the amount of authentication information that your browser is required to maintain. The amount of necessary information is reduced from hundreds or thousands of sites to just a small number of third-party authentication centers.

For example, SSL and third-party authentication provide the mechanisms to allow a trusted third-party, such as your ISP, to vouch for the identify of a commercial Internet site. After being assured of its identity, you can safely provide credit card information to the site.

SSL Eavesdropping Protection

Another feature of the HTTPS (the secure version of HTTP) protocol permits the encryption of all data sent to or from the server to enables private communications. This encryption prevents an eavesdropper from learning potentially sensitive information from your transactions. However, this protection can only be achieved if encryption is supported by both the server and by the client's browser. The exchange of credit card information, for example, is usually protected by using encryption.

Realms with Users and Groups

As your server grows and the number of supported users increases, additional mechanisms are needed to make it easy to administer and maintain your server. One such mechanism forms groups of users with identical access rights. You can create different groups, each supported by different virtual hosts. Another possibility is to partition a server according applications, projects, or departments. Users with the same user name in two different realms are considered as two different users with different sets of access privileges. Using groups extends access privileges more efficiently than referencing a valid-user listing. You define groups using the AdminServlet. For example, you can define a group "admin" in which all members have access to the various administrative pages and servlets; giving a new user administrative privileges is as simple as making that user a member of the admin group.

ACLs Protect Web Pages

Jeeves provides access control lists (ACLs) to let your server's administrator control a user's access to individual document pages or directories. ACLs are also used to protect access to servlets. Servlets can use the supplied ACL mechanisms to implement additional servlet-specific access control policies and schemes. You define ACLs using the AdminServlet or by editing the acl.properties file.

Simple and Secure Administration

It is not often recognized that good tools to handle administrative tasks are big advantages in terms of security. Manual administration (editing text files by hand, for example) is extremely error prone; errors invariably reduce security. Jeeves provides administrative tools based around the AdminServlet that help avoid common administrative errors.

By default, access to the administration pages and servlets is controlled through the digest authentication method previously described. These pages and servlets also can be accessed through HTTPS so that the administrative operations are protected from tampering and disclosure. A user must provide the proper password to access administration functions.

Non-Root UID/GID

Servers on Unix systems have a special security problem. Unix only permits programs run as "root" to bind to the well-known ports from 1 to 1023. These ports are usually protected in multiuser systems to prevent ordinary users from running servers (such as a mailer or web server) on these standard ports. Because the default HTTP server TCP port is 80, Unix web servers need to start up as "root" just to bind to this port. However, permitting complex programs run as "root" is generally a big security risk.

The Unix version of Jeeves enables you to control which Unix user ID to use after your server binds to the TCP port. This facility enables you to run Jeeves as your default server without worries that a malicious servlet can exploit "root" access to system resources and disrupt your system. In fact, Jeeves can be set up so that "root" access is needed only when initially setting up the server. Then all normal administrative tasks can occur without requiring special access privileges. You must have a version of Jeeves that includes a special native library that supports the setUser() method.

Security Sandbox

For running untrusted servlets, Jeeves provides a secured environment that isolates the untrusted servlet from the rest of the HTTP server. The server administrator makes the decision of whether to trust a servlet. For example, the server could trust all local servlets and not trust any servlet loaded from the network. A server could trust servlets by verifying a digital signature of a trusted development source. Trusted servlets execute on a thread in the main server's thread group. Untrusted servlets execute in a thread group separate from the server's group. Using a separate thread group prevents a servlet from trying to interfere with the main task processing. The untrusted servlet environment limits access to network resources, files, and server configuration information by adding a servlet security manager which checks for risky operations and blocks them. Execution of untrusted servlets is shown in figure 16.3.

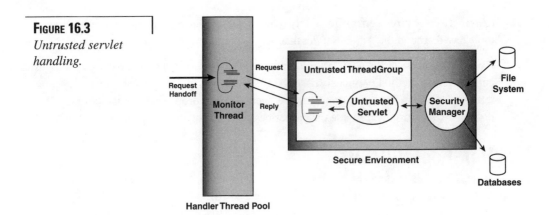

FIGURE 16.3
Untrusted servlet handling.

Built-in Servlets

Because the Servlet API is efficient and powerful, many of the features often coded directly into an HTTP server are implemented as Jeeves servlets. This use of servlets simplifies the HTTP server code and enables server administrators and users to customize server features by providing additional servlets. Jeeves includes several standard servlets to provide the functions commonly available in HTTP servers. These core servlets are as follows:

- File servlet (FileServlet) accesses files and directories
- Server-side include servlet (SSIncludeServlet) processes server-side include files
- Error servlet (ErrorServlet) creates custom error responses
- Invoker servlet (InvokerServlet) invokes an arbitrary servlet
- Imagemap servlet (ImagemapServlet) handles image maps on the server
- CGI invoker servlet (CGIServlet) runs CGI programs
- Administration servlet (AdminServlet) performs administrative tasks
- FTP proxy servlet (ProxyServlet) handles proxy requests
- Forms servlet (FormServlet) processes a form

Generally, the standard servlets are not designed to be subclassed; most provide only public service() and sendResponse() methods. However, the ErrorServlet and FormServlet are designed to be modified to provide custom error messages and perform custom forms processing.

FileServlet

The FileServlet provides the normal static content file serving functions expected of an HTTP server. The URL path translation rules are setup to default requests not handled by other servlets to the FileServlet. The FileServlet only supports GET and HEAD requests; an error is returned for any other HTTP method. If the requested file is a directory, the servlet returns the contents of a welcome file residing in the requested directory. The default name of the welcome file is index.html. If the welcome file is not found, the servlet returns a formatted directory listing. You can change the name of the welcome file by adding a welcome="pagename.html" entry to httpd.properties.

If a file is requested, the servlet determines the correct content type by matching the file extension against those in the mime.properties file. The FileServlet has an internal cache to hold the contents of frequently requested documents. If the file size is less than a configured value, the file is read into an internal buffer and cached. The file caching size is specified by the ramcache.entry.size entry in the httpd.properties file; the default value is 8,000 bytes.

If the MIME type of the file is java-internal/parsed-HTML, the content type is set to text/html, and the FileServlet calls the server-side include servlet for additional processing of the file. By default, the extension of files that contain server-side includes is .shtml, as specified in the mime.properties file.

Server-Side Include Servlet

If the MIME type of the file is java-internal/parsed-html, the SSIncludeServlet further processes the file to resolve any references to servlets embedded in the document. By default, these files have extensions of .shtml. As the document is written to the client, the SSIncludeServlet scans for the newly defined <servlet> HTML tag. When this tag is encountered, the servlet identified in the attributes of the tag is invoked and its output is sent to the client in place of the <servlet> </servlet> HTML element.

The server-side includes supported by SSIncludeServlet are not the same as that supported by many other HTTP servers, such as NCSA and Netscape, that embed server-side include commands inside HTML comments. Jeeves server-side includes can only be used to invoke servlets and insert the output into the current document. The syntax for invoking servlets follows:

```
<servlet name=Name code=Code.class codebase=CodeBase
initParam1=initArg1 initParam2=initArg2 ...>
<param name=param1 value=val1>
<param name=param2 value=val2>
```

continues

```
        .
        .
        .
</servlet>
```

The server first tries to invoke the servlet with the name provided in the name field. If this fails or if no name is provided, the server attempts to load the servlet based on the code and codebase fields. Any remaining attribute fields within the <servlet> tag are passed as initialization parameters to the servlet. If the server loads the servlet and a name was specified, the server keeps the servlet loaded so that the next time the servlet is accessed it is not reloaded. If no name is specified, the server reloads the servlet each time it is accessed.

After the servlet is ready to execute, the server calls the service() method of the servlet. The name/value pairs specified in the HTML file with the <param> tag are accessible to the servlet using the standard getParameter() and getParameters() methods on the ServletRequest object passed to the servlet in the service() method. Everything the servlet writes to ServletResponse.getOutputStream() gets written to the client as part of the client's requested document.

Error Response Servlet

When you call HttpServletResponse's sendError() method with only a status code to return an error to the requester, the ErrorServlet is actually invoked to create and send the error reply. The built-in ErrorServlet returns either a simple error reply message generated by translating the status number into a standard error text string, or it returns the contents of a file from the pre-configured error page directory (the error.directory servlet init() parameter). The files in the error directory are named by adding the .html extension to the status code; for example, the message for "not found" (code 404) is contained in the file 404.html.

By implementing the creation and transmission of error response pages as a servlet, Jeeves provides great flexibility in handling error responses. You can easily replace the built-in servlet with your own customized error response servlet.

InvokerServlet

The InvokerServlet processes HTTP requests to explicitly invoke a servlet instead of implicitly invoking a servlet as a result of path translation. In the default server configuration, the InvokerServlet is triggered by a /servlet in the requested URL. The rest of the URL characters occurring after /servlet is presumed to identify the name of the servlet to be executed.

ImagemapServlet

The ImagemapServlet handles the server-side processing of imagemaps that are specified using an extension of standard NCSA mapfiles. A server-side imagemap is specified in an HTML file by placing <IMG> inside the <A HREF=...> tag instead of text description of the link. For example, the following HTML is used to place an image map in a document:

```
<A HREF="http://<server-host-name>/imagemap/<map-file-name>">
<IMG SRC="<image-file>" ISMAP>
</A>
```

Imagemap files can reside anywhere HTML documents are permitted to reside. The ImagemapServlet supports imagemap files that are in standard NCSA format, with the addition of the following Jeeves-specific extensions:

- **Text menus.** Text-only browsers are presented with a menu of links when an imagemap is selected. An optional double-quoted string may be added to the end of each line in the imagemap file to add description to menus generated for text only browsers.

- **Base command.** Defines the base URL for relative URLs in the mapfile. The three valid values are "map" for map-relative URLs (the default), "referer" for URLs relative to the HTML page containing the imagemap, or any full URL.

- **Text command.** The double-quoted string following the text command is inserted into the menu generated for text-only browsers.

Each line in the imagemap file starts with a keyword that is a command or the name of a shape, followed by a URL, followed by the coordinates required to define the indicated shape, and ends with an optional text string used for creating a menu for text-only browsers. The URLs can be relative or full; relative URLs are resolved as specified by the base command. Coordinates for shapes are expressed as x and y values; the coordinates of the top, left of the image is 0,0. Valid keywords are

- **default.** Defines the URL when the user clicks on a location in the map that is not defined by a region.

- **base.** Defines the base URL used to resolve relative URL references made in defining shapes. Instead of specifying a URL as the argument of the base command, use "map" to indicate a URL relative to the imagemap file or "referer" to indicate a URL relative to the document containing the imagemap.

- **text.** Specifies a text string to be inserted into the menu generated for text-only browsers.

- **circle.** Specifies a circle defined by center and edge-point coordinates.
- **ploy.** Specifies a polygon with at most 100 vertices as defined by the coordinates.
- **rect.** Specifies a rectangle defined by upper-left and lower-right coordinates.
- **point.** Specifies a point defined by a single coordinate.

CGIServlet

To enable backward compatibility with existing CGI programs, Jeeves has a built-in servlet, CGIServlet, that functions as a bridge between the Servlet API and CGI. The translation of servlet requests to CGI is feasible because all the necessary information is available through the Servlet API.

AdminServlet

Online server administration is performed by AdminServlet. Using this servlet, the administrator can perform all the server's configuration functions without ever having to manually edit configuration files. Also, the use of an administration servlet ensures that changes to multiple configuration files are correctly completed.

The user interface of the administration servlet, like the rest of Jeeves, was not frozen when the JDK 1.1 APIs were finalized. Therefore, this section does not include screen shots nor provides detailed coverage of using the AdminServlet to administer Jeeves.

The following is a partial list of the functions performed using the AdminServlet:

- Restart or shut down the server
- Change operating parameters, such as the server port
- Vary parameters that affect server performance, such as timeouts and file cache size
- Control event logging
- Specify file and servlet name aliases
- Control virtual host properties
- Configure proxy operation
- Set up user and group access control information
- Administer access control lists

These functions and parameters are covered in more detail in the following section, "Running the Jeeves Server."

Running the Jeeves Server

After installing Jeeves, you must perform some initial configuration of the server. As with all servers, a variety of parameters need to be set for proper server operation. Maintenance of the configuration files is the only drawback of the flexibility of the Jeeves server. All configuration files are kept in the admin directory. Fortunately, much of this administrative burden is handled by the AdminServlet.

The Jeeves server uses a variety of files to set parameters and control its configuration; all files are in the Properties class file format. Properties is a subclass of Hashtable that defines a mechanism to load and store the contents of a hashtable to a file. Each line in the file corresponds to one key/value entry in a hashtable and is comprised of key string separated from a value string by the equality (=) character. For example, the server's TCP port is specified by the following entry:

```
server.port=8080
```

This line is located in the httpd.properties file.

The Jeeves HTTP server uses the following configuration information to support servlets:

- Server operational parameters—httpd.properties file
- Path translation rules—rules.properties file
- File alias table—aliases.properties file
- Servlet control and init parameters—servlet.properties file
- File suffix to MIME type translation—mime.properties file

The details of server administration are certain to change as Jeeves evolves into a shipping product. In this section you learn about the concepts being administered and with less emphasis on the actual administration mechanisms.

In addition to configuration information directly related to servlets, the Jeeves HTTP server supports virtual hosting and proxy operation. Virtual hosting enables the administrator to establish multiple, logically disjoint HTML document collections on one physical server. You are probably unaware that different virtual hosts are served by one physical server unless you closely inspect the IP address of the servers; compare IP addresses because even the IP host names of virtual hosts are indistinct. Proxy services supports operation through a security firewall and provide local caching for proxied files. This advanced server configuration information is stored in the following files:

- Proxy configuration—proxy.properties file
- Virtual hosting configuration—included in the httpd.properties file

The final aspect of server operation is security. In Jeeves, server security is supported by a complex scheme of security realms, users and groups, and access control lists. The related files are as follows:

- Access control lists—acl.properties file
- General security configuration—security.properties file
- User and group identification files stored within the realm directory

The next section focuses only on the configuration aspects related to servlets and not the virtual hosting, proxy, and security configuration information.

Server Operational Parameters

Most server operational parameters are defined in the "httpd.properties" files. The major parameters and their function are shown in table 16.3.

TABLE 16.3 **Server Operational Parameters**	Parameter	Function
	server.port	Defines the TCP port number used by the server. The standard system HTTP server runs on port 80, but 8080 is used as the default value for user-run servers.
	server.min.threads/ server.max.threads	Define the minimum and maximum number of threads in use by the server framework to handle HTTP requests. If a new request is received and all threads are currently busy, a new thread is created and used to process the request as long as the number of allocated threads is less than server.max.threads. Service threads that have been idle for a period of time are destroyed until the number of threads equals server.min.threads. You do not normally need to change these default values.
	server.grace	Specifies the period of time, in seconds, that server waits for pending requests to complete before the server closes the connection. The default value usually provides servlets with more than enough time to complete their request.

Parameter	Function
ramcache.entry.size	Specifies the maximum size of files, in bytes, that are read into the in-memory file cache. The default value (8000 bytes) should cover most circumstances. Setting the value to 0 disables operation of the in-memory file cache.
keepalive.count	Specifies the maximum number of transactions that can be exchanged over the TCP connection before the server closes the connection. This feature is used only for those connections that include the keep-alive HTTP request field. Setting the value to 0 disables this feature and the TCP connection is always closed after the response is sent.
keepalive.timeout	Specifies the maximum time, in seconds, that the TCP connection is kept open to accept additional requests. This feature is used only for those connections that include the keep-alive HTTP request field. The connection is closed when the keepalive.count is reached or the keepalive.timeout expires.
welcome	Specifies the file name of the default welcome file in a directory. The contents of this file is returned rather than the standard directory display. The default value is index.html.
rules.config	Defines the file path (directory and file name) of the property file that defines the rules that translate a URL to a servlet name. You change this file to add special URL-to-servlet mappings.
aliases.config	Defines the file path (directory and file name) of the property file that defines the file aliases.
servlets.config	Defines the file path (directory and file name) of the property file that specifies the loading and initialization information for all named servlets loaded at start-up.
mime.config	Defines the file path (directory and file name) of the property file that defines the mapping from file suffix to MIME type. You will need to change this file only to add an additional suffix to MIME type translation or to change the extension of the server-side include files from the default .shtml.

Path Translation Rules

The rules.properties file defines the translation rules for converting an URL request to the name of the servlet to handle the request. An example file is as follows:

```
/=file
/cgi-bin=cgi
/imagemap=imagemap
/servlet=invoker
/admin/adminservlet=admin
/admin/performanceservlet=performance
/admin/servletinfoservlet=servletinfo
/admin/aclServlet=aclServlet
/loganalyzer=loganalyzer
```

The string to the left of the equals sign (=) is matched against the requested URL; the longest match, starting from the left of the requested URL, is used in the translation. The string on the right of the = is the name of the servlet to handle the request. The string "/" to the left on the first line specifies the default mapping as "file," which provides the usual HTTP file and directory service.

If you want to replace one of the standard, built-in servlets, such as "file," with your own custom version, do not change the name of the servlet in the rules.properties file, but instead change the class to be loaded for the servlet named "file" in the servlet.properties file. Internally, the server code provides some special processing based on the name of the servlet. The name in the rules.properties file is treated as a description of the service.

Alias Table

Jeeves provides an aliasing mechanism to translate the requested path information into another string. For files, the FileServlet uses the rules in the alias.properties file to map the shorthand path name specified in an URL to a full file path name. Use aliases as a way to accomplish the following:

- Eliminate typing long URLs
- Hide your internal directory structure
- Temporarily fix broken links when reorganizing directories and moving files

An example alias.properties file follows:

```
/=public_html
/cgi-bin=cgi-bin
```

```
/admin=admin/html
/doc=doc
/applet=servlets
/icons=icons
/~user=/home/$user/public_html
```

The string to the left of the = is matched against the requested URL; the longest match, starting from the left of the requested URL, is used in the translation. The string to the right of the = is the file name of the file. The last line defines the familiar shorthand for a user's directory, "~user," which actually refers to "/home/user/public_html."

Servlet Control Parameters

The servlet.properties files contains all the information needed to load and initialize any named servlet. You can specify three different parameters for each servlet: these are a codebase, code class name, and initialization parameters. They take the form of the following entries, respectively:

- <servletname>.codebase=URL
- <servletname>.code=classname
- <servletname>.initArgs=name/value pairs

You need to specify the codebase if the class is not in the current CLASSPATH. The name/value pairs from initArgs can be accessed by the servlet by calling the getInitParameter() method to get the value of a specific parameter or getInitParameters() to get a hashtable of all arguments.

A special entry, servlets.startup, lists the servlets to be automatically loaded at server start-up time. An example of a servlet.properties file is as follows:

```
servlets.startup= file cgi invoker imagemap admin proxy error
file.code=sun.server.http.FileServlet
cgi.code=sun.server.http.CgiServlet
invoker.code=sun.server.http.InvokerServlet
imagemap.code=sun.server.http.ImagemapServlet
error.code=sun.server.http.ErrorServlet
myservlet.code=specialsyservlet.class
myservlet.initArgs=param1=value1, param2=value2,\
   param3=value3
```

You use the backslash (\) character to indicate a line continuation.

File Suffix to MIME Type Translation

Most servlets know the type of content that they are producing and can correctly set the contentType attribute of the response. However, the FileServlet has no such knowledge and thus needs a means to determine the likely content type from the file name. The convention is to use a consistent set of file name suffixes that can be mapped to MIME types. This mapping is stored in the mime.properties file. A small portion of this table is as follows:

```
*=text/plain
java=text/plain
html=text/html
htm=text/html
gif=image/gif
jpeg=image/jpeg
mpeg=video/mpeg
qt=video/quicktime
shtml=java-internal/parsed-html
```

Each line in the file indicates a given file name suffix representing a particular MIME type. The first line (*=text/plain) is the default rule that is applied when all other rules fail to match. The order of entries in this file is not important; the * character indicates the default content type if the file matches none of the suffixes. Note that the last line of the sample file defines a mapping of file names with suffixes of .shtml to the private MIME type java-internal/parsed-html. The File Servlet invokes the server-side include servlet to process any file with a content type of "java-internal/parsed-html" (which is converted to MIME-type text/plain when the file is sent). You only need to add entries to this table to reflect new applications or file types.

The Servlet API

The Servlet API is defined by the classes in the java.servlet, java.servlet.http, and java.servlet.html packages. Figure 16.4 shows the packages, classes, and their relationships. Together, these packages specify the following:

- The generic behavior of servlets independent from the web transport protocol
- Additional facilities available to HTTP-specific servlets
- Support for programmatic creation of HTML pages as a hierarchical structure of HTML elements

FIGURE 16.4

The servlet API classes.

Servlet API

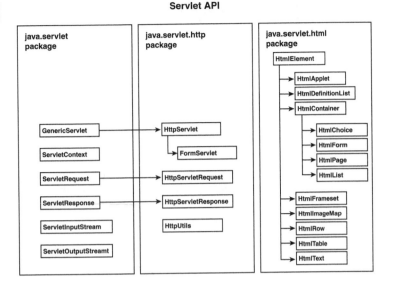

The following sections cover the methods that comprise the Servlet API. Where appropriate, the equivalent CGI variable is indicated. In addition to the Servlet API's availability on any server platform that supports servlets, developers may have access to vendor-specific classes and servlets that are proprietary to a given server and not part of the Servlet API. Any such extensions would be covered by server-specific documentation.

The java.servlet Package

The java.servlet package defines the operation of servlets from a protocol-independent perspective. At this level, the protocol used to access the servlets could be HTTP, a network file system protocol, or other transport protocol. Servlets that are designed to operate as a server-side include use the classes in this package. The four interfaces and three implementation classes in this package are described in more detail in the following sections.

Servlet Interface Class

Servlet is the highest level, generic interface class. It defines only four basic methods to accomplish the following: initialize the servlet, destroy the servlet, service a request, and return an information string:

- **init(ServletStub).** Automatically called by the system to initialize a servlet. Subclass this method if your servlet needs to perform any initialization after it is loaded. Access the initialization parameters specified for your servlet in the servlet.properties file by calling getInitParameter() or getInitParameters().

- **destroy().** Called by the system to free allocated resources when the servlet class is unloaded.

- **service(ServletRequest, ServletResponse).** Called to process the incoming request and create the outgoing response. You must code your service() method in a thread-safe manner because concurrent requests for the same servlet result in multiple threads executing your service() method. The easiest way to be thread-safe is to not modify any object instance variables and only use parameters of the service() call. Alternatively, you can add the "synchronized" modifier to your declaration of service() to restrict access to one thread at a time.

- **getServletInfo().** Called to get an information string that describes the servlet.

A subclass of Servlet uses a ServletContext object, described in the next section, to obtain information about the server's environment and to call various server utility routines.

ServletContext Interface Class

The ServletContext interface defines methods that the servlet can use to interact with its operating environment. The relationship between a servlet and the ServletContext is similar to how an applet is related to an AppletContext. The facilities provided to a servlet is limited to getting MIME types, translating path names, finding other servlets, and logging information. These methods are as follows:

- **getMimeType(String filename).** Returns the MIME type of the specified file by matching the file name suffix against entries in the mime.properties file.

- **getRealPath(String path).** Applies the alias rules in the alias.properties file to the specified virtual path and returns the corresponding real path; null is returned if the translation fails.

- **getServerInfo().** Returns a string identifying the name, version, and platform of the server software and is equivalent to the CGI variable SERVER_SOFTWARE.

- **getServlet(String).** Returns a servlet of the given name.

- **getServlets().** Returns an enumeration of all the servlets currently loaded in the server. This enumeration includes the calling servlet.

- **log(Servlet, String).** Writes a message to the servlet log for a given servlet.

ServletRequest Interface Class

The ServletRequest interface class defines method used to obtain information about the servlet request independent of the actual transport protocol used between the client and server. The request must be carried by an IP-based transport protocol, such as HTTP. Implementations of ServletRequest for specific transports, such as HTTP, must provide the following protocol-related methods:

- **getRemoteAddr().** Returns the IP address of the client that sent the request (its equivalent CGI variable is REMOTE_ADDR).

- **getRemoteHost().** Returns the fully qualified host name of the agent that sent the request (its equivalent CGI variable is REMOTE_HOST).

- **getServerName().** Returns the host name of the server that received the request (its equivalent CGI variable is SERVER_NAME).

- **getServerPort().** Returns the port number on which this request was received (the CGI variable is SERVER_PORT).

- **getProtocol().** Returns a string identifying the protocol and version (the CGI variable is SERVER_PROTOCOL).

The request can include parameters or content information. The servlet can determine the length of any content sent with the request using getContentLength(). The servlet can also obtain the content encoding type using getContentType(). When content is available, the servlet can read it using a HttpInputStream obtained from getInputStream(). Implementations of ServletRequest for specific transports, such as HTTP, must provide the following content-related methods:

- **getParameter(String).** Returns the value of the specified parameter for the request.

- **getParameters().** Returns a hashtable of all the parameters of this request.

- **getContentType().** Returns the MIME type of any data included with the request, or null if the MIME type is not specified in the request header.

- **getContentLength().** Returns the size of the data included with the request, or –1 if a length is not specified in the request header.

- **getInputStream().** Returns an input stream for reading any data included with the request.

ServletResponse Interface Class

The ServletResponse interface class defines a general way to create the response to the service request. At this generic level, the response is just content with a MIME identifier and optional length. To write the actual content of the response, the servlet calls getOutputStream() to get a ServletOutputStream and then makes the necessary print() calls to compose the response. The methods to create the response are as follows:

- **setContentType(String).** Sets the MIME type of the response.
- **setContentLength(int).** Sets the content length for the response.
- **getOutputStream().** Returns a ServletOutputStream used for writing response data to the client.

GenericServlet Class

In general, the GenericServlet class is a base implementation class for any transport-independent servlet, and specifically it is used for any servlet that can be invoked from a server-side include. GenericServlet implements the Servlet interface and provides convenient access to information from the servlet's ServletContext. In addition to implementing init(), destroy(), service(), and getServletInfo() methods required by the Servlet interface, GenericServlet provides the following methods:

- **init().** Called after the servlet is loaded to initialize the servlet. Override this method to accept initialization parameters or to perform other initialization functions. A servlet is initialized only once, when it is loaded.
- **getInitParameter(String name).** Gets the value of an initialization parameter of the servlet as specified in either the servlet.properties file or as an attribute in the <servlet> tag for server-side includes servlets.
- **getInitParameters().** Returns a name/value pair hashtable of the initialization parameters of the servlet.
- **getServletContext().** Returns the servlet context.
- **log(String).** Logs a message into the servlet log file.

ServletInputStream

ServletInputStream is an abstract subclass of InputStream that defines the readLine(byte[], int offset, int count) method, which reads bytes into the byte array starting at the offset until the array is filled or a newline character is read.

ServletOutputStream Abstract Class

ServletOutputStream is an abstract subclass of OutputStream that is similar to a PrintStream, but only defines methods to print the most commonly used network data types (ints, longs, and strings). The implementation of ServletOutputStream handles conversion from internal Unicode encoding of characters to US-ASCII, which is generally used by Internet protocols. This class also defines methods to print and terminate the line with the Internet-standard CR/LF combination. The output methods are as follows:

- print(int), println(int)
- print(long), println(long)
- print(String), println(String)
- println()

You must convert other data types using toString() before printing to the ServletOutputStream.

The java.servlet.http Package

The java.servlet.http package supports servlets that specifically use HTTP. This package contains two interface classes, two implementation classes, and the implementation of a servlet class intended to be subclassed. As the API matures, other standard servlets may be included into the Servlet API definition. The HTTP-specific classes are HttpServlet, HttpServletRequest, HttpServletResponse, FormServlet, and HttpUtils. All are described in the following sections.

HttpServlet Abstract Class

Subclass HttpServlet, an abstract subclass of GenericServlet, to implement your HTTP-specific servlets. HttpServlet handles the cast conversion between the generic ServletRequest and the ServletResponse objects and their HTTP-specific subclasses. You override the service(HttpServletRequest, HttpServletResponse) method in your servlet class to perform the servlet processing function. The HttpServlet methods are as follows:

- **service(ServletRequest, ServletResponse).** Performs the cast conversion between generic and HTTP-specific request and response objects. Normally do not override this method, but instead override the following HTTP-specific method.

- **service(HttpServletRequest, HttpServletResponse).** Override this abstract method to accept HTTP service requests.

HttpServletRequest Interface Class

HttpServletRequest is a subclass of ServletRequest that handles the extra request information, other than content identification, contained in an HTTP request header. The information available from HttpServletRequest, beyond that of the base ServletRequest, falls into four general categories:

- General information about the request
- Information concerning the URL
- Authentication-related information
- Access information to the original HTTP header

The exact information available using these calls is described in the following sections.

General Request Information

These methods provide general information about the request, including the name of the method used to access the data and any query information:

- **getMethod().** Returns a String containing the method used in the request, for example, "GET," "HEAD," or "POST" (the equivalent CGI variable is REQUEST_METHOD).

- **getQueryString().** Returns the query string part of the URI, or null if none; the query string follows the ? in the URI (the CGI equivalent is QUERY_STRING).

URL Information

These methods provide information about the requested URL, its major components, and its local translation:

- **getRequestURI().** Returns the request URI.

- **getServletPath().** Returns the part of the request URI that refers to the servlet being invoked.

- **getPathInfo().** Returns optional, extra path information following the servlet path, which immediately precedes the query string.

- **getPathTranslated().** Returns extra path information translated to a real path using the alias.properties rules (CGI's variable is PATH_TRANSLATED).

- **getRequestPath().** Returns the part of the request URI that corresponds to the servlet path plus the optional, extra path information.

Authentication-Related Information

The servlet can provide some very weak access control by using name and address information about the client as provided by getHostName() and getHostAddress(). The type of HTTP-level authentication in use is available using getAuthType(). Finally, for connections running in basic mode, getRemoteUser() returns the user identification:

- **getAuthType().** Returns the authentication scheme of the request, or null if none (CGI variable AUTH_TYPE).

- **getRemoteUser().** Returns the name of the user making this request; null is returned if the name is not supplied with the request (CGI's equivalent is REMOTE_USER).

Access to HTTP Request Header Fields

HttpServletRequest provides a means to get direct access to the HTTP request header fields to get information not explicitly supported by an HttpServletRequest method. Examples include user-agent, referer, preferred languages, accepted content encodings, and client-state (*cookie*) information, as well as all non-standard header fields.

Instead of using an enumerator, the following two methods to access the raw header take an index into the header. An index of 0 retrieves the first header field; null is returned if the index is greater than the number of fields available:

- **getHeader(int).** Returns the value of the nth header field; null is returned if there are fewer than *n* fields.

- **getHeaderName(int).** Returns the name of the nth header field; null is returned if there are fewer than *n* fields.

You can also access request header fields by name, which happens to be the easiest approach. In this case, the request header is searched for a matching field name and returns the field value. Use one of the following methods, depending on the desired data conversion:

- **getHeader(String fieldname).** Returns the value of a header field; if this method is not available, null is returned.

- **getIntHeader(String fieldname, int default).** Returns the value of an integer header field after converting the string to an int. If the field is not found, it returns the default value.

- **getDateHeader(String fieldname, long default).** Returns the value of a date header field after converting the string to a date. If the field is not found, it returns the default value.

HttpServletResponse Interface Class

The HttpServletResponse is a subclass of ServletResponse and provides the mechanisms to create an HTTP response header. These mechanisms are used for the following four purposes:

- To set the response status.
- To add arbitrary response header fields.
- To create an error response.
- To redirect the request to another URL.

Creating normal, error, and redirect responses using the HttpServletResponse object is described in the following sections.

Setting the Response Status

The return status defaults are 200 or OK. If an error is returned or OK is not the correct status, the servlet can specify both an error code and some descriptive text. If only an error code is given, the code is translated into a standard status text string. The two methods are as follows:

- **setStatus(statusCode).** Sets the status code in the returned HTTP header. The status code is translated into a text string using a standard definition of arguments.
- **setStatus(statusCode, messageString).** Sets the status code in the returned HTTP header.

Specifying Non-Standard Header Fields

Your servlet can add any field to the response header by using one of the setHeader() methods, leting you add non-standard header fields not supported by HttpServletResponse. Provide the name of the header field (without a colon) as the first argument and the data as the second argument. Variants of setHeader are defined for String, int, and date parameters. Successive calls to set the same header field overwrite the previous value and do not add multiple copies of the field. The four methods are as follows:

- **setHeader(String fieldname, String).** Sets the value of the named header field to the indicated value.
- **setIntHeader(String fieldname, int).** Sets the value of the named integer header field after converting the value to a string.

- **setDateHeader(String fieldname, long).** Set the value of the named date field after converting the long into an Internet-standard date-time string.

- **unsetHeader(String fieldname).** Removes the named header field from the response.

Returning Error Responses

HttpServletResponse provides two methods to create and send standard error responses. To return an error, your servlet calls sendError() with a status code and possibly an explanatory message. The page is titled and has a header that indicates the status code and a standard text message based on the status code. The optional explanatory message is inserted into the body of the returned page. Calling sendError(404, "Couldn't find it!") would create a returned page that has a title and H1 header of "404 Not Found" and "Couldn't find it!" as the text. These methods are

- **sendError(int).** Sends an error response to the client using the specified status code and no explanatory message.

- **sendError(int, String).** Sends an error response to the client using the specified status code and detailed explanatory message.

Returning Redirect Response

HttpServletResponse also provides a method to create and send a standard redirect response. Calling sendRedirect() creates and sends a "302" (Moved Temporarily) response. Pass a string that indicates the new location of the page. The string should be a URL because it is placed in the returned page as a link. However, sendRedirect() does not check to see whether the string is a correctly formatted URL. If you have a URL object already, convert it to a string using toString() before calling sendRedirect(). This method, sendRedirect(String), sends a redirect response to the client using the specified redirect location URL.

FormServlet Class

The FormServlet class is the only servlet class that is specified as part of the Servlet API, and hence it is available in all web servers that support servlets. Build forms processing servlets by subclassing FormServlet and overriding the sendResponse() method. The sendResponse() method handles form information and generates a response. As a subclass of HttpServlet, the following methods are defined for the FormServlet:

- **getServletInfo().** Override this method to return a String containing information (such as author and version) about your servlet.
- **service(HttpServletRequest, HttpServletResponse).** If special request processing is required, override this method in your servlet.
- **sendResponse(HttpServletResponse, Hashtable).** Override this method to supply code to process the form and generate a response.

An example construction of your own form processing servlet is provided in "Handling HTML Forms."

HttpUtils Class

The HttpUtils class is a set of static utility routines useful in building servlets. In Jeeves Alpha 2, the only method defined is parseQueryString(String). This method builds a Hashtable of name/value pairs based on parsing a query string. Your servlet can use the name (as the key) in the Hashtable.get() method to retrieve the value string.

The java.servlet.html Package

The third package that defines the Servlet API is java.servlet.html. This package includes 13 HTML support classes that provide operations for assembling HTML elements such as tables, imagemaps, and forms. From these elements, you can build an HTML page as a hierarchical list of HTML commands and text elements, and then you can write out the completed page to a ServletOutputStream. The classes are as follows:

- **HtmlElement.** Supports the basic interface definition
- **HtmlText.** Supports text enclosed by tags
- **HtmlContainer.** Supports a list of HtmlElements enclosed by tags
- **HtmlApplet.** Supports the applet HTML tag with width and height specification
- **HtmlChoice.** Supports the select HTML tag
- **HtmlDefinitionList.** Supports the dl, dt, and dd HTML tags
- **HtmlForm.** Supports building HTML forms comprised of input fields, check boxes, radio buttons, text areas, selections, and submit buttons
- **HtmlFrameset.** Supports frameset HTML tag
- **HtmlImageMap.** Supports client-side image map HTML tags
- **HtmlList.** Supports the ul and ol HTML list tags
- **HtmlPage.** Supports building a web page comprised of a header and body areas

- **HtmlTable.** Supports building of tables from row elements
- **HtmlRow.** Supports the HTML to define a row of a table

The methods in this package do not automatically add double quotes to enclose literal strings used as HTML attributes. You must add double quotes if your string has embedded spaces or other special control characters.

All the classes in this package implement the HtmlElement interface, which lets you specify text for the HTML tag and write the resulting HTML to an output stream. By creating objects that represent the various HTML tags and calling methods to add data and attributes to the tags, you can generate the most common HTML elements and avoid some simple errors, such as ending tags in the wrong order. However, it may be simpler to hand-generate the HTML, particularly for simple, static pages. The examples in the section "Writing Servlets" make use of the classes from the java.servlet.html package to generate dynamic response pages.

The parameter layout of these methods is similar for all classes. The first parameter is the information that is to be added to the HtmlElement. Methods are often defined to handle the addition of Strings, HtmlElements, or Vectors.

These HTML generation classes are new to the Jeeves Alpha 2 release. The contents of the java.servlet.html package and the API are likely to evolve in future releases. The final API may be significantly different from that discussed in this section.

The second parameter is eitherthe tag or attributes for a tag implied by the method. For example, addLink() implies an "a" tag, so the second parameter is interpreted as attributes of the tag. For tags, do not include the <, >, or / characters in the tag string; these characters are automatically supplied where needed. Multiple tags are specified using a comma-delimited string.

These HTML support classes do not check the actual HTML to verify that the tags and keys are legal and used correctly. It only ensures that tags are terminated in the correct order; for example, it verifies whether </body> occurs before the </html> command.

HtmlElement Interface

The HtmlElement interface defines two methods provided by all classes in the java.servlet.html package. These are as follows:

- **wrap().** Adds HTML tag pairs (such as <h1> and </h1>) to the element such that it follows previously added tags and encloses the text of the element. The tag or tags are specified as the argument to wrap(). Conceptually, an HtmlElement has beginning tags,text, and ending tags.
- **write().** Writes the HTML to an OutputStream.

HtmlText Class

HtmlText is a fundamental class in the package because it supports text enclosed by HTML tags.

- **add(String), add(String, String tag).** Adds the text, which can be optionally wrapped in the tag.
- **addTag(String), addTag(String, String).** Adds a single, non-paired tag, such as <p>, with optional tag attributes.

HtmlContainer Class

HtmlContainer is a base class for elements that herarchically contain other HTML elements. Conceptually, an HtmlContainer has beginning tags, a list of HtmlElements, and ending tags. For example, an HtmlPage is a subclass of HtmlContainer.

HtmlContainer supports wrap(), write(), and the various types of add() and addTag() methods. Unique to HtmlContainer are the following methods:

- **addImg(String).** Adds an <IMG> tag where the String is the URL of the image's source (SRC attribute).
- **addLink(String text, String URL).** Adds a link (anchor tag) where "text" is the text occuring between the tags and "URL" is the URL for the link (HREF attribute).

HtmlPage Class

The HtmlPage class represents a complete HTML page that has a header, title, and body sections. Create a new HtmlPage with a String that is the page's title. HtmlPage automatically creates the <html><head><title>, </title></head><body>, and </body></html> commands. All HtmlElements added to an HtmlPage are added into the body area of the page.

Writing Servlets

Together the Servlet API and the Jeeves HTTP server provide an environment that makes writing servlets very easy. All servlets must implement the java.servlet. Servlet interface by subclassing either GenericServlet or HttpServlet. When an HTTP request is received, the server translates the URL into a reference to a specific servlet class, as was previously described in the "Jeeves HTTP Server Overview" section. If this is the first request for the servlet, the servlet class is dynamically loaded, and its init() method is called to perform any necessary servlet-specific initialization. In most cases, the servlet has already been loaded in which case its service() method is just called.

Note that Jeeves is a multithreaded server and several different threads can concurrently executing the service() method of the same servlet object. For example, a single instance of the FileServlet object serves all requests to load files. Consequently, servlets must be designed to operate in multithreaded environment. The easiest way to ensure this is to store all information about the request being processed in local variables and not store it as instance variables in the object. For cases where access to a single resource must be controlled, you must use the standard Java synchronization techniques based on the "synchronized" keyword. In most cases, you can just add the "synchronized" modifier to the declaration for service() or sendResponse() and effectively modify the servlet to serve only one client at a time.

The following sections contain examples of a simple servlet, form processing servlets, an error response servlet, and a server-side include servlet.

Simple Servlet

To learn how to write a servlet, build a simple servlet that displays a table of the various HTTP information available from the request. Subclass HttpServlet and override the service() method as shown in the following code:

```
public class SimpleServlet extends HttpServlet {
  public void SimpleServlet() {
  }

  public void service (HttpServletRequest req, HttpServletResponse res)
    throws ServletException, IOException {
```

Your servlet can create its response using either the HttpServletResponse passed to the service() method or by resetting the HttpServletResponse and writing the response header directly to the ServletOutputStream.

Before calling service(), Jeeves sets the HttpServletResponse status to 200 or "OK," the "Date:" header field is set to the current date and time, and the "Server:" header field is set to identify the server. If there is an error or "OK" is not the correct status, the servlet can specify both an error code and some descriptive text. If only an error code is given, the code is translated into a standard status text string. Normally you would not change these values.

You do need to identify the type of data contained in the response by specifying the MIME type; and you may optionally specify the content length. To write the content, the servlet calls getOutputStream() to get a ServletOutputStream as follows:

```
res.setContentType("text/html");
ServletOutputStream out = res.getOutputStream();
```

You can create your HTML either manually by using print() statements or by using the HTML support package defined as part of the Servlet API. Use the HTML classes and create a new HtmlPage. The information from the request is displayed as a table. First, display the information available only through method calls:

```
HtmlPage page = new HtmlPage("HTTP Request Display");
page.add("HTTP Request Information", "h1");

HtmlTable tbl = new HtmlTable("Border");
tbl.addHeader("Parameter");
tbl.addHeader("Value");
nextRow(tbl, "Server name", req.getServerName());
nextRow(tbl, "Server port", Integer.toString(req.getServerPort()));
nextRow(tbl, "Client host", req.getRemoteHost());
nextRow(tbl, "Client addr", req.getRemoteAddr());
nextRow(tbl, "Method", req.getMethod());
nextRow(tbl, "Request URI", req.getRequestURI());
nextRow(tbl, "Path info", req.getPathInfo());
nextRow(tbl, "Path Xlated", req.getPathTranslated());
nextRow(tbl, "Query String", req.getQueryString());
```

Next, get a Hashtable containing all of the HTTP request header parameters and iterate through them, as follows:

```
Hashtable params = req.getParameters();
Enumeration enum = params.keys();
while (enum.hasMoreElements()) {
  String name = (String) enum.nextElement();
  String value = (String) params.get(name);
  tbl.newRow();
  tbl.addData("<strong>" + name + ":</strong>");
  tbl.addData("<em>" + value + "</em>");
}
```

Finally, write the HTML for the page to the ServletOutputStream. The response header that you create is automatically written to the ServletOutputStream before your first write is handled. This code completes the service() method:

```
    page.add(tbl);
    page.write(out);
    }
```

The nextRow() method formats each line of the response as follows:

```
    void nextRow(HtmlTable tbl, String name, String value) {
    tbl.newRow();
    tbl.addData("<strong>" + name + ":</strong>");
    tbl.addData("<em>" + value + "</em>");
    }
}
```

This completes the SmpleServlet class definition. The servlet can also use
ServletResponse to return a standard error or redirect response.

Handling HTML Forms

Many of the functions performed by CGI programs center around HTML forms handling.
When using HTML forms, the browser extracts the information entered into the form by
the user and sends it to the server as either a GET or POST request. Because form
processing is such a common servlet activity, the Servlet API includes a built-in Servlet
class specific for forms handling: The FormServlet extracts the form information from the
query string for GET requests or from the content for POST requests. The differences
between GET and POST are invisible to your subclass of FormServlet.

In the following example, FormServlet is subclassed to build a form-processing servlet
that simply reads and displays the contents of a form:

```
public class FormDisplayServlet extends FormServlet {
  public void FormDisplayServlet() {
  }
```

FormServlet's service() method has already accomplished the following:

- Verified the HTTP method as GET or POST
- Retrieved the form information from either the URL for a GET request or from the
  content of the request for a POST
- Stored the form information as a Hashtable of name/value pairs

Your subclass should override the sendResponse() method to do any request processing as
follows:

```
public void sendResponse(HttpServletResponse res, Hashtable params)
  throws IOException {
ServletOutputStream out = res.getOutputStream();
```

You must always specify the content-type on responses that include data. Allocate a HtmlPage to help construct the HTML response page and add a level-one header as shown in the following:

```
res.setContentType("text/html");
HtmlPage page = new HtmlPage("Form Display");
page.add("Form Display", "h1");
```

Because the FormServlet superclass has already stored the form information in a Hashtable, performing forms handling is a simple matter of retrieving data from the Hashtable and processing it. For this example, processing is simply formatting the forms data as a table that is returned to the browser. Access the data using an Enumerator and add a row to the table for each name/value pair in the form request as shown in the following:

```
HtmlTable tbl = new HtmlTable("Border");
tbl.addHeader("Input Element");
tbl.addHeader("Value");
int count = 0;
Enumeration enum = params.keys();
while (enum.hasMoreElements()) {
  String name = (String) enum.nextElement();
  String value = (String) params.get(name);
  count++;
  tbl.newRow();
  tbl.addData("<strong>" + name + "</strong>");
  tbl.addData(new HtmlText(value, "em"));
}
```

Note the two different ways to include HTTP format information in the table cells. The first involves manually creating a string that contains the desired HTML commands. The second uses the HTML support classes to generate a text element that is added to the table. The use of one approach instead of using the other is primarily a style issue, except in two cases. The HTML classes are a simplification of the complete language; you are required to manually create HTML code for attributes not supported by the classes. Alternatively, when your HTML processing is structured or repeating as in this example, it is easier to use the support classes because they reflect the hierarchical nature of HTML.

After you finish building the table, write a summary of the form information, add the table to the page, and then write the HTML for the complete page to the output stream. The first write to the ServletOutputStream triggers a write of the HTTP response header to the output stream. Even though the ServletOutputStream is buffered, you do not need to call the flush() method; the server automatically calls the stream's flush() method. The following code completes the sendResponse() method. Remember that the ➡ symbol indicates a line that normally fits on the previous line.

```
page.add("<p>This page contains " + Integer.toString(count) + " input
➡elements.\n");
page.add(tbl);
page.write(out);
}


}
```

This completes the definition of the FormDisplayServlet class.

Extending the FormServlet

One limitation of the standard FormServlet is that the subclasses that implement the forms processing do not have access to the request information contained in the HTTP header. Only the name/value pairs from the form are provided to FormServlet subclasses when performing form processing. The main reasons why the request information is needed is to obtain state information from the client (using cookies), to verify the client's ability to accept certain MIME types or to obtain the user's name when performing additional access control checks. The following modified version of FormServlet passes the HttpServletRequest information as an argument of the sendResponse() method:

```
public abstract class NewFormServlet extends HttpServlet {
  public void NewFormServlet() {
  }

  public void service (HttpServletRequest req, HttpServletResponse res)
    throws ServletException, IOException {
```

First determine the HTTP method being used. For GET requests, the form information is encoded into the URL after the servlet reference and can be obtained by calling getQueryString(). For POST methods, the processing is a bit more complex; the form information follows the request header and must be identified as being URL encoded. The getContents() method, which follows, reads the request content and returns a string.

The following code retrieves the query information:

```
String formdata;
String method = req.getMethod();
if ("GET".equals(method))
  formdata = req.getQueryString();
else if ("POST".equals(method)) {
  if (!"application/x-www-form-
urlencoded".equalsIgnoreCase(req.getContentType()))
    throw new IOException("illegal content type");
  formdata = getContents(req);
}
else
  throw new IOException("invalid method");
```

After you have the query information, call parseQueryString() to construct a Hashtable of name/value pairs. It decodes the special URL encoding where " " (the space character) is represented as "+," and non-printing characters are represented as a number preceded by a percent sign (%). Finally, call the servlet using the newly defined service() method as shown in the following:

```
Hashtable fd = HttpUtils.parseQueryString(formdata);
sendResponse(req, res, fd);
}
```

The NewFormServlet class defines a variant of the sendResponse() method that accepts information about the query in addition to information from the form. This new method is defined as follows:

```
public abstract void sendResponse(HttpServletRequest req,
➥HttpServletResponse res,
  Hashtable formdata);
```

The getContents() method reads the request content and returns it as a string. Note the loop structure around the read() call; this loop guarantees that the read() fully completes with all request information. The code to read the request content is as follows:

```
public String getContents(ServletRequest req) throws IOException {
InputStream in = req.getInputStream();
int count;
byte buf] = new bytereq.getContentLength()];
for (int index = 0; index < buf.length; index += count) {
  count = in.read(buf, index, buf.length - index);
  if (count == -1)
```

```
      throw new IOException();
  }
  return new String(buf, 0);
  }
}
```

This completes the definition of the NewFormServlet class.

Building Server-Side Includes Servlets

Jeeves provides support for a form of server-side includes that uses the newly defined <servlet> tags. Files whose MIME type is "java-internal/parsed-html" are further processed by the SSIncludeServlet to resolve any references to servlets embedded in the document. By default, files with the .shtml suffix are scanned.

As the document is written to the client, the SSIncludeServlet scans for the newly defined <servlet> HTML tag. When this tag is encountered, the servlet identified in the attributes of the tag is invoked and its output is sent to the client in place of the <servlet> </servlet> HTML element.

The server-side includes supported by SSIncludeServlet are not the same as those supported by many other HTTP servers, such as NCSA and Netscape; these embed server-side includes commands inside HTML comments.

The syntax for invoking servlets is as follows:

```
<servlet name=Name code=Code.class codebase=CodeBase
initParam1=initArg1 initParam2=initArg2 ...>
<param name=param1 value=val1>
<param name=param2 value=val2>
 .
 .
 .
</servlet>
```

The server first tries to invoke the servlet with the name provided in the name field. If this fails or if no name is provided, the server then attempts to load the servlet based on the code and codebase fields. Any remaining attribute fields within the <servlet> tag are passed as initialization parameters to the servlet. If the server loads the servlet and a name was specified, the server keeps the servlet loaded so that the next time the servlet is accessed, it is not reloaded. If no name is specified, the server reloads the servlet each time it is accessed.

After the servlet is ready to execute, the server calls the service() method of the servlet. The name/value pairs specified in the HTML file with the <param> tag are accessible to the servlet by using the standard getParameter() and getParameters() methods on the ServletRequest object that is passed to the servlet in the service() method. Everything the servlet writes to ServletResponse.getOutputStream() is also written to the client as part of the document that the client requested.

The following section contains an example server-side include servlet that inserts the current time (at the server) into a document.

DateSSIServlet

The DateSSIServlet is a servlet designed to work as a server-side include. This outputs the current date and time into the document that referenced this server-side include servlet. Servlets that can function as server-side include the GenericServlet subclass rather than the more common HttpServlet because HTTP information is not available. The class definition for DateSSIServlet and its service() method is as follows:

```
public class DateSSIServlet extends GenericServlet {
  public void service(ServletRequest req, ServletResponse res)
    throws ServletException, IOException {
  Date today = new Date();
  res.setContentType("text/plain");

  ServletOutputStream out = res.getOutputStream();
```

To enable the user to control whether to display the time in the local time-zone or in GMT, use an initialization parameter. For HttpServlets, the initialization parameters are obtained from the configuration file servlet.properties. For server-side includes, the user specifies initialization parameters as additional name/value pairs within the servlet tag. The following code determines the time format (local or GMT) and performs the indicated operation:

```
String zone = getInitParameter("date");
  if ("local".equalsIgnoreCase(zone))
    out.println(today.toString());
  else
    out.println(today.toGMTString());
  }

}
```

This completes the definition of the DateSSIServlet class. The HTML code to invoke this servlet to output local time to a document is as follows:

```
<servlet name=dateSSIServlet date=local></servlet>
```

The ending </servlet> tag is required even though this servlet does not take parameters. Note that this servlet can be invoked directly rather than just as a server-side include.

Subclassing ErrorServlet

When calling HttpServletResponse's sendError() method with only a status code to return an error to the requester, the ErrorServlet is actually called to create and send the error reply. The built-in ErrorServlet returns either a simple error reply message generated by translating the status number into a standard error text string, or it returns the contents of a file from the preconfigured error page directory. Calling sendError() with a status code and message string bypasses the ErrorServlet and returns a simple page that contains the error text message.

Assume that you have a busy site that is the target of many hypertext links. When files are moved to new directories, you will have many old links that will cause "not found" errors. By changing the entry in the servlet.properties file that specifies the class to be loaded for the "error" servlet, you can have your subclass of ErrorServlet invoked rather than the standard built-in version. By overriding the service() method, you can dynamically create custom error reply pages containing links to possible alternates to the requested URL.

In the following example, the service() method is overridden, but not init(), so that the original ErrorServlet will be properly initialized.

```
public class NewErrorServlet extends ErrorServlet {
  public NewErrorServlet() {
  }
```

Your service() method is called with the original request's HttpServletRequest object which has information about the requester; obtain the status code from the HttpServletResponse object. First determine whether the error is "not found," code 404. If not, just call super.service() to get the standard error reply page. The service() method is defined as follows:

```
public void service(HttpServletRequest req, HttpServletResponse res)
  throws IOException {
if (((HttpServletResponse)res).getStatusCode() != 404) {
  super.service(req, res);
  return;
}
```

If the status is 404, you use the URL request string to lookup a list of potential matches by calling getAlternates(). If no alternates are found, call super.service() for the standard error reply as shown in the following code:

```
String request = req.getRequestURI();
Vector alternates = getAlternates(request);
if (alternates.isEmpty()) {
  super.service(req, res);
  return;
}
```

The getAlternates() method returns a Vector of URL strings that are similar to the requested URL. This method might reference a hand-generated table, consult an automatically generated site index, or perform a real-time search of the file system; the exact mechanism is not defined for this example. The intent is to present a list of candidate links to the user. You can then construct the reply page with this information as shown in the following code:

```
res.setContentType("text/html");
res.setDateHeader("Date", System.currentTimeMillis());
ServletOutputStream out = res.getOutputStream();
HtmlPage page = new HtmlPage("404 File not Found");
page.add("404 - File not found", "h1");
page.add("The file <strong>" + request + "</strong> was not found. ");
page.add("You may have misspelled the URL or the file has moved. ");
page.add("Here is a list of possible links that are similar to your
⮑original request:");
```

After adding the initial message to the error reply page, construct a table of links to the candidate documents. When the table is complete, add it to the page and write the page's HTML to the ServletOutputStream. The first write to the ServletOutputStream causes the response header to be written to the ServletOutputStream. The following code completes the definition of the service() method:

```
HtmlTable tbl = new HtmlTable();
Enumeration enum = alternates.elements();
while (enum.hasMoreElements()) {
  String link = (String)(enum.nextElement());
  tbl.newRow();
  tbl.addData(new HtmlText(link, "a href=" + link));
}
page.add(tbl);
```

```
page.write(out);
}
```

The getAlternates() method is called to build a list of alternate URLs for the indicated file. The exact technique for constructing this list is undefined in this example. Depending on your application, this method could reference a manually constructed file or perform a search for similar file names. The following code is only the shell of the method:

```
Vector getAlternates(String file) {
Vector v = new Vector();

  .
  .
  .

return v;
}


}
```

This completes the definition of the NewErrorServlet class.

Summary

The Jeeves Alpha 2 release covered in this chapter is just a beginning step toward defining a radically new architecture for server software. Taken to its logical conclusion, servlets can evolve into the server-side equivalent of application components, and Jeeves can become the future of server software component architecture—a Java Beans for the server. This new architecture goes beyond simply replacing CGI programs to completely changing server implementations. Jeeves shows how an HTTP server can be remolded to use servlets to significantly increase flexibility and customization. As the servlet technology matures, more standard servlets will be defined, such as standard servlet bridges to databases, and new server-side technologies, such as JDBC, will be first introduced as servlets.

Chapter 17

JDBC

This chapter is intended to facilitate the development of database access applications using Java. The focus of this chapter is the Java Database Connectivity Application Programming Interface, or JDBC, as it is known. The features of this API are explored with relevant code examples. Alternative technologies for database access from Java applications are evaluated. In addition, the compelling reasons for the widespread acceptance of JDBC are presented.

What is JDBC?

With the widespread development and deployment of Java-based applications, developers and users require database connectivity that is easy and flexible. Powerful, yet simple, application code that is independent of any particular DBMS or database connectivity mechanism is often sought by developers. In March 1996, JavaSoft announced their step in this direction. The first specification for the JDBC API was made available as a draft for open analysis. Within months, leading commercial database vendors and third-party developers introduced JDBC-compliant drivers and products using JDBC.

JDBC is intended as a call-level SQL interface that provides Java programmers with a uniform interface to a wide range of relational databases. It is similar in concept to Microsoft's Open Database Connectivity (ODBC) API, which has become the standard for personal computers and LANs. JDBC provides a common base on which higher-level APIs and tools can be built. Using proprietary interfaces for Java applications is no longer necessary because the JDBC provides a standard DBMS-independent database access mechanism. This operates via a Driver Manager that can support multiple drivers connecting to different DBMSs.

What Does JDBC Do?

The primary function of JDBC is the execution of SQL statements and the retrieval of results. It defines Java classes to represent database connections, SQL statements, result sets, metadata, and so on. These classes, written completely in Java, enable a much closer interaction than what would normally be possible by embedding C language function calls in Java programs.

JDBC Release Information

Today, JDBC 1.1 is available. This version will be included in JDK 1.1 (Java Development Kit) and can be downloaded as a compressed .tar or .zip file from the following:

```
http://splash.javasoft.com/jdbc/jdbc./index.html
```

This includes the .java and the .html files for the API; however, this does not include any database drivers. The JDBC 1.1 specification is available from the JavaSoft site as a postscript or acrobat file.

The Application Programming Interface of JDBC

The Java core classes have been designed to use different methods to perform different tasks, instead of using methods that take many parameters to control a wide range of behavior. This pattern has been maintained in the JDBC API.

Components

The key components of the API are shown in figure 17.1.

FIGURE 17.1

JDBC in the application context.

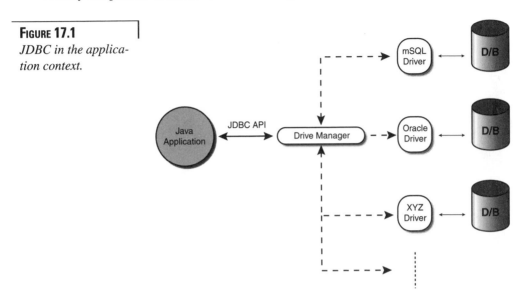

The components are discussed in the following sections.

Driver Manager

The Driver Manager controls the interaction between the application and the driver being used. It can support multiple drivers connecting to different DBMSs. It loads the requested driver and provides support for the managing database connections.

Drivers

Drivers provide the interface between the application and the vendor-specific DBMS. JDBC drivers are currently available from a number of vendors. A list is available at the following site:

```
http://splash.javasoft.com/jdbc/jdbc.drivers.html
```

Drivers can be written in Java so that they can be downloaded along with an applet. They can also be implemented using native methods to connect to database access libraries. JavaSoft requires that a driver support at least ANSI SQL-92 Entry Level functionality to pass the JDBC compliance tests.

In general, the drivers should provide implementations of the abstract classes that are specified in the JDBC API. Each database driver should provide a class that implements the java.sql.Driver interface. This interface is used by the java.sql.DriverManager class to locate a driver for a particular database URL. In addition, each driver must provide implementations of the following interfaces:

- java.sql.Connection
- java.sql.Statement
- java.sql.PreparedStatement
- java.sql.CallableStatement
- java.sql.ResultSet

Drivers can be classified as indicated in the following sections.

A Native-API Partly Java Driver

This type of driver maps JDBC calls to calls on the client API for Oracle, Sybase, Informix, DB2, or some other DBMS. It also requires some binary code to be loaded on each client machine. This driver is useful when corporations want to develop Java applications, and at the same time leverage their existing investment in DBMSs that do not have ODBC drivers. Because the driver maps the JDBC calls to client API calls, the Java application does not need to embed native DBMS access API in it.

A Net-Protocol All-Java Driver

This driver is considered to be the most flexible type. It translates JDBC calls to a DBMS-independent net protocol, which can then be translated to a vendor-specific DBMS protocol by a server. The net server middleware is capable of connecting its Java clients to a variety of different databases. Vendors that provide this type of driver probably provide products that are suitable for use in intranets. To support Internet access, these drivers must satisfy web-imposed security requirements. For example, they limit access across firewalls, among other things.

A Native-Protocol All-Java Driver

This driver translates JDBC calls to the network protocol used by the vendor-specific DBMSs. DBMS vendors are the source for these drivers because many of the protocols used in this scenario are proprietary. Using these drivers is a feasible solution for intranet access because they enable a direct call from the client machine to the DBMS server.

The JDBC-ODBC Bridge

The Open Database Connectivity (ODBC) interface is Microsoft's solution for DBMS-independent database access; however, ODBC is not appropriate for direct use from Java applications because it is a C interface. Calls from Java programs to native C code have a number of drawbacks that would impact the security, implementation, robustness, and automatic portability of these applications. Some ODBC binary code and, in some cases, database client code must be loaded on each client machine that uses this driver. As a result, this driver is a good choice on a corporate network or in a three-tiered architecture for application server code written in Java.

JDBC is based on the X/Open SQL Call Level Interface, which is also the basis for ODBC. Due to the similarities of the two specifications, the JDBC-ODBC bridge is quite small and efficient. The bridge translates JDBC calls to those that can be understood by ODBC clients at a C language level. The bridge is a joint development of JavaSoft and Intersolv.

The JDBC-ODBC bridge provides backward compatibility to a wide range of databases that have ODBC drivers, but no JDBC drivers yet. JDBC has been designed to be efficiently implemented on ODBC, so the bridge is a good way to use ODBC from Java. The name of the bridge package is sun.jdbc.odbc. It is available for the Solaris and NT/Win95 platforms and can be downloaded from:

```
http://splash.javasoft.com/jdbc/index.html
```

The JDBC Driver Test Suite

JavaSoft and Intersolv have jointly developed a JDBC driver test suite that nicely profiles the capabilities of a JDBC driver. This test suite is an attempt to ensure the portability of applications across different JDBC drivers. As of now, it is not intended as a driver certification.

The JDBC Test Harness version 0.03 and the JDBC Test Suite version 0.05 are available for download at the following:

```
http://splash.javasoft.com/jdbc/index.html
```

Both are needed to test a JDBC driver.

Interfaces and Classes

The JDBC API has a collection of interfaces that enable the primary functions of opening and managing connections to particular DBMSs, executing SQL statements, and processing the results. Added functionality in the form of cursors, transaction management, dynamic database access, and metadata is also provided. Exception handling is an essential part of any robust application. For this purpose, three exception handling classes are provided. The java.sql package contains the various interfaces and classes.

The interfaces follow:

- Driver
- Connection
- Statement
- CallableStatement
- PreparedStatement
- ResultSet
- DatabaseMetaData
- ResultSetMetaData

The classes follow:

- DriverManager
- DriverPropertyInfo
- Date
- Time
- Timestamp
- Types

The exception classes follow:

- DataTruncation
- SQLException
- SQlWarning

Figure 17.2 illustrates the interaction between the commonly used interfaces and classes.

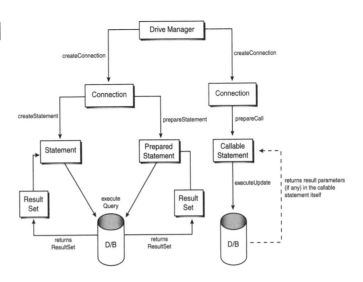

FIGURE 17.2

Interaction between interfaces and classes.

The following sections describe the interfaces and classes and explain their commonly used methods and data members. A complete listing of all the data members and methods is beyond the scope of this chapter.

To obtain a complete listing of all data members and methods, visit the following URL:

```
http://splash.javasoft.com/jdbc/html-0110/Package-java.sql.html
```

The java.sql.Driver Interface

As is the case with all Java interfaces and classes, the Driver interface extends the Object class. Each driver should provide a class that implements the Driver interface. When a Driver class is loaded, it should create an instance of itself and register with the DriverManager. In the following section, some of the commonly used methods of the Driver interface are discussed.

Boolean acceptsURL(String DatabaseURL) Method

This method returns true if the driver is capable of opening a connection to the given URL, or false otherwise. The method accepts the URL of the connecting database.

Connection Connect (String DatabaseUrl, Properties Props) Method

This method attempts to make a database connection to the given URL. It accepts the URL of the connecting database. Moreover, the Properties type parameter can be used to pass a list of name-value pairs as connection arguments. Usually, the user name and password are passed in the Properties parameter.

The driver should return null if it realizes that it cannot connect to the given URL. If it is successful, it returns a Connection object that represents a connection to the URL. The driver raises an SQLException if it has trouble connecting to the database.

int getMajorVersion() Method

This method obtains the major version number of the driver. Initially, the major version number of the driver should be 1.

int getMinorVersion() Method

This method obtains the minor version number of the driver. Initially, the minor version number should be 0.

DriverPropertyInfo[] getPropertyInfo(String DatabaseURL, Properties Props) Method

With this method, a user interface tool can get a list of properties to be obtained from the user, in order to connect to a database. It might be necessary to have more than one call to this method, depending on what the user has supplied so far.

This method accepts the URL of the connecting database and also a Properties type parameter that indicates the proposed information that will be sent while opening a connection.

The method returns an array, possibly empty, of DriverPropertyInfo objects, which describes the possible properties to be supplied by the user. It can throw a SQLException.

Boolean jdbcCompliant() Method

This method ascertains whether the Driver is a JDBC COMPLIANT™ driver. A driver should return a true value only if it passes the JDBC Compliance tests, otherwise it returns false. To be JDBC COMPLIANT™, a driver must provide full support for the JDBC API and SQL 92 Entry Level.

The java.sql.Connection Interface

The public interface Connection extends the Object class. A Connection represents a data access and manipulation session with a particular database. Within this session, SQL statements can be executed, returning result sets. Some widely used methods are described in the following sections.

void close() Method

Some situations may warrant an immediate release of the Connection's database resource and JDBC resources, instead of waiting for them to be automatically released. The close() method provides these functions. Errors occurring in this method throw a SQLException.

void commit() Method

By default, changes are automatically committed after each statement is executed. In case the auto-commit feature has been disabled, explicitly call commit() to save the changes to the database, or they will be lost. This method also releases any database locks currently held by the Connection. It throws a SQLException, in case of an error.

void rollback() Method

This method discards all the changes made since the last commit() or rollback() call. It also causes any database locks held by the Connection to be released.

Statement createStatement() Method

This method returns a new Statement object that can be used to execute SQL statements without parameters. This method throws a SQLException in case of an error.

PreparedStatement prepareStatement(String SQL_Statement) Method

This method returns a new PreparedStatement object containing the pre-compiled statement. This object can be used to execute the pre-compiled statement many times. This method accepts a SQL statement as a parameter that may contain more than one '?' IN parameter placeholder.

It throws a SQLException, in case of an error.

CallableStatement prepareCall(String SQL_Statement) Method

This method returns a new CallableStatement object containing the pre-compiled SQL statement. The SQL_Statement parameter is a SQL statement that may contain more than one '?' parameter placeholder. This method throws a SQLException, in case of an error.

void setAutoCommit(Boolean enableAutoCommit) Method

This method enables an application to specify whether its SQL statements should be automatically committed or grouped into transactions that are terminated by a commit()or rollback() call. The auto-commit mode is the default for new connections.

The java.sql.Statement Interface

The Statement interface extends the Object class. Statement objects execute SQL statements that are static by nature, and obtain results following their execution. Results are in the form of ResultSet objects; however, there can be only one ResultSet object open for each Statement object at any time. This means that if multiple ResultSets are required by the application, each must be generated by a corresponding Statement object.

The following sections discuss the most widely used methods of this interface.

void close() Method

This method can be used when it is necessary to release a Statement's database resource and other JDBC resources immediately, instead of waiting for this to occur when the Statement is automatically closed. The void close() method throws a SQLException when an error occurs.

Boolean execute(String SQL_Statement) Method

This method executes a SQL statement that can return multiple results. The return value indicates the form of the first result. If the return value is true, the next result is a ResultSet. A return value of false indicates either that there are no more results or that the next result is an update count. You can then use the getResultSet(), getMoreResults(), or getUpdateCount() methods to retrieve any subsequent results. A SQLException is thrown in case of an error.

ResultSet executeQuery(String SQL_Statement) Method

This method executes a SQL statement that returns a single ResultSet object. A SQLException is thrown, in case of an error.

int executeUpdate(String SQL_Statement) Method

This method executes SQL UPDATE, DELETE, or INSERT statements. A row count is returned for these statements. SQL statements that do not return anything, such as SQL DDL statements, can also be executed. These statements return a value of 0. In case of an error, a SQLException is thrown.

ResultSet getResultSet() Method

This method returns the result of the current Statement, in the form of a ResultSet object. This method should be called only once for each result. A SQLException is thrown, in case of an error.

Boolean getMoreResults() Method

This method moves to the next result of a Statement object. A value true is returned if the next result of the Statement is a ResultSet. If the next result is an update count or if there are no more results, a value false is returned.

The java.sql.PreparedStatement Interface

The public interface PreparedStatement extends the Statement interface. If the application requires multiple executions of a particular SQL statement, it is a good idea to pre-compile it and store it in a PreparedStatement object. The object can be used many times to execute the statement efficiently. Some of the most widely used methods of this interface are described in the following sections.

void clearParameters() Method

In general, parameter values persist during repeated executions of a Statement. Setting a parameter's value clears its previous value automatically. However, to immediately release the resources used by current parameter values, use the clearParameters() method. It throws a SQLException, in case of an error.

setXXX Methods

The setXXX methods that are used for setting the IN parameter values must specify types compatible with the defined SQL type of the input parameter. For example, setInt should be used if the SQL type of the IN parameter is Integer. "XXX" stands for the various data types that are supported.

The java.sql.CallableStatement Interface

The public interface CallableStatement extends the PreparedStatement interface. This interface provides the functions that execute SQL stored procedures.

A CallableStatement can return one or multiple ResultSets. JDBC provides a SQL escape for stored procedures; this enables a uniform call to all relational DBMSs. The escape syntax has a form that includes a result parameter, and it has a form that does not. The result parameter must be registered as an OUT parameter, if it is used. The other parameters may be used for input, output, or both.

Parameters are referred to by number in a sequential manner, beginning from 1.

The set methods inherited from PreparedStatement are used to set the IN parameter values. All OUT parameter types must be registered before the execution of the stored procedure. The most commonly used methods of the CallableStatement interface are described in the following sections.

getXXX Methods

The getXXX methods are used to obtain the values of the OUT parameters, after execution of the stored procedure.

void registerOutParameter(int parameterIndex,int sqlType) Method

This method must be called before executing a stored procedure call to register the java.sql.Type of each OUT parameter. The parameterIndex parameter indicates the number of the parameter. For example, 1 indicates the first parameter, 2 indicates the second parameter, and so on. The sqlType parameter is a SQL type code defined by java.sql.Types. This method throws a SQLException, in case of an error.

void registerOutParameter(int parameterIndex,int sqlType, int scale) Method

This version of the registerOutParameter method is used for registering Numeric or Decimal OUT parameters. The first two parameters are the same as in the previous version of the method. The scale parameter represents the number of digits to the right of the decimal point. Its value should be greater than or equal to zero. This method throws a SQLException, in case of an error.

Boolean wasNull() Method

An OUT parameter can have the value of SQL NULL. The wasNull() method returns true if the last value read was SQL NULL; otherwise, false is returned. This method throws a SQLException, in case of an error.

The java.sql.ResultSet Interface

The public interface ResultSet extends the Object class. The table of data that is generated by the execution of a Statement can be accessed through a ResultSet object.

The ResultSet object maintains a cursor that points to its current row of data. Initially, the cursor points to a location before the first row. Then, the table rows can be retrieved in sequence by using the "next" method.

The getXXX methods retrieve the values in the columns of a particular row. Within a row, the column values can be randomly accessed. The columns are numbered sequentially beginning from 1. Column index numbers or names can be used to retrieve the column values. The JDBC driver attempts to convert the data to the specified Java type and returns a suitable Java value for the getXXX methods. The section that describes the mappings between SQL types and Java types provides more details.

When a Statement is re-executed or is used to retrieve the next result from a sequence of results, the current ResultSet is automatically closed. This also happens when the Statement that generated the ResultSet is closed.

The ResultSet interface's most widely used methods are described in the following sections.

ResultSetMetaData getMetaData() Method

The ResultSetMetaData object, returned by the getMetaData method, provides the number, types, and properties of a ResultSet's columns. The getMetaData() method throws a SQLException, in case an error occurs.

Details of the ResultSetMetaData interface are provided later in the chapter.

void close() Method

This method is used when the application wants to release a ResultSet's database resource and JDBC resources immediately instead of waiting for this to happen when the ResultSet is automatically closed. This method throws a SQLException to indicate an error condition.

Boolean next() Method

Not all commercially available DBMSs support positioned updates and positioned deletes. So, it is up to the programmer to use the Database-MetaData. supports-Positioned Update() and DatabaseMeta-Data. supports-Positioned Delete() methods to confirm that the underlying DBMS does, in fact, support them. For example, the Oracle RDBMS supports positioned updates and deletes.

A ResultSet is initially positioned before its first row. To access the rows of the ResultSet, successive calls must be made to the next() method. It throws a SQLException, in case of an error. So, the first call to next()makes the first row of the ResultSet the current row.

The next() method returns true if the new, current row is a valid row. It returns false if no more rows exist. This functionality is achieved by the use of a cursor.

The idea of a cursor should be familiar to most programmers who have worked with a database. A cursor can be thought of as a pointer or iterator pointing to or indexing into a set of tuples. A *tuple* is a record in a database table. It has values for the fields in the table. In the JDBC API, a cursor is an iterator indexing into a ResultSet.

Cursors are very useful for dealing with multi-tupled ResultSets. Extracting information from each row in the ResultSet is facilitated through cursors. When a ResultSet is first created, the cursor points to the first row of data. The row that a cursor points to is referred to as the current row. The next() method of the ResultSet interface iterates through the ResultSet. The next() method advances the position of the cursor to the next row of data. The current version of JDBC provides only rudimentary support for cursors. The name of the cursor can be obtained by using ResultSet.getCursorName(), which returns a Java String object. The row of a ResultSet object, currently pointed to by a cursor, can be updated or deleted by a positioned update or delete, respectively, that uses the name of the cursor.

Developers who have worked with ODBC style cursors should be aware that JDBC does not support scrollable cursors or enable the placement of bookmarks. The use of cursors is illustrated in the "Querying the Database" section of the example scenario discussed later in this chapter.

The java.sql.ResultSetMetaData Interface

The public interface ResultSetMetaData extends the Object class. Information about the java.sql.ResultSetMetaData appears in the section, "Noteworthy Features in JDBC," later in the chapter.

The java.sql.DatabaseMetaData Interface

The public interface DatabaseMetaData extends the Object class. Information about the java.sql.DatabaseMetaData appears in the section, "Noteworthy Features in JDBC," later in the chapter.

The java.sql.DriverManager Class

The DriverManager class extends the Object class. It controls the interface between the application and a set of JDBC drivers. The DriverManager also provides a set of services for managing the drivers.

During its initialization, the DriverManager class tries to load the driver classes that are referenced in the "jdbc.drivers" system property. If this property exists, it should have a colon-separated list of driver names. The DriverManager class will attempt to load each named Driver class. By modifying this property, a user can choose the JDBC drivers to be used by his or her application. A program can also load JDBC drivers at run time. For example, a Driver class can be explicitly loaded using the standard Class.forName method. To load the imaginary.sql.iMsqldriver class, the following line of code can be used.

```
Class.forName("imaginary.sql.iMsqlDriver");
```

The methods of the DriverManager class are described in the sections that follow.

Connection getConnection() Method

The getConnection method attempts to establish a connection to the specified database URL. If it is successful, it returns a Connection object, which represents the connection to the database URL. If there is an error, a SQLException is thrown.

The method has three different forms:

- **Connection getConnection(String DatabaseURL).** This causes the DriverManager to try to select an appropriate JDBC driver from among those that are registered.
- **Connection getConnection(String DatabaseURL, Properties Props).** This form accepts a Properties type parameter, which specifies a list of string name-value pairs. Usually, a "user" and "password" property should be included.
- **Connection getConnection(String DatabaseURL, String UserName, String UserPassword).** With this form, the user name and password are explicitly passed as parameters, instead of being included in a Properties object.

void registerDriver(Driver newDriver) Method

To register itself with the DriverManager, a newly loaded Driver class should call this method. In the case of an error, a SQLException is thrown.

Driver getDriver(String DatabaseUrl) Method

This method causes the DriverManager to attempt to load a driver that understands a particular database URL. If such a driver is present and is registered, the method returns a Driver object. This Driver object represents a JDBC driver that can connect to the database URL. This method throws a SQLException, if an error occurs.

Enumeration getDrivers() Method

To get a list of JDBC drivers that the current caller can access, use the getDrivers() method. This method returns an Enumeration of all the currently loaded JDBC drivers that are accessible to the caller.

void deregisterDriver(Driver dropDriver) Method

The DriverManager can also de-register drivers from the list of registered drivers. This method drops the driver from the DriverManager's list. However, applets can only de-register drivers from their own class loader. In the event of an error, this method throws a SQLException.

The java.sql.DriverPropertyInfo Class

The DriverPropertyInfo class extends the Object class, and is primarily of interest to advanced programmers who require or wish to explore various connection properties. This method enables an interaction with a Driver and provides properties for connections.

The constructor of this class accepts the name of the property (as a String) and the current value of the property (as a String). The current value of the property may be null. The following list describes the variables for the DriverPropertyInfo class:

- **choices.** This is an array of possible values for a property, if the value can be selected from a set of values; otherwise it should be null.
- **description.** This provides a brief description of the property and may have a null value.
- **name.** This supplies the name of the property.
- **required.** If this is set to true, a value must be supplied for the property during Driver.connect. Otherwise the property is optional.
- **value.** This indicates the current value of the property. This may depend on a combination of the information supplied to getPropertyInfo, the Java environment, and driver-supplied default values. If no value is known, it may be null.

The java.sql.Date Class

This class is essentially an extension of the java.util.Date class. Functions have been added to enable JDBC to identify this class as a SQL DATE value. The class has formatting and parsing operations to support the JDBC escape syntax for date values.

The documentation provided by JavaSoft recommends against using the full facilities of the underlying java.util.Date class. For example, the setHours method would give a java.sql.Date value that would not compare properly with other SQL Date values because a SQL Date consists of just a day, a month, and a year. The following sections describe the methods and constructors of the java.sql.Date class.

Constructors for the java.sql.Date Class

The constructor for this class has the following two forms:

- **Date (int Year, int Month, int Day).** This constructs a date from the supplied parameters.
- **Date(long datevalue).** This constructs a date using a time value in milliseconds.

Methods of the java.sql.Date Class

The java.sql.Date class has the following methods:

- **String toString().** This method returns a String in the "yyyy-mm-dd" format.
- **Date valueOf(String datestring).** This method accepts a String in the form "yyyy-mm-dd" and returns a corresponding Date object.

The java.sql.Time Class

This class adds to the functionality provided by the java.util.Date class enabling JDBC to identify it as an SQL TIME value. Formatting and parsing operations have been added to support the JDBC escape syntax for time values.

Once again, the JavaSoft documentation recommends against using the full facilities of the underlying java.util.Date class. For example, the setMonth method obtains a java.sql.Time value that would not compare properly with other Time values. The constructors and methods of the java.sql.Time class are described in the following sections.

Constructors for the java.sql.Time Class

The constructor has the following two forms:

- **Time (int Hour, int Minute, int Second).** This constructs a Time object from the parameters.
- **Time (long timevalue).** This constructs a Time object using the timevalue, provided in milliseconds.

Methods of the java.sql.Time Class

The java.sql.Time class has two methods:

- **Time valueOf(String timevalue).** This method accepts a String in JDBC time escape format "hh:mm:ss" and converts it to a Time object.
- **String toString().** This method returns a String in "hh:mm:ss" format.

The java.sql.Timestamp Class

This class is an extension of the java.util.Date class. The modifications enable JDBC to identify this as a SQL TIMESTAMP value. The capability to hold the SQL TIMESTAMP nanos value has been added along with formatting and parsing operations to support the JDBC escape syntax for timestamp values.

This class is actually a combination of a java.util.Date and a separate nanos value. The nanos, which are fractional seconds, are separate from the integral seconds, which are stored in the java.util.Date component. To obtain a time value that includes the fractional seconds, convert the nanos to milliseconds and add this value to the value returned by the getTime() method.

Also, the hashcode() method uses the java.util.Date implementation and does not include the nanos in the result.

Constructors for the java.sql.Timestamp Class

The constructor for the java.sql.Timestamp class has the following two forms:

- **Timestamp(int Year, int Month, int Date, int Hour, int Minute, int Second, int nanosecond).** This constructs a Timestamp object using the values supplied as parameters.
- **Timestamp(long timevalue).** This constructs a Timestamp using a milliseconds time value.

Methods of the java.sql.Timestamp Class

The java.sql.Timestamp class has the following methods:

- **Timestamp valueOf(String timeStampStr).** Accepts a String in the timestamp format "yyyy-mm-dd hh:mm:ss.fffffffff" and returns a corresponding Timestamp object.
- **String toString().** Returns a String in the "yyyy-mm-dd hh:mm:ss.fffffffff" format.
- **int getNanos().** Returns the Timestamp's fractional seconds part.

- **void setNanos(int nanovalue).** Sets the Timestamp's nanos value.
- **Boolean equals(Timestamp ts).** Tests timestamp values for equality. This method compares the current Timestamp with the supplied Timestamp value. It returns true if they are equal or false if they are not.
- **Boolean before(Timestamp ts).** Determines whether the current Timestamp object is earlier than another Timestamp value. This method accepts the Timestamp value, ts, to compare with the current Timestamp object. It returns true if the current Timestamp object's value is before ts; otherwise, false.
- **Boolean after(Timestamp ts).** Determines whether the current Timestamp object is later than another Timestamp value. It accepts the Timestamp value, ts, to compare with the current Timestamp object. It returns true if the current Timestamp object's value is after ts.

The java.sql.Types Class

The Types class extends the java.lang.Object class and defines constants used to identify SQL types. The actual type constant values are equivalent to those in XOPEN.

A detailed mapping of SQL types to Java types is presented in the section, "Mapping SQL Data Types to Java Data Types," later in the chapter.

The java.sql.DataTruncation Class

The DataTruncation class extends the java.sql.SQLWarning class. When JDBC truncates a data value unexpectedly, it reports a DataTruncation warning for a read process, or throws a DataTruncation exception for a write process.

The SQL state for a DataTruncation is "01004."

The following sections describe the constructor and methods for the java.sql.DataTruncation class.

Constructors for the java.sql.DataTruncation

The constructor has the following form:

```
DataTruncation( int index, boolean param_truncated,
booleanread_truncated, int dataSize, int dataTransferredSize)
```

The "index" parameter is the index of the column or parameter value. The "parameter_-

truncated" parameter is true if a parameter value was truncated. If the truncation occurred for a read process, the "read_truncated" value is true. The "dataSize" variable indicates the original size of the data. The size of the data after truncation is indicated by "dataTransferredSize."

Methods of the java.sql.DataTruncation Class

The java.sql.DataTruncation class has the following methods:

- **int getIndex().** Returns the index of the column or parameter that was truncated. The return value is –1, if the column or parameter index is unknown. In this case, the "parameter" and "read" fields of the DataTruncation object should be ignored.

- **Boolean getParameter().** Returns true, if the truncated value was a parameter; if a column value was truncated, false is returned.

- **Boolean getRead().** Returns true if the value was truncated when read from the database. It returns false if the data was truncated during a write.

- **int getDataSize().** Returns the number of bytes that should have been transferred. The value is –1, if the size is unknown. If data conversions were being performed, the number returned may be an approximation.

- **int getTransferSize().** Returns the number of bytes that were actually transferred. If the size is unknown, the return value is –1.

The java.sql.SQLException Class

The java.sql.SQLException class extends the java.lang.Exception class. Information about a database access error is provided by the SQLException class.

Each SQLException class provides the following kinds of information:

- A string that describes the error. It is available via the getMessage() method. This string is used as the JavaException message.

- A vendor specific integer error code. This is usually the actual error code that is returned by the database being accessed.

- A SQLState string that is in accordance with the XOPEN SQLState conventions. The acceptable values of this string are described in the XOPEN SQL specification.

- A chain to the next Exception. This can be used to obtain more information about the error.

The constructors and methods for the java.sql.SQLException class are described in the following sections.

Constructors for the java.sql.SQLException Class

The constructors of this class follow:

- **SQLException().** This constructs an SQLException object. The reason and SQLState attributes of the object default to null, and the vendorCode attribute defaults to zero.

- **SQLException(String reasonForException).** This constructs an SQLException with a reason. However, the SQLState attribute defaults to null and the vendorCode attribute defaults to zero.

- **SQLException(String reasonForException, String SQLState).** This constructs an SQLException with a reason and a SQLState. The reasonForException attribute describes the exception, and the SQLState attribute is an XOPEN code for the exception. However, the vendorCode attribute is set to zero.

- **SQLException(String reasonForException, String SQLState, intvendor-Code).** This constructs a fully specified SQLException.

Methods of the java.sql.SQLException Class

The java.sql.SQLException class consists of the following methods:

- **int getErrorCode().** This returns the vendor-specific exception code.

- **String getSQLState().** This returns the SQLState, defined in the XOPEN specification.

- **SQLException getNextException().** Use this method to obtain the next exception that is chained to the current exception.

- **void setNextException(SQLException nextSQLException).** This adds a SQLException to the end of the chain.

The java.sql.SQLWarning Class

The java.sql.SQLWarning class extends the java.sql.SQLException class. The SQLWarning class provides information about a database access warning. When a method of an object causes a warning to be reported, the warning is chained to that object. The constructors and methods for the java.sql.SQLWarning class are described in the following sections.

Constructors for the java.sql.SQLWarning Class

The constructors for this class have the following forms:

- **SQLWarning().** This constructs an SQLWarning with the reason and SQLState attributes set to null, and the vendorCode attribute set to zero.

- **SQLWarning(String reasonForWarning).** This constructs a SQLWarning with a reason. However, the SQLState attribute defaults to null and the vendorCode attribute defaults to zero.

- **SQLWarning(String reasonForWarning, String SQLState).** This constructs a SQLWarning with values for the reason and SQLState attributes. The vendorCode attribute defaults to zero.

- **SQLWarning(String reasonForWarning, String SQLState, int vendorCode).** This constructs a SQLWarning object with a reason that describes the warning, a SQLState, which is an XOPEN code identifying the warning, and a vendorCode, which is a vendor-specific warning code.

Methods of the java.sql.SQLWarning Class

The java.sql.SQLWarning class consists of the following methods:

- **SQLWarning getNextWarning().** This returns the SQLWarning object chained to the current SQLWarning object.

- **void setNextWarning(SQLWarning nextWarning).** This adds a SQLWarning object to the end of the chain.

Mapping SQL Data Types to Java Data Types

Before assigning data that is retrieved from a database to application variables, be sure it is assigned to compatible types. Also, in order to store and retrieve parameters and recover results returned after the execution of SQL statements, enough type information should be made available to the program.

A mapping of SQL data types to Java data types makes this conversion clear. The default Java mapping for common SQL data types is shown in table 17.1.

SQL Type	Java Type
TINYINT	byte
SMALLINT	short
INTEGER	int
BIGINT	long
REAL	float
FLOAT, DOUBLE	double
NUMERIC, DECIMAL	java.lang.Bignum
BIT	Boolean
BINARY, VARBINARY, LONGVARBINARY	byte[]
CHAR, VARCHAR, LONGVARCHAR	String
DATE	java.sql.Date
TIME	java.sql.Time
TIMESTAMP	java.sql.Timestamp

TABLE 17.1

Common SQL Data Types

The documentation provided by JavaSoft mentions that the Java data type does not need to have exactly the same form as the SQL data type. For instance, Java does not have any fixed length arrays. So, variable length Java arrays can be used to represent both fixed and variable length SQL arrays.

Also, Java Strings have been used, although they do not match any of the SQL CHAR types exactly.

Some details of these mappings are discussed in the following list.

- TINYINT↔byte. Represents an 8 bit value, so it can be mapped to Java's byte type.
- SMALLINT↔short. SMALLINT represents a 16 bit value, so it can be mapped to Java's short type.
- INTEGER↔int. INTEGER represents a 32 bit value, so it can be mapped to Java's int type.
- BIGINT↔long.BIGINT represents a 64 bit value, so it can be mapped to Java's long type.
- REAL↔float. REAL has to support 7 digits of mantissa precision. It has been mapped to the float type in Java.
- FLOAT↔double. FLOAT has to support 15 digits of mantissa precision.

Both the NUMERIC and DECIMAL SQL data types are mapped to java.-lang.Bignum extended precision number type, which is provided in JDK 1.1. Moreover, simple Strings and arrays of chars can be used to access DECIMAL and NUMERIC values. In this way, Java programmers can use getString to receive a NUMERIC or DECIMAL result.

- DOUBLE↔double. DOUBLE has to support 15 digits of mantissa precision.

- NUMERIC↔java.lang.Bignum. NUMERIC represents fixed point numbers when absolute precision is required. This type is often used for currency values.

- DECIMAL↔java.lang.Bignum. DECIMAL also represents fixed point numbers when absolute precision is required. This type is often used for currency values.

- BIT↔Boolean. BIT is mapped directly to the Boolean type in Java. It can be used to indicate a 0 or 1 value.

- BINARY↔byte[]. BINARY can be expressed as a byte array in Java. Java programmers do not need to distinguish between the three SQL byte arrays: BINARY, VARBINARY, and LONGVARBINARY.

- VARBINARY↔byte[]. VARBINARY can be expressed as a byte array in Java.

- LONGVARBINARY↔byte[]: LONGVARBINARY can be expressed as a byte array in Java. The LONGVARBINARY SQL type can be used to return multi-megabyte data values. So, it can be retrieved as a Java input stream. Programmers can then read data from the stream, in the chunk size that they prefer.

- CHAR↔String. CHAR is expressed as a String type in Java. Java programmers do not need to distinguish between the CHAR, VARCHAR, and LONGVARCHAR SQL data types because they can be expressed identically in Java.

- VARCHAR↔String. VARCHAR is expressed as a String type in Java.

- LONGVARCHAR↔String. LONGVARCHAR is expressed as a String type in Java. The LONGVARCHAR SQL type can be used to store multi-megabyte strings. By retrieving a LONGVARCHAR value as a Java input stream, programmers can retrieve the value in chunks. Java streams can be used for Unicode, as well as ASCII data.

- DATE↔java.sql.Date. Consists of a day, month, and year. For SQL DATE information, java.sql.Date can be used. The hour, minute, second, and millisecond fields of the base class java.util.Date are set to zero.

- TIME↔java.sql.Time. Consists of hours, minutes, and seconds. For SQL TIME information, java.sql.Time can be used. The year, month, and day fields of the base class java.util.Date are set to 1970, January, and 1, respectively. This signifies the "zero" date in the Java epoch.

- TIMESTAMP↔java.sql.Timestamp. Comprises of both DATE and TIME, and also a nanosecond field. For SQL TIMESTAMP information, you can use java.sql.Timestamp. This class has a nanosecond field, too.

This section discusses the mapping of results and parameters whose types are known at compile time. Some applications may not have knowledge of the database schema that they access, at the time they are compiled. So, JDBC provides support for complete dynamically typed data access.

JDBC Metadata Capabilities

Metadata is information about the data in the database and the database itself. This information is invaluable when determining the nature of the data in the database, and the capabilities of the database. The initial design of JDBC used complex methods in core JDBC classes to implement metadata features. This approach was, however, discarded and replaced by two additional interfaces in JDBC release 1.10. JDBC provides database application programmers with two interfaces that provide a wide range of metadata functions. These interfaces are java.sql.DatabaseMetaData and java.sql.ResultSet-MetaData.

The DatabaseMetaData Interface

DatabaseMetaData provides metadata about the database itself. The methods of this interface generally return their results in java.sql.ResultSet objects. Only a few of the most commonly used features of DatabaseMetaData are discussed here. For a complete reference document, refer to the JavaSoft web site at the following:

```
http://splash.javasoft.com/jdbc/html-0110/
➥java.sql.DatabaseMetaData.html#_top
```

- **URL getURL().** Obtains the Uniform Resource Locator (URL) of the database. The URL is returned as a Java String object, if it can be determined. An SQLException is thrown if the URL cannot be determined.

- **String getUserName().** Returns the user name that is known to the database as a Java String object. It throws an SQLException if the user name cannot be determined.

- **int getMaxConnections().** Provides the maximum number of active connections that the database can support. An integer representing the maximum number of connections is returned.

- **ResultSet getTables(String CatalogName, String SchemaNamePattern, String TableNamePattern, String TableTypes).** Searches for tables matching the TableNamePattern and the specified TableTypes (for example, Table, System Table, View, and so on) in the catalog (specified by CatalogName). It also searches for all the schema matching SchemaNamePattern. It returns a ResultSet containing the descriptions of all the tables matching the above mentioned criteria. Each row in the ResultSet describes a single table. The user can iterate through the ResultSet to obtain table descriptions.

Not all the methods of this interface may be completely implemented by all database drivers. Database vendors or third-party driver providers may implement only the most commonly used methods. Any method that is not implemented throws an SQLException, if the method is invoked.

If you are wondering how to specify the catalog names and schema names, methods to obtain the catalog names and schema names from a database exist. Similarly, there are methods that determine the available table types and general database information (this includes the product name, product version, and information about the provided driver).

The ResultSetMetaData Interface

This metadata interface is probably more commonly used than the DatabaseMetaData interface. The ResultSetMetaData interface gives an application programmer information about the ResultSet obtained from a query. The programmer can use this interface to determine properties of the columns in a ResultSet.

The important methods of this interface are mentioned in the following list, along with a brief description:

- **int getColumnCount().** Obtains the number of columns in the ResultSet. It returns an integer that equals the number of columns.
- **String getColumnName(int Column_Number).** Obtains the actual name of a column, given the column number in a ResultSet.
- **int getColumnType(int Column_Number).** Returns the SQL type of the column indicated by Column_Number. SQL types are defined in java.sql.Types. Refer to table 17.1 for a list of SQL types and their mapping to corresponding Java data types.
- **Boolean isCurrency(int Column_Number).** Checks whether the value in the column specified using Column_Number is a currency (cash) value or not. This method is quite useful in financial applications. The method returns a true or false value.
- **String getTableName(int Column_Number).** Gets the name of the table to which the column represented by Column_Number belongs. It returns the name of the table in a Java String object.

There are other methods to determine whether a particular column can only be read or written, or whether a search can be specified using the column.

Implementation Scenario Using JDBC

H2O Inc. is an upcoming dealer in water pumps of all kinds, with offices in Atlanta and Macon, Georgia. With growing competition, H2O decided that they needed to target a wide market, including the entire state of Georgia, by using the World Wide Web. H2O was convinced that web shopping would bring in an unprecedented amount of revenue because their company would become more visible and more accessible from distant places.

However, they faced certain problems. The offices in Atlanta and Macon had grown independently, creating differences in the way each of the offices maintained information. The Atlanta office maintained its inventory database on Oracle, whereas the Macon office, being smaller, maintained its database on mSQL (Mini SQL—for full details refer to http://Hughes.com.au/product/msql/), a lightweight database engine.

To enable their web shoppers to see the entire inventory contained collectively within both offices, they designed an application using Java and JDBC.

The following sections demonstrate how JDBC and Java were used to create a web shopping site.

System Overview

From the system overview in figure 17.3, it is evident that the application must read the databases at both sites and combine the information to give a complete picture to the prospective customer.

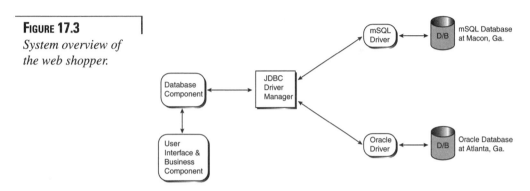

FIGURE 17.3
System overview of the web shopper.

It is assumed that the application uses JDBC API 1.10. H2O obtained Oracle and mSQL JDBC drivers from JDBC driver vendors. The application is logically composed of two units: a user interface combined with a business logic component coded using Java, and a database component coded using the JDBC API.

H2O's aim is to first provide a list of the available water pumps from which the shopper can choose. This can be followed by non-update types of operations (such as price inquiry, inventory inquiry, and so on) or update operations (such as ordering a particular water pump).

System Implementation

Because this chapter is mainly about JDBC, the discussion focuses on the database component of the system. The implementation can be done in a series of systematic steps, as shown in the following sections.

- **Connecting to the Databases.** This section explains two sample methods of establishing database connections.
- **Querying the Database.** After a connection is established, various query operations can be performed. This section explores commonly used query operations.
- **Update Operations.** In this section, you are introduced to some of the update operations provided by JDBC.
- **Cleaning up.** This section illustrates the closing of statements and connections.

Step One: Connecting to the Databases

The first step in any database application is to establish a connection to the databases that contain information pertinent to the application. The following code creates a connection to the database at Macon, Georgia.

Listing 17.1   Connecting to the Database at Macon

```
new imaginary.sql.iMsqlDriver();
String url = "jdbc:msql://www.H2OMacon.com:4333/Shopdb";
Connection con = DriverManager.getConnection(url, "nobody",
    "");
```

The first line of code creates an instance of the mSQL JDBC driver provided by Imaginary (refer to http://www.imaginary.com/~borg/Java). The application will communicate with the mSQL database using the previously mentioned mSQL JDBC driver. Another way to inform the DriverManager about a Driver class is to use the standard Class.for-Name method, in the following way:

```
Class.forName("imaginary.sql.iMsqlDriver");
```

4333 is the MSQL_-PORT for non-root access on Unix systems.

The second line of code creates a String object with the value of the location of the H2O Macon office database. This String object is required to create a Connection object and follows the naming convention defined in JDBC 1.10 specifications. Here, the substring "jdbc" informs the server that the protocol to be used is JDBC. The substring "msql" defines the subprotocol, and "//www.H2OMacon.com:4333/Shopdb" specifies the database name "Shopdb" and the server name.

The next line of code actually creates the connection by using the location specified by String url and logging in as user "nobody" with an empty password parameter. This whole section of code must be placed within a "try" block to catch any SQLException that might be caused by the execution of this code. A SQLException is thrown if a connection could not be established.

There are other ways to obtain a database connection. One way is to use the Driver interface to obtain a connection. The same effect as the previously defined piece of code can be achieved by implementing the code in listing 17.2.

Listing 17.2 Alternative Method of Connecting to a Database

```
    Properties props = new Properties();
        props.put("server","www.H2OMacon.com:4333");
        props.put("user","nobody");
        props.put("password","");
        Driver msqldr = new imaginary.sql.iMsqlDriver();
        String url = "jdbc:msql://www.H2OMacon.com:4333/Shopdb";
connection1 = msqldr.connect(url,props);
```

Here, the connection is obtained by asking the mSQL JDBC driver to create a connection to the given URL, using the given properties. In essence, both segments of code achieve the same result—they create a connection.

The next action is to create a connection to the database in the Atlanta office of H2O. This can be accomplished by using a JDBC driver for Oracle (refer to http://www.weblogic.com/—this is an Oracle JDBC driver offered by webLogic Technologies) or by using the JDBC-ODBC bridge. The code lines in listing 17.3 use jdbcKona, a JDBC driver offered by webLogic for connecting to Oracle, Sybase, and MS SQL databases.

Listing 17.3 Connecting to the Database at Atlanta

```
Properties props = new Properties();
props.put("user",     "nobody");
props.put("password", "");
props.put("server",   "www.H2OAtlanta.com/inventory");
try {
    Connection connection2 =
    ➥DriverManager.getConnection("jdbc:weblogic:oracle", props);
    }
catch (SQLException e) {
        System.out.println("Error message " + e.getMessage());
        }
```

Now that both the connections are set up, it is time for the next step.

Step Two: Querying the Database

H2O needs to present to the prospective customer the list of all the different kinds of water pumps available at both sites of the company. The solution is to run queries against both databases, and then combine the results to give an overall picture. The queries are shown in code listing 17.4.

Listing 17.4 Querying the Databases

```
Statement stmt1 = connection1.createStatement();
ResultSet set1 = stmt1.executeQuery("SELECT * from SHOP_MACON ORDER BY
  Pump_Id");
           // Pump_Id is the primary key which represents a unique pump
           // identification number
    Statement stmt2 = connection2.createStatement();
    ResultSet set2 = stmt2.executeQuery("SELECT * from SHOP_ATLANTA
ORDER
BY Pump_No");
           // Pump_No is essentially same as Pump_Id but was named
           // differently by the Atlanta database designers.
```

After the preceding two statements are executed, all the unique tuples from each site are stored in ResultSets, set1 and set2. The executeQuery method of Statement interface is usually used to execute a non-update query. You can also use java.sql.PreparedStatement for this purpose. A PreparedStatement can be used to specify IN parameters to query statements. IN parameters are used to dynamically change the query statement as required. For example, if the prospective shopper was interested only in pumps that cost less than a particular value, it might be efficient to have a PreparedStatement with IN parameters, as shown in the following line of code:

```
PreparedStatement stmt3 = connection1.prepareStatement("SELECT *FROM
  SHOP_MACON WHERE (Pump_Cost < ?)");
```

The question mark symbolizes an unknown IN parameter. To determine all the pumps whose cost is lower than 500 dollars, the following may be done:

```
stmt3.setInt(1, 500);
ResultSet set3 = stmt3.executeQuery();
```

The statement numbered 1, sets the value of the first IN parameter to an integer value of 500. If there had been more than one "?" symbols in the PrepapredStatement, it would mean that more than one IN parameters exist. The parameter number (the first argument that is sent to the setInt method) is used to set one of the IN parameter values while using one of the setXXX methods (XXX stands for either Int, String, Byte, and so on) that is defined for the PreparedStatement interface.

In order to modify the above query to search for pumps costing less than 1,000 dollars, all that needs to be done is to change the IN parameter as shown in the following lines of code:

```
stmt3.setInt(1, 1000);
ResultSet set4 = stmt3.executeQuery();
```

ResultSet set4 now contains all the pumps costing less than $1,000. As can be seen from the previous examples, PreparedStatements are an efficient way to code dynamically changing queries.

Getting back to H2O's web shopping system, the ResultSets from querying both databases have been obtained. These results have to be processed correctly in order to give the web shopper a complete picture. Now, it is perfectly possible that the number of attributes (columns) in ResultSets set1 and set2 vary and that the names of the corresponding attributes are different. So, the application programmer might need to obtain the names of the attributes for processing the obtained data. This can be achieved using the ResultSetMetaData interface as shown in the code listing 17.5.

Listing 17.5 Using ResultSetMetaData

```
ResultSetMetaData rset1 = set1.getMetaData();
int num_columns_in_set1 = rset1.getColumnCount();
 String[] col_names1 = new String[num_columns_in_set1];
 for (int iterator=0; iterator<num_columns_in_set1; iterator++) {
     try {
         col_names1[iterator] = rset1.getColumnName(iterator);
         }
     catch (SQLException e) {e.getMessage()}
     }
```

Listing 17.5 first defines a ResultSetMetaData object (in line 1) then uses the metadata object to obtain the number of columns in the result (in line 2). The application programmer can use the getColumnName method of the metadata object to determine the column names of the attributes in ResultSet set1. This information can be used for printing purposes; for example, in a report header.

Assume for simplicity that the web shopper is to be presented with three attributes from each table—Pump_Id in set1 and Pump_No in set2, Pump_Name in set1 and Pump_Label in set2, and Pump_Cost in set1 and Pump_Price in set2.

Furthermore, assume that these attributes are columns numbered one, two, and three, respectively, in the actual tables; hence, they are numbered similarly in the ResultSets.

The following code in listing 17.6 extracts the required information from the ResultSets set1 and set2.

JDBC

Listing 17.6 Navigating through the set1 ResultSet Object

```
while (set1.next()) {
    String  Pump_ID = set1.getString(1);
    String     Pump_NAME = set1.getString(2);
    float     Pump_COST = set1.getFloat(3);
    Process_Row(Pump_ID, Pump_NAME, Pump_COST);
    }
```

The ResultSet object is automatically assigned a cursor at the time of its creation. The name of the cursor can be obtained using the getCursorName() method of the ResultSet interface. To obtain the names and prices of the pumps satisfying the query, it is necessary to iterate through the ResultSet using the next() method, which advances the cursor's position by one. Similarly, the results from ResultSet set2 must also be read. This can be accomplished by implementing the code in listing 17.7.

Listing 17.7 Navigating through the set2 ResultSet Object

```
while (set2.next()) {
    String  Pump_ID = set2.getString("Pump_No");
    String     Pump_NAME = set1.getString("Pump_Label");
    float     Pump_COST = set1.getFloat("Pump_Price");
    Process_Row(Pump_ID, Pump_NAME, Pump_COST);
    // Process_Row is a method that combines the results
    // from the two tables.
    }
```

Note that the column names are used to index into each row in the ResultSet directly. Although this produces much more readable code, it is not as efficient as using column indexes to index into each row.

Step Three: Furthering the Scenario with Update Operations

The Java component of the system displays the information requested by the web shopper. It then offers the shopper an opportunity to place an order.

Assume, the web shopper decides to purchase two HG55-E (Pump Id) High Power Water Pumps. After carefully considering the buyer's location, the business logic component has decided that the pumps shall be delivered to the customer from the Atlanta unit of H2O. The database must be updated to reflect the potential sale. This is illustrated in listing 17.8.

Listing 17.8   Updating the Database at Atlanta

```
Statement stmt4 = connection2.createStatement();
String query = new String("UPDATE SHOP_ ATLANTA SET Pump_Units =
Pump_Units
- 2 WHERE Pump_Id = ");
    // Pump_Units represents the number of pumps available in
    // the inventory at that given instant.
query.concat(selected_Pump_Id);
        //Selected_Pump_Id represents the String object containing
        //the Id of the pump the shopper wants to buy
try {
    return_code = stmt4.executeUpdate(query);
    }
catch (SQLException e) {
    System.out.println(e.getMessage());
    }
```

As can be seen from the code in listing 17.8, the executeUpdate() method of Statement interface is used to execute SQL statements that may make some changes to the database. This includes UPDATE, INSERT, DELETE, and DDL (Data Definition Language) commands.

The execution of the code in listing 17.8 does not indicate that the transaction has been completed. The web shopper needs to be mailed an invoice, and the shipping office needs to be informed of the requested delivery. The entire logic associated with these processes may be handled by a stored procedure named "shipping_and_invoice" which takes these parameters: Selected_Pump_Id, Quantity_Purchased, User_Name, and User_Address.

The following code calls the stored shipping_and_invoice procedure.

Listing 17.9   Calling a Stored Procedure

```
try {
    CallableStatement call_stmt = connection1.prepareCall("{ ? = call
    ➥shipping_and_invoice(?, ?, ?, ?)}");
    }
catch (SQLException e) {}
call_stmt.registerOutParameter(1, java.sql.Types.Bit);
call_stmt.setString(2, Selected_Pump_Id);
call_stmt.setInt(3, Quantity_Purchased);
call_stmt.setString(4, User_Name);
```

continues

Listing 17.9   Continued

```
call_stmt.setString(5, User_Address);
try {
     call_stmt.executeUpdate();
     }
catch (SQLException e) {}
boolean successful = call_stmt.getBoolean(1);
if (successful)
     send_user_message("Transaction successful!");
          // send_user_message displays a message on the screen
else
          send_user_message("Transaction failed!");
```

It is possible that some drivers may send the call statement to the database when the prepareCall method is invoked. Others wait until the executeUpdate method of the CallableStatement is invoked. So, it is good programming practice to try to catch exceptions for both the prepareCall and executeUpdate methods.

To execute a stored procedure, it is necessary to use the Callable-Statement interface. The CallableStatement interface extends the PreparedStatement interface that was used earlier. The Callable-Statement object is created by using the prepareCall method of the Connection object. The prepareCall method takes a special escape sequence (refer to "{call ....}"). The curly braces form an escape sequence that instructs the driver and the driver manager that this is a stored procedure. The second line of code uses a version of the call statement that returns a result value. The result value is indicated by the first question mark. Every result value must be registered as an OUT parameter with the CallableStatement. This is accomplished by using the registerOutParameter as shown on the fifth line. The java.sql.Types.Bit data type has been used because the stored procedure is expected to return a Boolean value. The second line of code has several ? symbols apart from the result value. Here, these are used as IN parameters. Actually, these can be used as either IN or OUT parameters. If they are used as OUT parameters, they must be registered with the CallableStatement, in a manner similar to the result value. The IN parameters are specified by using the setXXX (XXX represents Int, String, and so on) methods of the PreparedStatement interface. The four IN parameters that are required for this procedure are set between the sixth and ninth lines. The command "call_stmt.executeUpdate();" actually executes the CallableStatement.

The statement "Boolean successful = call_stmt.getBoolean(1);" extracts the Boolean value returned by the stored procedure to check if the transaction was successful. The last four lines of code are fairly straightforward.

Step Four: Cleaning Up

Now that the transaction has been completed, it is good practice to release all resources that the application might have obtained. Each of the Statement objects used can be released using the close() method. For example, the following code releases the resources held by Statement object, stmt1:

```
stmt1.close();
```

This process should be repeated for each Statement object created by the application.

Finally, the database connections should be released. This is also achieved by using the close() method. For example, the following closes Connection object, connection1, and releases the resources held by this connection:

```
connection1.close();
```

Thus, JDBC aided H2O in creating the web shop that they desired. This was achieved by leveraging their system infrastructure using this modern technology.

Comparison of JDBC with Existing Database Access Technologies for the World Wide Web

The use of the World Wide Web as a medium for business brought into existence many technologies that enable database access over the web. Notable among these technologies is Common Gateway Interface, or CGI, as it is known. In this section, the JDBC approach is compared to some of the existing web-based database access technologies, namely the following:

- CGI scripts
- Java API for databases
- Vendor tools for database access from the web

CGI Scripts

Common Gateway Interface scripts are a common technology that can be used to access a database from the web. CGI is used to interact with databases on a server. These scripts can be implemented by using a variety of languages including C, C++, Perl, Python, and so on. They interact with a user through the medium of HTML documents. They present their output information by creating HTML documents on the fly.

Prior to Java and JDBC, CGI scripts epitomized the term "dynamic" web interaction. CGI scripts could communicate with a database on a server by using either an Application Programming Interface or an embedded SQL. They could present the required information to the user by using a well-understood and easy-to-use medium—HTML.

However, there are several shortcomings to using CGI scripts. CGI scripts are not truly "dynamic"; they actually run on the back-end server. So, the server bears the complete responsibility of all the required computation. This produces "fat" servers and "thin" clients, which are not desirable system characteristics. In contrast, the combination of JDBC and Java is a truly "dynamic" duo. The client performs a lot of processing while the server is used only when actual database access is required. Furthermore, the JavaAPI includes a package called java.awt, which is devoted to the creation and manipulation of graphical components. AWT stans for Abstract Windowing Toolkit. The java.awt package provides a very flexible and powerful means of designing user interfaces. HTML, though simple to use, lacks some of the features provided by java.awt.

Most importantly, CGI scripts are known to be weak security links in a system. There are several well-documented sources that describe the security concerns with CGI. In comparison, JDBC provides a more secure environment. However, it is only fair to say that the JDBC is relatively new—not everything is known about it yet.

Information regarding CGI security issues can be found at http://www.cerf. net/~paulp/cgi-security.

However, considering client/server design issues, JDBC is a much better approach than CGI scripts. Some of the important reasons are as follows:

- JDBC does not have the problem of a "fat" server and "thin" client.

- JDBC can be used with any DBMS that provides a JDBC driver. It can also be used with any DBMS that can be accessed through an ODBC driver. This can be accomplished by using the JDBC-ODBC bridge (provided by JavaSoft and Intersolv).

- JDBC provides metadata about the SQL query results.

Java API for Databases

An increasing number of database vendors might provide a Java API for database access. An example is MsqlJava (refer to `http://www.minmet.uq.oz.au/msqljava/`). MsqlJava is a Java API for mSQL databases.

Using a Java database API would produce a seamless integration of database access code within the application. Therefore, this is certainly a more desirable approach compared to CGI scripts.

However, using a Java database API restricts the application to the particular DBMS for which the Java API is provided. Therefore, JDBC is certainly a better option. Furthermore, not many DBMSs come with a Java API. (To this author's knowledge, mSQL is the only DBMS that provides a Java API.)

Vendor Tools for Database Access from the Web

Some DBMS vendors provide tools for web access; for example, Microsoft's SQL Server Web Assistant (refer to `http://www.microsoft.com/msdn/sdk/platforms/doc/ backoff/sqldrop/hydra/admin/src/adminwn_4.htm`). This is a non-CGI solution for database access from the web. The Web Assistant is mainly used to create HTML pages on a pre-scheduled basis, triggered basis, and so on. For more information on how Microsoft SQL Server can be used in the Internet environment, refer to `http:// www.microsoft.com/sql/sqlinet1.htm`.

However, using these kinds of tools limits the web application to a particular DBMS and a particular vendor. This is not a desirable characteristic of any application.

JDBC's Future Direction

JavaSoft intends to provide a higher level API over JDBC that will target transparent objects and relational mapping. This will enable the mapping of Java objects to one or more relational database tables. JavaSoft also plans to enhance the capabilities of the JDBC API to include increased cursor support and other useful features. Currently, there are plans for a Java Transaction Service API that will be designed to enable Java programs to complete transactions across multiple databases (refer to `http://splash.javasoft. com/jdbc/jdbc.databases.html`).

Other Database Access Technologies for Java

There may be other non-relational DBMS-based options available to Java application programmers who want to introduce persistence in their applications. The options presented in the following sections are Persistence through Object Serialization and ODMG Java Object Database Standard.

Object Persistence Using Object Serialization

Objects that exist beyond the life of the program they are created by are called *persistent* objects.

Serialization has been mainly utilized for serializing objects into a byte stream for communication via sockets in Java Remote Method Invocation. RMI is a registered trademark of Sun Microsystems, Inc.

For small applications, it is possible that the amount of data involved may not be sufficient to warrant the use of a DBMS. In such situations, it may be optimal to use Object Serialization to emulate database functions (such as persistence).

Object Serialization involves the mapping of objects into an object output stream and the subsequent reconstruction of objects from an object input stream.

Most common Java objects can be serialized by using the Object Serialization system (http://chatsubo.javasoft.com/current/serial/index.html). Serialization of user-defined classes requires the implementation of either the Serializable or Externizable interface. The difference between the two interfaces is that the object stream for Serializable objects contains sufficient information for reconstructing an object from the stream, whereas Externizable objects are solely responsible for their external formats and reconstruction.

Serialization can be used for persistence by creating files of objects. These files can be used instead of databases; however, it becomes the responsibility of the programmer to save all the objects in files (using serialization) before quitting the program and to read these objects from files before starting execution again. The overheads involved are quite considerable and increase rapidly with increasing numbers of application objects. An example of providing persistence for Java objects is Persistent Java (http://copeland.smartchoice.com/~laforge/index.html#Introduction), created by Bill la Forge. Serialization has been used for persistence in other languages such as C++ using products such as the Tools h++ Class Library from RogueWave Software, Inc. (refer to `http://www.roguewave.com/products/tools/toolsfund.html`).

ODMG Java Object Database Standard

Object Database Management Group (ODMG) and JavaSoft created a new working group in February 1996. The goal of this working group is to define an object database standard for Java. Object databases are ideally suitable to represent Java objects in a transparent and seamless manner. Key concepts of the standard include transparent persistence, persistence by reachability, multiple implementations of Java binding, and addition of classes to Java in order to implement the complete ODMG object model. Transparent persistence involves making active instances of Java objects persistent without any modifications to existing code. The requirement that all objects that can be reached from any root object be made persistent at commit-time is defined by "persistence by reachability." The Java environment must be enhanced to fully comply with the ODMG object model. This requires that classes and constructs such as collections, relationships, transactions and databases be added to Java.

Currently, there are some products designed for object database support for Java. They include ObjectStore PSE (persistent storage engine) from ObjectStore and POET for Java from POET. However, these products do not claim to be compliant with the new ODMG Java standard for object databases.

Online References

`http://splash.javasoft.com/jdbc`—This site provides the official JDBC documentation from JavaSoft. The JDBC 1.10 specification and API are available for download at this site.

`http://www.imaginary.com/~borg/Java`—The mSQL JDBC Driver is available at this site, along with documentation. This site also has links to MsqlJava and mSQL home pages.

`http://www.weblogic.com/`—This is the home page of webLogic, Inc. WebLogic provides JDBC drivers for several leading relational DBMSs such as Oracle, Sybase, and Microsoft SQL Server. WebLogic's JDBC drivers can be downloaded for trial use from this site.

Summary

This chapter provided you with an overview of the aims and functions of JDBC. The documentation of the JDBC API should prove to be a valuable guide. The real-world implementation scenario shows how JDBC is used to achieve better integration and flexibility for a corporate enterprise. The insight provided can be extended to other environments. A comparison of JDBC with competing technologies showed a perspective that may be used when making you make decisions. As it evolves to provide wider functionality, JDBC certainly is a technology worth watching and following.

Index

FWEListener
    implementing, 705
    interface, 700

G

garbage collection
    managing, 198
    speed degradation, 596
generateMoves() method, 43-48
GenericServlet
    class, 736
    HttpServlet, 737
    subclass, 752
genetic inheritance (metaphor), 52-53
GET requests, encoding form information, 749
get() method, 221
getAddress() method, 337
getAllByName() method, 337
getAllowUserInteraction() method, 333
getAlternates() method, 754
getAppletContext() method, 100
getAudioClip() method, 35
getAuthType() method, 739
getChecksum() method, 517, 548-550
getCodeBase() method, 97
getColumnName method, 789
getCommandString() method, 395
getConnection() method, 772
getContent() method, 329, 332
getContentEncoding() method, 332
getContentLength() method, 332, 735
getContents() method, 749-750
getContentType() method, 332, 735
getCursorName() method, 790
getDate() method, 332
getDateHeader() method, 739
getDocumentBase() method, 34, 97
getDoInput() method, 332
getDoOutput() method, 332
getDriver(String DatabaseUrl) method, 772
getDrivers() method, 772
getExpiration() method, 332
getFilePointer() method, 321
getHeader() method, 739
getHeaderField() method, 332
getHeaderFieldDate() method, 332
getHeaderFieldInt() method, 332
getHeaderName(int) method, 739
getHostName() method, 337
getIfModifiedSince() method, 332

getImage() method, 34, 97, 152
getIndex() method, 227-229
getInformation() method, 696
getInitParameter() method, 734
getInitParameter(String name) method, 736
getInitParameters() method, 734-736
getInputStream() method, 735
getIntHeader(String fieldname, int default)
    method, 739
getLastModified() method, 332
getLineNumber() method, 315
getLocalPort() method, 341
getMaildrop() method, 409-411
getMessage() method, 777
getMetaData() method, 770
getMethod() method, 738
getMimeType(String filename) method, 734
getMoreResults() method, 766
getMyQuantity() method, 238
getNextNode() method, 238
getNextQuantity() method, 238
getNextRandom() method, 686
getObjectOfClass() method, 66
getOutputStream() method, 736, 746
getParameter() method, 34, 96-97, 752
getParameter(String) method, 735
getParameters() method, 724, 735, 752
getPathInfo() method, 738
getPathTranslated() method, 738
getPriority() method, 525
getProtocol() method, 735
getQueryString() method, 738, 749
getRealPath(String path) method, 734
getRemoteAddr() method, 735
getRemoteHost() method, 735
getRemoteUser() method, 739
getRequestPath() method, 738
getRequestURI() method, 738
getResultSet() method, 766-767
getSelectedItem() method, 143-146
getSelectedItems() method, 146
getServerInfo() method, 734
getServerName() method, 735
getServerPort() method, 735
getServlet(String) method, 734
getServletContext() method, 736
getServletInfo() method, 734, 742
getServletPath() method, 738
getServlets() method, 734
getsetData() method, 333-334
getSource() method, 696
getText() method, 148

Runtime.exec() method, 598-601
runtime.waitFor() method, 601

S

Save dialog box, creating, 155-156
saveTo() method, 299-300
saving keyword tables as static variables, 394
scaling transparency, 450
scheduling threads, 526-530
    preemptive scheduling, 526-527
    yielding, 527-528
screens
    borders, 158
    building
        Canvas class, 123
        Frame class, 122-123
        GridBagLayout manager, 159-161
        layout managers, 156-160
        Panel class, 123
    grids, 159
Scrollbar class, 152
scrolling lists (pop-up menus), 145-147
ScrollingFrame class, 152
SecondSonOfCounter class, 76
Secure Sockets Layer (SSL), 718
security
    applets, 116-118
    CGI, 711
        scripts, 794
    Java applet sandbox, 91
    Jeeves, 718-721
        ACLs, 720
        administration tools, 720-721
        authentication, 719
        digest authentication, 719
        security sandbox, 721
        SSL eavesdropping protection, 720
        SSL server authentication, 719-720
        Unix, 721
        user groups, 720
    override protection (final access
      modifier), 79-84
    security manager, 116
    threads, 536-539
security manager applets, 116
security sandbox, 721
SecurityManager, 537
Semaphore class, 556-557
SemaphorePrinterAccess class, 558-560

semaphores, 556-563
    implementing in Java, 556-557
    synchronization, 560-562
    throttling, 562-563
sendError() method, 724, 741, 753
sendError() method, 741
sendRedirect() method, 741
sendResponse() method, 718, 722, 741
sendResponse(HttpServletResponse, Hashtable)
  method, 742
sendtoall() method, 365
sendtoone() method, 365
SequenceInputStream, 317-318
serial ports, 645-646
    accessing, 647-655
    changing settings, 673-675
    closing, 666
    defaults, 672-673
    events, 670
    opening, 667-668
    reading data, 671
    simplifying use of, 658-666
        Action class, 666
        SerialData class, 665-666
        SerialPortMonitor class, 658-661
        WaitForTokens class, 661-665
    writing data to, 671-672
SerialData class, 665-666
SerialDevice package, 645-675
    C code
        closing serial ports, 666
        opening serial ports, 667-668
    NativeSerial class, 647-653
    serial port events, 670
    serial ports, 671-675
    SerialDevice class, 653-655
    SerialPeer class, 655-656
    utility classes, 658-666
        Action, 666
        SerialData, 665-666
        SerialPortMonitor, 658-661
        WaitForTokens, 661-665
    wait masks, 668-670
    Win32sSerialPeer class, 656-657
serialization, 706, 796-797
SerialPortMonitor class, 658-661
server applications, 382-383
    chat server, 360-369
        AppletServer class, 361-365
        ClientConnect class, 365-367
        Watcher class, 368-369